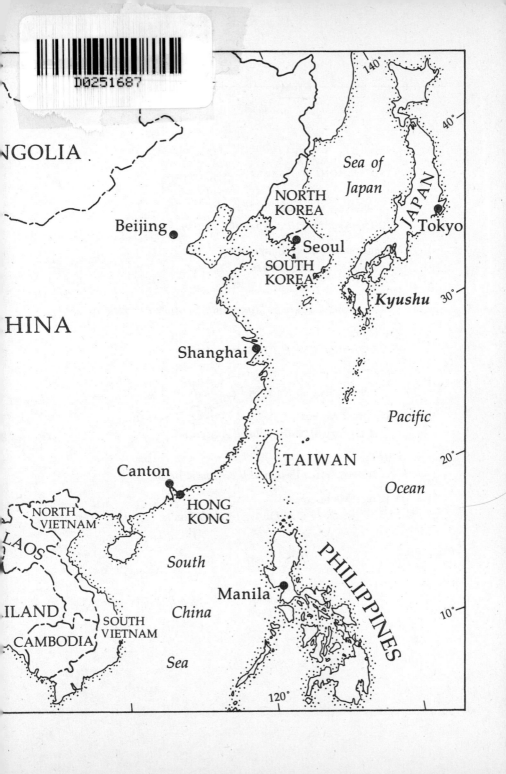

ALSO BY RONALD TAKAKI

A Pro-Slavery Crusade
The Agitation to Reopen the African Slave Trade

Violence in the Black Imagination
Essays and Documents

Iron Cages
Race and Culture in Nineteenth-Century America

Pau Hana
Plantation Life and Labor in Hawaii

From Different Shores
Perspectives on Race and Ethnicity in America

A Different Mirror
A History of Multicultural America

Hiroshima
Why America Dropped the Atomic Bomb

A Larger Memory
A History of Our Diversity, with Voices

Strangers from a Different Shore

A History of Asian Americans

Updated and Revised Edition

Ronald Takaki

Little, Brown and Company

Boston • New York • London

For
Carol,
Dana, Troy, *and* Todd

Originally published in hardcover by Little, Brown and Company, 1989
First Back Bay paperback edition, updated and revised, 1998

Excerpts from *America Is in the Heart* by Carlos Bulosan,
Copyright 1943, 1946 by Harcourt Brace Jovanovich, Inc.,
reprinted by permission of the publisher.

Excerpts from *Songs of Gold Mountain* by Marlon K. Hom,
Copyright © 1987 by The Regents of the University of California, are reprinted by permission of The University of California Press.

Library of Congress Cataloging-in-Publication Data
Takaki, Ronald T.
    Strangers from a different shore: a history of Asian Americans/
Ronald Takaki. — 1st ed.
        p.   cm.
    Includes index.
    ISBN 0-316-83109-3 (HC)   0-316-83130-1 (PB)
        1. Asian Americans — History.   2. Asian Americans — Social
conditions.   I. Title.
    E184.06T35 — 1989
    973'.0495 — DC19   89–2816

10   9   8   7   6   5   4

Q-MBG

PRINTED IN THE UNITED STATES OF AMERICA

Contents

IV. DIVERSITY

Preface to the New Edition

Confronting "Cultural Literacy"
The Redefining of America

When the first edition of *Strangers from a Different Shore* was published in 1989, I was invited to be a guest on NBC's *Today* show, with Jane Pauley. I flew to New York and checked into my hotel the night before my interview. Arrangements had been made for a limousine to pick me up at 8:00 A.M. and drive me to NBC for a live appearance at 8:20 A.M. But the limousine was late. Taking a taxi, I arrived just in time and had to be rushed into the studio. I was still trying to catch my breath and struggling to overcome my nervousness when Jane Pauley welcomed me to the *Today* show and then quickly asked, "Professor Takaki, I need to ask you some questions, you know, like an exam. Will you compare for us Ellis Island and Angel Island?"

What a perfect opening question, I thought. Here were forty million Americans watching the program, and most of them undoubtedly had never heard of Angel Island. Even if they lived in San Francisco, they probably viewed this scenic island in the middle of the bay as a recreational place to bike, hike, and picnic. In my answer, I said, "Jane, both of us have read E. D. Hirsch's book *Cultural Literacy: What Every American Needs to Know.*" This was a bestseller at the time, and Jane quickly nodded. "Well, in the back of the book, there's a long list of terms that every American should know, and this list includes Ellis Island but it omits Angel Island. Ellis Island was the entry point for European immigrants, and Angel Island was the location of the immigration station for 'strangers from a different shore' — for Chinese and Japanese immigrants."[1]

The point I was making was clear: cultural literacy, as defined by Hirsch as well as by educators and pundits like him, reflects a widely held but mistaken view that "American" means "white" or

European in origin. This ethnocentric notion leaves out many groups, including Asian Americans.

Two years later, Arthur Schlesinger reaffirmed this narrow view of American identity in his declaration of war against multiculturalism, a book provocatively entitled *The Disuniting of America*. Studying our racial and ethnic diversity, he warned, separates groups from one another and fragments our society. This "ethnic" ideology nourishes "a culture of victimization" and inculcates the "illusion" that membership in one or another "ethnic" group is "the basic American experience." He castigated the "multicultural zealots" for rejecting "the notion of a shared commitment to common ideals." The allegiance to "ethnicity," he warned, threatens "the brittle bonds of national identity" that hold "this diverse and fractious society together." As an alternative, Schlesinger urged Americans to renew their commitment to the nation's principles and to remember the origins of its political foundations. Aggressively, he asserted that the "unique source" of America's ideas of liberty, democracy, and the rule of law was Europe. These were *"European* ideas, not Asian, nor African, nor Middle Eastern."[2]

But Schlesinger's understanding of our diversity is mistaken and his fears of our expanding ethnicities are unwarranted. This is what the history of Asian Americans shows so clearly. Their experiences were "basically American" and reflected a "shared commitment to common ideals," re-visioning them in ways the Founding Fathers had not intended and would not have approved. They struggled to make our national principles racially more inclusive and therefore distinctly "American," no longer purely "European."

Indeed, the story of Asian Americans is woven into the history of America itself. The Chinese began coming here during the 1849 California gold rush, and my Japanese grandfather sailed across the Pacific in 1886, before the arrival of most Jewish, Italian, Hungarian, and Polish immigrants. Like Oscar Handlin's "uprooted," Asians also belonged to the "great migrations that made the American people."[3] Asians were members of what Walt Whitman called "the vast, surging, hopeful army of workers," who transformed the western deserts into farmlands, built the transcontinental railroad, and toiled in factories from San Francisco to North Adams, Massachusetts.[4]

More important, while Asian Americans experienced the "victimization" of discrimination and exploitation, they also fought against the exclusionisms designed to force them to remain strangers in America. When Thomas Jefferson wrote those powerful words "all men are created equal," entitled to "liberty" as an "unalienable right," he was not thinking that this would become the creed for a racially diverse America. For Jefferson, the new nation was to be a white republic, and this vision of America's "manifest destiny" led his fellow policymakers to enact the 1790 Naturalization Law, which restricted naturalized citizenship to "whites."[5] Thus, when Asians arrived, they found themselves politically excluded from their adopted country.

Facing discrimination, Asian Americans did what Abraham Lincoln wanted all of us to do: recognize America as a nation, "dedicated" to the "proposition" of equality, and pursue the "unfinished" work of making this ideal a reality.[6] After Congress enacted the Chinese Exclusion Law in 1882, an immigrant angrily scolded the policymakers. "No nation can afford to let go its high ideals," Yan Phou Lee wrote in the *North American Review.* "The founders of the American Republic asserted the principle that all men are created equal, and made this fair land a refuge for the world. Its manifest destiny, therefore, is to be the teacher and leader of nations in liberty. Its supremacy should be maintained by good faith and righteous dealing, and not by the display of selfishness and greed. But now, looking at the actions of this generation of Americans in their treatment of other races, who can get rid of the idea that that Nation, which Abraham Lincoln said was conceived in liberty, waxed great through oppression, and was really dedicated to the proposition that all men are created to prey on one another? How far this Republic has departed from its high ideal and reversed its traditional policy may be seen in the laws passed against the Chinese."[7]

While Lee's demands for inclusion and justice were easily dismissed at the time, they could not be forever denied. Protests continued, and a turning point came during World War II. By serving in the U.S. military during World War II, Asian Americans shared what Lincoln called "the mystic chords of memory" stretching from battlefields to patriot graves. In a letter written from the battlefront, a Japanese-American soldier explained to his family why he was ready to die for this country: "By virtue of the Japanese attack on our nation, we as American citizens of Japanese ancestry have been mercilessly flogged with criticism and accusations. But I'm not going to take it sitting down! I may not be able to come back. But that matters little. My family and friends — they are the ones who will be able to back their arguments with facts. . . . In fact, it is better that we are sent to the front and that a few of us do not return, for the testimony will be stronger in favor of the folks back home."[8] Many Japanese-American soldiers had left behind families unjustly evacuated and incarcerated in internment camps. Altogether, 33,000 Nisei served in the military; many of them did not "come back" to America. All of them had earned the right, through bloody sacrifices in defense of our democracy, to call upon their nation to rededicate itself to its founding principle of equality.

The victory over Nazism with its ideology of Aryan supremacy spurred Asian Americans to renew their claims on America. In 1952, they successfully helped lobby for the provision in the McCarran-Walter Law, which nullified the "white"-only restriction in the 1790 Naturalization Law. Harry Takagi explained the meaning of this victory: "It was the culmination of our dreams. I can't think of any other legislation that so united the JACL [Japanese American Citizens League]. The bill established our parents as the legal equal of other Americans; it gave the Japanese equality with all other immigrants, and that was a principle we had been struggling for from the very beginning."[9]

The Civil Rights Movement of the sixties stirred criticisms of the bias built into the U.S. immigration laws. When Congress passed the 1964 Civil Rights Act, Asian Americans raised a logical question: If racial discrimination was illegal, why was it still enforced in the laws regulating entry? "Everywhere else in our national life, we have eliminated discrimination based on national origins," Attorney General Robert Kennedy told Congress in 1964. "Yet, this system is still the foundation of our immigration law."[10] A year later, lawmakers abolished the national-origins restrictions and reopened the gates to Asian immigrants. Finally, racial restrictions had been removed from immigration legislation, and the Statue of Liberty had become a symbol of hope for all people.

The history of Asian Americans has much to teach us about how all of us might get along with one another in the twenty-first century. The importance of knowing this story was suddenly reinforced in my mind on a Monday morning in June 1997. While I was writing this preface, I received a phone call from the White House, inviting me to attend a meeting of scholars and civil rights leaders with President Bill Clinton. The purpose was to brainstorm ideas for his major speech on America's race relations in the coming century. I had already known from the newspapers that Clinton would be making his speech in California, where the population is 10 percent Asian American and where the university's flagship campus at Berkeley is 40 percent Asian American. I listened intently when the president's assistant said that Clinton wanted to recognize our society as "multiracial" and take the discourse on race "beyond black and white." "So," she stressed, "your presence as an Asian-American scholar at the meeting would be very important." I asked, "When is the meeting taking place?" She replied, "Tomorrow. So you have to catch a plane out of San Francisco today. Sorry, but that's the way we often do things around here. The speech is scheduled to be given this Saturday."

Within hours I was flying to Washington. As I looked down at the vast continent where peoples who had come from all over the world were working and living, I wondered what I would tell Clinton. I decided I would first describe the demographic face of America in the twenty-first century. Remembering Franklin D. Roosevelt's striking statement "the only thing we have to fear is fear itself," I came up with what I thought would work as a memorable phrase for Clinton's speech — "We will all be minorities."

This new identity will occur first in California within a few years and then in the entire nation by mid-century. Projected to become 10 percent of the U.S. population, Asian Americans will be part of this tremendous social and cultural transformation. This immense diversity ahead of us, I thought, could be viewed as a danger, sweeping us downward toward "the disuniting of America." But this coming "brave new world" of various cultures and ethnicities could also be seen as an opportunity for us to face our future by reaching toward a more inclusive and more accurate understanding of our past.

Here, I reflected, the history of Asian Americans offers an important lesson. In the telling and retelling of their stories, these immigrants and their descendants contribute to the creating of a larger memory of who we are as Americans. They reassure us that we can be ethnically diverse and still one people, restlessly and hopefully striving toward "a more perfect Union." Bursting with their varied visions of America, Asian Americans rebel against the ethnocentrisms embedded in Hirsch's enclosing cultural literacy and Schlesinger's exclusionist view of the past. Urging us to *rethink* the way we think about our nation's history, these "strangers from a different shore" tell us the time is opportune for the redefining of America.

Strangers from
a Different Shore

1

From a Different Shore

Their History Bursts with Telling

In Palolo Valley on the island of Oahu, Hawaii, where I lived as a child, my neighbors had names like Hamamoto, Kauhane, Wong, and Camara. Nearby, across the stream where we caught crayfish and roasted them over an open fire, there were Filipino and Puerto Rican families. Behind my house, Mrs. Alice Liu and her friends played mah-jongg late into the night, the clicking of the tiles lulling me to sleep. Next door to us the Miuras flew billowing and colorful carp kites on Japanese boys' day. I heard voices with different accents, different languages, and saw children of different colors. Together we went barefoot to school and played games like baseball and *jan ken po*. We spoke pidgin English. "Hey, da kind tako ono, you know," we would say, combining English, Japanese, and Hawaiian: "This octopus is delicious." As I grew up, I did not know why families representing such an array of nationalities from different shores were living together and sharing their cultures and a common language. My teachers and textbooks did not explain the diversity of our community or the sources of our unity. After graduation from high school, I attended a college in a midwestern town where I found myself invited to "dinners for foreign students" sponsored by local churches and clubs like the Rotary. I politely tried to explain to my kind hosts that I was not a "foreign student." My fellow students and even my professors would ask me how long I had been in America and where I had learned to speak English. "In this country," I would reply. And sometimes I would add: "I was born in America, and my family has been here for three generations."

Indeed, Asian Americans have been here for over 150 years.

Resting on benches in Portsmouth Square in San Francisco's Chinatown, old men know their presence in America reaches far into the
past. Wearing fedora hats, they wait for the chilly morning fog to
lift; asked how long they have been in this country, they say: "Me
longtime Californ'." Nearby, elderly Filipinos — *manongs* — point
to the vacant lot where the aging International Hotel had once offered
these retired farm workers a place to live out the rest of their lives.
They remember the night the police came to evict them and the
morning the bulldozers obliterated a part of their history. In the
California desert town of El Centro, bearded and gray-haired men
wearing turbans sit among the fallen leaves on the grounds of the
Sikh temple. One of them describes what life was like in California
decades ago: "In the early days it was hard. We had a hell of a time.
We had to face a lot of narrow mindedness."[1]

   Asian Americans are diverse, their roots reaching back to China,
Japan, Korea, the Philippines, India, Vietnam, Laos, and Cambodia.
Many of them live in Chinatowns, the colorful streets filled with
sidewalk vegetable stands and crowds of people carrying shopping
bags; their communities are also called Little Tokyo, Koreatown, and
Little Saigon. Asian Americans work in hot kitchens and bus tables
in restaurants with elegant names like Jade Pagoda and Bombay
Spice. In garment factories, Chinese and Korean women hunch over
whirling sewing machines, their babies sleeping nearby on blankets.
In the Silicon Valley of California, rows and rows of Vietnamese and
Laotian women serve as the eyes and hands of production assembly
lines for computer chips. Tough Chinese gang members strut on
Grant Avenue in San Francisco and Canal Street in New York's
Chinatown. In La Crosse, Wisconsin, welfare-dependent Hmong sit
and stare at the snowdrifts outside their windows. Holders of Ph.D.'s,
Asian-American engineers do complex research in the laboratories
of the high-technology industries along Route 128 in Massachusetts.
Asian Americans seem to be ubiquitous on university campuses: they
represent 11 percent of the students at Harvard, 10 percent at Princeton, 16 percent at Stanford, 21 percent at MIT, and 25 percent at
the University of California at Berkeley. From Scarsdale to the Pacific Palisades, "Yappies" — "young Asian professionals" — drive
BMWs, wear designer clothes, and congregate at continental restaurants; they read slick magazines like *AsiAm* and *Rice*. "I am Chinese,"
remarks Chester in David Hwang's play *Family Devotions*. "I live
in Bel Air. I drive a Mercedes. I go to a private prep school. I must
be Chinese."[2]

Recently Asian Americans have become very visible. While Asians have constituted a majority of Hawaii's people for nearly a century, they have become populous elsewhere in the country. Three hundred thousand Chinese live in New York City — the largest Chinese community outside of China. Describing the recent growth of New York's Chinatown, the *New York Times* observed in 1986: "With new arrivals squeezing in at a rate of nearly 2,000 a month, the district spread north through what was once a Jewish section on the Lower East Side and west across Little Italy, turning Yiddish into Mandarin and fettucine into won tons." Meanwhile, Flushing in Queens has become a "suburban" Chinatown, the home of 60,000 Chinese; resident Eileen Loh observed: "We are changing the face of Flushing." On the other side of the continent, Monterey Park in southern California has come to be called the "Chinese Beverly Hills." About a fourth of San Francisco's population is Asian, and Asians represent over 50 percent of the city's public-school students. In Los Angeles, there are 150,000 Koreans, and the Olympic Boulevard area between Crenshaw and Hoover has been designated Koreatown. Nearby, in an adjacent county, a new Vietnamese community has also suddenly appeared. "Along Garden Grove Boulevard in Orange County," the *New York Times* reported in 1986, "it is easier to lunch on pho, a Vietnamese noodle soup with beef, than on a hamburger." In California, Asian Americans represent nearly 9 percent of the state's population, surpassing blacks in number.[3]

Today Asian Americans belong to the fastest-growing ethnic minority group in the United States. In percentage, they are increasing more rapidly than Hispanics (between 1970 and 1980 the Hispanic population increased by 38 percent, compared to 143 percent for the Asian population). The target of immigration exclusion laws in the nineteenth and early twentieth centuries, Asians have recently been coming again to America. The Immigration Act of 1965 reopened the gates to immigrants from Asia, allowing a quota of 20,000 immigrants for each country and also the entry of family members on a nonquota basis. Currently half of all immigrants entering annually are Asian. The recent growth of the Asian-American population has been dramatic: in 1960, there were only 877,934 Asians in the United States, representing a mere one half of one percent of the country's population. Twenty-five years later, they numbered over five million, or 2.1 percent of the population, an increase of 577 percent (compared to 34 percent for the general population). They included

1,079,000 Chinese, 1,052,000 Filipinos, 766,000 Japanese, 634,000 Vietnamese, 542,000 Koreans, 526,000 Asian Indians, 70,000 Laotians, 10,000 Mien, 60,000 Hmong, 161,000 Cambodians, and 169,000 other Asians. By the year 2000, Asian Americans are projected to represent 4 percent of the total U.S. population.[4]

Yet very little is known about Asian Americans and their history. In fact, stereotypes and myths of Asians as aliens and foreigners are pervasive in American society. During Lieutenant Colonel Oliver North's testimony before the joint House-Senate committee investigating the Iran-Contra scandal in 1987, co-chair Senator Daniel Inouye became the target of racial slurs: some of the telegrams and phone calls received by the committee told the senator he should "go home to Japan where he belonged." But Senator Inouye was born in the United States and had been awarded a Distinguished Service Cross for his valor as an American soldier during World War II. The belief that Americans do not include people with Asian ancestries is usually expressed more innocently, more casually. A white woman from New Jersey, for example, once raved to William Wong of the *Oakland Tribune* about a wonderful new Vietnamese restaurant in her town: "We were there the other night and we were the only Americans there." Wong noted with regret: "She probably meant the only white people."[5]

But her remark reveals a widely shared assumption in American culture — one that reflects and is reinforced by a narrow view of American history. Many existing history books give Asian Americans only passing notice or overlook them altogether. "When one hears Americans tell of the immigrants who built this nation," Congressman Norman Mineta of California recently observed, "one is often led to believe that all our forebearers came from Europe. When one hears stories about the pioneers going West to shape the land, the Asian immigrant is rarely mentioned."[6]

Sometimes Asian pioneers are even excluded from history. In 1987, the editor of *The Californians,* a popular history magazine published in San Francisco, announced the "Pioneer Prize" for the best essay submitted on the "California pioneers." "By 'pioneers,' " the editor explained, "we mean those Americans and Europeans who settled permanently in California between 1823 and 1869 (the year the transcontinental Central Pacific was completed)." But actually, the "pioneers" also included Asians: thousands of them helped to build the very transcontinental railroad referred to in the magazine's announcement, and many settled permanently in California. Many classics in the field of American history have also equated "American" with "white" or "European" in origin. In his prizewinning study, *The Uprooted,* Harvard historian Oscar Handlin presented — to use the book's subtitle — "the Epic Story of the Great Migrations That Made the American People." But Handlin's "epic story" completely left out the "uprooted" from lands across the Pacific Ocean and the "great migrations" from Asia that also helped to make "the American people." Eurocentric history serves no one. It only shrouds the pluralism that is America and that makes our nation so unique, and thus the possibility of appreciating our rich racial and cultural diversity remains a dream deferred. Actually, as Americans, we come originally from many different shores — Europe, the Americas, Africa, and also Asia.[7]

We need to "re-vision" history to include Asians in the history of America, and to do so in a broad and comparative way. How and why, we must ask, were the experiences of the various Asian groups — Chinese, Japanese, Korean, Filipino, Asian Indian, and Southeast Asian — similar to and different from one another? Cross-national comparisons can help us to identify the experiences particular to a group and to highlight the experiences common to all of them. Why did Asian immigrants leave everything they knew and loved to come to a strange world so far away? They were "pushed" by hardships in the homelands and "pulled" here by America's demand for their labor. But what were their own fierce dreams — from the first enterprising Chinese miners of the 1850s in search of "Gold Mountain" to the recent refugees fleeing frantically on helicopters and leaking boats from the ravages of war in Vietnam? Besides their points of origin, we need to examine the experiences of Asian Americans in different geographical regions, especially in Hawaii as compared to the mainland. Time of arrival has also shaped the lives and communities of Asian Americans. About one million people entered between the California gold rush of 1849 and the Immigration Act of 1924, which cut off immigration from Asian countries, and, after a hiatus of some forty years, a second group numbering about three and a half million came between 1965 and 1985. How do we compare the two waves of Asian immigration?

To answer our questions, we must not study Asian Americans primarily in terms of statistics and what was done to them. They are entitled to be viewed as subjects — as men and women with minds, wills, and voices. By "voices" we mean their own words and stories as told in their oral histories, conversations, speeches, soliloquies, and songs, as well as in their own writings — diaries, letters, news-papers, magazines, pamphlets, placards, posters, flyers, court peti-tions, autobiographies, short stories, novels, and poems. Their voices contain particular expressions and phrases with their own meanings and nuances, the cuttings from the cloth of languages.

For a long time, Asians in this country were not allowed to tell their stories, sometimes even to talk. In Maxine Hong Kingston's novel *China Men,* Bak Goong goes to Hawaii, where he is told by a foreman that laborers are not permitted to talk while working. "If I knew I had to take a vow of silence," he says to himself, "I would have shaved off my hair and become a monk." In the cane fields, he hears the boss shout: "Shut up. Go work. Chinaman, go work. You stay go work. Shut up." He is not even supposed to scream when he feels the sting of the whip on his shoulder. After work, resting in the camp away from the ears of the foreman, Bak Goong tells his fellow workers: "I will talk again. Listen for me." Among themselves they curse the white man on horseback: "Take — that — white — demon. Take — that. Fall — to — the — ground — demon. Cut — you — into — pieces. Chop — off — your — legs. Die — snake." Then, one day, the workers dig a wide hole and they flop on the ground "with their faces over the edge of the hole and their legs like wheel spokes." Suddenly their words come tumbling out: "Hello down there in China!" "Hello, Mother!" "I've been working hard for you, and I hate it." "I've become an opium addict." "I don't even look Chinese anymore." "I'm coming home by and by." "I'm not coming home." The men had, Kingston writes, "dug an ear into the world, and were telling their secrets."[8]

Today we need to fill the shouting holes, to listen to the Bak Goongs of the past and learn their secrets. Their stories can enable us to understand Asians as actors in the making of history and can give us a view from below — the subjective world of the immigrant experience. Detained at the Angel Island Immigration Station in San Francisco Bay, Chinese immigrants carved over a hundred poems on the walls of the barracks. One of them wrote:

> *I used to admire the land of the Flowery*
> *Flag as a country of abundance.*
> *I immediately raised money and started my*
> *journey.*
> *For over a month, I have experienced enough*
> *wind and waves. . . .*

> *I look up and see Oakland so close by. . . .*
> *Discontent fills my belly and it is difficult for*
>   *me to sleep.*
> *I just write these few lines to express what is*
>   *on my mind.*[9]

We need to know what was on the "minds" of the people. As scholars of a new social history have noted recently, so much of history has been the story of kings and elites, rendering invisible and silent the "little people." An Asian American told an interviewer: "I am a second generation Korean American without any achievements in life and I have no education. What is it you want to hear from me? My life is not worth telling to anyone." Similarly, a Chinese immigrant said: "You know, it seems to me there's no use in me telling you all this! I was just a simple worker, a farmworker around here. My story is not going to interest anybody." But others realize they are worthy of scholarly attention. "What is it you want to know?" an old Filipino immigrant asked a researcher. "Talk about history. What's that . . . ah, the story of my life . . . and how people lived with each other in my time."

> *Ay, manong*
> *your old brown hands*
> *hold life, many lives*
> *within each crack*
> *a story.*[10]

When the people recount what happened, they become animated and their stories — to use Joy Kogawa's wonderful phrase — "burst with telling." They understand why their stories need to be shared. "I hope this survey do a lot of good for Chinese people," a Chinese man told an interviewer from Stanford University in the 1920s. "Make American people realize that Chinese people are humans. I think very few American people really know anything about Chinese." Remembering the discrimination he experienced, an old manong explained: "You cannot avoid racism, it is hanging over every Filipino-American. There are still too many ignorant people." In the telling and retelling of their stories, the elderly immigrants reclaim the authorship of their own history. They want the younger generations to know about their experiences. "Our stories should be listened to by many young people," said a ninety-one-year-old retired Japanese plantation laborer. "It's for their sake. We really had a hard

time, you know." And when the listeners learn about their roots,
they feel enriched — members of a "community of memory":

> *Your intimate life,*
> *The story of your fight,*
> *Though not recorded*
> *In any history book,*
> *Yet lives engraved on my heart.*[11]

Their stories belong to our country's history and need to be
recorded in our history books, for they reflect the making of America
as a nation of immigrants, as a place where men and women came
to find a new beginning. Initially many Asian immigrants, probably
most of them, saw themselves as sojourners. But so did European
immigrants. The view of Asian immigrants as "sojourners" and European immigrants as "settlers" is both a mistaken notion and a
widely held myth. Large numbers of newcomers from both Asia and
Europe, in the beginning at least, planned to stay here only temporarily; many sojourning laborers had left their wives and children
behind in their homelands, intending to work in America for a few
years and then return to their families. Chinese women staying behind
in Guangdong sang lyrics of loss:

> *Dear husband, ever since you sojourned in a*
> *   foreign land.*
> *I've lost interest in all matters.*
> *All day long, I stay inside the bedroom, my*
> *   brows knitted;*
> *Ten thousand thoughts bring me endless remorse.*
> *In grief, in silence.*
> *I cannot fall asleep on my lonely pillow.*

Migratory Polish men also sang about the experience of separation
from their families:

> *When I journeyed from Amer'ca,*
> *And the foundry where I labored. . . .*
> *Soon I came to New York City,*
> *To the agent for my passage. . . .*
> *Then I left Berlin for Krakow;*
> *There my wife was waiting for me.*
> *And my children did not know me,*
> *For they fled from me, a stranger.*

> *"My dear children, I'm your papa;*
> *Three long years I have not seen you."*[12]

Actually, migrants from Europe returned to their homelands in sizable numbers. Between 1895 and 1918, according to historian Rowland Berthoff, 55 percent as many Englishmen returned home as left for the United States; the proportion was 46 percent for the Scots and 42 percent for the Irish. The rate of return migration was very high for many groups of European sojourners — 40 percent for Polish and 50 percent for Italians. In "Home-Going Italians," published in *Survey* in 1912, Victor Von Borosini reported: "Most Italians remain in the United States from two to five years." Greek migration reflected a similar return pattern. Of the 366,454 Greeks who arrived in America between 1908 and 1923, 46 percent returned to Greece. "A very small percentage of the Greek emigrants go to foreign countries with the intention of remaining there," reported the U.S. consul in Athens in 1903. "They all go abroad with the intention to return to their native land sooner or later." But many Greeks eventually stayed. "It came gradually," said a Greek who became a settler. "I got married, began to raise a family and was immobilized." For this Greek immigrant and thousands of compatriots like him, explained historian Theodore Saloutos, the decision to remain in the United States permanently came as "an afterthought." Similarly, 55 percent of the 200,000 Japanese who went to Hawaii between 1886 and 1924 returned to Japan. Most of them had left Japan as *dekaseginin,* intending to work only for a few years in Hawaii. But significantly, almost half of the Japanese stayed, becoming *imin,* or people moving permanently to another country.[13]

But, coming here from Asia, many of America's immigrants found they were not allowed to feel at home in the United States, and even their grandchildren and great-grandchildren still find they are not viewed and accepted as Americans. "We feel that we're a guest in someone else's house," said third-generation Ron Wakabayashi, National Director of the Japanese American Citizens League, "that we can never really relax and put our feet on the table."[14]

Behind Wakabayashi's complaint is the question, Why have Asian Americans been viewed and treated as outsiders? In his essay "The Stranger," sociologist Georg Simmel develops a theory, based on the experiences of Jews, to explain the discrimination and estrangement experienced by a group entering another society. Not belonging in the new place initially, the intruders bring qualities that are not indigenous. Not bound by roots to the new place, they are in a state of detachment, viewed as clannish, rigidly attached to their old country and their old culture. Their "strangeness" stands out more sharply as they settle down in the new land and become traders and merchants, for they still lack organic and established ties of kinship and locality. What is stressed in the host society is not the individuality of the newcomers but their alien origin, the qualities they share with one another as "strangers."[15]

While Simmel's theory is heuristic and insightful for the study of Asian Americans, it needs to be grounded in history — the particularities of time and place. What transformed Asians into "strangers" in America was not simply their migration to a foreign land and their lack of indigenous and organic ties to American society, but also their point of origin and their specific reception. Their experiences here, as they turned out in historical reality, were profoundly different from the experiences of European immigrants. To be sure, the immigrants who crossed the Atlantic Ocean suffered hardships and anguish. As historian John Higham has described so powerfully in *Strangers in the Land,* the Italians, Jews, Irish, and other European-immigrant groups were victims of labor exploitation, social ostracism, and the sharp barbs of intolerant American nativism. Nevertheless, immigrants of European ancestry had certain advantages in America. The promise of this new world for them, as F. Scott Fitzgerald portrayed it, was mythic: here an individual could remake himself — Gatz could become Gatsby. They could give themselves new identities by changing their names as did Doris Kapplehoff to Doris Day, Bernie Schwartz to Tony Curtis, Issur Danielovitch to Kirk Douglas, and Edmund Marcizewski to Ed Muskie. "America represented a new life, new hope, new perspective," observed J. N. Hook in his book *Family Names.* "Why not enter it with a new name, an 'American' name that would have no association with the life forever left behind." A new "American" name also opened the way for economic opportunities. "Some immigrants believed, rightly in some instances, that their chances for material success would be improved if their name did not betray their origins." Others became "Americans" mainly by shedding their past, their ethnicity — the language, customs, dress, and culture of the old country. Physically indistinguishable from old-stock whites in America, they were able to blend into the society of their adopted country.[16]

Asian immigrants could not transform themselves as felicitously, for they had come "from a different shore." In the present study, the term "shore" has multiple meanings. These men and women came from Asia across the Pacific rather than from Europe across the Atlantic. They brought Asian cultures rather than the traditions and ideas originating in the Greco-Roman world. Moreover, they had qualities they could not change or hide — the shape of their eyes, the color of their hair, the complexion of their skin. They were subjected not only to cultural prejudice, or ethnocentrism, but also racism. They wore what University of Chicago sociologist Robert E. Park termed a "racial uniform." Unlike the Irish and other groups from Europe, Asian immigrants could not become "mere individuals, indistinguishable in the cosmopolitan mass of the population." Regardless of their personal merits, they sadly discovered, they could not gain acceptance in the larger society. They were judged not by the content of their character but by their complexion. "The trouble is not with the Japanese mind but with the Japanese skin," wrote Park as he observed American-white attitudes in 1913. "The Jap is not the right color."[17]

"Color" in America operated within an economic context. Asian immigrants came here to meet demands for labor — plantation workers, railroad crews, miners, factory operatives, cannery workers, and farm laborers. Employers developed a dual-wage system to pay Asian laborers less than white workers and pitted the groups against each other in order to depress wages for both. "Ethnic antagonism" — to use Edna Bonacich's phrase — led white laborers to demand the restriction of Asian workers already here in a segregated labor market of low-wage jobs and the exclusion of future Asian immigrants. Thus the class interests of white capital as well as white labor needed Asians as "strangers."[18]

Pushed out of competition for employment by racial discrimination and white working-class hostility, many Asian immigrants became shopkeepers, merchants, and small businessmen. "There wasn't any other opportunity open to the Chinese," explained the son of a Chinese storekeeper. "Probably opening a store was one of the few things that they could do other than opening a laundry." Self-employment was not an Asian "cultural trait" or an occupation peculiar to "strangers" but a means of survival, a response to racial discrimination and exclusion in the labor market. The early Chinese and Japanese immigrants had been peasants in their home countries. Excluded from employment in the general economy, they *became* shopkeepers and ethnic enterprisers. They also developed their own separate commercial enclaves, which served as an economic basis for ethnic solidarity, and their business and cultural separateness in turn reinforced both their image and condition as "strangers."[19]

Unlike European immigrants, Asians were also victimized by the institutionalized racial discrimination of public policies. The Chinese Exclusion Act of 1882 singled out the Chinese on a racial basis, and the National Origins Act of 1924 totally prohibited Japanese immigration while permitting the annual entry of 17,853 from Ireland, 5,802 from Italy, and 6,524 from Poland. Furthermore, the 1924 law supported the formation of families in European-immigrant communities, allowing European-immigrant men to return to their homelands and bring wives back to the United States. Their wives were accorded nonquota status, that is, there were no limits to the number of European women who could come here as wives. The law had the very opposite effect on Asian-immigrant communities. Seeking to prevent the development of Asian families here, it barred the entry of women from China, Japan, Korea, and India. Even U.S. citizens could not bring Asian wives into the country, for the latter were classified as "aliens ineligible to citizenship" and hence inadmissible. While the 1924 law did not apply to Filipino immigration (because the Philippines was a territory of the United States), the Tydings-McDuffie Act of 1934 provided for the independence of the Philippines and limited Filipino immigration to fifty persons a year.[20]

The laws not only determined who could come to the United States but also who could become citizens. Decades before Asian immigration had even begun, this country had already defined by law the complexion of its citizens. The Naturalization Law of 1790 had specified that naturalized citizenship was to be reserved for "whites." This law remained in effect until 1952. Though immigrants from countries like Ireland and Italy experienced discrimination and nativist reactions, they nonetheless could become citizens of the United States. Citizenship is a prerequisite for suffrage — political power essential for groups to defend and advance their rights and interests. Unlike their European counterparts, Asian immigrants were not permitted to exercise power through the ballot and their own Tammany Halls. As "aliens ineligible to citizenship," they were also prohibited by the laws of many states from land ownership — the condition Frederick Jackson Turner celebrated as the foundation of democracy in America. One of the laws went even further. The 1922 Cable Act provided that any American woman who married "an alien ineligible to citizenship shall cease to be a citizen of the United States."[21]

During a revealing moment in the history of American citizenship, the line between white and nonwhite blurred briefly. Fleeing from genocide in their homelands, 50,000 Armenians had come to America in the early twentieth century. In 1909 federal authorities classified Armenians as "Asiatics" and denied naturalized citizenship to Armenian immigrants. But shortly afterward, in the *Halladjian* decision, a U.S. circuit court of appeals ruled that Armenians were Caucasian because of their ethnography, history, and appearance. Four years later California passed its alien land law, but the restriction did not apply to Armenians. By 1930, some 18,000 Armenians lived in the state; their access to landownership enabled many Armenians to become farmers in Fresno County. They became wealthy farmers — owners of vast acreage and leading producers of raisins. "The Armenians, they like the Japanese," recalled a Japanese farmer of Fresno. "Lots speak only Armenian — just like Issei [immigrant Japanese]. They came about the same time too. But I think they learned a little bit more English than the Japanese did and they looked more American and I think it helped them a lot." The experience of the Armenians illustrated the immense difference it made to be Caucasian and not "Asiatic."[22]

But the most terrible and tragic instance of this difference occurred during World War II. Setting aside the Constitution of the United States, President Franklin D. Roosevelt issued Executive Order 9066, which targeted Japanese Americans for special persecution and deprived them of their rights of due process and equal protection of the law. Unlike German Americans and Italian Americans, Japanese Americans were incarcerated in internment camps by the federal government. Even possession of U.S. citizenship did not protect rights and liberties guaranteed by the Constitution: two thirds of the 120,000 internees were American citizens by birth.[23]

Behind state policy lay a powerful traditional vision of America as a "homogeneous" nation. In a sermon given aboard the *Arbella*, John Winthrop told his fellow Puritans as they sailed to America in 1630 that they would be establishing a "city upon a hill," with the "eyes of the world" upon them. Their colony was to be a "new" England. This conception of the character and purpose of the English "errand" to the New World embraced a racial identity. "In the settlement of this country," historian Winthrop Jordan noted, "the red and black peoples served white men as aids to navigation by which they would find their safe positions as they ventured into America." The question of the relationship between race and nationality became immensely important as the colonies struggled for independence and transformed themselves into a new nation. In 1751 Benjamin Franklin offered his thoughts on the future complexion of American society in his essay *Observations Concerning the Increase of Mankind.* All Africa was black or "tawney," he noted, and Asia was chiefly "tawney." The English were the "principle Body of white People," and Franklin wished there were more of them in America. Why should we, he asked, "darken" the people of America: "Why increase the Sons of Africa, by Planting them in America, where we have so fair an opportunity, by excluding all Blacks and Tawneys, of increasing the lovely White?" After independence, one of the *Federalist Papers* announced: "Providence [had] been pleased to give this one connected country to one united people — a people descended from the same ancestors, speaking the same language, professing the same religion, attached to the same principles of government, very similar in their manners and customs." In a letter to James Monroe, President Thomas Jefferson wrote that he looked forward to distant times when the American continent would be covered with such a people. Earlier, in his *Notes on the State of Virginia,* Jefferson had identified the particular people who should occupy the new continent, saying he recoiled with horror from the possibility of "either blot or mixture on that surface" and advocating the removal of blacks from the United States. America, for Jefferson, was to be a "sanctuary" where immigrants from Europe would establish a new society for themselves and their progeny. Jefferson's hope for America was articulated over a hundred years later by the United States Supreme Court in the 1923 decision of *U.S. v. Bhagat Singh Thind.* Denying naturalized citizenship to Asian Indians because they were not "white," the Court noted the assimilability of European immigrants: "The children of English, French, German, Italian, Scandinavian, and other European parentage, quickly merge into the mass of our population and lose the distinctive hallmarks of their European origin."[24]

But America also had a counter tradition and vision, springing from the reality of racial and cultural diversity. It had been, as Walt Whitman celebrated so lyrically, "a teeming Nation of nations" composed of a "vast, surging, hopeful army of workers," a new society where all should be welcomed, "Chinese, Irish, German — all, all, without exceptions."

> *Passage O soul to India! . . .*
> *Tying the Eastern to the Western sea,*
> *The road between Europe and Asia. . . .*
> *Lands found and nations born, thou born America,*
> *For purpose vast, man's long probation fill'd,*
> *Thou rondure of the world at last accomplish'd. . . .*
> *Europe to Asia, Africa join'd, and they to the New*
> *World.*

The new society's diversity was portrayed by Herman Melville in his novel about the chase for the great white whale. The crew of the *Pequod* is composed of whites, blacks, Indians, Pacific Islanders, and Asians. As they work together, they are integrated in the labor process and united in a relationship of dependency, mutual survival, and cooperation. Nowhere is this connectedness more graphically illustrated than in the "monkey-rope," which is fastened to both Ishmael and Queequeg. Lowered down to the water to secure the blubber hook onto the dead whale, with vicious sharks swirling around it, Queequeg is held by a rope tied to Ishmael. The process is perilous for both men. "We two, for the time," Ishmael tells us, "were wedded; and should poor Queequeg sink to rise no more, then both usage and honor demanded, that instead of cutting the cord, it should drag me down in his wake." There is a noble class unity among the crew, and the working class aboard the *Pequod* is saluted. An "ethereal light" shines on the "workman's arm," and the laborers are ascribed "high qualities" and "democratic dignity." In the early twentieth century, a Japanese immigrant described in poetry a lesson that had been learned by farm laborers of different nationalities — Japanese, Filipino, Mexican, and Asian Indian:

> *People harvesting*
> *Work together unaware*
> *Of racial problems.*

A Filipino-immigrant laborer in California expressed a similar hope and understanding. America was, Macario Bulosan told his brother Carlos, "not a land of one race or one class of men" but "a new world" of respect and unconditional opportunities for all who toiled and suffered from oppression, from "the first Indian that offered peace in Manhattan to the last Filipino pea pickers."[25]

Asians migrated east to America. For them, the first glimpse of what F. Scott Fitzgerald poetically described as this "fresh, green breast of the new world" was not the Statue of Liberty but the ancient volcanoes of Hawaii reaching from the ocean toward the sky, Mount Rainier rising majestically behind the port city of Seattle, and the brown hills of California sloping gently toward the sea touching Asia. For these arriving men and women, the immigration station was not on Ellis Island but Oahu, Hawaii, and Angel Island in San Francisco Bay. But like Fitzgerald's Dutch sailors seeing the new land for the first time in the seventeenth century, Asian immigrants, too, must have held their breath in the presence of this continent.[26]

America represented liminality, and the Asian immigrants' actions enabled them to make history even in conditions they did not choose. In their trans-Pacific odyssey, they "crossed boundaries not delineated in space." Their migration broke the "cake of custom" and placed them within a new dynamic and transitional context, an ambiguous situation "betwixt and between all fixed points of classification." They reached a kind of geographical and cultural margin where old norms became detached, and they found themselves free for new associations and new enterprises. In America, Asian immigrants encountered long hours of labor and racial discrimination, but they did not permit exterior demands to determine wholly the direction and quality of their lives. Energies, pent up in the old countries, were unleashed, and they found themselves pursuing urges and doing things they had thought beyond their capabilities. They had not read John Locke, but they, too, believed that "in the beginning, all the world was America." Like the immigrants from Europe, many Asians saw America as a place for a fresh start. They came here, as Filipino immigrant Carlos Bulosan expressed it, searching for "a door into America" and seeking "to build a new life with untried materials." "Would it be possible," he asked, "for an immigrant like me to become a part of the American dream?" The hopeful question also contained deep doubt, for Bulosan and his fellow Asian immigrants knew they were "strangers from a different shore."[27]

I

EXTRAVAGANCE

My first sight of the approaching land was an exhilarating experience. . . . Everything seemed familiar and kind — the white faces of the buildings melting into the soft afternoon sun, the gray contours of the surrounding valleys that seemed to vanish in the last periphery of light. With a sudden surge of joy, I knew that I must find a home in this new land.

Carlos Bulosan

My father sold me when I was seven years old; my mother cried. He seemed very sad, and when he went away he gave me a few cash, and wished me prosperity. That was the last time I saw him. I was sold four times. I came to California about five years ago.

Sing Kum

Day of spacious dreams!
I sailed for America,
Overblown with hope.

Ichiyo[1]

2

Overblown with Hope

The First Wave of Asian Immigration

"Get Labor First": The American Errand into the Wilderness

On the island of Kauai in 1835, a young man from Boston visited a small sugar mill where he noticed the presence of a few Chinese workers. William Hooper had been sent to this remote tropical island, still in a state of nature, by a Honolulu mercantile firm founded by New England businessmen. His mission was to establish the first sugar plantation in Hawaii. Hooper belonged to Euro-American efforts to colonize the islands, which had been unknown to whites until Captain James Cook had accidentally sailed across the archipelago in 1778. The Chinese laborers, the Yankee enterpriser reported to his company on March 28, worked six days a week, "making about 210 lb sugar per day & molasses by the cord. They could make four times as much by increasing the size of kettles. . . . They have to work *all* the time — and no regard is paid to their complaints for food, etc., etc. Slavery is nothing compared to it."[1]

A few months later, Hooper began operations for his plantation. Initially he hired twenty-five Hawaiian natives, and, on September 12, he noted in his diary: "Laid out a piece of land supposed to contain 12 acres to be cultivated with cane." He was pleased with his small but nonetheless portentous effort to transform the lush wilderness into ordered rows of cane fields. A year later, in his diary, he proudly listed his accomplishments: twenty houses for the natives, a house for the superintendent, a sugar mill, and twenty-five acres of cane under cultivation. He also recorded the moral purpose behind his energetic enterprise:

Just one year to day since I commenced work on this plantation, during which I have had more annoyances from the chiefs and difficulties with the natives (from the fact of this land being the first that has ever been cultivated, on the plan of *free* labour, at these islands) than I ever tho't it possible for one white man to bear, nevertheless I have succeeded in bringing about a place, which if followed up by other foreign residents, will eventually emancipate the natives from the miserable system of "chief labour" which has ever existed at these Islands, and which if not broken up, will be an effectual preventitive to the progress of civilization, industry and national prosperity. . . . The tract of land in Koloa was [developed] after much pain . . . for the purpose of breaking up the system aforesaid or in other words to serve as an entering wedge . . . [to] upset the whole system.[2]

A "white man" determined to advance the "progress of civilization," Hooper soon became frustrated by the inefficiency and recalcitrance of the Hawaiian laborers and began to employ a few Chinese. He quickly saw the enormous potential of an immigrant Chinese labor force. In a letter to Ladd and Company in 1836, he advised: "We may deem it at a future day, necessary to locate some halfdozen Chinese on the land, if the establishment grows it will require them. The superintendent cannot feed the mill, boil the juice, make sugar, etc., and to trust it to the natives is worse than nothing." Two years later, Hooper urged his company to import Chinese laborers. "A colony of Chinese would, probably, put the plantation in order," he predicted, "to be perpetuated, sooner and with less trouble than any other class of husbandmen."[3]

Ten years later, shortly after the war against Mexico and the annexation of California in 1848, an American policymaker called for the importation of Chinese laborers to the United States. In his plan submitted to Congress, Aaron H. Palmer recommended the development of steam transportation in the Pacific and the establishment of San Francisco as the center of American trade with China. Connected by railroad to the Atlantic states, San Francisco would become the "great emporium of our commerce on the Pacific." Chinese laborers, Palmer continued, should be imported to build the transcontinental railroad as well as to bring the fertile lands of California under cultivation. "No people in all the East are so well adapted for clearing wild lands and raising every species of agricultural product . . . as the Chinese."[4]

Both Hooper and Palmer shared a peculiarly white-American world view. Like John Winthrop before them, they felt a moral compulsion not to let the land "lie in waste." Their vision of Chinese cultivating cane in Hawaii and building railroads and clearing lands in the West reflected a significant theme of American history — what the perspicacious scholar Perry Miller described as "the errand into the wilderness." From the very beginning, the English settlement of America embraced a sense of mission. The colonists had come to remake the new world in their own image. The process, as it turned out, would be both ideological and economic, involving the cultural and physical transformation of the terrain. During the nineteenth century, the errand was extended westward across the Indian lands and Mexican territory to a new Pacific frontier. By 1848 the United States was poised on the western edge of the continent, ready to advance the "entering wedge" of its market civilization into Asia. Five years later, Commodore Matthew C. Perry sailed his warships into Edo Bay and coerced Japan at cannon point to open its doors to American "friendship" and "commerce." In 1898 the United States annexed the Republic of Hawaii and forcefully took the Philippines away from Spain.[5]

Like Mark Twain's Connecticut Yankee, Hooper and Palmer wielded both Protestant morality and technological power in the service of American "progress." In Twain's story, the Connecticut Yankee travels backward through time to King Arthur's court. He quickly takes command and transforms this idyllic and pre-industrial society into a modern world of railroads, steamboats, telegraph systems, and smoking factories. The Yankee also puts everyone to work, for in his new regime, imbued with a spirit of capitalism and armed with technological knowledge, there is to be no idleness. Even the religious hermit, standing all day on a pillar and constantly bowing his body to his feet in prayer, is not allowed to pray without being productive. A system of elastic cords is attached to him and his movements are utilized to power a sewing machine. "Necessity" would rule in the Yankee's kingdom. Similarly, Hooper and Palmer were representatives of an expansionist America. Determined to bring a modern industrial order of productivity to the Pacific frontier, they confidently thought America's "destiny" was "manifest": the West would become a great locus of "industry and national prosperity." Crucial for this transformation would be the entry of "strangers from a different shore" — from China as well as Japan, Korea, the Philippines, and India.[6]

*   *   *

"Get labor first," sugar planters in Hawaii calculated, "and capital will follow." During the second half of the nineteenth century, they ushered in a modern economy and made sugar "King." Mostly American businessmen and sons of American missionaries, the planters transformed this archipelago into a virtual economic colony of the United States. They were instrumental in arranging the 1875 Reciprocity Treaty between the governments of Hawaii and the United States, which permitted the island kingdom to export sugar to America duty free. Investments in cane growing became a "mania," and the production of sugar jumped from 9,392 tons in 1870 to 31,792 tons ten years later to nearly 300,000 tons in 1900. Between 1875 and 1910, cultivated plantation lands multiplied nearly eighteen times, or from 12,000 to 214,000 acres. Sugar was Hawaii's most important export: in 1897, a year before the United States annexed the islands, sugar exports accounted for $15.4 million out of an export total of $16.2 million.[7]

Before this tremendous growth of the sugar industry could occur, planters had to find labor. They were reluctant to invest capital in sugar production as long as they had to depend on Hawaiian labor. Native workers were not abundantly available because their population had been declining precipitously for several decades. Moreover, Hawaiian workers generally were not easily disciplined; farming and fishing offered them alternative means of survival. In 1850 planters founded the Royal Hawaiian Agricultural Society to introduce workers from China. Two years later, after the arrival of the first Chinese contract laborers, the president of the society predicted: "We shall find Coolie labor to be far more certain, systematic, and economic than that of the native. They are prompt at the call of the bell, steady in their work, quick to learn, and will accomplish more [than Hawaiian laborers]." To satisfy their demand for labor, planters scoured the world — mainly Asia, but also Europe — in search of workers.[8]

Planters viewed laborers as commodities necessary for the operation of the plantation. To their labor suppliers, the Honolulu mercantile houses such as Castle and Cooke and Theo. H. Davies and Company, they submitted requisitions for men and material. On July 2, 1890, for example, the Davies Company sent C. McLennan, manager of the Laupahoehoe Plantation, a memorandum acknowledging receipt of an order for

bonemeal
canvas
Japanese laborers
macaroni
a Chinaman

In another letter to McLennan, January 3, 1898, the Davis Company confirmed a list of orders, which included: "DRIED BLOOD [fertilizer]," "LABORERS. We will book your order for 75 Japanese to come as soon as possible," and "MULES & HORSES." On October 12, 1894, William G. Irwin and Company wrote to George C. Hewitt of the Hutchinson Plantation to acknowledge receipt of orders for pipe coverings, insulators, bolts, bone meal (three hundred tons), and Chinese laborers (forty men). On May 5, 1908, the vice president of H. Hackfeld and Company sent George Wilcox of the Grove Farm Plantation on Kauai a letter with itemized sections listing, alphabetically, orders for

Fertilizer
Filipinos. . . . [9]

In their orders for laborers, planters systematically developed an ethnically diverse work force as a mechanism of control. During the 1850s, they used Chinese laborers to set an "example" for the Hawaiian workers. Managers hoped the Hawaiians would be "naturally jealous" of the foreigners and "ambitious" to outdo them. They encouraged the Chinese to call the native workers "wahine! wahine!" [Hawaiian for "women! women!"][10]

Three decades later, realizing they had become too dependent on Chinese laborers, planters turned to Portuguese workers. "We need them," they explained, "especially as an offset to the Chinese. . . . We lay great stress on the necessity of having our labor mixed. By employing different nationalities, there is less danger of collusion among laborers, and the employers [are able to] secure better discipline." Meanwhile, planters initiated the importation of Japanese laborers as "the principle check upon the Chinese, in keeping down the price of labor." During the 1890s, planters recruited laborers from both China and Japan, thinking "discipline would be easier and labor more tractable if Chinese were present or obtainable in sufficient numbers to play off against the Japanese in case of disputes."[11]

Diversity was deliberately designed to break strikes and repress unions. Complaining about the frequency of strikes on plantations where the workers were mostly from the same country, plantation manager Robert Hall recommended a "judicious mixture [of nationalities] to modify the effect of a strike." Similarly manager George F. Renton advised his fellow planters to employ as many different nationalities as possible on each plantation in order to "offset" the power of any one nationality of workers. Bluntly stating the planters' divide-and-rule strategy, manager George H. Fairfield declared: "Keep a variety of laborers, that is different nationalities, and thus prevent any concerted action in case of strikes, for there are few, if any, cases of Japs, Chinese, and Portuguese entering into a strike as a unit." On September 26, 1896, in a letter to planter George Wilcox, H. Hackfield and Company stated confidentially: "Regarding the proportion of Chinese and Japanese laborers we beg to advise, that the Hawaiian Sugar Planters' Association and the Bureau of Immigration have agreed upon 2/3rd of the former and 1/3 of the latter. For your *private* information we mention, that the reason for this increasing the percentage of the Chinese laborers is due to the desire of breaking up the preponderance of the Japanese element."[12]

Four years later, however, planters could no longer import Chinese laborers, for Hawaii had been annexed to the United States and federal laws prohibiting Chinese immigration had been extended to the new territory. Worried the "Japs" were "getting too numerous," planters scrambled for new sources of labor. "There is a movement on foot [sic]," wrote the director of H. Hackfield and Company to planter Wilcox on December 22, 1900, "to introduce Puerto Rican laborers, and also some Italians, Portuguese, and Negroes from the South.... We would ask you to let us know at your earliest convenience how many laborers of each nationality you need." A year later, planters transported two hundred blacks from Tennessee to Hawaii.[13]

But planters preferred to "mix the labor races" by dividing the work force "about equally between two Oriental nationalities." Consequently, they turned to Korea as a new source of Asian labor, and they developed a plan to import Koreans and "pit" them against the "excess of Japanese." In 1903, they introduced Korean workers on the plantations, certain the Koreans were "not likely to combine with the Japanese at any attempt at strikes." An official of William G. Irwin and Company, a labor supplier, predicted: "The Korean immigration scheme which has been inaugurated will in due course give us an element which will go far towards not only assisting labor requirements but will be of great service in countering the evil effects in the labor market caused by too great a preponderance of Japanese." A planter, angry at Japanese workers for demanding higher wages, asked William G. Irwin and Company to send him a shipment of Korean laborers soon: "In our opinion, it would be advisable, as soon as circumstances permit, to get a large number of Koreans in the country . . . and drive the Japs out."[14]

But the Korean labor supply was cut off when the Korean government prohibited emigration to Hawaii in 1905. A year later, the planters began bringing laborers from the Philippines, a U.S. territory acquired from Spain after the 1898 war. Labor recruiter Albert F. Judd, displaying the first group of Filipino laborers on the dock in Honolulu, promised that if the Filipino were treated right, he would be a "first-class laborer," "possibly not as good as the Chinaman or the Jap, but steady, faithful and willing to do his best for any boss for whom he has a liking." Shortly afterward planters imported massive numbers of Filipino workers. The 1908 Gentlemen's Agreement restricted the emigration of Japanese laborers and the 1909 Japanese strike threatened planter control of the work force. During the strike, on July 28, 1909, the labor committee of the Hawaiian Sugar Planters' Association reported that several hundred Filipino laborers were en route to Hawaii: "It may be too soon to say that the Jap is to be supplanted, but it is certainly in order to take steps to clip his wings [and to give] encouragement to a new class [Filipinos] . . . to keep the more belligerent element in its proper place." Again, like the Chinese and Koreans, the Filipinos were used to control and discipline Japanese workers. One planter, for example, complained to C. Brewer and Company about the high wages demanded by the Japanese laborers on his plantation. On August 7, he wrote to the company: "If possible for you to arrange it I should very much like to get say 25 new Filipinos to put into our day gang. . . . In this way perhaps we can stir the Japs a bit." Twenty days later, he wrote again, stating that he was very pleased to receive the shipment of thirty Filipinos and that he hoped he could use them to bring the Japanese workers to "their senses."[15]

Like the planters in Hawaii, businessmen on the U.S. mainland were aware of the need to "get labor first." Many of them saw that advances in technology had transformed Asia into a new source of labor for American capitalism. Steam transportation had brought Asia to America's "door" and given American industries access to the "surplus" labor of "unnumbered millions" in Asia. "Cheap" Chinese labor was now "available." In an article entitled, "Our Manufacturing Era," published in the *Overland Monthly* in 1869, Henry Robinson described California's enormous economic potential: it had every variety of climate and soil for the production of raw material, a nearly completed railroad, an abundance of fuel and water power, markets in Asia and the Pacific, and an unlimited supply of low-wage labor from China. "If society must have 'mudsills,' it is certainly better to take them from a race which would be benefitted by even that position in a civilized community, than subject a portion of our own race to a position which they have outgrown." Robinson concluded: "If Chinese labor could be used to develop the industries of California, it would be the height of folly to forbid its entrance to the Golden Gate." A California farmer stated frankly that he could not get white labor to do stoop labor in the fields: "I must employ Chinamen or give up." Noting the need for Chinese workers for the railroads, agriculture, and manufacturing, San Francisco minister Otis Gibson reported in 1877 that there was a constant demand for Chinese labor all over the Pacific Coast because reliable white labor was not available at wages capital could afford to pay.[16]

Like the planters in Hawaii, employers of Chinese labor and their supporters had also devised a divide-and-control strategy. Railroad builder Charles Crocker described how Chinese workers could help to defuse the white labor movement by offering white workers hopes of becoming capitalists themselves: "I think that every white man who is intelligent and able to work . . . who has the capacity of being something else, can get to be something else by the presence of Chinese labor easier than he could without it. . . . After we got Chinamen to work, we took the more intelligent of the white laborers and made foremen of them. Several of them who never expected, never had a dream that they were going to be anything but shovelers of dirt, hewers of wood and drawers of water are now respectable farmers, owning farms. They got a start by controlling Chinese labor on our railroad."[17]

But the Chinese could also be pitted against and used to discipline white workers. E. L. Godkin of *The Nation* predicted that the importation of Chinese labor would become a favorite method of resisting white workers' strikes now that American capital had within its reach millions of Chinese "ready to work for small wages." In California, a traveler reported in 1870: "In the factories of San Francisco they had none but Irish, paying them three dollars a day in gold. They struck, and demanded four dollars. Immediately their places, numbering three hundred, were supplied by Chinamen at one dollar a day." Capital used Chinese laborers as a transnational industrial reserve army to weigh down white workers during periods of economic expansion and to hold white labor in check during periods of overproduction. Labor was a major cost of production, and employers saw how the importation of Chinese workers could boost the supply of labor and drive down the wages of both Chinese and white workers. The resulting racial antagonism generated between the two groups helped to ensure a divided working class and a dominant employer class.[18]

Six years after the Chinese Exclusion Act of 1882, Japanese labor was introduced: sixty Japanese were brought to Vacaville to pick fruit. During the 1890s, the demand for farm labor rose sharply with the development of sugar-beet agriculture. By the turn of the century, farmers in California were complaining about tons of fruit and vegetables rotting in the fields as a result of the labor shortage, and increasingly they were employing Japanese to meet their labor needs. Testifying before a congressional committee in 1907, sugar-beet king John Spreckels said: "If we do not have the Japs to do the field labor, we would be in a bad fix, because you know American labor will not go into the fields." Farmers saw another advantage in the use of Japanese labor. "The Japs just drift — we don't have to look out for them," explained an official of the California Fruit Growers' Exchange. "White laborers with families, if we could get them, would be liabilities."[19]

By then, however, farmers were facing demands for higher wages from Japanese workers. In 1907, the *California Fruit Grower* complained that "the labor problem" had become "extremely troublesome." Labor was in shortage and employers had been forced to increase wages. What was needed, the journal recommended, was the introduction of Asian-Indian laborers. "Not long ago a small colony of full-blooded Sikhs arrived from India, some of whom are now working in Fresno vineyards. . . . A report is current that a scheme is on foot [sic] to railroad these people into the United States by hordes. . . ." A year later California farmers employed Asian Indians as "a check on the Japanese," paying them twenty-five cents less per day. Shortly after the introduction of Sikh laborers in 1908, John Spreckels told a congressional committee that "if it had not been for the large number of these East Indians coming in there . . . we would have had to take all Japs."[20]

During the 1920s, farmers turned to Mexico as their main source of labor: at least 150,000 of California's 200,000 farm laborers were Mexican. An official for the California Fruit Growers' Association praised the Mexican workers. Unlike the Chinese and Japanese, they were "not aggressive." Instead they were "amenable to suggestions" and did their work obediently. Fearful Mexicans would be placed on a quota basis under the Immigration Act of 1924, growers began to import Filipino laborers, for the Philippines was a territory of the United States and represented an unimpeded supply of labor. "The Filipinos," reported the *Pacific Rural Press*, "are being rushed in as the Mexicans are being rushed out." In 1929 the Commonwealth Club of California stated that the "threat of Mexican exclusion" had created an "artificial demand for Filipino laborers," the "only remaining substitute in the cheap labor field." A representative of the Watsonville Chamber of Commerce told an interviewer in 1930: "We don't want the Filipino and Mexican excluded. Raising the crops that we do it is necessary to have a supply of this labor."[21]

Nor did California farmers want other groups of workers excluded, for a racially diverse labor force enabled them to exercise greater control over their workers. Frank Waterman of the state employment agency told an interviewer in 1930 how farmers could get a maximum amount of work out of Japanese and Chinese workers: "Put a gang of Chinese in one field and a gang of Japanese in the next, and each one works like hell to keep up with or keep ahead of the other." Noting the presence of Mexican, Chinese, Japanese, Asian Indian, Portuguese, Korean, Puerto Rican, and Filipino farm workers, the California Department of Industrial Relations reported that growers preferred to employ "a mixture of laborers of various races, speaking diverse languages, and not accustomed to mingling with each other. The practice [was] intended to avoid labor trouble which might result from having a homogeneous group of laborers of the same race or nationality. Laborers speaking different languages [were] not as likely to arrive at a mutual understanding which would lead to strikes."[22]

The Asian labor migrations to Hawaii and the United States represented an "industrial reserve army." But the actual operation of this labor supply was more complex than Karl Marx had imagined: it was transnational and racial. International labor migrations occurred within what Immanuel Wallerstein called the "modern world-system" of capitalism. Constituting the center of commerce and manufacturing production, "core" nations like the United States, England, France, Spain, and Portugal penetrated politically and economically the less-developed, "semi-peripheral" areas of Asia, Africa, and Latin America in their search for new markets, raw materials, and sources of labor. European and American colonialism disrupted economies there and also increased problems of poverty. The "necessities" of the "modern world-system" powered international labor migrations, "pushing" workers from Africa and Asia and "pulling" them to Latin America, the West Indies, and the United States. As Lucie Cheng and Edna Bonacich have argued, Asian labor immigration to America took place "under capitalism." Actually, so did the movement of European laborers to this country. But coming from "a different shore," Asian immigrants constituted a unique laboring army of "strangers," to use Georg Simmel's term: of alien origin, they were brought here to serve as an "internal colony" — nonwhites allowed to enter as "cheap" migratory laborers and members of a racially subordinated group, not future citizens of American society.[23]

But the context of the "modern world-system" and its economic forces only partly explains the Asian migrations to America. While the Asian immigrants did not choose the material circumstances of their times, most of them still made choices regarding the futures of their lives and therefore made history. The laborers themselves had their own view of "diversity": they did not come here to fill the "orders" of businessmen, which listed requisitions for labor and fertilizer. Nor did they come to be pitted against workers of other nationalities and to break strikes, nor to depress the wages of white workers, nor to be the "mudsills" of American society. Though driven by "necessity," they were also stirred by "extravagance." What were their "spacious dreams" and their "overblown hopes"?[24]

Tan Heung Shan and Gam Saan

They went as *wah gung*, Chinese laborers, as sojourners hopeful they would be able to work in a foreign country and return home rich in three to five years. They had given names to their lands of destination — *Tan Heung Shan* (the "Fragrant Sandalwood Hills") for the Hawaiian Islands and *Gam Saan* ("Gold Mountain") for California. Beginning in the 1840s and 1850s, they departed by the tens of thousands — about 46,000 to Hawaii in the second half of the nineteenth century and about 380,000 to the U.S. mainland between 1849 and 1930. The Chinese already had a long history of movement overseas. By the seventeenth century, there were 10,000 Chinese in Thailand and 20,000 in the Philippines. Chinese migrants defied the laws of the central governments of the Ming and Ch'ing dynasties, which prohibited overseas travel on pain of death. But the greatest outflow of Chinese occurred in the nineteenth century: between 1840 and 1900, an estimated two and a half million people left China. They went to Hawaii and the United States as well as to Canada, Australia, New Zealand, Southeast Asia, the West Indies, South America, and Africa.

Most of the Chinese migrants to the Kingdom of Hawaii and the United States were from Guangdong (Kwangtung province). Many of them sought sanctuary from intense conflicts — the British Opium Wars of 1839–1842 and 1856–1860, the peasant rebellions such as the Red Turban Rebellion (1854–1864), the bloody strife between the *Punti* ("Local People") and the *Hakkas* ("Guest People") over possession of the fertile delta lands, and class and family feuds within villages. "Ever since the disturbances caused by the Red [Turban] bandits and the Kejia bandits," a government report noted, "dealings with foreigners have increased greatly. The able-bodied go abroad. The fields are clogged with weeds." Forced to flee from the violence and turmoil, they felt "pushed" from their home country.[25]

One Chinese migrant described this expulsion:

> In a bloody feud between the Chang family and the Oo Shak village we lost our two steady workmen. Eighteen villagers were hired by Oo Shak to fight against the huge Chang family, and in the battle two men lost their lives protecting our pine forests. Our village, Wong Jook Long, had a few resident Changs. After the bloodshed, we were called for our men's lives, and the greedy, impoverished villagers grabbed fields, forest, food and everything, including newborn pigs, for payment. We were left with nothing, and in disillusion we went to Hong Kong to sell ourselves as contract laborers.

Another migrant remembered a battle "between our people and those called *Hakkas*. . . . These *Hakkas* had come from the far north many years ago and had settled in a village not far from ours. . . . They were quite different. They spoke a distinct dialect . . . and their women had natural feet and worked in the fields alongside of their men-folk. They were good fighters, and we had to flee for safety."[26]

But most of the migrants were driven by harsh economic conditions to seek survival elsewhere, in another country. Forced to pay large indemnities to the Western imperialist powers engaged in the Opium Wars, the Qing government imposed high taxes on the peasant farmers; unable to pay their taxes, many lost their lands. Displaced from the land, they were unable to find employment in the already-limited industrial sector as foreign competition, imposed on China after the Opium Wars, undermined domestic industries such as textile production. The hardships were particularly severe in Guangdong, where the population had increased by 76 percent — from sixteen million in 1787 to twenty-eight million in 1850. The population-land ratio in the province was worse than the national average: 1.67 *mou* (0.15 acres) per person compared to 2.19 *mou*. Floods intensified the problem of poverty and hunger. "The rains have been falling for forty days until the rivers, and the sea, and the lakes, and the streams have joined in one sheet over the land for several hundred *li* [a *li* being equal to one third of a mile]," the 1847 annual memorial to the emperor reported, "and there is no outlet by which the waters may retire." Behind the emigrating spirit, an observer explained in 1852, was starvation: "The population is extremely dense; the means of subsistence, in ordinary times, are seldom above the demand, and, consequently, the least failure of the rice crop produces wretchedness." One of the migrants gave his own account of the painful events leading to emigration:

> There were four in our family, my mother, my father, my sister and me. We lived in a two room house. Our sleeping room and the other served as parlor, kitchen and dining room. We were not rich enough to keep pigs or fowls, otherwise, our small house would have been more than overcrowded.
>
> How can we live on six baskets of rice which were paid twice a year for my father's duty as a night watchman? Sometimes the peasants have a poor crop then we go hungry. . . . Sometimes we went hungry for days. My mother and me would go over the harvested rice fields of the peasants to pick the grains they dropped. . . . We had only salt and water to eat with the rice.[27]

Learning about *Tan Heung Shan* and *Gam Saan,* many of the younger, more impatient, and more courageous men left their villages for the distant lands. The majority of them were married. The migrants were generally illiterate or had very little schooling, but they dreamed of new possibilities for themselves inspired by stories about the "gold hills." In 1848, shortly after the discovery of gold at John

Sutter's mill, a young man in Canton wrote to his brother engaged in the tea trade in Boston: "Good many Americans speak of California. Oh! Very rich country! I hear good many Americans and Europeans go there. Oh! They find gold very quickly, so I hear. . . . I feel as if I should like to go there very much. I think I shall go to California next summer." A witness in China described the excitement generated by the news of the gold rush: "Letters from Chinese in San Francisco and further in the country have been circulated through all this part of the province. The accounts of the successful adventurers who have returned would, had the inhabitants possessed the means of paying their way across, have gone far to depopulate considerable towns."[28]

Gam Saan promised not only gold to be mined but also opportunities for employment. In the port cities, circulars distributed by labor brokers announced: "Americans are very rich people. They want the Chinaman to come and make him very welcome. There you will have great pay, large houses, and food and clothing of the finest description. . . . It is a nice country, without mandarins or soldiers. . . . Money is in great plenty and to spare in America." The Chinese who returned to their villages with money made in Hawaii and America reinforced the excitement of emigration. Sixteen-year-old Lee Chew witnessed the triumphant return of a Chinese migrant from the "country of the American wizards." With the money he had earned overseas, he bought land as spacious as "four city blocks" and built a palace on it. He also invited his fellow villagers to a grand party where they were served a hundred roasted pigs, along with chickens, ducks, geese, and an abundance of dainties. The young Lee was inspired, eager to go to America himself.[29]

America seemed so beckoning. "After leaving the village," an immigrant said, "I went to Hong Kong and stayed at a *gam saan jong* ["golden mountain firm"] owned by people named Quan. I stayed there ten days to take care of the paper work for passage. At that time all I knew was that *gam saan haak* ["travelers to the golden mountain"] who came back were always rich." During the 1860s, a Chinese laborer might earn three to five dollars a month in South China; in California, he could work for the railroad and make thirty dollars a month. A popular saying of the time promised that if a sojourner could not save a thousand dollars, he would surely obtain at least eight hundred. But even with a saving of three hundred dollars he could return to China and become "a big, very big gentleman." A folk song expressed the emotions of many *gam saan haak*:

> *In the second reign year of Haamfung [1852], a trip*
> *to Gold Mountain was made.*
> *With a pillow on my shoulder, I began my perilous*
> *journey:*
> *Sailing a boat with bamboo poles across the sea,*
> *Leaving behind wife and sisters in search of money,*
> *No longer lingering with the woman in the bedroom,*
> *No longer paying respect to parents at home.*[30]

But how could poor peasants afford to go to the Kingdom of Hawaii and America? The Chinese migrants were told they did not need much money to get there. They could choose to go as contract laborers to Hawaii: under arrangements made by emigration brokers representing sugar planters, they could have "free passage" to the islands, where they would sign labor agreements to work for a planter for a term of five years and receive in return wages, shelter, food, and medical care.

Or they could go to the United States as free laborers under the credit-ticket system. Under this arrangement, a broker would loan money to a migrant for the ticket for passage, and the latter in turn would pay off the loan plus interest out of his earnings in the new country. Chung Kun Ai recalled how his grandfather went into such moneylending as a business venture: "One condition of his loan of $60 was that each borrower was to pay back $120 as soon as he was able to do so. In all, grandfather must have helped 70 young men from our village and nearby villages to migrate to North and South America and also Australia."[31]

Describing how the "Chinese poor" were able to come to California, Chinese merchants in San Francisco explained in 1852:

> Some have borrowed the small amount necessary, to be returned with unusual interest, on account of the risk; some have been furnished with money without interest by their friends and relations, and some again, but much the smaller portion, have received advances in money, to be returned out of the profits of the adventure. The usual apportionment of the profits is about three tenths to the lender of the money. . . . These arrangements, made at home, seldom bring them farther than San Francisco, and here the Chinese traders furnish them the means of getting to the mines.

Contrary to a popular stereotype and myth, the Chinese migrants were not "coolies." Thousands of Chinese were taken to Peru and

Cuba as "coolies" — unfree laborers who had been kidnapped or pressed into service by coercion and shipped to foreign countries. But the Chinese migrants in the United States came voluntarily. Some Chinese paid their own way, and probably most of them borrowed the necessary funding under the credit-ticket system. "The Chinese emigration to California," reported a British official stationed in Hong Kong in 1853, "was, by and large, free and voluntary. The Chinese emigration to California is now almost wholly confined to independent emigrants who pay their own passage money, and are in a condition to look to their arrangements." William Speer, who worked as a missionary in San Francisco's Chinatown for decades, beginning in the 1850s, never found evidence that Chinese laborers had been "brought over by capitalists and worked as slaves . . . against their will." The claim that the Chinese were "coolies," Speer declared, was a "fiction."[32]

The Chinese migration also included merchants — daring businessmen seeking new opportunities for enterprise in foreign lands. One of them was the father of Koon Keu Young, my stepfather. While maintaining his business operations in Guangdong, he went to Hawaii, where he opened two grocery stores in Honolulu, importing goods and foods from China. After he had successfully established both stores, he brought two of his sons to Hawaii to run the businesses and then returned to China. Koon Keu Young was only sixteen years old when he arrived in Honolulu and suddenly found himself responsible for the management of a store.

Almost all of the Chinese migrants were men. Single women did not travel alone to distant places, and married women generally stayed home. Len Mau Nin, for example, did not accompany her twenty-one-year-old husband, Len Wai, a contract laborer who went to Hawaii in 1882. She remained behind in Guangdong because one of her parents was blind and she was needed there. "Also most women didn't want to go to a strange place anyway," her grandson Raymond Len explained, "and leave the so-called comforts of an extended family." Moreover, Chinese tradition and culture limited the possibilities of migration for women. Confucianism defined the place of a Chinese woman: she was instructed to obey her father as a daughter, her husband as a wife, and her eldest son as a widow. In Chinese custom, the afterbirths of children were buried in different locations, depending on the sex of the baby — in the floor by the bed for boys and outside the window for girls. This practice signified what was expected to happen to a woman. She would leave the home of her family, marrying and joining the family of her husband. As a daughter-in-law, she was expected to take care of her husband's aging parents. "A boy is born facing in; a girl is born facing out," said a Chinese proverb. A daughter's name was not recorded in the family tree; it was entered later next to her husband's name in his genealogy.[33]

In Chinese culture, family and home were synonymous. They even shared the same character in the Chinese language. Women of all classes were regarded as inferior to men and were expected to remain at home, attentive to family and domestic responsibilities. The "bound feet" of Chinese women of "gentle birth," while indicating social rank and considered "beautiful," also symbolized their subordinate status as women and served to prevent them from wandering. In 1855 a Chinese merchant of San Francisco explained why many men did not bring their wives with them to America: the women of the "better families" generally had "compressed feet" and were "unused to winds and waves." But keeping women home was not a function of class. While peasant women did not have bound feet, they were also confined to a narrow world circumscribed by the "necessity" of gender. Tied to family and home, they stayed within the walls of their village.[34]

Chinese women were also left behind because it would have been too costly to accompany their husbands and the men thought they would be gone only temporarily. Moreover, according to an explanation sometimes known as the "hostage theory," women were kept home in order to ensure their absent husbands would not become prodigal sons in America. Chinese peasant culture was familialist; individual identity was based on family and lineage, and economic welfare and family were integrated. The Chinese system of patrilineal descent provided for the equal division of a family's household property and land among all adult sons and for them to share responsibility for the support of their elderly parents. By keeping the wives and children of their sons at home, parents hoped they would be able to buttress family ties and filial obligations. Their wandering sons would not forget their families in China and would send remittances home. "The mother wanted her son to come back," explained Len Mau Yun, married to Len Too Shing (one of Len Wai's sons). "If wife go to America, then son no go back home and no send money."[35]

Significantly, sons migrating to Hawaii were more likely to take their wives with them than their counterparts leaving for California.

In 1900, of the 25,767 Chinese in Hawaii, 3,471 or 13.5 percent were female, but of the 89,863 Chinese on the U.S. mainland, only 4,522, or 5 percent, were female. Why this difference in sex ratios between Hawaii and the continent?

One possible way to explain this pattern is to note the ethnic differences between the two groups of migrants. The Chinese in California were mostly Punti, whereas many of their counterparts in Hawaii were Hakka. The latter did not practice footbinding, and hence Hakka women had greater ability than many Punti women to travel and also to work abroad.

But conditions and circumstances in the receiving countries also determined the difference in sex ratios. In Hawaii, there were efforts to promote the migration of Chinese women. As early as 1864, the editor of the *Pacific Commercial Advertiser* anxiously noted the presence of the predominantly male Chinese population on the plantations and recommended the importation of Chinese women: "To throw in these islands, hundreds or thousands of laborers without their wives, to encourage their importation without that controlling and softening influence which women, by God's will, exercise over man, would be to encourage vice and urge on the fearful evils originated by dissolute habits." In 1877, as planters expanded sugar cultivation and recruited increasing numbers of Chinese laborers, the newspaper editor again expressed his concern about the influx of so many Chinese men in the prime of life and "full of the animal instincts natural" to youth. "No Chinamen," he insisted in an editorial, "should be allowed henceforth to come here . . . unless they are accompanied by their women." Meanwhile, missionaries also voiced alarm about this population of Chinese male laborers "without women and children" living like "animals" on the plantations. In his appeal to the planters to bring Chinese women to Hawaii, missionary Frank Damon declared: "No surer safeguard can be erected against the thousand possible ills which may arise from the indiscriminate herding together of thousands of men! Let the sweet and gentle influence of the mother, the wife, the sister, and the daughter be brought to bear upon the large and yearly increasing company of Chinese in our midst, and we shall soon see a change wrought, such as police regulations cannot produce."[36]

Planters themselves saw that Chinese women could be used to control the Chinese laborers. In a letter to Damon, planter H. M. Whitney wrote in 1881: "With Chinese families established on every plantation . . . there would be much less fear of riotous disturbances. . . . The influence of families especially *where settlers locate in a foreign country* — has always been a peaceful influence." Planters actively encouraged the immigration of Chinese women. In 1865, for example, the Hawaiian Board of Immigration commissioned Dr. William Hillebrand to recruit about five hundred Chinese laborers in Hong Kong, specifying a quota for women: 20 to 25 percent of them were to be married women. Under Hillebrand's program, Chinese men could afford to take their wives with them to Hawaii, for their spouses' passages would be paid for by the planters. Like the men, the women would sign labor contracts to work on the plantations. "It is understood," stated Hillebrand, "that the women be employed at light labor only, and *not be separated* from their husbands." But they were to be paid less than their male counterparts — three dollars rather than four dollars a month. Hillebrand's two shiploads of 528 Chinese laborers included ninety-six women and ten children.[37]

A similar combination of the missionary concern and employer self-interest that encouraged the immigration of Chinese women to Hawaii did not exist in California. In fact, the opposite occurred. Employers in California viewed Chinese laborers as temporary and migratory. They wanted a labor force of single men, a mobile work force ready to move to the next construction site or the next harvest. They did not want to have responsibility for families and did not care about the social needs of their workers. Their relationships with workers were contractual, businesslike: they were purchasing labor, nothing more, nothing less. Chinese male migrants could see that the work situation in the islands would be more settled. They would have employment for five years on a particular plantation where they would live in stable communities. But in California, as miners or railroad workers or migrant farm laborers, Chinese men would be entering a frontier society where conditions would be difficult for their wives and children.

The greater proportion of Chinese women in Hawaii than in the mainland United States was also influenced by the different ways the Chinese were viewed and received by whites in the two countries. In 1879, an editorial in the Hawaiian missionary paper *The Friend* described the difference between white attitudes toward the Chinese in California and Hawaii: "The California watchword may be 'The Chinese must go,' but that of Hawaii is 'The Chinese must come,' to work our cane and rice fields. Now let us treat them fairly, and do all in our power to introduce Chinese families and diffuse among them Christianity." Underlying this difference was, on the one hand, the large white working class in California that perceived Chinese laborers as competitors, and, on the other hand, the relatively small number of white workers in Hawaii. Chinese encountered greater racial discrimination and hostility, even violence, in California than in Hawaii. Moreover, whites in Hawaii did not see the islands as a place for extensive white settlement. Totaling only 6 percent of the population in 1878, they did not have a predominantly white society to preserve or defend. But whites in California, as early as 1850, or only two years after annexation, constituted 99 percent of the state's population. Thirty years later, on the eve of the enactment of the Chinese Exclusion Act, whites represented 87 percent of Californians. They felt the need to protect their white society and saw the entry of Chinese women and families as a threat to racial homogeneity and their view of America as a "white man's country."[38]

Significantly, Hawaii and the United States developed very different policies regarding the entry of Chinese women. Concerned about the increasing presence of a disorderly and overwhelmingly male Chinese population in the 1880s, the Hawaiian government limited Chinese immigration to 2,400 a year. But it exempted Chinese women and children from the quota in order to encourage them to come. The policies of the U.S. government, on the other hand, were designed to keep out Chinese women. The Page Law, passed in 1875 to prohibit the entry of prostitutes, was enforced so strictly and broadly it served not only to exclude Chinese prostitutes but also to discourage Chinese wives from coming here. Chinese women seeking to emigrate to the United States had to undergo rigorous interrogation and cross-examination by U.S. officials stationed in China. The Page Law intimidated all women considering emigration: the number of Chinese women entering the United States between 1876 and 1882 declined from the previous seven-year period by 68 percent. In 1882, during the interval of a few months between the passage of the Chinese Exclusion Act and its enforcement, 39,579 Chinese slipped into America. But this massive migration included only 136 women, testifying to the effectiveness of the Page Law.[39]

While the 1882 law prohibited the entry of "Chinese laborers," it was unclear whether it also restricted the entry of Chinese women. This question was tested two years later in the Circuit Court of California in *In Re Ah Moy, on Habeas Corpus*. In this case, Too Cheong, a Chinese laborer and resident of the United States, had returned to China in 1883 and had married Ah Moy. When he came back to the United States a year later, Too Cheong brought his wife with him. The court denied Ah Moy admission, declaring that the wife of a Chinese laborer, being herself a "Chinese laborer," could not lawfully enter the United States. Moreover, the court argued, a Chinese wife who was not a "Chinese laborer" in fact prior to her marriage took the "status" of her husband upon marriage and hence became a member of a "class" whose entry was prohibited. In 1888 Congress prohibited a Chinese "laborer" already here to leave and then return to the United States, and also made it unlawful for "any Chinese person" (except for merchants) to enter the country.[40]

The differences in state policies between Hawaii and the United States not only determined how many Chinese women went to each country but whether they migrated as wives or prostitutes. Generally, Chinese prostitutes were absent in Hawaii. Chinese men were allowed to have their wives accompany them to the islands or to join them there. Chinese immigration to Hawaii was carefully regulated by the government and the planters: usually Chinese migrants entered as contract laborers for the plantations, and this process screened out prostitutes. Furthermore, Chinese men could have relationships with Hawaiian women, and many of them married native women and raised families in the islands. Unlike their sisters in Hawaii, most of the Chinese women entering California before 1875 were prostitutes. In 1870, of the 3,536 Chinese women in California, 2,157, or 61 percent, had their occupations listed as "prostitute" in the population census manuscripts. Chinese could enter America voluntarily as immigrants; consequently the United States could not control the entry of prostitutes as effectively as the Kingdom of Hawaii. Furthermore the Chinese community in California was largely composed of migratory men dependent on prostitutes to satisfy their sexual needs.[41]

One of these prostitutes, Lilac Chen was only six years old when she was brought to San Francisco. Years later, at the age of eighty-four, she remembered the day her father said he was taking her to her grandmother's house: "And that worthless father, my own father, imagine . . . sold me on the ferry boat. Locked me in the cabin while he was negotiating my sale." Chen kicked and screamed; when she was finally let out, she could not find her father. "He had left me, you see, with a strange woman." Another prostitute, Wong Ah So, described her tragic experience: "I was nineteen when this man came to my mother and said that in America there was a great deal of gold. . . . He was a laundryman, but said he earned plenty of money. He was very nice to me, and my mother liked him, so my mother was glad to have me go with him as his wife. I thought that I was his wife, and was very grateful that he was taking me to such a grand, free country, where everyone was rich and happy." But two weeks after Wong Ah So had arrived in San Francisco, she was shocked to learn that her companion had taken her to America as a "slave" and that she would be forced to work as a prostitute.[42]

The transit of Chinese prostitutes reflected the nature of the Chinese migration to America: it was mainly the movement of men. Their plan was to be away temporarily. Waving good-bye, many sojourners heard their wives sing:

> *Right after we were wed, Husband, you set*
> *out on a journey.*
> *How was I to tell you how I felt?*
> *Wandering around a foreign country, when*
> *will you ever come home?*

> *I beg of you, after you depart, to come back soon,*
> *Our separation will be only a flash of time;*
> *I only wish that you would have good fortune,*
> *In three years you would be home again.*
> *Also, I beg of you that your heart won't change,*
> *That you keep your heart and mind on taking care*
> *of your family;*
> *Each month or half a month send a letter home,*
> *In two or three years my wish is to welcome*
> *you home.*[43]

"See you again, see you again," the men shouted. Turning away from their wives, they traveled on foot or in small boats to port cities like Canton and Hong Kong, where they boarded ships bound for Honolulu and San Francisco.

A Meiji Voice Crossing the Pacific

They came later than the Chinese immigrants, arriving in Hawaii in significant numbers beginning in the 1880s and then in the continental United States a decade later. But like the Chinese, the immigrants from Japan — the Issei, or "first generation" — carried a vision of hope.

> *Huge dreams of fortune*
> *Go with me to foreign lands,*
> *Across the ocean.*[44]

For over two centuries, the Japanese people had been forbidden by law from traveling to foreign lands. In 1639, Japan initiated an era of isolation from the West that remained effectively uninterrupted until Commodore Matthew C. Perry's intrusion in 1853. While Japan continued the ban on emigration, it experienced new difficulty enforcing the law. In 1868, the Hawaiian consul general in Japan secretly recruited and transported to Hawaii 148 Japanese contract laborers, and a year later, German merchant John Henry Schnell took some forty Japanese with him to found a silk farm in California. In 1884, the Japanese government permitted Hawaiian planters to recruit contract laborers.

The new policy ignited an emigration explosion. Internal pressures for overseas migration had been building for over a decade and were becoming intense in the 1880s. After the 1868 Meiji Restoration, Japan began fervently pursuing a program of modernization and westernization in order to protect itself against European and American imperialist powers. To finance the industrialization as well as militarization of Japan, the Meiji government required farmers to pay an annual fixed tax on land. During the 1880s, the government instituted deflationary policies that depressed the price of rice and caught farmers in a financial squeeze. Over 300,000 lost their lands because of their inability to pay the land taxes. "The depression of trade in Japan has increased month by month and year by year, showing no signs of abatement," the *Japan Weekly Mail* reported in 1884. "It seems to have come to a climax during the autumn of the present year, for the distress among the agricultural class has reached a point never before attained. Most of the farmers have been unable to pay their taxes, and hundreds of families in one village alone have been compelled to sell their property in order to liquidate their debts."[45]

Farmers all over Japan faced economic hardships. Many farmers in the northern prefectures moved north to the island of Hokkaido in search of opportunity. In the southwestern prefectures such as Kumamoto, Hiroshima, and Yamaguchi, farmers were in an especially dire situation. Hiroshima prefecture, for example, had the smallest amount of land per household. In 1885, a journalist described the worsening economic conditions in Yamaguchi prefecture: "What strikes me most is the hardships paupers are having in surviving. . . . Their regular fare consists of rice husk or buckwheat chaff ground into powder and the dregs of bean curd mixed with leaves and grass."[46]

Farmers in the southwestern prefectures were specifically targeted by the Hawaiian recruitment program. During the 1870s, Hawaiian consul R. W. Irwin had served as adviser to a large Japanese trading company headed by Masuda Takashi. Originally from Yamaguchi prefecture, Masuda was concerned about the people suffering there and advised Irwin to recruit laborers in the southwestern prefectures. Once emigration from this area was under way, it was fueled by stories, spread by word of mouth, about opportunities in Hawaii.[47]

The future in Japan seemed bleak for these financially distressed farmers, and thousands of them were seized by an emigration *netsu* — a "fever" to migrate to the Hawaiian Islands and the United States. They saw themselves as *dekaseginin* — laborers working temporarily in a foreign country. Their goal was to work hard in order to "return home in glory" after three years and use their savings to buy land or regain land lost to debtors.[48]

Many dekaseginin carried a responsibility to discharge family debts. One of them was the grandfather of Hawaii's Senator Daniel Inouye. A fire had broken out in the Inouye family home and spread to nearby houses; in order to pay for the damages, the family sent their eldest son, Asakichi, to Hawaii. Accompanied by his wife, Moyo, and four-year-old son, Hyotaro, he planned to return to Japan after the family debt had been paid. Some dekaseginin hoped to advance socially into a higher class by becoming a *yoshi* — a son-in-law adopted into the wife's family. "I planned to work three years in the United States to save 500 yen and then go back to Japan," a migrant explained, "because if I had 500 yen in Japan I could marry into a farmer's household, using it for my marriage portion." The migrants carried in their hearts the dream of striking it rich and coming back to Japan as *kin'i kikyo* — wealthy persons.[49]

Hawaii offered a chance to succeed. During the contract-labor period from 1885 to 1894, Japanese migrants signed agreements to have their passages paid for by planters and to work for three years for nine dollars a month plus food, lodging, and medical care. They clearly saw the wage advantage they would have in Hawaii: the higher wages in Hawaii and the favorable dollar-yen exchange rate could enable a plantation laborer in the islands to earn six times more than a day laborer in Japan. They were told they would be able to save four hundred yen — an amount a silk worker would be able to acquire only by working every day and saving all wages for ten years. Three years of separation from family and friends seemed a small sacrifice for such a huge sum.

When the Japanese government announced it would be filling six hundred emigrant slots for the first shipment of laborers to Hawaii in 1885, it received 28,000 applications. By 1894, some 30,000 Japanese had gone to the islands as *kan'yaku imin,* or government-sponsored contract laborers. After 1894, migrants went to the islands as private contract laborers through emigration companies, or as free laborers, drawing from their own resources or borrowing money to pay for their transportation.

> *Family fortunes*
> *Fall into the wicker trunk*
> *I carry abroad.*

"My father had put a mortgage on his property to get me the 200 yen I used when I sailed to Hawaii," said a migrant. "For the cost to come to Hawaii our land was placed under a mortgage," another one explained. "And we borrowed some money, about $100, from the moneylender. After we came to Hawaii we sent money back. If we didn't pay it back, our land would have been taken away."[50]

Beginning in the 1890s, Japanese migrants were also attracted to the U.S. mainland. American wages seemed fantastic: they were about a dollar a day — an amount equal to more than two yen. Inota Tawa calculated that as a laborer in America he could save in one year almost a thousand yen — an amount equal to the income of a governor in Japan. He begged his parents: "By all means let me go to America." In 1902, a carpenter in Japan could make only two thirds of a yen in wages for a day's work, while a railroad laborer in America was paid a dollar a day. To prospective Japanese migrants, "money grew on trees" in America.[51]

Between 1885 and 1924, 200,000 Japanese went to Hawaii and 180,000 to the U.S. mainland. They were predominantly young men: my grandfather Kasuke Okawa was only nineteen years old when he left home in 1886. Between 40 and 60 percent were in their twenties, and about 25 percent were in their thirties. Due to Japan's system of compulsory education, the migrants were comparatively well educated, with an average of eight years of schooling. In fact, Japanese migrants had a higher literacy rate than their European counterparts: according to the U.S. Census for 1910, only 9.2 percent of Japanese immigrants ten years of age and older were illiterate, compared to 12.7 percent of foreign-born whites in the same age group. Most Japanese migrants came from the farming class and were not desperately poor. The average Japanese-male immigrant arrived here with more money than his European counterpart.[52]

The Japanese migrants were a select group, more so than the Chinese. Unlike China, Japan was ruled by a strong central government. The Meiji Restoration had unified the country, and the new state was able to regulate emigration. Driven by a rising nationalism, the government viewed overseas Japanese as representatives of their homeland and required prospective emigrants to apply for permission to leave for Hawaii and the United States. Review boards screened them to ensure that they were healthy and literate and would creditably "maintain Japan's national honor." The Japanese government had received reports on the conditions of the Chinese in America and was determined to monitor carefully the quality of its emigrants. In 1884 Japanese Consul Takahashi Shinkichi had informed his Foreign Ministry: "It is indeed the ignominious conduct and behavior of indigent Chinese of inferior character . . . that brought upon the Chinese as a whole the contempt of the Westerners and resulted in the enactment of legislation to exclude them from the country." The Japanese government should deny indigent Japanese passage to the United States, he advised, or else the Japanese would soon follow "in the wake of the Chinese." Seven years later, as Japanese migrants began entering the United States, Japanese Consul Chinda Sutemi similarly warned that if the government permitted the emigration of "lower class Japanese," it would "unavoidably provide a pretext to the American working class and pseudo-politicians for their drive to exclude the Japanese from this country." The Chinese "failure" in America, Chinda stressed, must be a "lesson" for Japan.[53]

Seeking to avoid the problems of prostitution, gambling, and drunkenness generated by an itinerant bachelor society and to bring greater stability to the immigrant communities here, the Japanese government promoted the emigration of women. Japanese women went to America in much larger numbers than Chinese women. As early as 1905, females constituted over 22 percent of the Japanese population in Hawaii and about 7 percent on the mainland. Three years later, in the Gentlemen's Agreement, Japan restricted the emigration of Japanese "laborers," but strategically retained a loophole: parents, wives, and children of laborers already in America would be allowed to emigrate. This policy allowed my uncle Nobuyoshi Takaki, who came to Hawaii in 1904, to send for his father, Santaro, in 1912, and Santaro, in turn, to have his two remaining sons, Teizo and Toshio, join them in 1918. Moreover, thousands of women also entered Hawaii and the mainland through the same opening — 66,926 of them between 1908 and 1924. Between 1911 and 1920, women represented 39 percent of all Japanese immigrants. In fact, so many Japanese women emigrated that females represented 46 percent of the Japanese in Hawaii and 34.5 percent on the mainland in 1920, a year before the "Ladies' Agreement," in which Japan terminated the emigration of picture brides. But by then, some 20,000 picture brides, including my aunts Yukino Takaki and Mitsue Takaki, had already arrived here.[54]

The picture-bride system, or *shashin kekkon* ("photo-marriage") was based on the established custom of arranged marriage, *omiai-kekkon*. Marriage in Japanese society was not an individual matter but rather a family concern, and parents utilized go-betweens, *bais-hakunin*, to help them select partners for their sons and daughters. In situations involving families located a far distance from each other, the prospective bride and groom would often exchange photographs before the initial customary meeting, *omiai*. This traditional practice lent itself readily to the needs of Japanese migrants in America. "When I told my parents about my desire to go to a foreign land, the story spread throughout the town," picture bride Ai Miyasaki later recalled. "From here and there requests for marriage came pouring in just like rain!" Riyo Orite, who came here in 1913, also had a "picture marriage." Her marriage to a Japanese man in America had been arranged through a relative. "All agreed to our marriage," she said, "but I didn't get married immediately. I was engaged at the age of sixteen and didn't meet Orite until I was almost eighteen. I had seen him only in a picture at first."[55]

Japanese government policy for the emigration of women and the picture-bride practice operated within the context of internal economic developments that were transforming conditions for women. While women in China were restricted to the farm and the home, women in Japan in the nineteenth century were becoming wage-earning workers away from home in services such as inns and grogshops as well as in industries like tea processing and papermaking. Thousands of young women were engaged in the migration of labor, *dekasegi rodo,* within Japan and employed in industries away from home. During the 1880s, daughters of farming families constituted 80 percent of the labor force in the textile industry. Women were also hired regularly as construction laborers and employed in the coal mines, carrying heavy loads of coal out of the tunnels on their backs. By 1900, women composed 60 percent of Japan's industrial laborers. Women in rural areas were leaving home for work almost as commonly as men, and this pattern became increasingly widespread as the Meiji government accelerated modern capitalistic development in order to pursue *fukoku-kyohei* — a strong and prosperous nation ready to protect itself against expansionist Western powers. The movement of Japanese women to Hawaii and the United States was an extension of a proletarianization process already well under way in Japan.[56]

Japanese women were also more receptive to the idea of traveling overseas than Chinese women. The Meiji government required the education of female children, stipulating in the *Chakushu junjo (Procedures for Commencement)* of 1872 that "girls should be educated . . . alongside boys." The Emperor Meiji himself promoted female education. "My country is now undergoing a complete change from old to new ideas, which I completely desire," stated the emperor. Japanese youth, "boys as well as girls," should learn about foreign countries and become "enlightened as to ideas of the world." Japanese women, unlike their Chinese counterparts, were more likely to be literate. "I attended six years of elementary school: two years of Koto sho gakko [middle advanced elementary school], and four years of girls' middle school," said Michiko Tanaka. "We studied English and Japanese, mathematics, literature, writing, and religion." Under the reorganization of the school system in 1876, English was adopted as a major subject in middle school. Japanese women were also curious about the outside world. They had been told by their Emperor Meiji how women "should be allowed to go abroad" and how Japan would "benefit by the knowledge thus acquired." They also heard stories describing America as "heavenly," and many of them were more eager to see the new land than to meet their new husbands there. "I wanted to see foreign countries and besides I had consented to marriage with Papa because I had the dream of seeing America," Michiko Tanaka revealed to her daughter years later. "I wanted to see America and Papa was a way to get there." "I was bubbling over with great expectations," said another picture bride. "My young heart, 19 years and 8 months old, burned, not so much with the prospects of reuniting with my new husband, but with the thought of the New World." Informed they would be married and sent to husbands in America, many women secretly had their own extravagant reasons for going.[57]

The emigration of women was also influenced by views on gender and the system of land inheritance in Japanese society. A folk saying popular among Japanese farmers expressed their feelings about the respective places of their children: "One to sell, one to follow, and one in reserve." The "one to sell" was the daughter. She was expected to marry and enter her husband's family. "Once you become someone's wife you belong to his family," explained Tsuru Yamauchi. She found out she would be going to Hawaii somewhat abruptly: "I learned about the marriage proposal when we had to exchange pictures." Emigration for her was not a choice but rather an obligation as a wife. Whether a Japanese woman went to America depended on which son she married — the son "to follow" or the son "in reserve."[58]

Unlike the Chinese, Japanese farmers had an inheritance system based on the rule of impartible inheritance and primogeniture: only one of the sons in the family, usually the eldest, inherited the family's holding, or *ie*, thus keeping intact family ownership of the land and the means of the family's survival. In the mountainous island nation of Japan, arable land was limited, and most of the farm holdings were small, less than a single hectare, or about two and a half acres. Division of a tiny family holding would have led to disaster for the family. As the possessor of the family farm, the eldest son, the one "to follow," had responsibility for the care of the aged parents. The younger or noninheriting son or sons, "in reserve," had to find employment in towns. For them, the process and pattern of relocation within Japan were already in place, and could be easily applied to movement abroad. At the morning ceremonies of the elementary and middle schools, principals instructed their students: "First sons, stay in Japan and be men of Japan. Second sons, go abroad with great ambition as men of the world!" As they became dekaseginin, younger sons were not as tightly bound to their parents as their Chinese counterparts, and they were allowed to take their wives and children with them to distant lands.[59]

Actually, immigrant men also included first sons. My uncle Nobuyoshi Takaki was the oldest son; many first sons came when they were young, before they had responsibility for elderly and dependent parents, and others came to earn money to supplement the family incomes and to help defray family debts. In the village of Jigozen in Hiroshima prefecture, 30 percent of the emigrants between 1885 and 1899 were heads of families, 23 percent wives, 22 percent eldest sons, and 24 percent second and younger sons. The heads of families included both first and younger sons. While first-son heads of families sometimes took their wives with them, thinking their double incomes could enable them to pay off family debts more quickly and shorten their sojourn, younger-son heads of families were even more inclined to have wives accompany them, for they could stay away longer, perhaps even permanently.[60]

But whether Japanese women migrated depended also on the government policies and economic conditions of the receiving countries. Where the U.S. government had strictly prohibited the entry of Chinese women, it allowed Japanese women to come under the terms of the Gentlemen's Agreement. Furthermore, Japanese women entered California and other western states when society here was more stable and more developed than the earlier period of Chinese immigration. They were pulled by particular economic developments. As thousands of Japanese-immigrant men became shopkeepers and small farmers, they sent for their wives, thinking their spouses could assist as unpaid family labor. Wives were particularly useful on farms, where production was labor intensive. "Nearly all of these tenant farmers are married and have their families with them," H. A. Millis noted in his report on the Japanese in 1915. "The wives do much work in the fields."[61]

While the U.S. government permitted the entry of Japanese women, the Hawaiian government actively promoted their immigration. When it first opened negotiations for emigration with Japan in 1879, the Hawaiian government stipulated in its initial draft of the agreement that 40 percent of the immigrants were to be women. They were to come as contract laborers. Half of their expense for passage would be paid by the Hawaiian Bureau of Immigration, and they would receive six dollars per month in wages, compared to ten dollars for men. During the government-sponsored contract-labor period from 1885 to 1894, the Hawaii Bureau of Immigration systematically recruited Japanese women, who constituted 20 percent of the kan'yaku imin. Between 1894 and 1908, thousands of women sailed to Hawaii as private-contract laborers. One of them was my grandmother Katsu Okawa, who emigrated as a single woman in 1896. Unlike farmers on the U.S. mainland, who wanted a migratory male work force, planters in the islands saw Japanese women as workers, using them as cooks, seamstresses, and field laborers. Planters also viewed the family as a mechanism of labor control. In 1886, a year after the beginning of the Japanese movement to the islands, the Hawaii Inspector-General of Immigration, A. S. Cleghorn, reported that Japanese men did much better work and were more satisfied on plantations where they had their wives. "Several of the planters," he noted, "are desirous that each man [from Japan] should have his wife."[62]

After 1900, when Hawaii became a territory of the United States, planters became even more anxious to bring more Japanese women. Federal law prohibited the contract-labor system, and planters found they had to entice laborers to stay on the plantations. Realizing that men with wives were not as likely to leave the plantation as single men, planters asked their business agents in Honolulu to send "men with families." The manager of the Hutchinson Sugar Plantation, for example, wrote to William G. Irwin and Company in 1905: "Will you be kind enough to send us as soon as you are able to do so, forty Japanese married couples. We want them for the Hilea section of the Plantation where we have always had more or less trouble in keeping Japanese laborers, and believe that by having married couples only, the laborers would remain." In 1900 Shokichi and Matsu Fukuda left their six-month-old daughter, Fusayo, with her grandparents and migrated together as a married couple to work on the Puunene Plantation on Maui.[63]

Hundreds, possibly thousands of women were brought as prostitutes, most of them to the U.S. mainland. They were sold to *amegoro* (Japanese pimps) or were abducted or lured under false pretenses. One of them, the daughter of a farming family in Amakusa, later recounted her experience. In 1890, a "smooth-talking" salesman visiting Amakusa told her stories about foreign lands. He told her that "gold nuggets were waiting to be picked up on the riverbanks of America" and persuaded her to accompany him to nearby Nagasaki, where he showed her a foreign ship bound for America. After boarding the huge ship, she walked the decks enjoying the new experience. Then she was introduced to a seaman, who said: "Why don't you go to America on the ship?" "I'd like to go and see America," she replied, "but since I don't know anyone there, I can't." Just as she was "half thinking about wanting to go and half worrying," she suddenly heard a clanging bell as the ship hoisted anchor and sailed out of port. The salesman was nowhere to be seen. She was taken to a room by the sailor and warned: "I'll bring you meals; so don't leave the room. If by chance you're discovered, you'll be thrown into the sea." When the ship reached San Francisco, the seaman dressed her in Western clothes and took her off the ship. "Pulled by his hand in the pitch darkness of the night," she "trailed behind him" to "an unknown house" where she was forced to become a prostitute.[64]

Most Japanese migrants left voluntarily, looking forward to

their adventure. Still, as they prepared to leave their farms and villages, they felt the anxiety of separation. One of them remembered
how her husband's eldest brother had come to say farewell. "Don't
stay in the [United] States too long. Come back in five years and
farm with us." But her father then remarked: "Are you kidding?
They can't learn anything in five years. They'll even have a baby over
there. . . . Be patient for twenty years." Her father's words shocked
her so much she could not control her tears: suddenly she realized
how long the separation could be.

> With tears in my eyes
> I turn back to my homeland,
> Taking one last look.[65]

"My parents came to see me off at Kobe station," a woman
recalled many years later. "They did not join the crowd, but quietly
stood in front of the wall. They didn't say 'good luck,' or 'take care,'
or anything. They did not say one word of encouragement to me.
They couldn't say anything because they knew, as I did, that I would
never return." Perhaps, many migrants wondered, they would not
see Japan again, destined "to become the soil of the foreign land."
Realizing her stay in America would be a permanent one, another
migrant inscribed the moment and her feelings in poetry:

> Parting tearfully,
> Holding a one-way ticket
> I sailed for America.[66]

There were settlers among the migrants. "My father came here
as a non-sojourner," said Frank S. Miyamoto of Seattle. "He had
the idea that he would stay." His father had gone to Korea first and
then emigrated to the United States to become a merchant. He had
little reason to return to Japan, for he was the only son and both of
his parents had died. Similarly, Frank Tomori of Portland saw America as his new home: "I happened to see a Western movie, called
'Rodeo,' at the Golden Horse Theater in Okayama City, and was
completely obsessed with 'American fever' as a result of watching
cowboys dealing with tens of thousands of horses in the vast Western
plains. Enormous continent! Rich land! One could see a thousand
miles at a glance! Respect for freedom and equality! That must be
my permanent home, I decided." After the 1908 Gentlemen's Agreement there occurred a shift in the purpose of Japanese immigration
from the *dekasegi* (sojourning) to the *teiju* (settling) stage. "Stay in

America and make it your country" became the new slogan, as Japanese immigrants increasingly saw their stay as long-term, perhaps even permanent, and summoned their families to join them, *yobiyose*.[67]

As they left their homes, the migrants drew inspiration and strength from their legends. One of the stories was about Momotaro — the peach boy. An old, childless couple lived on a farm, and one day the woman went down to the stream to wash clothes. Suddenly she saw a large peach floating in the water. She brought it home and her husband cut the fruit open, and they were surprised to find a baby boy in the peach. Momotaro grew up to be a strong and brave warrior — an expert swordsman, a samurai for the people, and he went off to fight the demons who were threatening the village. After destroying the monsters, Momotaro returned home and took care of his parents for the rest of their lives. Most of the migrants promised they would return to Japan as they gathered within themselves a courage they did not fully realize they possessed.

> *Mine a Meiji voice,*
> *Crossing the Pacific sea,*
> *It has grown husky.*[68]

Leaving the Land of "Morning Calm"

Meanwhile, some 8,000 Koreans sailed to the United States between 1903 and 1920. Leaving the kingdom of *Choson* ("Morning Calm"), most of them migrated to the territory of Hawaii. Like the Chinese and Japanese, the Korean migrants were young: over 90 percent of the adults were between the ages of sixteen and forty-four. But unlike the first two groups of Asian immigrants, Koreans came from diverse walks of life. They were farmers, common laborers in the cities, government clerks, students, policemen, miners, domestic servants, and even Buddhist monks. Most of them were from urban areas rather than the country. In their level of education, they were more like the Japanese than the Chinese. About 70 percent of them were literate.

Converted to Christianity, many Koreans had been encouraged to emigrate by American missionaries. "I was born in Korea," said a migrant, "and was a Christian before I came to the United States." Significantly, 40 percent of all Korean immigrants were Christians. At large tent meetings in the seaport of Inchon, the Reverend George Heber Jones of the Methodist Episcopal Church preached to pro-

spective emigrants, inspiring them with "laudable ambitions." The
American missionaries, said Yi Tae-song of the Korean Christian
Movement of Hawaii, appeared in Korea and began telling "the
wonderful story of the Cross" and what it could do for those who
would accept it and carry it through life. The new converts were told
Hawaii represented a "haven of peace and plenty."[69]

The Korean migration was also driven by political reasons:
Hawaii represented a haven from Japanese imperialism. "There was
little or no opportunity for my grandfather to find a job in Korea in
those days," a Korean in Hawaii explained. "The Japanese imperial
government was controlling Korea at the time and the outlook toward the future was very poor." The Japanese were "cruel oppres-
sors." "When my grandfather learned that the Japanese government
was letting people out of the country to work in the islands, he was
happy to volunteer." Hawaii was also a place where Koreans could
struggle for national independence. "When I saw my country fall
into the hands of the Japanese aggressors," said a migrant, "I was
filled with sorrow, but, unable to do much to help, I applied for the
status of an immigrant and came to Hawaii hoping to learn something
in order to help my country."[70]

Some Korean migrants left as political refugees, escaping from
Japanese-government persecution. A high-school teacher in Korea
during the early years of the Japanese occupation, Whang Sa-sun
had joined the secret patriotic society, *Sinmin-hoe* (New People's Society). "At the time the Japanese military government persecuted the
people, especially the young people and took them to jail," said
Whang. In order to avoid arrest by the Japanese police for membership in the *Sinmin-hoe,* Whang left Korea. "My wife and I sneaked
out. . . . We crossed the Yalu River and from there rode the railroad
to Shanghai. At that time I wore Chinese clothes. The Japanese didn't
know I was Korean; they thought I was Chinese." In Shanghai,
Whang and his wife boarded a ship bound for America. "When I
left Korea, I felt like a free man. Korea was like a jail, and I was a
prisoner. I wanted to come to America. America was a free country."
Myung-ja Sur also felt politically compelled to leave Korea. "Because
the Japanese oppression was so severe for all Koreans, especially
Korean patriots, I had to flee to Shanghai," she told her grandson
years later. A schoolteacher, she had participated in the March First
Movement of 1919, distributing copies of the Declaration of Independence and Korean flags. "The Japanese went crazy. They beat up
people and killed thousands of Koreans while many were arrested

and later killed." In Shanghai, Sur was arrested by the Japanese secret police and imprisoned for a month. "When I returned to Korea the Japanese followed me everywhere so I decided to leave for America where I planned to continue my education. Before I left I sent my picture to this Korean man in the United States and he sent me his picture and then we were married."[71]

But, like the Chinese and Japanese, Korean migrants were also pushed from Choson by poverty. Famine and drought had inflicted economic suffering. One American missionary described the terrible conditions: "We have never known such unrest among the Koreans due to the excitement of so many going to the Hawaiian Islands to work on sugar plantations, and the dreadful hardtimes. . . . We can't blame them for wanting to go to America." In a letter to Governor Sanford Dole of Hawaii in 1902, Horace N. Allen of the U.S. legation in Seoul reported: "The severe famine of the past winter made the matter [of emigrating to Hawaii] seem all the more attractive to the people." The following year, on January 27, sugar-industry official C. M. Cooke reported the arrival of the first group of Korean immigrants: "We have just received about fifty laborers and their families from Korea. As the people there are in a starving condition we hope that we shall be able to get a number of them as they seem to be just what our plantations need."[72]

"Times were hard," a Korean immigrant recalled. "The country had been passing through a period of famine years. . . . My occupation as tax collector barely kept me from starvation's door as I travelled from village to village." His initial plan was to migrate alone and return to Korea after three years, but he finally decided to take his family with him to America. "We left Korea because we were too poor," another Korean recounted. Unable to restrain tears evoked by memories of the suffering, she added: "We had nothing to eat. There was absolutely no way we could survive." Echoing a similar story, a Korean migrant said: "There were no opportunities for work of any kind and conditions were bad. It was then that we heard of a man who was talking a lot about the opportunities in Hawaii. He said it was a land of opportunity where everybody was rich."[73]

From newspaper advertisements and posters, Koreans learned that plantation laborers in Hawaii received free housing, medical care, and sixteen dollars a month for a sixty-hour work week — a sum equal to about sixty-four won (Korean dollars), a small fortune to Koreans. Koreans were told by the labor recruiters that Hawaii was a "paradise" where "clothing grew on trees, free to be picked," and where "gold dollars were blossoming on every bush." They were given descriptions of America as a "land of gold" and a "land of dreams." Lured by fantasy and hope, Koreans borrowed money from a bank in Korea financed by the Hawaiian sugar planters. They agreed that the hundred-dollar loan for the transportation expense would be deducted by the plantation manager from their monthly pay over a three-year period.[74]

The Korean migration included many women: of the 6,685 adults who entered between 1903 and 1906, nearly 10 percent were women. Guaranteed employment and housing on the plantations, Korean men saw the islands as a place where family life was possible. But many took their wives and children with them because they were afraid that they would not be able to return to a Korea under Japanese domination. An additional 1,066 Korean women came as picture brides during the next seventeen years. Whereas the families of Japanese immigrants had arranged their children's picture-bride marriages, Korean migrants relied on Japanese agents to make the necessary arrangements for them. In their offices in the port cities, impersonal agents displayed photographs of grooms and gathered applications from interested young Korean women. At the time of their marriages, the men were generally twenty years older than their wives. Korean picture brides entered the United States with Japanese passports issued to them as colonial subjects of Japan under the terms of the Gentlemen's Agreement. By 1920, Korean women constituted 21 percent of the total Korean-adult immigrant population in the United States.[75]

For many Korean picture brides, Hawaii promised a better life. "My parents were very poor," said a Korean woman. "One year, a heavy rain came, a flood; the crops all washed down. Oh, it was a very hard time. . . . Under the Japanese, no freedom. Not even free talking." She had heard stories about the islands. "Hawaii's a free place, everybody living well. Hawaii had freedom, so if you like talk, you can talk; you like work, you can work. I wanted to come, so, I sent my picture. Ah, marriage! Then I could get to America! That land of freedom with streets paved of gold! Since I became ten, I've been forbidden to step outside our gates, just like the rest of the girls of my days. So becoming a picture bride would be my answer and release."[76]

Anxious to seek greater opportunities and freedom in America, many more Korean men and women would have left Choson had

Korean emigration not been so short-lived. In 1905, only two years after the arrival of the first Korean plantation laborers in Hawaii, Japan began to formalize its control over Korea by declaring it a "protectorate." The Japanese government then prohibited Korean emigration to Hawaii in order to curb Korean labor competition with Japanese workers in Hawaii and to cut off the source of Korean-independence activities in the United States. Consequently, Korean migrants came in much smaller numbers than the Chinese and Japanese.

Yet, like the other Asian migrants, the Koreans carried an expectation. As they crossed the Pacific Ocean to Hawaii, they said to themselves: *Kaeguk chinch wi* — "the country is open, go forward."[77]

Manongs in Movement

Unlike the Chinese, Japanese, and Koreans, Filipino migrants came from a territory of the United States. They went by the tens of thousands after the U.S. annexation of the Philippines — first to Hawaii in the early 1900s and then to the mainland in the 1920s. Ninety percent of the migrants were Catholic, reflecting the presence of the Catholic Church in the Philippines during centuries of Spanish colonial rule. Unlike the Chinese and Japanese, Filipinos had been in contact with European culture for a long time through the church. "The Filipinos were brought up under Christianity for 400 years," explained immigrant Phillip V. Vera Cruz. "They have a different upbringing and were more attached to the western people."[78]

They were also American in their outlook. Many had been educated in schools established by Americans. "From the time of kindergarten on our islands," said Salvadore del Fierro, "we stood in our short pants and saluted the Stars and Stripes which waved over our schoolyards." In their classrooms they looked at pictures of Washington and Lincoln, studied the Declaration of Independence, and read about the "home of the free and the brave" in their English-language textbooks. "We said the 'Pledge of Allegiance' to the American flag each morning," recalled Angeles Amoroso, who emigrated to the United States in 1923. "We also sang 'The Star Spangled Banner.' All of the classes were taught in English." Hundreds, thousands of American teachers had gone there to Americanize the Filipinos. "I studied under American teachers [in the Philippines], learning American history and English, being inspired by those teachers and American ideals," a Filipino told an interviewer in California in 1930. "It's no wonder that I have always wanted to come here."[79]

By 1930, some 110,000 Filipinos had gone to Hawaii and another 40,000 to the mainland. Some of them — several hundred, possibly a few thousand — were *pensionados,* or government-sponsored students. The vast majority of the migrants were laborers from poor and uneducated farming families. The Filipino migration was overwhelmingly composed of young men: of the 31,092 Filipinos who entered California between 1920 and 1929, 84 percent were under thirty years of age. Genevieve Laigo of Seattle never forgot how the Filipino men greatly outnumbered the Filipino women on the ship carrying them to America in 1929: "There were three hundred men and only two women!" In 1930, only 10,486 or 16.6 percent of the 63,052 Filipinos in Hawaii were female. The imbalance between Filipino men and women was even greater on the mainland, where only 2,941 or 6.5 percent of the 45,208 Filipinos were female.[80]

The greater percentage of Filipino women in Hawaii as compared to the mainland was influenced by the different labor conditions waiting for them in each region. A Filipino laborer would more likely consider taking his wife with him to Hawaii than to the mainland. In the islands, he would be employed on a plantation where he would live in a permanent and stable plantation community. On the mainland, he would be a migratory farm laborer, moving from field to field and from one temporary camp to another, even from one state to another. Furthermore, planters in Hawaii saw how it was in their interest to promote the emigration of Filipino women. The Hawaiian Sugar Planters' Association, which governed the sugar industry in the islands, determined that men with families were steadier workers than single men. In a study conducted in 1916, the association produced evidence demonstrating the positive "influence of family responsibility": Japanese men, many of them married, worked an average of 21.9 days a month (84 percent of full-time), while Filipino men, mostly single, worked only eighteen days a month (69 percent). To encourage Filipino men to have families on the plantation and thus become more reliable workers, the association approved a plan for the importation of Filipino women. In a letter to H. Hackfield and Company in 1916, a director of the association announced a new program to encourage the Filipinos on the plantations to secure wives from the Philippines. "If these men will furnish us with letters to their wives or prospective wives, photographs of themselves and letters from the managers and from some Filipino women in the camps recommending the men as being desirable husbands," the director stated, "we will endeavor to induce the wives or prospective wives to come to Hawaii, and will see that they reach the men who send for them."[81]

But the gender composition of the Filipino migration was not determined wholly or even mainly by employers and their needs. Filipino culture with its Spanish and Catholic traditions placed restrictions on the possibilities of travel for women, requiring them to be accompanied by their husbands or fathers. Moreover, Filipino migrants generally viewed themselves as sojourners; they did not see America as a place to bring families and to settle. Unlike the Chinese and Japanese, most of the migrating Filipino men were unmarried. Only 18 percent of the Filipino men on the U.S. mainland were married, and most of these had left their wives in the Philippines, thinking their stay in America would be only temporary.

Whether single or married, thousands of Filipino men felt forced to leave home. Had they remained in the Philippines, many migrants said, they would have found themselves "sinking down into the toilet." Life was getting harder, and people were forced to "reach farther and farther away to make ends meet." Times had not always been so terrible. In a poem about his early childhood in the Philippines, an immigrant in California depicted a moment of felicity and plenty:

> *My father was a working man*
> *In the land of the big rains,*
> *The water glistened on his arms*
> *Like the cool dew in the morning*
> *When the rice was growing tall. . . .*

"In the forest behind us," a plantation laborer in Hawaii recalled as he talked about his childhood in the Philippines, "we got so much to live on. I would go hunting there with a string trap once a month and you would have to call me clumsy if I brought down less than four wild chickens. We used to trap wild pigs there too and deer." But then "the rich people" from town came to hunt with guns. "Those lazy bastards would even come at night when the animals and birds were asleep and blind them with their flashlights. And boom! No miss. Boom! They fell like shaken mangoes to the ground."[82]

Increasingly the peasants discovered that the rich rice lands they cultivated were becoming owned by men who never saw their property, by "names on pieces of paper." Each year they had to give a larger share of their crops to distant landlords and were driven into debt. A Filipino immigrant remembered his father saying to his brother Luciano:

> "The moneylender has taken my land, son."
> "How much more do you owe him, Father?" asked Luciano.
> "It is one hundred pesos," said my father. "I promised to pay in three weeks, but he won't listen to me. I'd thought that by that time the rice would be harvested and I could sell some of it; then I would be able to pay him. He sent two policemen to Mangusmana to see that I do not touch the rice. It is my own rice and land. Is it possible, son? Can a stranger take away what we have molded with our hands?"
> "Yes, Father," said Luciano. "It is possible under the present government."

Many years after he had left the Philippines, another Filipino immigrant sadly described this process of dispossession: "There was a time when my ancestors owned almost the whole town of Bulac and the surrounding villages. But when the Americans came conditions changed. Little by little my father's lands were sold. My share was mortgaged finally to keep the family from starvation and I soon found myself tilling the soil as did the poor Filipino peasants."[83]

As the farmers experienced increasing hardships, they also sometimes encountered personal abuse from the Filipino elite. A young boy never forgot one such incident. One day he had gone with his mother into town to sell *mongo* beans. There they noticed an elegantly dressed young woman walking down the street. Irritated by their stares, the woman raised her silk umbrella. "What are you looking at, poor woman?" snapped the wealthy woman contemptuously as she struck the basket of beans, scattering them on the pavement. Crawling on her knees, his mother scooped the beans into the basket. "It is all right. It is all right," she tried to reassure her son. Confused and stunned, the boy knew it was not all right as he knelt on the wet cement and picked out the dirt and pebbles from the beans.[84]

But there was a way out of poverty, Filipinos believed. They could go to America — Hawaii and California. "*Kasla glorya ti Hawaii,*" they said, "Hawaii is like a land of glory." They could find work on the sugar plantations and "pick up" money. Then they could return home triumphantly as successful migrants, as *balikbayans* and *Hawaiianos*. Like peacocks, they could strut down the dusty streets of their villages, proudly showing off their "Amerikana" suits, silk shirts, sport shoes, and Stetson hats. They fancied themselves looking so rich with their "money to blow." "Everyone," reported a Filipino immigrant, "became fascinated by the tales told of Hawaii," seized by what was commonly known as the "Hawaiian fever."[85]

Called "drummers," labor agents sent to the Philippines by the Hawaiian sugar planters helped to spread the fever. They traveled from town to town, showing movies that depicted the "glorious adventure and the beautiful opportunities" awaiting Filipino workers in Hawaii. "One scene [in one of the movies] shows the handing out of checks," said a provincial school officer. "The movie is free and is usually shown in the town plaza, so that everyone has a chance to see it." The labor agents "dazzled the Filipino eyes" with the sum of two dollars a day, an attractive wage compared with the fifteen cents a man could earn daily by hard labor in the Philippines. "The migrating Filipino," reported the *Manila Times,* "sees no opportunity for him in the Philippines. Advertise in a Manila paper and offer a job at 25 pesos a month, not a living wage in Manila, and you will get a thousand applicants. Make the same offer in any provincial town, and the response will be twice as great, comparatively. Is it any wonder, then, that the lure of pay four to ten times as great, in Hawaii or the United States, draws the Filipino like a magnet?" Lured here in the 1920s, Ted Tomol told an interviewer half a century later, when he was eighty-three years old: "Back home, we thought California was the Eldorado."[86]

Trying to climb out of peonage, Filipinos signed labor contracts, agreeing to labor for three years in exchange for transportation to Hawaii and wages of eighteen dollars a month plus housing, water, fuel, and medical care. Decades later, a Filipino vividly remembered the day he signed his labor contract:

The agent was just coming down the steps when I halted my horse in front of the recruiter's office. He was a fellow Filipino, but a Hawaiian.

"Where are you going?" he asked.

"I would like to present myself for Hawaii, Apo," I answered as I came down from my horse.

"Wait, I'll go see if I can place you on the next load," he said, and turned back up into the door.

When he came out, he had a paper in his hand. "Come up, so we can fill in the forms," he waved; so I went in.

"You write?" he asked.

"No," I said; so he filled in for me.

"Come back Monday for the doctor to check you up," he

said, patting me on the back. "When you come back, bring *beinte cinco*, twenty-five, and I'll make sure of your papers for a place," he said, shaking my hand.

It was like that. "Tip" is what we call it here. But that is our custom to *pasoksok*, slipsome, for a favor.[87]

The migrants promised to be gone for only three years, for they believed it would be easy to earn and save money in America. Returning with rolls of cash bulging in their pockets, they would pay off the mortgages on their lands and recover their family homes. "My sole ambition was to save enough money to pay back the mortgage on my land," explained a Filipino. "In the Philippines a man is considered independent and is looked upon with respect by his neighbors if he possesses land." As he said farewell to his brother in the Philippines, a Filipino laborer promised: "I will come back and buy that house. I will buy it and build a high cement wall around it. I will come back with lots of money and put on a new roof. . . . Wait and see!"[88]

But not all of the departing Filipinos were sojourners. Rufina Clemente Jenkins had met an American soldier in the Philippines during the Spanish-American War and married him in 1900, when she was only fourteen years old. Two years later she sailed to America with her daughter, Francesca, to join her husband and make her home here. Pete Silifan of Seattle said that he had come to the United States "to look for a better living. Down there [the Philippines] we didn't have any future." Aware of the limited opportunities for education and employment in the islands, especially for women, Angeles Amoroso decided to search for a new future in the United States: "My father had the impression I would be away only for seven years, but I knew in my heart that I would be making America my permanent home."[89]

From the Plains of the Punjab

In 1907, a year after the first group of Filipinos had landed in Hawaii, workers from India began arriving on the West Coast. The period of Asian-Indian immigration was extremely short. Immigration officials began placing restrictions in 1909 and Congress prohibited immigration from India eight years later. Altogether only sixty-four hundred came to America. The Asian-Indian migrants were even more disproportionately male than the other groups of Asian immigrants: less than one percent were women. Generally they were young men, between sixteen and thirty-five years of age; many, perhaps most, were married. In 1907, Fred Lockley interviewed many of the Asian-Indian migrants and reported that "practically all" of the newcomers were married and had families in India. The migrants possessed little or no education: 47 percent were illiterate. Most had been unskilled laborers and agricultural workers in India, coming here in small groups, networks of *pindi* (village men) and *got* (cousins).[90]

They had left the fertile plains of the Punjab, the "land of five rivers," a rectangular-shaped province. Originally from the districts of Ludhiana, Jullunder, and Hoshiarpur, most of the migrants were Sikhs. Based on a doctrine of equality that challenged the Hindu caste system, Sikhism was a reform religion representing a syncretism of Islam and Hinduism. To demonstrate their religious commitment, the men never shaved their beards or cut their hair. They wore turbans, for the rules required them to cover their heads in the temple. Of all the immigrants in America, observed immigrant Saint N. Singh in 1909, none surpassed the Sikhs in "picturesqueness." They could be seen "clad in countless curious styles." Yards upon yards of cotton, calico, or silk were swathed about their heads, forming turbans, cone-shaped or round like a mushroom button, with waves or points directly in the middle of their foreheads or to the right or left, "as variable as the styles of American women's pompadours."[91]

The emigration of Asian Indians to this country was conditioned by British colonialism in India. Seeking to develop capitalist agriculture in India, the British government instituted changes in the land-tenure system and the production of agriculture that placed small landholders in an extremely vulnerable situation. In order to pay their debts, many of them had to mortgage their lands. Moneylenders unscrupulously required peasant farmers to sign mortgage contracts that charged 18 to 36 percent interest and contained clauses specifying the sale of the land in the event of late payments. Furthermore, a famine from 1899 to 1902 decimated the cattle owned by the peasants and forced them deeper into debt. Within this context, Indians by the hundreds and thousands left their homeland to work in the British West Indies, Uganda, Maritius, and British Guiana. Several thousand went to Canada and the United States. "Do you wonder when you look at India, with its low wages and high taxes, its famines and plagues, its absence of all incentive toward advancement, that the dam which for so long has held the people in check is weakening?"

observed a writer in the *Pacific Monthly Magazine* in 1907. "Do you
wonder that the East Indians are turning their faces westward toward
the land of progress and opportunity?"[92]

Canada was the destination for many Asian Indians, but they
found themselves unwelcome there. "British Columbians are proud
of India . . . proud of East Indians as boys of the flag," declared the
Vancouver World in 1906. "But an East Indian in Canada is out of
place." White workers also voiced their opposition to the entry of
Asian Indians: "British Columbia is a white man's country. The
coming hordes of Asiatic laborers will keep wages down and crowd
the white man to the wall, since a white man cannot nor will not
come down to the Asiatic laborer's low standard of living." A letter
written in 1914 on behalf of six hundred Sikhs in Hong Kong, addressed to their friends in America, expressed their fear of a Canadian
immigration restriction law: "For God's sake, help us get to the
United States or Canada. The new Canadian law will go into effect
on 5 March 1914 after which time few Hindus will be admitted into
Canada. It has been much more difficult for the past six months to
get into Manila than heretofore. We are shut out of Australia and
New Zealand. For God's sake, come to our assistance so that we
will be able to get into the United States or Canada."[93]

When asked why he had left the Punjab, Deal Singh Madhas
told an interviewer: "To make money and then return to the Punjab
and farm for myself instead of on the ancestral property." As Sikh
soldiers in the British army, many migrants had gone initially to China
to help suppress the 1900 Boxer Rebellion; others had been recruited
as policemen to be stationed in Hong Kong. "I was born in the
Punjabi district of India and served on the police force in Hong Kong,
China, for some years," Sucha Singh told an interviewer in 1924.
"While I was in China several Hindus returned and reported on the
ease with which they could make money in America and so I decided
to go." Many migrants had first served in the Indian Army. After
three years of military service, eighteen-year-old Puna Singh migrated
in 1906, having heard as a soldier exciting stories about America.
Generally the migrants were the second or youngest sons, sent by
their fathers to earn money to pay off debts and the mortgage. They
went abroad under the sponsorship of their families. Their decision
to emigrate was not a solitary one, reflecting personal desires or
hopes, but a collective conclusion based on kinship obligations and
the need to supplement the family income. To pay for their transportation to Vancouver and San Francisco, many Punjabis mortgaged

one or two acres of their land in India. Even if they had to become debtors to get to America, they thought the promise of getting ahead in the new land was worth the sacrifice. Paid ten to fifteen cents a day in India, they were told they could earn two dollars for a day's work in America. A Sikh migrant later recalled how California seemed "enchanted."[94]

The plan for virtually all migrants was to return to their villages. Moola Singh, for example, was only fifteen years old when he came here in 1911. He had recently been married by his father to a young woman, and they had spent only three months together when he left her with his relatives. "You're leaving me here?" she asked him. "Yes," he replied, "my mother is here." "What do I need a mother for? You started love; I need you." Moola promised: "I'll come back in six years." And his young bride countered: "I'll give you three years."[95]

Pacific Passages

Pushed from their homelands and pulled to America, the migrants left family, friends, and loved ones in China, Japan, Korea, the Philippines, and India. The groups were enormously diverse. They ranged in number — from approximately 430,000 Chinese, 380,000 Japanese, and 150,000 Filipinos to only about 8,000 Koreans and a similar number of Asian Indians. They brought a rich variety of religions including Taoism, Buddhism, Shintoism, Hinduism, Islam, Sikhism, and Christianity. They differed in gender composition: overwhelmingly the Chinese, Filipino, and Asian-Indian migrants were men, but among the Koreans and Japanese were significant numbers of women. Even within each group the ratio of men to women varied according to destination: proportionately more Chinese, Japanese, and Filipino women emigrated to Hawaii than to the U.S. mainland. While the men generally chose to go, many women had no choice; their husbands had decided for them or they were brought as prostitutes. "Necessity" drove their migration to America.

Most of the migrants in each group came as sojourners. Still some, even many, came thinking they would or might stay. Intention of permanent settlement increased for the Chinese after the 1882 exclusion act and for the Japanese after the 1908 Gentlemen's Agreement. Entering through loopholes in the exclusionist policies, Chinese and Japanese came to join family members and make their homes in America. The migrants also brought with them differing amounts of education. While the Japanese and Koreans were largely literate, most of the other groups had very limited or no schooling. Educated in American schools in the islands and able to speak some English, Filipinos were somewhat familiar with U.S. culture. While the Koreans came from urban areas, the migrants of the other groups originated generally from agricultural communities. Leaving a country with a weak central government, the Chinese lacked a strong sense of nationalism, while the Japanese embraced the patriotism of Meiji Japan. Witnessing Japanese penetration of their country, Korean migrants nurtured a defensive nationalism.

Still, what was equally, perhaps even more striking about most of the migrants was how they were stirred by a common discontent and how they came searching for a new start. "Poverty hurt," but hunger and want were not what essentially defined the migrants, for "necessity" also powered men and women who stayed home. The migrants were unique in a felicitous way: they were the dreamers. They could imagine what they could do in an unformed America, and their dreams inspired them to take risks. They wondered what they could become, unfurled before the winds of change and challenge. Possibilities exploded in their heads. They went to bed in the evenings, ideas and calculations roaring in their brains, and woke up in the mornings shivering with euphoric excitement and feeling a restless empowerment. They decided to be "extravagant." Scenarios of a brighter future, racing in their minds, swept them away relentlessly toward a rupturing experience, a radical break from the "cake of custom" and their old homelands. Ah, but the world is big, others warned them: Do you know the meaning of immensity? And they answered: We will tell you someday when we get back. The migrants felt their hearts tugging them toward an alluring America as they separated themselves from the graves of their ancestors and from a world where there were common points of cultural reference and where people looked like them and spoke their language. They reached for "what persisted."[96]

Many of the migrants had never before even stepped beyond the boundaries of their farms or villages. Entering the port cities, they were confused and frightened by the noises and the crowds. At the docks, they said final good-byes. "When I departed Naha Harbor [in Okinawa]," a migrant remembered, "my mother sang loudly and danced with other women relatives until my ship went out of sight. Her song went like this: 'My beloved child, on this auspicious ship, may your journey be as safe and straight as if linked by a silk thread.' " Another mother told her departing daughter: "I am going to miss you very much when you leave, but I'll always be with you. We won't be separated even for a moment." The daughter did not understand what her mother meant until that night when dressing for bed she found a piece of the Buddhist altar ornament in the breast of her kimono. A young Filipina accompanied her uncle who wanted her to be educated in the United States; waving good-bye to her mother, she said she would be back in seven years. "But I knew," she told her granddaughter many years later, "I was never coming back."[97]

Then there was a surge toward the moored ships, and the travelers began struggling through a sea of people. "Everyone was afraid that he would be left behind," said a Chinese migrant, "so as soon as the way was opened everyone just rushed to get on board and when he was finally aboard he was all out of breath." The ship pulled away from the dock, stretching and snapping off the streamers one after another.

> *Ribbons of farewell*
> *I hold between my fingers*
> *Feeling blood flow through.*

As she felt her ship sail away from Yokohama, a woman watched the city disappear behind the waves. "The ship gained speed heartlessly out into the open sea," she said. "I could see nothing but water, when suddenly, and so unexpectedly, I sighted Mount Fuji poking its head above the horizon. I thought that Mount Fuji was stretching itself up to say, 'Goodbye,' to me. 'Ah! Fuji-san,' was all I could utter." From the ships, Filipinos looked at pretty young women waving good-bye from the docks and giving them "remember me manong" smiles.

> *You were still waving, beloved*
> *When I left you*
> *To journey to another land*
> *A white kerchief*
> *You held*
> *Drenched with tears*
> *You couldn't help crying*
> *I promised it'll be short*
> *   while perhaps*
> *And I will be back home. . . .*

Gazing at the distant shores of Manila and holding his rattan suitcase, a manong felt a deep emptiness within: "I knew that I was going away from everything I had loved and known. I waved my hat and went into the vestibule that led to the filthy hold below."[98]

In the steerage, the voyagers were packed together. "It was crowded below deck," a Filipina later recalled. "I think there were more than 300 of us; my husband was in a different section while the women and children were in another section. During the long voyage I would often sit on deck, holding my youngest child. . . . My husband and my other child, who was four, would often go and watch through the fence the first-class passengers playing in the swimming pool." The smell of freight, oil, and machines filled the air of the stifling steerage. The passengers would try to climb out onto the deck where they could breathe fresh air and sun themselves. But "the first-class passengers were annoyed," a Filipino said, "and an official of the boat came down and drove us back into the dark haven below." On another occasion, a young white woman, wearing a brief bathing suit, was walking on the deck with a companion. Noticing the Filipinos sunning themselves, she remarked scornfully: "Look at those half-naked savages from the Philippines, Roger! Haven't they any idea of decency?"[99]

The passengers found the food terrible and monotonous. "The food was different from that which I had been used to, and I did not like it at all," a Chinese passenger complained. "When I got to San Francisco I was half starved because I was afraid to eat the provisions of the barbarians." A Japanese traveler remembered that "the cooks and the ship's boys were Chinese, and every day we had curry rice only." Time and again Japanese passengers grumbled about the food: "The soup served every morning contained only two or three small pieces of dried tofu (bean curd) and was watery and tasteless." "Breakfast and lunch consisted of bean paste soup and pickled radish. For supper we were served fat-back. Though rice was served, it was so hard it wouldn't go down the throat. There was no soy sauce, and everything was literally awful." Traveling in the steerage class of the steamship *President Pierce*, a Filipino passenger could not "stomach" the food — "wilted pechay (Chinese cabbage) and rotten vegetables; putrified fish, salted pork, and stale hamburger for meats; and foul-smelling brew of tea and coffee made from sea water for drinks." "Food was served in great buckets," another Filipino traveler reported, and Filipinos were disappointed to find them filled with bread rather than rice. They missed their daily rice — "food which every hardworking Filipino cannot do without, especially in the morning." Sometimes it did not matter what the passengers ate, for the seas were so rough that they could not keep their food down.[100]

On the ship, their world seemed to be in constant motion, swaying and rocking.

> *I ate wind and tasted waves for more than*
> *twenty days,*

a Chinese traveler wrote in a poem he had carved on the walls of the Angel Island immigration station in San Francisco Bay. "Day after day the weather was bad and the sea stormy," a Japanese passenger said. "The hatch was tightly closed and there was no circulation of air, so we were all tortured by the bad odor. As the boat was small, whenever a high wave hit us the top deck was submerged and the sound of the screw grinding in empty space chilled us."

> *One third-class porthole*
> *Against which from time to time*
> *Waves crested and broke.*

The passengers felt disoriented, unbalanced, nauseous. "After boarding, when we got close to the Mokpo River, the turbulence was heavy," a Korean immigrant recalled. "We felt the ship rocking and the people in the ship moved like a football and threw up." Confined below deck during stormy weather, Filipino voyagers on the *S.S. President Cleveland* sailing to San Francisco in 1926 were almost overwhelmed by the stench of vomited food, finding the steerage smelling like a "store of dried fish."[101]

The passengers felt grimy, but they had no place to wash hands and faces, no place to bathe. On one ship, the crew put a long row of bowls on deck, filled half full of water for the passengers to rinse out their mouths and wash their faces. Always the travelers faced the danger of epidemics sweeping through the steerages. On one occasion, 597 Chinese were forced to remain on their disease-infected ship for two months after it had reached Honolulu. A Filipino migrant never forgot the horror of a meningitis epidemic on board his ship: "The Chinese waiters stopped coming into our dining room, because so many of us had been attacked by the disease. They pushed the tin plates under the door of the kitchen and ran back to their rooms, afraid of being contaminated. Those hungry enough crawled miserably on their bellies and reached for their plates." Every now and then, he added, a young doctor and his assistant descended below deck to "check the number of deaths and to examine those about to die."[102]

In the steerage, the passengers slept on bunk beds in rows resembling the inside of an army barracks. "We were packed into the ship in one big room. There was no privacy, no comforts, no nothing. We were like silkworms on a tray, eating and sleeping." Sleep did not come easily, due to the congestion, excitement, and anxiety. "I could not sleep a few nights," explained Yang Choo-en, who left Korea in 1902, "because so many things were in my mind and I worried so much since I did not know what would happen in the new, strange land in Hawaii. I did not know how to speak English and I did not know anything about sugar plantation work either." The crossing was tedious. Japanese travelers tried to occupy themselves by presenting traditional dramas and holding talent shows for *noh* singing, *shigin* (the chanting of Chinese poems), and *biwa* (Japanese guitar) solos. Passengers had time for reflection. As he lay on his bunk in the dark hole of the steerage, a Filipino traveler felt seasick and lonely. "I was restless at night," he said, "and many disturbing thoughts came to my mind." Perhaps he had made a mistake, but it was too late. He could not turn back now.[103]

Theirs was a long, weary, and trying trans-Pacific traverse.

> *Island soul of me*
> *Cast off to cross the ocean.*
> *Ah, the world is big!*

The surging, swirling ocean around them seemed to emblematize their feelings — the cresting and crashing of their emotions and thoughts. They were in movement, with nothing solid and stable beneath them. They were awash with questions about their future: what would life be like in the new and foreign land, so far away? What would they become there? Would they ever see their homelands and families again? Would it be worth risking everything they had?

> *Loud waves rise and fall*
> *On the North Pacific sea*
> *Voyaging abroad*
> *I stand on froth-washed decks*
> *And am wet with salty spray.*[104]

Then, finally, after four to eight weeks of confinement, the tired and homesick passengers saw, in the distant horizon, the land of their destiny. "Gazing in silent wonder at the new land," the Chinese passengers on board the *Great Republic* arriving in San Francisco in 1869 were "packed" on the main deck, reported an observer. Then down the gangway they came, "a living stream of the blue-coated men of Asia," bending long bamboo poles across their shoulders to carry their bedding, matting, and clothing. They were dressed in new cotton blouses and loose baggy breeches, slippers or shoes with heavy wooden soles, and broad-brimmed hats of split bamboo. "For two mortal hours," the witness wrote, "the blue stream pours down from the steamer upon the wharf; a regiment has landed already, and still they come." Eight years later, another witness described the arrival of Chinese migrants in San Francisco: a thousand men were on the deck of the ship, "huddled together," all getting ready to go ashore, "washing and combing, talking and laughing, looking and wondering, scolding and quarreling, pushing and crowding; concealing opium in one part of their clothing, and silk handkerchiefs in another."[105]

The moment of arrival was engraved in the memories of the passengers. When Ahn Ch'ang-ho of Korea first saw the volcanic mountains of Hawaii rising from the sea before him, he was so deeply moved and overjoyed he later gave himself the pen name, *To San* (Island Mountain). Describing the day of his landing in Hawaii, Bonipasyo said: "At 8 A.M. we pulled into the immigration station of Honolulu. There was a band playing. We disembarked alphabetically and as we came down the gangplank, they [the immigration officials] asked us where we were going and we shouted the plantation of our destiny. 'Waialua Sugar Company!' 'Puunene Maui!' people shouted. I shouted, 'Naalehu, Hawaii.' " Then Bonipasyo and his fellow Filipino laborers heard their names called. They were ordered to step forward individually, and a plantation official then placed a *bango*, a numbered metal tag on a chain, around the neck of each man. "On a clear, crisp, September morning in 1868," after a sixty-day voyage from Guangdong, Huie Kin sighted land. "To be actually at the 'Golden Gate' of the land of our dreams! The feeling that welled up in us was indescribable," he recalled. After Huie and the other passengers had landed, "out of the general babble, some one called out in our local dialect, and, like sheep recognizing the voice only, we blindly followed, and soon were piling into one of the waiting wagons. Everything was so strange and so exciting. . . . The wagon made its way heavily over the cobblestones, turned some corners, ascended a steep climb, and stopped at a clubhouse, where we spent the night."[106]

Married to men they had not yet met, brides felt a special sense of anticipation and anxiety. "A month after the marriage," a Chinese woman said, "I sailed for America with my husband's relative, a distant clan cousin." Her family had arranged her marriage by proxy to a man she had never seen. "On the day that the boat docked at Port Townsend, the cousin who brought me to America came to escort me on the deck. Standing beside me at the rail, he pointed to a figure walking up and down the wharf. He said, 'See that man smoking a big cigar? He is your husband!' " A Japanese woman remembered how most of the passengers on her ship were picture brides: "When the boat anchored, one girl took out a picture from her kimono sleeve and said to me, 'Mrs. Inouye, will you let me know if you see this face?' " After arriving in San Francisco in 1919, Fusayo Fukuda was placed in a large waiting room with other picture brides; all the husbands except hers came and a panic swept through her as she looked around the empty room. She was wishing she had not come and she could reboard the ship for Japan when finally her husband, Yokichi Kaya, arrived.[107]

Most of the picture brides were much younger than their husbands. "When I first saw my fiancé, I could not believe my eyes," said Anna Choi, who was fifteen years old when she became a picture bride. "His hair was grey and I could not see any resemblance to the picture I had. He was forty-six years old." Surprised and shocked to find older men waiting for them on the dock in Honolulu, many Korean picture brides cried: "*Aigo omani*" — "Oh dear me, what shall I do?" One of these disconcerted picture brides was Woo Hong Pong Yun. Arriving in the islands at the age of twenty-three, she saw a thirty-six-year-old man greeting her as her new husband. "When I see him," she said years later, "he skinny and black. I no like. No look like picture. But no can go home." Another Korean picture bride, finding that her prospective husband did not look like his picture, was "so disappointed." "I cry for eight days," she said, "and don't come out of my room. But I knew that if I don't get married, I have to go back to Korea on the next ship. So on the ninth day I came out and married him. But I don't talk to him for three months." Still wearing kimonos and sandals as they disembarked from the ships, Japanese picture brides often found themselves immediately taken by their husbands to a clothing store and outfitted with Western dress. One young woman remembered how she put on a high-necked blouse, a long skirt, high-laced shoes, "and, of course, for the first time in my life, a brassiere and hip pads." But she had trouble with the underwear. "Japanese women used only a 'koshimaki' [a sarong-like underskirt]," she explained. "Wearing Western-style underwear for the first time, I would forget to take it down when I went to the toilet. And I frequently committed the blunder."[108]

The migrants wondered how they would be received by Americans. Would we find ourselves, Chinese newcomers asked apprehensively, "eating bitterness" in Gam Saan? In China, they had been warned about the "red-haired, green-eyed" whites with "hairy faces." Now, in San Francisco, as they were driven through the streets in wagons, Chinese were often pelted with bricks thrown by white hoodlums. Then, crossing Kearny Street and entering Chinatown, the tired and now bruised travelers were relieved to get away from the *fan qui* ("foreign devils") and glad to find "Chinese faces delighting the vision, and Chinese voices greeting the ear." After they had landed in San Francisco in 1900, John Jeong and several others were put in a carriage to be taken to Chinatown. "It was an open carriage with standing room only," recalled Jeong years later. "Halfway there some white boys came up and started throwing rocks at us. The driver was a white man, too, but he stopped the carriage and chased them away." After a group of Japanese had arrived in San Francisco in 1905, they saw a gang of twenty white youngsters on the dock. "The Japs have come!" they shouted and threw horse dung. "I was baptized with horse dung," a newcomer commented later. "This was my very first impression of America." When they landed in San Francisco in 1906, several Koreans saw a group of white men standing around the gangplank. "One guy stuck his foot out," one of the migrants said, "and kicked up my mother's skirt. He spit on my face, and I asked my father, 'Why did we come to such a place? I want to go home to Korea.' " A year later, a traveler from India reached Seattle, where he and his fellow Sikhs received "strange looks" as people peered at their turbans and beards and listened curiously to their Hindustani language.[109]

A wind came up behind the "strangers." Shortly after she had arrived in the San Joaquin Valley, a young Japanese bride stood alone in the darkness outside of her house: "If I looked really hard I could see, faintly glowing in the distance, one tiny light. And over there, I could see another. And over there another. And I knew that that was where people lived. More than feeling 'sabishii' [lonely], I felt 'samui' [cold]. It was so lonely it was beyond loneliness. It was cold." The migrants began to sense they had traversed new boundaries, some of them not defined by geography, and they anxiously gathered memory around themselves.

> Alone I watch
> The world moving in space, looking back into
> Childhood for the words that meant so much,
> The voices that had gone with the years.
> This is the hour of memory.[110]

They tried to remember the familiar places they had left behind — their homes, the neighbor's fruit tree sagging pregnantly with clusters of red *li-chi* fruit, the nearby stream where they caught shrimp with nets, the favorite footpath where delicious *kilins,* or mountain bamboo shoots, grew everywhere, and the secret places where they picked *matsutake* mushrooms. The farther they went from their village the more "vivid" it seemed to become in their minds. "There are mountains on one side, and there is the wide river on the other side," said a migrant remembering his village. "A tongue of land extends into the river and on this land are hills that are covered with guava trees. Now is the time for the guavas to bloom. I used to go there when I was a child and the smell of the blossoms followed me down into the valley."

> Chasing them in dreams,
> Mountains and rivers of home.

"Why had I left home?" a newcomer asked. "What would I do in America? I looked into the faces of my companions for a comforting answer, but they were as young and bewildered as I, and my only consolation was their proximity and the familiarity of their dialects." They could feel the liminality of the land awaiting them. Would everything be "familiar and kind"? the newcomers wondered. Or were they merely seeing illusions, harboring hopes that would "vanish," too?

> Illusion and I
> Travelled over the ocean
> Hunting money-trees.

> *Looking and looking . . .*
> *Even in America*
> *What? No money-trees?*

And so they entered a new and alien world where they would become a racial minority, seen as different and inferior, and where they would become "strangers."[111]

II

STRANGERS

A paper was presented to me yesterday for inspection, and I found it to be specially drawn up for subscription among my countrymen toward the Pedestal Fund of the Barthodi Statue of Liberty. Seeing that the heading is an appeal to American citizens, to their love of country and liberty, I feel that my countrymen and myself are honored in being thus appealed to as citizens in the cause of liberty. But the word liberty makes me think of the fact that this country is the land of liberty for men of all nations except the Chinese.

Saum Song Bo[1]

3

Gam Saan Haak

The Chinese in Nineteenth-Century America

Among the thousands of pioneers flocking to California during the gold rush were 325 forty-niners "from a different shore" — China. Like their counterparts from the eastern United States and elsewhere, they came to search for gold. A year later, 450 more Chinese arrived in California; then suddenly, they came in greatly increasing numbers — 2,716 in 1851 and 20,026 in 1852. By 1870, there were 63,000 Chinese in the United States. Most of them — 77 percent — were in California, but they were also elsewhere in the West as well as in the Southwest, New England, and the South. The Chinese constituted a sizable proportion of the population in certain areas: 29 percent in Idaho, 10 percent in Montana, and 9 percent in California. Virtually all adult males, they had a greater economic significance than their numbers would indicate: in California, the Chinese represented 25 percent of the entire work force.

During the nineteenth century, Chinese communities in the United States were diverse and in transition. The Chinese were predominantly a rural population for several decades: in 1870, only 24 percent of California's Chinese population lived in San Francisco. But increasingly the Chinese became an urban population. They lived in San Francisco (*Dai Fou,* or "Big City"), Sacramento (*Yee Fou,* or "Second City"), Stockton (*Sam Fou,* or "Third City"), Marysville, and Los Angeles. By 1900, 45 percent of all Chinese in California lived in San Francisco and the Bay Area, and two thirds of the state's Chinese were urban dwellers. The Chinese represented a wide range of classes. Between 1870 and 1900, approximately 40 percent of the Chinese in San Francisco and Sacramento were businessmen such as

shopkeepers and merchants, 5 to 12 percent professionals and arti-
sans, and the remainder wage-earning workers. In the rural regions,
farmers, labor contractors, and merchants constituted only about 15
percent of the Chinese population, while over 80 percent were service
workers and farm laborers. By the end of the nineteenth century, the
Chinese had spread geographically: only 51 percent of the total
Chinese population resided in California, and 14,693, or 16 percent,
lived in the North Atlantic region, representing the beginnings of
Chinatowns in Boston and New York City.

    As the first Asian group to enter America, the Chinese merit
our close attention. What happened to them in the nineteenth century
represented the beginning of a pattern for the ways Asians would be
viewed and treated here — their transformation into Georg Simmel's
"strangers." But their identity as outsiders was determined not only
by their entry but also by a complex combination of economic, ideological, and political developments in American society. New "necessities" drove the Chinese after they arrived in Gold Mountain.[1]

Searching for Gold Mountain

Initially, the Chinese were welcomed in California. "Quite a large
number of the Celestials have arrived among us of late, enticed thither
by the golden romance that has filled the world," the *Daily Alta
California* reported in 1852. "Scarcely a ship arrives that does not
bring an increase to this worthy integer of our population." The
paper then predicted that "the China boys will yet vote at the same
polls, study at the same schools and bow at the same altar as our
own countrymen." Three years later, San Francisco merchant Lai
Chun-Chuen sanguinely observed that "the people of the Flowery
land were received like guests," and "greeted with favor. Each treated
the other with politeness. From far and near we came and were
pleased."[2]

    Lai and his fellow *gam saan haak* ("travelers to Gold Moun-
tain") had reason to be pleased. At the celebration of California's
admission into the Union in 1850, the Chinese participated in the
ceremonies, along with American citizens. Happily acknowledging
the presence of the Chinese and other foreigners in California, Justice
Nathaniel Bennett declared: "Born and reared under different Governments and speaking different tongues, we nevertheless meet here
to-day as brothers. . . . You stand among us in all respects as
equals. . . . Henceforth we have one country, one hope, one destiny."
In August, Mayor John W. Geary of San Francisco invited the Chinese

to join with the citizens of the city in a memorial for the late President Zachary Taylor. "The China Boys feel proud of the distinction you have shown them," wrote As-sing and A-he on behalf of the Chinese to the mayor, "and will always endeavor to merit your good opinion and the good opinion of the citizens of their adopted country." Two years later, at the celebration of George Washington's birthday in San Francisco, "all countries" were represented in the ceremonies, observed a visitor. In the parade passed the "French, Spanish and Hebrew Societies" and then "some two hundred Celestials, or, as their banner termed them 'China boys of San Francisco.' Preceded by their mandarins and a band of music, straggling and evidently amused with their position, came this large delegation of our most orderly and industrious citizens." The Chinese future in America seemed auspicious. In his January 1852 address to the California legislature, Governor John McDougal declared that more Chinese migrants would be needed to help drain the state's swamplands, praising them as "one of the most worthy classes of our newly adopted citizens — to whom the climate and the character of these lands are peculiarly suited."[3]

But Governor McDougal failed to sense the rapidly changing political climate that had begun to turn against the Chinese. Coming down from the foothills and gathering force as it reached Sacramento emerged a nativist cry, "California for Americans." Seeking to drive out the French, Mexican, Hawaiian, Chilean, and especially the Chinese from the gold fields, American white miners demanded that the state eliminate competition from foreign miners. Four months later, after John Bigler had been installed as the new governor, a committee of the California Assembly issued a report on the problems generated by the presence of Chinese miners. "The concentration, within our State limits, of vast numbers of the Asiatic races, and of the inhabitants of the Pacific Islands, and of many others dissimilar from ourselves in customs, language and education" threatened the well-being of the mining districts, the committee stated. Most of the Asian laborers were "servile contract laborers"; not seeking to become American citizens, they degraded the American white workers already in the state and discouraged other Americans from coming to California. To halt the threat, the committee recommended the enactment of a foreign miners' license tax. A week later, in his special message to the legislature, Governor Bigler suggested that the state use its police power to prohibit the immigration of Chinese into California. Calling for extraordinary measures to check the "tide of Asiatic immigration," Bigler recommended legislation to prohibit contract labor and to impose heavy taxes on the Chinese in California.[4]

In May of 1852, the legislature passed the foreign miners' license tax. The racial purpose of this new tax was transparent: aimed mainly at the Chinese, this new tax required a monthly payment of three dollars from every foreign miner who did not desire to become a citizen. Even had they so desired, the Chinese could not have become citizens, for they had been rendered ineligible to citizenship by the 1790 federal law that reserved naturalized citizenship to "white" persons. The California tax law provided that the revenues raised be shared equally by the state and the counties where the mines were located. The foreign miners' tax remained in force until it was voided by the federal Civil Rights Act of 1870. By then California had collected $5 million from the Chinese, a sum representing between 25 and 50 percent of all state revenue. In 1855, the legislature passed a law entitled, "An Act to Discourage the Immigration to this State of Persons Who Cannot Become Citizens Thereof." This law imposed on the master or owner of a ship a landing tax of fifty dollars for each passenger ineligible to naturalized citizenship. Seven years later the legislature went even further, enacting a law "to protect Free White Labor against competition with Chinese Coolie Labor, and to Discourage the Immigration of the Chinese into the State of California." This law levied a capitation tax of $2.50 per month on all Chinese residing in the state, excepting Chinese operating businesses, licensed to work in the mines, or engaged in the production of sugar, rice, coffee, or tea. Clearly all of this legislation was seeking not revenue but Chinese exclusion.[5]

By then, 24,000 Chinese, two thirds of the Chinese population in America, were working in California mines. Most Chinese miners in the 1860s were independent prospectors. Many of them organized themselves into small groups, consisting of as many as forty partners, and formed their own companies. Many Chinese miners in Yuba County, historian Sucheng Chan has discovered, obtained their placer claims through preemption rather than purchase. Under a preemption claim, the miner filed the required application in the county record's office and marked the boundaries of the claim. Thus in 1856 Ah Louie and Company claimed 240 feet at Buckeye Bar along the Yuba River, and Sham Kee 4,200 feet along the same river eight miles outside of Marysville. Many of the companies did well, renewing their claims annually and often even purchasing them. Ah Chung and Company, for example, purchased two claims, sixty feet each, from Frederick Antenheimer and John Lawrence, paying $620 for the claims, two wheelbarrows, and some running planks.[6]

Chinese miners worked mainly placer claims. To extract the gold, they shoveled sand from the stream into a pan or rocker, then washed away the sand and dirt to allow any heavy particles of gold to remain on the bottom. A traveler in the Sierra Nevada saw "long files of Chinamen alone" breaking the "monotony of the landscape" as they scraped and washed "the sands in the nearby dry beds of the torrents." The Chinese miners in El Dorado County, the *Mountain Democrat* reported, generally worked in "old deserted claims" where they realized only about two to three dollars a day, and when they found a good claim, they would "buy it and pay liberally for it."[7]

Chinese miners became a common sight in the California foothills, especially along the Yuba River and its tributaries and in townships like Long Bar, North-east Bar, and Foster Bar. They wore blue cotton blouses, broad trousers, wooden shoes, and wide-brimmed hats, their hair closely cropped with long, jet black queues hanging down behind. A newspaper correspondent described companies of twenty to thirty Chinese "inhabiting close cabins, so small that one . . . would not be of sufficient size to allow a couple of Americans to breathe in it. Chinamen, stools, tables, cooking utensils, bunks, etc., all huddled up together in indiscriminate confusion, and enwreathed with dense smoke, presented a spectacle."[7] Day-to-day life for the Chinese miners was competitive and anxious. Telegrams sent from Downieville captured much of the tenseness in their lives:

Quong Chung Shing & Co   Downieville, Cal.,
724 Com'cl St., San Francisco   March 2, 1874

    Git Wo. I want you pay your cousin Ah Hoey expenses to come Downieville quick attend to claim. Am afraid there will be big fight. Answer.

                              Fong Sing / Kim Bayo

Ah Chu   Downieville, Cal.,
                              March 4, 1874

    Trouble about mining claims. I owe a share and all the company want you come. I want you come. Ans yes or no.

                              Fong Sing / Ah Jake

Yu Wo & Co   Downieville, Cal.,
717 Dupont St., San Francisco   March 28, 1874

    What the price of opium. Answer.

                                      Fong Wo & Co[8]

During the mid 1860s, profits in gold mining decreased, and Chinese miners began leaving the gold fields. By 1870 there were only 16,000 Chinese miners, a third of the Chinese population. Some of them had become wage earners, working in quartz mines. Chinese found they generally could not enter quartz mining except as laborers employed by whites because they lacked capital to purchase the heavy equipment and machinery necessary to remove the gold deposits from the hard-rock quartz. White owners of the quartz mines realized the Chinese would enable them to drive downward the wages of white workers. In 1869, the *Daily Alta California* enthusiastically supported the use of the Chinese in quartz mining: "The Chinamen are ploughmen, laundrymen, placer miners, woolen spinners and weavers, domestic servants, cigar makers, shoemakers, and railroad builders to the great benefit of the State, and why should they not be quartz miners?"[9]

What the *Daily Alta California* observed was part of a larger development — the transformation of Chinese immigrants from entrepreneurs to wage earners, from independent prospectors with their own claims to workers dependent on capitalists for their livelihood. Increasingly, their employers were white. By 1880, as historian Chan has noted, 70 percent of the Chinese in Sacramento City and 67 percent in Marysville were dependent on white employers. This pattern could be found elsewhere, becoming pronounced as the Chinese moved out of mining and as they became wage earners in the industrial sector of the economy.[10]

One of the most important areas of Chinese industrial employment was railroad construction. In February of 1865, fifty Chinese workers were hired by the Central Pacific Railroad to help lay the tracks for the transcontinental line leading east from Sacramento; shortly afterward fifty more Chinese were hired. The new laborers were praised by company president Leland Stanford as "quiet, peaceable, industrious, economical — ready and apt to learn all the different kinds of work" required in railroad building. "They prove nearly equal to white men in the amount of labor they perform, and are much more reliable," the company superintendent Charles

Crocker reported. "No danger of strikes among them. We are training them to all kinds of labor: blasting, driving horses, handling rock as well as pick and shovel." The white workers demanded that the company stop hiring Chinese laborers, and Crocker retorted: "We can't get enough white labor to build this railroad, and build it we must, so we're forced to hire them. If you can't get along with them, we have only one alternative. We'll let you go and hire nobody but them." Within two years, 12,000 Chinese were employed by the Central Pacific Railroad, representing 90 percent of the entire work force. The savings derived from the employment of Chinese rather than white workers was enormous. The company paid the Chinese workers thirty-one dollars a month; had it used white workers it would have had to pay them the same wages plus board and lodging, which would have increased labor costs by one third.[11]

The construction of the Central Pacific Railroad line was a Chinese achievement. Not only did they perform the physical labor required to clear trees and lay tracks; they also provided important technical labor by operating power drills and handling explosives for boring tunnels through the Donner Summit. In his account of the summit's penetration, superintendent Crocker stated: "We had a shaft down in the center. We were cutting both ways from the bottom of that shaft. . . . [We] got some Cornish miners [from Virginia City] and paid them extra wages. We put them into one side of the shaft . . . and we had Chinamen on the other side. We measured the work every Sunday morning; and the Chinamen without fail, always outmeasured the Cornish miners. . . . The Chinese are skilled in using the hammer and drill; and they proved themselves equal to the best Cornish miners in that work."[12]

The Chinese workers were, in one observer's description, "a great army laying siege to Nature in her strongest citadel. The rugged mountains looked like stupendous ant-hills. They swarmed with Celestials, shoveling, wheeling, carting, drilling and blasting rocks and earth." Time was critical to the company's interest, for the amount of payment it received in land and subsidy from the federal government was based on the miles of track it built. Determined to accelerate construction, the Central Pacific managers forced the Chinese laborers to work through the winter of 1866. The snowdrifts, over sixty feet in height, covered construction operations. The Chinese workers lived and worked in tunnels under the snow, with shafts to give them air and lanterns to light the way. Snowslides occasionally buried camps and crews; in the spring, workers found the thawing corpses, still upright, their cold hands gripping shovels and picks and their mouths twisted in frozen terror. "The snow slides carried away our camps and we lost a good many men in those slides," a company official reported matter-of-factly; "many of them we did not find until the next season when the snow melted."[13]

The Chinese workers struck that spring. Demanding wages of forty-five dollars a month and an eight-hour day, 5,000 laborers walked out "as one man." The company offered to raise wages from thirty-one to thirty-five dollars a month, but the strikers spurned the offer and stood by their original demands. "Eight hours a day good for white men, all the same good for Chinamen," they declared. The *San Francisco Alta* condemned the strike as a conspiracy: "The foundation of this strike appears to have been a circular, printed in the Chinese language, sent among them by designing persons for the purpose of destroying their efficiency as laborers." The insinuation was transparent: the strikers' demands had been merely drummed up, and agents of the competing Union Pacific were behind the Chinese protest. The intent was to nullify the possibility that the Chinese workers had minds and wills of their own and were capable of acting in their own interests. Meanwhile, the Central Pacific managers moved to break the Chinese strike. They wired New York to inquire about the feasibility of transporting 10,000 blacks to replace the striking Chinese. Superintendent Crocker isolated the strikers and cut off their food supply. "I stopped the provisions on them," he stated, "stopped the butchers from butchering, and used such coercive measures." Coercion worked. Virtually imprisoned in their camps in the Sierras and forced into starvation, the strikers surrendered within a week.[14]

Beaten, the Chinese returned to work and completed the railroad, the "new highway to the commerce of Asia." The crucial participation of the Chinese was widely admitted. In an essay on "Manifest Destiny in the West," a writer for the *Overland Monthly* exclaimed: "The dream of Thomas Jefferson, and the desires of Thomas H. Benton's heart, have been wonderfully fulfilled, so far as the Pacific Railroad and the trade with the old world of the East is concerned. But even they did not prophesy that Chinamen should build the Pacificward end of the road." In 1869, at Promontory Point, where the last two railroad tracks were finally connected, fifteen hundred people, including prominent individuals from across the country, gathered to celebrate the historic moment. Attending the great event, one witness captured the scene:

> One fact . . . forcibly impressed me at the laying of the last nail. Two lengths of rails, fifty-six feet, had been omitted. The Union Pacific people brought up their pair of rails, and the work of placing them was done by Europeans. The Central Pacific people then laid their pair of rails, the labor being performed by Mongolians. The foremen, in both cases, were Americans. Here, near the center of the American Continent, were the united efforts of representatives of the continents of Europe, Asia, and America — America directing and controlling.[15]

Released from employment after the completion of the transcontinental railroad, thousands of the Chinese laborers went to San Francisco, where their compatriots were already heavily involved in manufacturing. The formation of an urban Chinese community and the industrial development of the city paralleled each other. In 1860, only 2,719 Chinese resided in San Francisco, representing only 7.8 percent of the Chinese population in California, compared to 70 percent in the mining region. The Chinese saw San Francisco as a port of entry, a way station en route to the gold fields. Ten years later, the Chinese population in the city had zoomed to 12,022, a 343 percent increase. Meanwhile, San Francisco had begun to develop as a locus of industry. In 1860, it had about two hundred manufacturing firms employing some fifteen hundred workers. Ten years later, with nearly one fourth of California's Chinese population living there, San Francisco had over 12,000 laborers employed in industrial production and was the ninth-leading manufacturing city in the United States.[16]

During the 1860s, as Chinese ex-miners moved to San Francisco, they found limited employment opportunities in the Chinese ethnic economy, which was based on retail businesses, service, vice, and entertainment. But jobs were available elsewhere in the city, and the Chinese laborers quickly became part of the larger manufacturing economy. Chinese workers represented 46 percent of the labor force in the city's four key industries — boots and shoes, woolens, cigars and tobacco, and sewing. The *San Francisco Morning Call* reported in 1872 that nearly half the workingmen employed in the city's factories were Chinese.[17]

The exodus of Chinese from the mining regions to San Francisco was timely. The Civil War had disrupted the flow of manufactured goods to the West, and capitalists in San Francisco were eagerly venturing into manufacturing. In this emerging economy, Chinese workers were concentrated in the low-wage industries. Cigar workers, for example, received only $287 in annual wages, and 92 percent of them were Chinese. By contrast, tailors and seamsters earned $588 a year, and only 9 percent of them were Chinese. Chinese workers were also segregated within individual industries and paid less than white workers. In the garment industry, Chinese workers were employed mainly in factories producing women's clothing and received an annual average wage of $364, compared to $597 paid to the mostly white workers in factories making men's clothing. In factories where the labor force was racially mixed, whites occupied the skilled positions and Chinese the menial ones. In these firms, white foremen directed the labor of Chinese crews. And where Chinese were assigned to the same tasks as whites, they were paid less than their white counterparts in an ethnically based differential-wage system: the work was equal but the wages were not.[18]

The significant role of Chinese labor in the industrial development of California was widely recognized. A. W. Loomis, in his article "How Our Chinamen Are Employed," counted thousands of Chinese factory operatives working in woolen mills, knitting mills, paper mills, powder mills, tanneries, shoe factories, and garment industries. In his essay *Chinaman or White Man, Which?* the Reverend O. Gibson argued that California's manufacturing interests could "not be maintained a single day" without the low rate of Chinese labor. In *The Golden State,* published in 1876, R. G. McClellan described the state's economic dependency on Chinese labor: "In mining, farming, in factories and in the labor generally of California the employment of the Chinese has been found most desirable; and much of the labor done by these people if performed by white men at higher wages could not be continued nor made possible."[19]

Meanwhile, in the rural regions, the Chinese were participating in the development of California's agriculture, which was turning from wheat to fruit acreage. "They were a vital factor," historian Carey McWilliams writes, "one is inclined to state *the* vital factor, in making the transition possible." Formerly farmers in the Pearl River Delta in Guangdong, the Chinese shared their agricultural experience and knowledge. They "taught their overlords how to plant, cultivate, and harvest orchard and garden crops." Their contributions extended beyond California: Ah Bing in Oregon bred the famous

Bing cherry, and Lue Gim Gong in Florida developed the frost-resistant orange that bore his name and that gave the state its citrus industry.[20]

California was the locus of Chinese advances in agriculture. In the San Joaquin and Sacramento River deltas, the Chinese constructed networks of irrigation channels and miles of levees, dikes, and ditches. Wielding shovels and working waist-deep in water, they drained the tule swamps and marshes and transformed them into agricultural lands. In 1869, a writer for the *Overland Monthly* acknowledged the change in the landscape the Chinese had wrought: "The ditches and dykes which at present protect only a few little patches here and there of the most fruitful soil that the sun shines on, may be made to perform a like service all over the Tulare swamps; and the descendants of the people who drained those almost limitless marshes on either side of their own swiftly-flowing Yellow River, and turned them into luxuriant fields, are able to do the same thing on the banks of the Sacramento and the San Joaquin." In Salinas, Chinese laborers dug six miles of ditches to drain the land, cutting the peat soil "with huge knife-like spades and pitching it out with steel forks and hooks." Their work boosted the value of the land from twenty-eight dollars an acre in 1875 to one hundred dollars an acre two years later.[21]

Landowners like Reuben Kercheval and P. J. van Loben Sels employed Chinese extensively for reclamation work. The workers were paid by the cubic yard of earth dug and used as filler for the levees; sometimes they resorted to tricks to increase their wages. To calculate how much his Chinese laborers should be paid, van Loben Sels would measure the size of the hole in the borrow pit every four or five days. But it was difficult to make accurate measurements due to the unevenness of the terrain. In order to show the depth of the hole they had dug and a record of their labor, the Chinese workers left a column of dirt in the middle of each pit to serve as a ruler. They tended, van Loben Sels noticed, to use the highest point of ground for their column before digging the hole. In addition, occasionally they gave their column an "operation" during the night, surgically cutting the column crosswise somewhere in the middle and inserting a new layer of dirt. In the morning, the pit appeared deeper, and the laborers quietly expected their boss to measure the hole and pay them accordingly. Whenever they were caught making nocturnal adjustments on their columns, they were fined.[22]

The Chinese laborers wanted to be more than low-paid diggers: many wanted to be farmers themselves, working the land for their own profits. In Sacramento, Yuba, and San Joaquin counties, where concentrations of Chinese were large and where agricultural development was extensive, the number of Chinese truck gardeners jumped from 119 to 375 and the number of Chinese farmers from none to 538 between 1860 and 1880. Tenant farming offered the Chinese a way to enter the business with minimal capital. They could sign agreements with white landowners. In exchange for the use of the land, equipment, and the marketing of crops, Chinese tenant farmers would raise fruit and vegetables and then divide the profits with the landowners. In 1873, for example, Chou Ying and Wee Ying signed a contract with George D. Roberts, leasing 551 acres in three tracts. The lease stipulated that they would pay eight dollars an acre for one of the tracts and give Roberts a fourth of the crops produced on the remaining two tracts or pay ten dollars an acre if they chose to grow Chinese vegetables on them. Many of the Chinese tenant-farming enterprises represented partnerships, forming companies known as *yuen* ("garden"). Collectively the partners were responsible for the lease and the operation of a farm. "We found the broad fields apportioned off and rented to separate companies of Chinamen who were working them upon shares — each little company having its own cabin," an observer reported in 1869. "Teams being furnished them, they do all the working, preparing the ground, seeding, tending the crop, and gathering the fruit, leaving nothing for the proprietor to do but to attend to the marketing, and to put into his own pocket half of the proceeds."[23]

Most of the Chinese in agriculture were laborers, however. Describing how he had come to employ Chinese, a white farmer explained that he had initially used white workers but found they would work for only a few days and then would quit. "I then went to a Chinaman," he said, "and told him I wanted to contract for binding and stacking wheat. . . . Several hundred of them came. We had one or two hundred acres that had been reaped, and needed putting up very badly; and the next morning it was all stacked. The Chinamen did the work that night. They did the work well and faithfully, and of course we abandoned white labor." In 1869, the *Overland Monthly* described the ubiquitous presence of Chinese laborers in California agriculture: "Visit a hop plantation in the picking season, and count its 50, 60, or 70 pickers in the garb of the eastern Asiatics, working steadily and noiselessly on from morning till night, gathering, curing and sacking the crop. . . . Go through the fields of strawberries . . . the vineyards and orchards, and you will learn that most

of these fruits are gathered or boxed for market by this same people."
The Chinese were also working in the vineyards and wineries of the
Sonoma Valley. There Hungarian-immigrant Colonel Agoston
Harszthy, who would come to be known as "the father of California
viticulture," employed Chinese laborers to clear land and plant grapevines on his Buena Vista Ranch. A visitor to Harszthy's Buena Vista
winery in 1863 found Chinese working in the vineyards and also in
the press house, "filling, corking, wiring, etc. Champagne bottles."
He also saw Chinese workers blasting and excavating three wine
cellars, each to be twenty-six feet wide, thirteen feet in height, and
three hundred feet long.[24]

In 1870, the Chinese constituted 18 percent of all farm laborers
in California and were especially numerous in Sacramento (45 percent), Alameda (25 percent), and San Mateo (25 percent) counties.
Ten years later, Chinese farm workers represented 86 percent of the
agricultural labor force in Sacramento County, 85 percent in Yuba,
67 percent in Solano, 55 percent in Santa Clara, 46 percent in Yolo,
and 43 percent in Tehema. Polish journalist Henryk Sienkiewicz reported that the work in the hop fields and fruit orchards of northern
California was done "almost exclusively by hired Chinese." In 1893,
the *Pacific Rural Press* repeatedly acknowledged the contribution of
the Chinese as laborers to California agriculture: "The Chinese are
the mainstay of the orchardist and thus far it must be said, form the
only supply of labor which he can depend on. They are expert pickers
and packers of fruit. It is difficult to see how our annual fruit crop
could be harvested and prepared for market without the Chinaman."[25]

Employers of Chinese labor also realized they could pay especially low wages. Chinese laborers were paid only thirty dollars a
month — ten to twenty dollars less than the wages paid to white
workers. The Chinese were trapped in a racially based dual-wage
system. What enabled them to make ends meet was the fact that they
had left their families in China where the cost of living was much
lower than the United States and where their California earnings
went further in covering family expenses. However, low wages also
meant keeping their families in China even if they wished to have
their wives and children join them in America.[26]

Chinese farm laborers did not always quietly accept what their
employers offered them. In 1880, Chinese pickers in Santa Clara
County went out on strike seeking increased compensation for the
fruit they harvested. After the 1882 Chinese Exclusion Act had re-

duced the supply of Chinese farm labor, Chinese agricultural workers recognized the increased need for their labor and demanded higher wages. In 1900, the Bureau of Labor Statistics reported: "Relieved, by the operation of the Exclusion Acts, in great measure from the pressing competition of his fellow-countrymen, the Chinese worker was not slow to take advantage of circumstances and demand in exchange for his labor a higher price, and, as time went on, even becoming Americanized to the extent of enforcing such demands in some cases through the medium of labor organization."[27]

But the racially divided farm-labor force generated ethnic antagonism, and Chinese became targets of white-labor resentment, especially during hard times. "White men and women who desire to earn a living," the *Los Angeles Times* reported on August 14, 1893, "have for some time been entering quiet protests against vineyardists and packers employing Chinese in preference to whites." Their protests did not remain quiet as economic depression led to violent anti-Chinese riots by unemployed white workers throughout California. From Ukiah to the Napa Valley to Fresno to Redlands, Chinese were beaten and shot by white workers; they were herded to railroad stations and loaded onto trains. The Chinese bitterly remember this violence and expulsion as the "driving out."[28]

"Ethnic antagonism" in the mines, factories, and fields reinforced the movement of Chinese into self-employment — stores, restaurants, and especially laundries. Chinese wash-houses were a common sight as early as the 1850s. A journalist visiting California in 1853 commented on the hardworking Chinese laundrymen: "What a truly industrious people they are! At work, cheerfully and briskly, at ten o'clock at night." By 1870, there were 2,899 Chinese laundry workers in California, 72 percent of all laborers in this occupation. Twenty years later their number had more than doubled to 6,400, or 69 percent of all laundry workers. During this period, the ratio of laundry workers to all workers in the Chinese population jumped from one out of every seventeen to one out of every twelve. Nearly half of Sacramento's 103 Chinese establishments listed in the *Directory of Chinese Business Houses* in 1878 were laundries.[29]

The "Chinese laundryman" was an American phenomenon. "The Chinese laundryman does not learn his trade in China; there are no laundries in China," stated Lee Chew, who came to America in the early 1860s. "The women there do the washing in tubs and have no washboards or flat irons. All the Chinese laundrymen here [in America] were taught in the first place by American women just as I was taught." In China, wrote Wong Chin Foo of New York in *The Cosmopolitan* in 1888, laundry work was a "woman's occupation," and men did not "step into it for fear of losing their social standing."[30]

But why in America did Chinese men enter this line of work? Unlike the retail or restaurant business, a laundry could be opened with a small capital outlay of seventy-five to two hundred dollars. The requirements were minimal: a stove, trough, dry-room, sleeping apartment, and sign. A Chinese laundryman also did not need to speak much English to operate his business. "In this sort of menial labor," said one, "I can get along speaking only 'yes' and 'no.' " And he could manage without knowing numbers. "Being illiterate, he could not write the numbers," another laundryman said describing a fellow operator. "He had a way and what a way! See, he would draw a circle as big as a half dollar coin to represent a half dollar, and a circle as big as a dime for a dime, and so on. When the customers came in to call for their laundry, they would catch on to the meaning of the circles and pay accordingly."[31]

But "Chinese laundrymen" were also "pushed" into their occupation: laundry work was one of the few opportunities that were "open" to Chinese. "Men of other nationalities who are jealous of the Chinese have raised such a great outcry about Chinese cheap labor that they have shut him out of working on farms or in factories or building railroads or making streets or digging sewers," explained Lee Chew. "So he opens a laundry." Thus the "Chinese laundry" represented a retreat into self-employment from a narrowly restricted labor market. "You couldn't work in the cigar factories or the jute or woolen mills any more — all the Chinese had been driven out," old Chinese men later remembered sadly. "About all they could be was laundrymen or vegetable peddlers then." Crowded into laundry work, one out of four employed Chinese males in the United States in 1900 was a laundryman.[32]

In a laundry there were usually two workers, one doing the washing and a second the ironing. Their work began about seven o'clock in the morning on Monday. "The man who irons does not start in till Tuesday," Lee Chew said, "as the clothes are not ready for him to begin until that time. So he has Sundays and Mondays as holidays. The man who does the washing finishes up on Friday night, and so he has Saturday and Sunday off. Each works only five days a week, but those are long days — from seven o'clock in the morning till midnight." They washed and ironed clothes for white miners and workers; frequently mistreated and harassed by their customers, they were forced to scream and curse in silence. "We had to put up with many insults and some frauds," complained Lee Chew, "as men would come in [to the laundry] and claim parcels that did not belong to them, saying they had lost their tickets, and would fight if they did not get what they asked for." In the mining country, Lee said, "we made plenty of money in gold dust, but had a hard time, for many of the miners were wild men who carried revolvers and after drinking would come into our place to shoot and steal shirts."[33]

While most of the Chinese resided in the West, they were also present elsewhere in the United States, including the South. The Chinese presence below the Mason-Dixon line developed within a different context: there they entered a biracial society composed of whites and blacks. The era of Reconstruction was a troublesome time for southern planters. "Emancipation has spoiled the negro and carried him away from the fields of agriculture," the editor of the *Vicksburg Times* in Mississippi complained in 1869. "Our prosperity depends entirely upon the recovery of lost ground, and we therefore say let the Coolies come." That same year the southern planters' convention in Memphis announced that it was "desirable and necessary to look to the teeming population of Asia for assistance in the cultivation of our soil and the development of our industrial interests." In his address to the convention, labor contractor Cornelius Koopmanshoop said his company had imported 30,000 Chinese laborers into California, and offered to make them available in the South.[34]

Planters quickly saw that the Chinese could be employed as models for black workers: hardworking and economical, the Chinese could be the "educators" of the former slaves. Louisiana and Mississippi planters imported Chinese laborers and pitted them against black workers during the 1870s. They praised the workers from Asia for outproducing blacks in per-worker competition, and used the Chinese to "regulate" the "detestable system of black labor." A southern governor frankly explained: "Undoubtedly the underlying motive for this effort to bring in Chinese laborers was to punish the negro for having abandoned the control of his old master, and to regulate the conditions of his employment and the scale of wages to be paid him."[35]

In Mississippi a newspaper reported the successful introduction of Chinese laborers in 1870: "Messrs. Ferris and Estell, who are cultivating on the Hughs place, near Prentiss, recently imported direct from Hong Kong, a lot of Chinese, sixteen in number, with whom as laborers, they are well pleased." Meanwhile in Louisiana, A. B. Merrill, owner of the Milloudon plantation outside of New Orleans, had a work force of 140 Chinese. A traveling correspondent described them in his vivid account:

> Mounting horses and spreading our umbrellas, we rode out a mile or more through the fields, past countless negroes and mule-teams ploughing, to the spot off by themselves where the picturesque heathens were hoeing cane. . . . Apart, in the middle of the field stood the imperturbable sinecurist who made a faint show of overseeing his countrymen . . . Ah Sing. . . . The Chinamen went on with their work, hoeing the young cane, and doing it very carefully and precisely. Occasionally they would look up at us, but in a very stolid, careless way. Ah Sing approached and greeted us with a polite, "Hallo, how do?" On learning that we were well, he observed . . . , "Belly hot to-day."

The wife of a Louisiana planter, in a letter to her daughter, described the Chinese workers as very good hands: "Yesterday was their Christmas day and they asked for half the day and had prepared themselves a good dinner." One day, she continued, one of the "Chinamen" had come into the yard and asked for her. "I went to the porch to see what he wanted. He took off his hat, got down on his knees, and bowed himself his head touching the ground four times very stately then got up. I thought he was drunk but it was a mark of respect he was showing."[36]

But the Chinese did not stay long on the plantations. As early as 1871, the *New Orleans Times* noted that the Chinese preferred to work in the small trades and industries in the city rather than the "plodding work of the plantations." By 1880, there were fifty Chinese in Mississippi, 133 in Arkansas, and 489 in Louisiana. Ninety-five of them lived in New Orleans, working as laundrymen, cigarmakers, shoemakers, cooks, and woodcarvers. By then the southern planters had overthrown Reconstruction; their political power over blacks restored, they quickly lost interest in Chinese labor.[37]

In 1870, while southern planters were experimenting with the introduction of Chinese laborers, New England businessmen were attentively watching a new development in a small town in Massachusetts. After a long ride on the recently completed transcontinental railroad, seventy-five Chinese had arrived in North Adams to work in one of its shoe factories. Hidden in the western mountains of the state, North Adams immediately became the subject of national interest.

Between 1840 and 1870, North Adams had been transformed from an isolated rural village into an industrialized town. According to *Harper's New Monthly Magazine,* it was "one of the busiest little towns, humming and smoking with various industries, and nestled in the most picturesque and mountainous part of the valley of the Housatonic." The economic takeoff for this town occurred after the railroad had connected North Adams with Pittsfield in 1846 and opened new market possibilities. The impact was dramatic. Within thirty years, dwellings had increased from one hundred to more than four hundred, and the number of cotton looms had multiplied ten times, from twenty-two to more than two hundred. In 1869, the town's 4,000 workers produced $7 million worth of goods. Between 1860 and 1870, the population nearly doubled from 6,924 to 12,090; almost one third of the population were European immigrants, particularly Irish. North Adams had become the locus of thirty-eight factories — cotton mills, woolen mills, carriage manufactories, paper mills, and shoe factories.[38]

The owner of one of these busy factories, Calvin T. Sampson, personified the new manufacturing era of North Adams. A descendant of the original settlers of Plymouth Colony, he had established "A Model Shoe Factory." His factory produced more than 300,000 pairs annually; the local press praised it as a successful business, "built up from small beginnings, by persistent energy, industry, economy, and judgment." Actually, Sampson's success depended more on the use of machinery and the exploitation of labor. Three years after he had founded his factory in 1858, Sampson introduced the first of Well's pegging machines in shoe manufacturing. The new technology, a newspaper reported, increased both efficiency and profits: "Each machine performs the labor of six men, and effects a saving of two cents on every pair of shoes made." The machine also reduced workers from craftsmen to low-paid, unskilled tenders of the machine. Sampson's increasing reliance on capital-intensive production reflected a general pattern in New England manufacturing.[39]

Workers in New England recognized the need to protect themselves against labor-eliminating machines and low wages, and in 1867 they organized the Secret Order of the Knights of St. Crispin. Within three years, the Crispins became the largest labor organization in the United States; 50,000 strong in membership, the union was especially active in the shoemaking industries of Massachusetts. In 1870 the Crispins at Sampson's shoe factory in North Adams struck. They demanded higher wages, an eight-hour day, and access to the company's account books in order to fix wages in accordance with profits. Sampson fired the striking workers. Unsuccessful in his effort to hire scabs from a nearby town, he decided to declare total war against the Crispins and drive a "wedge" into the conflict.[40]

The "wedge" was a contingent of Chinese workers from San Francisco. Sampson had been considering the employment of Chinese labor: a year before the strike, the official organ of shoe manufacturers, *Hide and Leather Interest,* had condemned the Crispins and urged employers to import Chinese workers as strikebreakers. Sampson had also read a newspaper article on the effectiveness of Chinese labor in a San Francisco shoe factory. Shortly after the strike began at his factory, Sampson sent his superintendent to San Francisco, where he signed a contract with a Chinese labor supplier. According to the terms of the agreement, Sampson would pay the company a commission for the Chinese workers and transport them to Massachusetts; he would pay each worker twenty-three dollars a month for the first year and twenty-six dollars a month for the next two years, plus room and fuel. The workers would labor for three years and pay for their own clothing and food.

The arrival of the seventy-five Chinese workers in North Adams on June 13 was a moment of great interest in the East. "A large and hostile crowd met them at the depot, hooted them, hustled them somewhat, and threw stones at them," *The Nation* reported. Thirty plainclothes policemen marched the newcomers to dormitories at Sampson's factory, where they were placed behind locked and guarded gates. A few days later, the *Boston Commonwealth* announced: "They are with us! the 'Celestials' — with almond eyes, pigtails, rare industry, quick adaptation, high morality, and all — seventy-five of them — hard at work in the town of North Adams." The *Springfield Republican* predicted the "van of the invading army of Celestials" would free Sampson from "the cramping tyranny of that worst of American trades-unions, the 'Knights of St. Crispin.' " White workers as well as white employers watched as Sampson opened his factory again and began production.[41]

They did not have to wait long for results. Within three months, the Chinese workers were producing more shoes than the same number of white workers would have made. The success of Sampson's experiment was reported in the press. "The Chinese, and this especially annoys the Crispins," the editor of *The Nation* wrote, "show the usual quickness of their race in learning the process of their new business, and already do creditable hand and machine work." The editor of *Harper's New Monthly Magazine* visited Sampson's factory and described the new workers in felicitous terms: "They are generally small. . . . [A]bout sixty of the Chinese workmen [are] in the room, and there can be nowhere . . . a busier, more orderly group of workmen." Writing for *Scribner's Monthly,* William Shanks agreed. The Chinese "labored regularly and constantly, losing no blue Mondays on account of Sunday's dissipations nor wasting hours on idle holidays," he reported. "The quality of the work was found to be fully equal to that of the Crispins." Through the use of Chinese labor, Sampson had widened the margin of his profits: the saving in the cost of production for a week's work was $840, which totaled $40,000 a year. These figures inspired Shanks to calculate: "There are 115 establishments in the State, employing 5,415 men . . . capable of producing 7,942 cases of shoes per week. Under the Chinese system of Mr. Sampson, a saving of $69,594 per week, or say $3,500,000 a year, would be effected, thus revolutionizing the trade."[42]

In their struggle against Sampson, the striking Crispins tried to promote working-class solidarity by organizing a Chinese lodge of St. Crispin. Although little is known about this effort, it was probably conditioned by pragmatic concerns: the recruitment of the Chinese workers into the St. Crispin union would have undermined Sampson's "wedge." Watching the Crispin outreach to the Chinese, the editor of *The Nation* commented: "Chinese lodges and strikes will come in time when enough Chinamen are collected together in any given place; but the prospect appears not immediately flattering at North Adams." Based on practical self-interests rather than an ideological commitment to class solidarity, the Crispin attempt to unionize the Chinese workers quickly collapsed. At a meeting in Boston in July 1870, white workers turned against the Chinese laborers, condemning Sampson for reducing "American labor" to "the Chinese standard of rice and rats."[43]

Sampson's daring action had sobering effects on white workers in other North Adams shoe factories. Ten days after the arrival of Sampson's "Mongolian battery," Parker Brothers, Cady Brothers, Millard and Whitman, and E. R. and N. L. Millard forced laborers to return to work with a 10 percent wage reduction. Commenting frankly on the significance of Sampson's experiment of employing Chinese labor, a writer for *Scribner's Monthly* wrote: "If for no other purpose than the breaking up of the incipient steps toward labor combinations and 'Trade Unions' . . . the advent of Chinese labor should be hailed with warm welcome." The "heathen Chinee," he concluded, could be the "final solution" to the labor problem in America.[44]

Sampson's experiment also impressed capitalists elsewhere in the East. Three months after the arrival of the Chinese in North Adams, James B. Hervey brought sixty-eight Chinese to Belleville, New Jersey, to work in his Passaic Steam Laundry. Like Sampson, with whom he had consulted, Hervey had secured them through a labor supplier in San Francisco. Eventually he employed three hundred Chinese workers and used them to meet his labor needs and counter strikes by Irish workers. Meanwhile, in Beaver Falls, Pennsylvania, the Beaver Falls Cutlery Company had also begun hiring Chinese laborers to help discipline striking white workers. Within a year, the cutlery company increased the number of its Chinese workers from seventy to 190.

The promise of Chinese labor had been proven in the West and its potential had been demonstrated in the South and the East. But, from the very beginning, the Chinese presence represented a dilemma. "What we shall do with them is not quite clear yet," remarked Samuel Bowles in 1869 in his book *Our New West*. "How they are to rank, socially, civilly, and politically, among us is one of the nuts for our social science students to crack, — if they can." And what would be the future of white workers in this country as its industrial development depended more and more on Chinese labor?[45]

The Heathen Chinee

One answer to both questions was a proposal to reduce the Chinese into a permanently degraded caste-labor force: they would be in effect a unique, transnational industrial reserve army of migrant laborers forced to be foreigners forever. They would be what sociologist Robert Blauner has termed an "internal colony," a racially subordinated group. Unlike white immigrants such as the Irish, Italians, and Poles, the Chinese would be a politically proscribed group. Part of America's process of production, they would not be allowed to become part of her body politic. "I do not believe they are going to remain here long enough to become good citizens," Central Pacific official Charles Crocker told a legislative committee, "and I would not admit them to citizenship."[46]

For Crocker and other employers of Chinese labor, the Chinese would be allowed to enter and work temporarily, then return to their homeland while others would come here as replacements. The Chinese would be used to service the labor needs of America's industry without threatening the racial homogeneity of the country's citizenry. The migrant workers would be inducted into a labor-supply process that would move labor between China and the United States in a circular pattern. Anti-Chinese laws, economic exploitation, and racial antagonism would assist in this process, compelling the Chinese to leave America after a limited period of employment. They would remain "strangers."[47]

But what enabled capitalists like Crocker to degrade the Chinese into a subservient caste of laborers was a particular ideology. Historically, whites generally perceived America as a racially homogeneous society and Americans as white. Long before the Chinese arrived, they had already been predetermined for exclusion by this set of ideas; the Chinese future in America could be seen in the black and Indian past. The entrance of a new nonwhite group provided an occasion for the reaffirmation of the "errand into the wilderness" in an industrializing America that would soon no longer have a frontier.

Not surprisingly, when the Chinese began coming to California they almost immediately provoked widespread concerns about the relationship between race and national identity. One of the first Americans to address the issue was Hinton Helper of North Carolina. A critic of slavery, he urged his fellow white farmers in the South to overthrow the planter class and remove blacks from the country. While visiting California in 1851, Helper had been surprised and disturbed to find so many Chinese working and living in the new state. "Certain it is," he predicted in his book *The Land of Gold*, published in 1855, "that the greater the diversity of colors and qualities of men, the greater will be the strife and conflict of feeling." Helper insisted that America should be a homogeneous white society. Comparing the entry of the Chinese in the West to the existence of blacks in the East, he protested: "Our population was already too heterogeneous before the Chinese came. I should not wonder at all, if the copper of the Pacific yet becomes as great a subject of discord and dissension as the ebony of the Atlantic."[48]

Helper's comparison between the two groups prefigured a stereotyping process: the Chinese were associated with blacks in the racial imagination of white society. Shortly after the Civil War, the *New York Times* issued a warning that depicted the newly freed blacks and the newly arrived Chinese as threats to the American political system: "We have four millions of degraded negroes in the South . . . and if there were to be a flood-tide of Chinese population — a population befouled with all the social vices, with no knowledge or appreciation of free institutions or constitutional liberty, with heathenish souls and heathenish propensities . . . we should be prepared to bid farewell to republicanism." The *San Francisco Chronicle* compared the Chinese "coolie" to the black slave, and condemned both as antagonistic to free labor: "When the coolie arrives here he is as rigidly under the control of the contractor who brought him as ever an African slave was under his master in South Carolina or Louisiana." Like blacks, the Chinese were viewed as antagonistic to republican and free-labor society.[49]

The Chinese migrants found that racial qualities previously assigned to blacks quickly became "Chinese" characteristics. Calling for Chinese exclusion, the *San Francisco Alta* warned: "Every reason that exists against the toleration of free blacks in Illinois may be argued against that of the Chinese here." White workers referred to the Chinese as "nagurs," and a magazine cartoon depicted the Chinese as a bloodsucking vampire with slanted eyes, a pigtail, dark skin, and thick lips. Like blacks, the Chinese were described as heathen, morally inferior, savage, childlike, and lustful. Chinese women were condemned as a "depraved class," and their depravity was associated with their physical appearance, which seemed to show "but a slight removal from the African race." Chinese men were seen as sensuous creatures, especially interested in white women. A writer for the *New York Times* reported that he noticed "a handsome but squalidly dressed young white girl" in an opium den and inquired about her. The owner replied: "Oh, hard time in New York. Young girl hungry. Plenty come here. Chinaman always have something to eat, and he like young white girl. He! He!"[50]

Like blacks, the Chinese were viewed as threats to white racial purity. As early as 1661, Maryland had enacted the first antimiscegenation law prohibiting marriage between whites and blacks, and by the nineteenth century, laws against miscegenation existed in most states. But the California law was designed to include the Chinese. At the state's constitutional convention of 1878, John F. Miller warned: "Were the Chinese to amalgamate at all with our people, it would be the lowest, most vile and degraded of our race, and the result of that amalgamation would be a hybrid of the most despicable, a mongrel of the most detestable that has ever afflicted the earth." Two years later, California lawmakers enacted legislation to prohibit the issuance of a license authorizing the marriage of a white person with a "negro, mulatto, or Mongolian."[51]

In the white imagination, the Chinese were also sometimes related to Indians. The editor of the *California Marin Journal* declared that the winning of the West from the "red man" would be in vain, if whites were now to surrender the conquered land to a "horde of Chinese." The association between Indians and Chinese suggested one way to solve the "Chinese Problem." "We do not let the Indian stand in the way of civilization," stated former Governor Horatio Seymour of New York, "so why let the Chinese barbarian?" In his letter published in the *New York Times,* Seymour continued: "Today we are dividing the lands of the native Indians into states, counties, and townships. We are driving off from their property the game upon which they live, by railroads. We tell them plainly, they must give up their homes and property, and live upon corners of their own territories, because they are in the way of our civilization. If we can do this, then we can keep away another form of barbarism which has no right to be here." A U.S. senator from Alabama "likened" the Chinese to the Indians, "inferior" socially and subject to federal government control. The government, he argued, should do to the Chinese what it had already done to the Indians — put them on reservations.[52]

What all three groups — blacks, Indians, and Chinese — shared seemed singularly striking: they were all nonwhite. This perception went beyond a matter of prejudice. In the 1854 California Supreme Court decision of *People v. Hall,* it became a basis for public policy. A year before, George W. Hall and two others were tried for murdering Ling Sing. During the trial, one Caucasian and three Chinese witnesses testified for the prosecution. After the jury had returned a guilty verdict, the judge sentenced Hall to be hanged. Hall's lawyer then appealed the verdict, arguing that the Chinese witnesses should not have been permitted to testify against Hall. An existing California statute provided that "no black or mulatto person, or Indian, shall be permitted to give evidence in favor of, or against, any white person," and the question was whether this restriction included the Chinese. In its review, the California Supreme Court reversed Hall's conviction, declaring that the words "Indian, Negro, Black, and White" were "generic terms, designating races," and that therefore "Chinese and other people not white" could not testify against whites.[53]

In 1859, the California superintendent of education applied the color line to the public schools. The integration of blacks, Indians, and Chinese would lead to the ruin of the schools, the superintendent warned. "The great mass of our citizens will not associate on terms of equality with these inferior races; nor will they consent that their children should do so." A year later, the California legislature established segregated schools, authorizing school officials to withhold public funds from any school that admitted the proscribed groups. In 1879 President Rutherford Hayes placed the "Chinese Problem" within the broad context of race in American society. The "present Chinese invasion," he argued, was "pernicious and should be discouraged. Our experience in dealing with the weaker races — the Negroes and Indians . . . — is not encouraging. . . . I would consider with favor any suitable measures to discourage the Chinese from coming to our shores."[54]

In the exclusionist imagination, however, the "strangers" from Asia seemed to pose a greater threat than did blacks and Indians. Unlike blacks, the Chinese were seen as intelligent and competitive; unlike Indians, they represented an increasing rather than a decreasing population. As an industrial army of aliens from the East, they threatened to displace and force white workers into poverty. During the 1870s, white workers expressed their fear of the Chinese in a popular song:

O workingmen dear, and did you hear
The news that's goin' around?
Another China steamer
Has been landed here in town.
Today I read the papers,
And it grieved my heart full sore
To see upon the title page,
"O, just 'Twelve Hundred More!'"

O, California's coming down,
As you can plainly see.
They are hiring all the Chinamen
and discharging you and me;
But strife will be in every town
Throughout the Pacific shore,
And the cry of old and young shall be,
"O, damn, 'Twelve Hundred More.'"[55]

Similarly, in the play *"The Chinese Must Go"* by Henry Grimm of San Francisco, the racial anxieties of white workers were acted out on the stage. Two Chinese characters conspire to destroy white labor:

> Ah Coy. By and by white man catchee no money; Chinaman catchee heap money; Chinaman workee cheap, plenty work; white man workee dear, no work — sabee?
>
> Sam Gin. Me heep sabee.
>
> Ah Coy. White man damn fools; keep wifee and children — cost plenty money; Chinaman no wifee, no children, save plenty money. By and by, no more white workingmen in California; all Chinamen — sabee?[56]

White workers have reason to be alarmed, for the sinister Chinese are planning to take away their jobs and even their country. One of the characters, Frank B., says to a friend:

> You wasted your dimes in a candy store, I see. Let me tell you, if I take a four-bit piece, buy meat and flour with it, digest it, it turns into blood; therefore, money is blood. Now, what would you think of a man who would allow a lot of parasites to suck every day a certain quantity of blood out of his body, when he knows that his whole constitution is endangered by this sucking process; mustn't he be either an idiot or intend self-destruction? And suppose those Chinese parasites should suck as much blood out of every State in the Union, destroying Uncle Sam's sinews and muscles, how many years do you think it would take to put him in his grave?[57]

The most powerful articulation of anti-Chinese fears and anxieties was presented by Bret Harte in a poem, "The Heathen Chinee." Published in the *Overland Monthly* in 1870, the poem became instantly and immensely popular as newspaper after newspaper across the country reprinted it and as the phrase "heathen Chinee" became a household word in white America. The *New York Globe* had to publish Harte's poem twice in order to satisfy the demands of its readership. "Certainly nothing has been printed of late, if ever, which has run through the newspapers of this country as this has," the editor of the *Springfield Republican* observed in his review of the poem. "Part of this effect is owing to the temporary excitement of the public about the Chinese question, — but the combination of delicate humor, and force of expression, both plain and grotesque, seen in these verses would have made them famous at any time."[58]

The publication of Harte's poem was timely. The transcontinental railroad had been completed in 1869, and thousands of Chinese, released from railroad employment, were moving into the cities and becoming very visible. The railroad made transportation to California both inexpensive and easy for thousands of white workers from the East, and it opened California markets to competition from eastern manufacturers. White workers in California increasingly saw the Chinese as competitors in the job market. By the end of 1870, there were three workers — two white and one Chinese — for every job in San Francisco. But fear of Chinese labor competition was no longer confined to the West, for Chinese laborers had begun working in a New England shoe factory three months before Harte's poem reverberated in the print media. The poem helped to crystallize and focus anti-Chinese anxieties and paranoia, its rhymes evoking from white America a nervous chuckle.

"The Heathen Chinee" describes a card game between Ah Sin and William Nye. Determined to beat his opponent, Nye has cards stuffed up his sleeves; yet, even with his extra cards, the Irishman loses time and again. Ah Sin has a "childlike" smile, but the reader learns

> *That for ways that are dark*
> *And for tricks that are vain*
> *The heathen Chinee is peculiar.*

Suddenly, Nye catches Ah Sin cheating. As he beats Ah Sin with his fists, he notices cards hidden in Ah Sin's sleeves falling to the floor around them. And Nye shouts: "We are ruined by Chinese cheap labour."[59]

Clearly, the poem is ambiguous. While it negatively stereotypes the Chinese, it portrays Nye as a cheater too. Yet, what most impressed Harte's readers, feeling amused and anxious at once, was the "heathen Chinee's" "peculiar" ways, his deceptiveness and slyness, his "sin"-fulness, and his ability to "ruin" white labor in America. Harte regarded himself as a friend of the Chinese and actually regretted the racist effect of his poem. His feeling of guilt led him to remark privately to a friend: "Perhaps you can have little respect for a poet who wrote such trash as the *Heathen Chinee*."[60]

Yet, after the publication of the poem, Harte continued to write about the Chinese in America. While he protested against the injustices committed against them, he perpetuated anti-Chinese racism through his images of them as "heathens" and threats to white America. This contradiction may be found in two of Harte's short stories — "Wan Lee, the Pagan" and "See Yup."

In "Wan Lee, the Pagan," the narrator Harte begins by telling the readers about his visit to the Chinese merchant Hop Sing, a "grave, decorous, handsome gentleman" with a pigtail. Harte reports that Hop Sing's warehouse has a "deliciously commingled mysterious foreign odor." There he is offered tea and a snack of sweetmeats from a "mysterious jar" that looks as if it might contain "a preserved mouse."

The principal character in the story is Wan Lee, a twelve-year-old boy living with Hop Sing in San Francisco. Wan Lee is quite impish, good at "imitation" and "superstitious," carrying around his neck "a hideous little porcelain god." The boy "knows but little of Confucius, and absolutely nothing of Mencius," says Hop Sing. "Owing to the negligence of his father, he associated, perhaps too much with American children." Partially acculturated, Wan Lee falls in love with a white girl.

Their relationship is a touching one. "Bright," "cheery," and "innocent," the white girl awakens "a depth in the boy's nature that hitherto had been unsuspected." When she goes to school, Wan Lee walks behind her, carrying her books and defending himself against the racist attacks of "Caucasian Christian" boys. He also makes beautiful presents for her, and she reciprocates. She reads and sings to him; she teaches him "a thousand little prettinesses and refinements only known to girls"; gives him a "yellow" ribbon for his pigtail, as best suiting his "complexion"; shows him wherein he is "original and valuable"; and takes him to Sunday school with her, against the "precedents" of the school. "Small-womanlike," she triumphs. They get along very well together — "this little Christian girl, with her shining cross hanging around her plump, white, little neck, and this dark little Pagan, with his hideous porcelain god hidden away in his blouse." But tragedy awaits them. At the end of the story, Wan Lee is killed during two days of anti-Chinese mob violence in San Francisco — "two days when a mob of her citizens set upon and killed unarmed, defenseless foreigners, because they were foreigners and of another race, religion, and color, and worked for what wages they could get."

Despite his condemnation of the "Christian" murderers of Wan Lee, Harte had presented an ambiguous message to white America. The Chinese, in the characters of Hop Sing and Wan Lee, were described as unfortunate victims of white working-class hatred and cruel racism; yet they were also depicted as mice-eaters, "pagan," "dark," "impish," "superstitious," "yellow," and subversive to white labor and white racial purity.[61]

Like "Wan Lee, the Pagan," the story of See Yup was intended to express moral disapproval of anti-Chinese racism. Yet, again Harte's writing warred against itself. In this story, See Yup is a laundryman in a small mining town; he is a "heathen" and exudes a "peculiar odor" — half ginger, half opium — called the "Chinese smell." See Yup is victimized by the white miners. "Subject to the persecutions of the more ignorant and brutal," he is "always" a "source of amusement" to whites. White boys would tie his pigtails to a window, and white miners would take their dirty clothes to his laundry and pick up their cleaned clothes without paying for them. The unhappy target of racial abuse and exploitation, See Yup knows he can find no justice or recourse in the courts.

One Saturday, See Yup enters the Wells Fargo office and asks the clerk to send a bag of gold dust valued at $500 to San Francisco. He had gathered the gold, it seems, while working the tailings of an abandoned mine. He has gold sent to San Francisco three Saturdays in a row, and the clerk at the Wells Fargo office notices See Yup's good fortune and spreads the news that See Yup has made a strike. The white miners then organize themselves into a committee and visit See Yup's mine. In two hours, they witness See Yup and his fellow Chinese miners extract twenty dollars worth of gold dust from the sand and gravel. The work is being performed in the "stupidest, clumsiest, yet *patient* Chinese way." And the white miners exclaim: "What might not white men do with better appointed machinery!" The miners form a syndicate and force See Yup to sell his mine for a meager $20,000. After he yields to the miners, See Yup leaves town. The white miners take over operations, bringing in "new machinery" to assist them. Some gold is taken in the first week, but nothing is found the next week. Suspicious, the miners learn what had happened. See Yup had borrowed $500 in gold dust from a friend, openly sent the gold to San Francisco, and had Chinese runners secretly return it to him so he could send it out again. After he had been coerced into selling his mine, he had salted the mine with some gold dust and disappeared with the money his oppressors had forced him to accept.

Harte's point again was not entirely clear. The white miners certainly got what they deserved. But See Yup was a trickster, and his deception reflected a perceived Chinese propensity to be clandestine and clannish. "We knew," Harte had his narrator remark in the story, "that the Chinese themselves possessed some means of secretly and quickly communicating with one another." So armed, See Yup turned out to be a formidable and dangerous threat to white men in America.[62]

What Harte described in his literary efforts to entertain and amuse became the focus of serious scholarly reflections for Henry George. Pondering the "Chinese question," George developed a deep and disturbing analysis of American capitalism. The issue had first confronted him as a young man in California during the 1850s: he had been sitting in the gallery of the American Theatre in San Francisco on New Year's Eve when suddenly the curtain fell and the people in the audience sprang to their feet. On the curtain they saw depicted "what was then a dream of the far future — the overland train coming into San Francisco." But the celebration caused George to wonder whether the railroad would benefit workers, and he remembered what a miner had said to him during a discussion on the Chinese presence in the gold fields of California. What harm were the Chinese doing, he had asked, if they were only working the cheap diggings? "No harm now," the old miner replied, "but wages will not always be as high as they are today in California. As the country grows, as people come in, wages will go down, and some day or other white men will be glad to get those diggings that the Chinamen are now working."[63]

The miner's answer led George to address the problem of progress and poverty in America. The railroad, depicted there on the curtain before him, seemed to symbolize the paradox. Increasingly George focused on the Chinese as a clue to understanding the contradiction emerging in industrial America. The development of his analysis was not entirely abstract. His diary contains several references to the "Chinaman" and his visits to the "Chinese quarter." On February 21, 1865, he recorded: "Worked for Ike. Did two cards for $1. . . . In evening had row with Chinaman. Foolish." The next day, he wrote: "Hand very sore. Did not go down till late. Went to work in 'Bulletin' at 12. Got $3. Went to library in evening. Thinking of economy."[64]

Three years later, George expounded his initial critique of industrial capitalism in an essay on "What the Railroad Will Bring Us." He predicted that the transcontinental railroad would enable Americans to convert the wilderness into a "populous empire." But it would also bring population into the West and boost land values. While the owners of land would become wealthy, the workers would be forced to compete for low wages. Class divisions would deepen within white society. Much of this transformation, George noted, could already be seen in the mining business, where the "honest miner" had passed away, succeeded by the "millowner" with his "Chinese" work force.[65]

A year later, George presented his analysis of the "Chinese Problem" in an article published in the *New York Tribune*. The advances in transportation by steamship had made possible the mass migration of Chinese to the United States. The Chinese were crowding into the labor market of California and becoming the new "peons" of the captains of industry. "The superintendents of the cotton and woolen mills on the Pacific prefer the Chinese to the other operatives," George noted, "and in the same terms the railroad people speak of their Chinese graders, saying they are steadier, work longer, require less watching, and do not get up strikes or go on drunks." Comparing the Chinese workers of modern industrial America to the black slaves of antebellum America, George warned that the Chinese constituted a more serious peril. Blacks, when brought to this country, were "simple barbarians with nothing to unlearn"; they were "docile" and capable of accepting white ways. But the Chinese migrants could not be "assimilated." They had "habits of thought rendered permanent by being stamped upon countless generations." Strangers in America, the yellow workers were a "population born in China, reared in China, expecting to return to China, living while here in a little China of its own, and without the slightest attachment to the country — utter heathens, treacherous, sensual, cowardly and cruel."[66]

Many of the issues intellectually agitating George in his analysis of the "Chinese question" — land, labor, and industrialization — led directly to the writing of his most important book, *Progress and Poverty: An Inquiry into the Cause of Industrial Depressions and of Increase of Want with Increase of Wealth. The Remedy*. Published in 1879, the book was immediately thrust into the national debate on Chinese immigration restriction. In fact, George's publisher deliberately issued a "cheap edition," predicting the book would have an "enormous" sale due to its timely connection to the demand for Chinese exclusion.[67]

Progress and Poverty represented the culmination of ten years of research and reflection — George's final analysis of the problem of poverty in America and his remedy. The paradox, he argued, was the existence of poverty amid material progress. The cause of this contradiction was the discrepancy between wages and the cost of living. Wages constantly tended to remain minimal and to provide but a bare living. While the productive power of labor increased, rents increased faster and thus forced down wages. In order to extirpate poverty, George continued, land would have to be placed under "common" ownership. This could be accomplished through a "single tax" on all "unearned increment" — the increased value of land generated from the increase of population and productivity. The public domain and the availability of land in America had been the "transmuting force," which had turned the "thriftless, unambitious European peasant into the self-reliant Western farmer." But the frontier was gone, for the American advance had reached the Pacific Ocean. Unemployment had become a problem: "It is because men cannot find employment in the country that there are so many unemployed in the city." Within the context of this progress and poverty, the Chinese immigrants represented a disturbing development: they were peculiar aliens in America. While whites had progressed from a savage state to that of nineteenth-century civilization, the Chinese had stood still. Unlike the European peasant, the Chinese immigrant could not be transformed into an American. As a result of the "Chinese environment," George concluded, the immigrants from the East remained "Chinese" and were "unassimilable."[68]

Three years after the publication of *Progress and Poverty,* Congress prohibited the immigration of Chinese laborers. During the congressional debate on the proposed legislation, the editor of *The Nation* noted that the law would appeal to white workers, particularly the "hard-working" "Bill Nyes" of the Pacific Coast. But actually the action of Congress reflected a broader concern and anxiety than simply the Chinese presence. In fact there was very little objective basis for the Congress to be worried about Chinese immigrants as a threat to white labor. The Chinese constituted a mere .002 percent of the U.S. population in 1880. Behind the exclusion act were fears and forces that had little or no relationship to the Chinese. Congress was responding to the stressful reality of class tensions and conflict within white society during an era of economic crisis. George had identified the problem in his book: something had gone wrong and an age of opportunity seemed to be coming to an end. America had been a place where an abundance of land and jobs had always been available. The problem for employers had always been the need for more labor. But suddenly, during the closing decades of the nineteenth century, society experienced what historian John A. Garraty called "the discovery of unemployment." Unemployment had become a national crisis. The enormous expansions of the economy were followed by intense and painful contractions, which in turn generated social convulsions such as the violent Railroad Strike of 1877.[69]

Within this context of economic crisis and social strife, Congress voted to make it unlawful for Chinese laborers to enter the United States for the next ten years and denied naturalized citizenship to the Chinese already here. Support for the law was overwhelming. The House vote was 201 yeas, thirty-seven nays, and fifty-one absent. While congressmen from the West and South gave it unanimous support, a large majority from the East (fifty-three out of seventy-seven) and the Midwest (fifty-nine out of seventy-two) also voted for the prohibition. Significantly, support for the anti-Chinese legislation was national, coming not only from the western states but also from states where there were few or no Chinese. In the debate, congressmen revealed fears that were much deeper than race. The exclusionists warned that the presence of an "industrial army of Asiatic laborers" was exacerbating the class conflict between white labor and white capital. White workers had been "forced to the wall" by Chinese labor. The struggle between labor unions and the industrial "nabobs" and "grandees" was erupting into "disorder, strikes, riot and bloodshed" in the industrial cities of America. Congressmen still remembered the armed clashes between troops and striking railroad workers in 1877, and were aware of the labor unrest that would shortly erupt in Chicago's Haymarket Riot of 1886 and the Homestead and Pullman strikes of the 1890s. "The gate," exclusionists in Congress declared, "must be closed." The Chinese Exclusion Act was in actuality symptomatic of a larger conflict between white labor and white capital: removal of the Chinese was designed not only to defuse an issue agitating white workers but also to alleviate class tensions within white society.[70]

Aimed initially at Chinese "laborers," the prohibition was broadened in 1888 to include "all persons of the Chinese race"; exemptions were provided for Chinese officials, teachers, students, tourists, and merchants. Renewed in 1892, the Chinese Exclusion Act was extended indefinitely in 1902. The exclusionist legislation led to a sharp decline in the Chinese population — from 105,465 in

1880 to 89,863 in 1900 to 61,639 in 1920. For Congress, one way to solve the "Chinese problem" was to legislate the disappearance of the Chinese presence in America.[71]

But how was exclusion viewed through the eyes of the Chinese "strangers"?

Letters from the "Colony"

In a letter to a white friend written in the 1850s, a Chinese migrant asked, Why did whites in "your country" treat the Chinese with "contempt"? Many Chinese had been killed by "lawless wretches," and Chinese witnesses of the crimes had not been allowed to testify in courts. The "first root" of this problem was the degradation of the Chinese as "a race" in America. "Now, what injury have we Chinese done to your honorable people," he angrily questioned, "that they should thus turn upon us and make us drink the cup of wrong even to its last poisonous dregs?"[72]

To the Chinese, white prejudice and discrimination were both uninformed and insulting. In an open letter to Governor John Bigler, published in the *Daily Alta California* in 1852, Norman Asing chastised the governor for his inflammatory and anti-Chinese message to the legislature:

> The effect of your late message has been thus far to prejudice the public mind against my people, to enable those who wait the opportunity to hunt them down, and rob them of the rewards of their toil. . . . We would beg to remind you that when your nation was a wilderness, and the nation from which you sprung *barbarous,* we exercised most of the arts and virtues of civilized life; that we are possessed of a language and a literature, and that men skilled in science and the arts are numerous among us; that the productions of our manufactories, our sail, and work-shops, form no small commerce of the world. . . . We are not the degraded race you would make us.

Three years later, speaking for the Chinese merchants of San Francisco, Lai Chun-Chuen chided white Americans for viewing the Chinese as "the same as Indians and Negroes." The Indians knew "nothing about the relations of society," wearing neither clothes nor shoes and living in caves. By contrast, the Chinese had their philosophers, thousands of years of transmitted wisdom, the civil government of successive dynasties of emperors, and a wealthy civilization. "Can it be possible that we are classed as equals with this uncivilized race of men? . . . We doubt whether such be the decision of enlightened intelligence."[73]

The Chinese Six Companies, the most important association representing the Chinese community to the larger society, challenged the discriminatory laws and protested against anti-Chinese harassment and violence. In a letter to President Ulysses Grant sent in 1876, the Chinese Six Companies declared that the United States had always welcomed emigration from all countries to its shores and that the Chinese had responded by crossing the ocean to this land. Noting the contributions of the Chinese here, the Chinese Six Companies asked: "Are the railroads built by Chinese labor no benefit to the country? Are the manufacturing establishments, largely worked by Chinese, no benefit to this country? Do not the results of the daily toil of a hundred thousand men increase the riches of this country?" A year later, the Chinese Six Companies denounced the mob violence committed against the Chinese in "this *Christian civilization.*" "We are not ignorant that self-defence is the common right of all men," the organization warned in a letter to the mayor of San Francisco. "Should a riotous attack be made upon the Chinese quarter, we should have neither the power nor disposition to restrain our countrymen from defending themselves to the last extremity and selling their lives as dearly as possible."[74]

The Chinese protest went beyond words. Time and again, they took into court their struggle for civil rights. Insisting on the right of Chinese immigrants to become citizens, Chan Yong applied for citizenship in San Francisco's federal district court in 1855. Chan Yong, the local newspapers noted, was more "white" in appearance than most Chinese, but the court denied him citizenship, ruling that the 1790 Naturalization Law restricted citizenship to "whites" only and that the Chinese were not "white." Seven years later, Ling Sing sued the San Francisco tax collector, challenging the $2.50 capitation tax levied on Chinese. In *Ling Sing v. Washburn,* the California Supreme Court ruled that while the Chinese could be taxed as other residents, they could not be set apart as special subjects of taxation. Significantly, in this case, Ling Sing successfully invalidated a state law on the grounds that it violated the U.S. Constitution.[75]

The *Ling Sing* decision underscored the need for federal protection of civil rights for Chinese. During the 1868 negotiations between the United States and China regarding a treaty between the two countries, the Chinese Six Companies lobbied for the inclusion of provisions to protect the Chinese immigrant. They contacted Daniel Cleveland, a San Francisco lawyer and adviser to the federal officials involved in the treaty negotiations, and explained to him that federal legislation was greatly needed to "free" the Chinese in the United States from "wrongs" and protect Chinese lives and property. Federal protection of Chinese property would also encourage Chinese investments in this country, and would promote American trade with China. The outcome of the negotiations was a major victory for the Chinese Six Companies. The 1868 Burlingame Treaty recognized the "free migration and emigration" of the Chinese to the United States as visitors, traders or "permanent residents," and the rights of Chinese in the United States to "enjoy the same privileges, immunities, and exemptions in respect to travel or residence, as may there be enjoyed as the citizens or subjects of the most favored nation."[76]

Buoyed by their success in the Burlingame Treaty, Chinese merchants sought federal legislation to abolish discriminatory state laws. In 1869, accompanied by several supporting white merchants and bankers, representatives of the Chinese community met with a congressional delegation in San Francisco. At this meeting, merchant Fung Tang asked the congressmen to give the Chinese the just and equal protection guaranteed to them by the treaty and to provide federal protection from state injustices like the foreign miners' tax and the exclusion of Chinese testimony in courts. "We think your special tax, collected *only* from Chinese miners, is not according to our treaty with your government," Tang argued. "We are willing to pay taxes cheerfully, when taxed equally with others. . . . Most of all — we feel the want of protection to life and property when Courts of Justice refuse our testimony, and thus leave us defenseless, and unable to obtain justice for ourselves." Again the Chinese struggle for civil rights was effective. The 1870 Civil Rights Act, well known for its protection of blacks, also contained language and provisions for civil rights for the Chinese: "all persons," it read, within the jurisdiction of the United States shall have "the same right" to "make and enforce contracts, to sue, be parties, give evidence, and to the full and equal benefit of all laws and proceedings for the security of person and property as is enjoyed by white citizens . . . any law, statute . . . to the contrary notwithstanding." Furthermore "no tax" shall be imposed "by any State upon any person immigrating thereto from a foreign country which is not equally imposed and enforced upon every person emigrating to such State from any other foreign country, and any law of any State from any other foreign country is hereby declared null and void."[77]

But guarantees of equal protection by treaty and by federal law had little or no effect on what happened in society. There the Chinese remained vulnerable, victims of racial discrimination and violence. "The cheap labor cry was always a falsehood," protested Lee Chew. Our labor was "never cheap" and "always commanded the highest market price." But "it was the jealousy of laboring men of other nationalities — especially the Irish — that raised all the outcry against the Chinese. No one would hire an Irishman, German, Englishman or Italian when he could get a Chinese, because our countrymen [were] so much more honest, industrious, steady, sober, and painstaking. Chinese were persecuted, not for their vices, but for their virtues." Blamed as "the source of the troubles" of the American working class, the Chinese suffered from racial attacks. They had to flee from American boys who screamed, "God Damn Chinamen!" and threw rocks at them. "When I first came," Andrew Kan told an interviewer in 1924, forty-four years after his arrival, "Chinese treated worse than dog. Oh, it was terrible, terrible. At that time all Chinese have queue and dress same as in China. The hoodlums, roughnecks and young boys pull your queue, slap your face, throw all kind of old vegetables and rotten eggs at you." "The Chinese were in a pitiable condition in those days," recalled Huie Kin in his account of San Francisco's Chinatown during the 1870s. "We were simply terrified; we kept indoors after dark for fear of being shot in the back. Children spit upon us as we passed by and called us rats."[78]

Chinese saw the source of their oppression was white racism, for they were treated very differently from the European immigrants. "Up to 800,000 Europeans enter the United States per year, yet the labor unions hardly cared," the Chinese Six Companies noted. "A few thousands of the Chinese arrivals would irritate American workers . . . and European immigrants get citizenships and voting rights often immediately after their arrival in the United States." Similarly, laundryman Lee Chew complained: "Irish fill the almshouses and prisons and orphan asylums, Italians are among the most dangerous of men, Jews are unclean and ignorant. Yet they are all let in, while Chinese, who are sober, or duly law abiding, clean, educated and industrious, are shut out. . . . More than half the Chinese in this country would become citizens if allowed to do so, and would be patriotic Americans."[79]

Immigrants with white skins did not remain "strangers" in America. Ginn Wall painfully understood this reality. He had come here in the 1870s to work on the railroad and brought his wife, hoping they would be able to make a home for themselves in California. Many years later he cursed America for denying him the fulfillment of his dream. "Let's just fold up here," he told his son. "You come with me and we'll go back home. This is a white man's country. You go back to China when you make your money, that is where you belong. If you stay here, the white man will kill you."[80]

Other Chinese laborers shared Wall's apprehension and fear. Few Chinese men had come with their wives, and Chinese were generally afraid to raise families and make their homes in America. In 1855, a Chinese merchant of San Francisco explained that the Chinese had been "warned" not to come to America and that consequently they did not find "peace in their hearts in regard to bringing families." Noting how the Chinese were victims of racial violence and robbery, the merchant sadly concluded: "If the rabble are to harass us, we wish to return to our former homes." The record of Chinese departing from the San Francisco Custom House reflected a return mentality. The numbers of migrants returning to China even exceeded the numbers entering this country during the years 1864, 1866, and 1867, and remained constantly high during the years before the Chinese Exclusion Act. Between 1850 and 1882, 330,000 Chinese migrants entered the United States, and 150,000, or 47 percent, returned to China.[81]

But thousands of Chinese sojourners decided to stay, or found they could not return to their homeland. For many Chinese migrants, America turned out to be not "Gold Mountain" but a mountain of debt. "From the proceeds of a hard day's toil, after the pay for food and clothes, very little remains," explained the Chinese Six Companies in a protest against the foreign miners' tax in the late 1850s. Chinese migrants had borrowed money for their passage or perhaps had sold all of their property to come to America. How "bitter" they now felt, unable to go home. "In the course of four years, out of each ten men that have come over scarcely more than one or two get back again." In 1876, the Chinese Six Companies again complained in an address to Congress:

> Many Chinamen have come; few have returned. Why is this?
> Because among our Chinese people a few in California have
> acquired a fortune and returned home with joy. . . . They have
> expected to come here for one or two years and make a little
> fortune and return. Who among them ever thought of all these
> difficulties? Expensive rents, expensive living. A day without
> work means a day without food. For this reason, though wages

are low, yet they are compelled to labor and live in poverty, quite unable to return to their native land.[82]

Still, though they considered themselves sojourners, Chinese migrants showed signs of settlement from the very beginning. In San Francisco during the 1850s, they built a Chinatown, a bustling colony of thirty-three general merchandise stores, fifteen apothecaries, five restaurants, five herb shops, three boarding houses, five butcher stores, and three tailor shops. "The majority of the houses were of Chinese importation," observed a traveler, "and were stores, stocked with hams, tea, dried fish, dried ducks, and other Chinese eatables, besides copper pots and kettles, fans, shawls, chessmen, and all sorts of curiosities. Suspended over the doors were brilliantly-colored boards covered with Chinese characters, and with several yards of red ribbon streaming from them; while the streets thronged with Celestials, chattering vociferously as they rushed about from store to store." A Chinese immigrant, arriving in San Francisco in 1868, found a thriving and colorful Chinatown, "made up of stores catering to the Chinese only." The Chinese were "all in their native costume, with queues down their backs," and the entire street fronts of the stores were open, with groceries and vegetables overflowing on the sidewalks. Every morning in the streets could be seen Chinese vegetable peddlers, "in loose pajamalike pants and coats carrying two deep baskets of greens, fruits, and melons, balanced on their shoulders with the help of a pole."[83]

Nine years later, the Chinese quarter of San Francisco was six blocks long, running from California Street to Broadway. All day long and often until late at night, the streets were crowded with Chinese. According to the Reverend Otis Gibson, they had shaven crowns and neatly braided queues, and they sauntered "lazily along, talking, visiting, trading, laughing, and scolding in the strangest, and, to an American, the most discordant jargon." Here and there they gathered in groups on street corners. Frequently "a group of these fellows" would amuse themselves for a long time at "the expense of some party of 'white people,' who, passing through 'Chinatown' to see the sights, all unconscious to themselves," presented to the Chinese "a show quite as novel as they themselves [could] boast of seeing."[84]

Everywhere in the colony were signboards in Chinese characters, giving the stores and shops euphonious and poetic names. Adorning the entrances of wholesale houses were signs for Wung Wo Shang ("everlasting harmony, producing wealth"), Tung Cheung ("unitedly prospering"), Wa Yung ("the flowery fountain"), and Man Li ("ten thousand profits"). Apothecary shops had signboards that read: "The hall of the approved medicines of every province and of every land." Restaurants had signboards describing the culinary delights they offered: "Fragrant almond chamber," "Chamber of the odors of distant lands," "Fragrant tea chamber." A store of foreign goods carried the signboard Chai Lung Shing, or "abundant relief." Fan Tan saloons had signboards promising: "Get rich, please come in," "Straight enter the winning doors," "Riches ever flowing." On the glass windows and doors of their stalls, opium dealers pasted red cards announcing: "Opium dipped up in fractional quantities, Foreign smoke in broken parcels, No. 2 Opium to be sold at all times." Hung on the walls of stores were scrolls that stated "Profit coming in like rushing waters, Customers coming like clouds" and "Ten thousand customers constantly arriving, Let rich customers continually come."[85]

The immigrants also built Chinatowns in rural towns like Sacramento, Marysville, and Stockton. Business communities there were formed to service the needs of Chinese miners and farmers. By 1860, there were 121 Chinese merchants, storekeepers, and grocers in the three counties of Sacramento, Yuba, and San Joaquin. Twenty years later, their number had increased by 44 percent to 174. In addition, there were twenty-two restaurant keepers, fifty-four butchers and fish sellers, and 564 laundrymen and laundresses. Meanwhile, Chinatowns also developed in Fresno and Los Angeles, and by 1890 these had Chinese populations of 2,736 and 4,224 respectively.[86]

Organizations abounded in Chinatowns. Tongs were present almost from the very beginning: the first secret society, the Kwangtek-tong, was founded in California in 1852. Originally underground anti-government movements in Guangdong, the tongs served a particular need in Chinese America. "We are strangers in a strange country," said a tong member. "We must have an organization (tong) to control our country fellows and develop our friendship." A laundry worker said he decided to join a tong because he believed it would help the Chinese to cultivate friendship and to help one another while they were in "a strange land." Tongs offered their members protection. "Occasionally members of the tongs use their organization to take advantage of non-members of tongs," said a Chinese. "For example, a Chinese leased a building and found it necessary to raise his rent to pay for the advanced rent on his new lease; the renters threatened to bring trouble to the non-tong member who held the lease, unless he let them have the old rate of rent." Meeting the needs of immigrants, tongs proliferated in the United States; extending their activities beyond mutual assistance, they came to control the opium trade as well as gambling and prostitution in the Chinese communities. The tongs had amusingly high-sounding names; for example, the On Leong Society or "Chamber of Tranquil Conscientiousness" and the Kwang-tek-Tong or "Chamber of Far-Reaching Virtue" were prostitution organizations. Tongs were colorful and visible organizations in Chinatown. After the death of a tong leader, the tong would hire bands, "both American and Chinese, and have a long parade — not just for mourning, but to show its glory."[87]

Chinese immigrants also formed *fongs* composed of close family and village members, and "clans," larger groupings of village associations. The family associations maintained clubhouses, functioning as residences and social centers. The clans established temples, transmitted letters to the villages in the homeland, and shipped home the bodies or bones of the deceased. In San Francisco's Chinatown, they also provided police and garbage service. Transcending the fongs and clans were the *huiguan,* district associations based on the districts or regions from which the migrants had originated, such as Toishan, Yanping, or Namhoi. These associations were responsible for receiving the migrants, providing initial housing, and finding employment. They also administered the "credit-ticket" system, checking migrants seeking return passage to make certain all their debts had been paid. In San Francisco during the 1850s, the district associations were the Sze Yup, Ning Yeung, Sam Yup, Yeong Wo, Hop Wo, and Yan Wo; they later organized themselves into the "Chung Wai Wui Koon." Known popularly as the Chinese Six Companies, the organization helped settle interdistrict conflicts and provided educational and health services to the community. The leaders of the Chinese Six Companies were merchants. They interacted with the city's white business community. They had access to public officials and also regularly arranged to have influential Americans advise and speak for the Chinese community.

Gradually the Chinese were creating their own communities in America. They built altars to honor their gods — Kwan Kung, god of literature and war; Bak Ti, god of the north; Hou Wang, the monkey god; Kwan Yin, goddess of mercy. They also celebrated traditional holidays. During Chinese New Year in January or February, they first did their *Dah Faw Hom Muy,* or housecleaning. "Everything is cleansed to prepare for welcoming the coming year,"

A. W. Loomis reported in 1869. "The house is almost turned inside out; ceiling, floors and furniture are scrubbed." The house could not be cleaned again until after the celebration, or else the good fortune arriving with the new year would be swept away. "Oh yes — we cleaned the house upside down," a Chinese immigrant remembered. "You know it was good luck to have plenty at the start of the New Year. We couldn't buy too much, but a bit of everything. And then there would be oranges and lishee [gifts of money wrapped in red paper for good luck]. We didn't have money for the lishee — we used dried nuts for money." Then the Chinese ushered in the New Year with lion dances and firecrackers. During the celebration, whites also joined the festive throngs in Chinatown. "The merchants," said Loomis, "appear highly delighted to see and to welcome all of our citizens whom they can recognize as friends, and all with whom they have had any kind of business connections," offering liquors and cigars to the *"white people."* As soon as the clock tolled off the last minute of the departing year, firecrackers exploded in a roaring, crackling din, filling entire streets with columns of smoke and sheets of flames, covering the ground red with the shreds of spent fireworks, and frightening away the evil spirits for the coming year. A Cantonese poem described this time of celebration:

> New Year's Day starts a new calendar year.
> The scent of spice fills the air beyond the front
>   door.
> Everywhere, we Chinese sojourners greet each other
>   with auspicious sayings.
> In joyous laughter,
> We wish good luck to others, and to ourselves.
> May this year be prosperous for all walks of life;
> So that, clothed silk, we can together bid the
>   Flowery Flag [America] farewell.[88]

In the spring, the Chinese held their "Pure Brightness Festival," or *Qing Ming*. This was memorial day for the Chinese in America. Unable to visit the family graves in China, they went to local Chinese cemeteries where they prayed before "spirit" shrines. In the fall, the Chinese celebrated the Moon Festival to thank the gods for good harvests. During this celebration, they enjoyed moon cakes, a pastry shaped like a moon filled with delicacies like salted duck egg yolks and sweetened soybean paste.[89]

For recreation, the Chinese attended the Chinese theater. The first Chinese play in America was presented in 1852 when 123 actors of the Hong Fook Tong performed at the American Theatre in San Francisco. In 1879, a Chinese theater was erected in the city. "It is a three-story brick building, 92 feet deep, with a frontage of 52 feet," the *San Francisco Chronicle* reported. "The height of the ceiling from the floor in front of the stage is 35 feet. It has an iron front, a large main gallery in the center of the auditorium, and two hanging side galleries. Its seating capacity is to be for 2500 people. . . . Thirty-five cents is the price of admission." During performances in the Chinese theater, the men — sometimes a few hundred, sometimes a thousand — sat on benches in the gallery. Smoking cigars and cigarettes and eating mandarin oranges and Chinese melon seeds, they listened to the Chinese orchestra and watched the Chinese drama on stage. In the dark smoke-filled theater, sitting in a segregated section, could be seen Chinese women.

In America, Chinese women found themselves in a world of men. In 1852, of the 11,794 Chinese in California, only seven were women — a ratio of 1,685 males to every one female. Eighteen years later, of 63,199 Chinese in the United States only 4,566 were female — a ratio of fourteen to one. Chinese women worked in a variety of occupations: they were housekeepers, servants, laundresses, seamstresses, shoemakers, cooks, miners, and fisherwomen. But overwhelmingly, especially in the early years, Chinese women were prostitutes. In the 1870 census manuscripts, 61 percent of the 3,536 Chinese women in California had occupations listed as "prostitute." Most of the Chinese prostitutes were in a condition of debt peonage, under contracts like this one signed by Xin Jin:

> The contractee Xin Jin became indebted to her master/mistress for food and passage from China to San Francisco. Since she is without funds, she will voluntarily work as a prostitute at Tan Fu's place for four and one-half years for an advance of 1,205 yuan (U.S. $524) to pay this debt. There shall be no interest on the money and Xin Jin shall receive no wages. At the expiration of the contract, Xin Jin shall be free to do as she pleases. Until then, she shall first secure the master/mistress's permission if a customer asks to take her out. If she has the four loathsome diseases she shall be returned within 100 days; beyond that time the procurer has no responsibility. Menstruation disorder is limited to one month's rest only. If Xin Jin becomes sick at any time for more than 15 days, she shall work one month extra; if she becomes pregnant, she shall work one year extra. Should

Xin Jin run away before her term is out, she shall pay whatever expense is incurred in finding and returning her to the brothel. This is a contract to be retained by the master/mistress as evidence of the agreement. Receipt of 1205 yuan by Ah Yo. Thumb print of Xin Jin in the contractee. Eighth month 11th day of the 12th year of Guang-zu (1886).[90]

Called *lougeui* ("always holding her legs up") and *baak haak chai* ("hundred men's wife"), Chinese prostitutes worked in the mining outposts, railroad camps, agricultural villages, and Chinatowns like Sacramento, Marysville, and San Francisco. Dressed in fancy clothes and wearing jewelry, some prostitutes worked in high-class brothels. "And every night, seven o'clock, all these girls were dressed in silk and satin, and sat in front of a big window," recalled Lilac Chen, who had been brought here in 1893 by a brothel owner, "and the men would look in and choose their girls who they'd want for the night." Most of the prostitutes worked in lower-grade brothels or in "cribs" — street-level compartments four feet wide and six feet deep with windowed doors covered with bars or heavy screens facing dim alleys. Dressed in cotton tunics and trousers, women peered out from the windows, promising men pleasure for twenty-five or fifty cents: "Lookee two bits, feelee floor bits, doee six bits." They were fed two or three times a day, their dinner usually consisting of rice and a stew of pork, eggs, liver, and kidneys. They were enormously profitable for their owners. "At an average of 38 cents per customer and seven customers per day," Lucie Cheng Hirata has calculated, "a lower-grade prostitute would earn about 850 dollars per year and 3,404 dollars after four years of servitude. Since women in the inferior dens were kept at the subsistence level, the cost of maintaining them must not have exceeded 8 dollars per month or 96 dollars per year per person." The average capital outlay or purchase price of a woman was usually about $530. As Lucie Cheng Hirata wryly noted, "These calculations indicate that the owner would begin to make a profit from the prostitute's labor in the first year of her service!"[91]

Virtual slaves, many of the prostitutes became opium addicts, seeking in the drug a psychic sanctuary from the daily abuse and degradation. "My owners were never satisfied, no matter how much money I made," a prostitute complained. When they were angry, her owners would often beat her with wooden clubs, and once they threatened her with a pistol. "My last mistress was very cruel to me," another prostitute said; "she used to whip me, pull my hair, and pinch the inside of my cheeks." Disease was a constant threat: syphilis

and gonorrhea were widespread. Life for the prostitute was dangerous and sometimes short. Occasionally they were beaten to death by
their customers or owners, and others committed suicide by taking
overdoses of drugs or drowning themselves in San Francisco Bay.
Prostitute Wong Ah So was luckier. She was at a "party given by
the Tong men" where "slave girls" sat and drank with the men.
"Suddenly I saw a friend of my father's come in, a man who had
seen me less than a year ago," she recalled. "Although I was all
dressed up so grand he recognized me, and the first chance he had,
he came and asked me, 'Are you not so and so's daughter?' " Ten
days later, thanks to the man's efforts, Wong Ah So was rescued and
taken to a Christian mission.[92]

Chinese prostitutes in California decreased in number significantly after 1870. By 1880, only 24 percent of the 3,171 Chinese
women in the state were designated as prostitutes in the census manuscripts. The number of adult Chinese females listed in the manuscript
census as "housekeepers" — women performing household chores
without pay and reporting no other occupations — doubled from
753, or 21 percent of the total population of this group in 1870, to
1,445, or 46 percent, in 1880. In that year, 72 percent of married
Chinese women were housekeepers. A Chinese folk song urged
Chinese prostitutes to seek husbands and a safer life:

> *Prostitution ruins the body most harmfully.*
> *Come ashore, the sooner the better.*
> *My advice is to get hitched to a man, and don't*
> *ever forget, dear young lass:*
> *It's no shame to have a decent meal with plain tea.*
> *All in all —*
> *You'd also gain a husband.*
> *We've all witnessed the frequent raids of brothels*
> *in the Golden Gate;*
> *You need not to worry about these roughnecks once*
> *you live with a man.*[93]

Meanwhile Chinese men had begun bringing wives with them
to America or arranging to have women sent here to become their
wives. Ah Chew came to California around 1854 when he was about
fifteen years old and worked in the gold mines; driven from mining
by white miners, he found work in the Sacramento delta in levee
construction. "Levee building was very hard work, but at least it was
steady," his grandson stated. "After my grandfather had decided to

settle down in the Sacramento Delta, he went back to China on a sailboat to marry, and then brought his wife over here." In 1862, at the age of eighteen, Chin Gee-Hee came to America and worked in a lumber mill in Washington. He saved his earnings, and within a few years he sent for a wife and secured for her a job as a cook in the mill's cookhouse. In 1875, Mrs. Chin gave birth to their son, Chin Lem, believed to be the first Chinese born in the Washington Territory. In 1869, A. W. Loomis reported the case of "a wife coming all the way alone across the stormy sea" to be with her husband. "Friends at home besought her not to do a thing so in conflict with Chinese custom; the husband and his relatives in this country, when they heard of her purpose, wrote entreating her not to expose herself to the hardships and perils on the sea, and to the trials which would be liable to befall her here; but she answered that where the husband was there she had a right to be." She came to California, where she supported herself and her child by sewing garments and making cigarettes, while her husband worked for a mining company in the Kern River area.[94]

In Washington, California, and elsewhere Chinese families were gradually forming as men began to leave mining and railroad construction and to enter more stable pursuits like farming and shopkeeping. One area of enterprise that encouraged the formation of Chinese families was the fishing industry in Monterey. In the fishing village of Point Alones, for example, nearly half of the Chinese were female. According to a description published in the 1870s, the village was organized into "companies," but most of these companies were actually families: "Man Lee Company, three men and three women; Sun Sing Lee Company, three men, two women and three children. . . ." As early as 1876, in its memorial to President Ulysses Grant, the Chinese Six Companies noted the presence of "a few hundred Chinese families" in the country, and added: "There are also among us a few hundred, perhaps a thousand, Chinese children born in America."[95]

Increasingly, Chinese men wanted to find wives and settle down. But they discovered that sometimes getting a wife could be vexatious and expensive. Fook Sing of Downieville, California, for example, went through a trying ordeal. He had been informed about a Chinese woman named Min Que who was in Wadsworth, Nevada. On July 25, 1874, he sent a telegraph to Kaw Chung in Wadsworth: "Don't you let her go. I will come tomorrow and see her. I want to bring her to Downieville to live with me. What time does the train start?

Answer quick." The next day he sent another message to Chung: "I will start for Wadsworth today and meet her. . . . Tell her to wait for me to come and if she wants to go I will let her. Don't care. Answer." But she went off with or was taken by another man. On August 12, Ah Tom sent a telegram to Ting Yeu of Downieville: "Fook Sing's woman has gone to Marysville." The next day the disappointed and anxious Fook Sing sent telegrams to Sing Lung in Marysville: "Bring woman up right away will pay three hundred dollars. Answer." "Is man who took woman there? Answer." At 11:05 A.M. the same day, Sing Lung wired Tie Yuen in Downieville: "Tell Fook Sing Min Que is here. What you going to do? Answer quick." Fook Sing had found the woman, but would Min Que agree to marry him? At 4:20 P.M. Sing Lung telegraphed Fook Sing: "She wants you to come right away and get warrant with officer, friends will help. You don't be afraid. We will get her sure." Fook Sing rushed to Marysville, and on August 15, he wired Tie Yuen: "I saw the woman but have not arrested her. Send marriage certificate." Immediately Tie Yuen responded: "Will send the certificate next stage."[96]

Fook Sing, it seems, was able to get himself a wife; but he was one of the lucky few. "In all New York there are less than forty Chinese women," Lee Chew commented bitterly, "and it is impossible to get a Chinese woman out here [to the United States] unless one goes to China and marries her there, and then he must collect affidavits to prove that she is really his wife. That is in the case of a merchant. A laundryman can't bring his wife here under any circumstances." Most Chinese men were trapped in a womanless world. "You know Chinese no allowed to marry white girl in California and Oregon. Only in Washington and up here make lots of trouble," Woo Gen of Seattle told an interviewer. Protesting the legislation prohibiting the entry of Chinese women, Woo asked: "What Chinese going do for wife?"[97]

Cut off from women from their homeland, a few of them developed relationships with white women. In a letter to Lung On, Markie Tom wrote about two white women: "There are two barbarian girls here, very nice, and who do not look down on our Chinese." He added that they would like to meet Chen Shih. In 1886 the San Francisco Board of Supervisors reported several white-Chinese couples living in Chinatown: "At No. 900 and at 902 Dupont Street, one white woman living with a Chinaman on the third floor; at 613 Jackson Street, second floor; at 708 Commercial Street, third story; at 710 Commercial Street, third story. . . ." In New York, Wong Chin Foo wrote in *Cosmopolitan,* Chinese men were married to "Irish, German, or Italian wives," most of them "poor working girls." "The Chinamen often make them better husbands than men of their own nation," Wong stated, "as quite a number of them who ran away from their former husbands to marry Chinamen have openly declared. The Chinaman never beats his wife, gives her plenty to eat and wear, and generally adopts her mode of life. Their children speak the English language, and adopt the American ways and dress." Among "the white women of Chinatown," Lee Chew reported, were "many excellent and faithful wives and mothers."[98]

In an interview conducted in 1924, a Chinese merchant in Portland told a story about a disappointment he had experienced. He had arrived here in 1880 and had married a Chinese woman in 1893. But he did not marry the woman he loved. Some years before he had known a missionary's wife whose husband had been ill. "I had helped them, and finally he died, and I used to go and see her, to help her, and then she used to come and see me. This went on more often than before, and pretty soon we had what you might call love. She very often would hold my hand and make love very much like the Americans do. I was a young fellow and I liked this. I also knew that she was white and I was Chinese." She agreed to marry him, but she wanted first to take a little trip to her home in eastern Canada before the wedding. While he waited for her to return, he received a letter from her every day initially, then after a silence of three weeks, he got a "very cool letter." Confused, he went to find her in Canada. "She nearly refuse to see me," he said. "I was very surprised at this. My heart was very heavy. Oh, I feel so badly, my mind was all upset." He returned to Portland, where his friends advised him to forget her. "But I was very fond of her. I think she would have made a much better wife than the no-good woman I married." The marriage was an unhappy one, and his wife had moved to Detroit with one of their sons.[99]

For the overwhelming majority of Chinese men, the future would not include the possibility of a family in their new land. "Pathetic the lonely bachelors stranded in a foreign land," reflected a Chinese migrant in a Cantonese rhyme. On Sundays, most Chinese men had no families to take on outings. They had "no *homes* in this country," observed Otis Gibson of San Francisco, and nearly all the common laborers lived on the streets on Sundays simply because they

had "nothing to do, and nowhere else to go." Sitting at tables or
lying on beds, they reviewed the "classics" or skimmed "the pages
of some cheap novel." "Yes, go to theater," a waiter at a Chinese
restaurant replied when asked about his free time. "When I no work?
I sleep. Sometimes gamble a little." At night and during the weekends,
men played mah-jongg, fan-tan, and *baakgapbiu,* a game similar to
keno. "Gambling is mostly fan tan," reported Lee Chew, "but there
is a good deal of poker, which the Chinese have learned from Americans and can play very well. They also gamble with dominoes and
dice." Tom Lee, a cook and houseboy, said: "No get lonely for home
China, many China boys all same one family. Sometime have holiday.
Put on Merican hat, shoe, tie, all same White man, walk to Stockton
have good time." Men also tried to find release in the brothels or
escape in the opium parlors: inhaling deeply from ivory opium pipes,
they "mounted the dragon" and rode into fantastic worlds far away
from their dreary reality.[100]

Mostly the men spent their leisure hours in the back rooms of
Chinese stores. There "all Chinese came," a migrant recalled. "Not
just relatives. They all just like to get together. They talk together. . . . Sometimes they even get some idea from China. Our village had something to do — they send a letter over here, we get
together and talk it over — and send it back. We communicate, see,
otherwise you're alone. You know nothing."[101]

A uniquely *Chinese-American* social institution, the store was
a center of life in the Chinese community, the "resort of all the
Chinese in the colony" and "a place of call." There they were able
to purchase Chinese foods, books in Chinese, firecrackers, incense,
ceremonial paper, Chinese herbs, and other Chinese sundries. There
they escaped from the "strangeness and fierceness of their everyday
world" and recalled "happier days at home when they crowded the
village inns . . . to drink tea and exchange gossip, or to listen to
vagrant minstrels chant ballads." In the back rooms of stores, men
spent many pleasant hours telling Chinese folktales and especially
ghost stories, like the one about the sound of the slippers:

> In China many years ago the father of a certain woman
> died. . . . The daughter had cared a great deal for him and when
> he died she grieved deeply. Not long after his death she was
> awakened one night by a familiar sound, the sound of her father's
> slippers walking across the floor. She was not afraid of ghosts
> or of darkness, so she got up to look, but she could not discover

anything unusual. Many nights after that she heard the sound, always at the same time, and always she would wake up and investigate, but never did she discover what it meant.

Shortly afterwards the daughter was married and her husband took her over here, to America. She arrived in America and had forgotten all about the sound of the slippers. But one day she heard it again, here in her new home in America. She was very much surprised at this. She did not think it strange when she heard it in China. But here in America! The sound was exactly the same as that she had heard when she lived in her little house in the village. And, even today, ever so often always at the same hour, she hears it and she knows, that it is the sound of her dead father's slippers scratching across the floor.[102]

In the back rooms of stores, as the Chinese gathered around the stove for warmth, they challenged each other at chess and checkers, played musical instruments, listened to the phonograph, and read newspapers. Some of them also taught each other English, struggling through *An English-Chinese Phrase Book,* compiled by Wong Sam and Assistants in San Francisco in 1875. The phrases reflected their everyday lives — the broad range of experiences, anxieties, and hopes of the Chinese in America. From this indispensable manual, they could learn the English sentences necessary to guide them in the strange new land:

> He took it from me by violence.
> The men are striking for wages.
> He claimed my mine.
> When will the lease expire?
> He cheated me out of my wages.
> He was choked to death with a lasso, by a robber.
> Can I sleep here tonight?
> Have you any food for me?
> She is a good-for-nothing huzzy [sic].
> The passage money is $50 from Hong Kong to California.
> The steamer will leave to-morrow.
> How long have you been in California?
> She is my wife.
> An unmarried man is called a bachelor.
> I received a letter from China.
> The United States have many immigrants.
> The immigration will soon be stopped.[103]

In the back rooms, the men found out what was happening in town and also in the homeland. "Letters for the colony" were directed in care of the store and public notices were written on "tablets of red paper and posted beside the door." Chinese newspapers were available, and interpreters were there to conduct negotiations and adjust differences with "the outside world." The store was a community "post office" where proprietors like Lung On of the Kam Wah Chung Store used their calligraphy skills to write letters for illiterate Chinese workers.[104]

One sojourner received a letter from his mother, a wailing reminder to fulfill his filial obligations:

> I hear that you, _____, my son, are acting the prodigal. . . . For many months there has arrived no letter, nor money. My supplies are exhausted. I am old; too infirm to work; too lame to beg. Your father in the mines of the mountains suffers from a crushed foot. He is weak, and unable to accumulate money. Hereafter, my son, change your course; be industrious and frugal, and remit to me your earnings; and within the year let me welcome home both your father and yourself.

She had also written to an older relative, whom she had appointed to act as guardian:

> I hear that my son is playing the prodigal, being idle, or spending his earnings for unnecessary articles of clothing and in other forms of self-indulgence. I authorize you, his near relative and senior in years, to strenuously admonish him. If moderate chastisement fails, then call to your aid one or more of your brothers, (relatives) and sorely beat him, not pitying his body.[105]

But returning home was not easy for many sojourners. Ing Weh-teh, for example, had worked hard and saved his money, but had lost the money when a friend in Oregon had invested it without his consent. "Because you took away that money," he wrote to Ing Pang-chi, "I could not return home. I came to America — to labor, to suffer, floating from one place to another, persecuted by the whites, for more than twenty years. . . . Do you know that both the old and the young at my home are awaiting me to deliver them out of starvation and cold?" Liang Kau-tsi had also been in America for two decades and was scolded by his brother in a letter: "Because of our family's poverty, you went out of the country to make a living. You still haven't made any money during all of these twenty years? I am afraid that you are Americanized and totally forget about us."[106]

Something had happened to Ing Weh-teh and Liang Kau-tsi and thousands of their fellow Chinese in the new land. They had come to America "extravagantly" in search of Gam Saan, but found themselves "eating bitterness," *hec fu.* For many of the Gold Mountain men, the venture was a sad failure.

> *My life's half gone, but I'm still unsettled;*
> *I've erred, I'm an expert at whoring and*
>   *gambling.*
> *Syphilis almost ended my life.*
> *I turned to friends for a loan, but no one took*
>   *pity on me.*
> *Ashamed, frightened —*
> *Now, I must wake up after this long nightmare.* . . . [107]

In America the Chinese were forced to become "strangers" by economic interests — the demands of white capitalists for a colonized labor force and the "ethnic antagonism" of white workers — as well as by an ideology defining America as a homogeneous white society. The Chinese found new conditions of "necessity" circumscribing their lives. As "strangers from a different shore," they were denied equality of opportunity and separated from their homeland by the *keli* — the "tyrannical laws" of exclusion. "They call us 'Chink,' " complained an old laundryman in 1924, cursing the "white demons." "They think we no good! America cut us off. No more come now, too bad!" Determined to find their Gold Mountain, they created their own "colonies," their Chinatowns, and they also struggled for their civil rights in the larger society. Coming from a society dominated by authoritarian political structures where social change through law and established political channels was unknown, they had become involved in the processes of democratic political institutions in America. They could not become citizens, but they knew they were worthy of citizenship. "Since I have lived and made money in this country," Andrew Kan argued in 1924, after forty-four years of working in America, "I should be able to become an American citizen."[108]

Before they had come here, the Chinese could not have fully anticipated what they would do to the new land and America to them. Gam Saan represented liminality. Years after their arrival, they could marvel at what they had achieved and wonder at what they had become. Mostly peasants in the old country, the Chinese had become pioneering prospectors in the foothills of the Sierras, railroad workers blasting tunnels through the granite mountains of California and laying tracks across the salt deserts of Utah, agricultural laborers in the fruit orchards of California and the cotton fields of Louisiana, enterprising farmers in the San Joaquin and Sacramento valley, tory workers in San Francisco and North Adams, laundrymen and shopkeepers from New York to Washington. *"Jo lui jai,"* they said, "we worked like mules." They had entered America and changed the land, their achievements trumpeting their presence. In turn, many found themselves transformed: looking at themselves in the mirror, they saw tall people. The Gold Mountain men and women had also created a world of Chinese America, rendering society on this side of the Pacific Ocean racially and culturally more diverse. No longer sojourners, they still found themselves viewed and treated as "strangers" by the *fan qui* ("foreign devils"). Though they had come across a different ocean than the European immigrants, they knew they had earned their claim to settlement, to be Chinese Americans.[109]

4

Raising Cane

The World of Plantation Hawaii

Paralleling the migration of Chinese to California was the movement of Chinese, Japanese, Korean, and Filipino laborers to Hawaii, an American economic colony that became a territory of the United States in 1900. Over 300,000 Asians entered the islands between 1850 and 1920. Brought here as "cheap labor," they filled the requisitions itemizing the needs of the plantations. Their labor enabled the planters to transform sugar production into Hawaii's leading industry. "It is apparent," declared the *Hawaiian Gazette* excitedly in 1877, "that Sugar is destined most emphatically to be 'King.'" But to be "King" the sugar industry required the constant importation of workers whose increasing numbers led to the ethnic diversification of society in the islands. For example, in 1853, Hawaiians and part-Hawaiians represented 97 percent of the population of 73,137 inhabitants, while Caucasians constituted only 2 percent and Chinese only half a percent. Seventy years later, Hawaiians and part-Hawaiians made up only 16.3 percent of the population, while Caucasians represented 7.7 percent, Chinese 9.2 percent, Japanese 42.7 percent, Portuguese 10.6 percent, Puerto Ricans 2.2 percent, Koreans 1.9 percent, and Filipinos 8.2 percent.[1]

Hawaii was ethnically very different from the mainland. In 1920, Asians totaled 62 percent of the island population, compared to only 3.5 percent of the California population and only 0.17 percent of the continental population. Constituting a majority of the population in Hawaii, Asians were able to choose a different course than their mainland brethren. Powered by "necessity" yet buoyed by "ex-

travagance," they responded in their own unique ways to the world
of plantation Hawaii.

Hana-hana: Working

> *Hawaii, Hawaii*
> *Like a dream*
> *So I came*
> *But my tears*
> *Are flowing now*
> *In the canefields.*[2]

Asian immigrants were not prepared for their experiences as
plantation workers in Hawaii. They had come from societies where
they labored to provide for their families within a context of traditions and established rules and obligations. They had greater control
over their time and activities, working with family members and
people they knew. "In Japan," a plantation laborer said, "we could
say, 'It's okay to take the day off today,' since it was our own work.
We were free to do what we wanted. We didn't have that freedom
on the plantation. We had to work ten hours every day." The Filipino
tao, or peasant farmer, followed the rhythm of the day, the weather,
and the seasons in the Philippines. He worked in the fields with his
wife and children, driving the carabao before him and urging his
family workers to keep pace with him. *Hana-hana* — working on
the plantation in Hawaii — was profoundly different.[3]

Though laborers still awoke early as they did in the old country,
they were now aroused by the loud screams of a plantation siren at
five in the morning. A plantation work song captured this moment:

> *"Awake! stir your bones! Rouse up!*
> *Shrieks the Five o'Clock Whistle.*
> *"Don't dream you can nestle*
> *For one more sweet nap.*
> *Or your ear-drums I'll rap*
> *With my steam-hammer tap*
> *Till they burst.*
> *Br-r-row-aw-i-e-ur-ur-rup!*
> *Wake up! wake up! wake up! w-a-k-e-u-u-u-up!*
>
> *Filipino and Japanee;*
> *Porto Rican and Portugee;*

Korean, Kanaka and Chinese;
Everybody whoever you be
On the whole plantation —
Wake up! wake up! wake up! w-a-k-e-u-u-u-up!
Br-r-row-aw-i-e-ur-ur-rup![4]

After the 5:00 A.M. plantation whistle had blown, the *lunas* (foremen) and company policemen strode through the camps. "Get up, get up," they shouted as they knocked on the doors of the cottages and the barracks. "Hana-hana, hana-hana, work, work." A Korean remembered the morning her mother failed to hear the work whistle and overslept: "We were all asleep — my brother and his wife, my older sister, and myself. Suddenly the door swung open, and a big burly luna burst in, screaming and cursing, 'Get up, get to work.' The luna ran around the room, ripping off the covers, not caring whether my family was dressed or not." "You must wake up," a Filipino laborer said, or else a policeman would kick open the door of your room and chase you out of bed. "I got one companion, he like lay off one morning," he added smiling. "Oh, the policeman come, and my friend was so scared that he ran to work in his underpants."[5]

"All the workers on a plantation in all their tongues and kindreds, 'rolled out' sometime in the early morn, before the break of day," reported a visitor. One by one and two by two, laborers appeared from "the shadows, like a brigade of ghosts." From an outlying camp, they came on a train, "car after car of silent figures," their cigarettes glowing in the darkness. In front of the mill they lined up, shouldering their hoes. As the sun rose, its rays striking the tall mill stack, "quietly the word was passed from somewhere in the dimness. Suddenly and silently the gang started for its work, dividing themselves with one accord to the four quarters of the compass, each heading toward his daily task." The workers were grouped by the foremen into gangs of twenty to thirty workers and were marched or transported by wagons and trains to the fields. Each gang was watched by a luna, who was "almost always a white man." The ethnicity of the gangs varied. Some of them were composed of one nationality, while others were mixed. One luna said he had workers of all races in his gang, including Hawaiians, Filipinos, Puerto Ricans, Chinese, Japanese, Portuguese, and Koreans.[6]

There were gangs of women workers, too, for women were part of the plantation work force — about 7 percent of all workers in

1894 and 14 percent in 1920. Most of the women workers — over 80 percent of them — were Japanese. Women were concentrated in field operations, such as hoeing, stripping leaves, and harvesting. My grandmother Katsu Okawa was a cane cutter on the Hana Plantation, and my aunt Yukino Takaki was an *hapaiko* worker, or cane loader, on the Puunene Plantation. Though women were given many of the same work assignments as men, they were paid less than their male counterparts. Japanese-female field hands, for example, received an average wage of only fifty-five cents per day in 1915, compared to the seventy-eight cents Japanese-male field hands received.[7]

Women also worked in the camps: they washed laundry, cooked, and sewed clothes. "I made custom shirts with hand-bound button holes for 25 cents," recalled a Korean woman. "My mother and sister-in-law took in laundry. They scrubbed, ironed and mended shirts for a nickel a piece. It was pitiful! Their knuckles became swollen and raw from using the harsh yellow soap." On the Hawi Plantation, my grandmother Katsu Okawa operated a boarding house where she fed her husband and eight children as well as fifteen men every day. On the Honokaa Plantation, Mrs. Tai Yoo Kim prepared meals for her husband and twenty bachelors. Every morning at five o'clock, she fed them a breakfast of rice, broth, and kimchi. For six days a week, she packed twenty-one lunch tins with rice and dried salt fish. Then for dinner she prepared soup, rice, and a soy-seasoned dish of vegetables, meat, or fish, or a dish of corned beef and onions.[8]

The most regimented work was in the fields. "We worked like machines," a laborer complained. "For 200 of us workers, there were seven or eight lunas and above them was a field boss on a horse. We were watched constantly." A Japanese woman, interviewed years later at the age of ninety-one, said: "We had to work in the canefields, cutting cane, being afraid, not knowing the language. When any *haole* [white] or Portuguese luna came, we got frightened and thought we had to work harder or get fired." "The *luna* carried a whip and rode a horse," another Japanese laborer recalled. "If we talked too much the man swung the whip. He did not actually whip us but just swung his whip so that we would work harder." A Korean woman fumed: "I'll never forget the foreman. He said we worked like 'lazy.' He wanted us to work faster. He would gallop around on horseback and crack and snap his whip."[9]

One of the most tedious and backbreaking tasks was hoeing weeds. Laborers had to "hoe hoe hoe . . . for four hours in a straight line and no talking," said a worker. "Hoe every weed along the way to your three rows. Hoe — chop chop chop, one chop for one small weed, two for all big ones." They had to keep their bodies bent over. They wanted to stand up and stretch, unknotting twisted bodies and feeling the freedom of arched backs. The laborers cursed the lunas, "talking stink" about the driving pace of the work: "It burns us up to have an ignorant *luna* stand around and holler and swear at us all the time for not working fast enough. Every so often, just to show how good he is, he'll come up and grab a hoe and work like hell for about two minutes and then say sarcastically, 'Why you no work like that?' He knows and we know he couldn't work for ten minutes at that pace." The lunas were just plain mean "buggas." Laborers also did "hole hole" work, the stripping of the dead leaves from the cane stalks. To protect themselves against the needles of the cane leaves, they wore heavy clothing. Still, as they left the fields each day, they found their hands badly cut by the cane leaves. In a plantation work song, Japanese laborers lamented:

> *Hawaii, Hawaii*
> *But when I came*
> *What I saw*
> *Was hell*
> *The boss was Satan*
> *The lunas*
> *His helpers.*[10]

As they worked, laborers wore *bangos* hanging on chains around their necks — small brass disks with their identification numbers stamped on them. In the old country, they had names, and their names told them who they were, connecting them to family and community; in Hawaii, they were given numbers. The workers resented this new impersonal identity. Laborers were "treated no better than cows or horses," one of them recalled. "Every worker was called by number, never by name." The lunas "never called a man by his name," another worker grumbled. "Always by the bango, 7209 or 6508 in that manner. And that was the thing I objected to. I wanted my name, not the number."[11]

When the cane was ripe, lunas on horseback led the workers out into the fields to harvest the crop. Describing the harvesting process, a visitor wrote: "Just beyond these Chinese huts were canefields, an intense yellow-green, the long, slender leaves tossing in the breeze like a maize-field before the harvest. There were great bands of Japanese at work in the field." They worked with "incredible rapidity, the line of men crossing a field, levelling the cane."[12]

Cutting the ripe cane was dirty and exhausting work. As the workers mechanically swung their machetes, they felt the pain of the blisters on their hands and the scratches on their arms. "When you cutting the cane and you pulling the cane back," a worker said, "sometimes you get scratched with the leaves from the cane because they have a little edge just like a saw blade." Their heavy arms, their bent backs begged for a break, a moment of rest.

> *Becoming weary*
> *I sit for a while to rest*
> *In the cane field,*
> *And whistle*
> *To call the breezes.*[13]

But the breezes did not always come. Twelve feet in height, the cane enclosed and dwarfed the Asian workers. As they cleared the cane "forests," cutting the stalks close to the ground, they felt the heat of the sun, the humidity of the air, and found themselves surrounded by iron red clouds of dust. They covered their faces with handkerchiefs; still they breathed the dust and the mucus they cleared from their noses appeared blood red. "The sugar cane fields were endless and the stalks were twice the height of myself," a Korean woman sighed. "Now that I look back, I thank goodness for the height, for if I had seen how far the fields stretched, I probably would have fainted from knowing how much work was ahead. My waistline got slimmer and my back ached from bending over all the time to cut the sugar cane."

> *My husband cuts the cane stalks*
> *And I trim their leaves*
> *With sweat and tears we both work*
> *For our means.*[14]

Collecting the cane stalks, the workers tied them into bundles and loaded them onto railway cars. A train then pulled the cane to the mill where engines, presses, furnaces, boilers, vacuum pans, centrifugal drums, and other machines crushed the cane and boiled its juices into molasses and sugar. Inside the mill, laborers like my uncle Nobuyoshi Takaki felt like they were in the "hold of a steamer." The constant loud clanking and whirring of the machinery were deafening. "It was so hot with steam in the mill," Bashiro Tamashiro recalled, "that I became just like *pupule* [crazy]."[15]

At four-thirty in the afternoon, the workers again heard the blast of the plantation whistle, the signal to stop working. "Pau hana," they sighed, "finished working." Though they were exhausted and though they thought they were too tired to hoe another row of cane or carry another bundle of stalks, they suddenly felt a final burst of energy and eagerly scrambled to the camps.

> *In the rush at pau hana*
> *I get caught in cane leaves,*
> *When I stumble and fall,*
> *They prickle, they jab.*[16]

Planters claimed they treated their workers with "consideration and humanity," seeking "in every possible way to advance their comfort and make them contented and happy." But their purpose was not entirely humanitarian. Planters understood clearly that it was "good business" to have their laborers "properly fed": it "paid" to have a "contented lot of laborers," for they would then be able to extract a "good day's work" from them.[17]

The paternalism of the planters was also intended to defuse the organizing efforts of the workers. A plantation manager explained how laborers were "capable of comprehending the difference between kind words, kind acts, kind wages generally and ruffian roughness and abuse." Paternalism was designed to pacify labor unrest. "We should avail to get our house in order before a storm breaks," planters told themselves. "Once the great majority of the laboring classes are busy under conditions which breed contentment . . . we can expect a gradual and effectual diminution of the power of the agitating [labor] element." Planters agreed that "humanity in industry pays."[18]

Plantation paternalism also served to maintain a racial and class hierarchy. White plantation managers and foremen supervised Asians, constituting 70 to 85 percent of the work force. They saw their role as "parental" and described Koreans as "childlike" and Filipinos as "more or less like children" "by nature." The vice president of H. Hackfield and Company sent managers a circular informing them that the Filipino was "very incapable of caring for himself." Left entirely to his own resources, the Filipino was likely to spend his money on "fancy groceries" and consequently to be insufficiently nourished. Managers should "look after" Filipino laborers. Planters explained their paternalism in terms of white racial superiority. They had spread "Caucasian civilization" to Hawaii, where they as members of "a stronger race" had to supervise and care for Asian and Hawaiian laborers. "Where there is a drop of the Anglo-Saxon blood, it is sure to rule."[19]

Behind paternalism was the "necessity" of coercion. Planters believed that they should control their workers with "the strong hand." "There is one word which holds the lower classes . . . in check," they declared, "and that is Authority." The plantation organization resembled a system of military discipline. A plantation bulletin explicitly drew an analogy between the army and the plantation work force:

> To gain a picture of the plantation organization, as it directly affects irrigation, one may compare it roughly to a military organization, as follows:
>
> Plantation Manager . . . . The General
> Department of Agriculture:
>   Control and Research . . . . The Staff
> Plantation Head Overseer . . . . Lieutenant General Head
> Irrigation Overseer . . . . Major Section
> Overseers . . . . Captains
> Reservoir Men . . . . Supply Sergeants
> Ditchmen . . . . Corporals
> Irrigation Men . . . . The Troops[20]

As "generals," plantation managers devised an intricate system of rules and regulations for their "troops." They required their workers to be "industrious and docile and obedient," "regular and cleanly in their personal habits," punctual for work and rest, and present on the plantation at all times. To punish workers for violating the rules, planters developed an elaborate system of fines, which specified a charge for virtually every kind of misconduct. On one plantation, for example, workers were fined for

> breaking wagon through negligence — $5.00
> refusal to do work as ordered — $.25
> trespass — $.50
> cutting harness — $2.00
> insubordination — $1.00
> neglect of duty — $.50
> drunkenness — $.50
> drunken brawling — $5.00
> gambling in Japanese or Chinese camps — $5.00.[21]

Where fines did not work, harsher penalties were employed. Asked how he would punish a contract laborer for idleness, a planter replied: "We dock him; we give him one one-half or three quarters of a day of wages; and if he keeps it up we resort to the law and have him arrested for refusing to work." Sometimes planters used physical punishment to intimidate the workers. Chinese workers on the Olowalu Plantation were allowed five to fifteen minutes for lunch and were "kicked" if they did not return promptly to work. Lee Hong-ki complained about the strictness of a German luna: "If anyone violated his orders, he was punished, usually with a slap on the face." The Hawaiian government had outlawed whipping, but the law did not always reflect reality. "It is well known that many are the stripes inflicted and borne because the sufferer is ignorant of the law," the editor of the *Pacific Commercial Advertiser* noted in 1868, "or if he knows it, knows also that it is next to useless to seek redress." A plantation manager said disobedient "Japs" should be whipped, for "this class of people [has] no feelings except through the hide." In a letter to his agent, William G. Irwin, dated August 22, 1879, planter George Dole inquired about a "black snake whip" he had ordered for one of his overseers: "If you have received it, please forward it." Kim Hyung-soon bitterly recalled how he and his fellow Korean workers were not allowed to talk, smoke, or even stretch their backs as they labored in the fields: "A foreman kept his eyes on his workers at all times. When he found anyone violating working regulations, he whipped the violator without mercy." A worker graphically described the tiered structure of strict supervision: "Really, life on the plantation is one of restrictions, unwritten rules and regulations imposed upon the inhabitants by the manager who is assisted by his various ranks of overseers and lunas to see to it that the people obey these regulations and do the amount and nature of the work that is expected of them. . . . In conclusion I say that life on a plantation is much like life in a prison."[22]

To strengthen their authority over their ethnically diverse work force, planters developed an occupational structure stratifying employment according to race. Skilled and supervisory positions were predominantly occupied by whites. In 1882, for example, 88 percent of all lunas and clerks were white, while 28.5 percent of the laborers were Hawaiian and 48.3 percent were Chinese. None of the lunas were Chinese. In 1904, the Hawaiian Sugar Planters' Association passed a resolution that restricted skilled positions to "American citizens, or those eligible for citizenship." This restriction had a racial function: it excluded Asians from skilled occupations. They were not "white" according to federal law and hence ineligible to become naturalized citizens. In 1915, Japanese laborers were mostly field hands and mill laborers. There were only one Japanese, one Hawaiian, and two part-Hawaiian mill engineers; the remaining forty-one mill engineers (89 percent) were of European ancestry. A racial division was particularly evident in supervisory positions: of the 377 overseers, only two were Chinese and seventeen Japanese; 313 of all overseers (83 percent) were white. A Japanese worker bluntly explained why he and other Japanese would never be able to get ahead on the plantation. Told by an interviewer that he would be promoted, become a "big shot" if he had "the stuff," the worker retorted: "Don't kid me. You know yourself I haven't got a chance. You can't go very high up and get big money unless your skin is white. You can work here all your life and yet a haole who doesn't know a thing about the work can be ahead of you in no time."[23]

After federal law terminated the contract-labor system in 1900, planters used their centralized organization, the Hawaiian Sugar Planters' Association, to institute mechanisms to keep wages low. In a "Confidential Letter" to plantation managers on July 24, 1901, the association called for island conventions of managers to form wage-fixing agreements: "The deliberations of Island conventions at which managers would meet should be behind closed doors as it would be embarrassing to have such proceedings published." To carry out this plan, the association established a central labor bureau to coordinate all employment of Asian laborers and to set wage rates. Laborers were warned they should not try to leave their assigned plantations to bargain for higher wages, for they would not be hired by another plantation unless they could show a certificate of discharge. To provide incentives for their workers to increase their productivity, the association introduced a "bonus system" in 1910. "The Hawaiian sugar plantations are actuated in granting a bonus by the principle of desiring to compensate their employees for loyal labor," the association explained. "It is a reward for faithful service and a spur to productivity. And the bonus payments actually amount to profit sharing with the laborers." But the bonus also kept the workers from leaving the plantation. The bonus was paid only once a year, and workers forfeited it if they left the plantation before bonus time. In a letter to C. Brewer and Company, the manager of the Hawaiian

Agricultural Company Plantation stated frankly: "I wanted to have a string on them by their being on the annual bonus list."[24]

To control their workers, planters tied other "strings." They utilized a multitiered wage system, paying different wage rates to different nationalities for the same work. Japanese cane cutters, for example, were paid ninety-nine cents a day, while Filipino cane cutters received only sixty-nine cents. Planters also cultivated nationalistic consciousness among the laborers in order to divide them. They appealed to the "race pride" of the Filipino laborers to urge them to work as hard as the Japanese laborers. One Filipino workgang leader, giving instructions in Ilocano, declared to his men: "We are all Filipinos, brothers. We all know how to hoe. So, let's do a good job and show the people of other nations what we can do. Let us not shame our skin!" The planters' divide-and-control strategy promoted interethnic tensions that sometimes erupted into fistfights in the fields and riots in the camps. On the Spreckelsville Plantation on Maui in 1898, for example, three hundred Japanese, wielding sticks and clubs, drove a hundred Chinese laborers from the camps. A year later, during a riot involving Chinese and Japanese workers on the Kahuku Plantation on Oahu, sixty Chinese were wounded and four killed.[25]

Politics: Seasons of Rebellion

But plantation workers did not concentrate their discontent against each other; rather, they usually directed their rage outward against their bosses and the system, seeking to gain greater control over the conditions of their labor and a greater share of the profits they had produced. Not passive and docile as the managers wanted them to be, they actively struggled to improve the quality of their lives on the plantation in many different ways.

Occasionally workers fought back violently. They retaliated against mean overseers for physical abuse and mistreatment. Numerous instances of workers assaulting and beating up cruel and unfair lunas can be found in the records. On a Maui plantation in 1903, for example, after an Irish luna had hit a laborer, he was attacked by a gang of Chinese workers and buried under a ten-foot pile of cane stalks. In 1904, on the Waipahu Plantation, two hundred Korean laborers mobbed the plantation physician, claiming he had killed a Korean patient with a kick to the abdomen. Sometimes workers aimed their anger at property, especially the dry cane fields that were easy targets for arson. After the police had broken up a demonstration of protesting Chinese laborers on the Waianae Plantation in 1899, a fire swept through its cane fields.

But while planters worried about direct labor resistance, they also had to watch for subtle and ingenious actions. On the Koloa Plantation in the 1830s, William Hooper used script, or coupons, to pay his Hawaiian and Chinese workers: he wrote amounts for twelve and a half, twenty-five, and fifty cents on pieces of cardboard and told his workers they could exchange the coupons for goods at his plantation store. In 1836, Hooper was dismayed to discover that his workers had learned how to read and write from a young schoolmaster in the village, and some of them had utilized their newly acquired knowledge and skills to make artful reproductions of his coupons. The counterfeit coupons, according to a white neighbor, were "so strikingly like the original, imitating the signatures with scrupulous exactness, that it was some time before the fraud was detected." When he uncovered the deception, Hooper nervously scribbled into his diary: "Some native has attempted to counterfeit the papers which I issued for dollars." He then found that even the Chinese workers were forging his signature. In 1839, Hooper sent some of the counterfeit coupons to Ladd and Company in Honolulu: "I send you up a specimen of what I suppose to be *native* ingenuity in the shape of counterfeit money." Acknowledging its genuine appearance, Hooper admitted: "I would not swear it was not mine." By then, however, he had asked his company to have currency printed from a copper plate in order to be certain it could not be duplicated, and he had given specific instructions for its design: "If the ground work is fine waved lines, or a delicate net work, and the border highly wrought, we doubt if we shall be troubled with counterfeits from the Chinese or any other source."[26]

But the counterfeit conspiracy was only one moment in a long history of plantation labor struggles. Everywhere workers engaged in day-to-day resistance, trying to minimize the amount of labor their bosses extracted from them. Many workers feigned illness in order to be released from work. A visitor to a plantation near Hilo noticed the prevalence of various ailments among the laborers and commented: "It reminds me very much of plantation life in Georgia in the old days of slavery. I never elsewhere heard of so many headaches, sore hands, and other trifling ailments. It is very amusing to see the attempts which the would-be-invalids make to lengthen their brief smiling faces into lugubriousness, and the sudden relaxation into naturalness when they are allowed a holiday." Laborers had little incentive to work hard, and discipline was a constant problem for the planters. In one of their songs, field hands described their attitude toward work:

> When it rains I sleep;
> When it's sunny I stay away from work;
> And, when cloudy, I spend the day
> In drinking wine.

Laborers became skilled practitioners in the art of pretending to be working. On the Kohala Plantation on the island of Hawaii, a luna discovered that supervising Japanese women in the fields could be frustrating. In his diary, supervisor Jack Hall complained: "It always seemed impossible to keep them together, especially if the fields were not level. The consequence was that these damsels were usually scattered all over the place and as many as possible were out of sight in the gulches or dips in the field where they could not be seen, where they would calmly sit and smoke their little metal pipes until the luna appeared on the skyline, when they would be busy as bees."[27]

To escape from work and daily drudgery, sliding numbly into recalcitrance, many plantation laborers resorted to drugs — opium and alcohol. Visiting a Hilo plantation in 1873, Isabella Bird noted that the Chinese laborers smoked opium. A Chinese plantation worker recalled how the cook for his gang would bring their hot lunches to the field: "In the top of the bucket [lunch pail] was a little paper or envelope with the dope in it. All the men took their dope that way with their dinner." Drinking was extensive on the plantation. In the Japanese camps on Saturdays, "drinking bouts began everywhere" and an "uproar was made with drinking and singing" until late at night. A Filipino worker remembered how "drinks were readily available because just about everyone knew how to make 'swipe wine.' You just ferment molasses with water and yeast and in a week it's ready. And if you distilled that, you got clear liquor ten times stronger than any gin you could buy from the store."[28]

Planters complained that the use of drugs made it "impossible" to get from their laborers "anything like a fair day's work." "No employees can drink booze and do six honest days' work in a week," managers grumbled. "They are not 'up to scratch,' even if they can keep awake. . . . Their brains are muddled by booze." After saturating themselves with opium or alcohol on the weekends, laborers were "unfit for work" on Monday. Inspecting the camps on Mondays, plantation managers sometimes found a third of their men "dead drunk."[29]

Drugs eased, perhaps made more bearable, the emptiness plantation laborers felt on the weekends as well as the boredom of their meaningless and routine work during the week. "There was very little to do when work was over," recalled a Chinese laborer, "and the other fellows who were having a good time smoking asked me to join them, so then in order to be a good sport I took up opium smoking, not realizing that I would probably have to die with it." "If we don't smoke," another Chinese worker said, "we feel as if something were gnawing at our insides. The opium fumes will drive away that feeling and lift us out of our misery into a heaven of blissful rest and peace." Momentarily at least, drugs enabled workers to escape the reality of the plantation and to enter a dream world where they could hear again the voices of fathers, mothers, and other loved ones. They smoked opium and drank to "get their feelings up." "Drinking killed time and made the work day seem to go faster," a Filipino plantation hand explained. "At least, it helped feeling like everything was together. So swipe wine was our coffee in the mornings. And swipe was our milk for lunch. Swipe was our evening juice. And swipe was for sleeping. And the next morning again, swipe was for work. Woozy with swipe was the only way I could stay down with patience for work."[30]

But drugs were self-destructive and offered only temporary euphoria, and plantation workers often sought a more permanent form of escape — *ha'alele hana,* desertion from service. Until Hawaii became a U.S. territory in 1900, the contract-labor system was legal in the islands and plantation laborers under contract were bound by law to serve three-to-five-year terms. In one of their work songs, Japanese laborers urged each other to desert:

> *I hate 'hole hole' work*
> *Let's finish cutting cane*
> *And go to Honolulu.*

Thousands of contract laborers fled from their assigned plantations before the completion of their contracts. In 1892, Marshal Charles B. Wilson calculated that 5,706 arrests, or one third of the total arrests made between 1890 and 1892, were for desertion.[31]

Planters constantly worried about their contract laborers running away. "On the island of Maui," the *Pacific Commercial Advertiser* observed in 1880, "scarcely a day passes which does not bring along some member of the police force in search of absconding Chinese plantation laborers, who are making quite a business of shipping [signing a labor contract], drawing large advances, and then 'clearing out' causing their employers much inconvenience and expense." References to runaway contract laborers filled many pages of the diaries of plantation managers. On page four of his diary, manager Anton Cropp of the Koloa Plantation wrote: "On Saturday and Monday [December 12 and 14, 1891] Mr. Kahl-Cannu went as far as Mana for Jap. Deserters, and found Yosida 17 and Yosiwa 22. Before the District Judge in Koloa, they were found guilty and sent to jail." On page twelve, manager Cropp listed the "Deserters Japanese":

#5	Nakajin recaught & redeserted
#8	Kaneki
#12	Murohisa recaught & redeserted
#16	Kako
#17	Toshida recaught
#19	Iwamoto
#21	Iamamoto Furokishi
#24	Murakami
#323	Asahare recaught
#326	Hayashi
#400	Imatzu
#418	Saito recaught
#409	Uyeda
#416	Murakami recaught
#655	Nakane
#685	Fukushima Kaisaku recaught
#619	Seto
#621	Kuba recaught Honolulu

On the next page of his diary, manager Cropp recorded the action of a Japanese woman who had abandoned both her boss and her husband: "Ura, wife of Fujinaka #700 deserted on January 1892. Ura was under contract with the K.S.C. [Koloa Sugar Company] to work for 3 years commencing in May 1891 and therefore was bound to work until May 1894. Having worked on 2/3 of a year the K.S.C. charges Fujinaka #700 for passage and expenses for balance of term of Ura:

$$
\begin{array}{rr}
\text{passage} & \$15 \\
& 2 \text{ to plantation} \\
\text{pro-rata exp} & \underline{2} \\
\text{total} & 19 \\
\end{array}
$$

Interest percent of
same for 2⅓ years ___3___
$22
of this 2⅓ part of 3 to be charged to F.
charged payday — March 7, 1892.

Thus Fujinaka not only lost his wife but was required to reimburse the Koloa Sugar Company for her desertion.[32]

Most waited until their contracts expired and then left the plantations. In 1859 the editor of the *Polynesian* reported the massive movement of Chinese workers from the plantations: "In February next the last of the Coolie contracts expires, and we may then expect a still further increase of liberated laborers from the plantations on the other islands, to swell the crowd of Chinamen already prowling about Honolulu." On January 11, 1882, the manager of a plantation scribbled a worried note in his diary: "Most of our Chinamen gave notice today that they will leave after the end of this month." By 1882 only one third of the Chinese population of 15,000 were employed on the plantations. Generally staying on the plantations only as long as they were required by their contracts, Chinese workers moved in search of better employment opportunities. Many became rice farmers, making the swamplands yield rich harvests, and others settled in nearby villages and opened small stores. "My grandfather Len Wai worked on a plantation and operated a store during after-work hours," stated Raymond Len. "The store did well and he went full time into it after his contract was up." Most Chinese ex-plantation laborers went to Honolulu, where they lived in a bustling Chinatown.[33]

Thousands of Japanese workers also left the plantations after their contracts had been fulfilled. In 1900 the editor of the *Maui News* observed that a "traveling mania" had seized these workers: "Very many of the Japanese are leaving the plantation by every steamer for Honolulu." After annexation and the prohibition of contract labor in the Territory of Hawaii, laborers were no longer bound to the plantations, and planters anxiously witnessed an exodus of Japanese laborers to the mainland. In their camps, Japanese workers read circulars and advertisements about higher wages in California. In 1906 the *Hawaiian Star* reported: "The 'American fever,' as it is called among the Japs, appears to be causing a lot of agitation among them. Local Japanese papers contain the advertisement of Hasagawa, who recently got a license to solicit laborers, calling for 2,000 Japanese to go to the coast at once. The advertisement offers wages of from $1.35 per day up, stating that men who are good can make from $2 to $4 per day." In their efforts to stem the Japanese movement to the mainland, planters asked the Japanese Consul in Hawaii to issue circulars in Japanese instructing Japanese laborers to remain on the plantation. In 1903 the consul urged his countrymen to "stay at work steadily on the plantations and not go to an uncertainty on the mainland." Ignoring the consul's advice, Japanese laborers continued to migrate to the mainland in search of the highest bidder for their labor. By early 1907, 40,000 Japanese had left Hawaii for the West Coast.[34]

But in March President Theodore Roosevelt suddenly issued an executive order prohibiting the passage of Japanese from Hawaii to the mainland. Baishiro Tamashiro had been planning to move to the West Coast, and years later he vividly remembered the disappointment he felt when he learned about the executive order: "On March 20th there was a change in the law, and I was prohibited to go to [mainland] America. It was written all over in the newspapers. We were planning to go on April 9; however, the rule came on the 20th of March. So all my planning was *pau* [finished]." At a mass meeting in Honolulu, Japanese laborers angrily denounced Roosevelt's restriction: "It enslaves us permanently to Hawaii's capitalists!" Trapped by law in Hawaii, Japanese workers saw they had no choice but to struggle for a better life in the islands.[35]

Most of them saw that the struggle would have to be a collective one, and that their most powerful weapon was the strike. But they also realized the planters had the power to retaliate brutally. Past experiences had taught them some harsh lessons. In 1891, for example, two hundred striking Chinese laborers had protested unfair deductions from their wages and marched to the courthouse in Kapaau on the island of Hawaii. The plantation managers ordered them to return to their camps; late in the afternoon, the strikers left the courthouse. But as they were walking back to the camps, they were confronted by policemen armed with bullock whips. In fear, one or two of the strikers stooped to pick up stones. Suddenly, according to a newspaper report, the Chinese strikers found themselves "in the midst of a general onslaught," and were "ruthlessly overridden and welted with the bullock whips." Pursuing the fleeing Chinese strikers, the policemen attacked the Chinese camp. They "demolished every window, strewed the premises inside and out with stones, seized every

Chinaman they came across, and yanked forty or more by their queues. . . . Chinamen were seen with their tails twisted about the pommel of a saddle, dragged at a gallop."[36]

Planters believed their repression of strikes had been justifiable because contract laborers could not legally strike: they were bound by contract to work for a specified term of years and could be arrested and punished in the courts for violating the agreement. But the Organic Act of 1900, which established Hawaii as a territory of the United States on June 14, abolished the contract-labor system.

Months before the Organic Act took effect, plantation workers anticipated their freedom. On April 4, Japanese workers in Lahaina struck. Upset over the deaths of three mill hands who had been crushed under a collapsed sugar pan, the laborers blamed management carelessness for the accident and refused to work. The strikers seized the mill and the town. For ten days, they defiantly "continued to meet, to parade in the town under Japanese flags, to drill, and even, unhindered by anyone, demolished the house and property of a store clerk who would not give them credit." The Lahaina strikers successfully forced the manager to yield to most of their demands, including a five-hundred-dollar payment to the relatives of each accident victim and a nine-hour day for all workers. Meanwhile, Japanese workers elsewhere went out on strike. On the Spreckelsville Plantation, they demanded the termination of all labor contracts. Two hundred strikers, swinging clubs and throwing stones, fought a posse of sixty policemen and lunas armed with black snake whips. The strikers were "most thoroughly black snaked" and forced to retreat to their camps, but in the end they won the cancellation of their labor contracts.[37]

In 1900, over twenty strikes swept through the plantations as 8,000 workers withheld their labor from the bosses. While the strikes were led and supported mainly by Japanese workers, two of them involved interethnic cooperation. On June 22, Chinese and Japanese laborers on the Puehuehu Plantation struck to protest the retention of part of their wages, a provision contained in their original labor contracts. Five months later, forty-three Japanese and Portuguese women field hands on the Kilauea Plantation demanded that wages be raised from eight dollars to ten dollars a month. Though the striking women were locked out by the management, they stood together and won their wage increases.

After 1900, management-labor conflict became even more intense. As they organized themselves and initiated strike actions, workers found themselves facing the power of the state. This occurred during the 1906 Waipahu Plantation strike. Demanding higher wages, Japanese laborers struck, and plantation manager E. K. Bull immediately requested police assistance. Forty-seven policemen armed with rifles were assigned to the plantation. They functioned as Bull's private army. The policemen marched in review on the plantation grounds to intimidate the strikers with a show of force; patrolling the camps, they stopped and questioned all stragglers. During a tense moment of the negotiations, Bull threatened to use the police to evict the strikers from their homes in the camps. Unintimidated, the seventeen hundred Japanese strikers forced Bull to grant concessions in order to end the strike.

The Waipahu Plantation strike of 1906 underscored the importance of collective labor action. Labor violence and arson were individualistic as well as sporadic actions; they did not seriously undermine planter control. Recalcitrance and drunkenness represented resistance but did not change conditions in the workplace. Desertion enabled dissatisfied workers to escape, leaving intact the mechanisms of planter discipline and regimentation. But striking constituted a particularly effective expression of labor resistance, for it could lead to a positive transformation of the plantation structure. Moreover, striking could enable men and women of various nationalities to gain a deeper understanding of themselves as laborers, to develop a working-class identity and consciousness.

Divided by the political strategy of the planters and by their diverse national identities, workers initially tended to define their class interests in terms of their ethnicity. Thus, at first they organized themselves into "blood unions" — labor organizations based on ethnic membership: the Japanese belonged to the Japanese union and the Filipinos to the Filipino union.

The most important manifestation of "blood unionism" was the Japanese strike of 1909. Protesting against the differential-wage system based on ethnicity, the strikers demanded higher wages and equal pay for equal work. They noted angrily how Portuguese laborers were paid $22.50 per month while Japanese laborers earned only eighteen dollars a month for the same kind of work. "The wage is a reward for services done," they argued, "and a just wage is that which compensates the laborer to the full value of the service rendered by him. . . . If a laborer comes from Japan and he performs the same quantity of work of the same quality within the same period of time as those who hail from the opposite side of the world, what good reason is there to discriminate one as against the other? It is not the color of skin that grows cane in the field. It is labor that grows cane."[38]

The Japanese strikers struggled for four long months. The strike involved 7,000 Japanese plantation laborers on Oahu, and thousands of Japanese workers on the other islands supported their striking compatriots, sending them money and food. Japanese business organizations such as the Honolulu Retail Merchants' Association contributed financially to the strike fund, and the Japanese Physicians' Association gave free medical service to the strikers and their families. A strong sense of Japanese ethnic solidarity inspired the strikers. Stridently shouting banzai at rallies, they affirmed their commitment to the spirit of Japan — *yamato damashii*. They told themselves they must "stick together" as Japanese to win the strike.[39]

The strike reflected a new consciousness among Japanese workers, a transformation from sojourners to settlers, from Japanese to Japanese Americans. In their demand for a higher wage, the strikers explained: "We have decided to permanently settle here, to incorporate ourselves with the body politique [sic] of Hawaii — to unite our destiny with that of Hawaii, sharing the prosperity and adversity of Hawaii with other citizens of Hawaii." Gradually becoming settled laborers, they now had families to support, children to educate, and religious institutions to maintain. Hawaii was becoming home for the Japanese laborers, and they asked what kind of home Hawaii would be for them. The strikers argued that the unsatisfactory and deplorable conditions on the plantations perpetuated an "undemocratic and un-American," class-divided society of "plutocrats and coolies." Such a pattern of social inequality was injurious to Hawaii in general. Fair wages would encourage laborers to work more industriously and productively, and Hawaii would enjoy "perpetual peace and prosperity." The goal of the strike was to make possible the formation of "a thriving and contented middle class — the realization of the high ideal of Americanism."[40]

But the planters pressured the government to arrest the Japanese strike leaders for "conspiracy." Then they broke the strike by hiring Koreans, Hawaiians, Chinese, and Portuguese as scabs and began importing massive numbers of Filipinos to counterbalance the Japanese laborers. Three months after the strike, however, the planters eliminated the differential-wage system and raised the wages of the Japanese workers.

An ethnically based strike seemed to make good political sense to Japanese plantation laborers in 1909, for they constituted about 70 percent of the entire work force. Filipinos represented less than one percent. But the very ethnic solidarity of the Japanese made it possible for planters to use laborers of other nationalities to break the "Japanese" strike. Eleven years later, Japanese workers found that they had been reduced proportionately to only 44 percent of the labor force, while Filipino workers had been increased to 30 percent. Organized into separate unions, workers of both nationalities came to realize that the labor movement in Hawaii and their strike actions would have to be based on interethnic working-class unity.

In December of 1919, the Japanese Federation of Labor and the Filipino Federation of Labor submitted separate demands to the Hawaiian Sugar Planters' Association. The workers wanted higher wages, an eight-hour day, an insurance fund for old retired employees, and paid maternity leaves. Their demands were promptly rejected by the planters. The Japanese Federation of Labor immediately asked the managers to reconsider their decision and agreed to declare a strike after all peaceful methods had been tried. The Japanese leaders knew there was "no other way but to strike." "Let's rise and open the eyes of the capitalists," they declared. "Let's cooperate with the Filipinos" — "back them up with our fund" and "our whole force." The Japanese leaders thought both labor federations should not act precipitously, however. Rather, both unions should prepare for a long strike and plan a successful strategy.[41]

But the Filipino Federation of Labor felt the time for action had arrived. Consequently, on January 19, 1920, Pablo Manlapit, head of the Filipino union, unilaterally issued an order for the Filipinos to strike and urged the Japanese to join them. In his appeal to the Japanese Federation of Labor, Manlapit eloquently called for interethnic working-class solidarity: "This is the opportunity that the Japanese should grasp, to show that they are in harmony with and willing to cooperate with other nationalities in this territory, concerning the principles of organized labor. . . . We should work on this strike shoulder to shoulder."[42]

Meanwhile, 3,000 Filipino workers on the plantations of Oahu went out on strike. They set up picket lines and urged Japanese laborers to join them. "What's the matter? Why you hanahana [work]?" the Filipino strikers asked their Japanese co-workers. Several Japanese newspapers issued clarion calls for Japanese cooperation with the striking Filipinos. The *Hawaii Shimpo* scolded Japanese workers for their hesitation: "Our sincere and desperate voices are also their voices. Their righteous indignation is our righteous indignation. . . . Fellow Japanese laborers! Don't be a race of unreliable dishonest people! Their problem is your problem!" The *Hawaii Hochi* advised Japanese laborers to strike immediately: "Laborers from different countries" should take "action together." Between Filipinos and Japanese, the *Hawaii Choho* declared, there should be "no barriers of nationality, race, or color." On January 26, the Japanese Federation of Labor ordered the strike to begin on February 1. United in struggle, 8,300 Filipino and Japanese strikers — 77 percent of the entire plantation work force on Oahu — brought plantation operations to a sudden stop. "Pau hana," they told one another, "no go work." "Pau hana," they declared defiantly, "we on strike."[43]

Aware of the seriousness of the challenge they faced and determined to break the strike, planters quickly turned to their time-tested strategy of divide and control. The president of C. Brewer and Company, one of the corporate owners of the sugar plantations, informed a plantation manager: "We are inclined to think that the best prospect, in connection with this strike, is the fact that two organizations, not entirely in harmony with each other, are connected with it, and if either of them falls out of line, the end will be in sight." The planters isolated the Filipino leadership from the Japanese Federation of Labor and created distrust between the two unions. They offered Manlapit a bribe, and suddenly, to the surprise of both the Filipino and Japanese strikers, Manlapit called off the strike, condemning it as a Japanese action to cripple the industries of Hawaii. But, on the rank-and-file level, many Filipinos continued to remain on strike with the Japanese. Escalating their attack on the Japanese, the planters slandered the Japanese strikers as puppets of Japan and claimed they were seeking to "Japanise" the islands. In a letter to a plantation manager, the Director of the Bureau of Labor of the Hawaiian Sugar Planters' Association described the plan for the ideological war to be waged against the Japanese strike leaders: "In order to let the plantation laborers know they are being duped and to make them realize what they are losing by allowing themselves to be misled by the agitating newspapers and strike leaders, we have commenced a program of propaganda. . . . There is absolutely no race so susceptible to ridicule as the Japanese."[44]

To break the strike directly, planters enlisted Hawaiians, Portuguese, and Koreans as strikebreakers. They knew that Koreans had a particular enmity for the Japanese, and the planters had consistently used Koreans to help break Japanese strikes. During the 1920 strike, Korean laborers under the leadership of the Korean National Association announced: "We place ourselves irrevocably against the Japanese and the present strike. We don't wish to be looked upon as strikebreakers, but we shall continue to work . . . and we are opposed to the Japanese in everything." More than one hundred Korean men and women organized themselves into a Strikebreakers' Association and offered their services to the Hawaiian Sugar Planters' Association.[45]

Planters served forty-eight-hour eviction notices to the strikers, forcing them to leave their homes and find shelters in empty lots in Honolulu. Crowded into encampments during the height of the influenza epidemic, thousands of workers and their family members fell ill and 150 died. "My brother and mother had a high fever," Tadao Okada recalled, "but all of us were kicked out of our home." Under such punishing and chaotic conditions, the strikers could not hold out indefinitely and were compelled to call off the strike in July.[46]

Though they had been soundly beaten, the workers had learned a valuable lesson from the 1920 strike. Filipinos and Japanese, joined by Spanish, Portuguese, and Chinese laborers, had participated in the first major interethnic working-class struggle in Hawaii. Men and women of different ethnicities, realizing how the 5:00 A.M. whistle had awakened all of them and how they had labored together in the fields and mills, had fought together for a common goal. And as they walked the picket lines and protested at mass rallies together, they understood more deeply the contribution they had made as workers to the transformation of Hawaii into a wealthy and profitable place. "When we first came to Hawaii," they proudly declared, "these islands were covered with ohia forests, guava fields and areas of wild grass. Day and night did we work, cutting trees and burning grass, clearing lands and cultivating fields until we made the plantations what they are today."[47]

During the strike, as the workers reached for a new unity transcending ethnic boundaries, leaders of the Japanese Federation of Labor questioned the existence of two separate unions — one for the Japanese and one for the Filipinos — and suggested the consolidation of the two federations into one union. They insisted that Japanese workers must affiliate with Filipino, "American," and Hawaiian workers, for as long as all of them were laborers they should mutually cooperate in safeguarding their standard of living. On April 23, the

Japanese Federation of Labor decided to become an interracial union and to call the organization the Hawaii Laborers' Association — a new name trumpeting a feeling of multiethnic class camaraderie.

One of the leaders of the Hawaii Laborers' Association articulated this new and developing class perspective. The fact that the "capitalists" were "haoles" and the laborers Japanese and Filipinos was a "mere coincidence," explained Takashi Tsutsumi. Japanese and Filipinos had acted as "laborers" in "a solid body" during the 1920 strike. What the workers had learned from their struggle, Tsutsumi continued, was the need to build "a big, powerful and non-racial labor organization" that could "effectively cope with the capitalists." Such a union would bring together "laborers of all nationalities." The 1920 strike had provided the vision — the basis for a new union: in this struggle, Japanese and Filipino workers had cooperated against the planter class. "This is the feature that distinguishes the recent movement from all others." Tsutsumi observed. "There is no labor movement that surpasses the recent movement of Japanese and Filipinos." Tsutsumi predicted that a "big" interracial union would emerge within ten years, springing from a "Hawaiian-born" leadership. "When that day comes," he concluded, "the strike of 1920 would surely be looked upon as most significant."[48]

This possibility of class unity in a multiethnic working class was explored by the son of a plantation laborer — Milton Murayama. In his novel *All I Asking for Is My Body*, Murayama describes an incident that occurs on a Maui plantation. During a strike of Filipino workers, the manager tries to recruit Japanese boys as scabs, and the youngsters view the situation as a chance to make extra money. But one day a discussion on the strike erupts in an eighth-grade class. "What's freedom?" asks Tubby Takeshita, and the teacher and students agree that freedom means being your "own boss," not "part of a pecking order." And they see that workers are at the bottom of the pecking order and getting a "raw deal." "You gotta stick together even more if you the underdog." Tubby says. And the teacher asks: "How much together? Filipino labor, period? Japanese labor, period? Or all labor?"[49]

Plantation Camps: Culture and Community

The plantation pecking order, Murayama observes, was reinforced by a plantation housing pattern resembling a "pyramid." At the top of the hill was the big house, the luxurious home of the manager; below were the nice-looking homes of the Portuguese, Spanish, and

Japanese lunas; then the identical wooden-frame houses of Japanese Camp; and finally the more run-down Filipino Camp. Moreover, the organization of the housing hierarchy was planned and built around its sewage system. The concrete ditches that serviced the toilets and outhouses ran from the manager's house on the highest slope down to the Filipino Camp on the lowest perimeter of the plantation. The tiered housing pattern and sewage system seemed emblematic: "Shit too was organized according to the plantation pyramid."[50]

Murayama's description is insightful. The physical organization of its housing reflected the social hierarchy of the plantation community. The manager lived in a mansion with spacious verandas and white columns overlooking the plantation; his foremen and the technical employees were housed in handsome bungalow cottages surrounded by well-kept lawns and flower gardens. "This section of houses on this tree-lined street was called 'lunas row,' " my cousin Minoru Takaki pointed out as he drove me around the Puunene Plantation on Maui in 1985. "Only the white lunas could live here, in the houses." As we then passed a recreational hall, he said: "That's 'haole club.' In the old days, only haoles were allowed to go there. It was segregated." He chuckled. "But you know what, my mother could go there. She was the maid." A Korean worker said that his three haole bosses lived in "big houses" far away from the laborers' camps. A government inspector found that the kind of housing varied with the class of labor: European laborers (either a family or two single men) were assigned two rooms in a four-room cottage, while Chinese workers were placed in barracks with from six to forty men in one room.[51]

Workers of different nationalities were usually housed in separate camps. "There were the Japanese camps," said my uncle Richard Okawa, describing to me the Hawi Plantation on the Big Island of Hawaii, "and the Chinese and Filipino camps, and one camp for the Puerto Ricans. Our family used to sell fish on the side, and your mother and I when we were young kids had to go from camp to camp on payday and collect the money the workers owed for the fish." The Puunene Plantation on Maui had sixteen camps, including many Japanese as well as Filipino camps and also "Young Hee Camp," "Ah Fong Camp," "Spanish A Camp," "Spanish B Camp," and "Alabama Camp." "Yeah," explained Minoru Takaki, formerly of "McGerrow Camp" (named after one of the lunas), "we used to have Negroes on the plantation."[52]

The organization of camps into different nationalities supported the planters' strategy of dividing and controlling their work force. But it may not have sprung from a consciously designed planter policy of residential ethnic segregation. Rather, the formation of segregated camps reflected the wave pattern of labor recruitment and immigration. As planters recruited groups of workers from different countries, they constructed new camps for them. Living together in ethnically separated camps, laborers found they could practice the customs and traditions of their homelands and speak their native languages. A Filipino worker, describing the development of separate camps for different nationalities on the Ewa Plantation, said: "At that time nearly everyone who worked at all in this plantation lived in one camp. There were Puerto Ricans, Spanish, a handful of Portuguese, Chinese, a few Japanese and a few Koreans. Each nationality group more or less constituted an exclusive group of its own; no group seemed to mingle with any other. . . . Every year there were many Filipino immigrants who joined our camp. There were so many Filipinos that a separate camp was given to them. The other nationalities soon had a camp of their own too, a thing which pleased everyone, as not only work was thought of but also parties among the laborers could be held."[53]

But not all plantations had separate ethnic camps, and a few planters even deliberately assigned their workers to integrated camps. The manager of the Waialua Plantation, for example, placed Korean workers in a "detached camp" after they arrived in 1903 in order to avoid the "danger of race troubles of any kind with Japanese, Chinese or Portuguese." This arrangement, however, was intended to be only temporary. His plan was to locate Koreans eventually in the "regular plantation camps where they will be subject to the same rules . . . and thereby lose their identity as Koreans and be merged into the plantation community as a whole." Describing one of the camps on the Waipahu Plantation, a Japanese laborer said: "In those days, we were living in a part of Waipahu called Pake [Chinese] Camp. In that camp, Pake and Japanese were all mixed up. We didn't have any trouble with the Pake." In his *Plantation Sketches*, Jared C. Smith praised the integrated camps of the Hawaiian Commercial and Sugar Company on Maui: "None of the camps are given over to one race exclusively, and equal treatment is given to all. The result of this mixing of all races in one village has been the disappearance of racial antagonisms and jealousies and the development of mutual respect."[54]

Housing conditions for workers varied from plantation to plantation. In 1899 Dr. Charles A. Peterson of the Bureau of Immigration found model camps where every house was weatherproof and where the surrounding space was clean and well drained. But he also visited camps that were "decrepit and dilapidated rookeries with roofs leaking and danger and disease threatening the occupants, with masses of filth blocking the drains and decaying refuse all about and beneath the houses." Seventeen years later, another investigator also reported a wide range of housing conditions. Some plantations had "splendid camps," "very clean" and "well-planted" with flowers. But other plantations had very dirty camps with houses in "a rotten condition."[55]

Generally, plantation laborers lived in crowded and unsanitary camps. Yasutaro Soga reported that workers were housed in dwellings resembling pig sties, and that several hundred laborers "swarmed together" in one-story "tenements." A Japanese laborer recalled: "Fifty of us, both bachelors and married couples, lived together in a humble shed — a long ten-foot-wide hallway made of wattle and lined along the sides with a slightly raised floor covered with a grass rug, and two *tatami* mats to be shared among us." Another worker described the "large partitioned house" she inhabited: "The type of room for married people was small, no bed or anything. . . . It was just a space to lay the futon down and sleep. We didn't have any household things, only our one wicker trunk, not even a closet. We just pounded a nail by the place we slept, a hook where I hung my muumuu, the old kanaka [Hawaiian] style." Chinese laborers on the Paia Plantation were crowded into "big warehouses filled with bunks stacked four or five high, steamer style. Two or three hundred lived in a building." Visiting the camps of Korean laborers, Hyon Sun found his compatriots living in tenements: "The married men each occupy one room, but single ones are put in compartments in groups of five or six people. The filth and uncleanliness of their living quarters are beyond description." An investigator for the Hawaiian Sugar Planters' Association in 1916 reported that Filipinos on one plantation were housed in congested camps. In many instances, six men occupied a small eight-by-twelve-foot room and two families had to share a single room. Due to the lack of privacy and space, workers often became tense and nervous. "Ten of us shared a small house and in such a cramped space we were constantly brushing against each other," a Filipino worker said. "We were often irritated at each other. Small annoyances led to quarrels. Endless arguments arose as to whose turn it was to prepare supper, wash dishes or buy the food.

An innocent remark or comment, interpreted wrongly, might result in a fight."[56]

After the 1909 strike, planters increasingly acknowledged the need to improve the squalid conditions of the camps. In September 1910, the Hawaiian Sugar Planters' Association advised planters to award cash prizes to workers who had the best-kept yards and gardens around their homes. The association wanted to prettify the plantation. "An attractive camp," the association stated, "is something which always attracts visitors, and which always gives them a favorable impression of the treatment of laborers by the plantations. When taking visitors around we always show them camps that are well kept in preference to those that are barren. . . . The plantations should also see to it that trees are furnished to laborers and that they are encouraged to plant and care for them."[57]

As planters employed men with families rather than single men, they began to abandon the barrack system and to provide cottages for families. In a letter to the manager of the Hawaiian Agricultural Company Plantation in 1916, C. Brewer and Company wrote that "dependable married men" were "preferred" as workers and authorized the building of cottages for married laborers. In 1920 the Hawaiian Sugar Planters' Association promoted the development of family-housing units: "Housing conditions on the plantations have changed greatly during the past few years, lately on account of the change in labor from single to married men." Planters had self-interested reasons for their camp-improvement program. They wanted to "stimulate" the "home feeling" in the camps in order to make workers happier and more productive. "Pleasant surroundings, with some of the modern comforts and conveniences," explained a plantation official, "go a long way to make the worker healthier and more efficient in his work."[58]

The laborers had their own reasons for beautifying their camp. Seeking to add a small bit of "extravagance" and a reminder of their homeland, Japanese workers placed bonsai plants on the steps of their cottages. They also developed artistic gardens; a mainland visitor observed that the flowers and "miniature gardens with little rocky pools and goldfish" suggested "a corner of Japan." Determined to have their traditional hot baths, Japanese workers also built *furos*. "The bath was communal," Tokusuke Oshiro said. "We all took a bath together. If, however, you got in last, it would be very dirty." Ko Shigeta recalled how men and women shared the furo on the Ewa plantation, and how he washed himself with the wives of other men stepping over him matter-of-factly as if he were "a dog or cat in their path," "the cold drops from the ends of their hair" falling on his bare back. A plantation manager reported that the Japanese camp had separate bathhouses for men and women. "But we find that both men and women are still making use of both tubs," he noted. "It will be difficult to break the Japs of this time worn custom."[59]

Workers cultivated vegetable gardens on plots assigned to them by the plantation manager. During his investigation of welfare conditions on the Grove Farm Plantation, a plantation official found an extensive system of vegetable gardens: "Each family is given a plot . . . and given water for the purpose of irrigation. These gardens have been very successful and supply a large part of the vegetable need of the family." A Japanese laborer recalled how he cultivated his garden even after ten hours of hard work in the cane fields: "After we came home from the field, it was dark especially in the winter months but we tilled our little vegetable garden with the help of the kerosene lamp light to raise the vegetables we ate."[60]

Gradually over the years, the workers transformed the camps into communities as cottages for families replaced barracks for single men. As they landscaped their yards and planted vegetable gardens, they developed a "home feeling" in their camps. People began to know and care for one another. "There was another thing I'd come to like about the camp," remarks Kiyoshi in Murayama's novel about plantation life. "The hundred Japanese families were like one big family. Everybody knew everybody else, everybody was friendly."[61]

Still, life on the plantation was largely an isolated and drab existence. "For the first two and a half years here," a Filipino plantation worker recounted, "I lived pretty much the same. Six days a week I worked from siren to siren." To escape from the plantation routine, laborers found ways to entertain themselves. Many of them went fishing. A Filipino worker said that he "went with friends to the rocky edge of the ocean" to "throw net" for fish on Sundays. "After *pau hana* . . . we caught small shrimp for fish bait," a Japanese laborer recalled. "There were a lot of fish there. We could catch as many *papio* [jack] as we wanted in those days."[62]

Lonely, far away from the families they had left behind in their homelands, many workers sought solace and entertainment in card playing and gambling. "Here and there gambling was in favor," reported Yasutaro Soga on the Waipahu Plantation. "On the Saturday evening following pay day, questionable women and professional gamblers from Honolulu came on business to the camp. . . . And the visitors wrung from the workers the fruits of their painstaking toil." Chinese gamblers traveled from plantation to plantation, and gambling in the Chinese camps became so intense it sometimes interfered with the plantation work schedule. On September 2, 1881, an annoyed plantation manager scribbled into his diary: "There are only a few Chinamen carrying cane. O. Otto [a foreman] went to the China house and drove the gambler outsiders out and told those who did not come to get their money and leave." According to the Japanese Consul in 1888, gambling among Japanese workers had reached a point where "all night sessions" were "common." Baishiro Tamashiro said he became so involved in gambling that he stopped working: "When I won, I would pay for my cook charge first of all. If not, I had to borrow money. I spent about half a year on gambling." Cockfight gambling was popular among Filipino laborers. "On Sundays I just sat around playing Sakura [a Japanese card game] and talking stories," said Bonipasyo. "But mostly, I watched the cockfights. It felt good to see blood spilled regularly." Many workers spent their weekends and nights gambling to help them forget their hardships, hoping to win big — perhaps even enough money to return home rich. Usually they lost, and in the fields the next day, they would sing:

> The thirty-five cents
> That I earned and saved
> Is gone by night
> From gambling.[63]

Many Filipino laborers found their wages gone by the end of the evening, spent at taxi-dance halls. There were few Filipino women on the plantations, and Filipino men crowded the taxi-dance halls, craving the company of women. On paydays, Filipino string bands, traveling from plantation to plantation, played music at dances. On the dance floor, Filipino men eagerly purchased tickets that offered them momentary joy, three minutes to hold, touch, and dance with a woman. "Some guys, they spend $50, $30, one man, one night," recalled Dorotio Allianic, a string-band player. "Go for broke, the men."[64]

After the 1909 strike, planters recognized the need to develop recreational programs and facilities for their workers. In 1910 the Hawaiian Sugar Planters' Association advised managers to provide amusements on the plantations. Such a "welfare program" of athletics, music, and movie entertainment, explained a sugar-industry official, would offer plantation managers "magnificent results." The program would not only hold the laborer on the plantation but also help to prevent strikes. "Leaving out of consideration the humanitarian side of any such welfare work," he added, "we believe it would be to the financial benefit of the plantation to endeavor to cultivate a spirit of contentment among the laborers." Sports, especially baseball, should be promoted: "A baseball ground well laid out and grassed, could be afforded by every plantation, and to encourage this sport, which every nationality of laborers is keen for, prizes could be offered to winning teams." Musical activities should be supported: "Every plantation could afford to encourage a band or a stringed orchestra; instruments could be provided by the plantation, and concerts and dances would become a feature of plantation life." Films and movies should be shown regularly on the plantation: "A moving picture show is something all nationalities enjoy. . . . Carefully selected films which would give the most satisfaction could be shown on every plantation." Nine years later, a plantation manager wrote to the Hawaiian Sugar Planters' Association: "Every Sunday we have baseball games between the Filipino laborers and our young Japanese and Portuguese boys in which our timekeepers and some of our overseers join. . . . In looking around at the almost universal unrest amongst labor and thinking of the absence of it upon these Islands, we feel that an unremitting endeavor should be made to keep our laborers content and happy."[65]

Planters also supported religious activities: they understood the usefulness of Christian churches and Buddhist temples as mediating institutions, and they permitted and sometimes even promoted religion on the plantation. Baptized by Lutheran missionaries in China, some of the Chinese laborers had come to Hawaii as Christians. Others were converted to Christianity by missionaries in Hawaii. On the plantations, Chinese laborers were given Chinese translations of the Bible and encouraged by the missionaries and the planters to organize congregations of Chinese Christians. In Paia, missionary Frank Damon was pleased to report in 1882: "A most suitable and commodious church has recently been erected here, which is used by . . . the natives in the morning and the Chinese in the afternoon." In Kohala, Luke Ah Seu became a lay reader at St. Paul's Episcopal Church, where he continued missionary work until 1898, and Kong Tet Yin served the Chinese members of the Congregational Church under the direction of the Reverend Elias Bond.[66]

The most energetic evangelist to the Chinese plantation laborers was S. P. Aheong. A contract laborer, Aheong had arrived in Hawaii in 1854 and worked on the Makawao Plantation on Maui. Converted to Christianity by the Reverend Jonathan Green, he was asked by the Hawaiian Evangelical Association to distribute religious literature to Chinese plantation workers. In 1868 Aheong plunged into a whirlpool of evangelical activity. He traveled from island to island, visiting plantations and holding religious meetings for his fellow Chinese. During his first ten months of religious work, he gave seventy-five sermons in Chinese. On August 18, 1868, Aheong wrote to the Reverend L. H. Glick from Lahaina: "My work was commenced the same day which you pointed out and I hold a Chinese meeting here at last Sabbath. Five out of 13 Chinamen came. I gave them some books to read which know how to read. One of them says how can a man say that China's idols are not the God because if a man say a bad word to the idol, then he shall have pain in the whole body. I say to him that he has by all mistaking, for I am since the great many years refuse the idol; and speak bad word to them but I do not pain my body at all, and I told him good deal about our heavenly father is the true God." A few weeks later, Aheong was in Hilo, where he wrote to the Reverend S. C. Damon: "I am glad to tell you about the Hilo Chinamen. Some of them been in this country more than 40 or 30 years, and never been to church since they been in these Islands, until I came here."[67]

Koreans gave Christianity a visible presence on the plantations. Many had been converted in Korea, and they began to found churches on the plantations shortly after their arrival in Hawaii. Visiting plantations in 1905, missionary Homer Hulbert reported the construction of seven plantation chapels for Koreans: "The Koreans themselves subscribed generously toward the erection of these edifices. A good part of the money was subscribed by the plantation proprietors who are keen to encourage all agencies looking toward peace and order and morality." Christianity spread rapidly among the Koreans, and in 1906 a visiting missionary was delighted to find "little congregations" of Koreans everywhere in the islands. "In the evening," he reported, "the sound of their hymns can be heard in most camps." He estimated that one third of all the Koreans in Hawaii were Christians and commended them for the moral influence they had on the camp community in stamping out gambling and intoxication. Planters considered their support for Korean churches was a "paying investment." One of them wrote to a Korean missionary: "These

Koreans make the most sincere Christians I have ever known. They are becoming more and more the most desirable and efficient laborers. . . . Your work among them [at the Mission] is showing excellent results. I shall certainly build a school house for their children as you request. They are among my most faithful employees."[68]

Japanese plantation laborers carried Buddhism with them to Hawaii. On every plantation, they established Buddhist temples; planters themselves often donated lands for temples and even subsidized Buddhist programs and priests, for they viewed Buddhism as a stabilizing influence on their workers. The Waipahu and Kahuku plantations financially supported Buddhist temples and schools; the Ewa, Aiea, Waialua, Waianae, and Waimanalo plantations on Oahu, and many plantations on the other islands, also provided grants of rent-free lands and monetary subsidies to Buddhist temples. In a letter to a plantation manager in 1902, a sugar-industry director encouraged planters to give financial support to Japanese-Buddhist schools and added: "The Directors are quite in sympathy with any movement on the part of the Japanese which should have good influence amongst them."[69]

The churches and temples reflected not only a spiritual requirement but also a broad need for ethnicity — a deeply felt urge of plantation laborers. Separated from their homelands, workers strove to retain their national identities; in the camps, they celebrated traditional festivals and recreated in Hawaii the familiar scenes of the old countries. One of the most colorful and noisy festivals was Chinese New Year. "The explosion of fire crackers throughout the day," reported the *Hawaiian Gazette* in 1867, "demonstrated that the great day of the Chinese year was being properly remembered." On their New Year's Day, Chinese plantation laborers took off from work; the manager of a plantation recorded in his diary on February 17, 1882: "No work on account of the Chinese New Year." To celebrate the important event, the Chinese trimmed the roofs of their joss houses with "long lines of small flags of every hue" and hung colored lanterns on the verandas of their barracks and cottages. Then they exchanged cards or slips of paper to wish one another good luck. Celebrators strummed Chinese musical instruments that resembled "a cross between a banjo and a guitar." The highlight of a traveler's visit to a plantation in 1888 was the Chinese New Year's festival: "Ah See was, apparently, something of a fire-worshipper, as one morning, when a Chinese feast was in progress on the plantation, we heard a tremendous cracking and fizzing, and on going out . . . we found he had lighted two bundles of firecrackers, which were going off in every direction, and Ah See, with his hands to his forehead, was bowing and grimacing to the crackers, as though they were so many spirits, and muttering what I suppose were charms against evil." During festival time on the Kohala Plantation, two rival Chinese benevolent societies, within view of each other across the Kapaau Gulch, competed to see which one could burn the longest or loudest string of firecrackers.[70]

During the midsummer, Japanese plantation laborers held their traditional *obon*, or festival of souls. Dressed in kimonos, they danced in circles to the beat of *taiko* drums in celebration of the reunion of the living with the spirits of the dead. In early November they observed the Mikado's birthday as a holiday. Irritated by the interruption of the plantation production schedule, plantation managers found they had no choice but to let their Japanese workers have the day off. "There is an old custom here among the Japs of observing the 3rd of November as a holiday," a plantation manager unhappily reported to C. Brewer and Company in 1911. "The Emperor's Birthday was celebrated everywhere," Tokusuke Oshiro recalled. "Mainly there was *sumo*. . . . Several young men, usually the good ones, got together at a camp and had Japanese-style *sumo* matches." Seichin Nagayama said that on the emperor's birthday or "Tenchosetsu," the "Okinawans would rest from work and order *bento* [lunch] from the *meshiya* [eating place]. At night the Okinawans would play *shamisens* [three-stringed musical instruments] made out of *tengara* [tin cans] on which they put strings. So we had music with the *tengara shamisen* — '*jara-jara, jan-jan, chan-chan*' — and we danced Okinawan dances."[71]

The most important celebration of Filipino plantation laborers was Rizal Day — December 30, the day the Spanish executed the famous revolutionary leader Jose Rizal in 1896. To honor Rizal, Filipino plantation bands played mandolins and guitars at outdoor concerts. As the Filipino laborers remembered Rizal, they told one another tales of his heroic deeds. "The Kastilas could not kill him, because the bullets bounced off his chest," a worker would declare. And a compatriot would "tell it up one notch" and quickly add: "He caught them [the bullets] with his bare hands!" Filipinos repeatedly told the story about how the revolutionary leader actually did not die: "After he was buried, his wife poured his love potion on his freshly filled grave, and in the night — he rose, Apo Rizal rose from the grave."[72]

Asian plantation workers carried to Hawaii not only their festivals and myths but also their foods. In the camps could be found
an interesting and unique variety of Asian ethnic foods — Chinese
char siu (barbecued pork) and *maunapua,* or *bao* (bun with pork
stuffing), Korean kimchi (pickled cabbage laced with garlic and hot
red pepper), Filipino adobo (stewed garlic pork and chicken), Japanese sashimi (raw fish) and sushi (rice cakes with seafood). Tofu
(Japanese bean curd) was in great demand on the plantations. "My
wife and I made the tofu and I would go out and sell it in the camps,"
Tokusuke Oshiro said. "The farthest I went to sell is Olaa's Ju-
yonri — the camp at the 14 mile marker in Olaa plantation. I had
regular customers who knew the days I would come. So when I
honked my horn, people would come out with container in hand."
Japanese families made *mochi* (sweet rice cakes), especially on New
Year's Day. For their lunch, Japanese laborers ate *musubi,* rice balls
with *ume* (pickled red plums) inside, and Filipinos spread *boggoong*
(salted fish) over their rice.[73]

As the laborers and their families mingled together in the camps,
they began to exchange their different ethnic foods, including not
only various Asian dishes but also Hawaiian *kalua* pig (baked in the
ground) and *lau lau* (fish and pork wrapped in ti leaves) and Portuguese hot sausage and sweet bread. The daughter of a Portuguese
laborer remembered how her mother would make gifts of her bread
and "little buns for the children in the camp. The Japanese families
gave us sushis and the Hawaiians would give us fish." "Everybody
took their own lunches" to school, Lucy Robello of the Waialua
Plantation said. "And like the Japanese used to take their little rice-
balls with an ume inside and little *daikon* [radish]. . . . And us Portuguese, we used to take bread with butter and jelly or bread with
cheese inside." Then, at noontime, Japanese and Portuguese children
would trade their *kaukaus* (lunches) with one another. Meanwhile,
in the fields, their parents were also sharing lunches. "We get in a
group," William Rego recalled. "We pick from this guy's lunch and
that guy'll pick from my lunch and so forth." Crossing ethnic lines,
workers would taste each other's foods and exclaim in Hawaiian:
"*Ono, ono!*" "Tasty, tasty!"[74]

Sitting on the ground in the cane fields and eating their kaukaus,
workers of different nationalities also began talking to one another.
Initially, the laborers of each ethnic group had spoken only their
native language. The language of their home country provided an
essential basis for their particular ethnic identity and culture. Lan-

guage gave each ethnic group a sense of community within the plantation camps by enabling its members to maintain ties with one another as they shared memories of their distant homeland and stories of their experiences in the new country. Japanese and Korean parents sent their children to Japanese- and Korean-language schools respectively; thus their children had to attend public school all day and then spend another hour or two in language school.

Gradually, however, workers of different nationalities began to acquire a common language. Working on the plantation required cross-ethnic communication, and planters used English as the "language of command." Plantation managers wanted the immigrant laborers to be taught a functional spoken English. "By this," explained a planter, "we do not mean the English of Shakespeare but the terms used in everyday plantation life. A great many of the small troubles arise from the imperfect understanding between overseers and laborers." Over the years a plantation dialect called "pidgin English" developed: incorporating peculiarly Hawaiian, Japanese, Portuguese, Chinese, and other elements, it grew out of management's need to give commands to a multilingual work force. On the plantation, a foreman was able to give instructions to an ethnically diverse gang of workers in pidgin English and communicate to all of them at once, and workers were able to respond in a pidgin English.[75]

Isolated on the plantations, workers sometimes came to think pidgin was the English language. On one occasion, Chinese workers found they could not understand their new field boss. A recent arrival in Hawaii, he had given his instructions to the men in "pure English." He explained to them that he wanted them to cut the cane close to the ground and to lop off the tops and throw them between the furrows for fertilizer. But his men found his language strange and unintelligible. A bystander noticed the confusion and translated the instructions in pidgin: "*Luna,* big boss speak, all men down below cutch; suppose too much *mauka* (uphill, high) cutch, too mucha sugar *poho* (wasted) — *keiki* (shoots) no use. Savvy? All men *opala* (trash) cutch, one side t'row — byenby mule men come, *lepo* (dirt) too mucha guru (good). Savvy?" "Savvy," the Chinese men replied and added in disgust: "Huy! wasamalla dis *Haole* — he no can taok *haole!*"[76]

"Our English in those days was really funny," a Japanese plantation worker recalled amusingly. "A contract worker in Lahaina Plantation was asked by his superiors, 'How many people are working here?' He answered, 'Ten, ten, wan burooku' (Ten, ten, one broke), in loud voice. The supervisor said, 'All right, boys,' and galloped away. What the worker meant to say is that ten plus ten minus one, 19." The workers also happily and promiscuously combined words from different languages. "You like hemo [Hawaiian] coppe ka [Japanese]?" (Will you pick coffee?) "Chicken he too much makee [Hawaiian]." (Many chickens died.) "No more hana hana [Hawaiian], no can kaukau [Hawaiian]." (I have no work, therefore I cannot eat.) They also invented their own expressions such as "mo betta": "Cow he mo betta come home." Newspapers even carried advertisements in pidgin English:

> Me — P. Y. Chong plenty smile any time now. Anybody too muchee kokua Me — P. Y. Chong new chop sui lestlunt fix up Hotel Stleet between Nuuanu and Smith. Too many person come Hotel Stleet Lau Yee Chai, catchem Me — P. Y. Chong Numbeh One kaukau lunch time, dinneah time, afteh-theateh suppeh time, any time catchem.
>
> Disee new Lau Yee Chai chop sui place no so hard to find, Chinee red and Chinee jade paint all oveh. Numbeh One lestlunt, no so muchee money cost kaukau. You come looksee, eh?
>
> Me — P. Y. Chong tank you so muchee.

A worker said lunas and workers would mix Japanese and Hawaiian words with hand gestures. "The Portuguese luna used to speak a little Japanese. 'Ni-ban (number two) dis you ditchee,' and the luna would pantomime with his hands and feet what we were supposed to do. We somehow managed to communicate." They more than managed, creating a new language of luxuriant cadences and expressive hand gestures.[77]

As pidgin English became the common language in the camps, it enabled people from different countries to communicate with one another and helped them create a new identity associated with Hawaii. "The language we used had to be either pidgin English or broken English," explained Faustino Baysa of the Waialua Plantation on the island of Oahu. "And when we don't understand each other, we had to add some other words that would help to explain ourselves. That's how this pidgin English comes out beautiful." A Korean mother recalled how she noticed her children were growing up as "Hawaiians," for they spoke "Hawaiian English" much more fluently than their native tongue. Speaking pidgin English, the immigrants and their children were no longer just Chinese, Japanese, Korean, or

Filipino; they were now embracing a local or regional identity transcending their particular ethnicity.[78]

Their acquisition of a new language reflected a deeper change in their outlook toward themselves and their new land. Most of the Asian laborers initially saw themselves as sojourners rather than settlers. They had come to Hawaii to earn money as wage laborers and then return to their homelands. Between 1852 and 1887, 26,000 Chinese arrived in the islands and 10,000, or 38 percent, went back to China. Of the 200,000 Japanese who entered Hawaii between 1885 and 1924, 110,000, or 55 percent, returned to Japan, including my grandfather Santaro Takaki. (Years later, after World War II, my uncle Nobuyoshi Takaki would also move back to Kumamoto.) Between 1903 and 1910, 7,300 Koreans arrived in Hawaii and 1,200, or 16 percent, saw their homeland again. Of the 112,800 Filipinos who came to the islands between 1909 and 1931, 18,600 remigrated to the mainland and 38,900, or 36 percent, returned to the Philippines. But what is so striking and so significant is the fact that so many sojourners stayed.[79]

Gradually, Asian-immigrant workers found themselves becoming settlers, establishing families in the new land. Married Chinese women increased from 559 in 1890 to 1,555 in 1910 to 3,212 in 1930. By then, 39 percent of the Chinese population was female. Many Chinese men married Hawaiian women. In 1871, colporteur Samuel P. Aheong of the Hawaiian Board Mission estimated a total of 1,201 Chinese men living in the islands and reported that 121 of them had "taken unto themselves" Hawaiian wives and their unions had produced ninety-one boys and seventy-six girls. By 1900, about 1,500 Chinese men married or lived with Hawaiian women, and their children represented the first Chinese-Hawaiian generation.[80]

Some Chinese men had two families: they were married to Hawaiian women but also had Chinese wives living in the old country. Len Wai, for example, had left his wife Len Mau Nin in China when he sailed to Hawaii as a contract laborer in 1882. "Every seven years after his initial arrival in the islands," reported his grandson Raymond Len, "he returned to China. My uncle was born there in 1889, my auntie in 1896, and my father, Len Too Shing, in 1903. While in Hawaii, my grandfather also had an Hawaiian wife and they adopted two Hawaiian children." When Raymond's father came to the islands, he became part of this Chinese-Hawaiian family. "I was ten years old when I came to Hawaii," explained Len Too Shing.

"The Hawaiian wife, Julia Kuli, became like my own mother. She was a big *wahinee* [woman]. My father was 5'6" and she was 5'11" and over 200 pounds. They spoke Hawaiian to each other. I spoke to my father in Chinese and my new mother in Hawaiian." Asked whether he saw himself as Chinese or Hawaiian, Len Too Shing replied: "I didn't think of myself as anything. I was just a 'local' kid." His Hawaiian mother died in 1930, and his father returned to his wife in China in 1932 — fifty years after he had first landed in the islands.[81]

Born in Hawaii, sons of Chinese-Hawaiian parents sometimes migrated to China. One of them remembered how he had been taken to China by his father when he was eight years old and discovered he had "two mothers." His father's Chinese wife treated him "just like her own son." "Hawaiian mother good too, treat me good," he said, "but China mother very, very good." A few Chinese men took their Hawaiian wives to China. "There were Hawaiian women in our villages in Quangdong," remembered Len Mau Yun. Some Chinese men eventually brought their Chinese wives to the islands, where they maintained both their "Chinese family" and their "Hawaiian family." In the Chinese-Hawaiian family, languages, customs, and foods were "mixed." "When my mother just married my father she didn't know any Chinese," said the daughter of one such family. "Later she picked up Chinese and now she can speak enough to carry on conversation. She speaks Chinese to our Chinese relatives and friends. My father speaks Chinese mostly, but some Hawaiian. We have a mixture of food at home. . . . Every time we have Hawaiian food we also have rice and other cooked vegetables."[82]

Families were also forming among the other Asian groups. By 1920, 46 percent of the Japanese and 30 percent of the Koreans in Hawaii were female. Between 1909 and 1924, 61,649 Filipinos entered Hawaii through the Hawaiian Sugar Planters' Association: 7,322 of them were women and 4,651 were children, representing together 19 percent of all Filipino immigrants. A new generation of Asian Americans was taking root in Hawaii. By 1920, 39 percent of the Chinese population in the islands were nineteen years old and younger, compared to only 20 percent on the mainland, and 45 percent of the island Japanese compared to only 32 percent of their continental counterparts. Meanwhile, minors constituted 32 percent of the Korean population in Hawaii and 29 percent of the Filipino. A plantation work song expressed a new sense of belonging springing from the presence of children:

> *With one woven basket*
> *Alone I came*
> *Now I have children*
> *And even grandchildren too.*[83]

Sojourners when they arrived in the islands, immigrant plantation laborers gradually found themselves becoming settlers. My grandparents Kasuke and Katsu Okawa had eight children who were born in Hawaii; in 1922 they left the Hawi Plantation on the Big Island and bought a house in Honolulu. In a letter to his brother Yahei, Asakichi Inouye explained why he had decided not to return to Japan: "My children are here, and my grandson [Daniel], and it is here that I have passed most of the days of my life. I do not believe that my wife and I, in our last years, could find contentment in Yokoyama, which has become for us a strange place." In his autobiographical novel, *Hawaii: End of the Rainbow*, Kazuo Miyamoto describes the process that led Seikichi Arata to stay in the new land: "With the passage of the years, he came to love Kauai as a place to live and possibly raise a family. The carefree atmosphere of this new country, not tied down by century-old traditions and taboos, and an immense opportunity that existed for those that could settle and seek their fortune, changed Seikichi's original intention of returning to this homeland at the expiration of the three year contract." A second-generation Korean, born on the Kahuku Plantation in 1905, told a similar story: "My parents . . . left Korea in the early part of 1903 and came to the Hawaiian Islands. Their intention was to return to their land as soon as they had saved money. In this hope they were disappointed, for they soon found out that it was not so easy to save money as they thought it would be. However, they became so used to the climate, freedom and advantages of this land that they no longer desired to leave this land permanently." When Shokichi and Matsu Fukuda migrated to Maui in 1900, they were sojourners; in fact they had left behind their six-month-old baby, Fusayo, with her grandparents. Some twenty years later, after Fusayo had emigrated to California as a picture bride, they decided they would return to Japan and take their Hawaiian-born children with them. But their son, Minoru, was a teenager by then, and Hawaii was home, the only world he knew and loved. "He refused to go," remembered his niece Aiko Mifune. "Japan was a foreign country to him. He was very adamant that the family should stay in Hawaii."[84]

After working and living in Hawaii for nine years, Tsuru Ya-

mauchi took her four children to Okinawa, a southern island of
Japan. She had been away from her birthplace for so long and wanted
her Hawaiian-born children to see her homeland and to meet their
family in Okinawa. But she found Okinawa "very different from
Hawaii: the climate, the food, the inconvenient things, such as closed
windows even in the summertime. . . . Even if we said Hawaii was
bad or something like that, there wasn't any place as good as Hawaii
for climate and sanitation. Okinawa hadn't changed a bit since before. That's why the children didn't like it, either. So I thought I
couldn't stay there too long."[85]

My aunt Mitsue Takaki also found herself planting new roots
in Hawaii. She had come as a picture bride in 1920 to marry my
uncle Teizo; eleven years later, her husband injured his knee at work
and returned to Japan for medical treatment. When he tried to reenter
Hawaii, however, the immigration authorities refused to grant him
permission. Mitsue chose to remain in the islands with her three
small children — Minoru, Susumu, and Kimiyo. She went to night
school to learn English and worked on the Puunene Plantation to
support her children. She wanted them to be educated and to have
opportunities in the land of their birth.[86]

But planters did not want the children of immigrant workers
to have opportunities: they needed the second generation as plantation laborers and saw Asians as a racial underclass. Several white
boys from Punahou High School, an elite institution for the children
of the planter class, were asked in 1928 to discuss their career plans.
"What do we care about these vocational discussions?" one of them
snapped. "Yes," agreed another. And referring to the school attended
mainly by Asian students, he added: "It's all settled; we, the Punahou
boys, will be the lunas and the McKinley fellows will carry the cane."
But young Asian Americans did not want to be cane carriers, and
worried planters stated candidly: "Sheer necessity, in order to prevent
starvation, may ultimately cause the island youth to return to plantation work."[87]

Many planters did not want the children of plantation laborers
to be educated beyond the sixth or eighth grade. They wanted the
schools to offer vocational training, not literature courses. Richard
Cooke, president of C. Brewer and Company, a major producer of
sugar, said that the public-school teachers should not keep their
students from working on the plantations. If the schools continued
to give students high career aspirations, Cooke warned, "we had
better change our educational system here as soon as possible." Not-

ing the need for agricultural labor, planter John Hind complained that the public-school system was too expensive: "Why blindly continue a ruinous system that keeps a boy and girl in school at the taxpayers' expense long after they have mastered more than sufficient learning for all ordinary purposes?" A visitor from the mainland noticed the increasing presence of Japanese children on the plantations and asked a Maui planter whether he thought the coming generation of Japanese would make intelligent citizens. "Oh, yes," he replied, "they'll make intelligent citizens all right enough, but not plantation laborers — and that's what we want."[88]

But many schools were not educating them to be plantation laborers. From teachers who had come from the mainland to the islands, children of immigrant workers learned about freedom and equality, reciting the Gettysburg Address and the Declaration of Independence. "Here the children learned about democracy or at least the theory of it," said a University of Hawaii student in 1947. They were taught that honest labor, fair play, and industriousness were virtues. But they "saw that it wasn't so on the plantation." They saw haoles on top and Asians on the bottom: "If you were a haole applying for a job, you didn't have to worry too much." Returning from school to their homes on the plantation, the students noticed the wide "disparity between theory and practice." Something was wrong they felt. "The public school system perhaps without realizing it," the university student observed, "created unrest and disorganization."[89]

Seeing their parents suffer from drudgery, low wages, and discriminatory barriers, many second-generation Asians did not want to be tracked into plantation employment. They disliked the "plantation pyramid," the structure of racial hierarchy, and they aspired to be something more than field laborers. My father, Toshio Takaki, who had come to the Puunene Plantation from Japan at the age of thirteen, felt the same restlessness as many Nisei. Initially, he worked as a field laborer, but he had an artistic passion and developed an interest in photography. He certainly was an "extravagant" young man. "The cottages in camp were small and he used the closet as a darkroom," an old friend, Ellen Kasai, recalled. He went around the plantation carrying a camera and taking pictures, and he impressed the people of McGerrow Camp as an odd and interesting individual. The plantation could not hold him down, and sometime in the 1920s he left to study with the photographer Jerome Baker in Honolulu. My father went toward "what persisted," an urge to be creative and "the freeing of beauty" through photography. The 1926 Honolulu city directory's entry for Toshio Takaki listed him as a finisher for the Honolulu Photo Supply Company; six years later he was listed as Harry T. Takaki, photographer. His studio was on Bethel Street.[90]

In 1922, the boys at McKinley High School in Honolulu were asked what they hoped to be in the future: 15 percent wanted to become professionals, 50 percent skilled workers, 5 percent farmers, and only half of one percent laborers. Presumably the others were undecided. In a 1929 survey of seventeen plantation schools, junior-high-school boys charted similar figures for themselves: of those who had considered careers, 8 percent wanted to become engineers, 11 percent doctors or teachers, 8 percent farmers, 12 percent business-men, and only 1.7 percent laborers. "My father was a common laborer on a plantation, who worked every day from six in the morn-ing to four o'clock in the afternoon," said a Japanese youth. "When-ever I saw some businessman in town, well dressed and gentle, my ambition was to become a businessman, and I was jealous of those who had high positions." A Korean student explained that young Asians had been born with "yellow skins and educated as if their skins were white." To send a young man through high school and then ask him to labor in the fields, he added, was an "absurdity." Second-generation Asians said they were American citizens and re-sented being told that they were "not fit to be anything but plantation laborers." At a conference of social workers in 1928, the governor of Hawaii urged them to direct the youth back to agriculture. In response to the governor, a young Chinese declared: "You cannot force the oriental youth with a high school education to go back to the plantations. He will not do it. We realize that our parents started on the plantations, but you cannot expect us to go back."[91]

Education, many Asians believed, was the key to employment opportunities and freedom from the plantation. "Father made up his mind to send his children to school so far as he possibly could," said the daughter of a Japanese plantation worker. "Yet he had no idea of forcing us. Instead he employed different methods which made us want to go to school. We were made to work in the cane fields at a very early age. . . . After a day's work in the fields dad used to ask: 'Are you tired? Would you want to work in the fields when you are old enough to leave school?' . . . My father did everything in his power to make us realize that going to school would be to our advantage."[92]

Education also seemed to promise opportunities for the second generation and their children to enter a world of words and ideas. A Nisei mother wrote to her son, who had gone away to college on the mainland: "It's 8:00 P.M. as I sit writing to you. About 1 A.M. in Ohio and I imagine you are snug in bed. We are still down at the store since Dad has to catch up soaking the teriyaki steak, etc. This week has been very busy and I am exhausted." She and her husband worked long, twelve-hour days, seven days a week. To send their son away to a college on the mainland was extravagant. She herself had to quit school after the eighth grade in order to work and help her parents pay for the needs of the family. "I never went to school much and you can say that again," she wrote in other letters. "What I do know is from reading. . . . In my small way I am trying and doing my best (working) so that you being an exception *can and must* be above our intellectual level. At times I yearn for rest (6 years without a vacation)."[93]

Her parents and other immigrants had labored as plantation workers to build the great industry of Hawaii and had laid the foundations for the American-born generations to have greater educational and employment opportunities. Years earlier, when they had first seen the plantations and the dreary camps, they had been uncertain about their future in the islands. "Here you couldn't see anything, no view, no landscape, just fields and hills," one of them complained. "Ah, such a place. Is Hawaii a place like this?" Confused, many migrants had asked in quiet moments of reflection:

> *Should I return to Japan?*
> *I'm lost in thoughts*
> *Here in Hawaii.*

And what would happen if they stayed too long?

> *Two contract periods*
> *Have gone by*
> *Those who do not return*
> *Will end up as fertilizer*
> *For the cane.*[94]

In the evenings, sitting on their porches in the camps, the workers "talked stink" about the howling haole lunas, the way they were called by their bango numbers rather than their names, the regimentation of daily labor, and the "shit system" of social hierarchy on the plantation. But, powered by the liminality of the islands, they refused to allow the "necessity" of the plantation to determine their lives, and over the years, their feelings toward the place had begun to change. As they worked in the fields, they saw how their labor had transformed and enriched the new land. "With my bare hands and calloused heart and patience," a Filipino worker boasted, "I helped build Hawaii." As Asian workers went out on strike, they realized the need to improve the conditions of their communities, to turn the camps into homes for their families. Japanese workers struck for higher wages, saying their action was *kodomo no tami ni*, or "for the sake of the children." And as Asian workers transplanted their customs and traditions and foods to the camps, as they erected new churches and temples and planted gardens near their cottages, as they spoke to fellow workers from other countries in a new language, and as they watched their children grow up and play in the camps, they began thinking of themselves as settlers and of Hawaii as their home.[95]

"Lucky come Hawaii," some of them whispered as they stood breathless before rainbows arching over ancient volcanoes, the steep sides of the mountains hanging vertically from the clouds like corrugated curtains. The opportunities to make a place for themselves in the islands were greater for them than for their brethren on the mainland. They lived in a society where the elite included Hawaiians, people with dark skin, and where racial divisions could not be drawn as sharply as on the continent. With a greater proportion of women among their number, they were able to establish families sooner than their continental counterparts. They lived in stationary communities — in plantation camps where they formed critical masses enabling them to transplant large parts of their traditional cultures. Moreover, unlike Asians on the mainland, they constituted a majority of the population. They did not compete with a large white working class or arouse "ethnic antagonism" between Asian and white labor. They did not become victims of white working-class racism and violence. By their numerical preponderance, they had greater opportunities to weave themselves and their cultures into the very fabric of Hawaii and to seek to transform their adopted land into a society of rich diversity where they and their children would no longer be "strangers from a different shore."[96]

III

NECESSITY

Positively No Filipinos Allowed.

Sign on hotel door

From our tree tops we would see the boss coming 'way off in the distance and when he reached us he found us working very hard.

Dhan Gopal Mukerji

If we wanted to rent land, it had to be in a child's name that was born in this country — a citizen. It was impossible as a foreigner.

Do-Yun Yoon

Both my hands grimy,
Unable to wipe away
The sweat from my brow,
Using one arm as towel —
That I was . . . working . . . working.
Kimiko Ono[1]

5

Ethnic Solidarity

The Settling of Japanese America

During his visit to California in the 1920s, a young Japanese man from Hawaii was shocked by the pervasiveness and intensity of anti-Japanese hostility. He had heard "various rumors" about the terrible ways whites treated the Japanese there. "But I didn't realize the true situation until I had a personal experience," the Nisei said. "In one instance, I went to a barber shop to get my hair trimmed. On entering the shop, one of the barbers approached me and asked for my nationality. I answered that I was Japanese, and as soon as he heard that I was of the yellow race, he drove me out of the place as if he were driving away a cat or a dog."[1]

This Nisei had come from a vastly different place. In Hawaii, Japanese were needed as laborers, and they had been incorporated by the planters in a paternalistic racial hierarchy. A large white working class did not exist in the islands; in fact, most of the people in the islands were Asian and the Japanese alone represented 43 percent of the population. Their problems and difficulties were related mainly to their conditions as laborers. They were generally confined to the wage-earning plantation work force; possibilities for self-employment in shopkeeping and small farming were limited. The plantations operated retail stores for food, clothing, and other provisions, and most of the arable lands in the islands were owned by the government and the "Big Five" corporations. Aware they could not effectively advance themselves through individualism and small business, Japanese tended to emphasize a class strategy of unionization, politics, and collective action.

On the mainland, however, Japanese faced a fundamentally

different "necessity." As our Japanese youth discovered in California, here he was a member of a racial minority. Altogether, Asians were extremely few compared to whites, and the Japanese — the largest Asian group — totaled only 2 percent of the California population. While agricultural and railroad employers of Japanese laborers were willing to include Japanese in subordinate economic and social roles, whites generally scorned their very presence and white workers waged hostile and sometimes even violent campaigns to keep the Japanese out of the labor market. Ethnicity more than class tended to determine social relations on the mainland. The Japanese found certain possibilities that existed to a greater extent on the American continent than in Hawaii — the presence of economic niches for small shop-keeping and the availability of land for small farming. Consequently theirs would be a different path — ethnic solidarity and ethnic enterprise.[2]

Japanese ethnic solidarity — a shared identity as countrymen and common cultural values — contributed to the establishment of the Issei ethnic economy, which in turn provided an economic basis for ethnic cohesiveness. But both their ethnicity and their economy developed within an American context of what Edna Bonacich terms "ethnic antagonism." Racial exclusionism defined the Japanese as "strangers" and pushed the Issei into a defensive Japanese ethnicity and group self-reliance. Denied access to employment in the industrial and trade labor market, many Issei entered entrepreneurial activity, turning to self-employment as shopkeepers and farmers. "When I was in Japan, I was an apprentice to a carpenter," explained an Issei, "but in America at that time the carpenters' union wouldn't admit me, so I became a farmer." Thus the Issei developed a separate Japanese economy and community, making America a society of greater cultural diversity. But the very success of the Japanese in enterprise further aroused waves of exclusionist agitation, and their very withdrawal into their self-contained ethnic communities for survival and protection reinforced hostile claims of their unassimilability and their condition as "strangers."[3]

Ethnic Enterprise

Eight years after the Chinese Exclusion Act of 1882, there were only 2,039 Japanese on the U.S. mainland. But within two decades, the Japanese had surpassed the Chinese in number — 72,257 to 71,531. Twenty years later, while the Chinese population had remained virtually constant, the Japanese had nearly doubled to 138,834. They were concentrated in the Pacific Coast states, especially California, where 42 percent of the total continental Japanese population lived in 1900, and 70 percent thirty years later. By 1930, the Japanese were almost evenly divided between Issei, or first generation, and Nisei, second generation. Approximately 40 percent of the Japanese migrants had made America their permanent home, and together with their children they were ushering Japanese America into the *teiju* — the era of settlement.

Like the Chinese before them, the Japanese immigrants experienced racial discrimination. In fact, they inherited much of the resentment and prejudice that had been directed against the Chinese. Sometimes the Issei were even called "chinks." As a young boy, Minoru Iino attended a grammar school where his white classmates looked at him with curiosity. "Some of them asked me to talk in Chinese, not realizing that I was Japanese," he recalled. "When I talked Japanese, they all laughed." When he walked home from school, Iino was asked by the white boys to make "Chop-Suey" for them, and heard them singing, "Ching ching chinaman chopped off his tail."[4]

But the newcomers were usually viewed and treated as a distinct group. Racist curses repeatedly stung their ears: "Jap Go Home," "Goddamn Jap!" "Yellow Jap!" "Dirty Jap!" Ugly graffiti assaulted their eyes at railroad stations and in toilets: "Japs Go Away!" "Fire the Japs!" On the street corners of Santa Monica Boulevard and Sunset Boulevard in Los Angeles, scribblings on the sidewalks threatened: "Japs, we do not want you." Outside of a small town in the San Joaquin Valley, a sign on the highway warned: "No More Japs Wanted Here." The term "Jap" was so commonplace it was even used unwittingly. "Attorney Morton, who was one of my acquaintances," remembered Chohei Nishikata, "said, 'Hello, Jap,' or 'Hello, Mr. Jap,' in a friendly way whenever he saw us. Intellectual though he was, he didn't know that 'Jap' was not the correct word."[5]

But discrimination went beyond words. "People even spit on Japanese in the streets," Juhei Kono told an interviewer years later. "In fact, I myself, was spit upon more than a few times." "There was so much anti-Japanese feeling in those days!" exclaimed Choichi Nitta. "They called us 'Japs' and threw things at us. When I made a trip to Marysville to look for land, someone threw rocks." Entering barbershops operated by whites, Japanese were told: "We don't cut animal's hair." When the newcomers tried to rent or buy houses, they were turned down by realtors who explained: "If Japanese live around here, then the price of the land will go down." At theaters, Japanese were often refused admittance or seated in a segregated section. "I went to a theatre on Third Avenue with my wife and friends," an Issei recalled. "We were all led up to the second balcony with the Blacks." In the cities, they were pelted with stones and snowballs, and their businesses were vandalized — their store windows smashed and the sidewalks in front smeared with horse manure. In the country, Japanese labor camps were time and again attacked by whites, and Japanese-owned barns became targets for arson.

> For a little while
> Encountering a person
> Who was anti-Japanese,
> I rubbed against a spirit
> Out of harmony with mine.[6]

At times it was difficult for them to restrain their rage. "They called us 'Japs,' so we kicked them, and they ran away," growled Minejiro Shibata. "Whenever the whites looked down on me, I got really mad. . . . They must have thought of us as something like dogs." Victims of racial slurs in school, Japanese children sometimes lost their tempers. "During recess the white children all gathered round me and bullied me, calling out 'Jap! Jap!'" remembered Yoshito Kawachi. "I got to the point where I couldn't stand it anymore, so I bought candy and gave it out little by little to those who were friendly. After a while everybody started shaking hands with me — all except two girls who persisted in being hard on me. Finally my patience broke and I hit them one day."[7]

The Japanese on the mainland experienced not only more intense racial discrimination but also a more impersonal labor structure than their counterparts in Hawaii. During the early decades, most mainland Japanese were located in migratory labor; in 1909, there were 40,000 in agriculture, 10,000 in railroads, and 4,000 in canneries. Unlike plantation workers, they did not have a direct relationship with their employers: Japanese labor contractors, keiyakunin, operated as intermediaries between laborers and employers. They functioned as employment agents, recruiting laborers in the port cities, transporting them to the work sites in the country, and negotiating wages and labor conditions. They charged a fee or commission, to be deducted from wages. Contractor Kumamoto Hifume, for example, collected ten cents from the $1.10 daily wage of each worker he had recruited for the Northern Pacific Railroad. A contractor with a work force of a thousand men would have a lucrative income. A supplier of labor to employers, contractors also served as foremen or field bosses: they supervised the workers, translated instructions, and disbursed wages.[8]

Japanese workers found that their employers had virtually no interest in their welfare. The labor contract arrangement and the migratory nature of work precluded paternalism and employer responsibility. Constantly moving from field to field and carrying blankets for bedding, migratory farm laborers were called *burankekatsugi* — persons who shouldered blankets. They did not live in permanent camps where they could build stable communities: they were literally here today and gone tomorrow. Constantly shuttled from one construction site to another, railroad workers lived in boxcars, sleeping in double-decked bunks. "We slept in the freight cars, suffering a lot from troops of bedbugs. In order to protect ourselves from these despicable insects we each made a big sleeping sack out of cotton cloth, crawled in with our comforter and blanket, and then pulled the string tight at the top to close up the sack." Japanese cannery workers were shipped from the West Coast to Alaska then sent back after the fishing season.[9]

In the valleys during the summer, farm workers felt the hot wind blowing against their perspiring bodies as the temperature went up to 120 degrees and the field became as "hot as though it were paved with hot iron boards." In the mountains during the winter, railroad workers were whipped by frigid winds. "In winter . . . the temperature went down to 20 degrees below freezing," they recalled. "Because of the severe cold, our excrement froze immediately when we went to the toilet outside the tent." They tried to fight off the weather by singing:

> *A railroad worker —*
> *That's me!*
> *I am great.*
> *Yes, I am a railroad worker.*
>
> *Complaining:*
> *"It is too hot!"*
> *"It is too cold!"*
> *"It rains too often!"*
> *"It snows too much!"*
> *They all ran off.*

> *I alone remained.*
> *I am a railroad worker!*[10]

But the laborers were usually too tired to sing. Loading eight-foot ties onto freight cars from 7:00 A.M. to 6:00 P.M. every day was enough to make railroad workers "grit their teeth" and "scream." The square logs bit into their shoulders, leaving them in a "greasy sweat." In Alaska, Japanese cannery workers had to race furiously and frantically against the machinery. After the boats brought in the catch of salmon, conveyor belts carried as many as two hundred salmon per minute up to the deck. The men, holding hooks in both hands, had to sort this charging multitude of huge fish and did not have a single second to relax. The cannery workers suffered from a particular problem — the "Alaskan smell," "a nasal cocktail of rotten fish, salt, sweat and filth." They would strip to the skin, throw away their work clothes, and scrub themselves thoroughly in the shower. Still the smell "wouldn't come off, as if it had penetrated to their very guts." Bathed in dusty sweat, farm laborers worked in the fields from dawn to dust, harvesting the crops and hoeing the weeds, row after row, their bodies constantly bent. They cursed the compression of their lives:

> *All my living days*
> *Gripped tightly and pressed into*
> *That old hoe handle!*[11]

They also swore at the tasteless food and monotonous diet. Japanese farm laborers "drank river water brought in by irrigation ditches. When they felt hungry, they devoured fresh grapes. If they ate supper, it consisted of flour dumplings in a soup seasoned with salt." Railroad workers also ate dumpling soup, called *suiton*. "For breakfast and for supper we ate dumpling soup, and for lunch we had baked dumplings," said Kumaichi Horike. "Since we didn't have real soy sauce, we used home-made sauce concocted from burned flour, plus sugar, salt and water — a strange mixture indeed."

> *Sticky dumpling soup*
> *And immigrant episodes,*
> *Mixed into a stew!*

Many suffered from malnutrition and night blindness due to their poor diets. At the end of the month, after payday, the railroad workers would leave their mountain camps and travel to town. There they bought bourbon at one or two dollars a bottle, canned salmon, and rice. Homesick for Japanese food, the hungry men made "extravagant" rice balls covered with slices of salmon and gleefully consumed their improvised sushi.[12]

Getting drunk on cheap whiskey, the workers sang the songs of Japan and talked about home. Sometimes homesickness overwhelmed them. "After a while I finally became night-blind," a railroad worker recounted sadly. "I couldn't see things in the evening, so I quit working earlier than other people. One day I was standing in front of a shack, alone and lonely. I saw a woman approaching along the railroad from a distance. I felt it was strange and gazed at her, and discovered that the woman was my dear old grandma in my hometown. 'Oh, grandma!' Shouting, I ran toward her — but suddenly she disappeared. I was seized with a sharp homesickness, and in the middle of that wasteland I wept out loud."[13]

During their hours of leisure, Japanese laborers had little to do but gamble. A 1902 labor handbook warned them: "As a laborer in the countryside, you will toil from dawn to dusk with only shots of whiskey and cigarettes to enjoy. Beware of gambling! Why did you leave your home and cross the wide Pacific to endure hardships in this foreign land? It was of course to enrich your family and benefit the homeland. Then, why try to forget your long days of toil by gambling?" But the workers had to do something to pass the time, to help them forget. And they might, they hoped, even strike it rich. They retreated to Japanese pool halls, which seemed to be ubiquitous — forty-one in San Francisco, twenty-one in Sacramento, nineteen in Fresno, and thirty-five in Los Angeles in 1912. To find female companionship, lonely men went to Japanese bar-restaurants where *shakufu* (barmaids) served them familiar foods and spoke Japanese with charm and traditional deference.[14]

Perhaps we should stay in the city, the men wondered, and find work there. But work in the city was also demanding and exhausting. Restaurant worker Tadashi Yamaguchi remembered how he had to wake up at four o'clock in the morning in order to start the wood fire for the stove. "I began to serve guests at 6 A.M. At 11 A.M. when the chief cook prepared dinner, I was in charge of the pantry and arranged the salad orders. My work was finished at 8 P.M." Describing the daily labor and life of laundry workers, Tsuruyo Takami of Spokane detailed her long day: "My husband was running the Rainier Laundry. . . . At noon I had to prepare a meal for twelve. The employees worked from 8 A.M. to 5 P.M., but I began to fix the dinner at 5 P.M., cooking for five or six persons, and then after that I started my night work. The difficult ironing and pressing was left for me. . . . Frequently I had to work till twelve or one o'clock. Not only I, but all the ladies engaged in the laundry business had the same duties."[15]

In the cities, a separate Japanese economy of hotels, boarding houses, restaurants, shops, stores, and pool halls quickly sprang up to meet the immigrants' needs. In the *Nihonmachi,* or Little Tokyo section, Japanese could feel comfortable among compatriots while avoiding racial discrimination from white-owned businesses. There they could also make connections for employment. Newly arrived immigrants could stay at a hotel or boarding house where labor contractors helped them find employment outside of the city. The owner of three boarding houses and the Tamura Hotel in San Francisco, Tamura Tokunosuke provided lodging to Japanese immigrants and supplied laborers to contractors at the rate of three dollars per worker.[16]

By 1909, according to the Immigration Commission, there were between 3,000 and 3,500 Japanese-owned establishments in the western states, most of them in major cities like San Francisco, Seattle, Los Angeles, and Sacramento. In its survey of 2,277 Japanese businesses, the commission found that 337 were hotels and boarding houses, 381 restaurants, 187 barbershops, 136 poolrooms, 136 tailor and dye shops, 124 provision and supply stores, 97 laundries, and 105 shoe shops. This Japanese ethnic economy created jobs, especially for some 12,000 service workers.[17]

The formation of the Japanese urban economy was sudden and extensive. Between 1900 and 1909, the number of Japanese businesses jumped from ninety to 545 in San Francisco and from fifty-six to 473 in Los Angeles. By 1910, a sizable ethnic economy existed to service the Japanese community. There were 3,000 establishments and 68,150 Japanese in the western states — a ratio of one business per twenty-two persons. Generally the businesses were small in scale. In California in 1909, of the 2,548 enterprises, only sixty-four were owned by corporations and 550 by partnerships, while 1,934 represented individual proprietors. Fifty-eight percent of the establishments had capital investments of less than a thousand dollars each, and 55 percent of the proprietors operated their businesses without hired help.[18]

Japanese ethnic enterprise in America also included large-scale businesses. Masajiro Furuya was considered a top businessman

among Japanese on the Pacific Coast. Born in 1863, Furuya received
a teacher's credential and served in the military for three years. In
1890 he arrived in Seattle, where he worked as a tailor; two years
later, he opened a tailor shop and grocery store. His business expanded rapidly as more and more Japanese immigrants came to the
Northwest. His grocery store became a department store where Japanese customers could find ethnic foods such as sake and tofu as well
as Japanese art. Furuya established branch stores in Portland and
Tacoma, a post office, a labor supply agency, and the Japanese Com-
merical Bank.

Furuya was able to pay his Japanese workers low wages, for
they were unable to find employment in white-owned companies. He
organized a small army of traveling salesmen, dressing them in the
"Furuya style" dark blue suits and sending them into the back country
to take orders. "The job of travelling salesmen for Furuya wasn't
easy," said Chieto Morita. "As a salesman I travelled about in a truck
in Washington, Idaho, Montana, North Dakota and Wyoming with
loads of goods. . . . I travelled among roundhouses, sawmills, railroad sections and gangs where Japanese worked, to get orders."[19]

As an employer, Furuya imposed strict discipline on his workers
and expected loyalty from them. " 'Captain' Furuya always taught
us 'to be honest,' " one of his employees said years later. "I always
lived up to his teaching. I am truly grateful to my deceased master."
Another "Furuya man" recalled how every morning in the office they
had a *hibi no chikara* (inspirational meeting). After he had gathered
his fifty employees around him, Furuya instructed them to cultivate
the Christian faith and to convey Christian love to the customers.
His relationship to his workers was parental; in fact, he lodged many
of them in his boarding house, where they occupied the floor below
Furuya and his family. His men remembered him as a joyless and
stern businessman: "Mr. Furuya had never seen movies, plays or
baseball in all his life. . . . There were no vacations or Sundays off
for Mr. Furuya, so he gave no vacation to the employees." "Every
time he came around in the office, we felt stiff, as if a military officer
had come to inspect. Such was Mr. Furuya; but he had one bad habit.
While talking with others, he picked his nose and made a ball of it
with his thumb and little finger, and flipped it away. They called it
'Mr. Furuya's snot-shot.' "[20]

As a businessman, Furuya was in the right place at the right
time, possibly in more ways than one. The expansion of his ethnic
enterprise into a little empire required a considerable amount of

investment capital, and one account of its origin became widely known in the community. "It was an accepted opinion among us in the Japanese community," an Issei revealed, "that Furuya's success was attributable to Japanese prostitutes' money which had been entrusted to him." They worked, it was said, in three "pink hotels" on King Street in Seattle, and they asked Furuya to keep the money for them in the safe in his tailor shop. "But the women lived in such a precarious trade, and also, some of them may have died or moved away under certain circumstances without requesting the money back. As a result, Furuya, they say, made big money out of it."[21]

The Furuya Company was part of a growing service economy that paralleled increasing Japanese participation in agriculture. In the late 1880s, Issei had been employed initially as farm laborers in the Vaca Valley of California and on farms near Tacoma in Washington. Increasingly, as they left the railroads, mines, and lumber mills, Japanese immigrants entered agricultural employment — the apple orchards in Washington, the hop fields in Oregon, the vineyards and fruit farms in California, and the beet fields in Idaho, Utah, and Colorado. But they did not want to remain field laborers. By 1909, significantly, 6,000 Japanese had become farmers.[22]

The Japanese farmers had "practically all risen from the ranks of common laborers," the Immigration Commission observed in 1909. "Of 490 for whom personal data were secured, 10 upon their arrival in this country engaged in business for themselves and 18 became farmers, while 259 found employment as farm laborers, 103 as railroad laborers, 4 as laborers in sawmills, 54 as domestic servants, and 42 in other occupations." Most of the Japanese immigrants had been farmers in Japan. For centuries their families had cultivated small plots, irrigating the land and relying on intensive labor to make it yield harvests. Becoming a farmer in America was a fervent dream.[23]

To obtain land to farm, the Japanese utilized four methods — contract, share, lease, and ownership. In 1910, for example, of the total Japanese farm acreage, 37,898 acres were under contract, 50,400 under share, 89,464 under lease, and 16,980 under ownership. The contract system was a simple arrangement: the farmer agreed to plant and harvest a crop for a set amount to be paid by the landowner when the crop was sold. The share system involved greater risks as well as the possibility of greater remuneration; where the contract farmer was in effect paid a wage, the share farmer received a certain percentage of the crop's profit. The contract and share systems enabled Japanese immigrants to raise themselves from field laborers to farmers, even though they did not have the capital. Under both arrangements, the landowner provided the tools, seed, fertilizer, and everything else necessary for the production of the crop; the Japanese farmer, in turn, was responsible for the labor. In order to feed himself and his workers, he purchased supplies on credit from storekeepers and merchants. After the crop was harvested and sold, the farmer then paid off his expenses — his wages owed to his laborers and his bills owed to his mercantile creditors. Under the lease arrangement, the Japanese farmer rented the land: he assumed full responsibility for all the expenses for the crop and paid the landowner rent. He could secure capital or interest-based loans from brokers and shippers and could be advanced provisions by merchants by agreeing to pay 10 to 20 percent higher prices for the goods he purchased. At the end of the season, if he harvested a bountiful crop and received a good price for it, he would then pay his rent and clear his debts. The goal of Japanese farmers under the three systems was to accumulate enough capital to purchase land.[24]

But what enabled them to become farmers so rapidly was their timely entry into agriculture. Beginning in the late nineteenth century, industrialization and urbanization led to increased demands for fresh produce in the cities. The development of irrigation in California at this time opened the way for intensive agriculture and the shift from grain crops to fruit and vegetable production. Between 1879 and 1909, the value of crops representing intensive agriculture skyrocketed from only 4 percent to 50 percent of all crops grown in California. This tremendous expansion occurred under the stimulus of new market possibilities for fruit distribution created by two extremely important technological achievements — the completion of the national railroad lines and the invention of the refrigerator car. After 1880 the refrigerator car, observed historian Gerald Nash, generated a complicated chain of events, placing the lucrative eastern markets within reach of California fruit growers for the first time in history.[25]

Many of the fruit and vegetable farmers were Japanese. They concentrated on short-term crops like berries and truck vegetables. As early as 1910, they produced 70 percent of California's strawberries, and by 1940 they grew 95 percent of the state's fresh snap beans, 67 percent of its fresh tomatoes, 95 percent of its spring and summer celery, 44 percent of its onions, and 40 percent of its fresh green peas. Based on intensive cultivation, Japanese agriculture grew rapidly and flourished. In California, the Japanese owned or leased twenty-nine farms with a total of 4,698 acres in 1900. Within five years, the total acreage had jumped to 61,858 and increased again to 194,742 by 1910. Ten years later, the Japanese controlled a total of 458,056 acres.

As Japanese men entered farming, many sent for their wives or picture brides. The women found their new homes were often crude "huts" with oil lamps for light, boards nailed together with legs for tables, and straw-filled canvases for beds. Chiyo Hisayasu found a single house in the middle of the fields. "It was a dilapidated hovel said to have been a hunter's cabin. There was only one room, in which there were three beds." Her husband shared the tiny house with a young boy and an older man. They had stretched a thick rope across the room and hung clothes on it to make a kind of temporary curtain for the newlyweds. "What an inappropriate life for a bride and groom!" she later exclaimed. Another Issei wife described her house as a "shack" with "one room, barren, with one wooden bed and a cook-stove — nothing else. The wind blew in with a weird whistle through the cracks in the board walls."[26]

The workday on the farm was long and demanding. Stooped over the rows, husbands and wives worked side by side in the fields, their hands in constant motion as they felt the early-morning sun warm their backs and later the chilly air of dusk. Remembering the pace and punishment of farm work, Yoshiko Ueda said: "I got up at 4:30 A.M. and after preparing breakfast I went to the fields. I went with my husband to do jobs such as picking potatoes and sacking onions. Since I worked apace with ruffians I was tired out and limp as a rag, and when I went to the toilet I couldn't stoop down. Coming back from the fields, the first thing I had to do was start the fire [to cook dinner]." Ueda worked so hard she became extremely thin. "At one time I got down to 85 pounds, though my normal weight had been 150."

> Both my hands grimy,
> Unable to wipe away
> The sweat from my brow,
> Using one arm as towel —
> That I was . . . working . . . working.[27]

Women had double duty — field work and housework. "I got up before dawn with my husband and picked tomatoes in the greenhouse," Kimiko Ono recounted. "At around 6:30 A.M. I prepared breakfast, awakened the children, and all the family sat down at the breakfast table together. Then my husband took the tomatoes to Pike Market. I watered the plants in the greenhouses, taking the children along with me. . . . My husband came back at about 7 P.M. and I worked with him for a while, then we had dinner and put the children to bed. Then I sorted the tomatoes which I had picked in the morning and put them into boxes. When I was finally through with the boxing, it was midnight — if I finished early — or 1:30 A.M. if I did not."

> *Face black from the sun*
> *Even though creamed and powdered,*
> *No lighter for that!*[28]

Issei women divided their time into hatarite ita, or working, and asonderu, or keeping house. Often Issei women complained about their husbands as "Meiji men": "We worked from morning till night, blackened by the sun. My husband was a Meiji man; he didn't even glance at the house work or child care. No matter how busy I was, he would never change a diaper." "Since my husband was a 'Meiji man,' he didn't split firewood [in the morning] and help me as white husbands do." After working in the greenhouse and taking care of children all day, "I did miscellaneous chores until about midnight. However tired I was, the 'Meiji man' wouldn't let me sleep before him." A woman captured in poetry the feeling of numbing exhaustion many Issei sisters experienced:

> *Vexed beyond my strength,*
> *I wept. And then the wind came*
> *Drying up all tears.*[29]

Over the years, Issei men and women converted marginal lands like the hog wallow lands in the San Joaquin Valley, the dusty lands in the Sacramento Valley, and the desert lands in the Imperial Valley into lush and profitable agricultural fields and orchards. "Much of what you called willow forests then," farmer S. Nitta proudly told an interviewer in 1924, "Japanese took that land, cleared it and made it fine farming land." In 1920 the agricultural production of Japanese farms was valued at $67 million — approximately 10 percent of the total value of California's crops. A year later, in his report to Governor William Stephens, Colonel John P. Irish, president of the California Delta Association, described the Japanese triumph:

> They [the Californians] had seen the Japanese convert the barren land like that at Florin and Livingston into productive and prof-

itable fields, orchards and vineyards, by the persistence and intelligence of their industry. They had seen the hardpan and goose lands in the Sacramento Valley, gray and black with our two destructive alkalis, cursed with barrenness like the fig tree of Bethany, and not worth paying taxes on, until [K.] Ikuta, the Japanese, decided that those lands would raise rice. After years of persistent toil, enduring heartbreaking losses and disappointments, he conquered that rebellious soil and raised the first commercial crop of rice in California.[30]

One of the most successful Japanese farmers was Kinji Ushijima, better known as George Shima. After arriving in 1887, he worked initially as a potato picker in the San Joaquin Valley and then became a labor contractor, supplying Japanese workers to white farmers. Shima wanted to become a farmer himself and began by leasing fifteen acres. To expand his operations, he leased and purchased undeveloped swamplands in the delta; diking and draining his lands, he converted them into fertile farmlands. He rapidly expanded his farming operations near Stockton and used a fleet of a dozen steamboats, barges, tugboats, and launches, bearing the name "Shima," to transport his potato crops from Stockton to San Francisco. By 1912, Shima controlled 10,000 acres of potatoes valued at half a million dollars and was regarded as a Japanese Horatio Alger. Describing his smart business practice of selling crops when prices were high and storing them when prices were low, the *San Francisco Chronicle* praised Shima as a model: his success "pointed to the opportunities here to anybody with pluck and intelligence." Wealth did not immunize Shima from racism, however. When he purchased a house in an attractive residential section close to the university in Berkeley, he was told to move to an "Oriental" neighborhood by protesters led by a classics professor. The local newspapers announced: "Jap Invades Fashionable Quarters" and "Yellow Peril in College Town." But Shima refused to move. Raising his family in Berkeley, he had his children educated at the best colleges in the country — Vassar, Harvard, and Stanford. Widely known as "the Potato King," Shima had an estate worth $15 million when he died in 1926. His pallbearers included David Starr Jordan, the chancellor of Stanford University, and James Rolph, Jr., the mayor of San Francisco. Two years before his death, Shima told an interviewer that he had lived in this country so long he felt "more at home here than in Japan."[31]

The development of agriculture was central to the emergence of the Japanese ethnic economy. In 1925, approximately 25,000 out of 53,884 gainfully employed Japanese — 46 percent of the total — were engaged in agriculture. Most Japanese farmers were small operators, their farms usually under forty-nine acres. As truck farmers, they sold their crops to local markets in cities like Los Angeles, Sacramento, Fresno, and San Francisco. In the Los Angeles City Market in 1909, for example, 120 of the 180 produce stalls were owned by Japanese. As Japanese agriculture became important economically, it reinforced the development of the urban Japanese ethnic economy. Farmers relied on urban businessmen for their labor supply, capital, and provisions, and in turn, shopkeepers and produce distributors in cities received fruit and vegetables from the farmers.

The success of this Japanese-immigrant economy reflected the effectiveness of Japanese ethnic solidarity and the mutual-support systems they had developed in America. Japanese farmers belonged to *kenjinkai*, prefectural- (*ken*) based social associations (*kai*). A kenjinkai brought its members or people (*jin*) together for social activities such as annual picnics; more importantly, it provided a network of social relations buttressing economic cooperation and assistance for employment, housing, and credit. Frequently Issei farmers from the same kenjinkai formed a credit-rotating association, or *tanomoshi*, to pool resources and make capital available to individuals for initial investments on equipment and land. Farmers organized cooperatives — *kobai kumiai* for purchasing bulk foods and *sango kumiai* for marketing their crops. Farmers' associations, or *nogyo kumiai*, assisted members in renting and purchasing lands, settling disputes between tenants and landlords, obtaining supplies, disseminating information about agricultural techniques and produce prices, and selling crops in the city markets. The principle of group cooperation was embedded in Japanese culture. *Tanomu* denoted "dependable" and conveyed the sense of trust and honor that buttressed the cooperative-credit system. A *kumi* in Japan was a hamlet or neighborhood, signifying community and cohesiveness. An Issei farmer explained the idea of cooperation to his son: "If you hold *hashi* [chopsticks] individually, you can certainly break them all, but if you put them together, why you can't break a bunch of *hashi*. And so, like that, as a family we should stick together, but also as a community we should be sticking together."[32]

The very entry of the Japanese into agriculture, while drawing from their ancestral culture for success, transformed them from sojourning *dekaseginin* to settlers. The experience of Riichi Satow was the story of many fellow Issei farmers. He had leased a ranch outside of Sacramento and started growing strawberries. The harvest for the first year was "just stupendous," he said, and the harvest for the following year was again "wonderful." The yield was some 2,200 crates, and each crate sold for $2.25. "We hired only two workers during the picking time, and my brother and I did all the rest of the work. With the money from the harvest, about three thousand dollars, I bought this place and moved in. About that time I began to think of settling down in this country permanently. I was convinced that settling down here was a must."[33]

"Live permanently here, remain on the soil," many told themselves.

> *Resolved to become*
> *The soil of the foreign land,*
> *I settle down.*

Japanese farmers were raising not only crops but also children, the Nisei born in America, and they began to feel a deeper connection to the land they cultivated.

> *America — where*
> *My three sons grow lustily —*
> *More than a wayside stop.*

But their decision to remain here, to make their home in this foreign land, evoked ambivalence and memory:

> *Past dream spent chasing*
> *Rabbits — one called "Go Home!"*
> *The other, "Stay here!"*

> *Once decided to stay,*
> *In America I dream of*
> *My old native town!*[34]

Ethnic solidarity and agricultural enterprise enabled many Japanese immigrants to establish themselves, and as successful settlers they believed Issei could even become accepted in American society. This was the hopeful vision of Abiko Kyutaro. His mother had died giving birth to him in 1865, and Abiko was raised by his grandparents. When he was fourteen years old, he ran away to Tokyo, where he was converted to Christianity. Separated from his family, Abiko lacked the normal ties binding him to Japan. Feeling his "ambitions were stifled" in Japan, Abiko departed for America. In 1885 he arrived in San Francisco, with only a dollar in his pocket. While Abiko did menial jobs to make ends meet, he attended school and then enrolled in the University of California but did not complete his degree. By the early 1890s, Japanese immigrants were beginning to arrive in increasing numbers, and Abiko saw opportunity in the service enterprises. During the 1890s, he operated several different businesses including a restaurant and a laundry, and he began publishing a newspaper, the *Nichibei Shimbun*. Fluent in English and familiar with business, Abiko became a labor contractor and one of the founders of the Japanese American Industrial Corporation. His company, organized in 1902, quickly became one of the largest labor-contracting agencies in California, supplying Japanese labor to agriculture, mining, and railroads.[35]

A thoughtful man, Abiko worried about the future of the Japanese in America. They were coming as dekaseginin, and he believed that this mentality was the source of their problems. As sojourners, Japanese seemed to be driven by a single purpose — to make money and return to Japan as soon as possible. Thinking they would be here only temporarily, Issei did not seem to care about their shabby living conditions and their indiscrete behavior, which included drinking, gambling, and carousing with prostitutes. Neither did the dekaseginin feel a desire or a responsibility to contribute to American society. The sojourner identity, in turn, was contributing to the anti-Japanese exclusionist movement, for it confirmed hostile claims of their foreignness and unassimilability.

As dekaseginin, Issei were placing an albatross around their own necks, Abiko argued; but they should cast it away and strive to become settlers. They should abandon their life-style of bunkhouses and gambling houses and try to live respectfully, worthy of acceptance in American society. Issei should bring their wives and families to America and seek to become naturalized citizens. Abiko personally set an example for his teaching: in 1909 he returned to Japan to marry Yonako and brought his bride to his new homeland. But, Abiko believed, Japanese immigrants had to do more than establish families here. They had to develop economic and social stakes through farming. A student of American history and culture, Abiko was aware of the significance of agricultural land ownership in this country. Farming represented the path for the transformation of many Europeans from immigrants to Americans. A practical man,

Abiko was certain his fellow Japanese were ably suited to become Americans through agriculture, for most of them had been farmers or had come from farming families in the old country.

The realization of a Japanese-American community rooted in agriculture became Abiko's crusade. His newspaper, the *Nichibei Shimbun*, became the voice of his vision. The name of his newspaper, or *shimbun*, announced its perspective: *Nichi* for Japan and *Bei* for America. In the pages of this leading Japanese daily, Abiko proclaimed his message — *dochaku eiju*, settlement on land and permanent residency: Go into farming, own land, be productive, put down roots in America. Abiko also published the *Nichibei Nenkan*, the *Japanese American Yearbook*. A detailed record of Japanese agricultural holdings in California, his publication listed the names of all farmers, their form of land tenure, their acreage holdings, and their crop specialties. To assist potential farmers, the yearbook included examples of share and lease agreements and information about the cost of purchasing land and operating farms.[36]

An activist, Abiko took his crusade beyond words. He decided to create an actual model of his ideal Japanese farming community. In 1906, he founded the American Land and Produce Company. His company purchased 3,200 acres of undeveloped desert land near Livingston in the San Joaquin Valley, and the land was parceled into forty-acre lots and sold to Japanese farmers. "We believe that the Japanese must settle permanently with their countrymen on large pieces of land if they are to succeed in America," Abiko's company announced in an advertisement. "Those wishing to take advantage of this opportunity for success are welcome to visit one of our offices." The settlement was called the Yamato Colony. *Yamato*, the ancient name for Japan, was to be a "new Japan," Abiko's "city upon a hill" in the San Joaquin Valley of California.[37]

A handful of Issei pioneers responded to the invitation in 1907 and moved to the desolate site, where they were greeted by clouds of fine sand blown by the wind. Their actions told their purpose: the colonists settled as families and planted a variety of fruit trees and grapes — a long-term crop requiring four seasons to mature. They planted eucalyptus trees around their houses to shield them from the 110-degree summer heat and to break the force of the valley winds. Significantly, the pioneers chose a site for a cemetery. "If there was to be a permanent colony," pioneer Seinosuke Okuye wrote in his diary in 1907, "the spot for the cemetery should be chosen from the beginning." Abiko's faithful followers had left the graves of their ancestors behind in Japan and they were planning to stay, literally to become one with the soil of their adopted land.[38]

The nearby Merced River had been dammed and the Yamato colonists constructed a system of irrigation canals and ditches to tap this life-giving supply of water. While visiting Yosemite, the source of the Merced River, Okuye was struck by the breathtaking beauty of the Sierra Nevada Mountains, with their colossal white granite half domes reaching toward the heavens like cathedrals. There he experienced a moment of epiphany: "When I saw the magnificent scenery of Yosemite I felt as though I had been given a sign." The Yamato colonists irrigated the parched land, and by 1910, they had planted 1,064 acres of grapes, 507 acres of fruit trees, one hundred acres of alfalfa, and five hundred acres of hay. "In the eleven years since the Japanese founded their colony," reported the *San Francisco Chronicle* in 1918, "fruit shipments from Livingston have increased from nothing in 1906 to 260 carloads in 1917." By then, the Yamato Colony was home for forty-two Issei farmers, all with families. They were owners of the land, mixing their labor with the soil and becoming Americans.

> *A wasted grassland*
> *Turned to fertile fields by sweat*
> *Of cultivation:*
> *But I, made dry and fallow*
> *By tolerating insults.*

Fertile fields moistened by sweat, Abiko hoped, would bring respect to the Japanese and an end to the insults directed against them as "strangers"; lands transformed would trumpet Japanese dreams of settlement in America.[39]

The Exclusionist Basis of Ethnicity

By the time Japanese immigrants began coming to the United States, they could see what had happened to the Chinese: the presence of Chinese in the manufacturing and trades occupations had provoked stormy protests from white workers and led to exclusionary laws and the immigrant retreat into Chinese ethnic enclaves. Initially, Issei laborers, like the Chinese immigrants before them, tried to pursue employment opportunities in the general economy. In 1890, fifteen Japanese workers began producing shoes for a white manufacturer in San Francisco; they then lost their jobs because of pressure from the Boot and Shoemakers' White Labor League. Driven out of shoe manufacturing, the Japanese workers adopted a strategy designed to avoid ethnic antagonism in the labor market. They withdrew from shoe production and specialized instead in shoe repairing, where they would not be competing with white laborers. But the Japanese shoe-makers did not clearly understand the problem they faced: white workers resented not only Japanese competition but their very pres-ence in America. This message was conveyed to the Issei during the 1903 strike in Oxnard, California.

Japanese farm laborers were first employed in the sugar-beet industry of Oxnard in 1899. Within three years, there were nine Japanese labor contractors supplying workers to farmers in the area. In 1902, a group of Oxnard businessmen, including the presidents of the Bank of Oxnard and Bank of A. Levy and the manager of the American Sugar Beet Company, organized a new labor contracting company, the Western Agricultural Contracting Company. Its pur-pose was to undercut the independent Japanese labor contractors while at the same time lowering labor costs. Within a year, the WACC had gained control of approximately 90 percent of the contracting business. Under the WACC, workers suffered severe reductions in wages as the piecework rate for thinning beets dropped from five dollars to $3.75 per acre.

In response to the WACC and wage cuts, five hundred Japanese and two hundred Mexican agricultural laborers organized the Jap-anese-Mexican Labor Association in February, 1903. The association elected Kosaburo Baba as president, Y. Yamaguchi as secretary of the Japanese branch, and J. M. Lizarras as secretary of the Mexican branch. At the meetings of the JMLA, discussions were conducted in both Spanish and Japanese, with English serving as a common language for both groups. For the first time in the history of Cali-fornia, two minority groups had come together to form a union. Demanding the right of independent labor contractors to contract directly with the growers, the JMLA led twelve hundred workers — 90 percent of the labor force — out on strike in early March.

The leadership of the JMLA defined the struggle in broad class terms. In a statement written jointly by Yamaguchi and Lizarras, the union declared: "Many of us have family, were born in the country, and are lawfully seeking to protect the only property that we have — our labor. It is just as necessary for the welfare of the valley that we get a decent living wage, as it is that the machines in the great sugar factory be properly oiled — if the machines stop, the wealth of the valley stops, and likewise if the laborers are not given a decent wage, they too, must stop work and the whole people of this country suffer with them." The strike was effective. The WACC had only sixty men under contract. The farmers saw that the JMLA controlled the labor they needed, and a settlement was reached by the end of the month: the WACC agreed to cancel all existing contracts, except one, and farmers agreed to pay union laborers a piecework rate of five dollars an acre for thinning beets. The JMLA had emerged as a victorious and powerful force for organizing farm laborers.[40]

The strike seized the attention of American labor and raised two fundamental questions of policy: should the American labor movement organize farm workers, and should it admit racial minorities into its ranks? In its support for the JMLA and the strike, the Los Angeles County Council of Labor answered both questions affirmatively. Organized labor on the Pacific Coast must seize this opportunity to organize agricultural laborers, the council declared, for the most effective method of protecting American workers and their standard of living was by the universal organization of all workers. The Council specifically called for the inclusion of the Japanese: "While we are utterly opposed to the unrestricted immigration of the various Oriental races, we heartily favor the thorough organization of those now here, and believe that the fact that men are able to do our work when we strike is sufficient reason why they should be organized, regardless of race or color."[41]

A very significant moment in the history of organized labor had occurred. Here was an opportunity to bring together workers of different ethnicities on the basis of class solidarity. The Mexican secretary of the JMLA, J. M. Lizarras realized this, and petitioned the American Federation of Labor to charter his organization as the Sugar Beet Farm Laborers' Union of Oxnard. But this movement to build interracial unity was suddenly thwarted. Samuel Gompers, the president of the federation, agreed to issue a charter to Lizarras only on one condition: "Your union will under no circumstance accept membership of any Chinese or Japanese." Gompers's requirement was racist and contradicted the very principles of the Oxnard strike. Refusing the charter, Lizarras protested:

> We beg to say in reply that our Japanese brothers here were the first to recognize the importance of cooperating and uniting in demanding a fair wage scale. . . . In the past we have counseled, fought and lived on very short rations with our Japanese brothers, and toiled with them in the fields, and they have been uniformly kind and considerate. We would be false to them and to

ourselves and to the cause of unionism if we now accepted privileges for ourselves which are not accorded to them. . . . We will refuse any other kind of charter, except one which will wipe out race prejudice and recognize our fellow workers as being as good as ourselves. I am ordered by the Mexican union to write this letter to you and they fully approve its words.[42]

The JMLA stood by its principles, but without the AFL charter and the general support of organized labor, the Japanese and Mexican union passed out of existence within a few years. Tragically for the American labor movement, Gompers had drawn a color line for Asians. Earlier he had led the movement against the Chinese. Again, in 1903, under Gompers's leadership, the American Federation of Labor turned away from the possibility of class solidarity. A year after the Oxnard strike, the AFL called for amending the Chinese Exclusion Act and extending the prohibition to the Japanese. The *American Federationist*, its official publication, explained the reasons why organized labor in America needed to be racially exclusionary. White workers, including ignorant ones and the newcomers from southern and eastern Europe, possessed qualities enabling them to join and contribute to the labor movement. They could be taught the fundamentals of unionism and would stand shoulder to shoulder with faithful workers. But, the *American Federationist* argued, Japanese immigrants lacked this capacity. They did not share the white workers' "God," their "hopes, their ambitions, their love of this country." Unable to be "assimilated," the Japanese could not become "union men." Carrying to America a different culture and coming here only to make money, they would remain "strangers."[43]

Meanwhile, in San Francisco, which had been the storm center of the anti-Chinese agitation, white workers had already initiated a political campaign for Japanese exclusion. Demanding the renewal of the Chinese Exclusion Act, scheduled to expire in 1902, white workers assembled at a mass meeting and urged Congress to extend the ban to the Japanese. The Japanese peril, they anxiously stated in their resolution, was uniquely threatening to white labor. Unlike the Chinese, the Japanese had a particular "virtue" — their "partial adoption of American customs" — that made them "more dangerous" than the Chinese had been as "competitors." The protest in San Francisco soon had reverberations in Sacramento. In his 1901 message to the legislature, Governor Henry Gage warned that the unrestricted immigration of Japanese laborers constituted a "menace" to American labor similar to the earlier "peril from Chinese labor." Under Governor Gage's leadership, the legislature sent Congress a memorial requesting legislation for Japanese exclusion. Four years later, white workers formed the Asiatic Exclusion League. "The Caucasian and Asiatic races are unassimilable," they stated in their constitution. "The preservation of the Caucasian race upon American soil . . . necessitates the adoption of all possible measures to prevent or minimize the immigration of Asiatics to America." Meanwhile, newspapers like the *San Francisco Chronicle* and patriotic organizations like the Native Sons of the Golden West joined the anti-Japanese exclusionist clamor. "Would you like your daughter to marry a Japanese?" asked the Native Sons in their publication, the *Grizzly Bear*. "If not, demand that your representative in the Legislature vote for segregation of whites and Asiatics in the public schools."[44]

Washington seemed unresponsive to the pleas from California, but suddenly, the federal government was forced to address the issue of Japanese immigration. On October 11, 1906, the San Francisco Board of Education directed school prinicipals to send "all Chinese, Japanese and Korean children to the Oriental School." This segregation decision sent political waves across the Pacific. The government of Japan quickly sent a protest to Washington, angrily claiming that the school board action violated a treaty provision guaranteeing Japanese children in the United States equal educational opportunities.[45]

The action of the school board precipitated an international crisis. President Theodore Roosevelt had respect as well as concern for Japan's military power. Japan had demonstrated "feats of heroism" in the war against Russia in 1905, and he was determined to treat Japan with "scrupulous courtesy and friendliness." Anxious to avoid a confrontation between the United States and Japan, Roosevelt scolded the school board for the segregation of Japanese children: "The cry against them is simply nonsense." In a letter to Secretary of State Elihu Root, he complained about how "our people wantonly and foolishly insulted the Japanese in San Francisco." To protect the Japanese against mob violence, federal troops had been deployed in the city. "As you know we now have plenty of troops in the neighborhood of San Francisco, so that in the event of riot we can interfere effectively should the State and municipal authorities be unwilling or unable to afford the protection which we are bound to give the

Japanese." In his December 1906 message to Congress, President Roosevelt urged his fellow Americans to accept the Japanese immigrants:

> Here and there a most unworthy feeling has manifested itself toward the Japanese — the feeling that has been shown in shutting them out from the common schools of San Francisco and mutterings against them in one or two other places because of their efficiency as workers. To shut them out from the public schools is a wicked absurdity. . . . I ask fair treatment for the Japanese as I would ask fair treatment for Germans or Englishmen, Frenchmen, Russians, or Italians.[46]

But President Roosevelt's concern for the Japanese in San Francisco was merely strategic, shrouding for the moment his personal racial attitudes. American expansionism in the past, he had written in 1894, had enabled the "white race" to keep the "best portions of the New World's surface." The incorporation of Hawaii into the United States prompted Roosevelt to criticize the planters there for importing massive numbers of Japanese laborers. The newly acquired islands, Roosevelt argued, should be "filled" with a "white population" representing "American civilization." Committed to the preservation of America as "a heritage for the white people," Roosevelt personally favored the restriction of Japanese immigration. After he left the presidency and was no longer responsible for maintaining peaceful relations between the United States and Japan, Roosevelt became increasingly shrill in his advocacy of Japanese exclusion. "To permit the Japanese to come in large numbers into this country," he argued, "would be to cause a race problem and invite and insure a race contest." Japanese and whites represented "wholly different types of civilization." While both civilizations were "equally high," they represented thousands of years of separate lines of development, and the mixing together of peoples from the "culminating points of two such lines of divergent cultural development would be fraught with peril."[47]

Seeking to resolve the school controversy in San Francisco and to reduce international tensions, President Roosevelt invited Mayor Eugene Schmitz and the members of the school board to Washington. The compromise reached by President Roosevelt and the San Francisco officials revealed the purpose behind the segregation order. Actually it seemed hardly necessary to place Japanese students in the "Oriental School," for there were only ninety-three of them. The real and larger agenda of the school board's action was Japanese exclusion. The strategy, seeking to create an incident and force Washington's hand, worked. Emerging from their discussions with the president, the officials stated: "We have every reason to believe that the administration now shares, and that it will share, our way of looking at the problem, and that the result we desire — the cessation of the immigration of Japanese laborers, skilled or unskilled, to this country, will be speedily achieved." Satisfied by assurances from the president, the school board members returned to San Francisco and rescinded the segregation order, "excepting in so far as it applied to Chinese and Korean children." President Roosevelt, in turn, issued an executive order prohibiting the remigration of Japanese immigrants from Hawaii to the mainland and also entered into negotiations with Japan to limit Japanese immigration. Under the terms of the 1908 Gentlemen's Agreement, Roosevelt extracted an understanding that Japan would not permit the emigration of laborers to the United States.[48]

The school board controversy intensified anti-Japanese hatred and violence. "The persecutions became intolerable," a Japanese laundry operator said. "My drivers were constantly attacked on the highway, my place of business defiled by rotten eggs and fruit; windows were smashed several times. . . . The miscreants are generally young men, 17 or 18 years old."

> *Immigrant records —*
> *Now and then a bloody page*
> *Indicates the pain!*[49]

While the Japanese were hurt by the violence and vandalism of hoodlums in the streets, they suffered even more from the actions of legislators in Sacramento. In 1907, the California legislature began discussions on a bill designed to deny landownership to Japanese immigrants. The bill was introduced repeatedly in sessions of the legislature and became law in 1913. Support for the anti-Japanese legislation was overwhelming — thirty-five to two in the Senate and seventy-two to three in the Assembly. While the law did not specifically refer to the Japanese, it was aimed at them, declaring unlawful the ownership of "real property" by "aliens ineligible to citizenship." The law also stipulated that such aliens would be allowed to lease agricultural land for terms of no longer than three years.[50]

The supporters of the alien land law freely acknowledged its racial intent. Referring to what had happened in Hawaii, where Asian immigrants had become a majority of the population, Fresno *Republican* editor Chester Rowell wrote to Governor Hiram Johnson: "The law must be passed ultimately, if California is not to be Hawaiianized." State Attorney General Ulysses S. Webb explained that the legislative restriction targeting the Japanese was based on a concern for "race undesirability." The law sought to limit their presence by curtailing their privileges, he continued, for they would not come in large numbers and stay if they could not acquire land.[51]

Urging the legislature to pass the legislation, a California farmer described the Japanese threat:

> Near my home is an eighty-acre tract of as fine land as there is in California. On that tract lives a Japanese. With that Japanese lives a white woman. In that woman's arms is a baby. What is that baby? It isn't Japanese. It isn't white. I'll tell you what that baby is. It is a germ of the mightiest problem that ever faced this state; a problem that will make the black problem of the South look white. All about us the Asiatics are gaining a foothold.

The concern of many exclusionists was not so much miscegenation as settlement. As Japanese immigrants became landholders, they increasingly became settlers — immigrants with families. The 1908 Gentlemen's Agreement contained a loophole for the entry of picture brides and other family members. "As soon as a Jap can produce a lease," the *Sacramento Bee* warned, "he is entitled to a wife. He sends a copy of his lease back home and gets a picture bride and they increase like rats. Florin [a valley farming town] is producing 85 American-born Japs a year." Seeking reelection a few years later, Senator James Phelan put it more bluntly when he campaigned on the slogan "Keep California White." (Issei farmers responded by saying, "Keep California green.")[52]

The legislative proscription provoked angry protests from the Japanese government and the immigrant community. The Issei denounced it as the "height of discriminatory treatment," for it accorded the people of a first-rate power "worse treatment than people of third-rate southern and eastern European nations living in the United States." But they lacked political power to protect themselves against the unfair law. Feeling their hope of permanent settlement in America had been shattered, many Issei farmers were forced to organize their lives and work around three-year leases. Aware they could not stay in one place, they concentrated on short-term crops.

Issei farmers were also reluctant to make long-term investments for houses and buildings on their lands. Shortly after the passage of the act, journalist Kiyoshi Kawakami asked an Issei farmer why he did not build a modest farmhouse on his property. "Because the place doesn't belong to us," the farmer answered. "We are just tenants and our term of lease is never longer than a year or two. And, besides, you know what the labor unions at San Francisco and the politicians at Sacramento are talking about us year in year out. We may have to get out any time. . . . We don't know what is going to become of us next year." The farmer calculated it would be "foolish" to invest his "hard-earned" money in housing, like "dumping" the money "in the mud!"[53]

But Japanese farmers found loopholes in the 1913 law. They were able to own and lease land under the names of their American-born children. "If you wanted to lease or own land for any purpose," recalled I. K. Ishimatsu of San Jose, "you had to use your children's name. . . . A set of books had to be set up for inspection by the state authorities in order to prove that you were an employee working for a wage." Japanese farmers also operated their farms through land corporations in which they held a substantial but minor financial interest. "I bought the land under the name of a corporation," a farmer explained, "because Issei couldn't buy land at that time. The land registration was then switched from the corporation's into our children's names when they came of age. That's how we handled this matter, and I continued growing strawberries." The names of many Issei corporations reflected their hopes — Grace Farm, Truth Farm, Peace Farm, Eden Farm, and Lucky Farm. Seven years after the 1913 law, Japanese farmers had increased their lands under lease from 155,488 to 192,150 acres and their lands under ownership from 26,707 to 74,769 acres.[54]

Japanese farmers soon found themselves facing new and tighter restrictions. Under a 1920 law, aliens ineligible to citizenship were not even allowed to lease agricultural land nor to acquire agricultural land under the names of native-born minors or stock in any corporation owning real property. Three years later, the law was amended, making it illegal for aliens ineligible to citizenship to "acquire, possess, enjoy, use, cultivate, occupy, and transfer real property." "Because of the Alien Land Law," an Issei stated, "there were many who changed their occupations, swallowing their tears." The tighter law, combined with the post–World War I agricultural depression, led to a drop in Japanese landholdings: between 1920 and 1925, Japanese-owned lands declined from 74,769 to 41,898 acres and Japanese-leased lands from 192,150 to 76,397 acres.[55]

To circumvent the laws, many farmers entered into unwritten arrangements with white landlords. The farmer would actually lease the land but would appear to serve as a salaried manager. An Issei recounted how eight Japanese farmers in town "made arrangements with their children or friends who were citizens and obtained white sponsors in order to run their farms legally. But a couple of them were exposed for violation of the Land Law and their land was confiscated by the State. Really, every farmer lived in fear and trembling. . . . We were all walking a tightrope."[56]

Issei farmers also evaded the law by "borrowing the names" of American citizens. L. M. Landsborough, for example, purchased six lots of land for Japanese farmers with the deeds in his name, and Carl Lindsay held one share out of the twenty-three sold by the Tanji brothers in the Yamato Colony. One of the three directors of the Yamato Produce and Land Company was Guy Calden, a San Francisco lawyer who specialized in the laws affecting the Japanese. Kazuo Miyamoto, a U.S. citizen born in Hawaii, was a senior at Stanford when a distant relative offered to pay his expenses for medical school in exchange for leasing farmland under his name. "Nobody could have planned anything more convenient at such an opportune time," remarked Miyamoto, who went on to graduate from medical school. An Issei farmer explained how many fellow farmers used this practice: "I asked a Nisei nearby to be the nominal owner of the land, and pretended that I worked for the boy. I presume about 80% or 90% of the Japanese farmers in the Auburn district quietly went about their business in this way." But he realized that all of them would be helpless if the law were strictly applied. "It was truly nerve-wracking to live under this heavy pressure of wondering and waiting." An Issei woman said that her son was the nominal owner of the family's farm: "Every time some kind of difficulty arose, we had to pay a lawyer's fee to go through the legal process. I was in dire distress on account of the lawyer's fee. Every day was insecure like this, and whenever we had unfamiliar white visitors, I was scared to death suspecting that they might have come to investigate our land."[57]

California's alien land laws threatened to turn the immigrant's dream of settlement into a chimera. An Issei from Santa Paula, California, called the land law a "death sentence" for the Japanese. Similar laws were also enacted in Washington, Arizona, Oregon,

Idaho, Nebraska, Texas, Kansas, Louisiana, Montana, New Mexico, Minnesota, and Missouri.[58]

The restrictive land laws were based on the ineligibility of the Japanese to naturalized citizenship. Actually, however, their status related to citizenship was not completely clear. The 1790 law granted naturalized citizenship to "white" immigrants only, and the 1882 law restricting Chinese immigration had withheld this privilege from the Chinese. But the laws did not specifically exclude Japanese, and consequently, several hundred Japanese immigrants were able to secure citizenship in the lower federal courts. This practice came to an end in 1906 when the U.S. Attorney General ordered the federal courts to deny naturalized citizenship to Japanese aliens. But the Attorney General's action only sharpened the discussion over citizenship for the Japanese. In his 1906 annual message to Congress, President Roosevelt tried to resolve the issue by recommending legislation to extend naturalized citizenship to Japanese immigrants.[59]

The California alien land act underscored the necessity of citizenship. Newspapers like the *Nichibei Shimbun* and the *Shin Sekai* editorialized that the acquisition of naturalization rights would be "the basic solution" to the harsh and unfair 1913 law. But the naturalization issue involved the larger question of the immigrant's assimilability into American society. "The Japanese are intensely distinct and self-conscious as a race and nation," charged the *Review of Reviews* in 1913. "Those who come here, come as Japanese. They have no thought of becoming Americans." But Issei settlers realized Japanese eligibility to naturalized citizenship could concretely refute such false perceptions and open the way for Japanese immigrants to be transformed from unwanted strangers to welcomed settlers. "Foreign people living within our jurisdiction with no hope of becoming American citizens, constitute a floating unstable element in our national existence," wrote Issei journalist Kiyoshi Kawakami in 1914. "When [Americans] single out aliens of a certain race or nationality as objects of discrimination in the matter of naturalization [they] fix upon them the odium of inferiority and thus instill in their hearts a feeling of resentment." Viewed with contempt and suspicion, Japanese immigrants reciprocated with disdain. "The remedy is obvious," argued Kawakami. "Open the doors of citizenship to them, encourage them to become worthy members of the commonwealth, and their hearts will glow with hope and they will strive to prove their right and fitness to become American citizens."[60]

But the naturalization issue only stirred fears of Japanese immigration, which in turn precluded the possibility for the Issei to gain citizenship. The two questions were suddenly separated from each other in 1921: in the "Ladies' Agreement," Japan barred the emigration of picture brides and virtually ended Japanese immigration to America. This new development, explained Kiichi Kanzaki of the Japanese Association of America, meant that Japanese immigration was really nothing for Americans to worry about anymore. The problem was how to make the Japanese already here an integral part of American society. The only way to make certain they would not remain a foreign and isolated group would be to grant them American citizenship.[61]

In 1922, the U.S. Supreme Court decided the question of Japanese eligibility to citizenship in the *Ozawa* case. Determined to prove his right and fitness for citizenship, Takao Ozawa had filed an application for U.S. citizenship on October 14, 1914. Ozawa was confident he was qualified. After arriving here as a student in 1894, he had graduated from high school in Berkeley, California, and had attended the University of California for three years. He then moved to Honolulu, where he worked for an American company and settled down to raise a family. After his application was denied, Ozawa challenged the rejection in the U.S. District Court for the Territory of Hawaii in 1916. But the court ruled that Ozawa was not eligible for naturalized citizenship. The petitioner was, the court declared, "in every way eminently qualified under the statutes to become an American citizen," "except" one — he was not white.[62]

Six years later, the case went before the Supreme Court. Ozawa informed the Court that he was a person of good character. Honest and industrious, he did not drink liquor, smoke, or gamble. More importantly, "at heart" he was "a true American." He did not have any connection with the government of Japan or with any Japanese churches, schools, or organizations. His family belonged to an American church and his children attended an American school. He spoke the "American [English] language" at home so that his children could not speak Japanese. He even chose for a wife a woman educated in American schools instead of one educated in Japan. Loyal to the United States, Ozawa stated he was indebted to "our Uncle Sam" for the opportunity the country had given him. But Ozawa lost his petition: Ozawa was not entitled to naturalized citizenship, the Supreme Court held, because he was "clearly" "not Caucasian." Commenting on the Court's decision, the *Shin Sekai* expressed the rage and disappointment of the Japanese community: "The slim hope that we had entertained . . . has been shattered completely."[63]

An even more devastating development soon occurred. In 1924, Congress enacted a general immigration law that included a provision prohibiting the entry of aliens ineligible to citizenship. Although they had not been named explicitly, the Japanese had been singled out for special discriminatory treatment, for the Chinese and Asian Indians had already been excluded by other legislation. "This new law is very unjust," observed Chinese immigrant Andrew Kan in 1924. "This law I think really made for Japanese, but they are afraid to say only Japanese, because Japan is a very strong nation, might make great deal of trouble. So they have to include Chinese, too, but it is not necessary for the Chinese, because they have [the Chinese exclusion] law." But the anti-Japanese exclusionists did not hesitate to state explicitly the law's purpose. In his testimony to Congress shortly before its passage, V. S. McClatchy of California declared: "Of all races ineligible to citizenship, the Japanese are the least assimilable and the most dangerous to this country. . . . With great pride of race, they have no idea of assimilating in the sense of amalgamation. They do not come to this country with any desire or any intent to lose their racial or national identity. They come here specifically and professedly for the purpose of colonizing and establishing here permanently the proud Yamato race. They never cease to be Japanese."[64]

Actually the exclusionist provision for the Japanese was totally unnecessary. The 1924 law provided for immigration based on nationality quotas: the number of immigrants to be admitted annually was limited to 2 percent of the foreign-born individuals of each nationality residing in the United States in 1890. At that time, there were only 2,039 Japanese in this country. Two percent would have been only forty, and for its quota, Japan would have been entitled only to the minimum allowance of one hundred immigrants. In 1920, the Japanese "colony" that supposedly threatened McClatchy's America actually amounted to no more than one hundredth of one percent of the U.S. population.

In an editorial on the 1924 law, the *Rafu Shimpo* of Los Angeles scolded the lawmakers for betraying America's own ideals and dishonoring its best tradition. The Congress had "planted the seeds" of possible future "cataclysmic racial strife," the newspaper warned, by "branding" the Japanese people as inferior. In a "Message from Japan to America," the *Japan Times and Mail* made a distinction between restriction and discrimination: if the immigration law had excluded all immigration or had placed Japan on the same basis as other nations, Japan would not have resented it. "But Japan does resent a clause that, while not mentioning Japanese specifically, affects Japanese alone of all the races . . . and stamps Japanese as of an inferior race." When R. Ode, a Japanese foreman at a lumber company, was asked by an interviewer in 1924 what he thought about the new exclusion law, he exploded: "That's not right. It's all right if they treat all countries like that, but just Japan, that's not right." Due to the unjust law, many Issei protested, the Japanese were "no longer men but dogs."[65]

The 1924 restriction seemed to complete a cycle. The Issei had initially come as sojourners and had kept their cultural and national ties to Japan. "Necessity," the usual difficulties and circumstances of trying to start new lives in America, encouraged them to promote intragroup cooperation and assistance. But, as they began to settle here, they encountered racism that drove them into ethnic enclaves and strengthened their sense of ethnic solidarity. They were scorned as "strangers from a different shore": unlike European immigrants, the "Japs," as Robert E. Park put it in 1913, did not have "the right color." Rejected and isolated, Issei came to rely heavily on one another as Japanese in order to survive — to find employment, invest in shops and farms, and protect themselves against an antagonistic white society. The very cohesiveness of the Japanese refueled reactions against "diversity" and confirmed hostile claims of Japanese unassimilability. Reacting to the exclusionist agitation of the larger society, Issei turned inward, sheltering themselves in their separate ethnic communities.[66]

"The Japanese cannot say," an Issei admitted, "they are not clannish. But if they have become more so . . . it is because of restraint, economic deprivation, social ostracism, and political discrimination." Condemning the new law as discrimination based on race, the Japanese government explained the reasons for the Japanese reluctance to assimilate: "The process of assimilation can thrive only in a genial atmosphere of just and equitable treatment. Its natural growth is bound to be hampered under such a pressure of invidious discriminations as that to which Japanese residents in some states of the American Union have been subjected, at law and in practice, for nearly twenty years. It seems hardly fair to complain of the failure of foreign elements to merge in a community, while the community chooses to keep them apart from the rest of its membership." Spurned by the larger society, Japanese immigrants had retreated into their own communities, and whites were now blaming the victims of racial discrimination for being "strangers."[67]

Waves of despair and anger swept through Japanese-immigrant communities. The Issei had come all the way to America, and scanning the land here, they had seen the deserts, the sagebrush, and the "sand in the windy air." They had been told "nobody could transform it." But, inspired by the liminality of the place, the pioneers had moistened the land with their sweat and had "turned these wide wilderness fields into fertile land," "fresh green rows of strawberries reaching as far as the eye could see." My, what extravagance, they could whisper to themselves. They felt an earned ebullience, a sense of satisfaction as they gazed upon the earth, pregnant with crops. Kneeling to the ground, they lovingly rubbed the dirt between their calloused fingers. Issei lives "decorated the land" as "history." But, after the Ozawa decision and the 1924 immigration act, their lives seemed to be coming to "nothing." Over thirty years of hard work were "ending darkly," their accomplishments inconsequential, their fields ruins for melancholy ruminations. Alone Issei would sip their bitter sake, mumbling into their cups:

America . . . once
A dream of hope and longing,
Now a life of tears.

One immigrant concentrated all of his deep interior grief in poetry:

Issei's common past —
Gritting of one's teeth
Against exclusion.[68]

Dispirited by prejudice and "so much of dark side of life" in America, a few Issei decided to return to Japan. Some reacted to the setbacks by sobbing, "*shikataganai*" ("it cannot be helped") and facing their situation stoically. Perhaps, they thought, they were destined to look back in sorrow at their achievements, their very success decreeing their exclusion. They withdrew into a world of mute despair, saying they were "pioneers" and therefore had to "suffer the hardships." Others also gave up trying to become Americans but did so bitterly. "We try hard to be American but Americans always say you always Japanese," one of them explained in anger. "Irish become American and all time talk about Ireland; Italians become Americans even if do all time like in Italy; but Japanese can never be anything but Jap." He felt the Japanese had been denied the equality of opportunity offered to immigrants from Europe. "I know I am not wanted," he continued. "No use try to be American, we all have to go back to Japan some day."[69]

But other Issei refused to let "necessity" dictate their future and to sigh *"shikataganai,"* sealing their disappointment in tongues of stone and shrouding their rage behind curtains of silence. They knew the dream of America should have delivered more, for they were no longer dekaseginin and they spoke loudly of their expectations and their rights. "We live here," declared George Shima, a farmer and president of the Japanese Association of America. "We have cast our lot with California. Our interest is here, and our fortune is irrevocably wedded to the state in which we have been privileged to toil and make a modest contribution to the development of its resources." More importantly, many Issei had in fact become Americans. "We have unconsciously adapted ourselves to the ideals and manners and customs of our adopted country, and we no longer entertain the slightest desire to return to our native country." We have "drifted farther and farther away from the traditions and ideas" of Japan, and "our sons and daughters do not know them at all. They do not care to know them. They regard America as their home."[70]

The 1924 law was a turning point in the lives of the Issei generation. They saw the handwriting on the wall: they had no future in their adopted land, except through their children — the Nisei. The Issei could see they had been doomed to be foreigners forever, their dreams destroyed and their sweat soaked up in an expanse called America. Denied land ownership and citizenship, the Issei placed their "only one hope left" in their American-born children.

> Hope for my children
> Helps me endure much from it,
> This alien land.

Like the carp, which they admired for its inner strength and intrepid spirit, the immigrants had swum against the currents of adversity; still, struggling upstream and climbing waterfalls in search of a calm pool where Japanese might live peacefully in America, they found themselves driven backward.[71]

Hyphenated Americans: The Nisei Generation

But theirs had been a life of constant struggle, *ganbatte.* And many Issei became even more determined to help their children succeed.

Through the Nisei, the parents hoped, Japanese would no longer be forced to be "strangers" in America. English speaking and educated in American schools, the second-generation Japanese would be "ambassadors" for the Issei. They would teach white Americans about the culture of Japan and the hopes and history of the immigrant generation. As "intermediaries," they would "interpret" the East to the West and the West to the East. "I think it is very good idea for Orientals and Occidentals to meet and exchange the good customs in each," explained Issei farmer S. Nitta. "It is good for the people of different races to know each other. Now the Japanese do not look like Americans, their face is a different color, their hair is different, and maybe we do not have so nice an appearance." But if whites were taught about the Japanese and their culture, they would treat them with tolerance. The Nisei would be the "bridge" (*kakehashi*) to the larger society.[72]

Issei tried to give the second generation strength and confidence for their mission by teaching them the Japanese principles of *ko* (duty to parent), *giri* (mutual obligation), *on* (ascriptive obligation), and *gamanzuyoi* (strength and endurance). The Nisei must be taught the "precious records" of the "truth," the "history" of the "aches and pains and exclusion."

> *My son, remember!*
> *Your parents struggled fiercely*
> *To build their life work*
> *Under the stigma, "Immigrant!"*

Their children were Americans by birth, free from the dark mark, and the Issei hoped the next generation would be able to secure the dignity and the equality of opportunity denied to them.[73]

The immigrants worked hard and saved their money in order to send their children to college so that they would not be "inferior to Americans." They stressed the need for the Nisei to excel in education, for it would be the key to overcoming the "handicap" of discrimination and "the racial mark of the Mongolian face." "You are American citizens," Issei reminded their children time and again as though repeating a litany. "You have an opportunity your parents never had. Go to school and study. Don't miss that opportunity when it comes." Education would give the second generation access to employment opportunities denied to the immigrants. The parents were willing to give up their own comforts, even necessities, for the education of their children, for the future of the Nisei generation.

"*Kodomo no tami ni,*" they whispered in their hearts, "for the sake of the children."

> *Working together*
> *Making effort faithfully*
> *Till they all grow up.*

> *Alien hardships*
> *Made bearable by the hope*
> *I hold for my children.*[74]

Representing a rapidly growing group within the Japanese community, the Nisei constituted 27 percent of the mainland Japanese population in 1920 and a majority, or 52 percent, ten years later. By 1940, on the eve of World War II, 63 percent of the community were Nisei. As a result of the abrupt 1908 cessation of immigration of Japanese men, the age gap between the two generations was wider than usual. In 1930, the average age of the Nisei was ten, compared to forty-two for Issei men and thirty-five for Issei women. A significant proportion of Nisei grew up in families where their parents were farmers or shopkeepers. In 1930, sizable percentages of the Issei population were self-employed — 47 percent in northern California, 79 percent in southern California, 55 percent in Washington, and 48 percent in Oregon.[75]

The Nisei had their own peculiar view of the world. They spoke to each other in English and to their parents in Japanese. "My father only spoke Japanese," recalled Noriko Bridges. "One day, when I was young, I had been with a boy and didn't come home for lunch. My father asked me what Roy and I had been doing. 'We were fucking,' I replied in English, thinking he wouldn't understand what I said. Suddenly his face turned white. I felt betrayed. He knew more English than he had been letting on." But if some Issei did know only a little English, most Nisei possessed a very limited knowledge of Japanese. "Nisei spoke poor Japanese," said Frank Miyamoto. "We could only talk about everyday things with our parents. While Nisei picked up some Japanese culture, they didn't understand Japanese concepts the way Issei understood them." Language was a barrier between parents and their children, and second-generation Japanese had difficulty grasping the subtleties and the finer points of their ancestral culture.[76]

The Nisei always seemed to feel their "twoness" — as both Japanese and American. Their lives and their identities were bifurcated between the land of their parents and the land of their birth, folk stories about the peach boy Momotaro and children's tales about Jack and the Beanstalk, the Japanese love songs their mothers sang in the kitchen and the popular songs they heard on the radio, the summer *obon* dances and the weekend jitterbug dances, Japanese New Year's Day and Christmas, the annual *kenjinkai* picnics and high-school outings, banzai to the emperor's health and the pledge of allegiance to the flag of the United States. Their foods reflected both cultures: even at home they ate *tsukemono* (Japanese pickled vegetables) and *udon* noodles as well as dill pickles and spaghetti. "My children no like Japanese food," Mrs. J. Nakashima of Seattle said. "I only fix it about every other Sunday, and the children say, 'Oh mama. You going fix it in Japanese way?' They all time want American food." Nisei names reflected their dual identities. Many changed, shortened, or Americanized their Japanese first names — for example, from Makoto to Mac, Isamu to Sam, and Chiyoji to George. They also gave themselves English translations of their Japanese names such as Lily for Yuriko, Violet for Sumire, and Victor for Katsu ("victory"). Others simply gave themselves or one another American names and they became Marie, Thomas, Doris, Ralph. "My parents named me Futaye, but when I was a teenager I took an American name," said Betty Yamaguchi. "I also gave my sister Nobuye the name Grace when she was eight years old." Many Nisei had two names — their Japanese names at home and their American names in school and on the playground.[77]

The second generation learned about America at school and Japan at home. "My lessons at school taught me about the lives and character of George Washington, Thomas Jefferson, and Abraham Lincoln," recalled Togo Tanaka, "but at home my father taught me *Shushin*, the Japanese code of ethics, and he instilled in me the values of honor, loyalty, service, and obligation that had been taught to him by his forebearers in Japan." Most Nisei attended two schools — American school and Japanese-language school, and their educational experience seemed to split their culture and personality. "At Bailey Gatzert School I was a jumping, screaming, roustabout Yankee," wrote a Nisei describing herself as a student. "But Nihon Gakko [Japanese school] was so different from grammar school I found myself switching my personality back and forth daily like a chameleon. . . . I suddenly became a modest, faltering, earnest little Japanese girl with a small, timid voice."[78]

Something deep and dividing was developing within the consciousness of the Nisei. They were like Ichiro, the protagonist in John Okada's novel *No-No Boy.* "There was a time when I was your son," Ichiro says to himself, trying to describe his relation to his mother and to figure out who he is:

> There was a time that I no longer remember when you used to smile a mother's smile and tell me stories about gallant and fierce warriors who protected their lords with blades of shining steel and about the old woman who found a peach in the stream and took it home and, when her husband split it in half, a husky little boy tumbled out to fill their hearts with boundless joy. I was that boy in the peach and you were the old woman and we were Japanese with Japanese feelings and Japanese pride and Japanese thoughts because it was all right then to be Japanese and feel and think all the things that Japanese do even if we lived in America. Then there came a time when I was only half Japanese because one is not born in America and raised in America and taught in America and one does not speak and swear and drink and smoke and play and fight and see and hear in America among Americans in American streets without becoming American and loving it.[79]

What sharpened the edges of the duality Nisei experienced was the condition of their parents as "strangers" in America. Forced to be aliens forever in their adopted country, many Issei parents retained their ties to Japan. They registered their children as citizens of Japan. In 1926, in the Pacific Coast and Rocky Mountain states, 84 percent of the Nisei were registered as Japanese nationals; by 1940 over 50 percent of the Nisei in the United States had Japanese citizenship. They were literally citizens of two countries — American by birth and Japanese by registration. Actually, although it was not commonly known, thousands of American-born children of European-immigrant parents were also dual citizens. But Issei parents wanted their children to have dual citizenship for a special reason: they were afraid they might be forced to return to their homeland and wanted to be able to take their children with them. They also worried about the difficult future of racial discrimination their children faced here and wanted to give their children the option of moving to Japan. Many parents actually sent their children to Japan to be educated and to learn Japanese ways. Called *kibei,* these second-generation Japanese lived in Japan for several years and then returned to America. Fearful that Nisei would be forced to seek employment in Japan, immigrants sent their children to Japanese-language schools in America. "I am going to encourage him to learn the Japanese language," Yamato Ichihashi said describing the education planned for his six-year-old son, "so that he can to go Japan if he meets too many obstacles here." Nisei Togo Tanaka remembered his father saying, "Spend more time studying Japanese. If you have any ability, there is no future for you in this country."[80]

But most Issei parents saw America as their new home and Japan as a fallback, a potential refuge for the Nisei if the situation became intolerable. The immigrants wanted their children to study hard and learn English, the language representing a key to their acceptance in the *hakujin* (white) society as well as a means to livelihood. They were told repeatedly by their parents: "If I could only speak English like you, I would have amounted to something." Their parents urged them to try their best to be the head of the class, insisting they study at home daily. "I studied hard because I felt it was the thing to do," a Nisei explained. "It was important to succeed in school. I enjoyed seeing those A's on my report card, but a big part of the pleasure came in seeing how pleased my parents were. I guess you might say I worked for good grades because it made my parents happy."[81]

Seiko, success, could be achieved through education. "We Nisei were told over and over about the importance of school and education — how knowledge in one's mind could never be taken away and that learning could be the ladder toward success and security and equality," remembered Yori Wada, who would later be appointed a regent of the University of California. In the 1920s a survey of Nisei found that although 65 percent of the Japanese in California lived on farms, less than 10 percent of the Japanese children reported that they intended to stay there. Through education, many Nisei hoped they would be able to advance beyond their parents economically and socially. "Why do I want to go to college?" one of them said. "Because I don't want to get stuck on the farm. I don't want to spend my life in stoop labor like my folks." The Nisei drive to succeed was fueled by the equality of opportunity denied to their parents.[82]

But citizenship and education, the second generation soon discovered, did not immunize them from racial discrimination. Like their immigrant parents, they, too, were regarded as strangers. They, too, were forced to sit in segregated sections in theaters and refused service by white barbers. "White barbers wouldn't cut my hair," recalled Fred Korematsu, who grew up in San Leandro, California. "So I went to a Japanese barber, but the line was long. There were about twelve Japanese ahead of me." The Nisei were also told to "go back" to Japan and called "Japs." A white teacher at the Los Feliz Elementary School in Hollywood referred to a six-year-old Nisei student as "that Jap boy." Walking home from school, Japanese children were often attacked by stone-throwing white boys. Nisei winced when they were asked: "You speak English well; how long have you been in this country?" As citizens, they were legally allowed to own land and homes but experienced widespread housing discrimination. When Togo Tanaka tried to purchase a home in Los Angeles, he made 119 inquiries about houses for sale, and in 114 instances he was told: "You cannot live here. Your money is not good enough. The deed has a racially restrictive covenant, and only members of the Caucasian race may reside here."[83]

But Nisei were determined they would not be "Japs" forever. They would prove their worth and force whites to accept them "on the basis of merit, and merit alone." They would overcome prejudice by trying harder, especially at school. Not expecting equal treatment, the second generation knew they had to be better than average if they hoped to overcome the handicap of discrimination. "We will show them [whites] that we can do something," declared a Nisei, "but we will have to fit ourselves better than the ordinary American." The second generation strove to be exceptionally well educated. "Race prejudice in California," observed Nisei college student S. Morris Morishita, "is producing an unusual phenomenon. It is creating an educated class among the second-generation Japanese the like of which is not duplicated anywhere else in the world."[84]

Young Japanese Americans graduated from high school with good grades, even honors, and many completed college. The average educational level of Nisei was two years of college — well above the national average. Still, they found themselves cut off from employment opportunities. Many came of age during the Great Depression — a time of massive unemployment in the country. But, because of racial discrimination, job possibilities were especially restricted for the Nisei. A study of 161 Nisei who graduated from the University of California between 1925 and 1935 found that only 25 percent were employed in professional vocations for which they had been trained. Twenty-five percent worked in family businesses or trades that did not require a college education, and 40 percent had "blind alley" jobs. University job-placement offices repeatedly reported virtually no employment prospects for Japanese-American graduates. "Our experience with employment for Japanese and Chinese has been most unsatisfactory," the University of California at Berkeley stated. "Many of these students have taken the engineering courses and we have found a distinct prejudice against foreigners existing in the public utilities and manufacturing companies." Similarly, Stanford University observed: "It is almost impossible to place a Chinese or Japanese of either the first or second generation in any kind of position, engineering, manufacturing, or business."[85]

Proudly holding college degrees, Nisei saw dead-end futures waiting for them. "Practically no employment except domestic," said a Nisei YWCA worker in Oakland in 1927, "is open to Japanese people, even though they be University graduates, except employment by their own people." One Nisei who graduated with honors in electrical engineering had difficulty finding employment, while his white classmates were able to step right into their professional field upon graduation. He drifted to Los Angeles and then to Honolulu, where he was finally able to secure a minor position in a small electrical shop that offered practically no chance for advancement. Yoshiko Uchida reported that her sister, a Mills College graduate with a major in child development, could find no employment in her field as a certified nursery-school teacher and had to work as a nursemaid. "My sister . . . was not alone in facing such bleak employment opportunities," Uchida added. "Before World War II, most of the Nisei men who graduated from the university as engineers, pharmacists, accountants, or whatever seldom found employment in their field of study." Civil-service employment was virtually closed to Nisei: in 1940 Los Angeles did not have a single Japanese fireman, policeman, mailman, or public-school teacher.[86]

Changing their names would not have opened employment opportunities to the Nisei: one of them, Kelly Ohara, had a Japanese surname that matched his Irish given name. Ohara had a bachelor's degree and had also completed graduate work in engineering with good grades and strong recommendations: still he was unable to find a job in an American company. His Japanese family name might have seemed and sounded Irish, but Ohara did not look Irish.[87]

Like their Chinese-American counterparts, Nisei found themselves trapped in an ethnic labor market. Only a very tiny percentage of them worked for white employers: in Los Angeles in 1940, only 5 percent were employed in white-owned businesses. The vast majority of Nisei worked in small Japanese shops, laundries, hotels, fruit stands, and produce stores. After graduating from the University of California at Berkeley in 1940, Yori Wada tried to find a job, driving from Eureka to Ventura; unsuccessful, he returned to his hometown to work as a clerk in a Japanese grocery store. Some Nisei became doctors and dentists, serving Japanese exclusively; many more became "Japanese gardeners." As a senior in college, a Nisei woman described her restricted career future: "After I graduate, what can I do here? No American firm will employ me. All I can hope to become here is a bookkeeper in one of the little Japanese dry goods stores in the Little Tokyo section of Los Angeles, or else be a stenographer to the Japanese lawyer here." Denied equal employment opportunities in the larger economy, the Nisei were confined to "the Japanese colony."[88]

Unable to find employment in their chosen careers, college-educated Nisei were often asked: Why don't you "go back" to Japan to work? "Well," they snapped, "what do you mean by going *back* to our old country? We've never been there in the first place." Annoyed, they added: "Most of us were born here, and we know no other country. This is 'our country' right here." Many Nisei became discouraged. "No matter what our qualifications may be," they complained, "evidently the only place where we are wanted is in the positions that no American would care to fill — menial positions as house-servants, gardeners, vegetable peddlers, continually 'yes, ma'am'ing. . . . Why try to be anything at all?" Some Nisei resigned themselves to their limited employment prospects. "What's the use of going to college?" one of them argued. "I have a little fruit stand, and I give the American customers the kind of service they want. I have a comfortable income. I am happy."[89]

But actually, as historian John Modell has noted, "for hemmed-in Nisei, the fruitstand was the bitterest of all symbols of their frustration." In 1940, one out of five Nisei in Los Angeles worked in Japanese-owned retail produce stands, and half of the Japanese retail produce proprietors and managers were Nisei. Produce work was hard and the hours long — up to seventy-two a week. "I am a fruit-stand worker," wrote one Nisei in a local newspaper. "It is not a very attractive nor distinguished occupation, and most certainly unappealing in print. I would much rather it were doctor or lawyer . . . but my aspirations of developing into such [were] frustrated long ago by circumstances . . . [and] I am only what I am, a professional carrot washer."[90]

The problem, the Nisei saw, went far beyond the mere matter of jobs. It was profoundly cultural, involving the very definition of who was an American. In his reflective essay, "The Rising Son of the Rising Sun" published in *New Outlook* in 1934, Aiji Tashiro questioned why Japanese Americans were viewed as strangers. "The Jablioskis, Idovitches, and Johannsmanns streaming over from Europe," he noted, "[were able] to slip unobtrusively into the clothes of 'dyed-in-the-wool' Americans by the simple expedient of dropping their guttural speech and changing their names to Jones, Brown or Smith." Tashiro knew it would make no difference for him to change his name to Taylor. He spoke English fluently and had even adopted American slang, dress, and mannerisms. But "outwardly" he "possessed the marked characteristics of the race." To be accepted as an American seemed hopeless. "The voice of the flute has long been the unfathomable voice of the East beating upon the West with futility."[91]

But most young Japanese Americans were unwilling to retreat in philosophical resignation. As citizens, Nisei could do what had been denied to their parents — they could vote and seek to exercise power within the body politic in order to protect their rights. During the 1930s, some Nisei organized Japanese-American Democratic Clubs in San Francisco, Oakland, and Los Angeles. Calling themselves "progressives," they had multiple goals — support for the New Deal, election of progressive Democrats, and the promotion of legislation to outlaw racial discrimination. They tended to come from the working classes rather than the professional or petite bourgeoisie. Their monthly *Nisei Democrat* and the Los Angeles *Doho* carried news of their activities and helped to broaden the base of Nisei political participation. As Japanese Americans, the progressives struggled against racism. At the 1938 state conference of the Young Democrats of California, for example, Ruth Kurata and her fellow Nisei delegates from the Los Angeles club presented demands for federal legislation to make acts of racial discrimination punishable misdemeanors and for the establishment of a council within the Young Democrats to be responsible for eliminating discriminatory laws. A year later, Nisei progressives circulated a petition supporting legislation guaranteeing equal rights in employment, housing, and civil liberties to racial minorities in California. They also supported the labor movement, especially the activities of the Congress of Industrial Organizations, and urged Japanese-American laborers to struggle for higher wages and improved working conditions through unionization.[92]

Paralleling the activities of the Nisei progressives was the emer-

gence of another response, led by Nisei professionals and small businessmen. One of the leaders, James Sakamoto, editor of the *Japanese
American Courier,* expressed their vision:

> The future is bright for residents of this community, but the
> brightness depends upon their intent to settle here and to make
> homes here that they may take their rightful part in the growth
> of the city. The time is here to give a little sober thought to the
> future. The second generation are American citizens and through
> them will be reaped the harvests of tomorrow. Home, institu-
> tions, and inalienable rights to live the life of an American, is
> the cry of the second generation and will be the cry of posterity.
> It is high time to lower the anchor.

By "lowering the anchor," Sakamoto referred to the full identification
of Nisei with America. They were born in the United States and
would stay permanently; they should not think of themselves as
Japanese but as Japanese Americans. In fact, the problem was their
very dual identity, their hyphenated status. The solution was simple:
Nisei should seek to become "one hundred percent Americans."[93]
     To promote this perspective, Sakamoto and like-minded Nisei
saw the need for a national organization. Second-generation professionals had formed local Nisei civic clubs, such as the American
Loyalty League in San Francisco and Fresno and similar organizations
in Seattle and Portland. The leaders included Dr. Thomas Yatabe of
Fresno and lawyers Saburo Kido of San Francisco and Clarence Arai
of Seattle. Within the community, they were respected as prominent
young men, and they felt a sense of responsibility for the community.
In 1930, they gathered at a convention in Seattle and established the
Japanese American Citizens League. Significantly, at the meeting, a
debate exploded over the name of the new organization. Their name,
they realized, would carry their message. Should they use a hyphen
between "Japanese" and "American"? they asked. Or should they
drop all reference to "Japanese"? In the end, the convention agreed
to subordinate "Japanese" as an adjective to modify "American."[94]
     The JACL struck a chord in the hearts of many Nisei. Between
1930 and 1940, the organization expanded dramatically from eight
charter affiliates to fifty chapters, with some fifty-six hundred dues-
paying members. The JACL met the needs of Nisei professionals and
small businessmen. Through the JACL, they could claim their identity
as Americans. They could educate the larger society, disseminating

information about the educational and business achievements of the Japanese-American community. Through JACL conferences, banquets, dances, and social activities, they could also satisfy their needs for ethnic community. Ironically, ethnic solidarity seemed to offer a way for Japanese Americans to be accepted by white society.

The JACL focused on the conservative and accommodationist strategies of enterprise and self-help. "Agitation begets agitation," Sakamoto insisted, "and this can never lead to the best results." The "seeds of discrimination," the editor continued, could be completely uprooted only through the cultivation of friendship and understanding. Economic success in the form of small business and independent professions such as medicine and law would be the "sledgehammer blow" driving the Nisei "stake" into American society. Self-improvement, not political militancy, should be the Nisei approach. While acknowledging the existence of discrimination in employment, the *Nikkei Shimin* (*Japanese American Citizen*) published by Kido urged Nisei not to protest and complain: "In technical or commercial vocations, we cannot afford to work with talents *inferior* to Americans. It is not enough even to be their *equals;* we must *surpass* them — by developing our powers to the point of genius if necessary. We believe that the complaints against race prejudice in the matter of vocational opportunities *are not justified*. They only show that something is lacking in the initiative or ability of the one who complains."[95]

"Patriotism" would be the key to open the door to acceptance. "Only if the second generation as a whole works to inculcate in all its members the true spirit of American patriotism can the group escape the unhappy fate of being a clan apart from the rest of American life," Sakamoto argued. "Instead of worrying about anti-Japanese activity or legislation, we must exert our efforts to building the abilities and character of the second generation so they will become loyal and useful citizens who, some day, will make their contribution to the greatness of American life." The crucial word was "loyal." Japanese Americans, both Issei and Nisei, had already proven their usefulness in the American economy. What the Nisei had to demonstrate was their worth as patriotic sons. The 1936 JACL convention denounced dual citizenship, and its newly elected president, James Sakamoto, launched the JACL's "Second Generation Development Program." Nisei were urged to demonstrate their American loyalty by:

- Contributing to the social life of the nation, living with other citizens in a common community of interests and activities to promote the national welfare.
- Contributing to the economic welfare of the nation by taking key roles in agriculture, industry, and commerce.
- Contributing to the civic welfare as intelligent voters and public-spirited citizens.[96]

Both the "progressives" and the JACL members were struggling over their identity, trying to find and make a place for themselves in America. Politically, the Nisei generally viewed themselves as American citizens. They had chosen not to be dual citizens, and many felt this decision should entitle them to "just as many, if not more, rights than a native-born American." "I am a citizen by choice," explained a Nisei, "but a native-born person is a citizen of the United States because he cannot help it."[97]

Moreover, Nisei had cultivated an American cultural outlook. An editorial in the 1939 English holiday edition of the San Francisco *Japanese American News (Nichi Bei)* celebrated the American consciousness of the Nisei: "Once upon a time, and surely it was a long time ago, someone had the magnificent idea of the Nisei bridging the Pacific" to establish an understanding between Japan and America. But the time had come to "burn a few of our bridges behind us." The Nisei did not really have actual or spiritual ties to "the homeland of their parents." Their true culture was not one of Japanese art and music and literature but was essentially "middle-class American." Young Nisei listened to Bob Hope and Fred Allen, sang the songs of Bing Crosby, read *Collier's,* the *Saturday Evening Post,* and the *American Magazine.* They enjoyed "swing, the Sunday funnies, and Myrna Loy."[98]

But the editorial had simplified the feelings of the Nisei. Actually, many of them experienced profound cultural confusion — what a Nisei described as the "queer mixture of the Occident and the Orient":

> I sat down to American breakfasts and Japanese lunches. My palate developed a fondness for rice along with corned beef and cabbage. I became equally adept with knife and fork and with chopsticks. I said grace at mealtimes in Japanese, and recited the Lord's prayer at night in English. I hung my stocking over the fireplace at Christmas, and toasted *mochi* at Japanese New Year. . . . I was spoken to by both parents in Japanese or in

English. I answered in whichever was convenient or in a curious mixture of both.

The Nisei were both "Occident" and "Orient," but they felt they would always be Japanese and could never be American. "I wanted to be an American," a Nisei explained. "I wondered why God had not made me an American. If I couldn't be an American, then what was I? A Japanese? No. But not an American either. My life background is American. . . . [But] my looks made me Japanese."[99]

Deep in their hearts, many Nisei did not want to be completely assimilated, to become simply "American." They felt they were heirs to a complex combination of two cultures and that they should be allowed to embrace their "twoness." Everything they had learned at school about their country had taken "root" and they felt they were Americans. But the second-generation Japanese did not want to have to reject the culture of their parents, which had also become a part of themselves. Even JACL theoretician James Sakamoto explained how the Nisei had a "natural love for the country of their birth" as well as for the land of their parents. In their view, Japan was "a nation, complete in itself, great, wonderful, with a glorious future." Within themselves the Nisei experienced "the clash and the adjustment and the synthesis of the East and the West." They stood on the "border line" that separated the Orient from the Occident, the "streams of two great civilizations — the old Japanese culture with its formal traditions and customs and the newer American civilization with its freedom and individualism" flowing on either side of them.[100]

Monica Sone felt this division within and described the ways it pulled her in her autobiography, *Nisei Daughter*. After arriving in America in 1904, her father had worked with a railroad gang, harvested potatoes in Washington's Yakima Valley, and cooked in the galleys of ships sailing between Seattle and Alaska. With his savings, he opened a small laundry and thought about marrying and settling down. Through a go-between he asked for the hand of the seventeen-year-old daughter of a Japanese Congregationalist minister who had emigrated with his family to Seattle. Shortly after the birth of the first child in 1918, he sold his shop and bought a hotel in the skidrow district. A year later Kazuko Monica was born. Her Japanese name meant "peace," and her American name came from Saint Monica, the mother of Saint Augustine. Two of her siblings also had both Japanese and American names — Henry Seiichi and Kenji William.[101]

The world of Monica's childhood reflected this cultural duality. In her home there were the *North American Times*, Seattle's Japanese-community newspaper, "its printing resembling rows of black multiple-legged insects," as well as back issues of *National Geographic*. She ate pickled daikon and rice as well as ham and eggs. Monica played games like *jan ken po* and jacks, and she studied both Japanese *odori* dance and ballet.[102]

At the age of six, Monica had made the "shocking discovery" that she had "Japanese blood" when her parents told her that she would be attending Japanese school. Suddenly she had to figure out who she was and looked at the society around her for clues. In Seattle, she wandered past Japanese shops and stores, "past the cafes and barbershops filled with Filipino men, and through Chinatown." She noticed "some pale-looking children who spoke a strange dialect of English, rapidly like gunfire," and her friend Matsuko told her they were *hakujin*. Then Monica saw children who, with their black hair and black eyes, looked very much like her. But they spoke in "high, musical voices," and Matsuko whispered to her that they were "Chinese." Monica wondered what it meant to be Japanese.[103]

To be Japanese, Monica learned, involved an identity with Japan. Seattle's Japanese celebrated *Tenchosetsu*, the Emperor's birthday, shouting "banzai, banzai, banzai" and singing *Kimi gayo*, the Japanese national anthem. When the Japanese community knew a Japanese training ship would be arriving, it would "burst into sudden activity, tidying up store fronts, hanging out colorful welcome banners." During their visit, the Japanese sailors would be invited to dinner in the homes of Issei families. Everyone would attend sumo wrestling matches and performances of Japanese classical plays. Every June Seattle's Japanese held a community gathering — the Nihon Gakko picnic, where they played games, sang *naniya bushi* songs, danced, and stuffed themselves with sushi, barbecued teriyaki meats, and *musubi* rice balls.[104]

But Monica knew she was not only Japanese. While she enjoyed many of the activities of her parents, she also experienced other feelings. She shouted banzais, but did so "self-consciously." She sang the *Kimi gayo*, but did so "slowly and low" as if she were reluctant to part with each note, feeling "heavy-eyed and weary." Monica shared the sentiments expressed by a Nisei boy. After one of the seemingly tedious celebrations of *Tenchosetsu*, he shouted to a friend: "Thank God, that's over! Come on, Bozo, let's get going." Monica thought she had more interesting things to do. She was a "rabid" fan of Mickey Mouse and a member of the Mickey Mouse Club that met every Saturday morning at the Coliseum Theater. "We sang Mickey Mouse songs," she recalled, "we saw Mickey Mouse pictures, we wore Mickey Mouse sweaters, we owned Mickey Mouse wrist watches."[105]

When Monica was about seven years old, she was taken on a family visit to Japan, where she met "real Japanese." At the port, her uncle greeted them by "bowing stiffly," and her father and mother, "not to be outdone, bowed their heads and plunged into an elaborate greeting." Before entering the hotel dining room, Monica and her siblings were instructed to take off their shoes; inside, they had to sit on the floor, their legs tucked beneath them, "tailor fashion." On one occasion Monica made a remark in English, and her cousin teased her: "You talk so funny." Neighborhood children also mocked the young visitors, whispering aloud, "Look, they must be from America. They certainly wear odd clothes."[106]

Monica's parents had taken their children to Japan to meet their aging grandfather. When it came time for the family to return to America, the children tried to persuade their grandfather to come to Seattle and live with them. "There's plenty of room for you, Ojih-chan," pleaded Henry. "You could share my room. I wish you'd live with me, Ojih-chan!" But Ojih-chan smiled tenderly and said he was too old to go to America. Many years later Monica learned the real reason why he could not accompany them: in 1924, the United States had prohibited all Japanese immigration. "That was why Father had taken us to Japan, so Grandfather could see us and say farewell to his son who had decided to make his home across the sea. The children who had been born in America belonged there and there he and Mother would stay."[107]

But, as she grew up, Monica found that the Japanese were not always welcome in America, even though they had become settlers and even though many of them like herself were citizens by birth. She heard whites call her father "Shorty" and "Jap." When her parents tried to rent a summer cottage near the beach, they were told: "I'm sorry, but we don't want Japs around here." Stunned by the rejection and the remark, Monica blurted out: "But, Mama, is it so terrible to be a Japanese?" Even the second-generation Japanese, Monica noticed painfully, were denied a claim to the land of their birth. As a teenager, she had driven to the country with some friends to swim at the Antler's Lodge. But the manager blocked their entrance, saying, "Sorry, we don't want any Japs around here." "We're not Japs. We're American citizens," the teenagers retorted as they sped away in their car. A Nisei friend, Dick Matsui, was working at the Pike Public Market one summer when a white man selling vegetables at a nearby stall shouted at him: "Ah, why don't all of ya Japs go back to where ya belong, and stop cluttering up the joint." Dick snarled back: "Don't call me 'Jap.' I'm an American."[108]

The most anxious problem Monica and her fellow Nisei faced was employment discrimination. Issei parents painted grim prospects for them. "A future here! Bah!" exploded one of her father's friends. "How many sons of ours with a beautiful bachelor's degree are accepted into American life? Name me one young man who is now working in an American firm on equal terms with his white colleagues. Our Nisei engineeers push lawn mowers. Men with degrees in chemistry and physics do research in the fruit stands of the public market. And they all rot away inside." After graduation from high school, Monica applied for secretarial training at the Washington State Vocational School and was told by the counselor: "We are accepting six of you Japanese-American girls this year. I don't want you to think that we are discriminating against people of your ancestry, but from our past experiences, we have found it next to impossible to find jobs for you in the business offices downtown."[109]

Actually, Monica had been admitted to the university and had her heart set on going to college in the fall. Her parents had allowed her brother Henry to attend the university, but they suddenly said she should enroll in business school. "But why?" she asked, confused and distressed. "There's something in the air I don't like," her father replied hesitantly. "Some hotheads have been talking about war between America and Japan for some time now." And he added: "From a purely practical point of view, I want to see you acquire an office skill of some sort so you can step into a job and be independent, just in case." A dutiful daughter, Monica went to business school and graduated within a year.[110]

Like many Nisei, Monica often felt despair and wondered if she would have to beat her head against the wall of racial discrimination all of her life. But she swallowed her pride, determined to endure the injustices, bound to America by "an elemental instinct." After a bout with tuberculosis, Monica returned to her family. Her parents had bought a new house, a "marvelous big barn of a house on lovely Beacon Hill," where they could see "the early morning mist rising from Lake Washington in the east, a panoramic view of Puget Sound and the city in the west." Monica felt a surge of energy and optimism.

"In such a setting, my future rolled out in front of me, blazing with happiness. Nothing could possibly go wrong now." But had Monica looked more closely, as did some worried fellow Nisei, she would have discerned on the western horizon the terrible storm cloud of war that was sweeping ominously toward America from across the Pacific and that would show the fragility and vulnerability of the separate Japanese economy and community.[111]

6

Ethnic Islands

The Emergence of Urban Chinese America

During the 1920s, a Chinese college student from Hawaii was distressed to discover how differently the Chinese were viewed and treated in California. In the islands she had grown up in a world where the majority of the people looked like her and where she had become accustomed to a "friendly, democratic, cosmopolitan spirit and atmosphere." She saw herself as an American, a citizen by birth. "I did not stop to think of myself as being distinctly a Chinese and of my friends as being distinctly Americans, or Japanese, or some other nationality," she wrote in a response to a questionnaire. "It never occurred to me that I am only a Chinese — made American in spirit." After arriving in Los Angeles, she was "thrilled" to be on the mainland; however, when she went to the university to register, she noticed people staring at her as though she were "a strange being": "I realized very soon that I was not an American in spite of the fact that I had citizenship privileges. At the University, I was referred to as a FOREIGN STUDENT. I objected to being called such at first; I insisted that I was an American. . . . But soon I learned that was laughed at. . . ." Mocked by whites, she was "disappointed and deeply hurt" by their stares and sneers. She learned painfully that she was "a foreigner — a Chinese." Lonely and homesick for Hawaii, she felt "humiliated and chagrined" to think that she had prided her American citizenship above her ethnicity when in reality her citizenship meant "nothing — nothing in the United States."[1]

By the "United States," she was referring to the mainland, where the Chinese had been forced to retreat into ethnic islands — their own separate economic and cultural colonies. During the early decades of the twentieth century, the Chinese became increasingly urban and employed in restaurants, laundries, and garment factories. Isolated from American society, their communities in the cities became places of curiosity for white tourists, and a new industry began to develop in Chinatowns. Tourism became a new "necessity," reinforcing both the image and condition of the Chinese as "strangers" in America.

Angel Island

"Rather than banish the Chinaman," Jacob Riis recommended in 1890 in *How the Other Half Lives*, "I would have the door opened wider — for his wife; make it a condition of his coming or staying that he bring his wife with him. Then, at least, he might not be what he now is and remains, a homeless stranger among us." But the door to Chinese immigration had been closed by the government here, creating an isolated, predominantly male community. The exclusion law and the *Ah Moy* court decision had prohibited the entry of Chinese women, including the wives of Chinese laborers already in the United States.[2]

Cut off from their wives, Chinese men spent endless hours talking about their lives. The future had seemed so promising when they had left their villages for Gam Saan:

> *If you have a daughter, marry her quickly to a*
> *traveller to Gold Mountain,*
> *For when he gets off the boat, he will bring*
> *hundreds of pieces of silver.*

But many Gold Mountain men found their dreams of wealth dashed in America. Their return delayed, they now remembered the warning of an old Taishan folk rhyme:

> *If you have a daughter, do not marry her to a*
> *traveller to Gold Mountain,*
> *For he will leave her and forget her.*[3]

Perhaps they should not have been so "extravagant." Meanwhile, lonely wives in China longed for the warmth and presence of their men far away in the land of Gam Saan:

> *You bid farewell to the village well, setting out for*
> *overseas.*
> *It's been eight years, or is it already ten, and*
> *you haven't thought of home.*

*Willow branches are now brilliant, fields exuberantly
  green.
In her bedroom, the young woman's bosom is filled with
  frustration and grief.*[4]

The women had become "widows" of men living in America.
They sent the stranded sojourners, their husbands, "letters of love,
soaked with tears." One Chinese migrant in Oregon responded, writing a letter that began, "My Beloved Wife":

> It has been several autumns now since your dull husband left
> you for a far remote alien land. Thanks to my hearty body I am
> all right. Therefore stop your embroidering worries about me.
>   Yesterday I received another of your letters. I could not
> keep tears from running down my cheeks when thinking about
> the miserable and needy circumstances of our home, and thinking
> back to the time of our separation.
>   Because of our destitution I went out, trying to make a
> living. Who could know that the Fate is always opposite to man's
> design? Because I can get no gold, I am detained in this secluded
> corner of a strange land. Furthermore, my beauty, you are im-
> plicated in an endless misfortune. I wish this paper would console
> you a little. This is all what I can do for now. . . .

This letter was never finished and never mailed, left in a desk drawer
of the Kam Wah Chung Store in Oregon.[5]
     What happened to the nameless writer of this unmailed letter
might have paralleled the life stories of the owners of the Kam Wah
Chung Store — Lung On and Ing Hay. They had come to America
as sojourners in the 1880s. They worked first as wage earners and
then opened their own merchandise store. Gradually, over the years,
as they built their business and developed personal and social ties to
their new community, they felt a detachment from their homeland
and their families. In 1899, Lung's father instructed his son in a
letter: "Come home as soon as you can. Don't say 'no' to me any
more. . . . You are my only son. You have no brothers and your age
is near forty. . . . You have been away from home for seventeen years,
you know nothing about our domestic situation. . . . Come back, let
our family be reunited and enjoy the rest of our lives." In a letter to
"My Husband-lord," Lung's wife scolded her absent mate: "According to Mr. Wang, you are indulging in sensuality, and have no
desire to return home. On hearing this I am shocked and pained. I

have been expecting your return day after day. . . . But, alas, I don't know what kind of substance your heart is made of. . . . Your daughter is now at the age of betrothal and it is your responsibility to arrange her marriage." Her appeal must have moved her husband, for Lung wrote to his cousin Liang Kwang-jin on March 2, 1905: "We are fine here, thank you. Tell my family that I will go back as soon as I accumulate enough money to pay the fare." But a few weeks later, Lung learned from a letter written by his cousin, dated March 4, that certain events in the life history of his family in China had already passed him by: "Two years ago your mother died. Last year your daughter married. Your aged father is immobile. He will pass away any time now. Your wife feels left out and hurt. . . . Come back as soon as you receive this message." Meanwhile, Ing's father had also written to his son in 1903: "Men go abroad so that they might make money for support of their families, but you have sent neither money nor a letter since you left."[6]

Separated from their families in China, the men missed the company of their own small children — their sounds and laughter. Perhaps this was why Lung On and Ing Hay regularly saved pictures of children cut from calendars, advertisements, and newspapers and placed them safely in a box. Discovered decades later in one of the desk drawers of the abandoned store, this box of pictures told sad tales of Chinese-immigrant fathers living far away from their children. The two shopkeepers also pampered the white children in the neighborhood. Years later, one of them, Mrs. John W. Murray recalled: "Doc Hay always gave us children Chinese candy, oranges and other goodies."[7]

Back home, Chinese women fingered and studied old yellowing photographs of their men, so young and so handsome. Look at these dreamers and the twinkle in their eyes, filled with possibilities and promises, they said proudly. But, aiya, what did they look like now, after twenty years in Gam Saan? A folk song conveyed the widening emotional distances that had developed between Chinese men in America and their wives in China:

> *Pitiful is the twenty-year sojourner,*
> *Unable to make it home.*
> *Having been everywhere — north, south, east,*
> *west —*
> *Always obstacles along the way, pain*
> *knitting my brows.*

Worried, in silence.
Ashamed, wishes unfulfilled.
A reflection on the mirror, a sudden fright:
  hair, half frost-white.
Frequent letters from home, all filled with much
  complaint.[8]

Desperate to be reunited with their loved ones, some men looked for loopholes in the law. Aware Chinese merchants were permitted to bring their families here, Chinese laundrymen, restaurant owners, and even common laborers sometimes tried to pose as "paper merchants." A Chinese who had sworn in his oath to the immigration authorities that he was a "merchant" turned out to be a hotel cook; another was actually a gardener. Other Chinese would bribe merchants to list them as partners or would buy business shares in order to claim they were merchants. "A number of the stores in the cities are organized just for that purpose," explained an immigration commissioner. "They are organized just to give the Chinese a chance to be a merchant."[9]

Most Chinese men, however, believed they would never be able to bring their wives to America. Then suddenly a natural disaster occurred that changed the course of Chinese-American history. Early in the morning of April 18, 1906, an earthquake shook San Francisco. "*Aih yah, dai loong jen, aih yah dai loong jen,*" residents of Chinatown screamed, "the earth dragon is wriggling." In terror, they jumped out of their beds, fled from collapsing buildings, and ran down buckling streets. "I remember how everything fell off the shelf," said eighty-three-year-old Alice Fun, who was born in San Francisco in 1899. "We had one of those stoves made out of brick and the stove had crumbled. So my father was going to put it back together again. But very soon we had to evacuate the place." Leland Chin was asleep when the earthquake hit: "I wake up, and here everything is shaking. Then here went everything tumbling down!" He looked out onto California Street and saw "a big crack" in the earth. Then came the fires, roaring down along Montgomery Street and the financial district.[10]

The fires destroyed almost all of the municipal records and opened the way for a new Chinese immigration. Chinese men could now claim they had been born in San Francisco, and as citizens they could bring their wives to the United States. Before the earthquake, the number of women had consistently remained at 5 percent or less of the Chinese population. In 1900 there were only 4,522 Chinese females in America. Only handfuls of them entered the country each year: between 1900 and 1906, their numbers ranged from twelve to 145 annually. But after the catastrophe in San Francisco, they began arriving in increasing numbers — from 219 in 1910 to 356 in 1915 to 573 in 1920 to 1,050 in 1922 and 1,893 two years later. One out of every four Chinese immigrants was female during this period, compared to only one out of twenty during the nineteenth century. Some 10,000 Chinese females came between 1907 and 1924. But this immigration was halted suddenly by that year's immigration act. One of the law's provisions prohibited the entry of aliens ineligible to citizenship. "The necessity [for this provision]," a congressman stated, "arises from the fact that we do not want to establish additional Oriental families here." This restriction closed tightly the gates for the immigration of Chinese women. "We were beginning to repopulate a little now," a Chinese man said bitterly, "so they passed this law to make us die out altogether." The law was cruel punishment for American men of Chinese ancestry. "It breaks up families, will not let the wife of a citizen come in, that is not right," a Chinese protested. "One's wife should be able to join him. The baby is able to come in while the mother is not." The provision applying the restriction to wives of citizens was repealed in 1930. By then, women represented 20 percent of the Chinese population, providing the beginning of a viable base for the formation of Chinese-American families.[11]

Meanwhile, Chinese sons had also begun coming to America. According to U.S. law, the children of Americans were automatically citizens of the United States, even if they were born in a foreign country. Thus children fathered by Chinese Americans visiting China were American citizens by birth and eligible for entry to their country. Many young men came to the United States as sons of American citizens of Chinese ancestry. Others came as imposters: known as "paper sons," they had purchased the birth certificates of American citizens born in China and then claimed they were citizens in order to enter the United States. Hay Ming Lee explained how the process worked: "In the beginning my father came in as a laborer. But the 1906 earthquake came along and destroyed all those immigration things. So that was a big chance for a lot of Chinese. They forged themselves certificates saying they were born in this country, and then when the time came, they could go back to China and bring back four or five sons, just like that!" Exactly how many Chinese men falsely claimed citizenship as "paper sons" will never be known, but it was later calculated that if every claim to natural-born citizenship were valid, every Chinese woman living in San Francisco before 1906 would have had to have borne eight hundred children.[12]

But the purchase of a birth certificate did not mean entry, for the "paper sons" were detained at the immigration station on Angel Island in San Francisco, where they had to pass an examination and prove their American identity. To prepare for the examination, they studied "crib sheets," or *Hau-Kung,* and memorized information about the families of their "fathers": they had to remember "everyone's name, the birthday, and if they passed away, when." When they approached the Golden Gate, they tore up their crib sheets and threw them overboard. Paper son Jim Quock said that his grandfather had gone to America in the 1860s and had accumulated a fortune in gold. But he was robbed and murdered. "They never found the body or anything," Quock said. Inspired by the possibility of making money in America, he decided to follow his grandfather's path. "The only way I could come was to buy a paper, buy a citizen paper. I paid quite a bit of money, too. I paid $102 gold!" Quock was given a two-hundred-page book about his "paper" family to study. After his arrival at the Angel Island Immigration Station, he was detained for three weeks for the interrogation. "They ask you questions like how many steps in your house?" Quock recalled. "Your house had a clock? Where do you sleep at your house? I said, 'I sleep with my grandmother and brother.' They say, 'Okay, which position do you sleep?' All kinds of questions; you got to think." Sometimes "paper sons" had to think quickly during the examination. Two young men, seeking admission as the sons of a merchant, were questioned separately by the inspectors. The first applicant was asked if there had been a dog in the house and he answered, "Yes." Later, they asked the second applicant the same question and he said, "No, no dog." The inspectors then recalled the first applicant, pressing him about the existence of the dog. "Yes," he replied smartly, "well, we had a dog, but we knew we were coming to the United States, so we ate the dog."[13]

The presence of "paper sons" often led to confusing situations in families. A father named Wong could have two sons, each with a "paper name," or *Tze-ming,* such as Chan or Chang, having entered as "sons" of other men. A Mr. Lee could come here as "Mr. Woo," his wife would use the name "Mrs. Woo," and his children would register for school and the selective service as Woos. But to their family and in the Chinese community they would be Lees. Chinese often would refer to their *gaa-lo-dau* (false father) and offer explanations for their names: "According to the paper, I am supposed to be his brother" or "I share the same paper with him." Sen Hin Yung, who entered America as a sixteen-year-old son of a merchant in 1921, was actually Yip Jing Tom. On his gravestone, Yip Jing Tom is written in Chinese and Sen Hin Yung in English. After arriving in San Francisco in January 1910, Bing Mak passed the examination at Angel Island and was admitted to America as Bing Lai, the son of his mother's cousin, Poon Lai. Ack Pon Yee, the nephew of Boston merchant Tze Chun Wong, came here as his uncle's "paper son." One of Wong's sons had died as a baby and Ack Pon filled the slot as a Wong, becoming here the "paper brother" of Alfred Wong, who was born in the United States.[14]

There was a "paper son" in our family. My stepfather, Koon Keu Young, had entered America as the son of a merchant; his father had gone back to China and died there. Many years later a "Cousin Bobby" appeared. As a child I was told he was my stepfather's cousin, the son of another merchant. Cousin Bobby was a cook and he often helped in our family restaurant. The two cousins were very close; I can still remember them talking stories loudly in Cantonese and laughing as they flashed their spatulas over sizzling woks. After I had graduated from college, I was surprised to learn from my stepfather that the two of them were brothers: born after his father had returned to China, "Cousin Bobby" was actually "Uncle Bobby."

By the thousands, Chinese had begun entering the United States again. After sailing through the Golden Gate and disembarking on Angel Island, the newcomers were placed in the barracks of the immigration station. Their quarters were crowded and unsanitary, resembling a slum. "When we arrived," said one of them, "they locked us up like criminals in compartments like the cages in the zoo. They counted us and then took us upstairs to our rooms. There were two to three rooms in the women's section. . . . Each of the rooms could fit twenty or thirty persons." The men were placed in one large room. There were 190 "small boys up to old men, all together in the same room," a visitor reported in 1922. "Some were sleeping in the hammock like beds with their belongings hanging in every possible way . . . while others were smoking or gambling." The days were long and tedious, and "lights went out at a certain hour, about 9 P.M." But their "intestines agitated," many could not fall asleep. The inmates could see San Francisco to the west and Oakland to the east;

they had journeyed so far to come to America and yet they had not been allowed to enter. As they waited and waited, many expressed their rage and frustration in poems carved in silence on the walls of the barracks:

> Imprisoned in the wooden building day after
>   day,
> My freedom withheld; how can I bear to talk
>   about it?
> The days are long and the bottle constantly
>   empty; my sad mood, even so, is not
>   dispelled.
> Nights are long, and the pillow cold; who can
>   pity my loneliness?[15]

But the newcomers were not released until they had convinced the authorities their papers were legitimate. And not everyone passed the examination. Approximately 10 percent of all the Chinese who landed on Angel Island were forced to board oceangoing ships and sent back to China.

> Barred from land, I really am to be pitied.
> My heart trembles at being deported back to
>   China. . . .
> I came to seek wealth but instead reaped
>   poverty.

Some, in anger, vowed revenge. They promised in their poems, still defiantly visible on the walls of the barracks, to punish the "barbarians," "the heartless white devils," and to destroy the racial barriers of exclusion.

> It is unbearable to relate the stories
>   accumulated on the Island slopes.
> Wait till the day I become successful and
>   fulfill my wish!
> I will not speak of love when I level the
>   immigration station![16]

The lucky ones were allowed to hurry onto ferries and to sail happily to San Francisco. By 1943, some 50,000 Chinese had entered America through Angel Island. But they did not then go to the California foothills to become miners, the Sierra Nevada Mountains to work on the railroad, or the valleys of San Joaquin and Sacramento to join the migrant farm laborers. Unlike the earlier pioneers from China, they went to the cities, seeking shelter and employment in Chinatowns.

Gilded Ghettos: Chinatowns in the Early Twentieth Century

The geographical distribution of the Chinese in America changed significantly during the early decades of the twentieth century. By 1940, of the 77,504 Chinese on the mainland, 43,987, or 57 percent, resided in the Pacific states and 16,404, or 21 percent, in the Middle Atlantic states. Between 1900 and 1940, Chinatowns in the mountain and western regional cities like Butte, Boise, Rock Springs, Denver, and Salt Lake City were in decline. While the percentage of the Chinese population residing in cities with 100,000 or more inhabitants was only 22 percent in 1880 and 33 percent in 1900, it rose rapidly to 56 percent within twenty years and to 71 percent by 1940. Predominantly a rural people in the nineteenth century, the Chinese became mainly an urban group. By 1940, 91 percent of the Chinese population, compared to only 55 percent of the Japanese (and 57 percent of the total U.S. population), was classified by the Census Bureau as "urban."[17]

The urbanization of the Chinese population reflected several different developments. A Chinatown could survive, as Rose Hum Lee noted, only in a city with a population of at least 50,000, in an area with a diversified rather than a single industry, and in a state with a Chinese population of at least 250. Most of the Chinatowns in small western towns did not have these requirements. Secondly, the decline of the small Chinatowns was a consequence of the immigration exclusion laws and the absence of Chinese women. "Well, there they were, with three hundred Chinese workers, and except for my mother, not a single woman," explained Johnny Ginn, describing the disappearance of a Chinese community. "That was the whole Chinese settlement in Sebastopol [California]. All those old guys thought about was how they wanted to go back to China. . . . And the reason there's no Chinese in Sebastopol today is that eventually they all died off because there was no reproduction."[18]

Pushed from the small towns, the Chinese were pulled to the metropolitan cities where employment was available in an ethnic-labor market. In the nineteenth century, Chinese laborers could be found in every sector of the American economy — agriculture, mining, manufacturing, and transportation. By 1920, they had virtually vanished from these areas of employment. The mainstay of California agriculture in the late nineteenth century, Chinese farm laborers did less than one percent of the harvesting in 1920. By then, there were only 151 Chinese miners, compared to 17,609 in 1870; only one hundred Chinese workers in cigar making and boot and shoe manufacturing, compared to more than 2,000 in 1870; only 488 Chinese railroad workers, compared to over 10,000 Chinese employed by the Central Pacific Railroad in the 1860s.

The Chinese were located in a different sector of the labor market from whites. By 1920, 58 percent of the Chinese were in services, most of them in restaurant and laundry work, compared to only 5 percent for native whites and 10 percent for foreign whites. Only 9 percent of Chinese were employed in manufacturing, compared to 26 percent for native whites and 47 percent for foreign whites. "In all my life," said Peter Wong, who immigrated in 1921, "I always worked for the Chinese, never for Americans. I worked in a laundry. I worked in a restaurant, I worked in a Chinese store." Wong and his fellow Chinese workers had been crowded into a Chinese ethnic economy. The Chinese had been driven out of the general labor market and forced to withdraw to those occupations "where no bitter voice" would be raised against them.[19]

"The Chinks are all right if they remain in their place," said a white worker. "I don't mind their working in the laundry business, but they should not go any higher than that. After all, there aren't even enough jobs for us whites, without them butting in." Explaining why so many Chinese had entered the laundry business, one of them said: "It is a very hard job, sure enough. But there is nothing else to do. This is the kind of life we have to take in America. I, as one of the many, do not like to work in the laundry, but what else can I do? You've got to take it; that's all." The Chinese laundryman personified the forced withdrawal of the Chinese into a segregated ethnic-labor market. They had not always been laundrymen; in fact, in 1870 of the 46,274 Chinese in all occupations, only 3,653, or 8 percent were laundry workers. By 1920, of 45,614 gainfully employed Chinese, 12,559, or 28 percent (nearly one out of three) were laundry workers. The number of Chinese laundries soared in the first half of the twentieth century. In Chicago, for example, there were 209 of them in 1903 and 704 twenty-five years later. In New York City by 1940, 38 percent of all gainfully employed Chinese were engaged in laundry work; Chinese laundries were "located on almost every street corner." Chinese laundrymen had to spread themselves out, to Chicago, New York, Baltimore, Los Angeles, and other cities, and to different districts within a city, where there were not too many laundries. "If you are the only laundry located in the country or small city, people will bring their clothes to you," said a laundry operator. "If there were two laundries, you will not find enough to eat."[20]

But as the "Chinese laundryman" seemed to become ubiquitous in American cities, he became the object of ridicule and stereotyping. He talked "funny" and was fond of eating a strange delicacy — "dead rats." According to a chant of white children, he was

> *Chinkie, Chinkie, Chinaman.*
> *Sitting on the fence;*
> *Trying to make a dollar*
> *Out of fifteen cents.*

The Chinese laundryman chased white children with a red-hot iron and did all kinds of "mysterious and sinister things" in the back room of the laundry. He was a kidnapper of bad little boys, carrying them away in bags to unknown places. He became the neighborhood's Fu Manchu — the spooky crook, the bad guy, associated with murder and the darkness of night.[21]

Actually, Chinese laundrymen were too busy trying to earn a living and survive. The little capital required to start a laundry was often borrowed from relatives. For example, the December 2, 1927 entry of a laundryman's personal account showed that for a "new shop" he had borrowed one hundred dollars from Cousin T. H., one hundred dollars from Uncle H. K., twenty dollars from Uncle S. K., and twenty dollars from Cousin W. T. On February 2, 1928, he borrowed ten dollars from Uncle S. L. to "pay rent." The capital could also come from the *woi,* a sort of "loan of the month club." Meaning "get together" or "put together," the *woi* was a collective loan fund organized by a small family or clan group composed of fifteen to thirty members and was one of the ways, possibly the "main way," for Chinese to finance their laundry enterprises. In the *woi,* each member placed an equal amount of money into a pool at the beginning of the first month of the year, and the total sum was then loaned to a member based on an interest rate ranging from 5 to 20 percent. This process was repeated each month for a year. Every member made his regular contribution, and members with loans added the interest due.[22]

Once he had secured his loan and opened his business, the Chinese laundryman found himself working long hours. During his visit to a Chinese laundry, sociologist Paul Siu recorded the activities of the day. Like most laundrymen, Tong and his partners lived in the back of the shop, and they woke early in the morning. At 8:00 A.M., Tong went out to collect the laundry. Hong and Wah worked inside, attending the steam boiler and washtub. Ming sorted and marked laundry in the office. The noise of the washing machine drowned out their conversation. Tong returned with a load of dirty laundry in a wooden trunk and left again. The first wash was done, and Hong and Wah rinsed and wrung it then hung it to dry. About ten Tong was back, bringing a second load with him. It took an hour and a half to wash, rinse, wring, and then hang the clothes in the drying rooms. Around ten-thirty, Hong began to cook lunch. For lunch on busy days, they had cold meats and cakes with coffee. In the afternoon, they turned to the next set of tasks: Hong and Ming did most of the starching work, while Wah and Tong did the damping and ironing. Afterward Hong set the collars and cuffs on a machine, a chore that took him the whole afternoon and deep into the night. At eleven thirty, all the men ate their dinner. After supper, they all sat in the yard to cool off before they went to bed, and they finally were able to fall asleep at one in the morning.[23]

"Ah, those days were hard ones," a retired laundry operator sighed. "It is very hard to work at the laundry. They don't call it 'Eight Pound Livelihood' for nothing." The weight of the iron, filled with red-hot charcoal, seemed to symbolize their burdensome toil. Laundrymen had to stand all day. "My feet bothered me," an old man said. "I could no longer stand too long on my feet." But even younger men felt the daily wear and tear on their bodies. "I don't like this kind of life; it is not human life. To be a laundryman is to be just a slave. I work because I have to," one of them moaned. "I feel backaches all the time and headaches. I am not an old man yet, but I feel old." Their lives seemed to be measured by the pieces washed and ironed.

> One piece, two pieces, three pieces,
> The clothes must be washed cleanly,
> Four pieces, five pieces, six pieces,
> The clothes must be ironed smoothly. . . .
> You say laundry is really cheap work;
> And only the Chinamen are willing to be so
>   low. . . .
> Really, I, too, don't believe there is a future in it,

> *Washing people's sweat with your own blood*
> *and sweat.*
> *Would you do that? Wouldn't you do that?*
> *Year after year, with a nostalgic drop of tear;*
> *Deep at night, by the flickering laundry light.*[24]

Working and living in their small shops located in white neighborhoods, the laundrymen felt caged. "Nobody can imagine such a life as ours in the 'Golden Mountain,'" a laundryman lamented in frustration. "I have been confined in this room for more than two years. Sometimes I feel so lonesome in this small jail, I just want to go back to China." Many of them led lives of quiet resignation, working to earn enough money for a place to sleep and something to eat and taking life as it was: "I can't expect a life better than this and it is no use to try."[25]

Their loneliness was underscored by the absence of Chinese women. There were still few Chinese women in America; 80 percent of the Chinese population was male in 1930. But there were women in the world of the laundrymen: many were their customers. "There are two sisters [white] in this neighborhood, pretty and good natured," confided a laundryman. "When they come to call for their laundry, they act very friendly. I know they are just working girls, employed in a downtown department store as saleswomen. Some people may get sentimental ideas about the girls, but I, no matter how friendly they are, just look upon them as customers." Chinese laundrymen knew they had to keep socially distant from white women in their shops or else they would be run out of town. Some visited prostitutes. "They are just instruments to relieve sex tension," observed one laundryman. The men could find prostitutes on the street (*cheeh-gai*) or in certain hotels (*tsu-ga*, or "home town"). But then they had to worry about venereal disease; they said it would be better to have a secret liaison with a *lao-kai*, a sweetheart. The long separation from their wives in China made it difficult for many laundrymen to remain faithful. "My wife in China? Oh, she can go and look for a lover too," a laundryman confessed to an interviewer. "I can't blame her. Of all the things I am doing here, I have no right to blame her if she does the same. She is also human, see."[26]

But perhaps, some laundrymen thought, hardships here would be only temporary, a stepping-stone to a better life in the homeland. "I have no other hope but to get my money and get back to China.

What is the use of staying here; you can't be an American here. We Chinese are not even allowed to become citizens. If we were allowed, that might be a different story. In that case, I think many of us Chinese would not think so much of going back to China."[27]

Not permitted to make America their home, laundrymen daydreamed about the land they had left. Their motto was *"Fu-quai-re-quai-ku-shiung"* — to return to the native village with wealth and distinction. In their imagination, they saw themselves going home with presents — with perfumed toilet soap (*gum shan shee* — "Golden Mountain fragrance"), a sewing machine, and even a radio for their wives. They would be admired by the villagers. Aiya, they would be so fancy, so "extravagant." They would swagger down the village streets and show off by speaking to one another in English. They would describe their *Yee-Sheong Kuan* ("clothing house" — their euphemism for laundry) and would build a *Chuo-sai-kai* (wealthy home) and sponsor "big affairs" like the weddings of their children.[28]

But most laundrymen did not make it back to China. Instead they became *Lo Wah Kiu* — old overseas Chinese who had stayed in America too long and had little chance of returning home. "We Chinese who are in this country are like convicts serving a term," protested a laundryman who had been here for over twenty years. To shorten their terms some tried gambling. One laundryman worked hard to save about fifteen hundred dollars and planned to use the money to open a restaurant. But his plan fell apart when his partner-to-be pulled out of the business scheme. Lacking sufficient funding for the restaurant, the laundryman decided to take a chance by gambling. "I thought if I could win about three more thousands," he later said regretfully, "I would go back to China instead of opening a restaurant. I kept on gambling until I lost everything, within two weeks."[29]

But Chinese laundrymen were not only mired in the fantasies and problems of being sojourners: they also engaged in acts of resistance, claiming their rights as members of their adopted society. In New York during the early 1930s, for example, large-scale laundries owned by whites introduced washing machines and steam presses to cut costs. Lacking the capital required to mechanize, Chinese laundries offered lower prices and extra services such as free mending and pickup and delivery. The white laundry operators responded by forming a citywide trade organization and setting minimum prices for laundrywork. Unable to force their Chinese competitors to raise their rates, they called for a boycott of Chinese laundries. Then, in 1933, they persuaded the New York Board of Aldermen to pass a laundry ordinance requiring a twenty-five-dollar annual registration fee and that one-person laundries applying for a license post a thousand-dollar bond. The bond requirement was clearly intended to drive small Chinese operators out of the laundry business, for they simply could not pay such a large sum of money.[30]

Anxious and angry, hundreds of Chinese laundrymen protested against the new ordinance. On April 16, 1933, they attended a mass meeting sponsored by the Chinese Consolidated Benevolent Association. But they quickly saw that the CCBA was more interested in collecting so-called "fees" from them than in fighting for their rights. Shortly afterward some of the laundrymen organized an independent laundry association — the Chinese Hand Laundry Alliance. More than twenty-four hundred joined this trade organization. Its leadership was democratically elected by the membership and its purpose was to unite Chinese laundrymen in a collective effort to defend and advance their interests. "Most of us had no capital to start a successful business," the CHLA declared. "Thus we ended up selling our labor in the laundry trade. This trade became the mainstay of Chinese survival in the United States." Employing the expertise of two lawyers, the CHLA challenged the bond ordinance: the alliance argued that the bond discriminated against small laundries and successfully pressured the Board of Aldermen to reduce the bond to one hundred dollars.[31]

Isolated in white neighborhoods, Chinese laundries were connected to larger segregated ethnic islands in American cities — the Chinatowns. In 1920, concentrations of Chinese were present in Los Angeles, Oakland, Chicago, Seattle, Portland, Sacramento, and Boston. Forty percent of all Chinese lived in two cities — San Francisco and New York. The metropolitan Chinatowns developed a different character and purpose from the initial nineteenth-century Chinatowns. They were no longer way stations to service single-male workers in transit to the gold fields, farms, and railroads. While they remained a place of refuge for a bachelor society, Chinatowns became residential communities for families, Chinese economic enclaves, and tourist centers.[32]

The Chinese had been residentially restricted to the "colony" for a long time. In the nineteenth century San Francisco's Chinatown had been a male rookery. According to an 1885 investigation, there were 14,552 bunks for single men in ten blocks of Chinatown. After 1900, as families increasingly occupied one-room units in Chinatown, problems of overcrowding became even more severe. "A Chinaman cannot secure a residence outside of Chinatown, in San Francisco, no matter how much he may offer for it," said Ng Poon Chew, editor of *Chung Sai Yat Po*. "I endeavored to obtain a home nearer my newspaper office in San Francisco but found it utterly impossible and have always been compelled to live in the Chinese quarters." "Only a very few Chinese could find houses in American districts," Mills College student Esther Wong wrote in 1924, "for most house owners do not want Chinese tenants. They are forced to live in close quarters. The buildings are . . . dark and gloomy, with no bath rooms and no privacy." Single men had to share a room. "In 1913, all the cousins from the Liu family in my village had one big room so all the members could fit in it," recalled Wei Bat Liu, "and we slept in that room, cooked in that room, one room." During the depression of the 1930s, congestion in Chinatown intensified as unemployed and relief-seeking Chinese from rural areas migrated to San Francisco.[33]

In Chinatown in 1934, 276 families lived in 652 rooms, or cubicles, or 2.4 rooms per family. They had seventy bathrooms, or four families per bathroom, and 114 kitchens, or 2.4 families per kitchen. The average number of persons per bathroom was 20.4 and per kitchen 12.3. Six years later, 15,000 Chinese lived in a confined area only five blocks by four blocks in size, their residential spaces wedged between, above, and below shops, restaurants, and stores. Of the 3,830 dwelling units in Chinatown, a city housing authority report revealed, approximately 3,000 had no heating. "Buildings constructed after the fire to house single men on a bare existence basis — that is, containing tiny windowless rooms with hall toilets and kitchens and often no bath facilities anywhere — now housed families." Chinatown was a slum. Eighty-two percent of Chinese dwellings were substandard, compared to only 20 percent for the rest of the city's population. The tuberculosis rate in Chinatown was three times higher than the rate for the other residential areas of San Francisco. The children were forced to play in the streets, for Chinatown had no parks.[34]

A ghetto, Chinatown confirmed views of the Chinese as unhealthy, unassimilable, and undesirable immigrants, yet this same negative imagery opened the way to the development of Chinatown as a tourist center — a "quaint" and "mysterious" section of the city, a "foreign colony" in America. There, advertisements promised, white tourists could experience the "sounds, the sights, and the smells of Canton" and imagine themselves in "some hoary Mongolian city in the distant land of Cathay." They could "wander in the midst of the Orient while still in the Occident" and see throngs of people with "strange faces" in the streets and also "a few Ah Sins, bland and childlike as Bret Harte's immortal hero," sitting in restaurants and eating "chop suey."[35]

Behind the glitter of Chinatown's exotic image was the tourist economy. The importance of tourist profits was highlighted even as early as 1900 when rumors of an outbreak of bubonic plague in Chinatown were circulated and the Chinese Merchants' Association quickly passed resolutions to support the Dragon Festival scheduled for the summer and to reassure frightened tourists. After the 1906 earthquake, Chinatown had to be completely rebuilt, and many city merchants were worried when they saw that the first structures appeared to be cream-colored nonentities. They wanted the section to have an "Oriental atmosphere," and were pleased that the new building for the telephone company in Chinatown resembled a Chinese temple. Aware of the profits tourism promised, the Chinese Six Companies began an active campaign to promote this new economic development. In 1909 they published a guidebook, *San Francisco's Chinatown*, which gave tourists information about the community and offered assurances they would be safe: "Visitors in Chinatown need fear no harm from members of the Chinese race."[36]

The mainstream media joined the promotional campaign. In a series of articles on "Historic Chinatown" published in 1917, the *San Francisco Chronicle* predicted that the "Oriental Quarter" with its "exotic atmosphere" stood on the "threshold of the greatest era of development it [had] ever known." Thanks to the great fire of 1906, the newspaper stated, Chinatown had been rebuilt: the new quarter was "thoroughly modern" while retaining its "Oriental charm and attractiveness." Moreover, the fire had destroyed the resorts and habitats of the Chinese underworld. "Some persons, those not familiar with the district, have the mistaken idea that when one enters Chinatown, particularly at night, one is in imminent danger of losing either one's life or one's purse." Such a fear was unwarranted, for the "Oriental colony" was well policed. But the "greatest safeguard" was the fact that the Chinese people were "honest and law-abiding," glad to be visited by their "American neighbors." Newspapers assured tourists that they could comfortably experience the culinary art of the Chinese. "Patrons of the Chinese cafes and restaurants who may not be familiar with the Chinese method of ordering," the *San Francisco Chronicle* informed its readers encouragingly, "find it is the policy of the management to aid visitors in selecting a repast without going to any great expense."[37]

A leading force behind the development of Chinatown's tourist business, the San Francisco Chamber of Commerce disseminated full-page illustrated advertisements extolling "the exotic beauty and alluring features of its Chinese colony." The promotional campaign made Chinatown "the chief jewel in San Francisco's starry diadem of tourist attractions." The Grayline Bus Company also participated in the Chinatown tourist trade; in 1935 it proudly announced it had introduced more than 10,000 tourists to Chinatown that year. In 1938 Chinatown merchants formed the Chinese Factors Incorporated and spearheaded a plan for increasing the flow of tourist dollars into Chinatown and the city. Their plan included recommendations for the conversion of back alleys into picturesque lanes, the proliferation of Chinese architecture and decorations in Chinatown, and the revival of Chinese pageantry. The Chinese New Year, celebrated in February, became a great "tourist catcher." By 1938 San Francisco was drawing a tourist trade of $28 million, of which nearly one fifth was spent in Chinatown. This "little ward of Canton," the *Chinese Digest* proclaimed in an editorial, had become the city's second most attractive and unique spot, next to Golden Gate Park. Grant Avenue merchants promoted the "exotic Oriental charm of Chinatown" because it made "good business talk." Tourism led to the introduction of a new dessert — the Chinese fortune cookie. White tourists expected some sort of dessert in Chinese restaurants, and a worker in the Kay Heong Noodle Factory developed an ear-shaped cookie containing a small slip of paper with a Chinese proverb.[38]

Tourism reflected the development of Chinatown's ethnic economy, where employment was available to Chinese workers. The labor unions and discrimination had forced Chinese workers out of the general labor market. "The Chinese kept existing because they were still used as domestic labor, because they were able to make a living among themselves, and also by selling art objects and relics," said Jack Wong. During the Great Depression of the thirties, tourism was viewed as a solution to the problem of unemployment among the Chinese. Thousands of Chinese had been driven onto the relief rolls: in 1931, some 2,300 Chinese in San Francisco, almost one sixth of the city's entire Chinese population, received assistance from the State Relief Administration. Meanwhile young Chinese faced increasingly limited employment prospects. In 1935, the editor of the *Chinese Digest* noted how the tourist trade had become Chinatown's main source of revenue and urged the community to do everything it could to protect its "golden goose." "Where will our bazaars be within a few years, if no visitors come to Chinatown?" he asked. "Where will our fancy chop suey neon signs end up? . . . Where can the younger generation turn to, to find any employment outside of Chinatown?" Tourism had become the economic lifeblood of the community, and the strategy for Chinatown was clear: "Make tourists WANT to come; and when they come, let us have something to SHOW them!"[39]

Tourists were shown a fantasy land, a strange place they had read about in Bret Harte's stories and had seen in Hollywood movies about Fu Manchu and Charlie Chan. Guided through the narrow alleys of this "wicked Orient," tourists were warned by white guides to stick together and not to stray from the group lest a hatchet man get them. The visitors peered into the dark shadows of the dimly lighted alleys "lit by flickering gas jets, which increased the sense of mystery" and saw "evil-looking Chinamen, in the employ of the guides, slink back and forth, carrying knives and hatchets and providing atmosphere and local color." The tourists were told about dark, underground tunnels filled with opium dens, gambling joints, and brothels where slave girls were imprisoned. They were even taken to fake opium dens, led down ladders to a strange subterranean world where smokers were "sunk in the bestial lethargy or the ecstatic dreams inspired by the drug." They were also shown "false lepers," and as they toured the markets of Chinatown, they were told that certain cuts of meat in the Chinese butcher shops were "carcasses of rats."[40]

"You read about underground tunnels in old Chinatown?" Gim Chang, who had grown up in Chinatown and then operated a business there for decades, told an interviewer in the 1970s. "I know nothing about them. I'm quite sure they didn't exist at all." But the tourist business fostered and exploited this sensational image of Chinatown. "Much to the opposition of the respectable Chinese," Florence Chinn observed in 1920, "the horrors and vices of the San Francisco Chinatown were heralded to the world" and "misrepresentations" were "forced" upon the Chinese by the tourist industry. Chinese children also resented the tourist invasions and the distortions presented to the visitors and would follow the tours and shout "liar" at the guides. "Many of the guides created false impressions in the minds of tourists, concerning Chinese habits and life," com-

plained Esther Wong in 1924. Once a tourist had wandered into the
Chinese YWCA and asked "in broken English for the location of the
underground dungeons and opium dens." Told that no such places
existed, he "was quite disappointed and 'Chinatown' lost its glamour
to him."[41]

The second largest Chinatown was in New York City. "The
Chinatown began with the establishment some thirty-five years ago
of the Wo Kee Company's tea store in Mott Street," a writer for
Harper's Weekly reported in 1907. "At that time a Chinaman was
a sight to be stared at in the streets of New York." The Chinese
population increased from 120 in 1870 to 853 in 1880 to 2,559 ten
years later. As Chinese newcomers gathered in the city, they expanded
their colony to Doyers, Pell, Bayard, and Canal streets and moved
into tenements previously inhabited by Irish and German families.
Directly east of Chinatown was Third Avenue and the Bowery. After
the turn of the century, the Chinese population in New York rose
rapidly from 4,614 in 1910 to 12,753 thirty years later, with half of
them living in three tracts of Chinatown. The ratio of males to females
among the Chinese in New York was a high six to one, compared
to only two to one in San Francisco. New York's Chinatown was
mainly a community of bachelors living in small, crowded rooms
and apartments. "The Engs, we are all cousins, so we grouped up,"
said Gene Eng. "Six to ten of us chipped in for this apartment. All
the expenses are paid by the whole group but those who are out of
work can stay there too." In 1940, only 28 percent of the Chinese
in New York City were American-born, compared to 58 percent in
San Francisco. The Chinese community in New York, still largely
composed of a bachelor and immigrant population, had not advanced
as far as San Francisco's Chinatown in becoming a settled and family
society.[42]

But New York's Chinatown had also become a gilded ghetto.
Originally its inhabitants were mainly involved in cigar manufacturing, and its grocery stores, herb shops, barbershops, and restaurants
catered to Chinese. During the 1890s, the area began to attract tourists. They read in *King's Handbook of New York City:* "Mott, Pell
and Doyers streets and vicinity are now given over to the Chinese. . . .
The district is a veritable 'Chinatown' with all the filth, immorality,
and picturesque foreignness which that name implies." After the turn
of the century, the tourist trade in New York's Chinatown became
a booming business. Chuck Connors, known as the "mayor of
Chinatown," guided tourists around the district, which he called his

"reservation." Connors and his thuggish guides lured visitors into their tours, saying they would be escorted safely through the menacing dark alleys. The guides hired Chinese and put on shows for their guests: in one performance, "opium crazed" Chinese men fought with knives in a battle over a slave girl. Soon bus companies entered the tourist trade, conducting tours through Chinatown's curved narrow streets lined with curio shops, stores, and restaurants. As the gawking tourists rode by in sightseeing buses, they listened to lurid tales about "tong murders," "opium dens," and "slave girls"; they also visited the Joss House, an attraction maintained by the bus company. While tourists were shown the filthy alleys and told stories about the peculiar Chinese habit of eating rats, they were also encouraged to dine in Chinatown and reassured they did not have to worry about unsanitary conditions. "A visit to Chinatown," the *New York City Guide* of 1939 recommended, "should include dinner at one of the numerous restaurants declared by the Board of Health to be among the cleanest in the city."[43]

Chinatowns in San Francisco and New York and across the country were cultural islands, cut off from the mainland of American society, perceived by whites as strange places to visit as tourists. By the 1930s, many of the sensational practices of the tourist trade were gone. But still the economy of Chinatowns was mainly a service one, much of it dependent on the external society. "Wherever the Chinese are," observed Rose Hum Lee in 1942, "it has been possible to count the variations in the ways they can earn their living on the fingers of the hand — chop suey and chow mein restaurants, Chinese art and gift shops, native grocery stores that sell foodstuffs imported from China to the local Chinese community and Chinese laundries."[44]

One Chinese-American business did become a huge financial success. While it was not dependent on tourism and not located in Chinatown, Joe Shoong's enterprise was connected to Chinatown, especially its labor supply. In 1903 Shoong opened the China Toggery dry-goods store in Vallejo, California. After the 1906 earthquake, he moved his store to San Francisco; his business did well and Shoong added branch stores in California, Oregon, and Washington. In 1928, he had sixteen stores and renamed his enterprise the National Dollar Stores. "Do you know why they call it the National Dollar Store?" said Kenneth Lim, a manager for over thirty years. "In the beginning they sold the goods for nothing over a dollar. That's how they started out. . . . Clothing, everything, was under one dollar." Lim described the early and exciting success of the store: "It's just crowded like anything, because they sold at a pretty low margin. Sometimes, even if it was just a little over a dollar, they sold it for a dollar, and when we had that kind of a sale (famous quality sheets), we used to open up a box, with so many hundred sheets. We collect the money and ring it up, so it was fast. Oh, everything was really fast." All of the National Dollar Stores stockholders were Chinese, with Shoong owning 51 percent of the stocks. His stores had Chinese managers, but 90 percent of the workers were white and nearly all of the customers were white.[45]

But, while the workers up front in the stores were white, the workers behind the scene were Chinese. In fact, Shoong's business relied heavily on the exploitation of Chinese labor: the women's dresses sold in the National Dollar Stores were manufactured by low-paid unorganized Chinese garment workers employed in San Francisco's Chinatown. In 1937 they organized themselves into the Chinese Ladies Garment Workers, an affiliate of the International Ladies Garment Workers Union, and struck against the garment factory owned by the National Dollar Store. Their strike lasted thirteen weeks, the longest in Chinatown's history, but the workers lost when their employer closed the factory rather than yielding to their demands. Shoong could simply open a new factory elsewhere, for his success had made him very wealthy. By then he was the owner of thirty-seven stores, one as far east as Kansas City, and their sales totaled $7 million. Shoong himself received $141,000 in salary and $40,000 in dividends and was described by *Time* magazine as "the richest, best-known Chinese business man in the U.S."[46]

But Shoong and a few other wealthy Chinese businessmen were exceptional. The overwhelming majority of Chinese were trapped in Chinatowns and in dead-end jobs. Excluded from areas of employment reserved for whites, Chinese workers were forced to work for Chinese employers. According to the 1940 U.S. Census, 61 percent of the Chinese in the labor force were manual laborers, almost all of them working in laundries, garment factories, and restaurants. They were concentrated in the service industry — 36 percent compared to only 7 percent for whites in this sector. "We overseas Chinese live in a coop twenty-four hours a day," wrote Lao Mei, describing the lives of restaurant workers in 1940. "We work long hours, our physical body takes the toll, and we must also deal with a dry and boring emotional life." Very few Chinese were in crafts — only one percent compared to 20 percent for whites. Twenty-nine percent of

Chinese women workers were in domestic service, 26 percent in clerical and sales, and 26 percent in manufacturing. U.S. citizenship and an American education did not offer much advantage to workers of Chinese ancestry: 59 percent of them were in manual labor. Sizable numbers of both American-born and foreign-born Chinese were managers and owners of small businesses — 19 percent and 21 percent respectively. The Chinese community was divided into laborers and merchants.[47]

Viewed from within, Chinatown was not a quaint ghetto, an attraction for tourists. For the people living there, the colony was their home and community — a place where they could live "a warmer, freer, and more human life among their relatives and friends than among strangers." The grocery stores of their *wa fau*, or Chinese market town, stocked familiar foods — Chinese cabbage, dried mushrooms, salted fish (*hom yee*), canned lichees, soy sauce, sea cucumber (*hoy tom*), bamboo shoots, shark fins, "bird's nest," dried boned ducks' feet, salted duck eggs (*hom don*), bean sprouts, Chinese roast duck, and fresh ("alive") chicken shipped in daily by Chinese chicken farmers in the country. The clothing stores sold pants and shoes that fit the Chinese. In Chinatown, there were newspapers in Chinese available, herb shops, Chinese theaters, and barbershops where residents could have their hair cut and done properly. Chinatown restaurants served bachelors cheap but tasty food and offered lavish, nine-course dinners to wealthy Chinese families, especially on Sundays. In their community were their temples, Chinese-language schools, and centers for family associations. In Chinatown some of the stores served as post offices: "Folks in Canton usually wrote to their relatives in the United States in care of these stores." In the outside world, among whites, the Chinese felt they had to be reserved and silent. But among themselves in Chinatown they could untie their tongues, for they liked to "talk, and talk loudly." In Chinatown restaurants, after the lunch crowds had disappeared, waiters and cooks would gather around, "with a cup of tea or coffee, and shoot the breeze. One would say something; another would respond. Everybody would be yapping to his liking, freely and naively. There wasn't an agenda of topics, but it usually covered a variety of subject matters — from national news to world affairs. The subject of sex was the most talked about . . . everybody had his story to tell." Chinatown to its inhabitants was "a home away from home, where the Chinese felt at ease and the Americans became the foreigners."

Inside Chinatown, they could tell jokes and laugh among themselves and hear folktales told and retold, creating "the illusion" that Chinatown was "really China."[48]

Chinatown had also become a place where children lived. The immigration of Chinese women after the 1906 San Francisco earthquake led to the formation of families in the Chinese community. In 1900, only 11 percent of the Chinese population were American-born. Children were rare: only 3.5 percent of the Chinese were under fifteen years of age, compared to 34.7 percent of the general population. "The greatest impression I have of my childhood in those days was that at that time there were very few families in Chinatown," recalled a resident. "Babies were looked on with a kind of wonder." Children were "petted" by the Chinese bachelors. But the American-born Chinese group grew quickly to 41 percent of the population in 1930 and 52 percent ten years later. The exclusion laws and the proportionately few Chinese women in America had delayed the formation of Chinese families in America: a second generation existed in the nineteeth century but a sizable American-born Chinese population did not really emerge until the twentieth century.[49]

To make space for their children, parents tore down the walls of rooms and transformed old bachelors' quarters into apartments for families. "Our room was designed for the old bachelors who used to come over here," said a second-generation Chinese."All my father did was break down some of the walls and we lived there over the store." As a child growing up in San Francisco's Chinatown, Frank Eng lived with his parents and seven siblings in "one big room" attached to the family store: "What they did, you see, was divide the whole room. There was a high ceiling and they just built another floor between the ceiling and the regular floor, and we lived on top." Effie Lai's family lived in their garment factory: "When we lived on Clay Street in San Francisco my father rented a store there. The front was the factory, the back was where we lived. . . . And my father had the long cutting table. We slept there too. Daytime it was a cutting table, nighttime it was our bed."[50]

In their Chinatown world, children watched their parents at work — laundrymen expertly wielding hot irons over *hong-choong* (ironing beds), seamstresses operating sewing machines in noisy garment factories, and cooks chopping carrots and celery in cramped restaurant kitchens. "Always cut them like this [at a forty-five-degree angle]," they told the children. The youngsters noticed how their parents were powered by "necessity," working long hours: "My father would get up and leave the house about six in the morning and not close the store until almost nine at night. So what's that? Fifteen hours?" The children worked, too. "If your parents had a business definitely you're going to stay around to help. You don't even demand to be paid because it's your duty to do so." After school each day, the children did their share of work, peeling shrimp and cutting onions in the alley behind the family restaurant and loading dirty clothes into the washing machines of the family laundry. "I began by helping my parents fold towels and handkerchiefs, very simple things," one of them said years later. "When I got to be eight or nine years old they showed me how to work the presses and I went from T-shirts and handkerchiefs to complicated things like shirts." Younger children accompanied their mothers to the factory. "My mother tied me to her back and sewed," recalled Victor Wong, who was a child in San Francisco's Chinatown during the 1930s. "The constant drum of sewing machines. The chatter of Cantonese. The F car rolling and rumbling from somewhere through Stockton Street near the tunnel. Stop; screeching and ding-ding off again to somewhere not Chinatown."[51]

That "somewhere," the children discovered, could be very unfriendly. "In those days, the boundaries were from Kearny to Powell, and from California to Broadway," an old-timer remembered. "If you ever passed them and went out there, the white kids would throw stones at you." Chinese parents repeatedly warned their children about "the whites out there," the "foreign devils" (the *fan qui*), and the "western people" (the *sai yen*): "Don't go too far because the white people are against you. They may throw a rock or do something to hurt you." Japanese immigration was already under way by the time the Chinese second generation had begun to form, and Chinese-American youth were sometimes called "Japs." Mistaken for Japanese, Chinese children were also told to get out of white-owned barbershops. "How do you know we're Japs?" they sometimes snapped. More often they were denounced as "Chinks" and "Chinamen."[52]

Their parents tried to prepare them for the anti-Chinese prejudice they would experience in the larger society. "Be proud that you're Chinese," they told their children. "Yes, legally you are Americans, but you will not be accepted. Look at your face — it is Chinese. But don't worry, just show them how smart you are because you have a superior heritage." "Don't pay any attention to the names the white children call you. They're just barbarians! Just be as nice as possible to them, because you have a superior culture."[53]

Still the racial slurs stung and the rejection hurt. "The children weren't nice to us at all," recalled Alice Fong Yu. "They yelled these obscenities to us each time we would be approaching the school: 'Ching Chong Chinamen sitting on a rail,' and oh, funny sounds, like 'eeyauyau-yauyau!' — things like that." Lillie Leung remembered how she was called a "Chink" and "resented it bitterly." Him Mark Lai said he was never near whites until he had entered junior high school and there they made him feel "uncomfortable," like an "outsider." High-school student Sun Lee told a Stanford interviewer in 1924 that the boys talked "rudely" to him and charged he was "not a citizen." "Even though their words hurt me I have never been ashamed of being a Chinese and never have I wished I were a white man." Called "chink" by the other students, a Chinese youth said: "It didn't anger me. I just thought, well, there are people in this world who are ignorant, so why get into a fight?" But other Chinese boys saw it differently. "When someone would call me 'Chink,' " Jack Don snarled, "I didn't like that. So, big or small, I didn't care what you were, I'd straighten that up right now." On one occasion during a study period in high school, Jack was approached by a white student who wanted to know how to work on a problem: "Hey, Chink, how do you do this?" Jack promptly gave him an answer with his fist. The teacher came over and asked what had happened, and Jack replied: "Well, he wanted some help with a problem and I'm showing him the chinky way of doing it."[54]

But the children were often instructed by their parents to absorb the abuse and concentrate instead on their studies. The immigrant generation hoped their children would help them recover their dignity. "Our parents *used* the children to vent their frustration on, trying to get us all to *get ahead*," Victor Wong explained. "And there was a lot of frustration inside of Chinatown, too, because the Chinese felt themselves to be such noble creatures, and yet they were subjugated, they were discriminated against, they couldn't leave the area, they couldn't buy houses, they couldn't get any kind of job."[55]

Though they had come from a "different shore" than their European counterparts and had been forced to be "strangers" in America, many immigrants began to feel a new closeness to their adopted country as they became parents of children born here. "America is my new home because she has become my children's home," said a mother. "She is my country now because she is the mother country of my children." Through their children they had connected themselves to the land here, and many parents sacrificed for their children to make it possible for them to have what had been denied to the immigrant generation. They urged their children to study hard so that they would not be victimized by racism as the first generation had been, suffering indignities and "eating bitterness," *hec fu.* "I've worked my fingers to the bones for you boys to get yourself an education," an immigrant father told his son. "If you cannot be better than they [whites] are, try to be their equal anyway, because that way, one of these days, you can be up there too."[56]

Searching for Bridges: Second-Generation Chinese Americans

For the second-generation Chinese, education was viewed as the way to get "up there." In the old country, peasants were too poor to send their children to school; here the immigrants could enroll their children in public school. "Think of all the marvelous things you can learn here," Alice Yu's parents told her. "You can get one of the best educations here. This is a wonderful country. You can learn a lot here." The children went to the public schools, where they said the pledge of allegiance to the flag of the United States and learned about American culture. In American schools, they came under the influence of their teachers. Edward L. C. of San Francisco remembered how Mr. Weinstein first gave him the idea of citizenship and how Miss Davis and Mrs. Beck brought him "closer to American ideals and American patriotism." But to be American was to be acculturated. "In the English school they didn't believe in Chinese customs," recounted Victor Wong. The teachers tried to "dissuade us from speaking Cantonese; they tried to dissuade us from everything Chinese. Their view of the Chinese ways was that they were evil, heathen, non-Christian." One of his teachers scolded him: "If you're gonna be an American, ya might as well learn ta speak English."[57]

But to their parents, they were also Chinese and had to learn the Chinese language and the culture of the old country. Consequently, after attending American school all day, the children went to Chinese school. "My Chinese school career began when I was 5 years old," said Edward L. C. of San Francisco. "The school was on Grant Ave. We went to Chinese school immediately after American school which was about 4 or 5 P.M. and stayed there till about 7 or 8 P.M." They also had classes at Chinese school on Saturday from 9

A.M. to 1 P.M. There they learned Chinese language, history, literature, and philosophy. Many of the children thought Chinese school was burdensome. "In the American schools they are anxious to get ahead of their classmates, while their attitude toward the Chinese learning is indifferent," observed Julia I. Hsuan Chen, herself a second-generation Chinese. "Consequently, the only language which the majority of the Chinese-Americans can read and write is English." Growing up in San Francisco's Chinatown in the 1920s, Thomas W. Chinn was sent to Chinese school. "Somehow," recounted Chinn, who founded the *Chinese Digest* in 1935, "we never became proficient in reading or writing Chinese — probably because we never thought of ourselves as needing Chinese. After all, weren't we Americans?"[58]

Like the Nisei, the second-generation Chinese shuttled between the American school and their home. In the home, wrote Kit King Louis in an essay, "Problems of Second Generation Chinese" published in 1932, the two cultures met. There they also clashed. As they grew up, many second-generation Chinese saw America as their "permanent home" and China as "remote and foreign." Many changed their given names — from Soo Fei to Fay, Wei Lim to William, Teong to Ted, Mei Guen to Mae Gwen, Yim Jun to Jean, Yim Sunn to Shelley, and Yoon to June. They viewed themselves as Americans and wanted their first names to identify them as such. They also wanted to look American. Mrs. E. M. Findlay, who worked for the Congregational Mission in San Francisco's Chinatown for twenty-seven years, described the Chinese youth in 1924: "The Chinese girls bob their hair, wear sleeveless dresses, and look just like the little American flappers." In their "extravagance," Chinese teenagers did not think too much about their daily mixing of the two cultures: "On weekends we'd go eat *wonton* and drink orange freeze at the soda fountain." Many youngsters saw themselves as modern. "My parents wanted me to grow up a good Chinese girl, but I am an American and I can't accept all the old Chinese ways and ideas," explained Flora Belle Jan of Fresno in 1924. "A few years ago when my Mother took me to worship at the shrine of my ancestor and offer a plate of food, I decided it was time to stop this foolish custom. So I got up and slammed down the rice in front of the idol and said, 'So long Old Top, I don't believe in you anyway.'" Sometimes the break from their parents and Chinese culture also involved self-rejection: "When I was young, before thirteen," admitted Grace Wen, "I used to wish I had light hair and blue eyes."[59]

Second-generation Chinese were sometimes given derisive appellations by the immigrants: they were called *"t'oa jee doy"* (one who is ignorant about Chinese culture) and *chok sing,* or "bamboo pole," meaning empty inside. Second-generation girls were thoroughly "occidentalized," as American as "pink lemonade in a Kansas fair," reported an American-born Chinese in an essay published in the *Chinese Digest* of 1939. "If you were to close your eyes for a moment, you'd be certain they were *real* Americans."[60]

Many American-born Chinese, especially the more educated youngsters, simply wanted more independence and more choice for themselves than their parents allowed. Chinese girls found they had to challenge traditional Chinese attitudes toward women. "My parents do not believe in freedom of women and children," asserted one of them. "I believe in complete freedom of women. A woman should be responsible to no one but herself." Betty Lee Sung, the daughter of a Chinese laundryman in Baltimore, broke from the expectations of her father: "My father did not want me to go on to college at all. He thought girls shouldn't have an education. He wanted me to get married, he wanted to match me with all sorts of men. And I didn't want to do that. I wanted to go to school. And he said, 'If you want to go to school and you disobey me, I'll disown you.' And I said, 'Well, I'll just have to leave. Good-bye, papa.' " Independence meant the freedom to choose one's own spouse and to base one's marriage on love rather than family arrangement. When Naomi Jung turned eighteen years old, she resisted the efforts of her father to find a husband for her through a matchmaker. "Don't worry about me," she bluntly told him. Similarly, Stanford University student Lillie Leung said to an interviewer in 1924: "My parents wanted to hold to the idea of selecting a husband for me, but I would not accept their choices. . . . We younger Chinese make fun of the old Chinese idea according to which the parents made all arrangements for the marriage of their children."[61]

But in reality the choice — to be Chinese or to be American — was not so clear-cut. Analyzing the "problem of American-born Chinese," Kit King Louis described their plight: "With their American ideas, thoughts, attitudes, and customs, they cannot feel at home with the Chinese people though they have a Chinese appearance. Because of their physical appearance, they are denied the opportunities to achieve the better social and economic status which they desire in the American community." But even Louis had failed to detect the stormy and at times subtle ambivalence many second-generation Chinese experienced. "There was endless discussion about what to do about the dilemma of being *caught in between* . . . being loyal to the parents and their ways and yet trying to assess the good from both sides," commented Victor Wong. "We used to call ourselves just a 'marginal man,' caught between two cultures."[62]

In actuality, second-generation Chinese Americans felt the pushes and pulls of two worlds — Chinese and American. "I think that both sides are pulling equally — one the land of freedom which was my birthplace, my home — the other, my parents' home, my race's abode and my motherland," explained Edward L. C. thoughtfully. "To me they both hold the same attraction but sometimes America seems to get me more over China and I say that if any place shall be my home in the old age it *shall* be America. Now in regard to Americans — I love them just as well as my own race but they don't give us the same respect (this is just some, not all). They spite us, they hate us and they wish we were never in America." Like the Nisei, many second-generation Chinese felt isolated, as though they were islanded between two cultural continents.[63]

The tension between two identities was taut at times, especially for Chinese-American daughters. One of them was Jade Snow Wong, the fifth daughter in a Chinese family. She was not a typical second-generation Chinese American, for her father was a businessman and a Christian. Still she experienced many of the dilemmas of her contemporaries. For Jade Snow Wong, growing up and coming of age in the country of her birth involved a complicated and often contradictory process. She found herself searching for a bridge from Chinatown to the larger society and for an identity that would allow her to be both Chinese and American.

As a child, Jade Snow lived in San Francisco's Chinatown, a community separated from the outside, "foreign" American world. Her father operated a garment factory on Stockton between Clay and Sacramento streets, and her family occupied an apartment behind the business. The son of a merchant already here in America, her father had emigrated with his wife and children, arriving in San Francisco during the first decade of the twentieth century. Her mother, to whom her father referred as "my inferior woman," had "little, two-and-a-half inch, bound feet." Her father taught Jade Snow her first lessons from Chinese books, and her mother made her bright silk Chinese dresses for holidays such as Chinese New Year's Day, when she would sit on her father's shoulders to watch the lion dances. Her father believed that all Chinese children in America should learn their ancestral language, and one evening after dinner he announced to eight-year-old Jade Snow and the rest of the family that the time had come for her to be enrolled in a Chinese evening school. As his daughter, she was expected to know Chinese and to be familiar with China's great rivers, T'ang poetry, and the culture of the homeland. Jade Snow's ethnic identity was also framed by the family meals of rice and Chinese dishes, and, she discovered when her brother was born, by her gender.[64]

Forgiveness from Heaven had been preceded by six girls, and his birth was the occasion for festive celebration in the Wong family. Jade Snow realized that Forgiveness from Heaven was more important to her parents because he was a boy and that she was "unalterably less significant" than the new son. When Uncle Bing came to visit the family, he congratulated her father on the birth of a son, noting the boy's intelligent features. Jade Snow watched Uncle Bing tuck a coin into the baby's hand in accordance with customary practice. As a boy, Forgiveness was qualified to receive special gifts from relatives and friends. He was also entitled to special support from his parents. Later they encouraged and sent him to college but required Jade Snow to pay for her own college education. Her father explained the reasons for denying her request for help to meet college expenses. Sons perpetuated a family's ancestral heritage, and thus it was necessary that they have priority over daughters. Wong sons made pilgrimages to ancestral graves, while Wong daughters left home at marriage and joined their husband's families.[65]

But, by then, Jade Snow was no longer the "dutiful" daughter. She thought it was unfair to have gender determine her destiny, making her the carrier of the "heritage" for other names. She had been told by her mother that she should not pursue a career. To have "a natural or complete life" as a woman she should be a wife and mother. Jade Snow's life trajectory, as defined by her mother, had a particular Chinese meaning: women were extensions of men and had no existence apart from fathers and husbands and oldest sons. In the privacy of her bedroom, Jade Snow protested the unfairness of it all. "There are no ancestral pilgrimages to be made in the United States! I can't help being born a girl." She did not want to marry just to raise sons. "I am a person, besides being a female! Don't the Chinese admit that women also have feelings and minds?"[66]

Actually her father had cultivated a spirit of independence in Jade Snow. He was himself Western in many ways. Shortly after his arrival in San Francisco, he had been converted to Christianity by the Cumberland Presbyterian Chinese Mission. The mission taught him English at night school and educated him in a new doctrine of individualism, challenging his traditional Chinese thinking. These ideas extended to women. To his wife, who was still in China with their two oldest daughters, he had written: "Do not bind our daughters' feet. Here in America is an entirely different set of standards, which does not require that women sway helplessly on little feet to qualify them for good matches as well-born women who do not have to work. Here in Golden Mountain, the people, and even women, have individual dignity and rights of their own." He wanted Jade Snow to have an American education, including training in Western music, and sent her to take piano lessons from Mrs. Schumann so she could play Beethoven, Chopin, and Mozart. "Education is your path to freedom," he told her. "In China, you would have had little private tutoring and no free advanced schooling. Make the most of your American opportunity."67

Jade Snow followed her father's advice. But her American education reinforced a widening rift developing between herself and Chinese culture. In elementary school, she learned in the foreign language new songs such as "The Farmer in the Dell" and "London Bridge." She also memorized a poem about Jack and Jill. In the fourth grade, Jade Snow was struck by the loveliness of her new teacher: Miss Mullohand had wavy, blonde hair, fair skin, and blue eyes. One incident that Jade Snow would always remember occurred in the schoolyard. During a baseball game, she was accidentally hit on the hand by a carelessly flung bat. Hurt, she found herself held by her teacher, who gently rubbed her sore hand and wiped away her tears. Cuddled in a foreign lady's arms, she experienced a very strange feeling. She could not remember when her mother had embraced her to give her comfort. Jade Snow was now conscious that " foreign" American ways were different from Chinese ways not only generally but also specifically, and that the specific differences would involve a "choice of action." The comparison made her "uncomfortable."68

Young Jade Snow wove back and forth between her American and Chinese cultures. She "eagerly devoured" the comic strips — "Bringing Up Father," "Dick Tracy," and "The Katzenjammer Kids" — then did her Chinese lessons. She went to the nearby movie house, where she saw films about cowboys and Tarzan, and also attended plays at the Chinese theater. Still, there was a division between the two worlds — a racial one, as Jade Snow learned. At the beginning of her seventh-grade year, Jade Snow enrolled in a junior high school outside of her neighborhood because her father did not want his daughter to study at a school where there were "tough" boys. There she found she was the only Chinese student, and she felt hesitant to make friends with the "foreign" classmates. One day, after school, a boy named Richard approached her and shouted: "Chinky, Chinky, Chinaman." Then he threw an eraser at her. Dancing around her gleefully, he teased: "Look at the eraser mark on the yellow Chinaman. Chinky, Chinky, no tickee, no washee, no shirtee!" Jade Snow dismissed Richard as ignorant. "Everybody knew," she thought to herself, "that the Chinese people had a superior culture." Her ancestors had created great works of art and had invented the compass, gunpowder, and paper.[69]

In high school Jade Snow decided she wanted to enter college but she had no money. So she did housework, cleaning and cooking for white families, hopeful that her savings plus a scholarship would provide sufficient funding for her to attend the University of California at Berkeley. But she failed to win a scholarship and decided to attend San Francisco Junior College.[70]

At San Francisco Junior College, Jade Snow took Latin, chemistry, and sociology. The last course, taken simply to meet a requirement, "completely revolutionized her thinking, shattering her Wong-constructed conception of the order of things." One day, as Jade Snow sat casually in class, she heard her professor make what was for her a startling statement. During a lecture on the history of the family in American society, he argued that parents could no longer demand unquestioning obedience from their children and should recognize the individuality and rights of young people. Relating the idea to her own situation, Jade Snow asked: "Could it be that Daddy and Mama, although they were living in San Francisco in the year 1938, actually had not left the Chinese world of thirty years ago? Could it be that they were forgetting that Jade Snow would soon become a woman in a new America, not a woman in old China?" Shortly afterward, as Jade Snow was leaving her house for a date with a boy, she was stopped by her father and was asked whether she had his permission to go out. "I can now think for myself," she answered, "and you and Mama should not demand unquestioning obedience from me." Insisting that she had "rights" of her own, she argued that she was not only his daughter but also an individual. Her declaration of independence shocked her father. "Where did you learn such an unfilial theory?" he demanded. "Do not try to force foreign ideas into my home."[71]

After Jade Snow graduated from junior college, she transferred to Mills College. She no longer attempted to bring the new, Western learning into her Chinese home. She abided. Visiting her parents during the weekends, she would slip into her old pattern of withdrawal, performing her usual daughterly duties; back at school, she would again become an individual.[72]

Still Jade Snow wanted recognition from her father. When he came to Mills College for her graduation ceremony in 1942, he visited the college art gallery with his daughter. There he saw some pottery Jade Snow had created in an art class. Impressed with her work, he told his daughter that her grandfather was artistically inclined and would have been pleased to see her handwork. Knowing it would not have been becoming for a Chinese daughter to say "Thank you" for an indirect compliment, Jade Snow properly replied: "Is that so?" Finally she felt appreciated, accepted, noting her pottery was more meaningful to her father than her "hard-earned Phi Beta Kappa key." Jade Snow Wong did not realize at the time how much her father's remark would influence her choice of a career.[73]

After graduating from college, Wong began her search for employment, and during an interview she was told that she should try to find employment only in Chinese companies because American firms would discriminate against her. Later, while working as a secretary for the Navy, Wong decided she wanted to do something more interesting and important than answering the phone and typing letters. But she discovered she faced discrimination not only as a Chinese but also as a woman. When she asked her boss about possibilities for advancement, she was given "straight" advice and told bluntly that she should not compete for equal pay in a man's world.[74]

Discouraged and depressed, Wong did something "extravagant": she retreated to the Santa Cruz Mountains for a vacation. She had to think about who she was and wanted to be. One morning she rose early and hiked on a mountain trail; sitting on a log in the shade of a bay tree, she thought about how she wanted to silence the narrow thinking of all the "Richards" and the "placement officers." Suddenly she saw a new path opening before her. She would write about the Chinese experience, about herself; as a writer, a "woman would not be competing against men." In order to provide a living for herself, she would also sell her pottery. After Wong returned from the Santa Cruz Mountains, she wrote her autobiography, *Fifth Chinese Daughter*, published by Harper and Brothers in 1945, and also opened her own ceramics shop in Chinatown.[75]

Impressed by his daughter's business success, her father shared with Jade Snow a carbon copy of a letter he had written decades earlier. When he had first come to America, he had been urged by his cousin to return to China and had replied: "You do not realize the shameful and degraded position into which the Chinese culture has pushed its women. Here in America, the Christian concept allows women their freedom and individuality. I wish my daughters to have this Christian opportunity." After reading the letter to Jade Snow, he said: "It is good to have you home again!"[76]

Jade Snow Wong had made her own place in the world. But hers was a niche that reflected the limited opportunities available to second-generation Chinese Americans. Jade Snow Wong had graduated from Mills College, but she noticed that not one of her American-Chinese high-school classmates had gone to college. In 1940 American-born Chinese men had only 6.2 years of education, compared to 8.3 years for men in general. American-born Chinese women did as well as their female counterparts — 8.6 years compared to 8.5 years. "On account of economic pressures," explained Julia Chen in 1941, "the majority of second generation Chinese are forced to give up their studies after they finish high school. Most of their fathers are either restaurant keepers or laundrymen whose income is too small for sending children to colleges and universities."[77]

But second-generation Chinese did not want to follow their parents in "three-legged economic pursuits, such as being cooks or runners of chop-suey houses and laundries." They "detested working in Chinatown or manning the traditional Chinese trades." They wanted to break away from the immigrant status of their parents and hoped that education and employment in the professions and skilled occupations would advance them toward equality in American society. Some second-generation Chinese managed to pursue their education, but they encountered difficulties trying to get "up there." Educated, they were still unable to find employment in the higher-paying jobs and fields of their choices. Seeking to be judged on the basis of merit, they sadly discovered that employers were color conscious.[78]

"Even if you had an education, there was no other work than in a laundry or restaurant," explained David Chin, himself the owner of a laundry in New York. When Stanford University student Pardee Lowe applied for a job as a chauffeur for a retired banker and his wife, he was asked during the interview: "You Chinee boy or Jap boy?" "Chinese, of course, but born in this country," he replied, amazed. Then she told him: "Me no likee, me no wantee Chinee boy." Seized with a "huge desire to laugh" by her effort to speak to him in pidgin English, Lowe burst out: "Mrs. Bitterns, I understand perfectly." Two Chinese engineers wrote to fifty engineering companies applying for positions in their field and received only negative responses. Similarly, Peter Soohoo graduated from the University of Southern California with a degree in electrical engineering in 1923; two years later he told a Stanford University researcher: "I have tried to get into the engineering field but thus far have not been able to do so." After completely failing to find a job as an engineer, a Chinese graduate of the Massachusetts Institute of Technology became a waiter in a Chinese restaurant. In "Does My Future Lie in China or America," which was the winning essay for the Ging Hawk Club in 1936, Robert Dunn of Harvard University wrote that his brother, "a graduate of M.I.T. last year, failed to receive a single favorable reply from different companies to which he sent letters of application for employment." Second-generation Chinese wondered whether they had a future outside of Chinatown. The Great Depression had made matters worse for them. "With thousands of fair-minded, blue-eyed collegians at his elbows, looking for a job, with thousands of similar tinted fellows working for a raise, ready to take his place the moment he slips," asked a young Chinese American, "is there a chance for a person with a yellow skin?"[79]

Employment prospects for Chinese Americans were generally discouraging. In 1927, Laura McKeen, the executive secretary of the YWCA in San Francisco, informed a Stanford University researcher: "The employment situation is very difficult for the Chinese, particularly for the American born Chinese, trained in the schools here. There are so few openings for the Chinese in the line of work he or she may have trained. If there is an opening, preference is, of course, given to the white applicant regardless of ability." The registrar of San Francisco State College told a student that she could enroll in a course. "But after the course," the registrar candidly added, "don't expect to be placed, because you are Chinese." Sometimes Chinese were placed, but they were paid less than whites. A Stanford graduate had been considered for a job by an American company, said Kingway Jung. "The manager was willing to pay him $5,000 a year but one of his business associates said, '$4,000 is good enough. After all, he is a Chinese.' "[80]

Young Chinese workers were trapped in an ethnic and low-skilled labor market. "Chinese girls are employed in stores as stock girls, but not sales ladies." "They don't even hire you as a sales lady, except in those Chinese stores." Chinese women could get jobs as cigarette girls if they wore Chinese dresses, or as "atmosphere" in the theater lobby when a Charlie Chan movie was showing. In 1938, the Oriental Division of the U.S. Employment Service in San Francisco reported that 90 percent of its placements were in services, chiefly in the culinary trades, and that most firms discriminated against the Chinese, even well educated U.S. citizens. Three years later, as the defense program began to pull the economy out of the depression, the *Christian Science Monitor* observed: "Even though the Nation is crying for skilled workers, even though the California aircraft industry has combed the San Francisco market for skilled and semi-skilled workers, university-trained Chinese are passed by." Five thousand young Chinese in San Francisco seemed to have "no future worthy of their education," destined instead to "washing dishes, carrying trays, ironing shirts, cutting meat, drying fish, and selling herbs." After they had graduated from college, Chinese young people were told by some whites: "Go back to Chinatown where you belong." Through the assistance of the Catholic Church, Emilie Lau was able to get a job as a file clerk in a San Francisco insurance company during the 1920s. "You have no right here," some whites told her. "By rights you should be in Chinatown, doing laundry." American-born Chinese women faced both racial and gender discrimination: 32 percent of them were clerks, 32 percent service workers, and 18 percent operatives, most of them garment-factory workers.[81]

Noting the employment discrimination second-generation Chinese faced, the San Francisco Chinese newspaper *Chung Sai Yat Po* advised them to "return" to China. "In the fields of agriculture and aviation, China is much lacking in Western knowledge. Unlimited opportunities are ahead. . . . Indeed, your future lies with China, not with America." Compared to America, China seemed to be a place where they would not have to worry about being rejected for a job because they were Chinese. A University of Washington student complained that the better jobs and career advancement were not available to him in "this fair land." "Go Further West, Young Man," he thought, "yes, across the Pacific and to China." Louise Leung, a Stanford University student, told an interviewer in 1924: "The Chinese who are trained in the schools here do not expect to remain in the United States, but they are looking toward China for the future." Chinese college graduates had the education and qualifications — "everything but the color" — for professional employment in America. Some Chinese Americans actually did "return" to China.[82]

"We *were* all immigrants in those days, no matter where we were born," recalled Victor Wong bitterly. "Between the Chinese and the English education, we had no idea where we belonged. Even to this day, if I wanted to say, 'I'm going to China,' I would never say it that way; I would say '*go back* to China.' Because I was taught from the time I was born that this was not my country, that I would have to go to China to make my living as an adult." The problem, the second generation could see, was plain: they "looked Chinese." But America was their country. Citizens by birth, they had attended American schools, and many had even graduated from college. As citizens, they expected to have greater opportunities available to them. But increasingly they became aware of the racial barriers erected against them and they woke up from "an illusion." Many felt disappointed and plunged into "emotional disturbance," Kit King Louis reported. Some found "satisfaction in returning to their own group," insisting they were "very proud to belong to the Chinese race." Many decided they should struggle for their rights as citizens, while others gave up their hopes of becoming full and equal citizens. All of them felt they were "strangers."[83]

Chinese in America had realized for a long time how their situation here was tied to developments in China. The very political weakness of the Chinese government conditioned their treatment here and influenced the anti-Chinese immigration policies of the U.S. government. They supported the struggle for China's independence from foreign domination in order to free themselves in America. A strong China, they hoped, would mean greater protection and more rights for them here. But they watched their homeland increasingly victimized by imperialist powers, including Japan. In the Sino-Japanese War of 1894–95, China had been humiliated by Japan; then ten years later, in its victory over Russia, Japan buttressed its sphere of influence in China. During the 1930s, Chinese in the United States anxiously saw Japan systematically unveil its plan for control of China. On September 18, 1931, the Japanese army attacked Mukden, then marched into Manchuria. Five months later, Japan violently seized Shanghai.

As they witnessed the terrible acts of Japanese aggression, second-generation Chinese felt a surge of nationalism, a deep concern for the homeland of their parents. In Chinese school they listened to the principal give speeches about how Chiang Kai-shek should do more to fight the Japanese. There was "a whole string of National Humiliation Days" — "the day when Japan forced the Twenty-one demands on Yuan Shih-kai, that was on May 9, then September 28, the Mukden Incident, January 28, the Shanghai Incident." The murderous events were "all sloganized" so the children could memorize them by heart. "If you were Chinese-American, you certainly felt the fate of China was important," recounted James Low. "I remember the teachers would always complain, 'China is weak, and look at the treatment we get here.' "[84]

Large forces and international developments were under way that would have a profound impact on the place of the Chinese, especially the second generation, in American society. When Jade Snow Wong graduated from Mills College, she found herself worrying about future plans for her career. She had assumed she would enter graduate studies for a master's degree in social work. "But Pearl Harbor had been bombed," she wrote in her autobiography, "and the students, like everyone else, were caught in the war fever."[85]

7

Struggling Against Colonialism

Koreans in America

As they left their homeland for Hawaii, Koreans encouraged each other: *"Kaeguk chinch wi"* — "the country is open, go forward." But they found hardships and disappointments in the plantation world of Hawaii, and thus many of them moved on to the mainland. "Opportunities in the Hawaiian Islands were very limited," recalled Meung-son Paik. "We heard of unlimited opportunities on the mainland; so Dad arranged a loan for steam ship fare and landed in Frisco in 1906 right after the earthquake." By 1907, some one thousand Koreans had remigrated. Many went inland, working in the copper mines of Utah, the coal mines of Colorado and Wyoming, and on the railroads in Arizona. A few Koreans went north to the salmon fisheries in Alaska. Most of them settled in California — some eight hundred out of a total Korean population of twelve hundred in 1910. Their mainland community remained small: Koreans numbered 1,677 in 1920 and only 1,711 twenty years later.[1]

Unlike the Japanese and Chinese on the mainland, the Koreans did not have their own separate ethnic economy and community. They were too few in number to have developed their own colony — their own Koreatown with its own stores, wholesalers, restaurants, services, churches, schools, and commercial networks. But the Koreans felt a strong sense of ethnicity, even more intensely than the Japanese and the Chinese. Though they lacked an economic basis for ethnic solidarity, they had another source for community: powered by a unique "necessity," Koreans in America had to struggle against colonialism in Korea.

A People Without a Country

On the mainland, the Korean immigrants found whites associating them with the Japanese. "No matter where I appeared — whether the library, on the street car, or downtown," a Korean woman reported in 1924, "I perceived that their [whites] attention was fixed upon me and soon there followed a faint but audible whisper, 'Oh, she is a Jap!' " Similarly J. Lim complained: "During the first days of school life, children would call me 'Jap.' I would protest and sometimes resort to fists, but the most effective means would be total indifference." Another student, Kwang-son Lee, became annoyed by her high-school history teacher's snide remarks about "Japs." One day she got up in class. "How do you know I'm . . . a Jap?" Lee questioned, insisting she was not Japanese. The teacher then asked: "Who are you then?" Sarcastically Lee retorted: "Are you so ignorant you don't know what a Korean is? And you a history teacher?" When a Korean newcomer went to a barbershop in Los Angeles, he was told they did not want the "Japanese trade."[2]

Like other Asians, Korean immigrants were seen as "strangers from a different shore" and experienced widespread racial discrimination. When they tried to rent houses, they were often refused by white landlords. "In renting a place," Do-Yun Yoon recalled, "only the 'junk house' was available. None in the nicer areas in the 'white town.' Only in 'Mexican town' or 'Black town.' " "When we first came to Delano," she added, "the Americans would not let us sit anywhere in the theater. They permitted us to sit in one corner with the Mexicans but not with the Americans." Koreans were also refused service in public recreational facilities and restaurants. In Los Angeles, Chang Lee-wook went to a restaurant for lunch. "Although there were not many customers," he said later, "the waitress did not come to my table. After awhile, a young receptionist came to me and said with a low voice that 'we can't serve you lunch, because if we start serving lunch to the Orientals, white Americans will not come here.' "[3]

Koreans experienced "ethnic antagonism" — competition and conflict between Asian and white workers. In 1910, for example, Koreans, hired to pick oranges, camped on Mary Steward's farm in Upland, California. Suddenly, one night, they were attacked by white farm workers; under a barrage of stones and rocks, they were told to get out immediately or they would be killed. After she had called the police and received permission to purchase guns, Steward armed the Korean workers and instructed them to defend themselves with deadly force against the white rioters. They quickly quelled the riot. "The minority Korean people in this great country of America," Steward declared, "have a right to live and work just as the other nationalities. They are hard working, diligent and honest people who are struggling for a decent life."[4]

Moreover, Koreans were subjected to discrimination by the state. The Asiatic Exclusion League condemned both Korean and Japanese immigrants as undesirable aliens, and the San Francisco Building Trades Council demanded that the Chinese Exclusion Act be extended to the Japanese and Koreans. Support for this legislation was spearheaded by a new organization called the Japanese and Korean Exclusion League. Meanwhile, in San Francisco in 1906, the Board of Education specifically included "Koreans" as well as Japanese in its segregationist directive. In a 1907 executive order, President Theodore Roosevelt prohibited the remigration of Japanese and Korean laborers from Hawaii to the mainland. In 1912 the Democratic Party in California called for "immediate federal legislation for the exclusion of Japanese, Korean and Hindoo laborers."[5]

The Alien Land Act of 1913 prohibited Koreans from owning land and limited leases in California, for Koreans had been denied naturalized citizenship. A Korean immigrant remembered the passage of the restrictive legislation: "We left California because the state had passed the alien land act. You couldn't control your farm. Then we went to Washington. But after we lived there for a few years, Washington passed an anti-alien exclusion farm law, so we went to Utah where they did not have such a law." Another Korean described the restriction: "If we wanted to rent land, it had to be in a child's name that was born in this country — a citizen. It was impossible as a foreigner." The question of Korean eligibility was tested in the courts after World War I by Easurk Emsen Charr. He had been drafted into the U.S. Army in 1918, and consequently Charr petitioned for citizenship in a federal district court in 1921, arguing that his military service should entitle him to naturalized citizenship. But the court declared that Koreans were "admittedly of the Mongol family" and hence excluded from naturalized citizenship. "The provisions of the draft law," the court explained, "clearly did not contemplate the incorporation of those not eligible to citizenship" in the armed forces.[6]

Mainland Korean America was largely a community of *chong gak* (bachelors): of the 1,015 Koreans who arrived on the mainland from Hawaii between 1905 and 1910, only forty-five were female and twenty-nine were children. One hundred and fifteen Korean picture brides came after 1910, but an imbalance between men and women remained. In 1920, 75 percent of the mainland Korean population was male; ten years later, it was 66 percent. "Most of the Korean men were alone in those days," a Korean immigrant explained. "They left their families in Korea, so they were bachelors and single men." Many of the "bachelors" were actually married men, or *horlebees*, with wives in Korea. Of the seventy-four Korean laborers employed by a railroad company, for example, two were widowed, thirty were single, and forty-two were married but here without their wives. Korean men sang love songs from the old country:

> *Some loves are soft, others are rough.*
> *Some loves are deep like Kuwol Mountain.*
> *Other loves are so sad like the girl who sent her love to*
> *   the army.*
> *Some loves are secret.*
> *What a delight! What a pleasure!*
> *You can't help falling in love.*

But there were few Korean women in America to hear them sing.[7]

In the cities, employment opportunities were restricted for Korean men: they were restaurant workers, gardeners, janitors, and domestic workers. After his arrival in this country, Whang Sa Sun worked as a house servant. "I felt the discrimination and realized that America was not a free country. Everybody did not enjoy liberty. The American people saw the Asian people as a different race. They didn't respect the Asian people. I wanted some postal or factory work, but they didn't give it to me. I couldn't get a job." Outside the cities, Koreans were able to find employment as railroad laborers. Sometimes they worked in "gangs" with Japanese laborers; usually they formed their own gangs. "After talking with the foreman of a railroad company," a migrant recalled, "I entered into a contract with him to provide a 'gang' of Korean workers. The conditions were that we worked repairing railroad tracks, ate and slept in wagons." Railroad workers were moved from one place to another. "We lived there [in Reedley, California] for a period of months. Then we had connections in Redlands, and moved over there. . . . From Redlands we moved to Riverside where we had some Korean friends. There was a group of Koreans there with one man as a labor boss."[8]

The overwhelming majority of Koreans were farm laborers. Using a traditional Korean arrangement, they were organized into work teams or "gangs," usually ten men in a group supervised by a *sip-chang* ("ten-head"). A Korean ethnic identity guided them. They believed their productivity as workers would help to open employment opportunities for Koreans in general: "Our only capital today in this land is nothing but honesty; therefore, work diligently without wasting time whether your employer watches you or not; then you will be working not only today but tomorrow and even the whole year round. If your employer has confidence in you, then your friends, Kim, Lee, or Park will also get jobs, because of your hard and honest work. In this way, eventually all Koreans will get jobs anywhere and at any time." For the Korean immigrants, economic success was tied to ethnic solidarity.[9]

The teams of Korean farm workers moved from field to field, town to town, depending on where they could find work. Ten days after he had arrived in San Francisco in 1916, a Korean immigrant went to Stockton, where he joined a team headed by a Korean labor contractor and worked on a bean farm. "There were about 20 other Koreans working there," he said. "We were hoeing the bean fields and when we finished we went to another bean farm for hoeing. It was hard work. . . . Then we went to Dinuba picking grapes. I was flocking with other Koreans, and I went where they went for available farm jobs." The *New Korea*, a newspaper published in San Francisco, described this movement of Korean farm laborers: "There are not many Koreans in Dinuba, but when it is grape picking time, many Koreans will come. . . . Sacramento is a stopping place for Koreans who go back and forth to work on farms."[10]

The day for Korean farm laborers began early in the morning. Waking up at five o'clock, they ate breakfast and then gathered at a meeting place where the farmers delegated the work. "They told you where to go and who to work with in the fields," a Korean worker recalled. There were orchards of peaches, plums, and grapes, and the workers followed the group leaders to the orchard to be harvested. There "the men did the picking if the trees were too tall for the women," and the "women, boys, and girls waited on the ground to pack the fruit." Picking fruit was dangerous work. "If you picked grapes you had to be careful where you put your hand in the vines because black widow spiders and yellow-jacket hornets were all over the grapevines." Workers were often bitten and stung. "As soon as I was stung by yellow-jackets I used to make mud-packs and place them on the wound to prevent the bite from swelling." Picking peaches was tedious: workers had to dust each peach with a feather brush to knock the bugs off the peach fuzz. "All the peaches were sized as we picked them and we checked each fruit for holes or big marks and if they were good we packed them."[11]

As the sun rose, it became very hot and dry in the California fields. "The day starts out around seventy to eighty degrees and by noon time the temperature reaches around a hundred and five and a hundred and ten degrees." Usually there was "no breeze whatsoever." After working all morning in the hot sun, the laborers looked for a shady spot where they could eat their lunch at noontime. "Most of us took our lunch which consisted of rice, kimchi, and maybe some beef or chicken. Each of us picked our own tree and ate under the shade and after we finished we usually took a short nap." At one o'clock work began again and continued until five. "By the end of the day your arms and legs felt very heavy and your back really ached." Returning home about six o'clock, "everybody fought to take a bath because if you worked in the fields your whole body got covered with dirt from head to toe, especially if you picked grapes. When you packed peaches, the fuzz made you itchy."[12]

Work in the tomato fields was equally punishing and exhausting. Employed on a tomato farm in Stockton, Whang Sa-yong had been assigned to plant the tomato seeds. "Three men worked as a team; the first man dug the hole, the second planted tomato seeds, and the third covered the hole and watered it." As a member of a team, Whang had to keep up with his fellow workers. "Everybody was working faster than I was, and I had a hard time following the other two. I waited for lunch time to come so that I could rest for awhile." But when lunchtime came, Whang could not eat his lunch because the weather was so hot and he was so tired. "I laid down on the ground and rested until the others finished their lunch. When I finished my day's work, I hardly could walk back to my rooming house. . . . During the night I was unable to sleep, because my whole body was sore and I felt pains all over."[13]

Gradually some Koreans were able to become farmers themselves. Often several individuals would combine their financial resources to lease and farm land. They would organize a Korean *kae* — a credit-rotating system similar to the Chinese *woi* and the Japanese *tanomoshi* — in which a group of Koreans would individually contribute money and allow a member of the group to borrow from the fund. The first member would repay the loan plus interest, and the fund would then rotate to a second member. Interest rates for the loans would decrease each time around, and the last member of the *kae* would not be charged interest on his loan. "During the years that my father was working as a farm laborer," a Korean said, "he made up his mind that he had to own his own business in order to make money. So, he and a group of friends got together and formed a company and pooled their money together. They were making great profits in potato farming in Stockton." In 1918, Korean rice farmers in the Sacramento Valley alone produced 214,000 bushels of rice; Kim Chong-nim was so productive as a rice farmer that he was known as the "rice king" in the Korean community. By the 1920s, Korean farmers in Willows, California, were cultivating 43,000 acres of rice, and Korean farmers in the San Joaquin Valley were shipping fruit to Korean wholesale markets in Los Angeles.[14]

One of the most successful Korean agricultural entrepreneurs was Kim Hyung-soon. Eight years after his arrival in California in 1913, he formed a business partnership with Kim Ho in Reedley. Together the two men expanded their enterprise — the Kim Brothers Company — from a fruit wholesaler to a large operation of orchards, nurseries, and fruit-packing sheds. Kim Hyung-soon and an employee named Anderson developed new varieties of peaches, including a "fuzzless peach" that was later sold in the market as "Le Grand" and "Sun Grand." The nectarine, which resulted from the crossing of peaches and plums, boosted the fortunes of the Kim Brothers Company. "We felt," said Kim Hyung-soon, "that we were the first Orientals who invented a new fruit for the American people and would be the first Korean millionaires in the Korean community."[15]

Korean entrepreneurial activities extended beyond agriculture. Koreans became extensively involved in the hotel business. In 1906, Wu Kyong-sik opened the first Korean hotel in Sacramento, and by 1920, there were more than twenty Korean-owned hotels in Dinuba, San Francisco, Stockton, Los Angeles, Manteca, Riverside, Lompoc, and even Yakima, Washington, and Chicago, Illinois. Many Korean hotel proprietors were labor contractors, providing room and board to Korean workers and arranging work for them. Koreans also established restaurants and retail stores including groceries, tobacco shops, bakeries, and photo studios. But the two most popular enterprises were barbershops and laundries. In the Pacific Coast states, Koreans operated thirty barbershops and twenty-five laundries, labor-intensive enterprises requiring minimal capital investment and yielding good profits. A survey of six Korean barbershops and laundries in San Francisco in 1918 showed that annual net profits ranged from nine hundred dollars to $2,784 — respectable incomes at the time. Like the other Asian groups, Koreans turned to self-employment as a route around racial discrimination in the labor market.[16]

Economic success, for Korean migrants, was tied to an accommodationist strategy to overcome racial discrimination. They thought that the Chinese and Japanese immigrants before them had provoked white anti-Asian reactions by retaining their old ways and keeping to themselves. In a 1910 editorial, the Korean newspaper *Sinhan Minbo* explained:

> The reason for discrimination against the Asiatics stems from the unfortunate situation of the Chinese who came to this country without abandoning their filthy habits and customs. And, everywhere they go they create disorders. After that the Japanese who have entirely different habits from white society, could not mingle with the whites . . . but also they spend as little as they can for food and houses. . . . So they are becoming a target of hatred from white workers.[17]

"The reason why many Americans love Koreans and help us, while they hate Japanese more than ever," the Korean newspaper *Kongnip Sinmun* asserted, "is that we Koreans gave up old baseness, thought and behavior, and became more westernized." Korean immigrants tried to learn English and were told by their leaders to be "accepted and invited again and again to work by the whites," showing them that Koreans were trusty, hardworking, and worthy. They highlighted their adherence to Christianity and expressed their gratitude to America. The *Kongnip Sinmun* declared that America had been a "boon" to Korean immigrants and that Americans had shown them goodwill and friendship. "We came to this country with empty hands, but now we have made some money which enables us to build a new Korean society and send young Koreans to school. Thus, we are very grateful to (the owner of this land) America."[18]

Though they were building "a new Korean society" in America, they could not allow themselves to become settlers. At the heart of their community was the struggle for Korean independence from Japan. Sojourners when they had left Choson between 1903 and 1905, they had suddenly become *yumin*, drifting people, after their homeland had been annexed by Japan in 1910. The first generation of Koreans in America, explained Chang Lee-wook, "suffered more mentally . . . than the succeeding generations," for they had been brutally detached from their country. Shortly after annexation, the *Sinhan Minbo* cried: "Korea is dead and no person is as sad as the person without a country." The Korean National Association angrily called for a "complete cessation of any association with the Japanese because normally one does not associate with the murderer of one's parents, and Japan had murdered our fatherland." Grieving over their loss, they became even more tightly bound to their homeland and were driven by a new "necessity" — the need to free Korea from Japanese colonialism.[19]

Life in America, for Korean migrants, had to be organized around the independence movement. As Korean businessmen increased their profits, they also gave more to the patriotic cause. In 1918, for example, Korean rice farmers in the Sacramento Valley contributed $42,955 to the Korean National Association. Individual contributions were sometimes as high as thirty-four hundred dollars, and many of them were over a thousand dollars. Kim Hyung-soon had originally left Korea seeking freedom from Japanese rule, but he insistently maintained his Korean national identity. Interviewed in 1975, at the age of eighty-nine, he explained that he had fought for the restoration of Korean sovereignty and wanted to die as a Korean. Asked about his last wish, he replied: "I would like to go back to Korea and work for the country."[20]

The nationalist movement gave many migrants a profound sense of purpose. Korean "farmers, waiters, and domestic servants by day," observed scholar Elaine Kim, "became independence workers by night." They found community and identity in patriotic organizations. "I was earning money then," recalled a woman who lived in Dinuba in 1919, "and decided that I wanted to become a member of the Korean Nationalist Association, pay dues to support the Korean newspaper, and also to contribute to the patriotic fund. I gave one-tenth of my pay — which was optional for women, but I felt so good to be able to do so." Involvement in the struggle offered meaning to her life in a bleak and harsh America. "On work days, I put on my work clothes and worked in the fields with the men — a lunch bucket hung over my shoulder. Sundays, I would dress up in my clean Sunday clothes and go to worship. I felt no sadness, just lots of enthusiasm and happiness in just being able to do something."[21]

For this woman and her compatriots, the church was an important engine of Korean nationalism. "The Christian Church," the *Kongnip Sinmun* declared in 1906, would "guide the future of Korean civilization." Korean migrants felt they were a stranded people. "A people without a country must have something to believe in and to hold on to," a community leader told his compatriots. "In Christian principles we have found a pattern for our future — both as individuals and as a nation." The Korean Methodist Church of San Francisco held its first service in October 1905, and the Korean Presbyterian Church was established in Los Angeles a year later. Within ten years, there were twelve Korean churches in California. The churches functioned as the religious arm of patriotic political organizations. Ministers like the Reverends Yi Tae-wi, Hwang Sa-yong, and Min Ch'an-ho were presidents of the Korean National Association. The church was an important center for the dispersed rural Korean community. In Dinuba, for example, Koreans from the San Joaquin Valley gathered at church on Sundays to worship, socialize, and renew their commitment to the liberation of their homeland. Their churches became forums for nationalistic education, sponsoring debates on topics such as "Jesus Christ and the Future of Korea," "The Relationship of Korea and Christianity," and "The Duty of Koreans Abroad." "If the Koreans gathered together," a migrant observed, "it was usually to worship in church or to protest against the Japanese oppression in Korea." A nationalist who lived in Los Angles in the 1920s, Louise Yim similarly noted: "The Korean's social life in the United States consisted of two main activities: politics and religion." Actually both served a common purpose.[22]

The migrants' passionate patriotism also conditioned their commitment to education. "We can crush the enemy [Japan] with learning," argued the *Kongnip Sinmun,* "and without learning our land is not ours. . . . We can study a full week, through only 4–5 hours of labor, and only three summer months of work will finance a year of education. If we are unable to attend day school, we can always go to night school." By 1920, Koreans on the mainland had the lowest illiteracy rate of all Asian immigrant groups — only 8 percent compared to 11 percent for the Japanese and 20 percent for the Chinese. They were not far behind the 4 percent illiteracy rate for whites. Believing language was a vital basis for a Korean cultural and national identity, parents established Korean-language schools in Sacramento, San Francisco, Dinuba, Reedley, Delano, Stockton, Manteca, Riverside, Claremont, Upland, and Los Angeles. "Let us think of the future Korean community of ten years from now," urged a Korean writer in *Sinhan Minbo.* "If we want to start afresh our Korean community, we should give serious thought to our children's education and have schools that would give them a Korean education." The second generation attended Korean-language schools in addition to American schools. "The happiest moment for my parents," said a student, "was when I came home with the certificate of graduation from my Korean language school."[23]

Korean family life was organized around the movement for Korean independence. Korean mothers were determined to raise their children as Koreans. Children "spoke Korean at home and, when they were old enough, dated Koreans their own age," recalled American-born Gloria Hahn. They were sent to Korean churches and taken to Korean-independence meetings on March 1; they celebrated the Korean king's birthday. Home, family, church, and nation were organically integrated in the life of the Korean community. "My mother stayed home to raise a family," Hahn said, "breaking the monotony of homemaking by being a charter member of the Korean Women's Patriotic League, writing for Korean newspapers, and working actively in her church."[24]

Driving the nationalist movement in America were the political organizations. As early as 1903, Korean migrants in Hawaii organized the Sinmin-hoe, or New People's Association, to support the independent sovereignty of Korea; two years later, Koreans in San Francisco organized the Kongnip Hyop-hoe. This mutual-assistance association helped fellow newcomers find housing and employment and also spearheaded the resistance against Japanese colonialism. Korean political organizations quickly proliferated in Hawaii and on the mainland. There were fifteen in the islands, including the Ewa Chinmok-hoe, Waipahu Kongdong-hoe, Kungmin Tanhap-hoe, and Singan-hoe, and five on the mainland — the Kongnip Hyop-hoe, Taedong Kyoyuk-hoe, Seattle Sinhung Tongmang-hoe, Chicago Kongjae-hoe, and New York Kongjae-hoe. In 1909, the patriots founded the Tae-Hanin Kungmin-hoe (THK), or Korean National Association of North America, in order to consolidate and coordinate the resistance efforts of the many nationalist organizations. The purpose of this new organization was the preservation of a Korean national identity and "the regaining of the independence of the fatherland by promoting education and business, advocating freedom and equality, and enhancing the honor of our countrymen." Headquartered in San Francisco, the Tae-Hanin Kungmin-hoe had chapters on the mainland and in Hawaii and required all Korean migrants to become members and pay dues to the organization.[25]

The independence movement in America was divided in leadership and strategy. Park Yong-man represented the activist and militant approach, Syngman Rhee emphasized education and diplomacy, and Ahn Ch'ang-ho called for the development of a patriotic leadership. The movement spawned numerous publications — the *Sinhan Minbo* (*New Korea*), the *Kongnip Sinmun* (*Korean News*), the *T'aep'yongyang Chubo* (*Korean Pacific Weekly*), and the *Sin Han'guk po* (*New Korean News*). These newspapers and magazines informed Korean migrants about the nationalist activities in America and in the homeland and kept alive the spirit of *aeguk chongsin* (patriotism) and the dream of *kwangbok* (restoration of sovereignty for their homeland).

Many nationalists advocated armed resistance. "We shall overcome this crisis by resorting to arms and blood," editorialized the *Sinhan Minbo*. "In order to kill all traitors and to crush the Japanese, it is necessary to resort to pistols and sword and it can be accomplished only through spilling our blood and sacrificing our lives." Korean quasi-military training programs were established in the United States to prepare for armed struggle against the Japanese in Korea. In Hawaii, Park Yong-man formed a military corps composed of three hundred soldiers, and "military academies" were established in Claremont and Lompoc, California. In Willows, California, nationalists began operating the Pilot Training School in 1920. Staffed by six Korean teachers and an American engineer, it had nineteen students, training them in three airplanes donated by "rice king" Kim Chong-nim. "When Korea is armed to such an extent that she can meet the foe on something like an even footing, victory will be ours," declared a Korean community leader. "We Koreans want to be in the fight. Actually, all Koreans have a date with the Japs, and the sooner we are able to keep it, the better."[26]

"Singly and collectively they hate the Japanese; all Japanese," an observer reported in the 1930s. Anti-Japanese sentiments were pervasive in the Korean-immigrant community. "DON'T BUY THE JAP'S SOY SAUCE. Now we produce better soy sauce in taste and color. Order now," insisted an advertisement in a Korean newspaper. Korean migrants detested being associated with the Japanese. After the earthquake had destroyed the buildings of the Mutual Assistance Association and the Korean church in San Francisco, the association announced it did not want any assistance from the Japanese: "We are calling your attention to the fact that we are anti-Japanese, so we shall not accept any relief fund from the Japanese consulate. We shall reject interference of Japanese authorities in our community affairs in any manner. No matter how great a plight we are in, we must always refuse Japanese help. We'd rather die free than under Japanese jurisdiction." Again, seven years later, Koreans scorned Japanese assistance. After eleven Korean farm workers had been beaten by whites in Riverside, a Japanese consulate official from Los Angeles visited the victims and offered help. Immediately the THK protested the involvement of a Japanese government official in Korean-immigrant affairs. In a telegram sent to Secretary of State William Jennings Bryan, the nationalist organization explained: "Please regard us not as Japanese in the time of peace and war. We Koreans came to America before Japan's annexation of Korea and we will never submit to her so long as the sun remains in heaven."[27]

Korean hatred for Japan grew as the immigrants realized how they had been cut off from the land of their birth. "My mother longed to go back to Korea," a daughter said, "but the thought of the Japanese made her shudder." Under Japanese rule, Korea had become a "tiger's cage" and a "snake-hell." Korean migrants who had returned to their homeland were appalled by Japanese oppression and warned their countrymen in America to stay away from Korea. "It is very difficult to describe the situation at home," wrote Cho Mun-chan, a returnee, in a letter published in the *Sinhan Minbo* in 1911, "and it is awfully hard to live under these conditions. I am chained now, after having lived freely in America. . . . I have only one request of you — please arrange my passage to America."[28]

They could not go home again, not until Choson had been freed from Japanese imperialism. "Without National Independence," proclaimed an editorial in the *Sinhan Minbo,* "We Have No Country To Return To. We are a conquered people. Occasionally, Koreans in America think they can return home, but they are not thinking whether they have their country or home. How we Koreans in America dare to forget prison-like Korea! and try to return to that place! We must struggle in exile. Yes, we shall return when we have a freedom bell and a national flag."[29]

Grieving over the loss of his homeland, a migrant urged his compatriots in America to dedicate themselves to nationalistic resistance: they did not want to become "new world citizens." "Now our business should be for all Koreans and our activity should be based on the welfare of our mother country. Thus we are not sojourners, but political wanderers, and we are not laborers but righteous army soldiers." Korean nationalists elevated the THK into their government in exile, representing them in their relations with the

U.S. government. A stateless people, the migrants would create a sovereign Korea in America.[30]

In America, Koreans felt a special mission to redeem their violated country. Safe here, they admired the patriots struggling against Japanese colonialism in Korea and honored their brave armed resistance of 1907–1909. They would not allow themselves to forget the 14,556 Koreans killed and 32,993 wounded during the insurrection against Japanese imperialism. They kept alive stories of Japanese atrocities: "One lady said that her brother had died in Korea from back injuries suffered from persistent Japanese floggings. Another told of the burning of a Christian church filled with a worshipping congregation. A third told of Japanese wholesale mistreatment of Korean-Christians who were tied by the thumbs to the ceiling and left to die by painful hanging. Still another related in detail the brutal mistreatment of the women who were physically tortured and mutilated for the 'savage satisfaction' of the Japanese men." Koreans in America repeated such stories and drew from them the emotional sustenance they needed for their cause.[31]

The Korean rage against Japanese colonialism exploded in 1908 when a Korean nationalist assassinated Durham Stevens. An American, Stevens had been employed by the Japanese government. His mission was to calm American business fears of Japanese control of Korea and to convince the U.S. government that the Korean people themselves welcomed and benefited from the Japanese protectorate. To the Korean immigrants, Stevens was a traitor, a "Japanese dog." En route from Korea to Washington, Stevens had stopped in San Francisco, and statements by Stevens justifying Japanese rule over Korea had been published in the local newspaper. Infuriated, the Korean community demanded Stevens meet with Korean representatives and retract his statements.[32] On March 23, a group of angry Koreans directly confronted Stevens in front of the Ferry Building, and one of them, Chang In-hwan, shot Stevens. Stevens died in the hospital, and Chang was charged with murder and sent to prison.

Chang immediately became a national hero for many Korean migrants. He was honored as an *Uisa* — a righteous person or a martyr who engages in terrorism for the sake of national independence. Contributions for Chang's defense flowed generously from Korea, Japan, Siberia, Manchuria, Mexico, and the United States. Koreans here gave the most — $4,696 — many of them donating their entire week's earnings to the defense. In court, Chang declared:

"I was born on March 30, 1875, in a northern Korean province and became a baptized Christian in my early age. When I saw my country fall into the hands of the Japanese, I was filled with sorrow, but I was unable to do much to help. I came to Hawaii as an immigrant to learn something in order to help my country. . . . While hundreds of thousands of Koreans are dying at the hands of the Japanese invaders, Stevens has the effrontery to invent the lie that the Koreans are welcoming their Japanese aggressors. . . . As a traitor to Korea, Stevens . . . made the Japanese occupation of Korea possible. . . . To die for having shot a traitor is a glory, because I did it for my people." In an editorial entitled, "The Sound of Two Bullets Cry for the Spirit of Freedom," the San Francisco *Kongnip Sinmun* justified the assassination: "Come Patriots! Come Patriots! Let us wake by the sound of the pistol. If you have zeal and thought, you must see Chang In-hwan as a patriot. It is right to attack everyone who hurts our compatriots and our country, so that every one of our 20,000,000 people may fight for the liberty and independence of our country to the end." The Korean immigrants, a Korean woman commented, were "insane about independence."[33]

Many Korean nationalists were driven by a patriotic fury. They lived "in a narrow world, a small world in a large," immigrant Younghill Kang sadly wrote in his novel *East Goes West,* published in 1937. "No message came back and forth from the large world to the little nor from the little world to the large." A character in the novel epitomizes this restrictive realm.

> [Pak] was a most typical Korean, an exile only in body, not in soul. Western civilization had rolled over him as water over a rock. He was a very strong nationalist; so he always sat in at the Korean Christian services, because they had sometimes to do with nationalism. With his hard-earned money, he supported all societies for Korean revolution against Japan. Most of his relations had moved out of Korea since the Japanese occupation — into Manchuria and Russia — but Pak still lived believing that the time must come to go back, and even now, with a little money sent in care of a brother-in-law, he had bought a minute piece of land to the north of Seoul. For fifteen years his single ambition had been to get back there and settle down. On Korean land, he wanted to raise 100 percent Korean children, who would be just as patriotic as himself. . . .[34]

Korea had become, for Pak, a single-minded subject. Kang's protagonist Chungpa Han offers to read the newspaper to Pak, but

Pak is "only interested to know what had happened in the Korean revolution, which had already quieted down. At least in the American newspapers." Bound to their past by the loss of their home country, Korean migrants were unable to have a future in America. "With Korean culture at a dying gasp, being throttled wherever possible by the Japanese, with conditions at home ever tragic and uncertain, life for us [Koreans in America] was tied by a slenderer thread to the homeland than for the Chinese. Still it was tied. Koreans thought of themselves as exiles, not as immigrants."[35]

But Han himself does not share the patriotic zeal of his countrymen. "It was as if I saw Korea receding farther and farther from me," he says. The nationalistic passion of Koreans only "italicizes" his own loneliness in the Korean community where the homeland is "constantly" kept before migrants' eyes. Still Han sees they have a country and an identity, and he seems to have neither. He thinks he has been westernized and cannot go home, back to Korea, except for a "visit."[36]

But as a Korean, Han feels unwelcome in America. He is told by an American senator: "Young man, I can see you have come to America to stay, and I'm proud and glad. Now you must definitely make up your mind to *be* American. Don't say, 'I'm Korean' when you're asked. Say 'I'm an American.' " Han realizes that the senator has no understanding of his plight as an Asian immigrant. "But an Oriental has a hard time in America," responds Han. "He is not welcome much." The senator would have none of Han's explanation and loudly insists: "There shouldn't be any buts about it! Believe in America with all your heart. . . . I tell you, sir, you belong here. You should be one of us." And Han tries again in vain: "But legally I am denied."[37]

Han's estrangement from the land of his birth and the land he hopes would adopt him haunts him in a recurring dream. In this dream, Han climbs a tree and sees a "hairlike bridge" stretching across the ocean to Korea. "Creeping across this bridge and beckoning with eyes of glee" are Yunkoo and Chak-doo-shay — the boys he had played with as a child. Then he sees at the other end of the bridge "a paradise of wild and flowery magic, with mountains and waterfalls and little gushing streams." Han struggles to reach the bridge, which seems somehow attached to his tree, as he hears Yunkoo and Chak-doo-shay daring him to follow them. They are "standing up now and running back and forth like men on a tightrope across the little trembling bridge." Han almost reaches the bridge.

But suddenly, things begin tumbling out of his pockets, "money and keys, contracts and business letters. Especially the key to [his] car, [his] American car." Sliding down the tree, Han grubs in the leaves and sticks on the ground, anxiously looking for the car key. But then, still searching for the key, Han descends the steps into "a dark and cryptlike cellar" where he finds some "frightened-looking Negroes." The key to an American car, a symbol of success, is denied to him as he is driven downward into a degraded racial caste. Then, looking outside through an iron grating, Han sees a terrifying mob of red-faced men with clubs and knives, shouting "fire, bring fire."[38]

Growing Up Korean American

Like Han, many second-generation Koreans also found themselves floating "insecurely, in the rootless groping fashion of men hung between two worlds." They did not share the fierce nationalistic spirit of the *ilse*, their immigrant parents. They represented, in the eyes of many immigrant Koreans, the second-generation "problem" — the "hyphenized Koreans" who had "very little knowledge of and appreciation for their ancestral connections." They did not seem to give "a rap" for their Korean roots. "To them only the glimmer and comforts of American life appeal; nothing else matters," immigrant Koreans complained about the *ise*, or second generation. In his advice to his children and grandchildren, Whang Sa Sun declared: "Keep your Koreanness. Don't lose your Korean spirit. Even though you are an American citizen, you have to remember our ancestors, our people. I don't want my children's children to forget their own country. Even though they weren't born there, or don't know the history or customs, I want them to keep the Korean spirit."[39]

But second-generation Koreans found they could not easily keep something they never had. Born in California, Jean Park grew up in the San Joaquin Valley, and her story can give us a glimpse into the experiences of young Koreans in America and the formation of a Korean-American identity.

As a child, Jean Park lived in Taft. She noticed that the community was "predominantly Caucasian and Caucasians ran the town." The small town had a main street with "one big general store and a couple of other shops that were operated by Caucasians." "At that time," she said years later, "we were the only Orientals living in Taft. There were a few Mexicans . . . and they were looked down upon. The Caucasians used to call them 'Wetbacks.' " Jean, her brother, and her sister played together all of the time, for "nobody ever came by our house to call us out to play." When Jean and her family went to town, they became the targets of stares, as though they were "criminals or something." The Caucasian children would laugh and make faces at them. But their encounters with whites were not always negative. "One day I came home from school and found the Caucasian widow, who lived across the street, crying on my mother's shoulder," recalled Jean. "She had injured herself seriously and one of her daughters had died in an automobile accident. This lady was a warm-hearted person and she treated us like her family. The incident stands out in my memory because it was the only time that a Caucasian person had come to us for sympathy."[40]

Like most of the workers in Taft, Jean's father was employed by the Standard Oil Company. "Though I never heard him speak English in our home, I remember he used English when he spoke with Caucasians," she said. "He must have learned English from the missionaries in Korea." Her father was at least twenty years older than her mother. Jean's mother was as big as her husband, "about five feet ten inches," and weighed "at least a hundred and sixty-five pounds but none of it was fat." She did all the housework, raised the children, and also did laundry for Caucasians. She was extremely resourceful. Initially unable to speak English, she figured out how to ask for what she needed. "At the time I didn't speak a word of English," her mother said, "so it was hard to get around." One day her landowner, a Mr. Williams, asked her whether she needed anything at the grocery store. "I didn't know how to say 'egg,' so I crumpled a white handkerchief into a ball and I then imitated a chicken laying an egg. I moved my arms like a chicken and I made noises like a chicken. Then I tried to get some beef; so I imitated a cow who went 'moo-oo.' Mr. Williams got a real big kick when he saw what I did and he nearly fell over from laughing so hard."[41]

A Korean nationalist, Jean's mother constantly talked about "her hope for Korea's freedom from Japan. She devoted what time she had to Korea's fight for independence and even gave some of her savings to the movement. Her life-long ambition was to return to a free Korea." She loved Korean songs, and would often sing:

> *Ari-rang, Ari-rang, A-ra-ri-yo*
> *He is going over the Ari-rang Hill*
> *Since he leaves me all alone*
> *He'll have a pain in his foot without going very far.*

She taught her children how to speak, read, and write Korean, and she also introduced them to Korean customs. "Many of the books we used came from Korea," Jean remembered, "and some of the books were borrowed from other Koreans. My mother was very strict. We had to memorize everything perfectly. She taught us the numbers, 'hanna, tul, saette . . .' and the alphabets and we repeated after her."[42]

Korean bachelors from nearby towns often visited Jean's family in Taft. They sat around with her parents, always talking about Korea. One of the *chong gak* was a sort of uncle to Jean and her siblings — a Mr. Kim, who was forty years old and worked as a dishwasher. Whenever Mr. Kim visited her family, he played with the children, and together they spent afternoons extravagantly. "In his old black limousine that looked like a hearse," Jean lovingly recounted, "he would drive us everywhere. Sometimes he drove us to nearby towns and other times we went to the mountains. When he drove us to town he treated us to ice-cream, soda, and candy." They would take hikes in the mountains, and he would chase the children up and down the hills. "He was very generous and loved children even though he didn't have kids of his own."[43]

At an early age, Jean realized her parents preferred sons. "My father expected a boy but instead I was born. I felt sorry for my father and I tried hard to please him whenever I could." She also found that her mother "favored boys over girls too because when she had her next child, a son, she rejoiced happily. She even went out of her way to make my brother happy. Though she did little things for my brother, I noticed them."[44]

Jean never forgot the summer afternoon her father charged through the door of their house cursing in Korean. Jean knew something was wrong because he had never come home so early. "What happened? Why did you come home from work?" her mother asked apprehensively. "I'm fired!" he exploded. Jean overheard her father say that a "jealous Caucasian" did not like him because he was "Oriental" and had urged the supervisor to fire him. "When my mother heard the story she swore that she would kill this Caucasian man and then said that she would castrate the fellow."[45]

After her father's dismissal from Standard Oil, her mother "became the dominant one in the family. She wore the pants in the family and made all of the important decisions. My father and the rest of us listened to everything she told us to do." She decided to raise chickens, and the family built a large chicken coop for five hundred chicks. "The business prospered well for a few months," Jean said. "Then I remember we woke up one morning to feed the chickens but when we got to the chicken coop the fences were ripped apart." Most of the chickens were gone. Angrily they drove toward town. On the way they saw a truck with two Caucasian men in the front and chickens in the back. "We stared at them suspiciously but then we drove on. My mother and father were so upset they didn't stop the men in the truck but I knew they were the ones who stole our chickens and ruined the chicken coop. For a long time I remembered their faces. After this incident the whole family took a dislike to Caucasians and we never associated with them until we moved to Reedley."[46]

Reedley had a main street with gas stations, grocery and hardware stores, and two theaters. "The people in Reedley lived segregated according to race," Jean noticed. "One race lived in one section of town and another race lived in another section." There were Mexicans, Japanese, Chinese, Koreans, Germans, and Italians. "Most of the Chinese had private businesses like grocery stores and restaurants. They formed a tightly knit community of their own residing mainly in one section of the town." Similarly, the Japanese had their own little community of Japanese grocery stores, sundae shops, barbershops, and hardware stores. Many of the Japanese were farmers and lived on the edge of town. "There were ten to twelve Korean families who lived a mile or two apart from each other. Most of the Korean families worked as farm workers and they barely made a living." The Korean community in Reedley was continually growing, with Koreans migrating from Colorado and Montana as well as Oregon and Washington. "Every year the Korean community got bigger and bigger until there were at least a hundred or two hundred."[47]

Racial and ethnic boundaries were drawn sharply in Reedley. German parents never allowed their children to play with Koreans, and whenever Jean and other Korean children walked past their houses the German children would all stare and make faces at them. Similarly the Japanese shunned the Koreans. "On the whole the Japanese looked down upon the Koreans," Jean recalled. "They felt superior to us. Rarely was there a Japanese boy or girl who treated a Korean boy or girl equally." But the ethnic lines became loosened in places. "Most of the Japanese knew us well because my mother spoke Japanese fluently. Although we were poor the Japanese grocers gave us charge accounts because they all knew my mother." Jean and her family also found the Italian families "very friendly." The

Italian families, like the Koreans, lived "on the poor side of town," and Jean's family became good friends with the Buccis, who were recent immigrants.[48]

In Reedley, Jean's father worked as a farm laborer. He made very little money and the family continued to face financial hardships. Poverty among the Koreans created a sense of community as they reached out to one another for support. "One thing I'll never forget about the Lees is that they were very understanding and they always helped other Koreans," said Jean. "If ever a Korean needed financial or other help the Lees were the first to volunteer. I guess they lived such a hard life themselves that they were always willing to lend a helping hand."[49]

"The church was the center of the Korean community," Jean remembered, "and the independence movement seemed to unite the first generation immigrants." Reedley did not have a Korean church, so Koreans in the San Joaquin Valley traveled on Sundays to the Korean church in Dinuba to attend worship services and get together. The minister was from Korea. When he prayed, "he rocked up and down on the balls of his feet. . . . He baptized my brother, sister, and me at a nearby river in Dinuba. He dunked my head below the surface of the water and chanted a prayer. Meanwhile I must have swallowed at least a cup of water. I didn't like being christened at all." Later the Kim Brothers Company (of nectarine fame) donated the money to build a big church for the Koreans in Reedley. "They could afford to give the money because they owned a fruit and produce farm that prospered."[50]

Jean's family moved periodically, from Reedley to Sanger, then back to Reedley. "Like my family, most of the Koreans were poor and they had to move a lot so that they could improve their socio-economic status," she explained. "There was no choice. They had to keep moving until they could get firmly established." In Sanger, her mother was almost able to establish a profitable family business. She had learned to make liquor from the Italian landlady. "During the prohibition era," Jean said, "we prospered from the sale of liquor. We made the liquor in a bathtub in our basement. Then we bottled it and I tapped the bottles. Afterwards my brother, Bill, and I stacked the bottles. My mother sold the liquor to the men who lived in the boarding house but my father drank it too." Forty to fifty men, mostly Korean bachelors, lived in the boarding house. One of the men had a fifteen-year-old son living with him. The son did not go to school because he had to work, and his father used all the money they earned drinking liquor.[51]

With the money made from bootlegging, Jean's mother invested in a trucking business, shipping fruit and vegetables from farms in the San Joaquin Valley to the produce markets in Los Angeles. But meanwhile her father was drinking heavily. Soon he developed bleeding ulcers from drinking and was hospitalized. The hospital bills cost so much they had to close down the trucking business, and then they exhausted most of their savings. "One day we woke up and found my father hanging from the tree. He hung himself. After that night our dog howled every day at night and it bothered us because it reminded us of the hanging so we had to shoot the dog." Jean remembered how her mother was terribly distraught and how a Caucasian lady who lived across the street "came over every day to bring back my mother's faith. She was an understanding lady. Every single day she cooked food for my mother and saw to it that my mother gained her strength back. 'Now you have a family to take care of,' she told my mother. 'So you can't let this upset you. You've got to take care of all your children.'" Jean's mother recovered, but it was difficult, especially during the Great Depression: she had to depend on welfare and worked as a farm laborer whenever she could.[52]

At school in the San Joaquin Valley, Jean and other Korean children felt different, like strangers among the white children and teachers. "It took me several months before I could understand the English language and my teacher," Jean recounted. "Whenever my teacher said anything to me I just nodded my head and pretended as if I knew what she said. Most of the children ignored me in school until I began to pick up the English language; so I was a loner in the beginning." But the loneliness was not simply the result of language inadequacy. "I felt out of place because wherever I turned I saw kids with blonde hair and blue eyes." Jean and her sister wore dresses and her brother blue jeans, and they tried to look American. "During lunchtime we ate in the school cafeteria since my mother felt that it would embarrass us to take rice and kimchee." They were afraid the white children would call them "hot pepper eaters and garlic eaters."[53]

But gradually Jean and other Korean children developed friendships with Italian, Portuguese, Mexican, and even Japanese children. "I was lucky," said Jean after commenting on Japanese prejudice against Koreans, "because I found a Japanese girl friend who was very nice and we got along well." One of the daughters of the Bucci family was the same age as Jean, and the two became best friends. In the spring the two friends had fun picking berries and mushrooms at a nearby river. "We practically lived at each other's homes." One of her brother's close friends was a Mexican boy. The children of different ethnic groups would go swimming together in the river and attended vacation Bible school together. In junior high school they went to dances. "Sometimes we drove up to Visalia on Fridays," said Jean, "because Chinese boys held dances there." "All of us could jitter-bug very well," Jean boasted. Despite her mother's insistence that she date only Korean boys, Jean's sister had Japanese boyfriends, and she "dated an Italian boy who worked for Safeway Grocery and she also went out with a Mexican boy." Jean and other young Koreans also listened to the radio. "Sometimes we just stayed at home and listened to the radio programs such as Amos and Andy . . . Fibber McGee and Molly, and others. . . . We didn't have television at that time but we still enjoyed ourselves as we laughed throughout every funny radio program."[54]

Growing up in America, second-generation Koreans seemed to drift away from the determined nationalism of their parents. "My mother got involved in Korean politics and she was a real patriot," Jean recalled. "All of the first generation Koreans joined the independence movement and they donated their money to people like Mr. [Syngman] Rhee. Most of us second generation Koreans didn't join the independence movement but we just watched all the elderly Koreans." Jean Park and most of her fellow second-generation Koreans stayed on the sidelines. They had not even been to Korea. They had difficulty feeling the painful loss of the homeland and understanding the indignity of Japanese domination. They did not harbor a hatred for the Japanese; in school and on the playground, they even had Japanese friends. They did not sadly see themselves as drifting or abandoned people, as did the first generation.[55]

Young Korean Americans witnessed a widening division between the two generations. The "elders tried to influence the children with their native customs and ideas," but the younger generation "took to an American idea rapidly." "By law I am American and by heart I am American," said a Korean youth, "although I am not of the same color or race." They heard their parents talking about the struggle for Korean independence, but they did not "pay any attention to it." They read community newspapers like the *New Korea*, but "the news in the paper had little significance to them." A young Korean expressed the feelings of many second-generation Koreans: "So far I have read very little about my parents' native land. I have never felt a sense of pride in knowing about my parents' native land but I have pity and sympathy for them." Their future, as second-generation Koreans saw it, was in America, not Korea.[56]

8

"The Tide of Turbans"
Asian Indians in America

In 1865, the Hawaiian Board of Immigration sent labor agent William Hillebrand to China to recruit laborers, instructing him to proceed from China to the East Indies to investigate the possibility of India as a labor source. Hillebrand was not able to complete his mission, but Hawaiian planters continued to cultivate an interest in procuring laborers from India. "Where shall we look for the kind of immigrants we need to supply us with both a homogeneous population and labor?" asked the *Pacific Commercial Advertiser* in 1874. "We answer, to the East Indies. From the teeming millions of Bengal and other provinces of Hindostan." Seven years later, planters appealed to the Hawaiian Minister of Foreign Affairs for his "assistance in removing the obstacles in the way of introducing East Indian Coolies into these islands." In 1884, when they learned that Japan had decided to permit emigration to the islands, the planters turned away from India for their labor needs.[1]

Twenty years later, Asian Indians suddenly began appearing in the lumber towns of Washington and the agricultural fields of California. By 1920, some sixty-four hundred had entered the United States. Many of them had carried "extravagant" dreams to America, but all became "strangers," driven by a new "necessity" here. Like the Koreans, they did not develop a colony or distinct ethnic community with geographical boundaries. A small and somewhat dispersed group, they did not form an Indiatown. Theirs is an especially interesting and important story. Asian Indians represented a new diversity in the Asian migrations east to America. Though they were, like their Asian brethren, "strangers from a different shore," they were Caucasian.

Dark Caucasians: The "Hindoo Question"

The Asian Indians were, as one of them wrote in a description of his fellow newcomers, "picturesque":

> All Hindoos who come to America have hair varying in hue from brownish-black to purplish or an intense raven-black. . . . The hide of the Hindoo varies from the dull, pale, sallow-brown of a Mexican to the extreme black of an African. The man who hails from the highlands of northwestern Hindustan is a shade darker than olive. A few coming from Kashmir have fair skins, light hair and blue eyes. Those who come from the low plains have darker complexions and an extremely sun-burnt appearance. . . . They have intelligent faces, keen eyes, compressed lips and determined chins. This type of countenance is distinctly Aryan, as all Hindoos who come to the land of the Stars and Stripes are descended from the same branch of the human family as the Anglo-Saxons.[2]

Called "Hindus" in America, only a small fraction of the Asian-Indian immigrants were actually believers of Hinduism. One third were Muslim, and the majority were Sikhs. As believers of Sikhism, they were required to wear the "five *k*'s" — *kes* (unshorn hair and beard), *kacch* (trousers to the knee), *kara* (iron bangle), *kirpan* (sword) or *khanda* (dagger), and *khanga* (hair comb).[3]

Wearing their traditional headdress, the newcomers from India were described as "the tide of turbans." "Always the turban remains," a witness wrote, "the badge and symbol of their native land, their native customs and religion. Whether repairing tracks on the long stretches of the Northern Pacific railways, feeding logs into the screaming rotary saws of the lumber-mills, picking fruit in the luxuriant orchards or sunny hillsides of California, the twisted turban shows white or brilliant . . . an exotic thing in the western landscape." Their different dress and their dark skin provoked taunts and verbal abuse from whites. "I used to go to Marysville every Saturday," recounted a Sikh. "One day a drunk *ghora* (white man) came out of a bar and motioned to me saying, 'Come here, slave!' I said I was no slave man. He told me that his race ruled India and America, too. All we were slaves. He came close to me and I hit him and got away fast."[4]

While Asian-Indian immigrants found themselves called "niggers," they were more frequently associated with the Chinese and Japanese. "Sixty years' contact with the Chinese, and twenty-five years' experience with the Japanese and two or three years' acquaintance with Hindus," declared American Federation of Labor president Samuel Gompers in 1908, "should be sufficient to convince any ordinarily intelligent person that they have no standards . . . by which a Caucasian may judge them." The Asiatic Exclusion League agreed, blaming the Japanese and the Asian Indians for the violence directed against them: "In California the insolence and presumption of Japanese, and the immodest and filthy habits of the Hindoos are continually involving them in trouble, beatings. . . . In all these cases, we may say the Oriental is at fault." In 1910 *Collier's Weekly* claimed that the immigrants from India were "inferior workmen," differing from "the unobtrusive Chinaman by being sullen and uncompromising."[5]

In "The West and the Hindu Invasion" published in the *Overland Monthly* in 1908, Agnes Foster Buchanan described the waves of different Asian immigrants entering and threatening American society. First came the Chinese, but the exclusion laws barred the "coolies" from America. But while the Chinese "stood knocking at our outer doors," the Japanese, "not waiting for permission, crept stealthily past the suppliants, entered and took possession. When San Francisco awoke from her short sleep, she found herself face to face with the Japanese question, infinitely greater and more insidious in its influence than the Chinese problem had ever threatened to be. . . ." While white Americans wondered what should be done about the Japanese, they suddenly noticed another group of "strangers" — the "Hindus." "Tall of stature, straight of feature, swarthy of color," they were unlike the Chinese and Japanese in an important way: they were "brothers" of "our own race," "full-blooded Aryans," "men of like progenitors with us." But like the Chinese and Japanese, the "Hindus" were willing to work for "cheap" wages and able to "subsist on incomes that would be prohibitive to the white man." Calling for legislation to exclude Asian Indians from America, Buchanan urged white Americans "to tell our brothers of the East" that while the earth was large enough for everyone, there was no one part of it that could "comfortably accommodate both branches of the Aryan family."[6]

Two years later, in *Forum* magazine, Herman Scheffauer conveyed a similar message in sterner, more hysterical language. Asian

Indians, he warned, represented the spectre of a new "Yellow Peril." "This time the chimera is not the saturnine, almond-eyed mask, the shaven head, the snaky pig-tail of the multitudinous Chinese, nor the close-cropped bullet-heads of the suave and smiling Japanese, but a face of finer features, rising, turbaned out of the Pacific and bringing a new and anxious question. . . ." Noting how the Chinese had been kept within the "circle of their lowly labors," and how the "brown, busy little men from Nippon" were "gradually ceasing to be the servants of the Americans" and becoming "dangerous rivals," Scheffauer warned that the "Hindoo invasion" of this "dark, mystic race" was "yet in its infancy," only the "head of the long procession" entering the Golden Gate.[7]

Asian Indians were especially feared as labor competitors by white workers and were often victimized by white working-class antagonism and violence. In September 1907, several hundred white workers invaded the Asian-Indian community in Bellingham, Washington, and drove seven hundred Asian Indians across the border into Canada. Two months later, white workers forcibly rounded up Asian Indians in Everett and expelled them from the town. In San Francisco, the Asiatic Exclusion League issued warnings of the new "menace" from India. Addressing the "Hindoo question," the league denounced the immigrants as competitors of white labor and as dirty, lustful, and diseased. "From every part of the Coast," the league claimed, "complaints are made of the undesirability of the Hindoos, their lack of cleanliness, disregard of sanitary laws, petty pilfering, especially of chickens, and insolence to women."[8]

In response to exclusionist pressures, immigration officials targeted Asian Indians seeking admission to the United States. Between 1908 and 1920, they denied entry to some 3,453 Asian Indians, most of them on the grounds they would likely become public charges. In an article on "The Hindu, the Newest Immigration Problem," *Survey* magazine editorialized in 1910: "The civic and social question concerns the ability of the nation to assimilate this class of Hindus and their probable effect on the communities where they settle. Their habits, their intense caste feeling, their lack of home life — no women being among them — and their effect upon standards of labor and wages, all combine to raise a serious question as to whether the doors should be kept open or closed against this strange, new stream." Seven years later, Congress enacted an immigration restriction law which designated India as one of the Asian countries in the "barred zone" and prohibited the entry of Asian-Indian laborers. Asian Indians were not welcome in America. Even Rabindranath Tagore, the winner of the Nobel Prize for literature in 1913, unhappily discovered that his achievement did not mean greater acceptance. After lecturing in Victoria, British Columbia, in 1929, he decided to visit the United States. Tagore encountered bureaucratic problems when he applied to the American consul for entry, and then he experienced racial prejudice in Los Angeles. Canceling his tour and promptly returning to India, Tagore commented caustically: "Jesus could not get into America because, first of all, He would not have the necessary money, and secondly, He would be an Asiatic."[9]

After the enactment of the 1917 "barred zone" law, the question of the political status of Asian Indians already in the United States still remained. The federal law of 1790 had reserved naturalized citizenship to "whites" only, providing the basis for excluding Chinese, Japanese, and Korean immigrants from citizenship. But Asian Indians were Caucasian. Would they be entitled to naturalized citizenship in the United States? Seeking to set forth a distinction between Asian Indians and white Americans, the Asiatic Exclusion League conceded in 1910 that students of ethnology all agreed "the Hindus" were "members of the same family" as Americans of European ancestry. But, "as a matter of fact," the league argued, the people of the United States were "cousins, far removed, of the Hindus of the northwest provinces." The "forefathers" of white Americans "pressed to the west, in the everlasting march of conquest, progress, and civilization," while the "forefathers of the Hindus went east and became enslaved, effeminate, caste-ridden and degraded." The Western Aryans became the "Lords of Creation," while the Eastern Aryans became the "slaves of Creation." "And now we the people of the United States are asked to receive these members of a degraded race on terms of equality," the league protested. What would be the condition in California if they were allowed to become citizens and if "this horde of fanatics should be received in our midst?"[10]

Asked about Asian-Indian eligibility for citizenship, the U.S. Attorney General Charles J. Bonaparte replied in 1907: "It seems to me clear that under no construction of the law can natives of British India be regarded as white persons." But the question had to be determined in the courts. In the 1910 *U.S. v. Balsara* and the 1913 *Ajkoy Kumar Mazumdar* decisions, the courts held that Asian Indians were Caucasians and hence entitled to be considered "white persons" eligible to citizenship under the 1790 law. In the 1922 *Ozawa* decision, the Supreme Court declared that "white person" was synonymous with Caucasian and therefore that Japanese immigrants were not eligible to naturalized citizenship. Asian Indians thought that the *Ozawa* case had reinforced their status as Caucasians and their own claim for naturalized citizenship.[11]

But in 1923, their expectations were shattered: in *U.S. v. Bhagat Singh Thind*, the Supreme Court ruled that Asian Indians were ineligible to naturalization. Arguing that the definition of race had to be based on the "understanding of the common man," the Court held that the term "white person" meant an immigrant from northern or western Europe. For the "practical purposes" of the statute, the term "race" must be applied to "a group of living persons *now* possessing in common the requisite characteristics." "It may be true," the Court declared, "that the blond Scandinavian and the brown Hindu have a common ancestor in the dim reaches of antiquity, but the average man knows perfectly well that there are unmistakable and profound differences between them today." The law "does not employ the word 'Caucasian' but the words 'white persons,'" the Court explained, "and these are words of common speech and not of scientific origin. The word 'Caucasian' not only was not employed in the law but was probably wholly unfamiliar to the original framers of the statute in 1790." Thus Asian Indians, while they were "Caucasian," were not "white." The intention of the Founding Fathers was to "confer the privilege of citizenship upon that class of persons" they knew as "white."[12]

Shortly after the Supreme Court had issued its decision on the *Thind* case, an Asian-Indian immigrant wrote to Puna Singh, advising his friend to stay in India. Singh had emigrated to the United States in 1906. He became a naturalized citizen in 1920, and then returned to India and married Nand Kaur two years later. "My father's friend sent him a letter to tell him about the *Thind* decision and warn him not to try to return to America with his wife," Jane Singh said. "The decision meant my father was no longer a citizen and could not re-enter this country. But the letter did not arrive in time." As it turned out, Puna Singh managed to return with his bride. But shortly afterward, federal authorities canceled the citizenships of Singh and scores of other Asian Indians. Angrily Singh declared he had been forced to become "a citizen of no country." Fellow immigrant Vaisho Das Bagai protested the nullification of his citizenship. He had arrived here in 1915 with his family and had become a naturalized citizen. Distraught over the loss, Bagai took his life in 1928. In his suicide note, he wrote that he had tried to be "as American as possible."

"But now they come to me and say, I am no longer an American citizen. . . . What have I made of myself and my children? We cannot exercise our rights, we cannot leave this country. Humility and insults, who are responsible for all this? I do not choose to live a life of an interned person. . . . Is life worth living in a gilded cage? Obstacles this way, blockades that way, and the bridges burnt behind."[13]

A year after the *Thind* decision, Congress passed the 1924 Immigration Act, which denied immigration quotas to peoples ineligible for naturalization. The *Thind* decision also provided the basis for the application of anti-miscegenation laws to Asian-Indian men seeking to marry white women and the denial of landownership to Asian Indians under the restrictive terms of the California Alien Land Law. Within weeks after the decision, California Attorney General U. S. Webb began instituting proceedings to revoke Asian-Indian land purchases. In its editorial praising the *Thind* decision, the *Sacramento Bee* sternly supported the enforcement of the land law against Asian Indians: "The decree in a test case brings Hindu holders of land in this State, and likewise all descendants of Hindus, within the mandatory provisions of the California anti-alien land law. There must be no more leasing or sale of land to such immigrants from India."[14]

"Japanese and East Indians," an Asian Indian in California sadly observed, "either must take to day labor or get out of the country." Even before the *Thind* decision, Asian Indians had begun a return migration. Haji Muhammad Sharif Khan went back permanently in 1920. While serving in the British Police Force in Hong Kong, he had been told about opportunities in America and arrived in San Francisco in 1903. Khan first worked on a railroad near Sacramento, then became a farm laborer. In 1914, he leased land in Petaluma to raise poultry, and within a few years he had a flock of 14,000 chickens. Khan's entry into the poultry business was timely, for it became very profitable as World War I suddenly generated enormous demands for food. After the war, Khan purchased a one-way ticket for India. Between 1920 and 1940, some 3,000 Asian Indians returned to their homeland.[15]

Their exclusion from America and citizenship here underscored the importance of Indian independence from British rule. The independence movement, led by Asian-Indian students and expatriates, found support in Asian-Indian communities in the United States. In 1908, Taraknath Das, a student at the University of Washington, began publishing *Free Hindustan;* three years later, Asian-Indian intellectuals in San Francisco organized the Ghadr (meaning "revolution" or "mutiny") party. They disseminated their revolutionary message through their weekly newspaper, *Ghadr,* and visited Asian-Indian communities in Sacramento, Fresno, and Stockton, urging their countrymen to support the nationalist cause. "Most of the Indian students," noted an immigration official in 1914, "are infected with seditious ideas. Even Sikhs of the laboring class have not escaped their influence." The Ghadr movement inspired nationalism among Asian Indians in America. In their protest songs, they denounced British imperial domination of their "mother country."

Alas, dear country, to what condition hast thou been reduced!
Your whole shape has become deformed, your downfall is near.
Your whole house has been destroyed and the Goddess of Wealth
*   looted.*
Dear Mother, you are continuously robbed by the British.

The message of Ghadr had a particular appeal to Asian Indians in the United States, for they saw a relationship between the degradation of their homeland and their ill treatment here. In another protest song, the nationalists asked:

Some push us around, some curse us.
Where is your splendor and prestige today?
The whole world calls us black thieves,
The whole world calls us "coolie."
Why doesn't our flag fly anywhere?
Why do we feel low and humiliated?
Why is there no respect for us in the whole world?

But an independent and great India would bring respect for them as Asian Indians in America. In the fall of 1914, after the outbreak of World War I, some four hundred Asian Indians left America to participate in Ghadr activities in India. The uprising failed, and the movement quickly collapsed. The Ghadr base in the United States was effectively destroyed in 1917 when the federal government, under British pressure, prosecuted and imprisoned several Asian Indians for conspiracy to violate the neutrality laws.[16]

A Community of "Uncles"

While Asian-Indian immigrants were interested in political developments in their homeland, most of them were mainly concerned about their condition in America. They had come with high hopes.

"The Indian journals have been full of stories of the splendid opportunities to make money by ordinary work," reported the Reverend E. M. Wherry. "Men, receiving from 5 to 8 cents a day in India, were told that by emigrating to America they might become suddenly rich. . . . There are now thousands of these Hindu peasants who have pushed their way into America." They had hoped they would soon make their fortunes by working in the fruit orchards and sawmills at from seventy-five cents to two dollars a day.[17]

Most of the Asian-Indian immigrants had been farmers or farm laborers in the Punjab. Eighty percent came from the *jat,* or farmer caste. Shortly after their arrival, however, many Asian Indians were first employed as railroad workers. Seven hundred were reportedly involved in the construction of the Three-Mile Spring Garden Tunnel of the Western Pacific Railroad. In Tacoma, Washington, Asian Indians were used as replacements for Italian railroad strikers. "For miles their turbaned figures may be seen wielding crow-bar or shovel along the tracks," the *Forum* reported in 1910. "Hundreds of them are encountered in the mighty lumber-mills buried in the thick fir forests along the Columbia River."[18]

Increasingly Asian Indians found themselves driven from employment in the railroad and lumber industries by violent white workers, and they moved south, riding the Southern Pacific Railroad into California, where they found employment in agriculture. "Every train that comes from the North and passes this city," commented the *Red Bluff News* in 1907 in a report on the movement of Asian Indians into the state, "has from one to twenty and often more of this new pest." Many California farmers, however, were eager to hire Asian Indians. The Chinese Exclusion Act had prohibited the entry of Chinese workers, and the Gentlemen's Agreement had cut off the supply of Japanese labor, so farmers turned to Asian Indians to reduce the labor shortage. "With the number of Japanese and Chinese laborers diminishing as a result of the restrictions placed upon the immigration of these classes," observed Immigration Commission Superintendent H. A. Millis in 1912, "the East Indians with freer immigration might fall heir to the kinds of work which have been done in part by these other Asiatics; for employers are inclined to follow the line of least resistance in finding a supply of labor, and competition between races engaged in unskilled work apparently depends more upon the rate of wages than upon efficiency." Indeed, farmers paid Asian-Indian workers from twenty-five to fifty cents less per day than Japanese laborers and used them to keep wages down.[19]

In northern California, five hundred Punjabis initially worked in the Newcastle fruit district east of Sacramento in 1908, and three hundred compatriots picked fruit in the nearby Vaca Valley. Asian-Indian farm laborers quickly spread throughout the Sacramento Valley, working on fruit farms and rice farms near Marysville, Tudor, Willows, and Chico. They moved into the San Joaquin Valley, where they worked in the grape and celery fields and where they cleared lands for new fields. Some six hundred of them were employed on the Tulare citrus farms. From the San Joaquin Valley, Asian Indians entered the Imperial Valley, gathering cantaloupes and picking cotton. A grower told an interviewer in 1930: "We are using Hindus for cleaning our ditches. The Japs won't do it and the Chinese have gotten too old. You can't get the younger generations of these peoples into any of this common work. But the Hindus are very efficient at this work."[20]

Asian-Indian farm laborers were organized into gangs — three to fifty laborers in each group. The gang leader, usually the member most fluent in English, received a commission from the gang and was also paid a wage by the employer; in return, he found employment for the workers, negotiated the terms of labor, arranged board and shelter, and served as general supervisor.

Punjabi farm laborers followed the harvesting of the different crops; they also performed various tasks, depending on the time of the year — pruning in December and January, irrigation work from March through May, and fruit picking from July through October. The "turbaned" workers "were continually on the wing," reported Annette Thackwell Johnson for the *Independent* in 1922, "coming from the melon and cotton fields in the Imperial Valley, en route to the fig orchards and vineyards of Fresno, or the rice fields near Sacramento." The Asian Indians moved around a great deal during the year because they contracted farm work for cultivating and pruning grapes or fruit trees, planting and harvesting rice, picking grapes and fruit. "During the grape picking season great numbers of them are in Fresno County," a Stockton lawyer said. "At the time of rice harvesting there will be about a thousand of them near Willows; during the cotton season in Imperial Valley (this being when the weather is very hot), they go to that place for work."[21]

Traveling in gangs from farm to farm, Punjabi laborers worked from ten to fourteen hours a day, depending on the season and the type of crop. "We got up at half past three," said one of them describing work in the asparagus fields, "and before the first faint daylight was visible we were ready for work." The workers were given miles and miles of rows. Cutting asparagus was monotonous and repetitious. "As soon as I had knelt down with my knife and cut out one head and put it in the box, there would be another one sprouting before me. Then I would have to stoop again, and it was this continuous picking and stooping that made it a terrible form of exercise." All day long it was "walk and bend, bend and walk," from half past four in the morning until seven in the evening. Periodically the boss — "an American foreman" — would come into the asparagus fields and yell, "Hurry up! Hurry up!"[22]

But the workers initiated ways to set their own pace. "We had an extraordinary boss," "an Italian constantly swearing and spitting," an Asian Indian recalled. The boss thought that he could discipline his workers by shouting at them, and so they devised "a very clever trick." "Whenever he shouted we worked hard and as he stopped shouting we relaxed our speed." After shouting continuously for a half hour or so, the boss would leave the fields; the workers would then slow down while vigilantly watching for his return. "We nearly always heard him before we saw him for he was noisily drunk half the day and the other half he fretted because he was not drunk." While picking fruit, workers would "disappear" into the trees and rest. "From our tree tops we would see the boss coming 'way off in the distance and when he reached us he found us working very hard." Sometimes the Asian Indians worked in the fields alongside Japanese farm laborers. Tensions developed as the two groups were pitted against each other. The Japanese taunted the Sikhs as "English slaves," remembered Tuly Singh Johl, and also called them "poles," referring to their tallness. But, working side by side, Japanese and Asian Indians also came to realize their shared brotherhood as workers. On one occasion, a Punjabi saw the boss in the distance approaching and said to the Japanese co-workers: "Boss is coming, hurry up." And one of the Japanese replied: "Hurry up-o, hurry up-o no good, work too much, all work finished; our job gone. Work slow, and job last, savvy?" The Asian-Indian worker understood. So between the two of them "the work that should have taken a week lasted a fortnight."[23]

Another way to extract more wages for their work was to manipulate the account books. The gang leader would list in his book the names of sixty men instead of the fifty that actually worked, and he would ask the boss to pay for the work of sixty men. Or the Asian-Indian bookkeeper and gang leader would conspire to alter

A Chinese opera in San Francisco's Chinatown, circa 1880. In the dark, smoke-filled theater, sitting in a segregated section, could be seen Chinese women.

A Chinese laundry in the late nineteenth century. "The Chinese laundryman does not learn his trade in China; there are no laundries in China." (Courtesy Library of Congress.)

Chinese laborers on the Milloudon plantation in Louisiana, 1871. "Ah Sing approached and greeted us with a polite, 'Hallo, how do?' On learning that we were well, he observed . . . , 'Belly hot to-day,' "

Chinese railroad laborers in the High Sierras, circa 1866. "The snow slides carried away our camps and we lost a good many men in those slides. Many of them we did not find until the next season when the snow melted." (Courtesy Asian American Studies Library, University of California, Berkeley.)

A Chinese prostitute in San Francisco, circa 1880, trying to entice passersby into her cubicle. "Lookee two bits, feelee floor bits, doee six bits." (Courtesy Amon Carter Museum, Fort Worth, Texas.)

Inside of a Chinese store. A uniquely Chinese-American social institution, the store was the center of life in the Chinese community, the "resort of all the Chinese in the colony" (Courtesy Asian American Studies Library, University of California, Berkeley.)

San Francisco's Chinatown
shortly after the 1906 earthquake.
"I was up, and here everything
is shaking." Then came the fires,
roaring down along Montgomery
Street and the financial district.
Photo by Arnold Genthe.
(Courtesy Library of Congress)

Angel Island Immigration Station in the early twentieth century. "When we arrived,
they locked us up like criminals in compartments like the cages in the zoo."
(Courtesy National Archives)

New York's Chinatown in the early twentieth century. Behind the glitter of Chinatown's exotic image was the tourist economy. (Courtesy National Archives.)

Immigration passport photograph of my father, Toshio Takaki, 1918, Kumamoto prefecture. At thirteen years of age, he left his village to join his father in Hawaii.

Nobuyoshi Takaki and his picture bride. Yukino. Actually, immigrant men also included first sons. My uncle was the oldest son.

The Takaki family on the Puunene Plantation, Maui, 1919: (from left to right) my uncle Teizo, grandfather Santaro, aunt Yukino, cousin Tsutako, uncle Nobuyoshi, and father, Toshio. This photograph was given to me by Yukino's younger sister, Toshino Watanabe Utano, May 1986, in Kumamoto, Japan.

Filipino plantation laborers arriving at the dock in Honolulu. The tags around their necks identified the plantations of their destiny.
(Courtesy Hawaii State Archives)

Author's uncle Teizo Takaki (on far right) and fellow workers on the Puunene Plantation, Maui, circa 1920.

Strikers at a mass meeting in Honolulu, April 1920. "Even the laborers of the utterly
isolated islands of Hawaii were moved by this world spirit."

The 1946 Sugar Laborer's Strike: woman and children march to support the strike.
Photograph in author's possession, a gift from Saburo Fujisaki,
one of the strike leaders.

A sign in California in the early twentieth century.
(Courtesy Visual Communications, Los Angeles, California.)

A sign in West Coast hotel, circa
1930. (Photo by Sprague Talbott,
Look Magazine.)

Filipino Laborers. The pool hall was their world.
(Photo by Sprague Talbott, Look magazine.)

"White men can't do the work as well as these whort men who can get down on their hands and knees, or work all day long stooping over." "Many people think that we don't suffer from stoop labor, but we do." Photo by Dorothea Lange. (Courtesy Library of Congress.)

There, "waiting for the night," hundreds of Filipinos in magnificent suits" stood ion front of poolrooms, gambling houses, and dance halls. (Courtesy Visual Communications, Los Angeles, California.)

"We were treated like actresses. It didn't matter what you looked like. Just that we were Filipinas." (Courtesy Asian American Studies Library, University of California, Berkeley.)

Carlos Bulosan. "I know deep down in my heart that I am an exile in America." (Courtesy Visual Communications, Los Angeles, California.)

A Korean rice farmer in California. By the 1920s, Korean farmers in Willows, California, were cultivating 43,000 acres of rice. (Courtesy Asian American Studies Library, University of California, Berkeley.)

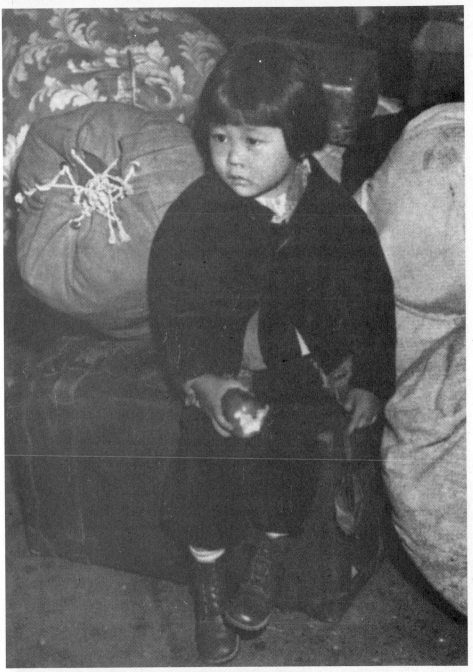

A Japanese-American child en route to a World War II internment camp. "How could I as a . . . child born in this country be declared by my own Government to be an enemy alien?" (Courtesy National Archives.)

The "turbaned" workers were continually on the wing, coming from the melon and cotton fields in the Imperial Valley, en route to the fig orchards and vineyards of Fresno, or the rice fields near Sacramento."

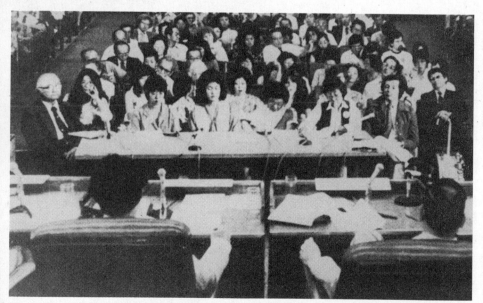

Redress and Reparations hearings before the Commission on Wartime Relocation and Internment of Civilians, 1981. Suddenly, during the commission hearings, scores of Issei and Nisei came forward to tell their stories. (Courtesy Visual Communications, Los Angeles, California.)

Nisei soldiers guarding captured German troops in Italy. The soldiers of the 442nd suffered 9,486 casualties, including 600 killed. "They brought an awful hunk of America with their blood." (Courtesy U.S. Army.)

Filipino-American soldiers in the Pacific front. The war gave Filipinos the chance to show themselves to America as "soldiers of democracy," as "men, not houseboys." (Army Signal Corps, photo from Commonwealth of Philippines.)

Hmong in Merced, California, 1988. "In America, we don't wear our traditional clothing . . . We only wear our traditional clothing on special days, and I will make my children only one set of clothes.' Photo by Chuong Chung.

Naturalization ceremony for Asian immigrants. Elderly Issei, forced to be "strangers" in America, were eager to become citizens in their adopted country. Photo by Tovo Miyatake.

the figures in the books. "Whenever the bookkeeper said thirty [men], the overseer translated thirty into forty," a worker revealed. "The bookkeeper would then make a profound bow as if the overseer's word were law, and there was no overseer on earth who could resist that bow. This form of cheating we later on called 'bonus' and we gave the name of 'bonus monger' to our bookkeeper."[24]

Camping near the fields, Asian-Indian migrant workers often slept under the stars or in tents. They were also housed in bunkhouses, barns, and sheds; twelve men could be found crowded into a single room, sleeping on the floor with blankets. Their religion determined their diet. The Muslims were not allowed to eat pork, and as a rule they would not purchase meat that had been prepared by other hands, which usually limited their meat to poultry and lamb butchered by themselves. The Hindus were vegetarians and usually had their own cooks in the camps. The Sikhs subsisted chiefly upon vegetables, fruit, milk, and *roti* (tortilla-like cakes of bread). Individual workers sometimes drank from one to two quarts of milk a day. Coming from a section of India where neither vegetable oil nor lard was commonly used, they consumed large quantities of butter, or *ghi,* amounting to at least fifteen pounds per person monthly. "Ghi bunanda salna," "It's the butter that makes the food," they said. The daughter of a Korean farmer in California remembered how much the Sikh laborers enjoyed their butter: "They would sit around a large pot of melted butter and garlic, dipping tortillas made with flour and water into it." The Asian Indians liked their foods heavily spiced with curry (*basar*), coriander seed (*dhania*), cumin seed (*zira*), cayenne (*lal mirch*), and black pepper (*kali mirch*). In one of the camps, an Asian Indian told a visiting lady: "We eat no meat, that is, no beef — the cow is sacred." "But you drink milk?" she snapped skeptically. "And your cow gives you the milk!" "Yes," he countered, "we drink our mother's milk also, but we do not eat her!"[25]

The gangs were, according to Bruce La Brack, "democratic bodies whose members shared a common religion, language, social background, set of values, and sense of purpose. Traditional patterns of leadership and cooperation as well as social distinctions found in the rural Punjab were frequently recreated within these work groups." In California the gangs became substitutes for families. Asian-Indian men, without wives and families, came to depend on the gangs for companionship and security. As members of a gang, they worked together, traveled together, lived and ate together, shared expenses and sorrows. They felt close bonds to one another. In the event one of them died, they collectively paid for the funeral and cremation costs, sent photographs of the body to India, and contributed money to the widow of the deceased.[26]

By the 1920s, Asian-Indian farm workers were able to negotiate for wages equal to those paid Japanese and white workers. By then a few Asian Indians had also become tenant farmers and even farm owners. "My experience in the labor camp inspection," reported a sanitary engineer for the State Commission of Immigration and Housing, "shows that the Hindus are rapidly leaving the employed list and are becoming employers." But many were pushed as well as pulled into farming. Due to racial discrimination, explained farmer Dalip S. Saund of the Imperial Valley, "few opportunities existed for me or people of my nationality in the state at the time. I was not a citizen and could not become one. The only way Indians in California could make a living . . . was to join with others who had settled in various parts of the state as farmers."[27]

Most of the Asian-Indian farmers probably had been gang bosses initially, and their education and ability to speak English as well as their higher income enabled them to enter agricultural enterprise. Partnership farming was very popular among the Punjabis: two to eight men would advance an equal amount of money for investment in a farm, becoming equal shareholders, and one partner would manage the business. Harnam Singh Sidhu, for example, formed a partnership with several other Sikhs to lease a thousand acres in Sutter County for rice farming. Their expenses were high, for they had to buy a thrasher, tractor, and other rice-harvesting machinery. But their first year's crop was very successful, enabling them to pay off their debts. The Punjabis were "excellent farmers, very industrious, willing to work under trying conditions," stated a white landlord. "In the heat of summer they got up at 4 o'clock, worked with their teams until about 10 A.M., then with the hoe until say 4 P.M. and then with their teams until 9 o'clock in the evening." In 1919, Asian Indians leased 86,315 acres and owned 2,077 acres in California. Their lands were located in the Sacramento Valley and the Imperial Valley, two areas accounting for nearly 90 percent of the total acreage farmed by Asian Indians. Many Punjabi farmers grew crops familiar to them in India, especially cotton and rice. In the Sacramento Valley, they devoted 45,000 out of the 59,000 acres under their cultivation to rice production. Other Asian-Indian farmers raised nuts, fruits, and potatoes; Jawala and Bisaka Singh became known as the "Potato Kings" of Holtville.[28]

After the enactment of the 1920 Alien Land Law and the 1923 *Thind* decision, Asian Indians were denied the right to own land in California. Some farmers were forced to become laborers again. "Since the Alien Land Laws were put into effect," said former landowner Sucha Singh, "I have been working for others near Holtville." Other Asian Indians continued to hold land by registering it under the names of their children born in the United States and therefore American citizens. The American-born sons of one Punjabi family held land for fellow countrymen for a commission of a dollar an acre. Most Asian Indians utilized a "front man" strategy, buying or leasing land and working out verbal agreements to have the property placed under the names of Anglo farmers, bankers, and lawyers. When Munshi Singh Thiara purchased twenty acres in Sutter County in 1918, he took an American as a "silent partner" who served as the legal owner of the property. In 1925, Imam Bakhash, his son Kalu Khan, and his partner, Atta Muhammad, leased two thousand acres near Willows, but their attorney, Duard Gies, actually leased the land in his own name and received a share of the crop for serving as the "front man." Similarly in 1928, Babu Khan and his brother Naimat Khan leased two thousand acres near Butte City in the name of their attorney, Jerry Barcelox of Chico. Harnam Singh Sidhu purchased forty-five acres of land under the name of an American whom he trusted, calling the arrangement a "dummy partnership." "Many of our American friends bought land for us under their names," recalled Bagga Singh Sunga of El Centro, "and so we were able to carry on farming." The director of the Holtville National Bank held lands for many Punjabi clients, and his bank became known as the "Hindu Bank." Punjabis also formed corporations with Anglos, an arrangement that enabled them to skirt the law and farm their own lands.[29]

Unlike Japanese farmers, Punjabi farmers developed a reliance on Anglos in their strategy to evade the Alien Land Law. Compared to the Japanese, few Punjabis had wives in the United States; hence they could not as easily as the Japanese register lands under the names of American-born children. Very few in number, Punjabis also were not able to form larger and more self-sufficient communities as were the Japanese. Consequently, they could not develop the vertical linkages that enabled the Japanese to produce, market, and distribute their crops within an ethnic organizational network. Unlike the Japanese, Punjabis had a low rate of literacy and needed assistance from Anglos to conduct their business.[30]

Asian-Indian landownership indicated a shift from sojourner to settler. Virtually all of the Asian Indians had come here initially to work temporarily and then return to their homeland. But even as early as 1910, according to a U.S. Immigration Report, only 46 percent of the Asian Indians interviewed expressed an intention to return to India; the others were either uncertain or had decided to remain permanently in the United States. An Asian-Indian immigrant told an interviewer in 1922 that he had left the Punjab "so long ago," meaning ten or twelve years. "Are you homesick?" he was then asked. "Not any longer, memsahib. One adjusts oneself." "Are you going back to the Punjab?" The immigrant shrugged, smiled, and then replied: "I make more money here."[31]

But even as settlers, very few had families in America. These immigrants were virtually all men: the ratio of Asian Indian men to women, calculated Bruce La Brack, was seventy-five to one at "its *most* favorable." But actually the ratio was even higher. In 1914 women represented only 0.24 percent of the 5,000 Asian Indians in California. Initially the men thought they would be here temporarily; moreover, many of them had already mortgaged their farms in India to pay for their transportation expenses and were too deeply in debt to consider bringing their wives and children with them. At least a third to half of the immigrants had left families behind in India. An Immigration Commission survey of 474 Asian Indians in 1909 showed that thirty-one were widowed, 228 were single, and 215 were married and had wives in India. That same year immigrant Saint Nihal Singh observed in an essay published in *Out West:*

> One of the chief points of difference between the emigrant from India and those hailing from Europe lies in the fact that the European brings along with him his family — his wife and children . . . — when he emigrates to America. Only one sex is represented among the Hindoo immigrants. Probably the greater percentage of them are married — for Hindoos marry young — but they leave their wives and children behind them and venture alone to find a fortune in the West. There is only one Hindoo woman on the North American continent. She lives with her husband, a doctor of Vedic medicine, in Vancouver, B.C.[32]

As Asian Indians established themselves here, they hoped to send for their families or to bring women to America to marry. A handful of women came as wives. Mrs. Nand Kaur Singh recalled her first home in an isolated apple orchard in Utah: "When we got there it was 11 at night. We went for a walk. . . . And then I started crying. I said, 'What's wrong with India?' And he said, 'You will like it here soon.' " But adjustment did not come easily. "I had come from a village where I was surrounded by family and friends, and here there was no one but my husband, who worked hard all day. . . . There were none of my countrywomen to speak with, and it was against our custom to talk with men who were not related."[33]

Altogether only a very few Asian-Indian women emigrated, and after the enactment of the 1917 Immigration Law, men with wives in India could not bring them here. Moola Singh had left his wife in the Punjab in 1911 and had saved enough money to pay for her passage to America. But by the time he had sent the money to her, the law had already been enacted. "She worry," Singh told an interviewer many years later. "She good, nice looking, healthy, but she love. You know love, person no eat, worry, then maybe die. Mother wrote one time letter, 'she sick, you gotta come home.' Then I write her letter from Arizona, to her I say, 'I'm coming, don't worry, I be there.' " But she passed away in 1921 before Singh could return. "Lots of time I dream," Singh said sadly, "she come close to me, she's with me now you know. No, she don't want come close, she go round, round, no come close in my dream . . . that's a life gone." Many Punjabi men thought about returning to India and bringing their wives back. "I knew that if I went back to India to join her, we would never be allowed to come back to the United States," said Bagga Singh Sunga of El Centro. "If we had our women here," said a fellow countryman, "our whole life would be different."[34]

Punjabi men were usually prohibited from marrying white women. County clerks in California often decided that the anti-miscegenation laws applied to Asian Indians and denied marriage licenses to Asian Indian–white couples. Consequently, Asian-Indian men seeking to marry Caucasian women had to travel to states like Arizona. One couple figured out an imaginative way to skirt the law: they were married at sea, outside of the three-mile limit of California. According to the *Sutter County Farmer* of May 29, 1923, "the groom was Sandar Din . . . and his bride, Berilla M. Nutter . . . both of Sutter County." After they had been refused a marriage license in Sutter County and then in Contra Costa County, the "Hindu took the prospective bride to San Francisco where he hired a launch . . . and when the boat reached the three-mile limit the captain performed the marriage ceremony and the party returned."[35]

Asian-Indian men frequently married Mexican women. In

northern California betwen 1913 and 1946, 47 percent of their wives
were Mexican. In central California, 76 percent were Mexican.
Meanwhile, in southern California, where most of the Asian Indians
with families resided, 92 percent of their spouses were Mexican.
"There have already been quite a few marriages between Mexican
women and Hindustani men," noted Taraknath Das in 1923. Over
50 percent of the Mexican spouses were immigrants themselves. Most
of the Mexican women were young, usually twelve to twenty years
younger than their husbands; like the Punjabi men, they were farm
laborers. They met each other while working and developed relations
leading to marriage. Such marriages were signs of Sikh settlement.
Lohar Bupara married Teresa, a Mexican immigrant, and purchased
land for farming near Delano under her name. Inder Singh, a farmer
in the Imperial Valley, told an interviewer in 1924: "Two years ago
I married a Mexican woman and through her I am able to secure
land for farming. Your land law can't get rid of me now; I am going
to stay." Many Punjabi-Mexican marriages involved sisters: one sister would marry an Asian-Indian man and then introduce her sister
to a friend of her husband. Mir Dad, for example, married Susana
Lopez in 1924: he had met her while visiting his friend Mir Alam
Khan, the husband of Susana's younger sister, Maria. Similarly,
Moola Singh married Maria La Tocharia in 1932, then her sister
Julia married Mota Singh and another sister, Hortencia, married
Natha Singh. Their marriages to Mexican women were generally not
approved by their families in India. "It used to be that our folks in
India objected to such marriages," said Sucha Singh in 1924. He
himself had not written to his family about his marriage to a Mexican.
"I suppose others have told them about it, but I do not care even if
they should be 'sour' about it."[36]

Asian Indian–Mexican marriages had their share of cultural
differences and conflicts. "My wife is inclined to be like the American
women to a certain degree," explained Inder Singh. "The American
woman is entirely too free; she is the boss. . . . My wife would like
to boss me, but I am not disturbed by that and we get along very
well." Apparently Singh had learned to make adjustments. At first
he had been "really shocked by the freedom of the women" in America. "I have now grown accustomed to the practice of men and women
going along the streets together. If I were to return to India, I believe
I would carry out this practice over there." But Singh also complained
that there was "entirely too much divorce here because the women
were so free." Referring to his wife, Singh said: "Should she at any

time want to leave me I would tell her, 'The road is wide; go ahead.' "
Many Asian Indian–Mexican marriages failed. In a study of 130 couples in the Imperial Valley, Karen Leonard found that thirty-five of the men had married more than once, a divorce ratio that was high for the time and that ran counter to general trends showing a lower ratio of divorces for people with rural, foreign-born, and Catholic backgrounds. As many men as women filed for divorce. In their petitions, the men claimed their wives had argued with them and cursed them, refused to cook and clean for their Punjabi friends, visited their mothers and sisters whenever they wished, and shopped in town where they purchased makeup. On the other hand, the women complained that their husbands drank heavily, physically abused them, committed adultery, and demanded domestic services beyond reason.[37]

In these Asian Indian–Mexican families cultural traditions were often melded. Foods, for example, were interchanged — tortillas for *rotis* or *chapattis* and jalapeños for Punjabi chili peppers. Languages were also mixed together. The Mexican wives generally understood some Punjabi, but the children spoke English and Spanish in the home. Punjabi fathers learned to speak Spanish. The children were usually given Spanish first names like Armando, Jose, and Rudolfo. A few of the sons had Indian names, but they went by their Spanish names or nicknames. Mexican mothers told Leonard: "Gurbachen? Oh, you mean Bacho," and "Kishen? That's Domingo." Lohar and Teresa Bupara named their three children Sarjit, Oscar, and Anna Luisa. The oldest, Sarjit, spoke Spanish, English, and Punjabi. Asian-Indian husbands and Mexican wives generally retained their respective religions. "There are several instances of a Sikh or Muslim husband going through a Catholic marriage ceremony so that the wife could continue to take communion in her church," reported Leonard. Moola Singh's wife, Susanna, said: "I'm a Catholic. . . . Well, God gives a lot of different languages . . . but I don't think so many Gods." The children were baptized Catholic, and were raised under the *compadrazgo* (godparents) system of the Spanish culture and the Catholic Church. In Asian Indian–Mexican families, the godparents were usually other Punjabi-Mexican couples. The godmother helped to give religious instruction, and the godfather provided advice and presents such as bicycles and confirmation dresses. In addition to godparents, the children also had many "uncles" — their fathers' Punjabi bachelor friends.[38]

There must have been many "uncles," for most of the Asian-

Indian immigrants were confined to bachelorhood. The "uncles" were often partners of the married men, and lived in the same household. They told the children stories about the Punjab and made them lemon pickles and sweet desserts like *lassi*. On Sundays, they gave them money for movies and ice cream. Many of these uncles were not really bachelors, for they had wives and children in India. Sometimes the men tried to joke about their situation, their lonely separation from their wives. One of their stories was about "a man who went away from his home and two years later his wife wrote him that a child had been born to her." Feeling very proud, the man showed the letter to his comrades. "They asked him how could she have a child while he was away so long? But the man shook his head wisely and answered, 'But I write her letters.' "[39]

The humor of this story highlighted the reality of a community of men cut off from women. Visits to prostitutes were "far from uncommon," historian Sucheta Mazumdar noted. Alcoholism was a pervasive problem, leading to brawls and even murders within the Asian-Indian community. Drinking was a "most common vice" among Asian Indians, observed Das, estimating that about a third to half of his countrymen drank. "Quite a few of them were in the habit of drinking strong liquors, such as whiskey and brandy, and very often got drunk." While working in the asparagus fields, Dhan Gopal Mukerji sadly witnessed his countrymen drinking themselves into "forgetfulness." They would buy liquor and hide in order to "indulge" their "appetites," "drinking up their wages in order to forget they were alive. All the old Indian bringing up was being swept away by a few months of inhumanly cruel work." The Yuba County death certificates show that syphilis and chronic alcoholism were leading causes of death among the immigrants in the early period.[40]

There was little available for the Punjabis to do during their leisure hours. Comparing his fellow countrymen to the Japanese and Chinese in America, Das observed: "While the Japanese play [in pool halls and bowling alleys] and the Chinese gamble, the Hindustanees debate." They "indulged in unnecessary discussion and debate, which, however it might sharpen their wits, often led to arguments and quarrels."[41]

Their religion, on the other hand, helped to give coherence and solace to their lives. Important religious events reinforced their sense of ethnicity and created a feeling of Asian-Indian community in America. Muslim Asian Indians observed the fast of Muharram. "They fasted from moon to moon and ate little at certain appointed hours,"

Mukerji observed. "With the hop pickers there was a priest whose name was Hadji, since he had done a 'hadji,' that is, a pilgrimage to Mecca." He was the only one in the group who could read the Koran in Arabic. Since the workers thought it would be sacrilegious to have Hadji read the Koran from the floor, they piled up bales of hay about eight feet high and had Hadji recite from the top of this edifice. For hours and hours, Hadji prayed loudly, his shrill voice praising "O Allah, the Almighty Allah, the Compassionate." After the period of fasting was over, the workers made preparations for the feast. "The Mohammedans would not buy the American butcher's meat, for animals whose flesh they eat must be killed by having their throats cut and in no other way. So they bought three big rams and after a great deal of prayer and benediction, cut their throats." During their feast, they beat tin cans and sang all night. Their songs had a common refrain:

> *Your hair is like a panther's shadow.*
> *Your eye brows are like the curve of a hawk's wings.*[42]

"Wherever there are 20 or 25 Sikhs," observed Das, "there is a temple also, which is sometimes nothing but a shack used for divine service." Each temple had a priest, usually one of the workers in the gang responsible on a part-time basis for the religious exercises and the care of the temple. Elected annually by vote, the priest received a salary as well as room and board. In Stockton, the Sikhs erected an elaborate temple. Two stories high, the building had a ground floor with a hall for meetings and rooms for the priest's residence. Upstairs was the prayer hall where the Granth, or sacred book of the Sikh Gurus, was kept on the altar. In this hall, decorated with rich carpets, a canopy, and pictures and texts on the walls, the priest would read the scriptures twice daily. Sikhs from throughout northern California visited the Stockton *Gurdwara* ("gateway of the guru") or temple four to six times annually, especially on the major festival days such as Baisakhi, Guru Arjun's Martyrdom Day, Guru Nanak's Birthday, and Guru Gobind Singh's Birthday. The temples functioned as important places where the immigrants could gather to worship and celebrate religious festivals; they were also community centers where the Asian Indians could socialize, settle quarrels, and assist newcomers.[43]

But the temples served a dwindling Punjabi population, a community of forgotten immigrants. By 1940, according to the U.S. Census, the Asian-Indian population in the United States had dropped to 2,405, most of them (60 percent) residing in California. The community was composed mostly of older people; 56 percent were over forty years of age and 32 percent over fifty. Occupationally, 65 percent were in agriculture — 15 percent as farmers and 50 percent as farm laborers. Only 4 percent were professionals. Of the sixteen hundred Asian Indians over twenty-five years of age, more than a third had not completed even a year of schooling. Their educational level was the lowest of all racial and ethnic groups reported in the census: the median number of school years completed by Asian Indians was only 3.7.

Five years later, in 1945, a lecturer of Oriental Studies at the University of Pennsylvania surveyed the Asian-Indian community in America. The community was "small and stable," observed Dr. S. Chandrasekhar. Men who had been on the move in search of jobs had settled down as heads of families. The improvement of their economic status was accompanied by the "Americanization" of their children. While the parents spoke Hindustani in the home, their children had begun to attend the local public schools and learned to speak English. For the American-born generation, India was "unreal and far away." But whether they were first- or second-generation Asian Indians, they felt isolated, not knowing for certain their place and future in America. In their identity, they seemed to be rooted neither here in America nor there in India. "Some would like to go to India, marry, and return to their adopted land; some would like relatives in India to come here and share the American way of life," explained Chandrasekhar. But their cultural ties to India had been "cut asunder," and "new blood" from the homeland could not be introduced.[44]

9

Dollar a Day, Dime a Dance

The Forgotten Filipinos

Technically, they were not foreigners, for they came from the Philippines, a territory acquired from Spain at the conclusion of the Spanish-American War. While they had not been granted citizenship, they were classified as "American nationals," which allowed them entry to the United States. The influx of Filipinos or "Pinoys," as they called themselves, was sudden and massive. In 1910, the mainland Filipino population was only 406, including seventeen in Washington and 109 in Louisiana — the descendants of Spanish-speaking Filipinos known as "Manilamen" who had deserted Spanish galleons in the eighteenth century. By 1920, there were 5,603 Filipinos on the mainland. Ten years later, their numbers had multiplied almost nine times to 45,208. Filipinos were almost everywhere: 3,480 in Washington, 1,066 in Oregon, 787 in Michigan, 2,011 in Illinois, 1,982 in New York, and hundreds of others in states like Colorado, Kansas, Virginia, Maryland, Pennsylvania, Mississippi, Montana, Idaho, Texas, and Arizona. Between 1910 and 1930, the Filipino population of California had jumped from five to 30,470.

The Filipinos on the mainland had very different experiences than their compatriots in Hawaii. In the islands, Filipinos did not face the presence of a racist white working class. They were pitted against Japanese workers on the plantations, but the managers carefully regulated this rivalry in order to prevent it from breaking into violence and disrupting the work schedule. On the mainland, however, Filipinos competed with white laborers and became the targets of violent white working-class backlash. A Filipino farm laborer who had moved from the islands to California explained: "Hawaii more

better than here. You would be in one place there and don't move
'round much. I here four years and not make anything — just enough
to buy some clothes and eat. If get a little money, maybe go back to
Hawaii. I scare myself when I hear that Filipino boy get killed by
white men. I don't know why dey do dat, but I scare myself."[1]

"*Isang magandang señora, libot na libot ng espada,*" the Tagalog riddle had warned the newcomers: "There is a beautiful lady
surrounded with swords." They had come here, thinking they were
Americans, pushed from the Philippines by poverty and pulled to
America by "extravagance." They found the land encircled by sharp
blades of white hostility and their lives by a new "necessity." "I have
been four years in America," a Filipino immigrant in California said
sadly, "and I am still a stranger. It is not because I want to be. I have
tried to be as 'American' as possible. I live like an American, eat like
American, and dress the same, and yet everywhere I find Americans
who remind me of the fact that I am a stranger." He and his fellow
Filipinos, like the Japanese and Chinese, had come from a "different
shore."[2]

Mabuhay Manong:
From the Fisheries of Alaska to the Fields of California

When Filipinos first arrived in San Francisco, they saw taxis waiting
for them near the docks, ready to drive them to Stockton. "*Mabu-
hay*" — "hooray," "good luck," shouted the *manongs* — first-
generation Filipinos — as they stepped from their ships. They could
have taken the bus or train to Stockton for two dollars, but most of
them found themselves swept into taxis, four or five Filipinos in each
taxi, together paying sixty-five to seventy-five dollars for the trip to
Stockton — the gathering place for Filipinos as they came to America.
"We landed in San Francisco," Alfonso Perales Dangaran recalled.
"An uncle met us and took us to Stockton because that was the center
of labor for our kind of people, that worked in the field." When
Manuel Buaken arrived in Stockton, he found the city "flooded with
Filipinos who had come in search of that big money they had heard
about, believing the same fantastic tales. . . . They were all waiting
for calls to work on the farms, and in the meantime, they had no
money and could only bum their way in and around the city." From
Stockton, the Filipinos fanned out into three areas of employment —
domestic service, the fisheries of the Northwest and Alaska, and
agriculture.[3]

Twenty-five percent of the Filipinos (11,400 out of 45,200) on the mainland in 1930 were service workers including janitors, valets, kitchen helpers, pantrymen, dishwashers and all kinds of service boys — chamberboys, bellboys, hallboys, houseboys, elevatorboys, yardboys, doorboys, and busboys. "My husband worked in a restaurant as a busboy. That's the only kind of job he was allowed to have," said Angeles Mendoza. According to Buaken, who worked as a dishwasher in Pasadena's Huntington Hotel, whites accepted unskilled jobs as dishwashers and porters only as a last resort, but Filipinos knew this was the only type of work open to them in the United States. Filipinos found themselves desired as servants. The manager of a San Jose hotel explained why the Filipino made "a wonderful servant," superior to a white one: "Being very susceptible to flattery, a pleasant word to the Filipino is as good as a coin. But not for the white boy: He must be tipped, and decently too. On receiving a tip in pennies one time, an American boy threw them down indignantly at the feet of the guest. A Filipino would never do this." Filipinos knew they had to wear the mask of docility. "I had to crawl on my knees to please them [white employers]," a Filipino busboy confided. "I had to be submissive and servile and eternally patient; had to be known for my whole-hearted willingness to serve others — or else! The laborer is not worthy of his hire, unless he also smiles."[4]

Working in the service industry sometimes had its amusing moments. Shortly after he arrived in San Francisco, Juan Dionisio found a job in a hotel on Stockton Street. The Italian landlady showed him how to make the beds and told him to stay in his room until she rang. "Then when nobody was there," he said, "I was supposed to go around and look and fix the rooms. . . . I was making dollar a day." Then some friends remarked: "Hey, you're making good job there . . . good-looking girls there. Maybe you're getting it free besides." But Dionisio did not understand what they were saying at first. "I didn't know. I was a virgin, you know, and then I realized it was a house of prostitution."[5]

Nine percent (4,200) of the Filipinos worked in the Alaska salmon fisheries. Recruited on the West Coast by Japanese and Filipino labor contractors, they were hired for the "long season" of seven months, beginning in April, or the "extra season" of three months from June through August. In 1930, Filipinos represented 15 percent of the Alaskan fishery work force. Called "Alaskeros," they cleaned salmon and packed them in boxes, working six days a week, from 6 A.M. to 6 P.M., or whenever there was salmon to pack.

Their leisure hours were times of loneliness, spent drinking or in whorehouses. In the "Song of the Alaskero," a worker describes the life and labor in the salmon industry:

> *It's a hard lonesome fate*
> *We face in Alaska.*
> *Oh! what a fate!*
> *Stale fat and ill-cooked fish,*
> *Our major, daily dish*
> *From the stingy, bossy Chink,*
> *Give us tummy-ache.*
>
> *We may curl and be bold*
> *Beneath some cover thick.*
> *Yet oh! how cold!*
> *And then ere the break of day*
> *Though dog tired we may be*
> *Up we must willy-nilly*
> *For another day.*[6]

After the season, the Alaskeros returned to Seattle and San Francisco, where they were usually disappointed to discover they had not actually made much money. A Filipino fishery worker in 1912 earned an average wage of $163, but he took home only $34.58 after $128.42 had been deducted for food and other expenses incurred in Alaska. Filipinos borrowed money from the contractor so they could go to Alaska and work. But then, when they came back to the West Coast, they were broke and had to draw meal tickets from contractors; in debt they had to sign up the following year for another stint in Alaska. They did "the same thing, year in and year out, season after season."[7]

Most of the Filipinos — 27,000, or 60 percent — worked in agriculture. They helped to fill the need for labor created by the exclusion of the Chinese, Japanese, Koreans, and Asian Indians. They were organized into gangs or crews, under the leadership of a Filipino labor contractor who located the jobs and negotiated the terms with the growers. "You would have one crew boss who would be in charge of all the 'boys,' " explained Joseph Ariola. "In the old days, he would go around to the different farmers and say, 'Do you need some work done? I can bring in my crew. My company comes out to over forty, fifty people.' " Riding old cars and trucks, they moved from field to field, area to area, following the ripening fruit and vegetables.

"We traveled. I mean we moved from camp to camp," a Filipino said. "You start out the year, January . . . you'd find a place and it was usually an asparagus camp. . . . From asparagus season, we would migrate to Fairfield, to Suisin and there the men worked out in the orchards picking fruits while the women and even children, as long as they could stand on their boxes, worked cutting fruits." Filipino farm laborers were shuttled from one place to another — Salinas, Manteca, Stockton, Lodi, Fresno, Delano, Dinuba, San Luis Obispo, Imperial, Sacramento, cutting spinach here, picking strawberries there, then to Montana, where they topped beets, to Idaho to dig potatoes, to the Yakima Valley in Washington to pick apples, and to Oregon to hoe hops.[8]

Work in the fields of California seemed to be harder than anything they had experienced in the Philippines. "I worked about six hours that first day," a Filipino laborer recalled, "and when my back was hurting I said to myself: 'Why did I come to this country? I was doing easy in the Philippines.' " But he kept saying to himself that he would become accustomed to the work. "But boy, the next day I could hardly sit down because my back and all of my body was sore." Always the workday was long: they moved into the fields at daybreak and returned after sundown. The temperature in the fields seemed hotter than it had ever been in the islands. A Filipino vividly described what it was like to work in the vineyards: "It was one hundred and thirteen degrees. I used to get two gallons of water to pour on my head. By the time it reached the ground, I was dry."[9]

Often, when they worked, Filipinos were enveloped in a fog of dust. Frank Waterman of the State Employment Agency told an interviewer in 1930 that the dust did not bother the Filipinos: "The white man can't stand the itch which results from working in the peat fields [the black soil] of the Delta. The dark skinned peoples are not affected by these conditions." But Filipino workers thought differently. "How dusty it was and itchy. Peat dirt even went inside your shoes, no matter how tight your shoes. If you wore hightops, when you took your shoes off, you saw about [an] inch of dust inside." In the fields, the dust, blowing in "clouds," settled in their ears, noses, and eyes. "I know from personal experience that when the sun beats down on the backs of the workers, the perspiration combined with the dust becomes almost unbearably itchy."[10]

While Filipinos harvested a wide variety of crops such as cotton, oranges, tomatoes, celery, onions, peas, melons, and lettuce, they were used extensively to pick asparagus. Josephine Romero Loable remembered how the Filipinos began working in the asparagus fields at four o'clock in the morning. They went out "with flashlights on their heads just like miners so they could get to the asparagus before it grew . . . the white heads." Organized in cutter crews, each gang numbered as many as three hundred workers. On hot, dry days they were surrounded by the fine soil ideal for asparagus cultivation; on rainy, wet days, they carried heavy loads of mud on their boots as they worked the rows, stooping to gather the delicate shoots. Filipinos also planted cauliflower, tiresome, backbreaking work. Laborers followed a wagon that stopped periodically to drop handfuls of the seedlings between the long furrows. Bent over, each worker picked up the seedlings with one hand and dug into the ground with the other; then, placing the seedling into the hole, the laborer moved on and dug another hole.[11]

Filipinos were viewed by farmers as ideally suited for "stoop labor." Commenting on the use of Filipinos as farm laborers, the editor of a California newspaper told an interviewer in 1930: "White men can't do the work as well as these short men who can get down on their hands and knees, or work all day long stooping over." Similarly, a Japanese farmer said that he assigned Mexicans to do the heavier work and to drive the tractors: "But the Fils do all the stoop labor. They are small and work fast." But a Filipino laborer told the same interviewer: "Many people think that we don't suffer from stoop labor, but we do."[12]

At six o'clock in the evening, the workers climbed into wagons and were taken away from the field. Always the Filipino workers returned to their camps covered with dirt; their bodies sweaty and itchy, they were hardly able to wait for their baths. But sometimes the wait was a long one. In the agricultural camp, a Filipino recalled, there was only one bathtub, a large individual galvanized can for the use of one hundred workers. Everyone took a bath each day after working, for it was impossible to sleep and rest well without bathing. Some five to ten people took a bath in the same water before it was changed and heated again. "So the job of bathing one hundred boys was an ordeal. It took six hours to heat enough water to wash one hundred dirty men." After dinner, the tired men went to bed, but many of them slept restlessly. "It was hard work," said a worker, "and at night, I'd feel all kinds of pain in my body — my back, my arm."[13]

Their camps were composed of dilapidated bunkhouses and shacks resembling "chicken houses." "The bunkhouse was made of old pieces of wood," one Pinoy remembered, "and was crowded with men. There was no sewage disposal. When I ate swarms of flies fought over my plate. . . . I slept on a dirty cot: the blanket was never washed." A Japanese grower told an interviewer in 1930 that he preferred to employ Filipinos because they were single men and could be housed inexpensively. "These Mexicans and Spaniards bring their families with them and I have to fix up houses; but," he said laughingly, "I can put a hundred Filipinos in that barn" (pointing to a large fire trap). Sometimes Filipinos were housed in temporary shelters, a cluster of tents. "We lived in tents with board flooring which was very convenient because when it rained, there was no mud," a Filipino said. "We slept in cot beds. They gave us enough blankets. It got cold at nights." Never did it get so cold back home. "Having just arrived from the Philippines it was hard to get used to the cooler climate. Oh man, sometimes I had to cover myself with the old mattress to stay warm through the night. It was cold, awful cold, and you could feel the wind blowing through the cracks in the wall." Other Filipino farm laborers had to be even more resourceful. "You made your own house, cooked your own food, you had to make your own stove out of anything. In the field, Filipinos, Oakies, and Mexicans — the farmer didn't supply you with shelter or anything."[14]

Resisting the daily punishment of agricultural labor, Filipino farm workers were not the docile and manageable laborers the farmers hoped they would be. One grower complained that the Filipinos he had hired in 1924 proved to be "most unsatisfactory," for they were "the essence of independence" and quarrelsome over contract prices. Three years later, during the peak season, this grower again hired a crew of Filipino laborers to pick the grapes. "These two weeks of harvest were the most bitter I have ever spent," he grumbled. "About the third day when we were in a great rush, the Filipinos evidently thinking we were in a tight place, struck for higher wages. We refused to meet their exorbitant demands whereupon general rioting ensued. The Filipinos became enraged and began destroying everything they could lay their hands on." Unwilling to meet the Filipino demands, the farmer hired a crew of Mexicans and harvested the crop "without any more difficulty and at a lower price." The Horticulture Commissioner of San Joaquin County in 1930 reported that the Filipinos arrived "green" but after they had been here a while they became "educated and sophisticated." Consequently they became "increasingly hard to manage."[15]

Filipino farm laborers became even more difficult to manage as the economic depression of the 1930s lowered wages. They saw they were trapped, as Buaken put it, in "a pit of economic slavery. . . . We are only allowed to do unskilled work, and in this work we must compete against Mexicans, Chinese, Japanese, and Negroes. . . . What are we to do to elevate ourselves?" The answer came from the fields. When the growers in the Imperial Valley tried to reduce wages in 1930, Filipino and Mexican field-workers struck. Separately, white packing-shed workers also went out on strike. In an effort to bring all of the workers together, the Trade Union Unity League formed the Agricultural Workers Industrial League. But the growers used the government to smash this new interethnic labor unity. Arresting over one hundred workers and setting the bail at $40,000, the authorities broke the strike.[16]

But the labor movement continued to gather strength and membership as farm workers resisted wage cuts. Filipinos in Stockton and Salinas formed the Filipino Labor Union. Believing they had to unionize in order to fight low wages and racial discrimination, 4,000 Filipinos joined the FLU. "*Ang lakas ay nasa pagkakaisa*," they said. "Strength is in union." Filipino farm workers constituted a potent political force in the labor movement, for they comprised 40 percent of the total agricultural work force in the Salinas Valley.

In August of 1933, the FLU led a one-day strike to protest the twenty-cent-an-hour wage. The growers brought in Mexican, Asian Indian, and Japanese laborers to replace the striking Filipinos and easily put down the Filipino walkout. But relations between the FLU and the growers remained tense. The FLU continued to expand its membership, while the growers countered by organizing the Filipino Labor Supply Association, composed of Filipino labor contractors opposed to the FLU. The showdown between the two forces occurred the following year when the FLU demanded that the growers recognize their right to collective bargaining as provided by the newly enacted National Industrial Recovery Act. In August, the FLU led Filipino lettuce workers in a strike, demanding forty to forty-five cents an hour, union recognition, and improved working conditions. Altogether 6,000 strikers were involved in the work stoppage as the Filipino strikers were joined by white laborers packing and storing the lettuce in the sheds. But the unity quickly disintegrated when the white strikers broke away from the striking Filipinos and agreed to arbitration.[17]

Facing the growers alone, the Filipino strikers felt the full force of grower opposition. The growers pitted the Filipino Labor Supply Association against the FLU and used Filipino laborers from the association to replace the strikers. They also increased the importation of Mexican laborers, deploying them as scabs against the Filipino strikers. Opening a propaganda front, the growers circulated stories claiming that Communists had infiltrated the leadership of the FLU. Meanwhile the growers, assisted by highway patrolmen, local special deputies, and armed vigilantes, drove off five hundred strikers. A sign on a street in Salinas warned the striking Filipinos: "This is a White Man's Country. Get Out of Here if You Don't Like What We Pay." The growers' war against the strikers came to a head in late September. Vigilantes attacked the camp of Rufo Canete, the president of the FLU. "Get going and don't come back," they shouted as they burned the camp to the ground and forced the strikers to flee for their lives. The police then raided the union headquarters in Salinas, arresting scores of strikers including their leader. The strategy of the growers was brutal and effective. Shortly after the raid, the captain of the state highway patrol telegraphed Sacramento: "Everything is quiet, I think the strike is over. Have leader in jail."[18]

The Filipino strikers held out. In the settlement to end the strike, the FLU extracted concessions: wages of forty cents an hour and recognition of the FLU as a legitimate farm workers' union. The FLU represented the emergence of ethnic labor unionism and the entrance of Filipinos into the labor movement in America. In 1936, the FLU organized another strike in the Salinas Valley, an action that led to a combined Mexican-Filipino agricultural union chartered by the American Federation of Labor — the Field Workers' Union Local No. 30326.

"The Filipino, militantly race-conscious, began to protest against his exploitation in California at an early date," observed Carey McWilliams sympathetically in 1935, "and has grown increasingly rebellious. . . . The Filipino is a real fighter and his strikes have been dangerous." The involvement of the Filipinos in the labor movement reflected a changing consciousness — a sober recognition of shattered dreams and a new sense of ethnic unity. "There was a need for us Filipinos to organize an independent union," said Antonio Gallego Rodrigo, "and force the growers to give us higher wages, better working and living conditions. . . . To me, it did not matter what island [in the Philippines] they came from or what dialect they spoke. They were all Filipinos like me." As Rodrigo and thousands of his *kababayan,* or countrymen, struggled for economic justice, they came to realize how determined they were in their "search for a door into America."[19]

The "Little Brown Brother" in America

But the door was not open to Filipinos. They quickly discovered that they were "little brown brothers" only in the Philippines; here, in continental America, their physical proximity exposed the limit of American-white paternalism and benevolence. Explaining how he had made the decision to approve the annexation of the Philippines, President William McKinley said he had gone down on his knees to pray for "light and guidance from the 'ruler of nations' " and had been told by God that it was America's duty to "educate" and "uplift" the Filipinos. The people of this new American possession were seen by their guardians as backward natives to be "civilized" by Americans seeking to carry the "white man's burden." Based on an ideology of racial supremacy, American expansionism abroad turned into exclusionism at home. "It must be realized that the Filipino is just the same as the manure that we put on the land — just the same," the secretary of an agricultural association told an interviewer in 1930. "He is not our 'little brown brother.' He is no brother at all! — he is not our social equal."[20]

Filipino immigrants encountered racial discrimination, often finding themselves identified with the Asian groups that had entered the country earlier. "Because of my color and race the white man mistakes me for either a Japanese or Chinese," a Pinoy said. When a Filipino tried to get a haircut, he was asked by a white barber: "Are you a Jap?" After he had been refused service in a white-owned barbershop, Magdaleno Abaya was filled with hurt and fear: "Whenever I wanted to go into an American barber shop I always hesitated for fear that I would be treated like a dog again." Filipinos were also sometimes thought to be black; staring at them whites asked, "Are they colored?" On the doors of hotels, Pinoys often read signs saying: "Positively No Filipinos Allowed." They sometimes were excluded from theaters or forced to sit in segregated sections. The Broadway Theater in Portland segregated "the Filipinos, Japanese, Chinese, Colored people on the balcony," allowing "only whites on the first floor." Filipinos were also frequently refused service in restaurants. Entering a coffee shop on Geary Street in San Francisco, Roberto Vallangca sat down, waiting to be served. "The two waitresses simply ignored me, laughing and joking with the other customers — acting like I was not there," he bitterly recalled. "Other customers came and went — some even sat beside me. The waitresses served them but did not even bother to even talk to or look at me. After about twenty-five minutes, I left the shop, feeling low, sad, ashamed; I realized then that I could not go anywhere because I was a Filipino."[21]

Finding a place to live was usually a frustrating ordeal. Filipinos were told by landlords and realtors: "Orientals are not allowed here." "Only whites are allowed in this neighborhood." "The reason why Orientals are not allowed to rent a place here is the fear that the place might be overcrowded with other nationalities. You were not the first one to try to rent a place here. I have other Filipinos, as well as Japanese, Chinese, and Mexicans in my office, and always I have to turn them away." Furthermore, Filipinos could not buy land because they, like the Japanese, Chinese, Koreans, and Asian Indians, were not "white" and thus not eligible to naturalized citizenship. "My folks were not citizens," Terry Rosal said, "so they could not buy a house. They bought the house, but the house was under my name and my brother, George, and still is. . . . They could never own a farm. They were just laborers, working in the agricultural fields." Not permitted by law to buy a house in Oakland, Antonio and Angeles Mendoza received special help from their landladies. They had been renting an apartment from two Irish sisters; concerned about the young Filipino couple, the sisters secretly saved the rent money each month and used it to buy a house for them as a gift. "That's how we got to own a house," explained Angeles Mendoza. "One of the white families tried to circulate a petition demanding we move out of the neighborhood, but no other families would sign it."[22]

Called names like "goo-goos" and "monkeys," Filipinos repeatedly encountered anti-Filipino stereotypes and images. Though the arrest rate for Filipino males compared favorably with that of white males (according to the Bureau of Census of Crimes, between 1910 and 1940 the number of felony commitments per thousand of the population was 4.4 percent for native whites and only one percent for Filipinos), Filipinos were often seen as "criminally-minded," as troublemakers, willing to "slash, cut or stab at the least provocation." They were called "headhunters" and "untamed" and primitive savages, on the "same level as the American Indians." Commenting on the overwhelmingly male Filipino migration, the President of the Immigration Study Commission stated: "These men are jungle folk, and their primitive moral code accentuates the race problem even more than the economic difficulty." In their protests against racial prejudice, Filipinos criticized the contradiction between America's ideals and reality: "We do not find that the United States government puts its theories into practice. In school in the Islands we learn from the Declaration of Independence that all men are created equal. But when we get over here we find people treating us as if we were inferior."[23]

White-nativist reactions against Filipinos were fueled by intensifying economic competition between white workers and Filipinos. Frequently this ethnic antagonism erupted into racial violence and riots. "We were better workers in the fields than the *puti* [white Americans]," a Filipino said. "We were driving them out of their jobs and they hated us. They'd gang up on us in the streets, shouting 'monkey, monkey.' " In the Yakima Valley in 1928, 150 white workers stopped two carloads of sixty Filipinos en route to apple farms. Then an infuriated mob escorted the Filipinos out of the area and told them to keep going or they would be shot. Elsewhere in Washington, Filipinos were assaulted and beaten by white mobs.[24]

Anti-Filipino hate and violence were most intense in California. Noting the increasing number of attacks on Filipino laborers in 1929, the *Evening Pajaronian* in the Salinas Valley predicted: "The Filipino labor question is likely to become as big a problem . . . as were the Chinese and Japanese problems, and the outbreaks [against Filipinos] were merely the scab coming off a slightly festering sore that, ere long, is likely to break forth in a nasty eruption." White working-class resentment against Filipino laborers intensified as the economy collapsed and as jobs became increasingly scarce. Afraid and angry, white workers turned to vigilante tactics. In August of 1930, for example, the Sunnyvale chief of police received a letter warning: "Get Rid of all Filipinos or we'll burn this town down." A farmer received a threatening handwritten message: "Work no Filipinos or we'll destroy your crop and you too." Meanwhile in Reedley, California, one hundred Filipino laborers sleeping in a camp on the H. C. Peterson ranch were the target of a dynamite bomb thrown by white men from a passing automobile. After the attack, Peterson said to an interviewer: "I told the boys in the camp to defend themselves if they had to." The interviewer recorded in his notebook: "They were all armed." Another farmer said that his Filipino men would not go to work without their guns. Four months later, in December, a bomb was thrown into a livery barn housing seventy-five Filipinos in Imperial, California: the explosion killed a laborer and wounded several others. One Filipino never forgot the moment of horror. "When we arrived home, we were bombarded with stones thrown by a white mob," recounted Richard Palma Loable. "They threw a stone into our kitchen. They didn't like Filipinos to stay in that town. [The next day] about nine o'clock, we went to bed. My gosh, about fifteen minutes, I heard a bomb . . . under the garage. Aresto Lande was killed. He was hit by the dynamite. His stomach was just a hole."[25]

Complaining about Filipino labor competition, a "common white laborer" told an interviewer in 1930: "Why, I applied just the other day for a job at a fruit ranch, and the superintendent told me: 'The hours are long, the pay is small, and you're not the right color anyway.' Can you beat that? . . . He said, 'I have orders to employ men — lots of 'em, but they have to be Mexicans and Filipinos.' " Fearful Filipinos were taking more than jobs away from white men, this frustrated white worker continued: "These Filipino boys are good dancers. They can dance circles around these 'white' boys, and the 'white' boys don't like it — especially when the Filipinos dance with 'white' girls. It's no telling what these Filipinos will do if they keep comin'; and it's no tellin' what the 'white' man will do either. Something is liable to happen."[26]

Something did happen at Watsonville, where the fusion of economic rivalry and sexual jealousy exploded in a bloody anti-Filipino race riot. In early December 1929, the police saw a Filipino man with a white teenage girl and arrested him. He was released from jail after the girl's mother explained to the authorities that her daughter and the Filipino were engaged and their relationship had her approval. On December 5, 1929, the town newspaper, the *Evening Pajaronian* published a photograph of the couple embracing each other. A month later, the local chamber of commerce protested against the presence of Filipino immigrants. In a resolution, the chamber declared that Filipinos represented "a moral and sanitary" threat and "a menace to white labor." In his endorsement of the resolution, Judge D. W. Rohrback described Filipinos as "little brown men about ten years removed from a bolo and breechcloth." Fifteen of them would live in "one room and content themselves with squatting on the floor eating rice and fish." "Attired like 'Solomon in all his glory,' " Filipino men were sensuous creatures, "strutting like peacocks and endeavoring to attract the eyes of young American and Mexican girls." Within this context of hysteria whipped up by local white leaders, four hundred white men attacked a Filipino dance hall. During four terrible days of rioting, many Filipinos were beaten and one was shot to death.[27]

Shortly after the riot, Judge Rohrback blamed the Filipinos for provoking the violence. "Damn the Filipino! He won't keep his place," the judge exclaimed in an interview. "The worst part of his being here is his mixing with young white girls from 13 to 17, buying them silk underwear and . . . keeping them out till all hours of the night. And some of these girls are carrying a Filipino's baby around inside them." In an article on the riot, a correspondent for the *Baltimore Sun* commented: "The Filipinos got into trouble at Watsonville because they wore 'sheikier' clothes, danced better, and spent their money more lavishly than their Nordic fellow farmhands and, therefore, appealed more than some of the latter to the local girls."[28]

The extreme violence of the anti-Filipino fury betrayed fears of Filipino sexuality. "The Japs and Chinese have never mixed with 'white' women to any extent," said a Stockton resident in 1930, "not to the extent that the Filipino does anyway." Unlike men from China, Japan, Korea, and India, men from the Philippines seemed to seek out white female companionship and to be attractive to white women. "The Filipinos are . . . a social menace as they will not leave our white girls alone and frequently intermarry," said a white man before the House Committee on Immigration and Naturalization in 1930. He added that he recently attended an automobile show in Washington, D.C., and saw a "sight" he had never expected to see: "As we were looking at some of the nicer cars along comes a Filipino and a nice looking white girl. We followed them around to be sure we were not mistaken. . . . I don't know what she saw in him."[29]

Explaining the "Filipinos' success with white women," the deputy labor commissioner said: "The love-making of the Filipino is primitive, even heathenish . . . more elaborate." A California businessman put it more bluntly: "The Filipinos are hot little rabbits, and many of these white women like them for this reason." In his remarks published in *Time* magazine, San Francisco Municipal Court Judge Sylvain Lazarus was very detailed in his description of the sexual prowess of Filipino men:

> It is a dreadful thing when these Filipinos, scarcely more than savages, come to San Francisco, work for practically nothing, and obtain the society of these [white] girls. . . . Some of these [Filipino] boys, with perfect candor, have told me bluntly and

boastfully that they practice the art of love with more perfection than white boys, and occasionally one of the [white] girls has supplied me with information to the same effect. In fact some of the disclosures in this regard are perfectly startling in nature.[30]

Organizations like the Native Sons of the Golden West and the Commonwealth Club hysterically portrayed Filipinos as sexual threats, and even prominent California leaders conjured up images of lascivious Filipino men. The former president of the University of California, Dr. David P. Barrows, testified before Congress that the social problems of the Filipino were "almost entirely based upon sexual passion." The Filipino, Barrows explained, "usually frequents the poorer quarters of our towns and spends the residues of his savings in brothels and dance halls, which in spite of our laws exist to minister to his lower nature."[31]

Beneath these sexual anxieties lay a fear of Filipino men as a threat to white racial purity. Relationships between Filipino men and white women represented "a hybridizing at the bottom, often under the most wretched circumstances, of the lower racial stocks." This "race mingling" would create a "new type of mulatto," an "American Mestizo." Judge Rohrback predicted that if the "present state of affairs" continued, there would be "40,000 half-breeds" in California within ten years. In congressional hearings on Filipino immigration, V. S. McClatchy testified: "You can realize, with the declared preference of the Filipino for white women and the willingness on the part of some white females to yield to that preference, the situation which arises." In his call for the restriction of Filipino immigration, McClatchy revealed, perhaps unwittingly, the sexual fears driving the exclusionist forces: "California in this matter [of exclusionist legislation] is seeking to protect the nation, as well as itself, against the peaceful penetration of another colored race."[32]

Reacting to Judge Lazarus's remarks, Quintin Paredes, Philippine Resident Commissioner in Washington, quipped: "Well the Judge admits that Filipinos are great lovers." And Ernest Ilustre in a letter to the editor of *Time* also accepted the judge's compliment: "We, Filipinos, however poor, are taught from the cradle up to respect and love our women. That's why our divorce rate is nil compared with the State of which Judge Lazarus is a proud son. If to respect and love womenfolks is savagery, then make the most of it, Judge. We plead guilty."[33]

But Filipino men could not so humorously and easily dismiss

the problem of white-male sexual jealousy. They had to worry about harassment and physical abuse from white men. "Once we went out with white people, white children, or especially the girls, we were in a dangerous spot. The life of the young Filipino at that time was very sad. We were not even allowed to go to the public dances without being bothered." "If you dated a white woman, you didn't know what was going to happen. You were scared in public." Filipino men were especially afraid of the police. "The law said we could not go out with white women. So you got to sneak. You hide, you sneak because the police will see you. They might put you in jail."[34]

The law in California prohibited marriages between whites and "Negroes, mulattoes, or Mongolians." The *Stockton Record* editorialized that Filipinos were not Caucasians and hence were "obviously" ineligible to intermarry with whites. "While the 'little brown brothers' may flock here," the newspaper continued, "they are unassimilable and miscegenation would be unthinkable." In a letter to the *Dinuba Sentinel,* a Californian compared the behavior of blacks and Filipinos: "Negroes usually understand how to act," but "these Fils" think they have "a perfect right to mingle with the white people and even to intermarry." Warning that biologically unassimilable races like the Filipinos should not be allowed to mingle with "the dominant race in this country," California Attorney General U. S. Webb insisted that the anti-miscegenation law be applied to Filipinos. "Race preservation," he argued, required this prohibition.[35]

But actually it was not clear whether the term "Mongolians" included Filipinos. Filipinos challenged the law: in 1933, Salvador Roldan successfully secured a California Court of Appeals decision allowing him to marry his white fiancée because he was Malay rather than Mongolian. The 1880 anti-miscegenation law, the court ruled, did not intend the classification "Mongolian" to be applied to a "Malay": "From 1862 to 1885 the history of California is replete with legislation to curb the so-called 'Chinese invasion,' and as we read we are impressed with the fact that the terms 'Asiatics,' 'coolies' and 'Mongolians' mean 'Chinese' to the people who discussed and legislated on the problem." However, the court then suggested a legislative remedy: "If the common thought of today is different from what it was at that time, the matter is one that addresses itself to the legislature and not to the courts." Almost immediately after the court ruling, the state legislature amended the anti-miscegenation law and added the "Malay race" to the restricted category. Twelve other states also prohibited marriages between whites and Filipinos.[36]

As Malays, Filipinos were not allowed to marry white women, but could they become U.S. citizens? In its answer to this question in 1934, the Supreme Court declared: " 'White persons' within the meaning of the statute [the Naturalization Law of 1790] are members of the Caucasian race, as Caucasian is defined in the understanding of the mass of men. The term excludes the Chinese, the Japanese, the Hindus, the American Indians and the Filipinos." Analyzing the exclusion of Filipinos from citizenship, Julian Ilar, a student at the University of Chicago, bitterly observed:

> Try as we will we cannot become Americans. We may go to the farthest extreme in our effort to identify ourselves with the ways of the Americans, straightening our noses, dressing like the American in the latest fashion, pasting our faces with bleaching cream, and our hair with stacomb — but nevertheless we are not able to shake off that tenacious psychology. Always we remain sensitive, always we retain at least a subconscious fear that we are being slighted because we are Filipinos. Always there lurks over us a trace of suspicion that perhaps after all, we do not "belong."[37]

Filipinos did not "belong" and should not be permitted to immigrate to the United States, the exclusionists believed. But the 1924 immigration law could not be applied to Filipinos because they came from an American territory. Filipinos presented California with "her latest race problem," explained Professor Donald Anthony in 1931. The Filipino "problem," however, was "unique," for Filipinos were not "aliens." Thus "our solution of the Oriental problem, exclusion," could not "very well be applied to people who, although not full citizens," were governed by the United States. The only way to exclude Filipinos, Anthony concluded, was to grant independence to the Philippines.[38]

Three years later, in 1934, Congress passed the Tydings-McDuffie Act, establishing the Philippines as a commonwealth and providing independence in ten years. "The Pacific coast states have resolved to bring about Filipino exclusion," the *Filipino Nation* of Los Angeles commented before the enactment of the new law. "Since they could not achieve that result except by giving the Philippines independence, they must now vote . . . for independence." The purpose of the Tydings-McDuffie Act was Filipino exclusion: as residents of an independent country rather than a U.S. territory, Filipinos would no longer have unrestricted entry to the United States. "It is absolutely illogical," argued Senator Millard Tydings, "to have an immigration policy to exclude Japanese and Chinese and permit Filipinos en masse to come into the country. . . . If they continue to settle in certain areas they will come in conflict with white labor . . . and increase the opportunity for more racial prejudice and bad feeling of all kinds." Under the new law, Filipino immigration was limited to only fifty persons annually, but additional Filipinos would be allowed to enter Hawaii as plantation laborers whenever the sugar planters required them. Filipinos in Hawaii were prohibited from remigrating to the mainland, and all Filipinos in the United States were classified as "aliens."[39]

Under the Tydings-McDuffie Act, Filipinos were reclassified as aliens, and suddenly they found themselves ineligible for assistance from New Deal programs such as the National Youth Administration and the Works Progress Administration. The Relief Appropriation Act of 1937 gave preference first to American citizens in need of relief and next to needy aliens who had declared their intention to become citizens. But Filipinos had been informed by the Supreme Court that they could not even apply for naturalized citizenship because they were not "white." Thousands of hungry and poor Filipinos were cut off from the federal relief rolls.[40]

Actually, exclusionist legislation was unnecessary by 1934, for Filipinos were no longer coming in significant numbers. America's image as the promised land had faded for Filipinos. "Widespread publicity has been given to the newspaper accounts of labor disturbances there," reported the Bureau of Labor in the Philippines in 1930, "and to the fact that there is a great deal of unemployment and suffering among the Filipinos in the western part of the United States. The true facts regarding the situation are now becoming generally known and there is much less tendency for adventurous young Filipinos to go to the United States." The numbers of Filipinos entering the country dropped suddenly and sharply from 11,360 in 1929 to 1,306 in 1932.[41]

Still, the exclusionists were not satisfied. They wanted the removal of Filipinos from America. In Los Angeles, County Supervisor Roger W. Jessup called for the deportation of some 7,000 indigent Filipinos on the welfare rolls. The cost of transporting a Filipino back to the Philippines, Jessup calculated in 1934, would be only eighty-seven dollars — an amount much less than maintaining him on welfare. A year later, the Congress responded to the demands of exclusionists by passing the Repatriation Act. Seeking to remove

"Filipino wards of public and private charitable organizations," this law offered Filipinos transportation to the Philippines at the expense of the federal government on the condition that they forfeit their right of reentry to the United States. The *Los Angeles Times* publicized the Repatriation Act and urged Filipinos to "go back home," for here was an opportunity to sail on "luxuriant ocean liners with Uncle Sam paying their passage and all expenses and wishing them bon voyage," and to be "greeted in Manila by brass bands and songs of welcome."[42]

The real purpose of the law, Carey McWilliams of the *Nation* pointed out, was Filipino exclusion. Originally allowed to enter the United States as "cheap labor," Filipino farm laborers had completed their "brief but strenuous period of service to American capital": they were no longer needed because of the availability of Mexican labor and no longer wanted because of their labor militancy. Employers now wanted Filipinos deported. Repatriation, McWilliams commented, was "a trick, and not a very clever trick, to get them out of this country."[43]

Support for Filipino repatriation, *Time* reported, came from Pacific Coast laborers: they saw the program as "a good excuse for inviting Filipino workers to go home rather than stay in the United States, selling their services for ten cents an hour, in competition with white men." Interest in "this subsidized exodus," the magazine added, was also stirred by white-male sexual jealousies. "To the intense dismay of many race-conscious Californians these little brown men not only have a preference for white girls, particularly blondes, but have established to many a white girl's satisfaction their superior male attractions." But the law failed to accomplish the purpose of Filipino removal: it was able to repatriate only 2,190 Filipinos.[44]

Filipinos were not rushing home. Letters from relatives and friends had given them a bleak picture of life at home: there were no jobs waiting for them in the Philippines. More importantly, they could not return, not yet, for their sense of pride would not permit them to do so. To be transported home at public expense as "wards" would be too humiliating. "*May puno'y walang sanga, may dahon walang bunga,*" they had been told by a Tagalog proverb, "It has a trunk without a branch, it has a leaf without fruit." They could not return, confessing failure. They knew they should not be blamed: "*Walang matalim na hasa kapag sa bato tumama,*" "No bolo knife is sharp when it strikes the rock." Still they felt "ashamed to go home without any surplus," unwilling to show themselves to their families once again unless they could sail to the Philippines under their "own steam" and with money in their pockets. One of the few returnees realized too late that he had made a mistake: "I have come home as a repatriate and that alone has given my name the stigma of failure as an adventurer."[45]

Originally Filipinos had migrated from the Philippines because they had found themselves facing grim futures and "sinking down into the toilet." Many of them had left wives and children behind, planning to return. In a letter to his wife, a Pinoy wrote: I am "working steady from sunrise to sunset, six days a week. . . . If I can keep up with the hard work, God willing, I should be returning home in two years. . . . Enclosed is a small amount of $45.00. Set aside part of it for Antonio's education, and keep paying Tata Iniong for that piece of land where someday, we will build our own house."

> *I promised it'll be a short*
> *while perhaps*
> *And I will be back home*
> *It's been only three months*
> *Since then*
> *To me, it means*
> *Three full years*
> *And I count*
> *Even the hours*
> *Because the heart*
> *Is filled with ache.*[46]

But most of the Filipino sojourners, four fifths of them, never returned. "If I had enough money, by golly! I'd go home," a migrant said. "I've been here 16 years and have saved nothing." Struggling for survival, Filipinos were forced to drift along, carried by the currents of the Great Depression. "For nine months the Filipino Social Relief Service in Los Angeles had been giving a free meal every Sunday to the unemployed Filipinos," wrote Midi Yanez in the *Filipino Nation* in 1932. "So many came — often as many as 300 in one day. . . . Walk down First Street or enter any of the Filipino pool halls and, if you are a Filipino, you will immediately be surrounded by a large number of your countrymen begging for a dime or a nickel for something to eat." The economic conditions of the depression had trapped Filipinos here. A Pinoy had written to his family in the Philippines: "We do not see any possibility at all of coming home. This depression has turned everything topsy-turvy. Wages are cut

70%. I have been out of work half of the time this year." Another Pinoy reflected: "I wanted to go back to the Philippines, to serve my country and my people as a teacher. But the Depression put the fire out of me so I stayed on, and on, and on." The depression, however, was only part of the story. "You shouldn't have come to America," a Filipino told his younger brother in California. "But you can't go back now. You can never go back, Allos."[47]

Bahala na: Men in McIntosh Suits

In America emerged a unique Filipino world. Growing up on the farms and in the villages of the Philippines, where traditions were strong and communities were stable, the migrants now found themselves moved from *campo* to *campo*. After work in the evening, they would stand in "the soft night air" outside the door of their bunkhouses and listen to their "loneliness breathing like a tired wind over the land." The wind seemed to whisper a Tagalog proverb: "*Ang kabayanihan ay bunga nang liboligong kahirapan,*" "Bravery brings many hardships." Relaxing together, they told each other about the girlfriends they had left behind in the Philippines. What were they doing tonight? they wondered. Were Epang, Maria, and the other women waiting faithfully for the men to return, or were they dancing with other men? During their hours of leisure, they would carry gallons of wine with them down to the river, where they would pick mushrooms and catch *kandole* (catfish) and have a fish fry. There, among *barkadas,* their close friends, they played guitars and sang old Filipino ballads:

> *Planting rice is never fun*
> *Bent from morn till the set of sun;*
> *Cannot stand and cannot sit*
> *Cannot rest for a little bit.*

They sang about coming to America and the conditions they found here:

> *Then why did I have to make*
> *A trip to this far place?*
> *Oh! what a mistake!*
> *At home it's easy life*
> *For there's no task nor strife*
> *Nor labor as hard to stand*
> *As that in this land.*

And they sang love songs:

> Will you remember
> Your pledge to me
> That your love
> Will never be diminished?

As they sang, they felt homesick, their voices becoming "so sad, so full of yesterday and the haunting presence of familiar seas."[48]

To escape from the loneliness they experienced in the campos, they went into town. Unlike the Chinese with their Chinatowns and the Japanese with their Little Tokyos and Nihonmachis, Filipinos did not develop their own ethnic sections in cities. The Filipino districts in Stockton and Los Angeles, for example, were mainly gathering centers for migratory workers. They were not places to live and build long-term communities. Unlike the Chinese and Japanese, Filipinos did not engage extensively in ethnic enterprise; in fact, there was only one Filipino grocery store in Los Angeles in 1933. Twenty years later there were only six. Filipino business activity tended to focus on services: in 1938, Los Angeles had sixteen Filipino restaurants and twelve barbershops.[49]

The notable lack of Filipino merchants in America was partly the result of centuries of Spanish colonialism in the Philippines. Primarily interested in the galleon trade between Manila and Acapulco, Spanish administrators in the Philippines did not develop a native capitalist economy and allowed Chinese merchants to service the retail needs of the local communities. Consequently, Filipinos did not bring to America a tradition of mercantile enterprise, or institutions such as the credit-rotating system. When they came here, they also found the Chinese and Japanese already established, with footholds in the retail trade that accommodated the needs of the Filipino newcomers and that preempted the entry of Filipino retailers. Pinoys arrived not only later, but at the beginning of the Great Depression, an inauspicious time to initiate new entrepreneurial ventures. Unlike their counterparts from China and Japan, most could speak English and had somewhat wider access to employment; not restricted by language barriers, they were thus not driven toward ethnic enterprise to the same extent.[50]

The lack of a Filipino town and the relatively low participation of Filipinos in business activity also reflected the transiency of the migrants. Most of them were single-male migratory workers shuttling back and forth from Seattle and San Francisco to Alaska and traveling constantly with the crops in Washington and California. Filipinos saw themselves as sojourners to a greater extent than did their counterparts from China and Japan, for they were from an American territory and thought they could come and go as they pleased. Young Filipinos saw themselves as Americans "born under the Stars and Stripes," observed Hilario Moncado of the Los Angeles *Filipino Nation* in 1931. As sojourning "nationals," they had even less inclination than the Chinese and Japanese migrants to bring families and institutions here, establish enterprises, and form communities replicating their homelands. Such possibilities were rendered remote by the 1934 Tydings-McDuffie Act, which cut off Filipino immigrants from their families in the Philippines. This Filipino exclusion law was even more severe than the immigration-restriction policies for the Chinese and Japanese. The Tydings-McDuffie Act did not have a provision allowing Filipino "merchants" to bring wives here as the 1888 law did for the Chinese, and it did not exempt family members and wives as the 1908 Gentlemen's Agreement did for the Japanese.[51]

Mostly young men without families, Filipino farm laborers usually went into town on weekends. "After being in the camp for a long time you go wild the first few days in the city," said Felix Tapiz. "We congregated in Chinatown. There were many happenings . . . dances, prostitution, whatever." There Filipinos hunted for excitement in the gambling joints and dance halls. Or they loitered on the streets in front of the Filipino barbershop, a community "focal point," where they could sit around and share stories. Or they hung out in the pool halls. For many of the Pinoys, the pool hall was "their world."[52]

In the Chinatowns and in the camps, gambling was a favorite pastime. "Most of these boys never gambled once or even knew what it was until they came here," a Filipino told an interviewer in 1930. "But, you see, there are few amusements open to them here." After work, sitting on blankets, they played poker and blackjack until late at night. They also gathered at cockfights, where they were swept away by the excitement and the flurry of violence, the betting, and the exchange of money. "Cockfights in Stockton was number one. Everybody used to love to go to the cockfights. . . . We used to do it in secret places. If we have fifty or one hundred Filipinos getting together, that's a good crowd for cockfighting." On weekends, especially after payday, Filipinos crowded into "Chinese" gambling houses, popularly known as *sikoy-sikoys*, where "chop suey was served free." There many of them lost not only the money they had earned that day but also their wages for the next few weeks and even months. "You work for one whole week, you go to the gambling house. You lose it all in one hour. Come Monday, you'll start all over again," said a Filipino. "Work, save your money, go to the gambling house on Saturday, lose your money, in sikoy-sikoy." "There were too many gambling houses," an unlucky Filipino regretted. "Sometimes I lost what I earned . . . eighty dollars, fifty dollars. . . . lost everything."[53]

Living in a world of men, many migrants spent their money on prostitutes. Often the services of the women were delivered to them in the camps. A taxi company in Stockton, reported the deputy labor commissioner of San Joaquin County, made five hundred dollars a month transporting prostitutes to the outlying areas. "These women must be white, weigh not over one hundred pounds, and be comparatively young — not over 24 or 25 years old." When Manuel Buaken was working in Stockton, he noticed a Cadillac sedan, driven by a man, stopping at his camp. The man had brought "three beautiful blondes," taking them into the Filipino quarters and making "fat collections" that night. He returned again within a week, with different women. "The frequency of such visits by these men who capitalize on the young bodies of innocent girls and on the sexual desires of Filipinos occurred twice a month," Buaken continued, "going from place to place, making the rounds of the camps at Stockton, Salinas, Bakersfield, Imperial Valley, Fresno, and San Joaquin Valley." Prostitutes "followed the seasons," a farm laborer stated, "the way Filipinos follow the crops." Far away from home, lonely and lacking the normal company of women, Filipino men paid $2.50, more than a whole day's earnings, for a moment of pleasure. "It's just natural for any young man — whether he's Italian or Filipino or American — to want to have some fun," a Filipino farm worker said. "The only chance we ever had was to go with all those prostitutes. We had to have somebody to enjoy ourselves with."[54]

One of their most popular pastimes was the taxi-dance hall. Filipinos flocked to dancelands with names like Pig and Whistle, Hippodrome, Mardong, Dreamland Saloon, Royal Palais, and Rizal Cabaret. There they danced to songs like "I Like Your Size, I Like Your Eyes," "Honey Bunch, You Know How Much I Love You," and "I Wish I Had My Old Girl Back Again." Filipino bands played lively music for favorite dances like the waltz, fox-trot, and polka. One band, the "Manila Serenaders" was an eighteen-piece orchestra. We "played in Oregon, Idaho, all middle states going up as far as

North Dakota and then South," recalled band member Carlos Malla. "We went to Missouri, Texas ... [playing in a] regular ballroom ... five hundred or a thousand [people dancing in] the hall."[55]

"*Bahala na*" — "Come what may," Filipino men shouted, for the dance hall was the place where they went to have a good time, to forget their problems. They were very extravagant. Exuding cologne, they had sticky pomades slicking down their jet black hair and wore fancy "McIntosh suits" — "expensive, highly tailored suits, sometimes white with padded shoulders, like suits Hollywood actors wear." "There were four main dancing cabarets in Los Angeles and I had a girlfriend in every hall," boasted Frank Coloma. "I usually went there after going to the pool halls or gambling places, and I always wore the very best suit — a McIntosh suit."[56]

In the glittering dance hall with hot music filling the night air, Filipino men were able to escape from the humdrum of their daily existence. There they could meet women, working as dance hostesses, "beautiful" ones — "all kinds, Italians, Mexicans, and Negroes, too." "The girls were always Americans, mostly blondes, and you couldn't dance with them without money." In the dance halls, the Filipino men were told by the women: "No money, no honey." They could dance with them — a dime a dance, a ten-cent ticket for one minute. They would buy rolls of tickets. "Most of the dime-a-dance halls had several dozen girls working there," a Filipino remembered. "Each dance cost a dime and was very short. Most of the boys bought a dollar's worth of dances." On the dance floor, the men would blow a whole day's wages in ten, twenty minutes. Many of them went to dance halls, trying to buy love, only to find their hearts broken and pockets empty. A Filipino recounted his sad story:

> My friend took me to the dance hall one night and there I met a beautiful girl. I fell in love with her. Night after night after finishing my work I could not help but go out to see her, and dance with her. For a while we were both very serious with one another. She finally asked me if I would marry her, and I consented to it, having spent a large sum of money for her already. My boss didn't seem to like the idea of my going out every night so she decided to get somebody to take my place. My girl friend felt that because of this sudden change I wasn't quite so generous to her as before, so she turned me down. Now all the money that I have been saving for years is all gone. My friends have deserted me. Now I am nothing but a helpless beggar.[57]

The loneliness of Filipino men, their craving for the company of women, often bordered on desperation. "We would not have led miserable lives, nor drifted from one shoulder to another, if, in the beginning, our women had come with us," a manong said. "We saw no point in growing roots — in making a home for ourselves." In 1930, 80 percent of Filipino men in California were under thirty years of age and unmarried. Statistically, it was unlikely many would be able to marry Filipinas: the ratio of Filipino males to females was fourteen to one.[58]

A Pinoy in Los Angeles wrote to his aunt in the Philippines asking her to find a wife for him: "Two days ago I received your most loving letter. . . . Tia (Auntie), why take so long a time to find a girl for me. Remember, I am not particular. As long as that dear one has a bit of everything (you know what I mean) that will serve the partnership. Have you anyone in mind?" Everywhere the few Pinays already in America attracted the attention of the Pinoys. "Back in the 1920s," recalled Terry Rosal, "there weren't that many Filipinas. One Pinay to one hundred Pinoys. And regardless of the shape or the age of the Pinay, she was a queen." Camila Carido smiled as she recounted the attention she received from the Filipino men when she was a teenager during the 1920s: "We were treated like actresses. The men treated us like royalty. It didn't matter what you looked like. Just that we were Filipinas." Similarly Belen de Guzman Braganza had no trouble getting dates in Seattle: "I could date anyone. You could count [the number of Filipino] women in your two hands. There were over one thousand five hundred Filipinos here. Imagine, they're all men." A popular song described the Filipina:

> The Filipino woman
> Like a star in the morning
> To see her brings joy
> There is a radiance
> And great beauty.[59]

But Filipino "queens," like the men, generally had to work. They cleaned homes as maids, harvested the vegetables and fruit in the fields, or cooked for the work crews. "My recollections of my mother," Teresa Romero Jamero said, "are those of her working so hard in the kitchen. She not only did the cooking for camp and family, she also worked in the fields." During his visit to a ranch in 1930, researcher James Wood noticed three Filipino women workers dressed in men's clothes and paid the same wages as the men. Pinays also helped to bring Filipino culture to America, introducing Filipino folk dances and foods to the United States. My mother "used to make that Filipino rice cake, that 'suman,' " said Hyacinth Camposano Ebat, "and my sister and I used to go around selling them."[60]

But there were too few Filipinas, and many Filipino men married outside the ethnic group — to Mexican, Chinese, Japanese, Eskimo, and Caucasian women. "If there were Filipino women here," commented a Filipino labor contractor in 1930, "I am sure that Filipinos would not seek white girls." Similarly Alfonso Perales Dangaran of Fresno explained that "there weren't many Filipino women" and thus the men married "white girls or Mexican girls." Most mixed couples in Los Angeles were Filipino-Mexican, and a popular song among Pinoys was "Mexicali Rose I Love You." Filipino men found they had much in common with Mexican women — including the Spanish language and the Catholic Church. They could also take Mexican women to public places without receiving inquisitive and disapproving glances, which they always experienced whenever they were with white women.[61]

Unlike Chinese and Japanese men, many Filipino men dated and married white women. Most Filipino men were single, and Filipino culture did not have the intricate system of arranged marriage practiced by the Japanese. "The picture bride idea won't work for the Filipino," remarked Luis Agudo in an interview in 1930. "He doesn't make love that way." Neither did Filipinos have the strong nationalism of their Japanese counterparts — a chauvinism requiring the preservation of ethnic purity. They had come from a society where mestizos, or persons of mixed ancestry, were present in large numbers and widely accepted. They had greater familiarity with Western culture than other Asian immigrants, for their homeland had been under Spanish colonial domination for over three hundred years. Educated in American schools in the islands and more or less proficient in English, they saw themselves as nationals rather than foreigners. Their Spanish or Mediterranean culture gave many Filipinos romantic qualities that made them attractive to women. They knew how to court women — how to dress sharply, how to give amorous attention, and how to sing love songs. Filipino men also entered American society during the 1920s, when young white women were experiencing greater freedom from traditional restraints, and when dance halls became popular places where Filipino men and white women could meet and socialize.[62]

Filipino men and white women who wished to marry encountered anti-miscegenation laws, especially in states like Oregon and California. They had to travel to states where such unions were not banned. "Intermarriage was not permitted in Portland," said George Pimentel. "We went to Washington where they allowed intermarriages." White women marrying Filipinos became targets of discrimination. In 1930, in a case involving German immigrant Mrs. Anne Podien-Jesena, who was married to Basalico Jesena, Monterey Superior Court Judge H. C. Jorgensen ruled that immigrant-white wives of Filipinos were not entitled to naturalized citizenship. The Federal District Director of Naturalization went even further, stating that American women marrying Filipinos would lose their U.S. citizenship.[63]

Filipino-white couples also experienced social ostracism. In restaurants, they often overheard hostile remarks: "There is a Filipino with a white woman." A Mr. Escalanta, the proprietor of the Manila Pool Hall in San Jose, told an interviewer in 1930: "I have advised the boys against being seen with white girls in public. This is one of the quickest ways to cause trouble. . . . I have a friend who is married to a white girl, and they never dare to go out together." "Even walking down the street with Filipino people," noted Lorraine Libadia, a white woman married to a Filipino, "you received comments, thrown at you more or less." The comments were crude, debasing: white women in the company of Filipino men were called "nigger lovers." "It was just as low as you can get," said Hazel Simbe. "My neighbors said all kinds of rude things to my mother. I realize now that she suffered a lot on account of me, of us. I cried bushels of tears." Many white wives tried to avoid being seen in public with their Filipino husbands: "My mother, who is white, seemed reluctant to go out with my father or as a family group."[64]

Filipino men and white women had to overcome cultural differences in their marriages. Filipino men often felt out of place in the social circles of their wives. "When among my wife's American friends I cannot make myself feel a part of the group," a Filipino said. "At times I am reluctant to talk, because of my peculiar accent. This makes me appear inferior. . . . I can also feel their seeming frigidity in their attitudes toward me." Their wives, in turn, also experienced awkward moments in the company of Filipino friends. "When my husband's friends speak in their dialect," an American wife recounted, "I listen to them with eagerness, trying to grasp the nature of their conversation. When the group laughs, I also 'giggle' with them just to make them feel that I am really a 'makabayan' [a member of the group]."[65]

Gradually a second generation began to emerge. In Stockton by the 1940s, there were about five hundred American-born Filipino and part-Filipino children. By 1946, more than half of the children of Filipino immigrants were offspring of biracial unions. "We have a second generation of mestizos," observed Sophie Bilbat. "A lot of [Filipino men] marry American [white]. They don't marry Filipino, very few if they do." The second-generation Filipinos grew up in a world of prejudice. They were frequently called "niggers" by white children and were also viewed as foreigners. Born in 1931, Liz Megino grew up in a white community in Oakland, California. "The students in the school I attended were white," she remembered. "I had many white friends but I never got invited to their parties." Another second-generation Filipino said: "When I was in seventh or eighth grade we went to a certain park in Stockton to play. And I remember some children screaming and yelling at us, 'Go back to where you come from. Go back to the country you come from. You don't belong here.' " But the Filipino children had been born here; they were from America.[66]

Most children had little time to go to the park, however, for they had to work. "I was nine years old," recalled Josephine Romero Loable. "I started washing clothes and taking care of other little things that my mother couldn't do because she worked." "Well, I really didn't have too much of a teenage life because, when I was fourteen, probably thirteen, I had to quit school," said Terry Rosal. "I had to go out in the fields and work. I worked on the asparagus farms as a cutter, as a shed boy, as a washer in the packing house." Stung by prejudice and saddled with work responsibilities, Filipino children often drew strength and comfort from their *compadres* — their godparents. "I have two godparents," said Ignacio Ladrido Balaba. "When my mother died, love was extended from these two families." Like the Punjabi children, Filipino children were also surrounded by bachelor friends of their parents, calling them "uncles."[67]

In the Heart of Filipino America

One of these thousands of Filipino bachelors was Carlos Bulosan, the son of a farmer in Binalonan on the island of Luzon. When he arrived in America in 1930, he was only a boy, just seventeen years old. He had promised his family: "I will come back someday." But Bulosan never returned to the Philippines; neither did he become an American citizen. "I know deep down in my heart," he wrote to a friend, "that I am an exile in America." Like most of his compatriots, this young Pinoy was a cannery worker, dishwasher, houseboy, and farm laborer. "Do you know what a Filipino feels in America?" he asked. In *America Is in the Heart*, published in 1946, he gave Filipinos their voices, allowing himself and his compatriots to describe their experiences and feelings and to make their claim on America. In this narrative, subtitled "A Personal History," Bulosan drew deeply from his own experiences and those of the Filipinos around him to create a moving and powerful story, a work of imagination and detail, a representation of the reality of Filipino America.[68]

Bulosan had journeyed to America in his mind long before he had actually stepped from the ship in Seattle. By the time he was born, the Philippines had been a colony of the United States for fifteen years. Under American rule, popular education was spreading throughout the archipelago and introducing ideas of opportunity and democracy. As a young boy, Bulosan felt this new stirring. One of his older brothers came home one day with a book filled with pictures and large letters. "If you learn to read this book," Amado said, "I will take you to school with me." "I will learn to read it in one day," Carlos replied boastfully. Years later he would remember how there was something moving in the way Amado had spoken to him: "His words seized my mind and nourished my life to the edge of the day. I was greatly fascinated with the idea of going to school, but did not know why, since there was no hope of my going beyond the third grade." What Carlos and other Filipino children learned in school seemed to contradict what was happening to Filipino farmers and peasants: while they learned about "ideas of social equality and of justice before the law," they watched their parents lose their farms to distant, faceless landlords.[69]

As a boy in the Philippines, Carlos encountered the American presence in the streets and marketplaces. American businessmen had begun their movement into the Philippines, living in "beautiful white houses" dotting the hills. American tourists crowded the markets, where they "took particular delight in photographing young Igorot girls with large breasts and robust mountain men whose genitals were nearly exposed, their G-strings bulging large and alive." One day, in the marketplace, Carlos was given ten centavos by an Amer-

ican lady tourist for undressing before her camera. "I had found,"
he said later, "a simple way to make a living."[70]

On another occasion, an American woman asked Carlos to carry
her groceries in a wheelbarrow. "I will never forget Miss Mary Strandon on the day I pushed the wheelbarrow to her apartment. When
I had carefully piled the vegetables and rice in the kitchen, she opened
her purse and offered me five centavos." Noticing the dirt on his
face, she had him wash his face with a bar of soap. "It was the first
time I had ever used soap." She had worked in a small-town library
in Iowa for fifteen years and had come to the Philippines, where she
worked in a library. Miss Strandon hired Carlos as a houseboy to
cook dinner and clean the house. During his free time, Carlos visited
Dalmacio, a houseboy working for another American woman living
in an adjacent apartment. Both boys talked about their plans to go
to America; they studied English, reading books about the country
of their dreams. One of the stories they read was about Abraham
Lincoln. "Who *is* this Abraham Lincoln?" Carlos asked his friend.
"He was a poor boy who became a president of the United States.
He was born in a log cabin and walked miles and miles to borrow
a book so that he would know more about his country." Fascinated
by the story, Carlos told Miss Strandon about what he had been
reading and asked her to tell him more about Lincoln. "I didn't know
you could read," she said and then described the great man who had
freed the black slaves. From that day onward this poor boy who
became president filled the thoughts of young Bulosan. Miss Strandon
brought him books from the library, and helped to open "a whole
new world" to the boy from Binalonan.[71]

But his readings and his expectations had not prepared him for
his experiences in America. When Bulosan arrived in Seattle, he had
only twenty cents. He was able to hitch a ride with four other Filipinos
to a hotel on King Street, "the heart of Filipino life in Seattle." The
proprietor glanced at their suitcases and asked for the rent. "We have
no money, sir," Bulosan admitted politely. "That is too bad," the
proprietor muttered, and walked outside, returning with "a short,
fat Filipino," who looked at the young men "stupidly with his dull,
small eyes, and spat his cigar out of the window." He pulled a fat
roll of bills from his pocket, giving twenty-five dollars to the proprietor, and shouted: "All right, Pinoys, you are working for me
now. Get your hats and follow me." In this way, Carlos and his
compatriots were "sold for five dollars each to work in the fish

canneries of Alaska." They were forced to sign a paper stating that each owed the labor contractor twenty dollars for bedding and another twenty for "luxuries." "What the luxuries were," Bulosan remarked later, "I have never found out."[72]

Shipped to Alaska, Bulosan and his four compatriots joined thousands of Filipinos, living in bunkhouses unfit for human habitation and working for the fishing industry. In the canneries, the lighting was inadequate and a strong smell of ammonia was pervasive. Work was exhausting and dangerous. Bulosan was assigned to a section called "wash lye," where he rinsed the beheaded fish that came down a small escalator. "One afternoon a cutter above me, working in the poor light, slashed off his right arm with the cutting machine. It happened so swiftly he did not cry out. I saw his arm floating down the water among the fish heads." When the season was over, Bulosan returned to Seattle, where he was paid. The labor contractor handed him a slip of paper, and he was amazed at the neatly itemized deductions he had supposedly incurred in Alaska: twenty-five dollars for withdrawals, one hundred for board and room, twenty for bedding, and another twenty for miscellaneous expenses. His take-home pay turned out to be only thirteen dollars.

So began his sojourn in America. After his stint in Alaska, Bulosan drifted from job to job and from unemployment line to unemployment line. He had entered the America of the Great Depression, and jobs were scarce and wages were low. Bulosan, like many Filipino farm laborers, followed the crops. He picked apples in the Yakima Valley of Washington; next he went down to California, where he harvested winter peas in Holtville, picked oranges in Riverside; then he rode a freight train to Idaho to pick peas and another train to Montana, where "the beet season was in full swing. Mexicans from Texas and New Mexico were everywhere; their jalopies dotted the highways. There were also Filipinos from California and Washington. Some of them had just come back from the fish canneries in Alaska." Bulosan rode the rails again, to Seattle, Portland, back to California — to Santa Maria, where he joined a crew planting cauliflower; from there he went to Nipomo and Lompoc. "It was cold in Lompoc, for the winter wind was beginning to invade the valley from Surf. The lettuce heads were heavy with frost. I worked with thick cotton gloves and a short knife. When the lettuce season was over the winter peas came next. I squatted between the long rows of peas and picked with both hands, putting the pods in a large petroleum can that I dragged with me." Bulosan sometimes worked as a dishwasher and a houseboy and did odd jobs here and there. Once, during a moment of desperation and hunger, he used a gun to rob a Japanese man, and on another occasion he stole a diamond ring from a house while a woman was upstairs taking a bath.[73]

Bulosan began to understand what Filipinos in America felt and why they had created "a wall around themselves in their little world." After the long work week in the fields, they retreated to Chinatowns in cities like Stockton and Seattle. There, "waiting for the night," hundreds of "Filipinos in magnificent suits" stood in front of poolrooms, gambling houses, and dance halls. Bulosan remembered the first time he went to a dance hall:

> I came to a building which brightly dressed white women were entering, lifting their diaphanous gowns as they climbed the stairs. I looked up and saw the huge sign:
>
> MANILA DANCE HALL
>
> The orchestra upstairs was playing; Filipinos were entering. I put my hands in my pockets and followed them, beginning to feel lonely for the sound of home.
> The dance hall was crowded with Filipino cannery workers and domestic servants. But the girls were very few, and the Filipinos fought over them. When a boy liked a girl he bought a roll of tickets from the hawker on the floor and kept dancing with her. . . . [My friend Marcelo] was dancing with a tall blonde in a green dress, a girl so tall that Marcelo looked like a dwarf climbing a tree. But the girl was pretty and her body was nicely curved and graceful, and she had a way of swaying that aroused confused sensations in me. . . . [Marcelo had a roll of tickets], and the girl was supposed to tear off one ticket every three minutes, but I noticed that she tore off a ticket for every minute. That was ten cents a minute.[74]

But every minute seemed worth it, helping Filipinos forget the humiliations, abuse, and racial violence they experienced. Bulosan saw how Filipinos were forced to live in skid row and the tenderloin. In Los Angeles, Bulosan and his brother Macario lived in the redlight district on Hope Street: "It was a noisy and tragic street, where suicides and murders were a daily occurrence, but it was the only place in the city where we could find a room. There was no other district where we were allowed to reside." When they tried to rent an apartment in the Vermont Avenue district, they noticed a landlady pulling down the For Rent sign as they approached, and they were told directly by another landlady: "We don't take Filipinos!" Feeling excluded and bitter, his brother said: "Well, there is nothing else to do but go back to *our* world."[75]

Once, while in Holtville, Bulosan saw a Filipino come into town with his American wife and their child. The couple entered a little restaurant and sat down at a table. Refused service, they left the restaurant; outside the child began to cry. The Filipino father returned to the restaurant, asking to buy a bottle of milk for the baby. "For *your* baby?" the proprietor shouted, coming out from behind the counter. "Yes, sir," replied the Filipino. "You goddamn brown monkeys have your nerve, marrying our women. Now get out of this town!" the proprietor yelled as he punched the Filipino between the eyes. In San Diego, Bulosan was turned away from all the hotels on Coronado Island and refused service at a drugstore fountain. In San Fernando, a citrus town near Los Angeles, a Filipino labor contractor who had planted lemon trees and helped to transform the valley into farmlands told Bulosan: "I have made this valley fruitful and famous. Some ten years ago I wanted to go into farming myself, so close I was to the soil, so familiar with the touch of clay and loam. But I found that I couldn't buy land in California." When he was ill in the Los Angeles County Hospital, Bulosan was told by a social worker: "You Filipinos ought to be shipped back to your jungle homes."[76]

At a farm in the Yakima Valley of Washington, Bulosan and his fellow Filipino farm laborers were driven into the darkness by white men carrying clubs and shooting guns. In Klamath Falls, Oregon, Bulosan was arrested by two policemen who called him a "brown monkey," robbed him of his two dollars, brutally beat him, and marched him to the California border. On another occasion, Bulosan and a Filipino friend were trying to organize farm laborers in Salinas. They were in the back room of a restaurant preparing a leaflet to be circulated among the workers when five white men kidnapped them at gunpoint. In the dark night they were driven across a beet field to some woods; there they were stripped naked, tarred and feathered, and viciously punched and kicked repeatedly. "The man on my right got out [of the car] and pulled me violently after him, hitting me on the jaw," Bulosan recounted. "Blood came out of my mouth. I raised my hand to wipe it off, but my attacker hit me again." Another man "kicked my left knee so violently that I fell on the grass, blinded with pain." Then a man called Lester "grabbed my testicles with his left hand and smashed them with his right fist."[77]

But while America could be cruel, Bulosan noticed, it could also be kind. Once, for example, he and some friends were trying to run away from white detectives in a railroad yard, and his friend Jose fell and had one of his legs amputated by the wheels of a moving train car. They carried Jose to the highway, seeking help, but the passing motorists looked scornfully and spat at them. Finally an old man came along in a Ford truck and drove them to the county hospital, where a kind doctor and two nurses did their best for Jose. "Walking down the marble stairway of the hospital," Bulosan began "to wonder at the paradox of America."[78]

The paradox puzzled and intrigued Bulosan. How could America be so profoundly contradictory? he questioned. In his search for answers, he thought about the white women he had come to know. One of them was Helen, a labor organizer he met during a farm laborers' strike in Oxnard. From the very beginning, he was suspicious of her, noticing how she used her "womanly ways" to attract and influence the strike leaders. At her suggestion, the strikers decided to block the trucks transporting the lettuce from the fields. Helen's strategy turned out to be a setup. When the strikers tried to stop the trucks, they were clubbed and beaten by the patrolmen, and their leaders were arrested. The next day the local newspaper reported that the strike was inspired by Communists. The power of the police and the propaganda of the press broke the strike. Helen disappeared after the strike, and Bulosan later learned that she was a professional strikebreaker, paid to undermine the labor movement. When Bulosan and a friend caught up with Helen in Los Angeles and accused her of being an agent of anti-union interests, she retorted angrily: "I hate Filipinos as deeply as I hate unions! You are all savages and you have no right to stay in this country!"[79]

But, while Helen represented America's mean and exclusionist spirit, there were other white women who personified America's sympathy and softness. After Bulosan had escaped from the vigilantes in Salinas, he found refuge in the home of a white woman. "What was the matter with this land?" he asked, confused. "Just a moment ago I was being beaten by white men. But here was another white person, a woman, giving me food and a place to rest. And her warmth! I sat on the couch and started talking. I wanted to explain what happened to me." "Lovely with long brown hair," Marian made Bulosan's heart ache, for "this woman was like my little sisters in Binalonan. I turned away from her, remembering how I had walked familiar roads with my mother." She drove Bulosan to Los Angeles, where she gave him some money she had earned as a prostitute: "Now you

can go to the university. Nearly three hundred dollars. All for you —
from Marian." Marian died shortly afterward. "She was," Bulosan
said lovingly, "the song of my dark hour." On another occasion,
Bulosan befriended a homeless young woman named Mary. "Her
hair was light brown, her skin milk-white. But her eyes were deep
blue and frightened." Mary became a member of the household,
cooking for Bulosan and his friends. She became a "symbol of goodness" and "purity," their "hope for a better America." When Bulosan
was in the hospital, he was visited weekly by Eileen Odell, who
brought flowers and paper sacks full of delicacies. For Bulosan, Eileen
was "undeniably the *America*" he had wanted to find in those "frantic
days of fear and flight, in those acute hours of hunger and loneliness.
This America was human, good, and real."[80]

As he traveled around the country looking for the America that
women like Eileen represented, Bulosan found his heart going out
not only to his poor fellow Pinoys but also to others in poverty and
trouble. Riding in a boxcar with a group of hobos, Bulosan kept
staring at a Negro boy because it was the first time he had ever seen
a black person. "Where are you going, boy?" he asked Bulosan.
"California, sir," Bulosan answered. "*Sir?*" the black laughed. "Boy,
you are far from California!" Bulosan began to understand how it
felt to be black in America. Also in the boxcar was a young white
woman. During the night, Bulosan heard her struggling with someone
in the dark. "I could hear the man fumbling at her. He was tearing
hungrily at her clothes." Responding to her anguished cries, Bulosan
was struck on the head and fell unconscious. Later he tried to comfort
the girl, feeling the tie between the two of them, "a bond of fear and
a common loneliness." In Montana, Bulosan met a Jewish girl in a
drugstore, and he remembered what she had said: "It is hard to be
a Jew!" In Los Angeles, Bulosan learned from Alice Odell about "her
starved childhood in Utah" and the farm her father had lost. In the
hospital, he became acquainted with a "poor American boy" from
Arkansas who had "never learned to write." Slowly Bulosan grew
to understand what his brother Macario had told him:

> America is not a land of one race or one class of men. We are
> all Americans that have toiled and suffered and known oppres-
> sion and defeat, from the first Indian that offered peace in Man-
> hattan to the last Filipino pea pickers. . . . America is also the
> nameless foreigner, the homeless refugee, the hungry boy begging
> for a job and the black body dangling on a tree. America is the

illiterate immigrant who is ashamed that the world of books and intellectual opportunities is closed to him.[81]

For Bulosan, the task was not only to understand America but also to make it a just society, to realize the America of his heart. There had been moments when Bulosan felt like lashing out violently against a cruel America. On one occasion two policemen, brandishing pistols, invaded a party at a Filipino restaurant and physically abused Bulosan, his friends, and their honored guest — a prominent educator from the Philippines. "I felt violated and outraged." He thought of his gun lying on the table of his room, and after the policemen left the restaurant, Bulosan rushed outside, running blindly toward his hotel. "I wanted my gun. With it I could challenge our common enemy bullet for bullet. It seemed my only friend and comfort in this alien country — this smooth little bit of metal." In the hotel room, Macario grabbed the gun from him; collapsing in rage on his bed, Bulosan lay face down, holding his chest against the "wild beating" of his heart. Still Bulosan was determined to strike back. Words would become his weapon.[82]

Writing, Bulosan understood, could be a political act. Even as a young boy in the Philippines, he had been encouraged by his brother Luciano to become a writer, wielding his pen for the people. In a discussion on politics, Luciano had told Carlos: "You must never stop reading good books. . . . Reading is food for the mind. Healthy ideas are food for the mind. Maybe someday you will be a journalist." Carlos wondered: *Journalist!* What did it mean? Many years later, lying in total darkness in a hospital in America, Bulosan remembered the hardships of his parents and the other impoverished peasants in the Philippines and sobbed: "Yes, I will be a writer and make all of you live again in my words."[83]

Bulosan turned to the writers of his own time for strength and found Younghill Kang, "a Korean who had immigrated to the United States as a boy" and whose "indomitable courage" rekindled in Bulosan "a fire of hope." Earlier, shortly after he had arrived in America, Bulosan had met an aspiring young Filipino writer named Estevan. Sickly and starving, Estevan declared: "I haven't become a writer in America in vain. Someday, my friends, I will write a great book about the Ilocano peasants in northern Luzon." Estevan had written stories and essays, but had not published any of them. Still he had impressed Bulosan: "He was the first writer I knew. . . . Thus it was that I began to rediscover my native land, and the cultural roots there that had nourished me, and I felt a great urge to identify myself with the social awakening of my people."[84]

The urge sprang from rage, and it expressed itself suddenly one day in a hotel room in San Luis Obispo. Bulosan had started writing a letter to his brother Macario, when he realized suddenly, "like a revelation," that he could "actually write understandable English." Swept away by the euphoria of empowerment, by the possession of a revolutionary tool, he wrote all night and when he finished his long letter, which was a story of his life, Bulosan jumped to his feet and shouted ebulliently through his tears: "They can't silence me anymore! I'll tell the world what they have done to me!" The next day he met Pascal, the socialist editor of a labor newspaper. Bulosan saw that the farm workers were "voiceless"; he would be a voice for them. He wrote prolifically for Pascal, seeking to tell the world about the travail and the political struggles of the laborers in the fields. "That's it, Carl," Pascal would shout, encouragingly. "Write your guts out! Write with thunder and blood!" "It is for the workers that we must write. We must interpret their hopes as a people desiring the fullest fulfillment of their potentialities."[85]

In his development as a writer and intellectual, Bulosan was also greatly influenced by several white women. While working as a dishwasher at a hotel in Solvang, Bulosan met Judith, who worked in a grocery store across the street. She had brown hair and blue eyes, and he would go to the store "pretending to buy something," but he "wanted only to look at her." When she asked him what he wanted, he fumbled for something to say. "Oh, you don't understand English well?" she said. "No, ma'am," he replied. "Oh, don't ma'am, me," she said. "I'm just a young girl. See? My name is Judith. I have some books. You'd like to read, perhaps?" Bulosan followed her through the back door and up into a house. In the living room, he saw books of many sizes and colors piled along the wall; enchanted, he was irresistibly drawn toward them and was overjoyed when she offered to share her books with him. "When my dishes were done, working faster, I ran to the store so Judith could read to me."[86]

Bulosan also received encouragement from Dora Travers. A member of the Young Communist League, she had come to visit his brother Macario in Los Angeles. She had fallen asleep in the room, and her presence evoked a poem from Bulosan. When he saw her again, he read the poem to her. "Write more poems, Carl," she said appreciatively. "I like your music. I think you will be a good *American* poet." Bulosan felt inspired. There was "music" in him, "stirring to be born." That evening, he wrote far into the night. The words came to him effortlessly as he wrote ten to fifteen poems in one sitting. Bulosan "could fight the world now with [his] mind, not merely with [his] hands."[87]

Besides Judith and Dora Travers there were others too. Harriet Monroe, editor of *Poetry: A Magazine of Verse*, noticed Bulosan's talent as a writer and began publishing his poems; she also offered to arrange a university scholarship for him. After reading Bulosan's poems, the writer Alice Odell introduced herself to him. She visited him regularly at the hospital during his two-year treatment for tuberculosis and read to him books including Thomas Wolfe's *Look Homeward, Angel*. After Alice Odell went to the Soviet Union, she asked her sister to visit Bulosan. Eileen Odell picked up where her sister had left off: she went to the hospital from week to week, and the two of them "found intimate conversations" in the books she had given him. When he became restless, he wrote letters to her. Every day the words poured from his pen. Bulosan began to "cultivate a taste for words, not so much for their meanings as their sounds and shapes." He tried to depend "only on the music of words" to express his ideas. "This procedure . . . was destructive to my grammar," Bulosan recalled, "but I can say that writing fumbling, vehement letters to Eileen was actually my course in English. What came after this apprenticeship — the structural presentation of ideas in pertinence to the composition and the anarchy between man's experience and ideals — was merely my formal search."[88]

As a writer, Bulosan wanted to help Filipinos, "my own kind," understand "this vast land" from their own experiences, enabling them to "piece together the mosaic of [their] lives in America." He wanted to help not only his compatriots but "all Americans" who had "toiled and suffered and known oppression and defeat" to see what he could see: they were all subjected to the "same forces" and were pitted against one another to be exploited. On a farm in Santa Maria, Bulosan had noticed how Japanese workers arriving from San Francisco were housed in another section of the farm. Years later he discovered that "this tactic was the only way in which the farmers could forestall any possible alliance between the Filipinos and the Japanese." In Salinas, Bulosan helped organize a Filipino strike in the lettuce fields and saw the companies import Mexican laborers to break the strike. During a strike in Oxnard, Bulosan noted that the Mexican and Filipino workers were split: "The companies would not recognize their separate demands, and although there were cultural and economic ties between them, they had not recognized one important point: that the beet companies conspired against their unity."[89]

But the common oppression of the workers, Bulosan saw, also taught them important lessons. "Our awakening was spontaneous: it grew from our experiences and our responses to them." In San Pedro, Bulosan attended a meeting of cannery workers — "Japanese, Mexicans, Filipinos, and white Americans." They were "politically informed" and spoke out "in broken English, but always with sincerity and passion." In Los Angeles, Bulosan met groups of workers in Macario's room. "They were ordinary laborers, but none of them was conscious of the kind of work the other did." Still they seemed "bound by a common understanding that shone in the room." Immigrants "from different shores," they knew that they were Americans, too, and had earned their right to claim their adopted country. But, though they had toiled in this land, America, for them, was still an "unfinished dream," still a society unwilling to embrace its own diversity.[90]

IV

DIVERSITY

When I went to Monterey I again found Jose. . . . He took me to a little wooden house not far from the sea. . . . I had not noticed that several men and women had come into the house. Some of the men were hanging electric bulbs in the yard. When everybody arrived, a Mexican girl distributed the gifts. . . . I saw a Chinese farmer coming toward me with a sack of rice. He dumped it laughingly in front of me and said:

"You! You! You!"

I laughed, too, because I knew that it was for me. I touched his rough hand.

"Thank you," I said.

He laughed and the sincere ring of his laughter filled the house. . . . I went outside and two Filipinos followed me. I walked down the block and stopped under a pepper tree. A Mexican came running to me with a jug of wine. He uncorked it. I took it from him.

"Good *vino*, no?" he said.

"First class," I shouted in the wind. . . . Then the orchestra in the yard began to play. The men and women started dancing. I could see the glow of their shiny heads in the pale light.

The Mexican was listening eagerly to the music.

"*Vamos* — dance!" he said suddenly.

Carlos Bulosan[1]

10
The Watershed
of World War II
Democracy and Race

One Sunday afternoon in Los Angeles, while sitting in a bar, Carlos Bulosan was suddenly stunned by a blaring newsbreak on the radio: "Japan bombs Pearl Harbor!" He rushed outside, trembling and looking for a familiar face. "It has come, Carlos!" his brother Macario shouted. The two men walked aimlessly in the streets. Memories of home and then apprehensions of the future swept through Bulosan like waves. "We had been but little boys when we left the Philippines," he thought. "And my mother! What would happen to her and my two sisters?" A few months later, Macario enlisted in the army, and as he watched his brother ride away on the bus, Bulosan sensed the significant impact the war would have on their lives and American society. "If I met him again, I would not be the same," he thought. "He would not be the same, either. Our world was this one, but a new one was being born."[1]

The war, Bulosan could see, would be a watershed, a crucial dividing line in the history of Filipinos as well as other Asians in America. Representing a new "necessity," the war came crashing down on Asian-American communities from Hawaii to New York: large international forces and developments were pulling Filipinos, Koreans, Asian Indians, Chinese, and Japanese into a whirlpool of chaos and change. The conflagration would require the immigrants and their offspring to determine more sharply than ever before their identities as Asians and as Americans. They had been viewed and treated as "strangers from a different shore," but now they would be asked to support their country in crisis and serve as Americans in the armed forces. The war would also challenge America's image of itself as a democracy. As the United States confronted the threat of Fascism in Asia and Europe, the nation would be asked to extend its democratic ideals to immigrants of color and acknowledge its diversity. The task would prove to be difficult, for it would require a critical scrutiny of American society and would expose the contradictions within.[2]

"On to Bataan"

The Japanese Zeros swooped down on Pearl Harbor, shattering the calm of this Sunday morning in Hawaii. "The airplanes looked like toys but they were shooting and dropping bombs on us," recalled Apolinaria Gusman Oclaray, who had left the Philippines with her husband Santiago in 1928. "I thought it was play, you know practice, and I asked my husband, 'How come the airplanes are firing?' And he said, 'Because this is a real war and a real war is like that.' " Seven hours later, Japanese forces invaded the Philippines. There, on the Bataan Peninsula, they encountered determined resistance from American and Filipino troops.[3]

Four long months later, on April 9, correspondent Frank Hewlett described the fall of Bataan: "The gallant United States and Philippine forces in Bataan peninsula surrendered today after enduring the tortures of hell. . . . They were beaten, but it was a fight that ought to make every American bow his head in tribute. . . . The Americans fought for everything they loved, as did the Filipinos, WITH THEIR FIERCE LOVE OF LIBERTY." Four days later, in her tribute to the brave men of Bataan, Eleanor Roosevelt highlighted the interracial brotherhood forged on the bloodstained battlefield: "Fighting in Bataan has been an excellent example of what happens when two different races respect each other. Men of different races and backgrounds have fought side by side and praised each other's heroism and courage." Carlos Bulosan conveyed in poetry the meaning of Bataan for Filipinos:

> Bataan has fallen.
> With heads bloody but unbowed, we yielded to the
>   enemy. . . .
> We have stood up uncomplaining.
> Beseiged on land and blockaded by sea,
> We have done all that human endurance could
>   bear. . . .
> Our defeat is our victory.[4]

At Bataan thousands of Filipinos had fought beside American soldiers, and the stories of Filipino military gallantry forced whites to view Filipinos in the United States more respectfully. Suddenly there was "something intangible in the air" that said America had learned to respect Filipinos, Manuel Buaken noticed. "No longer on the streetcar do I feel myself in the presence of my enemies. We Filipinos are the same — it is Americans that have changed in their recognition of us." A Filipino working in a Pullman car was pleasantly surprised by the abrupt change in the attitudes of white travelers. "I am very much embarrassed," he remarked. "They treat me as if I have just arrived from Bataan."[5]

Meanwhile, Filipinos in America worried about the Philippines and the loved ones they had left behind. They wanted to defend their homeland, and they immediately rushed to the recruiting offices to volunteer. They were refused, however, for they were classified as "nationals" and hence ineligible for service in the U.S. Armed Forces. When he learned his village of Binalonan had been crushed by Japanese tanks racing from Tayug toward Manila, Bulosan went to the nearest recruiting office: "As I stood in line waiting for my turn, I thought of a one-legged American Revolutionary patriot of whom I had read. But Filipinos were not being accepted."[6]

They had to get into this war, Filipinos insistently protested. President Franklin Roosevelt promptly changed the draft law to include Filipinos, and on February 19, 1942, Secretary of War Henry Stimson announced the organization of the First Filipino Infantry Regiment: "This new unit is formed in recognition of the intense loyalty and patriotism of those Filipinos who are now residing in the United States. It provides for them a means of serving in the armed forces of the United States, and the eventual opportunity of fighting on the soil of their homeland."[7]

Filipinos eagerly responded to the call to arms. In California alone 16,000 — 40 percent of the state's Filipino population — registered for the first draft. In 1942, the First Filipino Infantry Regiment and the Second Filipino Infantry Regiment were formed. Altogether more than 7,000 Filipinos served in these two regiments. "Their enthusiasm and discipline are far superior to any I have seen in my army career," declared their commander, Colonel Robert H. Offley. "The minute you put one of these boys in uniform he wants a rifle. The minute he gets a rifle he wants to get on a boat. He can't understand why we don't ship him out right away, so he can start shooting Japs." "To these pint-sized soldiers," stated the *American*

Legion Magazine describing the Filipinos, "this war is a personal grudge." Filipino-American soldiers had, as Doroteo Vite put it, "a personal reason to be training to fight the invaders." They wanted to defend their country. "My home and my family and all the things that were dear to me as a boy," explained Vite in 1942, "are there in the path of the Japanese war machine." A Filipino soldier said he met white men who were "thrilled" to see representatives of those "little fellows who were showing them dirty Japs how to fight."[8]

Filipinos wanted to get back to the Philippines to fight for the liberation of their homeland. "We wanted to be there" — in the Philippines, they later declared. The regimental song of the First Filipino Infantry was "On to Bataan." Shipped to the Pacific for duty, they were anxious for action. "After we came from Australia by submarine we went to the Philippines," said Magno Cabreros. "We trained in Australia under General MacArthur . . . learned how to roll parachutes, jump in combat . . . how to kill people noiselessly." Filipino soldiers made unique and valuable contributions to the war effort in the Pacific. They operated behind enemy lines, engaging in sabotage to destroy Japanese communications. The military intelligence gathered by Filipino soldiers, reported Lieutenant General R. K. Sutherland, proved to be "of the greatest assistance to impending military operations. By their loyalty, daring, and skillful performance of duty under hazardous conditions, they materially accelerated the campaign for the recapture of the Philippine Islands."[9]

But many Filipino-American soldiers were also fighting for their freedom on the home front. Their very wearing of a uniform was a political statement. "In a few months I will be wearing Uncle Sam's olive-drab army uniform," said a Filipino. "I am looking forward to that day, not with misgiving but with a boyish anticipation of doing something which up to now I have never been allowed to do — serving as an equal with American boys." The war, noted the wife of a Filipino soldier, gave Filipinos the chance to show themselves to America as "soldiers of democracy," as "men, not houseboys." To Filipinos, enlistment in the army gave them membership in American society. "In all the years I was here before the United States went into the war," a Filipino soldier observed, "I felt that I did not belong here. I was a stranger among a people who did not understand and had no good reason to understand me and my people. . . . In other words, it was a pretty difficult business to be a Filipino in the United States in the years preceding Pearl Harbor."[10]

But in many places it was still "difficult business" even after

Pearl Harbor, for they continued to be viewed as "strangers." Stationed at Camp Beale, soldiers of the First Filipino Infantry found they were unwelcome in Marysville, California. Dressed proudly in their U.S. Army uniforms, several Filipino soldiers went into the nearby town during their first weekend pass to have a good dinner and see the sights. They entered a restaurant and sat down, but no one came to serve them. After waiting for half an hour, one of them got up and asked for service and was told: "We don't serve Filipinos here." Filipino soldiers were turned away from theaters or were forced to sit in a segregated section, and their visiting wives were refused accommodations at the hotels. Informed about the discriminatory treatment his men were receiving, Colonel Robert H. Offley met with the Marysville Chamber of Commerce. "There," as Private First Class Manuel Buaken put it, "he laid down the law of cooperation with the army — or else. Then the merchants and the restaurant proprietors and the movie houses changed their tune," and opened their places to Filipinos. But the "soul of enjoyment" was gone for Buaken and his brothers. They knew that in their hearts those people were hating and ridiculing the Filipinos, laughing at their brown skins. And they hoped they would soon be gone from "these towns which hate built" and "this land of double-talk."[11]

But the war began to open the way for Filipinos. As members of the U.S. Armed Forces, they were allowed to become citizens, and on February 20, 1943, on the parade ground of Camp Beale, twelve hundred Filipino soldiers stood proudly and silently in V formation as citizenship was conferred on them. During the ceremony, the colonel in charge declared: "Officers who returned from Bataan have said there are no finer soldiers in the world than the Filipinos who fought and starved and died there shoulder to shoulder with our troops. I can well believe it as I look at the men before me. On those faces is quiet determination and a consciousness of training and discipline with a definite end in view. I congratulate them on their soldierly appearance and on their approaching citizenship." In the concluding speech, a judge welcomed the Filipinos: "Citizenship came to us who were born here as a heritage — it will come to you as a privilege. We have every faith you will become and remain loyal, devoted citizens of the United States."[12]

During the war, the California Attorney General reinterpreted the land laws and decided that Filipinos would be allowed to lease lands and encouraged them to take over holdings of the Japanese. "There were some Japanese children in our school," Liz Megino

remembered, "and all of a sudden they weren't there." Manuel
Buaken welcomed the internment of Japanese Americans and the
changes in discriminatory laws against Filipinos. The laws allowed
Filipinos to buy farms and become farmers. In the Imperial County
alone there were five hundred Filipino farmers "stopping" on the
"vacated farms of the Japs." Comparing Filipino qualities to what
he viewed as the unassimilability of Japanese, Buaken declared that
Filipinos always wanted nothing more than to learn from America,
to become "good Americans." They had developed no great banks
here in the United States, their savings going instead into American
banks. They had patronized American stores, "not stores devoted to
the selling of products from across the seas." They strove to learn
English, not to perpetuate foreign-language schools and to teach
foreign ideas to their children. Unfortunately Buaken based his own
Americanism on anti-Japanese sentiments rather than on the democratic ideals of America.[13]

Facing Fascism abroad, the United States felt compelled to make
good its claims to democracy. In 1941 President Franklin D. Roosevelt issued Executive Order 8802, prohibiting racial discrimination
in employment: "It is the duty of employers and labor organizations . . . to provide for full and equitable participation of all workers
in defense industries, without discrimination because of race, creed,
color, or national origin." The war opened employment to Filipinos
as war industries clamored for their labor. The employment of Filipinos in the defense factories prompted Fernando Taggaoa to remark
shortly before he left for the Pacific front in 1942: "In the United
States, the war is doing wonders for the resident Filipinos."[14]

Four years later, seeking to demonstrate American democracy
to people of color around the world, Congress passed a law that
extended citizenship to Filipino immigrants and permitted the entry
of one hundred Filipino immigrants annually. "It took a war and a
great calamity in our country to bring us [whites and Filipinos] together," observed Carlos Bulosan. Shortly after the war, sociologist
R. T. Feria assessed the impact of the war on the status of Filipinos.
He noted that as the Japanese left Los Angeles, Filipinos purchased
homes from them in the more desirable neighborhoods. Many Filipinos also bought small farms from the Japanese in the San Fernando
Valley and the Torrance-Gardena districts. Employment opportunities expanded for Filipinos as they entered the shipyards of Wil-
mington and San Pedro and the plants of Lockheed, Douglas, and
Vultee. "The majority became welders, technicians, assembly or office

workers, and a few became engineers." Most importantly, Feria observed, the war had forced Filipinos to make a decision — "to go home and help in the reconstruction of their homeland" or "to spend the rest of their days in America." Thousands of Filipinos, granted citizenship and feeling a sense of greater acceptance, chose to make America their permanent home. But would whites forget Bataan when the economic prosperity of the war began to slacken, Feria wondered, and would they invoke another "interminable era of dishwashing and asparagus cutting"?[15]

Filipinos had reason to be doubtful. They had been granted citizenship finally, but they knew the new political status did not mean acceptance. "What good would it do to become citizens of America," asked Private First Class Jose Trinidad, "if we are still brown-skin inferiors?" Filipinos could not change their complexions. Liz Megino recalled how Filipinos had to distinguish themselves from Japanese shortly after the beginning of the war: "My mother told me to make sure you say you're not Japanese if they ask you who you are. Filipinos wore buttons saying, 'I am a Filipino.' " Even before the end of the war, Filipinos in the Santa Maria Valley were reminded of their subordinate place in society. After Filipino farm laborers went on strike, the Economic Council of Santa Maria warned in an advertisement published in local newspapers that the wartime honeymoon for Filipinos was over: "At best, Filipinos are guests in the United States. . . . While Americans are dying to free their countrymen from Japanese slavery, the lavish expenditures of money by Filipinos on white women instead of assisting their countrymen is not promoting good-will among Americans. . . . Filipinos want America to build up their homeland and protect them, while their people conduct themselves as strikers in the Santa Maria Valley. . . . If the Filipinos act as they have recently, they should be classified with the Japanese; denied renting of land and such, as the Japanese were who also did not act properly as guests in America."[16]

"I Am Korean"

On the morning of December 7, 1941, several Koreans in Los Angeles were rehearsing for a play to be presented in the evening at a program sponsored by the Society for Aid to the Korean Volunteer Corps in China. The event was organized to raise funds for the relief of 200,000 refugee Korean families living in China and for the support of Korean volunteers engaged in armed struggle against the Japanese in China. During the rehearsal, they were suddenly interrupted by an electrifying announcement: "The Japanese have attacked Pearl Harbor." Then, spontaneously, everyone on the stage exploded: *"Taehan Toknip Manse!"* — "Long Live Korean Independence!" "No Korean, old and young alike, could control his emotions of joy," one of the players, Bong-Youn Choy, recalled movingly. "Some old Korean immigrants had tears in their eyes and kept silent. Every Korean felt that the long dream for national independence would soon become a reality." In the evening, the play was presented to an "enthusiastic and happy" audience of Koreans, Chinese, and whites.[17]

Also that night, Koreans gathered at the Korean National Association in Los Angeles and resolved:

1. Koreans shall promote unity during the war and act harmoniously.
2. Koreans shall work for the defense of the country where they reside and all those who are healthy should volunteer for national guard duty. Those who are financially capable should purchase war bonds, and those who are skilled should volunteer for appropriate duties.
3. Koreans shall wear a badge identifying them as Koreans, for security purposes.[18]

Korean nationalists welcomed the war, hopeful it would lead to the military destruction of Japan and the restoration of Korean independence. Even before the attack on Pearl Harbor, Syngman Rhee had recommended that America should initiate a war against Japan: "The United States should employ all her power, economic, moral, and military, now to check Japan in order to prevent an ultimate conflict with her." Rhee pictured Japan as a young bully. "Is it not equally clear, then, that your true policy should be to act quickly and keep him down by force before he grows too big, so that he can never get out of hand?" Koreans had been fighting Japan for decades in their homeland, and on April 20, 1941, the United Korean Committee, composed of representatives of nationalist organizations in the United States, issued the Declaration of the All-Korean Convention: "Hundreds and thousands of our brothers and sisters have died in the past on the battle fronts for the cause of national independence, and their sacrifices have become a living symbol for our guidance today. . . . We Koreans in America should unite together as one body and should support the Allied Powers until they bring a final victory of the present war against the Axis powers."

When the war came, Koreans in America were excited. "Korea for Victory with America," they shouted. The *Korean National Herald-Pacific Weekly* declared the "fact" that "every Korean born" was "an enemy born for Japan."[19]

Actually, for Koreans in America, the war years were also times of painful confusion. "When World War Two broke out," Jean Park remembered, "we were still living in Reedley." A few months after the attack on Pearl Harbor, she began to hear stories that the Japanese were being evacuated to internment camps. "People said that the Japanese were treated very cruelly and that they were dragged to unknown destinations." The evacuation of the Japanese opened opportunities for Koreans: her stepfather decided to move the family to southern California, where "the Japanese lost all their farms and many of the farms were being sold for very cheap prices." But when Jean and her family arrived at their new home, they found whites staring at them and shouting, "Japs go home!" "They were ready to stone us with rocks and descend on us because they had that evil look in their eyes."[20]

Government policies also failed to distinguish the Koreans from the Japanese. In 1940, the Alien Registration Act classified Korean immigrants as subjects of Japan; after the United States declared war against Japan, the government identified Koreans here as "enemy aliens." In February 1942, the *Korean National Herald-Pacific Weekly* insisted the government reclassify Koreans as Koreans. "The Korean is an enemy of Japan," the editorial declared, underscoring the torturous irony of the situation. "Since December 7, the Korean here is between the devil and the deep sea for the reason that the United States considers him a subject of Japan, which the Korean resents as an injustice to his true status. . . . What is the status of a Korean in the United States? Is he an enemy alien? Has any Korean ever been in Japanese espionage or in subversive activities against the land where he makes his home and rears his children as true Americans?" In Hawaii Koreans were classified by the territorial government as enemy aliens. Korean immigrants employed on defense projects in the islands experienced an even more painful insult: they were classified as Japanese. "For years we've been fighting the Japanese and now they tell us that we're Japs," Koreans snapped angrily. "It's an insult!" Placed in a restricted category, these Koreans had to wear badges with black borders. "Why in the hell do they pull a trick like this on us," the Korean workers screamed, "when we hate the Japanese more than anyone else in the world." After their protests, they were only allowed to have printed on their badges the statement "I am Korean."[21]

Some young Koreans, however, sympathized with Japanese Americans. "It made me feel sad to hear that their land was taken away from them [Japanese Americans on the West Coast]," said Jean Park, "and that they were imprisoned." Similarly second-generation Koreans in Hawaii did not see the local Japanese as the enemy. "It didn't make me feel any differently toward the Japanese," explained a Korean young man shortly after the bombing of Pearl Harbor. "We've lived with them all along and know them well and it didn't occur to me that they were responsible [for the attack]."[22]

But there were Korean nationalists who viewed the matter very differently. Kilsoo Haan, leader of the Sino-Korean People's League, charged in early 1941 that 35,000 to 50,000 Japanese in Hawaii were ready to assist Japan in a war against the United States. In 1942, Haan went to California, where he agitated for the forced evacuation of the Japanese from the West Coast. He claimed that the Japanese were engaged in military intelligence operations for Japan. "It is our conviction," Haan argued, "that the best way to prepare against the Japanese is to let the American people know the Japanese plans and what the Japs and the Japanese Americans are doing in this country."[23]

Like the Filipinos, Korean immigrants were anxious to become involved in the American war effort against Japan. Many Koreans possessed an invaluable weapon that the country needed: they knew the Japanese language. They were employed as Japanese-language teachers and as translators of Japanese secret documents; they served as propaganda broadcasters in the Pacific front and agents for underground activities in Japanese-occupied areas of Asia. An instructor in Oriental Languages at the University of California at Berkeley, Bong-Youn Choy also taught college-extension Japanese-language courses in Oakland and San Francisco two nights a week and worked for the Office of War Information in San Francisco on Saturdays and Sundays as a broadcaster to Korea. "I delivered lectures on Korean and Japanese politics to the Office of War Information for three months," he recalled. "In addition, I was asked to teach Japanese to the special Army Training Program classes." Commissioned as navy interpreters, Yi Jong-gun and Pak Yong-hak were sent to the Solomon Islands and participated in the Guadalcanal campaign.[24]

In Los Angeles, 109 Koreans — one fifth of the city's Korean population — joined the California National Guard. Ranging in ages from eighteen to sixty-five, they were organized into a Korean unit called the Tiger Brigade, *Manghokun*. They drilled regularly on Saturday and Sunday afternoons for three to four hours in Exposition Park, preparing to defend California against an enemy invasion. Congratulating them, an army official declared: "I myself have learned the real meaning of patriotism during my participation in this Tiger Brigade, and I cannot find adequate words to describe your contribution in winning this war." Meanwhile, elderly Korean women served in the Red Cross, and old Korean men volunteered as emergency fire wardens. Koreans everywhere bought defense bonds: between 1942 and 1943, they reportedly purchased more than $239,000 worth of defense bonds — an immense sum for a population of only ten thousand. Korean involvement in the war effort generated white-American respect for Koreans. At the celebration of the Korean National Flag Day on August 29, 1943, for example, the Los Angeles mayor raised the Korean flag to honor the uniformed men of the Tiger Brigade as they marched past City Hall. A year later, Hawaii territorial delegate Joseph R. Farrington introduced in Congress a bill for Korean immigration and naturalization. Farrington's bill did not pass, but Koreans had gained greater acceptance and had also helped to defeat Japan and free their homeland.[25]

Confronting Contradictions:
Nazi Nordic Superiority and American Exclusion of Asian Indians

On the eve of America's entry into World War II, Asian Indians were struggling for the right to become naturalized citizens, and the war to defend democracy buoyed their demand for equality on the home front. They had been denied eligibility to naturalized citizenship by the Supreme Court in the 1923 *Thind* decision and had been turned away from federal relief programs during the Great Depression because they were aliens ineligible to citizenship. Under the leadership of Mubarak Ali Khan, the India Welfare League denounced the discriminatory treatment accorded to Asian Indians and asked Congress to address the problem. In 1939, a bill was introduced in Congress providing citizenship to all Asian-Indian immigrants in residence since 1924. Leading an attack on the bill was Paul Scharrenberg of the American Federation of Labor. "First, it will be the people who are here in our country now, the Chinese, Japanese, and Hindus, who want to be naturalized," he warned in his testimony before Congress. "Then they will find some other means of breaking some other little hole in the immigration law here and there or elsewhere."

Unwilling to wait for congresssional action, Khairata Ram Samras decided to seek remedy in the courts. In 1940, he filed a petition in the federal court of San Francisco challenging the *Thind* decision. "Discrimination against Hindus in respect to naturalization," Samras argued, "is not only capricious and untenable but in violation of constitutional provisions."[26]

A year later, in August 1941, U.S. President Franklin Roosevelt and British Prime Minister Winston Churchill issued the Atlantic Charter, a broad statement of principles including the right of peoples to choose their own form of government. Asian Indians realized that the Atlantic Charter offered them an opportunity to press for their rights in the United States. Mubarak Ali Khan of the India Welfare League along with Sirdar Jagit Singh of the India League of America demanded both independence for India and naturalization rights for Asian Indians in the United States.

During the war, the American policymakers were forced to recognize the U.S. need for Indian cooperation in the war effort against Japan. They saw that India was strategic militarily, for Japan could push its campaign westward and try to join forces with Germany in the Near East. Japan could exploit Indian disaffection with British rule, create political chaos in Calcutta, and drive its military machinery across India. This Japanese military strategy and the necessity of Indian support prompted Congress to give attention to Indian-American demands: in March of 1944, the legislature considered a bill that would provide a quota for immigrants from India and naturalization rights for Asian Indians. A leading supporter of the proposed legislation, New York congressman Emmanuel Celler argued that oppressed people throughout the world looked to the United States for justice and equality and that "our breaking down of immigration and naturalization barriers" would "dull the edge of Jap propaganda."[27]

Four months later, in the *Far Eastern Survey*, S. Chandrasekhar of the University of Pennsylvania emphasized another reason for the bill's passage — the need to combat Nazi ideology:

> Today, more than ever, the United States is vitally interested in attitudes of Asiatic peoples toward this country. Hitler's justification of Nazi oppression in Europe is supposedly based on the right of the mythically superior Nordic to superimpose his *Kultur* on the other so-called inferior peoples of Europe. If the United States is successfully to combat such dangerous ideas, it can ill afford to practice racial discrimination in its relations with

Asiatic countries. The immigration policy of this country now excludes nearly a quarter of the human race. America cannot afford to say that she wants the people of India to fight on her side and at the same time maintain that she will not have them among her immigrant groups.

Clearly, the United States could not have it both ways. It could not oppose the racist ideology of Nazism and also "practice" racial discrimination. America had to put its "principle of equality" into its laws and policies, Chandrasekhar concluded, in order to reaffirm the faith of the millions in India looking to America for "justice and fair play."[28]

Two years later, Congress permitted India to have a small immigration quota and granted Asian Indians naturalization rights. During the next eighteen years, 12,000 Indians entered the United States. "Many of the older immigrants brought wives from India," wrote historian Gary Hess. "Had not immigration and naturalization laws changed in 1946, the East Indian community would almost certainly have eroded significantly perhaps to the point of extinction." The new law enabled Puna Singh, whose life we have been following, to become a naturalized citizen for the second time.[29]

Altogether 1,772 Asian Indians became U.S. citizens between 1947 and 1965. One of them was Dalip Singh Saund, a Punjabi Sikh who had come to California in 1919 and who had become a successful farmer in the Imperial Valley. For decades Saund had wanted to become a citizen. "I had married an American girl, and was the father of three American children," he explained in his autobiography. "I was making America my home. Thus it was only natural that I felt very uncomfortable not being able to become a citizen of the United States." Citizenship was more than a matter of political rights for Saund. It would also "nullify the effect of California's Alien Land Law, and thus eliminate one of the most oppressive handicaps to the workaday business life" of Asian Indians. Frustrated, Saund and his compatriots petitioned Congress to grant them eligibility to citizenship. To gain support for their proposal, they directed war-bond drives among Asian Indians, hoping to "earn" the "confidence" of Americans. "I saw that the bars of citizenship were shut tight against me," Saund remarked. "I knew if these bars were lifted I would see much wider gates of opportunity open to me, opportunity as existed for everybody else in the United States of America." Three years after he had helped to lobby their proposal successfully through Congress, Saund became a naturalized citizen. He went on to be elected to the

House of Representatives in 1956, serving for three terms. The war had opened the door of democracy to Asian-Indian Americans.[30]

The Repeal of Chinese Exclusion

"I remember December 7th so clearly," said Lonnie Quan of San Francisco four decades later. "I was living at Gum Moon Residence Club on Washington Street. It was Sunday. I didn't have a radio in the room." When her boyfriend arrived, he exclaimed: "This is it. Pearl Harbor was attacked!" The news was overwhelming: "I just couldn't believe it — it was a shock. I remember going to work in a restaurant, Cathay House, and everybody was just kinda glued to the radio."[31]

The next day, the United States and the Republic of China declared war on Japan, and the two countries became allies. Two weeks later, on December 22, *Time* magazine explained to its readers how they could distinguish the Chinese "friend" from the Japanese "enemy":

> HOW TO TELL YOUR FRIENDS FROM THE JAPS: Virtually all Japanese are short. Japanese are likely to be stockier and broader-hipped than short Chinese. Japanese are seldom fat; they often dry up and grow lean as they age. Although both have the typical epicanthic fold of the upper eyelid, Japanese eyes are usually set closer together. The Chinese expression is likely to be more placid, kindly, open; the Japanese more positive, dogmatic, arrogant. Japanese are hesitant, nervous in conversation, laugh loudly at the wrong time. Japanese walk stiffly erect, hard heeled. Chinese, more relaxed, have an easy gait, sometimes shuffle.

Two photographs — one of a Japanese and another of a Chinese — were used as illustrations. Previously maligned as the "heathen Chinee," "mice-eaters," and "Chinks," the Chinese were now friends and allies engaged in a heroic common effort against the "Japs."[32]

For a long time the Chinese had been viewed with scorn. "Then came Pearl Harbor, December 7," said a congressman in 1943. "All at once we discovered the saintly qualities of the Chinese people. If it had not been for December 7, I do not know if we would have ever found out how good they were." But the information distributed in *Time* and the chorus of praises for the Chinese gave them little assurance they would not still be mistaken for the enemy. They remembered how they had previously been called "Japs" and how many whites had lumped all Asians together. Fearful they would be targets of anti-Japanese hate and violence, many Chinese shopkeepers displayed signs announcing, "This is a Chinese shop." In the Chinese community thousands of buttons were distributed: "I am Chinese."

> *When World War II was declared*
> *on the morning radio,*
> *we glued our ears, widened our eyes.*
> *Our bodies shivered. . . .*
> *Shortly our Japanese neighbors vanished*
> *and my parents continued to whisper:*
> *We are Chinese, we are Chinese.*
> *We wore black arm bands,*
> *put up a sign*
> *in bold letters.*[33]

The outbreak of the war sharpened the attachment of Chinese immigrants to their homeland. They had been faithfully supporting the defense of their ancestral country against Japanese imperialism. Portland's Chinese community had sent a contingent of thirty-three trained Chinese-American pilots to Generalissimo Chiang Kai-shek. For years before the attack on Pearl Harbor, the Chinese in America had been deeply concerned about the war in Asia, especially China. They worried about loved ones they had left behind. A letter sent to America stated:

> Uncle, Venerable One, I write to you with respectful greeting:
> I received ten dollars from Hong Kong money from you lately. I thank you very much. How I would like to see you come home and be with us in the near future, too.
> Now Canton is captured by the Japs, our commodities here cannot be shipped to the village. For this reason, the prices of foodstuff in the village are high, very high. One bag of rice costs from eight to nine dollars. How can the poor families back home manage to live!
> However, everybody at home is well. I hope you are well, too, in America.
>
> Nephew

In a touching short story entitled, "One Mother's Day," published on May 15, 1941, in the *China Daily News* of New York, Lao Mei described the feelings of a Chinatown restaurant worker. Living as a "wanderer" in America, the worker suddenly one day is seized with nostalgic thoughts of home, thinking about his "invaded home village," especially his seventy-year-old mother. He anxiously wonders what had become of her as he walks the streets of New York City. "How about a fresh flower for your mother on Mother's Day?" asks an old woman with a basket full of fresh flowers. He is startled, "as if someone had discovered his inner secrets." He pauses momentarily, then takes out two dimes for a red one and a white one. And in the end of the story, he pins them together on his lapel and walks toward the park.[34]

Like this homesick restaurant worker, Chinese in America were reminded by the war of their deep family ties to their homeland, and America's entry into the war ignited patriotic explosions in Chinatowns across the country. In "A Memo to Mr. Hitler, Hirohito & Co.," the San Francisco Chinese community warned:

> Have you heard the bad news? America is out to get you. America has a grim, but enthusiastic bombing party started, and you're the target in the parlor game.
>
> San Francisco Chinatown, U.S.A., is joining the party. Chinatown will have fun blasting you to hell. Chinatown is proud to be a part of Freedom's legion in freeing all the decent people of the world from your spectacle.
>
> Chinatown's part of the party will cost $500,000. Admission price to the fun is purchase of a U.S. War Bond. We're all going to buy a War Bond for Victory.
>
> P.S. More bad news. Everyone in Chinatown is going to this party. We're NOT missing this one.

In San Francisco, the Chinese contributed generously to the defense of America. "San Francisco has gone over the top in its recent Red Cross drive," proudly announced K. S. Jue, president of the Shiu Hing Benevolent Society. "We raised $18,000 for the campaign. In the Defense Bond Drive, we bought over $30,000."[35]

In New York's Chinatown, excited crowds cheered themselves hoarse when the first draft numbers drawn were for Chinese Americans. According to a New York City survey, approximately 40 percent of the Chinese population were drafted, the highest of all national groupings. "The reason," historian Peter Kwong noted, "was an ironic one: because of the Exclusion Act, most Chinese had no dependents and according to the law were the first called." Actually, many had dependents, but they were in China. Still most Chinese here were male and of draft age, and many of them were eager to get into the fight against Fascism. Chinese boys, too young for the armed services, tried to enlist by giving the authorities their

"Chinese age," which was usually a year or two older than the age indicated on their birth certificates.[36]

Everyone in the Chinese community, including women and children, participated in the war effort. In an essay published in the *Chinese Press* in 1942, teenager Florence Gee proudly described the total involvement of her family in the war effort: "I am an American.... The war has hit home. I have an uncle in the army and one in the shipyard. My sisters are members of the civilian defense. My mother is taking first aid. I belong to a club where I learn better citizenship." Like many fellow Chinese young people, Florence collected tin cans and tin foil for war materials. In Minneapolis, the proprietor of the city's only Chinese gift shop closed his business during the height of the busy Christmas season to join his wife as a worker in a war-industry plant. Actress Anna May Wong signed up as an air-raid warden in Santa Monica. "As an American-born Chinese," she said, "I feel it is a privilege to be able to do my little bit in return for the many advantages bestowed upon me by a free democracy." In New York, Mrs. Emily Lee Shek became the first Chinese woman to join the WAACS. "She tried to join up right in the beginning [of the war]," the *Chinese Press* reported in September 1942, "but the 105-pound weight minimum barred her. When the requirement was dropped five pounds, she drank two gallons of water and lived on a special Chinese diet, and made it — yes, with one pound to spare."[37]

Young Chinese Americans wanted to be in U.S. military uniforms. "To men of my generation," explained Charlie Leong of San Francisco's Chinatown, "World War II was the most important historic event of our times. For the first time we felt we could make it in American society." The war had given them the opportunity to get out of Chinatown, don army uniforms, and be sent overseas, where they felt "they were part of the great patriotic United States war machine out to do battle with the enemy." Similarly Harold Liu of New York's Chinatown recalled: "In the 1940s for the first time Chinese were accepted by Americans as being friends because at that time, Chinese and Americans were fighting against the Japanese and the Germans and the Nazis. Therefore, all of a sudden, we became part of an American dream. We had heroes with Chiang Kai-shek and Madame Chiang Kai-shek and so on. It was just a whole different era and in the community we began to feel very good about ourselves. . . . My own brother went into the service. We were so proud that they were in uniform." Altogether 13,499 Chinese were drafted or enlisted in the U.S. Armed Forces — 22 percent of all Chinese adult males.[38]

Confined for decades in a Chinese ethnic-labor market composed mainly of restaurants and laundries, Chinese workers suddenly found the doors of employment opportunities opening to them, especially in the defense industries, where labor shortages were acute. Waiters left the restaurants and rushed to the higher-paying industrial jobs. In 1942 four restaurants in New York's Chinatown had to shut down because of a lack of waiters, and the proprietor of Li Po, a restaurant in Los Angeles, said: "I was just ready for another venture. But I can't now. No men to run it." In Los Angeles some three hundred Chinese laundryworkers closed their shops to work on the construction of the ship *China Victory*. "At Douglas, home of the A-20 attack planes and dive bombers," the *Chinese Press* noted in 1943, "there are approximately 100 Chinese working at its three plants — Santa Monica, Long Beach, and El Segundo." Chinese workers constituted 15 percent of the shipyard work force in the San Francisco Bay Area in 1943. Chinese also found employment in the defense industries at the Seattle-Tacoma Shipbuilding Corporation, the shipyards of Delaware and Mississippi, and the airplane factories on Long Island.[39]

One of these new defense-industry workers was Arthur Wong. After arriving in New York's Chinatown in 1930 at the age of seventeen, he found himself confined to the Chinese ethnic-labor market: "I worked five and a half days in the laundry and worked the whole weekend in the restaurant. And then came the war, and defense work opened up; and some of my friends went to work in a defense plant, and they recommended that I should apply for defense work. So I went to work for Curtiss-Wright, making airplanes. I started out as an assembler, as a riveter." Thousands of laundrymen and waiters like Wong were finally given opportunities to break away from the Chinatown economy. Describing the situation in New York City, the *Chinese Press* reported: "It is estimated about 30 percent of the Chinese-American young men here are employed in defense plants." Many college-educated Chinese were also now able to find employment in their fields of training, such as architecture and engineering. Between 1940 and 1950, the percentage of Chinese men in service occupations remained high, decreasing slightly from 38 to 36 percent (compared to only 6 percent for white men). But progress was evidenced elsewhere. Chinese men employed in craft occupations increased from 1.4 percent in 1940 to 3.5 percent in 1950 (compared to 23.3 percent for white men), and in professional and technical occupations from 2.5 percent in 1940 to 6.6 percent in 1950 (compared to 9.3 percent for white men).[40]

The war also opened employment opportunities for Chinese women. After she had graduated from college, Jade Snow Wong found that she could not find suitable employment because she was Chinese, but then the war industries began to demand workers. "By this time the trek to the shipyards was well underway," wrote Wong. "The patriotic fever to build as many ships as possible, together with boom wages, combined to attract people from all types of occupations." Wong was hired as a typist-clerk in a shipyard in Marin County. Several hundred "alert young Chinese-American girls," the *Chinese Press* reported in 1942, "have gone to the defense industries as office workers." The paper proudly presented a partial roster of these workers in the Bay Area — including Fannie Yee, Rosalind Woo, Jessie Wong of Bethlehem Steel and Anita Chew, Mildred Lew, and Evelyn Lee of Mare Island's Navy Yard: "They're part of the millions who stand behind the man behind the gun." A year later, in an article on "Women in the War," the *Chinese Press* informed its readers about Alice Yick, Boston Navy Yard's only Chinese woman mechanical trainee, who could run light lathes, grinders, shapers, planers, and other machine tools. "Helen Young, Lucy Young, and Hilda Lee," the paper continued, "were the first Chinese women aircraft workers in California. They help build B-24 bombers in San Diego."[41]

Writing for *Survey Graphic* in 1942, sociologist Rose Hum Lee happily recorded the ways the war was changing the lives of the Chinese on the home front: "They have gone in the army and navy, into shipbuilding and aircraft plants. Even the girls are getting jobs." But while the Chinese were participating in the war effort as Americans, Lee noted critically, they were not fully equal because of the exclusion laws and the denial of naturalized citizenship. The Chinese should be accorded the same treatment as European immigrants, she argued. Lee then linked the problem of Chinese inequality in the United States to the war, exposing America's hypocrisy: "Surely racial discrimination should not be directed against those who are America's Allies in the Far East and are helping her in every way to win the war. . . . To be fighting for freedom and democracy in the Far East, at the cost of seven million lives in five years of hard, long, bitter warfare, and to be denied equal opportunity in the greatest of democracies, seems the height of irony." The contradiction was too evident to be ignored and too embarrassing for the United States to be allowed to continue.[42]

The war abroad required reform at home, many Americans began to realize. In 1942, the California League of Women Voters of San Francisco launched an educational campaign to remove racial discrimination from the immigration laws. A year later, Congress began considering a bill to repeal the Chinese exclusion laws and to allow a quota for Chinese immigration. But the proposed legislation also fanned the embers of anti-Chinese fear and hostility. The American Federation of Labor again raised the specter of an invasion of a laboring army from China. An immigration quota for the Chinese, the union warned, would lead to pressures to open the gates even wider: if England with a population of less than 100 million had a quota of 65,000, then China and India, with populations of 400 million each, could demand and get annual quotas of over a million.[43]

Meanwhile, pressures for repeal mounted. In the spring, Madame Chiang Kai-shek toured the country and gave an eloquent speech on the war in Asia to a joint session of Congress. At a dinner party on May 15, she told several key congressmen that the repeal of the Chinese exclusion laws would boost Chinese morale and buttress her country's war effort. Chinese-American lobbying activities in support of the bill were widespread and intense. As president of the Chinese Women's Association of New York, Mrs. Theodora Chan Wang wrote a letter to Mrs. Franklin Roosevelt. What Chinese Americans wanted, wrote Mrs. Wang, was an immigration quota so that the Chinese would be accorded the privileges enjoyed by "our companions in ideology and arms." The reference to the war effort was clear and calculated. The Chinese Consolidated Benevolent Association of New York asked Congress to repeal the exclusion legislation, calling it a most serious violation of the fundamental principles of equality and friendly cooperation between the two nations. In Hawaii, Chinese Americans raised money to finance the campaign for repeal. At a conference in San Antonio in September 1943, more than seventy Chinese young people condemned the Exclusion Act as the stumbling block between China and America and urged their American friends to repeal it immediately, not to wait till the end of the war.[44]

Support for the repeal of the Chinese exclusion laws also came from the Korean and Asian-Indian communities. At a congressional committee hearing on the repeal bill, Kilsoo K. Haan of the Korean National Front Federation argued that Asians desired political and economic equality. In his testimony, Dr. Taraknath Das, an immigrant from India and a professor at the College of the City of New York, underscored the contradiction between American racist practices at home and proclamations of principles abroad: "As long as Anglo-American powers would continue to practice racial discrimination against the peoples of the Orient, a vast majority of the orientals will not have any genuine confidence in the professions of promotion of world democracy and world brotherhood." Plainly, America could not have it both ways.[45]

President Roosevelt felt the pressure, and sent Congress a message favoring the repeal bill. "China is our ally," Roosevelt wrote on October 11, 1943. "For many long years she stood alone in the fight against aggression. Today we fight at her side. She has continued her gallant struggle against very great odds." Aware the act would be essential to the war effort in Asia, the president urged Congress to "be big enough" to acknowledge an error of the past: "By the repeal of the Chinese exclusion laws, we can correct a historic mistake and silence the distorted Japanese propaganda."[46]

Japan had been appealing to Asia to unite in a race war against white America. Japanese propaganda had been condemning the United States for its discriminatory laws and for the segregation of the Chinese in ghettos where they had been relegated to "the most menial of occupations, despised and mistreated and at best patronizingly tolerated with a contemptuous humor." Tokyo broadcasts aimed at China described how the Chinese in the United States suffered from "a campaign of venomous villification of the character of the Chinese people." "Far from waging this war to liberate the oppressed peoples of the world," Tokyo argued on the airwaves, "the Anglo-American leaders are trying to restore the obsolete system of imperialism." In June 1943, after the House committee delayed action on the repeal bill, Japanese radio in Manila editorialized: "Agitation in the U.S. for the repeal of the Chinese Exclusion Act met an early death due to the opposition of anti-Asiatic congressmen, which bears out the fact it was never meant to be sincere, that it was only a gesture, empty words."[47]

Defeat of the repeal bill would have meant certain ridicule of America by Japan before a watching audience of millions in Asia.

Alarmed by the Japanese strategy, many U.S. policymakers felt the need to "spike" the propaganda guns of Japan. A retired Navy officer told a congressional committee holding hearings on the repeal bill that the Chinese exclusion laws were worth "twenty divisions" to the Japanese Army. Supporters of the bill argued: "It is time for us to realize that if nations cannot be gracious to each other, cannot respect each other's race, all talk of democracy is in vain." They also expressed fears of the war turning into a racial conflict. "The Japanese have been carrying on a propaganda campaign seeking to align the entire oriental world behind Japanese leadership, seeking to set the oriental world against the occidental world," one congressman warned. "They have called it a campaign of Asia for Asiatics." "Suppose the Chinese do capitulate and join Japan," another congressman predicted, "then all Asia is apt to go with her. Then you will have a race struggle in which we are hopelessly outnumbered that will last, not for 1 year or 5 years, but throughout generations to come." The handwriting seemed to be on the wall. The Chinese exclusion laws had to be repealed, for the "salvation of the white race" depended significantly on continued Chinese friendship and military cooperation. China, a Chicago newspaper declared, was America's "white hope" in the East.[48]

Shortly afterward, Congress repealed the exclusion acts and provided an annual quota for Chinese immigration. Actually the law did not open even a trickle of immigration: only 105 Chinese would be allowed to enter annually, and only an annual average of fifty-nine Chinese came to the United States during the first ten years of the law's operation. The law also extended the right of naturalized citizenship to Chinese immigrants. But it required applicants to present documentation of their legal entry in the United States and to pass tests for English competency and knowledge of American history and the Constitution. Between 1944 and 1952, only 1,428 Chinese were naturalized. Nevertheless Chinese immigrants could finally seek political membership in their adopted country. One of them was Jade Snow Wong's father. "At the age of seventy plus, after years of attending night classes in citizenship, he became naturalized," his daughter joyfully reported. "He embraced this status wholeheartedly. One day when we were discussing plans for his birthday celebration, which was usually observed on the tenth day of the fifth lunar month by the Chinese calendar, he announced, 'Now that I have become a United States citizen, I am going to change my birthday. Henceforth, it will be on the Fourth of July.' "[49]

The Myth of "Military Necessity" for Japanese-American Internment

"One morning — I think it was a Sunday — while I was working at Palama Shoe Factory I heard, '*Pon! pon! Pon! pon!*' " recalled Seichin Nagayama. He was only a few miles away from the navy base at Pearl Harbor. "I was drinking coffee and I thought, 'Strange. Are they having military practice?' At the corner of Liliha and Kuakini streets, a bomb fell in the back of a cement plant. We felt like going to see what happened, the noise was so loud. We found out that the war had started." The reverberations of the bombs falling near the Palama Shoe Factory and on Pearl Harbor were heard across the ocean; in a small Japanese farming community in California, Mary Tsukamoto was in church when she also suddenly felt the shocks of the explosions. "I do remember Pearl Harbor," she said years later as if it had happened that morning. "It was a December Sunday, so we were getting ready for our Christmas program. We were rehearsing and having Sunday school class, and I always played the piano for the adult Issei service. . . . After the service started, my husband ran in. He had been home that day and heard [the announcement] on the radio. We just couldn't believe it, but he told us that Japan attacked Pearl Harbor. I remember how stunned we were. And suddenly the whole world turned dark."[50]

As it turned out, Nagayama and Tsukamoto faced very different futures during World War II. Nagayama quit his job at the Palama Shoe Factory because the pay was too low and started work at Primo Beer. His life, like the lives of most of the 158,000 Japanese in the islands representing 37 percent of Hawaii's population, was not dramatically interrupted by the war. But Tsukamoto and 94,000 fellow Japanese in California, representing only one percent of the state's population, had their lives severely disrupted: along with some 25,000 Japanese from Washington and Oregon, they were forcefully placed in internment camps by the U.S. government. Everyone was given short notice for removal. "Signs had been nailed to the telephone poles saying that we had to report to various spots," Tsukamoto recalled. "They told us to register as families. We had to report to the Elk Grove Masonic Building where we were given our family number, No. 2076." While the Japanese in the islands had become "locals," members of the community in Hawaii, their brethren on the mainland had been forced to remain "strangers." Different histories were coming home to roost in Hawaii and in California.[51]

*   *   *

Shortly after inspecting the still-smoking ruins at Pearl Harbor, Navy Secretary Frank Knox issued a statement to the press: "I think the most effective fifth column work of the entire war was done in Hawaii, with the possible exception of Norway." Knox's assessment turned out to be inaccurate, for investigations by naval intelligence and the Federal Bureau of Investigation agreed that in fact no sabotage had occurred. But Knox's alarming announcement fueled rumors of sabotage committed by Japanese Americans in the islands — Japanese plantation laborers on Oahu had cut swaths in the sugar cane and pineapple fields to guide the Japanese bombers to the military installations, Japanese had parked cars across highways to block the traffic, and Japanese had given signals to enemy planes. At a cabinet meeting on December 19, Knox recommended the internment of all Japanese aliens on an outer island.[52]

But in a radio address aired two days later, General Delos Emmons, as military governor of Hawaii declared: "There is no intention or desire on the part of the federal authorities to operate mass concentration camps. No person, be he citizen or alien, need worry, provided he is not connected with subversive elements. . . . While we have been subjected to a serious attack by a ruthless and treacherous enemy, we must remember that this is America and we must do things the American Way. We must distinguish between loyalty and disloyalty among our people."[53]

A schism in policy was developing between Washington and Honolulu. Pursuant to Secretary Knox's recommendation, the War Department sent General Emmons a letter on January 10, 1942, asking for his view on the question of evacuating the Japanese from Oahu. Emmons replied that the proposed program would be dangerous and impractical. Such evacuation would require badly needed construction materials and shipping space, and would also tie up troop resources needed to guard the islands. Moreover, the mass evacuation of Japanese would severely disrupt both the economy and defense operations of Oahu, for the Japanese represented over 90 percent of the carpenters, nearly all of the transportation workers, and a significant proportion of the agricultural laborers. Japanese labor was "absolutely essential" for the rebuilding of the defenses destroyed at Pearl Harbor. A shrewd bureaucrat, General Emmons probably realized his analysis would fall on deaf ears in Washington and concluded his report by offering an alternative policy: if the War

Department should decide to evacuate the Japanese from Oahu, it should remove them to the mainland.[54]

In early February, Emmons informed Washington that he did not want to evacuate more than a few hundred Japanese until some 20,000 white-civilian women and children had first been transported to the mainland. He also estimated that 100,000 Japanese would have to be evacuated in order to remove all potentially disloyal Japanese, implying such a program would be impractical. On February 9, the War Department ordered General Emmons to suspend all Japanese workers employed by the army. But the order was rescinded after Emmons argued that the Japanese workers were indispensable and that the "Japanese question" should be handled "by those in direct contact with the situation."[55]

General Emmons was hoping his bureaucratic foot-dragging and his resistance against orders from Washington would wear down the War Department. His strategy seemed to be paying off: Washington agreed to scale down the number to be evacuated. On March 13, President Franklin Roosevelt, acting on the advice of his Joint Chiefs of Staff, approved a recommendation for the evacuation of 20,000 "dangerous" Japanese from Hawaii to the mainland. Two weeks later, General Emmons reduced the number drastically to only 1,550 Japanese who constituted a potential threat. But, on April 20, Secretary Knox again insisted that "all of the Japs" should be taken out of Oahu. The War Department then circulated a report received from the Justice Department warning of dangerous conditions in Hawaii. In a letter to Assistant Secretary of War John J. McCloy, Emmons angrily dismissed the report as "so fantastic it hardly needs refuting" and then directly attacked the credibility of the War Department and the Justice Department: "The feeling that an invasion is imminent is not the belief of most of the responsible people. . . . There have been no known acts of sabotage committed in Hawaii."[56]

The bureaucratic pushing and shoving between the War Department in Washington and the Hawaiian Department under the command of General Emmons continued. On October 29, Secretary of War Henry L. Stimson informed President Roosevelt that General Emmons intended to remove approximately 5,000 Japanese from Hawaii during the next six months as shipping facilities became available. "This, General Emmons believes, will greatly simplify his problem, and considering the labor needs in the islands, is about all that he has indicated any desire to move although he has been given authority to move up to fifteen thousand." Irritated by Emmons, President Roosevelt wrote to Stimson four days later: "I think that General Emmons should be told that the only consideration is that of the safety of the Islands and that the labor situation is not only a secondary matter but should not be given any consideration whatsoever."[57]

In the end, General Emmons had his way. He had seen no military necessity for mass evacuation and ordered the internment of only 1,444 Japanese (979 aliens and 525 citizens). Emmons saw that martial law had given the military government the authority to control Hawaii's Japanese population. But Emmons's success in resisting pressures from Washington depended not only on his administrative savvy and his ability to wage a waiting war of bureaucracy but also on widespread local opposition to mass internment.

In an article on "Hawaii's 150,000 Japanese" published in *The Nation* in July 1942, journalist Albert Horlings questioned whether the military authorities in Hawaii made their decision against mass internment based on their trust for the Japanese. He suspected "pressure" had been brought on the military, warning that the economic life of the islands would collapse without the Japanese. Horlings argued that businessmen appeared to favor "a liberal policy" toward the Japanese simply because they favored "business as usual."[58]

Indeed, economic pressure groups in Hawaii were advising General Emmons to resist relocation. A few isolated local businessmen favored mass internment. "At least 100,000 Japanese should be moved to inland mainland farming states," John A. Balch of the Hawaiian Telephone Company wrote to Admiral Chester Nimitz in August 1942. "If such a step as this was taken . . . not only the danger of internal trouble could be avoided, but the future of Hawaii would be secured against the sure political and economic domination by the Japanese within the next decade." But most of Hawaii's leading businessmen and *kamaaina haoles* (old-timer whites) opposed the proposal for mass internment. The president of the Honolulu Chamber of Commerce called for just treatment of the Japanese in Hawaii: "There are 160,000 of these people who want to live here because they like the country and like the American way of life. . . . The citizens of Japanese blood would fight as loyally for America as any other citizen. I have read or heard nothing in statements given out by the military, local police or F.B.I. since December 7 to change my opinion. And I have gone out of my way to ask for the facts." The kamaaina elite, possessing a sense of genteel paternalism and a long history of interaction with the Japanese in the islands, were unwilling to permit their mass uprooting. They also knew the evacuation of over one third of Hawaii's population would decimate their labor force and destroy the economy of the islands.[59]

Politicians and public officials also urged restraint and reason. Hawaii's congressional delegate, Sam King, advised the military that nothing should be done beyond apprehending known spies. Honolulu Police Captain John A. Burns refuted rumors of Japanese snipers firing on American soldiers during the attack on Pearl Harbor. "In spite of what . . . anyone . . . may have said about the fifth column activity in Hawaii," stated Robert L. Shivers, head of the FBI in Hawaii, "I want to emphasize that there was no such activity in Hawaii before, during or after the attack on Pearl Harbor. . . . I was in a position to know this fact. . . . Nowhere under the sun could there have been a more intelligent response to the needs of the hour than was given by the entire population of these islands." When schools were reopened in January 1942, the Superintendent of Public Instruction sent a directive to all teachers:

> Let us be perfectly frank in recognizing the fact that the most helpless victims, emotionally and psychologically, of the present situation in Hawaii will be children of Japanese ancestry and their parents. The position of loyal American citizens of Japanese ancestry and of aliens who are unable to become naturalized, but who are nonetheless loyal to the land of their adoption, is certainly not enviable. Teachers must do everything to help the morale of these people. Let us keep constantly in mind that America is not making war on citizens of the United States or on law-abiding aliens within America.[60]

The press in Hawaii behaved responsibly. Newspaper editors like Riley Allen of the Honolulu *Star Bulletin* and Mrs. Clarence Taylor of the Kauai *Garden Island* expressed confidence in the loyalty of the local Japanese and criticized the federal government's treatment of the Japanese on the mainland. "It was an invasion of the rights of the Japanese citizens on the Pacific coast to be picked up and shipped to the interior," editorialized the *Garden Island*. Newspapers also cautioned their readers not to spread or be influenced by rumors generated by the war situation. Within days after the attack on Pearl Harbor, the Honolulu *Star Bulletin* dismissed reports of Japanese subversion in the islands as "weird, amazing, and damaging untruths." "Beware of rumors always," urged the *Paradise of the Pacific* magazine in February 1942, "avoid them like a plague and, when possible, kill them as you would a reptile. Don't repeat for a fact anything you do not know is a fact."[61]

The reasons behind Hawaii's refusal to intern the Japanese were complex and did include the self-serving economic concern of the business community for the uninterrupted maintenance of its labor force. Still, in this moment of crisis an image of what Hawaii represented began to take a more definite form and content, drawing from the particular history of the islands and defining more sharply Hawaii's identity as a multiethnic community. Political and economic circumstances had provided an occasion for cultural development. In his radio message broadcast two weeks after the attack on Pearl Harbor, General Emmons declared: "Hawaii has always been an American outpost of friendliness and good will and now has calmly accepted its responsibility as an American outpost of war. In accepting these responsibilities, it is important that Hawaii prove that her traditional confidence in her cosmopolitan population has not been misplaced." While what Emmons described was a myth, it nonetheless also contained within it the possibility of an ideological counterpoint to the reality of racial hierarchy in the islands.[62]

The actions of the Japanese gave concreteness to the idea of Hawaii as a cosmopolitan community. During the morning of the attack, two thousand Nisei serving in the U.S. Army stationed in Hawaii fought to defend Pearl Harbor against enemy planes. Everywhere Japanese civilians participated in the island's defense. They rushed to their posts as volunteer truck drivers for Oahu's Citizens' Defense Committee. They stood in long lines in front of Queen's Hospital, waiting to give their blood to the wounded. Many of these civilians were Issei. "Most of us have lived longer in Hawaii than in Japan. We have an obligation to this country," they declared. "We are *yoshi* [adopted sons] of America. We want to do our part for America."[63]

Then that night, as the people of the islands tensely waited in the darkness for the expected invasion, thousands of Nisei members of the Hawaii Territorial Guard — youngsters from the high schools and the University of Hawaii ROTC program — guarded the power plants, reservoirs, and important waterfronts. For them, there was simply no doubt how they viewed the event: Japan had attacked their country. "As much as we would hate to see a war between the United States and Japan," Nisei Shigeo Yoshida had explained in 1937 during the hearings on statehood for Hawaii, "and as much as we would hate to see the day come when we would have to participate in such a conflict, it would be much easier, for us I think, if such an emergency should come, to face the enemy than to stand some of the suspicion and criticism, unjust in most cases, leveled against us. It is extremely difficult to bear up under the gaff of suspicion and expressions of doubt which have been leveled at us. It would be easier for me to pack a gun and face the enemy." Four years later, on December 7, that day did come and thousands of Nisei stood tall in defense of their country.[64]

"Japan's dastardly attack leaves us grim and resolute," declared Shunzo Sakamaki of the Oahu Citizens Committee for Home Defense on December 11. "There is no turning back now, no compromise with the enemy. Japan has chosen to fight us and we'll fight." The Japanese of Hawaii fought wholeheartedly. On June 5, 1942, more than seventeen hundred Japanese presented a check to the federal government for "bombs on Tokyo." In January 1943 General Emmons issued a call for fifteen hundred Nisei volunteers for the U.S. Army. "OK Tojo — you asked for it," announced a newspaper advertisement published in the Honolulu *Star Bulletin* on January 23 and signed by Akagi, Fukushima, Hiyama, Isoshima, Kanda, Kataoka, Kawashima, Komenaka, Musashiya, Ogata, Nagao, and Yamamoto. "You dished it out with a head start by treachery — now we're going to see how you can take it." In response to Emmons's call, 9,507 Nisei men volunteered for service. Many of them were sent to Camp Shelby, Mississippi, where they became members of the 442nd Regimental Combat Team and gave their unit the slogan, "Go for Broke," a pidgin-English phrase from the plantation gambling experience. "I wanted to show something, to contribute to America," explained Minoru Hinahara, who served as a Japanese-language interpreter in the U.S. 27th Army Division and participated in the invasion of Okinawa. "My parents could not become citizens but they told me, 'You fight for your country.' "[65]

If the Japanese in Hawaii were not interned, why were their brethren on the mainland evacuated and imprisoned in internment camps? Why did the mainland do "things the American Way" differently?

On the day after the attack on Pearl Harbor, Representative John M. Coffee declared in Congress: "It is my fervent hope and prayer that residents of the United States of Japanese extraction will not be made the victim of pogroms directed by self-proclaimed patriots and by hysterical self-anointed heroes. . . . Let us not make a mockery of our Bill of Rights by mistreating these folks. Let us rather regard them with understanding, remembering they are the victims of a Japanese war machine, with the making of the international policies of which they had nothing to do."[66]

Perhaps Coffee was overly hopeful and naive, but there were reasons to think Japanese Americans would not become victims of hysteria unleashed by the war. A confidential report on the question of Japanese-American loyalty had already been submitted to President Franklin Roosevelt. The president had secretly arranged to have Chicago businessman Curtis Munson gather intelligence on the Japanese in the United States and assess whether they constituted an internal military threat. After Roosevelt received the Munson report on November 7, 1941, he asked the War Department to review it. In his discussion on sabotage and espionage, Munson informed the President that there was no need to fear or worry about America's Japanese population: "There will be no armed uprising of Japanese [in this country]. . . . Japan will commit some sabotage largely depending on imported Japanese as they are afraid of and do not trust the Nisei. There will be no wholehearted response from Japanese in the United States. . . . For the most part the local Japanese are loyal to the United States or, at worst, hope that by remaining quiet they can avoid concentration camps or irresponsible mobs. We do not believe that they would be at least any more disloyal than any other racial group in the United States with whom we went to war."[67]

A month later the assessment of the Munson report was tested at Pearl Harbor. In his investigation of the Japanese in Hawaii and on the mainland, Lieutenant Commander K. D. Ringle of the Office of Naval Intelligence found that the large majority of them were at least passively loyal to the United States. In late January 1942, Ringle estimated that only about 3,500 Japanese could potentially be military threats and stated there was no need for mass action against the Japanese. Meanwhile, the FBI had also conducted its own investigation of the Japanese. On December 10, Director J. Edgar Hoover informed Washington that "practically all" suspected individuals whom he had initially planned to arrest were in custody: 1,291 Japanese (367 in Hawaii, 924 on the mainland), 857 Germans, and 147 Italians. In a report to the Attorney General submitted in early February, Hoover concluded that the proposed mass evacuation of the Japanese could not be justified for security reasons.[68]

Despite these intelligence findings, Lieutenant General John L. DeWitt, head of the Western Defense Command, behaved very differently from his counterpart General Emmons in Hawaii. Within two weeks after the attack on Pearl Harbor, General DeWitt requested approval to conduct search-and-seizure operations in order to prevent alien Japanese from making radio transmissions to Japanese ships. The Justice Department refused to issue search warrants without probable cause, and the FBI determined the problem was only a perceived one. In January, the Federal Communications Commission, which had been monitoring all broadcasts, reported that the army's fears were groundless. But the army continued pursuing plans based on the assumption of Japanese disloyalty. General DeWitt also wanted to be granted the power to exclude Japanese aliens as well as Americans of Japanese ancestry from restricted areas. On January 4, 1942, at a meeting of federal and state officials in his San Francisco headquarters, DeWitt argued that military necessity justified exclusion: "We are at war and this area — eight states — has been designated as a theater of operations. . . . [There are] approximately 288,000 enemy aliens . . . which we have to watch. . . . I have little confidence that the enemy aliens are law-abiding or loyal in any sense of the word. Some of them yes; many, no. Particularly the Japanese. I have no confidence in their loyalty whatsoever. I am speaking now of the native born Japanese — 117,000 — and 42,000 in California alone."[69]

The Western Defense Command ignored the Munson report as well as the information from the FCC and shunned Lieutenant Commander Ringle. Serving under DeWitt, Major General Joseph W. Stilwell had an insider's view of the situation at the Command's headquarters in San Francisco. In his diary, Stilwell described how DeWitt was responding irrationally to rumors: "Common sense is thrown to the winds and any absurdity is believed." But Stilwell did not understand the reasons for DeWitt's conduct. FBI director Hoover was more perceptive: while he also saw that the WDC's intelligence information reflected "hysteria and lack of judgment," he noticed that the claim of military necessity for mass evacuation was based "primarily upon public and political pressure rather than on factual data."[70]

Immediately after the press had been told by Navy Secretary Knox about Japanese subversive activity at Pearl Harbor, West Coast newspapers gave his claim headline attention: "Fifth Column Treachery Told" and "Secretary of Navy Blames 5th Column for Raid."

Nonetheless, newspapers were initially restrained, advising readers to remain calm and considerate toward the Japanese. But in early January, press sentiments began shifting suddenly. On January 5, John B. Hughes of the Mutual Broadcasting Company began firing a month-long salvo against the Japanese in California. The Japanese were engaged in espionage, he charged, and their dominance in produce production and control of the food supply were part of a master war plan. On January 19, *Time* reported Japanese fifth-column activities in Hawaii in an article entitled: "The Stranger within Our Gates." The next day, the *San Diego Union* stirred anti-Japanese hysteria: "In Hawaii . . . treachery by residents, who although of Japanese ancestry had been regarded as loyal, has played an important part in the success of Japanese attacks. . . . Every Japanese . . . should be moved out of the coastal area and to a point of safety far enough inland to nullify any inclination they may have to tamper with our safety here." Meanwhile the *Los Angeles Times* editorialized: "A viper is nonetheless a viper wherever the egg is hatched — so a Japanese American, born of Japanese parents — grows up to be a Japanese, not an American." On January 29, Henry McLemore blasted the Japanese in his syndicated column for the Hearst newspapers: "I am for immediate removal of every Japanese on the West Coast to a point deep in the interior. I don't mean a nice part of the interior either. Herd 'em up, pack 'em off and give 'em the inside room in the badlands." Two weeks later, in a *Washington Post* article entitled "The Fifth Column on the Coast," prominent columnist Walter Lippmann called for the mass removal of Japanese Americans: "The Pacific Coast is in imminent danger of a combined attack from within and without. . . . The Pacific Coast is officially a combat zone. . . . And nobody ought to be on a battlefield who has no good reason for being there. There is plenty of room elsewhere for him to exercise his rights."[71]

As the press mounted its campaign for Japanese removal, it was joined by patriotic organizations. In January the California Department of the American Legion began to demand that all Japanese known to possess dual citizenship be placed in "concentration camps." Shortly afterward American Legion posts in Washington and Oregon passed resolutions urging the evacuation of all Japanese. In the January issue of their publication, *The Grizzly Bear*, the Native Sons and Daughters of the Golden West told their fellow Californians: "We told you so. Had the warnings been heeded — had the federal and state authorities been 'on the alert,' and rigidly enforced the Exclusion Law and the Alien Land Law . . . had the legislation been enacted denying citizenship to offspring of all aliens ineligible to citizenship . . . had Japan been denied the privilege of using California as a breeding ground for dual-citizens (Nisei); — the treacherous Japs probably would not have attacked Pearl Harbor on December 7, 1941, and this country would not today be at war with Japan."[72]

Beginning in January and early February, the anti-Japanese chorus included voices from farming interests such as the Grower-Shipper Vegetable Association, the Western Growers Protective Association, and the California Farm Bureau Federation. "We've been charged with wanting to get rid of the Japs for selfish reasons," the Grower-Shipper Vegetable Association stated in the *Saturday Evening Post* in May. "We might as well be honest. We do. It's a question of whether the white man lives on the Pacific Coast or the brown man. They came into this valley to work, and they stayed to take over. . . . If all the Japs were removed tomorrow, we'd never miss them in two weeks, because the white farmers can take over and produce everything the Jap grows."[73]

Meanwhile, local and state politicians were already leading the movement for Japanese removal. The boards of supervisors of sixteen California counties, including Los Angeles County, passed resolutions urging removal. California Attorney General Earl Warren pressed federal authorities to remove Japanese from sensitive areas on the West Coast. The Japanese in California, he warned, "may well be the Achilles heel of the entire civilian defense effort. Unless something is done it may bring about a repetition of Pearl Harbor." On January 16, Congressman Leland Ford of Los Angeles wrote to the secretaries of the departments of War and the Navy and the FBI Director, insisting that "all Japanese, whether citizens or not, be placed in concentration camps." Two weeks later, several House members from the Pacific Coast states asked President Roosevelt to grant the War Department "immediate and complete control over all alien enemies, as well as United States citizens holding dual citizenship in any enemy country, with full power and authority" to evacuate and intern them.[74]

The Western Defense Command operated within the context of this clamor for Japanese removal. The situation was very different from Hawaii's. Economic interests in California did not need Japanese labor, and many white farmers viewed Japanese farmers as competitors. Representing a small, rather than numerically significant racial minority, the Japanese were more vulnerable to xenophobic attacks. Furthermore a mythology of California as a "cosmopolitan" society did not exist to protect its Japanese residents. In fact, the state's image as projected by politicians in the 1920 vote on the alien land law was "Keep California White." On February 1, in a telephone conversation with Provost Marshal General Allen Gullion, General DeWitt said he had "travelled up and down the West Coast," talked to "all the Governors and other local civil authorities," and decided to press for mass evacuation. Protection against sabotage, he said, "only can be made positive by removing those people who are aliens and who are Japs of American citizenship." On February 5, after he had received DeWitt's views in writing, Gullion drafted a War Department proposal for the exclusion of "all persons, whether aliens or citizens . . . deemed dangerous as potential saboteurs" from designated "military areas."[75]

But a decision on evacuation still had not been made in Washington. During lunch with President Roosevelt on February 7, Attorney General Francis Biddle said "there were no reasons for mass evacuation." In his diary on February 10, Secretary of War Henry L. Stimson wrote: "The second generation Japanese can only be evacuated either as part of a total evacuation . . . or by frankly trying to put them out on the ground that their racial characteristics are such that we cannot understand or trust even the citizen Japanese. This latter is the fact but I am afraid it will make a tremendous hole in our constitutional system to apply it."[76]

President Roosevelt was willing to make such a tremendous hole in the Constitution. In fact, he had been considering the internment of Japanese Americans for a long time. On August 10, 1936, President Roosevelt had written a memorandum to the Chief of Naval Operations: "One obvious thought occurs to me — that every Japanese citizen or non-citizen on the island of Oahu who meets these Japanese ships or has any connection with their officers or men should be secretly but definitely identified and his or her name placed on a special list of those who would be the first to be placed in a concentration camp in the event of trouble." Thus, five years before the attack on Pearl Harbor, Roosevelt was already devising a plan for the imprisonment of Japanese aliens and citizens in a "concentration camp" without due process of law.[77]

On February 11, 1942, Roosevelt met with Stimson, and shortly after the meeting, Assistant Secretary of War John J. McCloy telephoned the Provost Marshal General's office in San Francisco. "We talked to the President," McCloy said to Karl Bendetsen, chief of the Aliens Division, "and the President, in substance, says go ahead and do anything you think necessary. He says there will probably be some repercussions, but it has got to be dictated by military necessity. . . ." Three days after he had received his signal from Washington, General DeWitt sent Stimson his formal recommendation for removal, buttressing it with a racial justification: "In the war in which we are now engaged racial affinities are not severed by migration. The Japanese race is an enemy race and while many second and third generation Japanese born on United States soil, possessed of United States citizenship, have become 'Americanized,' the racial strains are undiluted. . . . It, therefore, follows that along the vital Pacific Coast over 112,000 potential enemies, of Japanese extraction, are at large today."[78]

Three days later, Attorney General Biddle wrote a memorandum to President Roosevelt, opposing DeWitt's recommendation for evacuation: "My last advice from the War Department is that there is no evidence of imminent attack and from the F.B.I. that there is no evidence of planned sabotage." Biddle tried to exercise reason and restraint, and his efforts to derail DeWitt's recommendation angered Congressman John Ford. "I phoned the Attorney General's office," said Ford, "and told them to stop fucking around. I gave them twenty-four hours notice that unless they would issue a mass evacuation notice I would drag the whole matter on the floor of the House and of the Senate and give the bastards everything we could with both barrels."[79]

The next day, February 18, Secretary of War Stimson met with Attorney General Biddle and several others from the Department of Justice and the War Department. In his autobiography, Biddle described the meeting: "The decision [for evacuation] had been made by the President. It was, he said, a matter of military judgment. I did not think I should oppose it any further." The following morning, President Roosevelt signed Executive Order 9066, which directed the Secretary of War to prescribe military areas "with respect to which, the right of any person to enter, remain in, or leave shall be subject to whatever restrictions the Secretary of War or the appropriate Military Commander may impose in his discretion." The order did not specify the Japanese as the group to be excluded. But they were the target: a few months later, when President Roosevelt learned about discussions in the War Department to apply the order to Germans and Italians on the East Coast, he wrote to inform Stimson that he considered enemy alien control to be "primarily a civilian matter except in the case of the Japanese mass evacuation on the Pacific Coast." Unlike the Germans and Italians, the Japanese were "strangers from a different shore."[80]

President Roosevelt had signed a blank check, giving full authority to General DeWitt to evacuate the Japanese and place them in assembly centers and eventually in internment camps. And so it happened, tragically for the Japanese and for the U.S. Constitution, for there was actually no "military necessity."

Under General DeWitt's command, the military ordered a curfew for all enemy aliens and all persons of Japanese ancestry and posted orders for evacuation: "Pursuant to the provisions of Civilian Exclusion Order No. 27, this Headquarters, dated April 30, 1942, all persons of Japanese ancestry, both alien and non-alien, will be evacuated from the above area by 12 o'clock noon, P. W. T., Thursday May 7, 1942." The evacuees were instructed to bring their bedding, toilet articles, extra clothing, and utensils. "No pets of any kind will be permitted." Japanese stood in silent numbness before the notices. Years later, Congressman Robert Matsui, who was a baby in 1942, asked: "How could I as a 6-month-old child born in this country be declared by my own Government to be an enemy alien?" But the order applied to everyone, including children. An American birthright made absolutely no difference. "Doesn't my citizenship mean a single blessed thing to anyone?" asked Monica Sone's brother in distress. "Several weeks before May, soldiers came around and posted notices on telephone poles," said Takae Washizu. "It was sad for me to leave the place where I had been living for such a long time. Staring at the ceiling in bed at night, I wondered who would take care of my cherry tree and my house after we moved out."

> Notice of evacuation
> One spring night
> The image of my wife
> Holding the hands of my mother.[81]

Believing the military orders were unconstitutional, Minoru Yasui of Portland refused to obey the curfew order: "It was my belief that no military authority has the right to subject any United States citizen to any requirement that does not equally apply to all other U.S. citizens. If we believe in America, if we believe in equality and democracy, if we believe in law and justice, then each of us, when we see or believe errors are being made, has an obligation to make every effort to correct them." Meanwhile Fred Korematsu in California and Gordon Hirabayashi in Washington refused to report to the evacuation center. "As an American citizen," Hirabayashi explained, "I wanted to uphold the principles of the Constitution, and the curfew and evacuation orders which singled out a group on the basis of ethnicity violated them. It was not acceptable to me to be less than a full citizen in a white man's country." The three men were arrested and convicted; sent to prison, they took their cases to the Supreme Court, which upheld their convictions, saying the government's policies were based on military necessity. Most Japanese, however, felt they had no choice but to comply with the evacuation orders.[82]

Instructed they would be allowed to take only what they could carry, evacuees had to sell most of their possessions — their refrigerators, cars, furniture, radios, pianos, and houses. "I remember how agonizing was my despair," recounted Tom Hayase, "to be given only about six days in which to dispose of our property." "It is difficult to describe the feeling of despair and humiliation experienced by all of us," said another evacuee, "as we watched the Caucasians coming to look over our possessions and offering such nominal amounts knowing we had no recourse but to accept whatever they were offering because we did not know what the future held for us."[83]

At the control centers, the evacuees were registered and each family was given a number. "Henry went to the Control Station to register the family," remembered Monica Sone. "He came home with twenty tags, all numbered '10710,' tags to be attached to each piece of baggage, and one to hang from our coat lapels. From then on, we were known as Family #10710." When they reported at the train stations, they found themselves surrounded by soldiers with rifles and bayonets.

> *Like a dog*
> *I am commanded*
> *At a bayonet point.*
> *My heart is inflamed*
> *With burning anguish.*

From there they were taken to the assembly centers. "I looked at Santa Clara's streets from the train over the subway," wrote Norman Mineta's father in a letter to friends in San Jose. "I thought this might be the last look at my loved home city. My heart almost broke, and suddenly hot tears just came pouring out. . . ." They knew that more than their homes and possessions had been taken from them. "On May 16, 1942, my mother, two sisters, niece, nephew, and I left . . . by train," said Teru Watanabe. "Father joined us later. Brother left earlier by bus. We took whatever we could carry. So much we left behind, but the most valuable thing I lost was my freedom."[84]

When they arrived, the evacuees were shocked to discover that they were to be housed at stockyards, fairgrounds, and race tracks. "The assembly center was filthy, smelly, and dirty. There were roughly two thousand people packed in one large building. No beds were provided, so they gave us gunny sacks to fill with straw, that was our bed." Stables served as housing. "Where a horse or cow had been kept, a Japanese American family was moved in." "Suddenly you realized that human beings were being put behind fences just like on the farm where we had horses and pigs in corrals."

If you live in a
Horse stable
The wind of cities
Blow through.

Conditions were crowded and noisy. "There was a constant buzzing — conversations, talk. Then, as the evening wore on, during the still of the night, things would get quiet, except for the occasional coughing, snoring, giggles. Then someone would get up to go to the bathroom. It was like a family of three thousand people camped out in a barn." Everywhere there were lines. "We lined up for mail, for checks, for meals, for showers, for washrooms, for laundry tubs, for toilets, for clinic service, for movies." There were curfews and roll calls, and "day and night camp police walked their beats within the center."[85]

After a brief stay in the assembly centers, the evacuees were herded into 171 special trains, five hundred in each train.

Snow in mountain pass
Unable to sleep
The prison train.

They had no idea where they were going. In their pockets, some carried photographs of themselves and the homes they had left behind, and they occasionally turned their gaze away from the landscape whizzing by them and pulled out their pictures.

Falling asleep with
A photograph,
Awakened by a dream,
Cold snowy wind of
Missoula.

The trains took them to ten internment camps — Topaz in Utah, Poston and Gila River in Arizona, Amache in Colorado, Jerome and Rohwer in Arkansas, Minidoka in Idaho, Manzanar and Tule Lake in California, and Heart Mountain in Wyoming.[86] Most of the camps were located in remote desert areas. "We did not know where we were," remembered an internee. "No houses were in sight, no trees or anything green — only scrubby sagebrush and an occasional low cactus, and mostly dry, baked earth." They looked around them and saw hundreds of miles of wasteland, "beyond the end of the horizon and again over the mountain — again, more wasteland." They were surrounded by dust and sand. At Minidoka, Monica Sone recalled, "we felt as if we were standing in a gigantic sand-mixing machine as the sixty-mile gale lifted the loose earth up into the sky, obliterating everything. Sand filled our mouths and nostrils and stung our faces and hands like a thousand darting needles."[87]

In the camps, the internees were assigned to barracks, each barrack about twenty by 120 feet, divided into four or six rooms. Usually a family was housed in one room, twenty by twenty feet. The room had "a pot bellied stove, a single electric light hanging from the ceiling, an Army cot for each person and a blanket for the bed."

Birds,
Living in a cage,
The human spirit.

The camp was linear, its barracks lined in orderly rows; barbed-wire fences with guard towers defined space for the internees. Some tried to resist the strictures of the new form of "necessity" by creating rock gardens with bonsai outside their drab barracks.[88]

Their little gardens provided relief in a world of military-like routine. "Camp life was highly regimented and it was rushing to the wash basin to beat the other groups, rushing to the mess hall for breakfast, lunch and dinner." Every morning at 7 A.M., the internees were awakened by a siren blast. After eating breakfast in a cafeteria,

the children went to school, where they began the day by saluting
the flag of the United States and then singing "My country, 'tis of
thee, sweet land of liberty." Looking beyond the flagpole, they saw
the barbed wire, the watchtowers, and the armed guards. "I was too
young to understand," stated George Takei years later, "but I remember soldiers carrying rifles, and I remember being afraid."[89]

Most adults went to work. Shopkeepers and farmers suddenly
found themselves working as wage earners for the government, forced
to abandon the virtues of self-reliance and independence that had
enabled them to survive in society. Government employees in camps
earned twelve dollars a month as unskilled laborers, sixteen dollars
as skilled, and nineteen dollars as professionals. Busy and active
people before the evacuation, many internees became bored and listless:

> Gazing at the barracks
> Where my wife exists,
> Beyond the barbed wire fence,
> I pluck and chew
> The leaves of grass.

Proud people before evacuation, they felt diminished, their dignity
destroyed. Some were overwhelmed by their despair.

> A fellow prisoner
> Takes his life with poison.
> In the evening darkness,
> Streaks of black blood
> Stain the camp road.[90]

In the camps, families no longer sat down to eat together. The
internees ate at long tables in large mess halls, and parents often sat
at separate tables from their children, especially the teenagers. People
were "crowded in a long line just like a snake," waiting "for a meal
in the dust and wind." Young married couples worried about having
children born in the camps. "When I was pregnant with my second
child, that's when I flipped," said a Nisei woman. "I guess that's
when the reality really hit me. I thought to myself, gosh, what am I
doing getting pregnant. I told my husband, 'This is crazy. You realize
there's no future for us and what are we having kids for?' "[91]

But the war had also begun to open a future for the Nisei. In
September 1942, the Selective Service had classified all young Japanese men as IV-C, or enemy aliens. A month later, however, the

Director of the Office of War Information urged President Roosevelt to authorize the enlistment of Nisei: "Loyal American citizens of Japanese descent should be permitted, after an individual test, to enlist in the Army and Navy. . . . This matter is of great interest to OWI. Japanese propaganda to the Philippines, Burma, and elsewhere insists that this is a racial war. We can combat this effectively with counter propaganda only if our deeds permit us to tell the truth." President Roosevelt understood the need to neutralize "Japanese propaganda": in December the army developed a plan for forming an all-Nisei combat team. On February 1, 1943, hypocritically ignoring the evacuation order he had signed a year earlier, Roosevelt wrote to Secretary of War Stimson: "No loyal citizen of the United States should be denied the democratic right to exercise the responsibilities of his citizenship, regardless of his ancestry. . . . Americanism is not, and never was, a matter of race or ancestry. Every loyal American citizen should be given the opportunity to serve this country . . . in the ranks of our armed forces. . . ."[92]

Five days later the government required all internees to answer loyalty questionnaires. The questionnaires had two purposes: (1) to enable camp authorities to process individual internees for work furloughs as well as for resettlement outside of the restricted zones, and (2) to register Nisei for the draft. Question 27 asked draft-age males: "Are you willing to serve in the armed forces of the United States on combat duty, wherever ordered?" Question 28 asked all internees: "Will you swear unqualified allegiance to the United States of America and faithfully defend the United States from any or all attack by foreign or domestic forces, and forswear any form of allegiance or obedience to the Japanese emperor, or any other foreign government, power or organization?"[93]

Forced to fill out and sign the loyalty questionnaire in the internment camps, Nisei stared at the form:

> *Loyalty, disloyalty,*
> *If asked,*
> *What should I answer?*

Some 4,600 or 22 percent of the 21,000 Nisei males eligible to register for the draft answered with a "no," a qualified answer, or no response. Many of them said they were not expressing disloyalty but were protesting against the internment. "Well, I am one of those that said 'no, no' on the questions, one of the 'no, no' boys," explained Albert Nakai, "and it is not that I was proud about it, it was just that our legal rights were violated and I wanted to fight back." When he was told the army wanted Nisei to volunteer for a special combat unit, Monica Sone's friend, Dunks Oshima retorted: "What do they take us for? Saps? First, they change my army status to 4-C because of my ancestry, run me out of town, and now they want me to volunteer for a suicide squad so I could get killed for this damn democracy. That's going some, for sheer brass!"[94]

At Heart Mountain internment camp, Frank Emi studied the questionnaire. "The more I looked at it the more disgusted I became," recalled Emi, who at the time was a twenty-seven-year-old Nisei with a wife and two children. "We were treated more like enemy aliens than American citizens. And now this [the loyalty questionnaire]." Emi decided to hand print his answer and post it on the mess hall doors: "Under the present conditions and circumstances, I am unable to answer these questions." Shortly afterward, he attended a mass meeting where he heard a stirring speech by Kiyoshi Okamoto. An educated soil-test engineer from Hawaii who had moved to the mainland and become a high-school teacher, Okamoto told his fellow Nisei that as American citizens they should stand up for the rights guaranteed to them under the Constitution. He referred to himself as the "Fair Play Committee of One." The fifty-year-old Okamoto moved the younger Nisei. "At first we were naive and just felt the questionnaire was unfair," said Emi. "But Okamoto taught us about the Constitution and it came to have great meaning as we began to resist."[95]

Though most Nisei answered Questions 27 and 28 affirmatively, they did not rush to join the army. The army was able to recruit only 1,208 volunteers — a small fraction of the 10,000 eligible Nisei. In January 1944, the Selective Service began reclassifying to I-A Nisei who had answered yes to the two questions and serving draft registration notices. At Heart Mountain, Emi and several fellow Nisei organized the Fair Play Committee and declared they would not cooperate with the draft unless their citizenship rights were restored first. Their movement spontaneously gathered widespread support. Four hundred Nisei attended their meetings and the Committee had two hundred dues-paying members. Draft resistance broke out in the other camps. Some three hundred Nisei refused to be inducted, protesting the violation of their Constitutional rights.[96]

Worried, government authorities acted quickly to repress the protest. Emi and six other leaders of the Heart Mountain Fair Play Committee were arrested and indicted for conspiracy to violate the

Selective Service Act and for counseling others to resist the draft. James Omura, editor of the Denver *Rocky Shimpo*, was also indicted on the same charges because his paper had published statements issued by the Committee and had offered editorial support. The cost of the trial bankrupted Omura's newspaper. Speaking over forty years later, Omura defended his actions: "The *Shimpo* took up the cudgel of Nisei rights under the Constitution." More important than silencing the *Shimpo*, for the government, was destroying the leadership of the Committee. During the trial, said Emi, "a surprise witness appeared in court. His name was Jack Nishimoto." Emi and Nishimoto had been friends. "When he took the stand," Emi recalled, "he began to tell wholesale lies about me, saying for example that I had told a resister's family not to worry because the Fair Play Committee would take care of him. I had not said such a thing. Years later, I learned from files released under the Freedom of Information Act that Nishimoto was an informer and had been instructed by the FBI to get close to me in order to gather information on the Fair Play Committee." In court Emi and his fellow leaders of the Committee argued that the draft law as applied to Japanese Americans in the internment camps was morally wrong and unconstitutional. "We, the members of the FPC are not afraid to go to war — we are not afraid to risk our lives for our country," they had declared in their statement of resistance. "We would gladly sacrifice our lives to protect and uphold the principles and ideals of our country as set forth in the Constitution and the Bill of Rights, for on its inviolability depends the freedom, liberty, justice, and protection of all people including Japanese-Americans and all other minority groups."[97]

Emi and the others were found guilty and sentenced to four years at Leavenworth Federal Penitentiary. "What you guys are doing is all right," a Nisei told Emi. "But I don't want to go to jail so I have to register for the draft." At Leavenworth they found themselves in a prison for hardened criminals. "They asked us, 'Why are you here?' " said Emi. "And we told them, and they replied, 'It don't make sense to put you in jail.' " Altogether some three hundred Nisei refused to be inducted and many of them were sent to prison. "Look, the government took my father away, and interned him someplace," explained a Nisei draft resister. "My mother is alone at the Grenada camp with my younger sister who is only fourteen. If the government would take care of them here in America, I'd feel like going out to fight for my country, but this country is treating us worse than shit!"[98]

During the war, 33,000 Nisei served in the U.S. Armed Forces.

They believed participation in the defense of their country was the best way to express their loyalty and to fulfill their obligation as citizens. Several thousand of them were members of the Military Intelligence Service, functioning as interpreters and translators on the Pacific front. Armed with Japanese language skills, they provided an invaluable service, translating captured Japanese documents, including battle plans, lists of Imperial Navy ships, and Japanese secret codes. Richard Sakakida's translation of Japanese plans for a landing on Bataan made it possible for American tanks to ambush the invaders as they landed. Nisei soldiers volunteered for service with Merrill's Marauders in Burma; one of their officers described their heroic work: "During battles they crawled up close enough to be able to hear Jap officers' commands and to make verbal translations to our soldiers. They tapped lines, listened in on radios, translated documents and papers, made spot translations of messages and field orders. . . ." As members of the MIS, Nisei soldiers participated in the invasion of Okinawa. Two of them, Hiroshi Kobashigawa and Frank Higashi were worried about their families in Okinawa. Both of them had been born in the United States and had parents who had returned to Okinawa before the outbreak of the war. When American soldiers landed in Okinawa, they found the people hiding in caves: Okinawans had been told by the Japanese military it would be better for them to be dead than to be captured, and the Okinawans were afraid they would be tortured, raped, and killed by the Americans. In his family's home village, Kobashigawa was relieved to find his mother, sister, and three younger brothers safe in a civilian refugee camp. Higashi found his father in the hills of northern Okinawa during a mop-up operation and carried him on his back to the village. Nisei soldiers like Kobashigawa and Higashi rescued their own families and also persuaded many Japanese soldiers to surrender. General Charles Willoughby, chief of intelligence in the Pacific, estimated that Nisei MIS contributions shortened the war by two years.[99]

Nisei soldiers also helped to win the war in Europe. In 1942, while General DeWitt evacuated the Japanese on the West Coast, General Emmons recommended the formation of a battalion of Hawaiian Nisei — the 100th Battalion. After training at Camp McCoy in Wisconsin and Camp Shelby in Mississippi, fourteen hundred Nisei of the 100th Battalion were sent to northern Africa and then to Italy in September 1943. They participated in the Italian campaign until the following March. Three hundred of them were killed and 650 wounded. The 100th was called the "Purple Heart Battalion." In

June, the 100th Battalion merged with the newly arrived 442nd Regimental Combat Team, composed of Nisei from Hawaii and from internment camps on the mainland. The Nisei soldiers experienced bloody fighting at Luciana, Livorno, and the Arno River, where casualties totaled 1,272 men — more than one fourth of the regiment. After the battle at the Arno River, they were sent to France, where they took the town of Bruyeres from the German troops in heavy house-to-house fighting. Then they were ordered to rescue the Texan "Lost Battalion," 211 men surrounded by German troops in the Vosges Mountains. "If we advanced a hundred yards, that was a good day's job," recalled a Nisei soldier describing the rescue mission. "We'd dig in again, move up another hundred yards, and dig in. That's how we went. It took us a whole week to get to the Lost Battalion. It was just a tree-to-tree fight." At the end of the week of fighting, the 442nd had suffered eight hundred casualties. When the trapped Texans finally saw the Nisei soldiers, some broke into sobs. One of the rescued soldiers remembered the moment: "[The Germans] would hit us from one flank and then the other, then from the front and the rear . . . we were never so glad to see anyone as those fighting Japanese Americans."[100]

Nisei soldiers went on to take the Gothic Line in northern Italy and then in April 1945 assaulted German troops on Mount Nebbione. "Come on, you guys, go for broke!" they shouted as they charged directly into the fire of enemy machine guns. Captain Daniel Inouye crawled to the flank of an emplacement and pulled the pin on his grenade. "As I drew my arm back, all in a flash of light and dark I saw him, that faceless German," he remembered.

> And even as I cocked my arm to throw, he fired and his rifle grenade smashed into my right elbow and exploded and all but tore my arm off. I looked at it, stunned and unbelieving. It dangled there by a few bloody shreds of tissue, my grenade still clenched in a fist that suddenly didn't belong to me any more. . . . I swung around to pry the grenade out of that dead fist with my left hand. Then I had it free and I turned to throw and the German was reloading his rifle. But this time I beat him. My grenade blew up in his face and I stumbled to my feet, closing on the bunker, firing my tommy gun left-handed, the useless right arm slapping red and wet against my side.[101]

The war, for the wounded Captain Inouye, was over. Two weeks later, in May 1945, the war in Europe came to an end for everyone. Nisei soldiers of the 442nd had suffered 9,486 casualties, including six hundred killed. "Just think of all those people — of the 990 that went over [with me], not more than 200 of them came back without getting hit," said 442nd veteran Shig Doi. "If you look at the 442nd boys, don't look at their faces, look at their bodies. They got hit hard, some lost their limbs." The 442nd, military observers agreed, was "probably the most decorated unit in United States military history." They had earned 18,143 individual decorations — including one Congressional Medal of Honor, forty-seven Distinguished Service Crosses, 350 Silver Stars, 810 Bronze Stars, and more than thirty-six hundred Purple Hearts. They had given their lives and limbs to prove their loyalty.[102]

One of the Nisei soldiers explained the meaning of their involvement and their sacrifice in the war. In a letter to a young Japanese woman in Hawaii, he wrote from the European battlefront during the war:

> My friends and my family — they mean everything to me. They are the most important reason why I am giving up my education and my happiness to go to fight a war that we never asked for. But our Country is involved in it. Not only that. By virtue of the Japanese attack on our nation, we as American citizens of Japanese ancestry have been mercilessly flogged with criticism and accusations. But I'm not going to take it sitting down! I may not be able to come back. But that matters little. My family and friends — they are the ones who will be able to back their arguments with facts. They are the ones who will be proud. In fact, it is better that we are sent to the front and that a few of us do not return, for the testimony will be stronger in favor of the folks back home.[103]

"They bought an awful hunk of America with their blood," declared General Joseph Stilwell. "You're damn right those Nisei boys have a place in the American heart, now and forever." After the war in 1945, General Stilwell flew to California to award the Distinguished Service Cross to Kazuo Masuda. Sergeant Masuda of the 442nd had single-handedly fired a mortar on Nazi positions and had been killed at Cassino, Italy. On the porch of a frame shack in Orange County, General Stilwell pinned the medal on Masuda's sister, Mary, who had recently returned from the internment camp. Several show-business personalities, including Robert Young and Will Rogers, participated in the ceremony, and a young actor, Ronald Reagan, paid tribute to the fallen Nisei soldier: "Blood that has soaked into the sands of a beach is all of one color. America stands unique in the world, the only country not founded on race, but on a way — an ideal. Not in spite of, but because of our polyglot background, we have had all the strength in the world. That is the American way."[104]

The Nisei soldiers had made an impact back home. A Filipino described how his attitude toward Japanese Americans had been turned around by the valor of the Nisei soldiers: "When Japan bombed Pearl Harbor, Manila, and all parts of the Philippines, I was entirely against the Japanese too. My feeling was 100% against them. But when those Japanese in the war showed their patriotism in favor of this country, I changed my mind. They should not have been taken [to internment camps]. Like the Italians and the Germans, all those born here are citizens. They should not have been suspected as spies." After the war, on July 15, 1946, on the lawn of the White House, President Harry Truman welcomed home the Nisei soldiers of the 442nd: "You fought for the free nations of the world . . . you fought not only the enemy, you fought prejudice — and you won."[105]

As they stood on the land of their birth, however, they could not be certain they had defeated prejudice in America. Captain Inouye soon discovered they had not won the war at home. He was on his way back to Hawaii in 1945 when he tried to get a haircut in San Francisco. Entering the barbershop with his empty right sleeve pinned to his army jacket covered with ribbons and medals for his military heroism, Captain Inouye was told: "We don't serve Japs here." Another Nisei soldier from Hawaii reflected on the future of his brothers in arms from the mainland. He and his Hawaiian buddies would be returning to the islands to take up "again the threads of life" where they had been left off. But the mainland Nisei soldiers had "no home to return to except the wire-enclosed relocation centers." "They have nothing to look forward to," he observed sadly, "except an even greater fight than that which they are undergoing here in Italy — to win their battle at home against the race-baiters and professional patriots."[106]

Meanwhile on the West Coast, General DeWitt had been succeeded by none other than General Emmons. On November 5, 1943, Assistant Secretary of War John J. McCloy wrote to Emmons after the new commander's transfer from Hawaii: "The situation in California is not the same [as in Hawaii]. You have no doubt become aware of the existence of active and powerful minority groups in California whose main interest in the war seems to take the form of a desire for permanent exclusion of all Japanese, loyal or disloyal, citizen or alien, from the West Coast or at least, from California. . . . This means that considerations other than of mere military necessity enter into any proposal for the removal of the present restrictions." California, General Emmons was learning quickly, had a different way of doing things than Hawaii.[107]

Even before the end of the war, the evacuation order had been rescinded and the War Relocation Authority had begun to close the internment camps. After administering the loyalty questionnaire, the War Relocation Authority had begun to permit internees who had responded affirmatively to Questions 27 and 28 of the loyalty questionnaire to leave the camps, allowing them to resettle in cities like Denver, Salt Lake City, and Chicago. "I felt wonderful the day I left camp," recalled Helen Murao. "We took a bus to the railroad siding and then stopped somewhere to transfer, and I went in and bought a Coke, a nickel Coke. It wasn't the Coke, but what it represented — that I was free to buy it, that feeling was so intense." But would the internees be free to return to the West Coast and rebuild their communities? At a press conference on November 21, 1944, President Roosevelt was asked this question. In his answer, Roosevelt offered his vision of a dispersed Japanese population:

> A good many of them . . . [have already left the camps and] have re-placed themselves, and in a great many parts of the country. And the example that I always cite, to take a unit, is the size of the county, whether it's the Hudson River or in western "Joegia" (Georgia) which we all know, in one of those counties, probably half a dozen or a dozen families could be scattered around on the farms and worked into the community. After all, they are American citizens, and we all know that American citizens have certain privileges. And they wouldn't — what's my favorite word? — discombobolate — (Laughter) — the existing population of those particular counties very much. After all — what? — 75 thousand families scattered all around the United States is not going to upset anybody.[108]

All of their rights guaranteed by the Constitution had been taken away, and now the Japanese were being told they were American citizens and had "certain privileges." Finally they could leave the internment camps but the President wanted them "scattered," for they should not be permitted to "discombobolate" American society. "My parents did not know what to do or where to go after they had been let out of camp," said Aiko Mifune. Her mother, Fusayo Fukuda

Kaya, had come to America as a picture bride in 1919; she and her husband, Yokichi, had been tenant farmers in California before they were interned in Poston, Arizona. "But everything they had worked for was gone; they seemed listless and they stayed in Arizona and tried to grow potatoes there." But most of the newly freed internees wanted to go home to the West Coast, and they boarded trains bound for Los Angeles, Seattle, and San Francisco. When a group of returning Japanese stepped from the train in San Jose, they were welcomed home by some black and white women led by Anne Peabody, Marjorie Pitman, Evelyn Settles, and Nina Wolters. The women gave them hot food and then transported them to their places of lodging. But often at other train stations, former internees were met with hostile signs: No Japs Allowed, No Japs Welcome. When they finally saw their homes again, many found their houses damaged and their fields ruined. An uncertain, fearful future seemed to await all of the returnees. They had suffered years of infamy — years they would never forget. Some were never able to return home: too old, too ill, or too brokenhearted, they died while in camp. Tragically, they had come all the way to America only to be buried in forlorn and windswept cemeteries of desert camps. Their "extravagance" did not deserve such an ending.

> *When the war is over*
> *And after we are gone*
> *Who will visit*
> *This lonely grave in the wild*
> *Where my friend lies buried?*[109]

11

"Strangers" at the Gates Again

Post-1965

While the winds of World War II destroyed Japanese-American communities on the West Coast, they also blew a fresh breath of democracy through America and opened the way toward greater
"diversity." The war against Nazism generated a greater awareness
of racism at home, and notions of white superiority became less
popular and less plausible. By an executive order in 1941, President
Franklin Roosevelt outlawed racial discrimination in defense-industry employment and created the Fair Employment Practices Commission. Six years later, President Harry Truman established the
Committee on Civil Rights. The courts also advanced civil rights for
racial minorities during this time. In 1948 the California Supreme
Court ruled that the anti-miscegenation laws were unconstitutional
because they violated the right of equal protection. Such laws, the
court stated in *Perez v. Sharp,* were based on racial distinctions that
were "by their very nature, odious to a free people" and to institutions
founded upon "the doctrine of equality." In the same year, the U.S.
Supreme Court decided that race-restrictive housing covenants constituted racial discrimination and a denial of equal protection of the
laws. Though they had come "from a different shore" than European
immigrants, Asians should be protected by the Constitution.[1]

Through the Rain at Night: Communities in Transition

But reforms came not only from above but also from below — from
the people themselves, especially in Hawaii, where a bloodless revolution occurred. For a long time, plantation workers had been demanding their rights and a fair share of the wealth created by their

labor. The war stirred unrest and agitation among them: as the laborers were told that America was defending democracy against Fascism, they became inspired to gain influence in the workplace through the exercise of democratic power.

Before World War II, Asian plantation laborers had been largely disfranchised. As aliens ineligible to citizenship, they could not use the suffrage to advance their interests and had to restrict their struggle to the workplace. But time had been on the side of the laborers. In 1920, only three out of every one hundred eligible voters in Hawaii were Japanese; twenty years later, as the Nisei generation came of age, thirty-one out of every one hundred eligible voters were Japanese, representing the largest ethnic block. By then, the International Longshoremen's and Warehousemen's Union (ILWU) had begun organizing workers in Hawaii, and its strategists soon recognized the laborers' potential political power. They saw the need to challenge the planter class at the ballot box first, then to confront the bosses at the negotiating table. Their political strategy was to conduct voter-registration drives on the plantations, elect their representatives to the legislature, and seize political power from the sugar interests. The ILWU predicted that union activity on "the political front" could easily swing the legislature from "plantation management control to plantation worker control." In a letter to the ILWU headquarters in San Francisco, regional director Jack Hall described the plan: "When card-indexing our members, classifying them by precincts and checking their registration, we found shockingly that less than 30 percent of our eligible members had registered. All emphasis at this time is on registration. We have a full time staff of four women in addition to some volunteer help for intensifying the registration drive. We can make a real dent in sugar control of our Legislature."[2]

Months before the 1944 election, the ILWU leaders introduced an idea developed by the Congress of Industrial Organizations — Political Action Committees. PACs raised money for candidates and made political endorsements in exchange for their commitments to the union and workers' demands. As such, they were powerful instruments for influencing the outcomes of elections. In July 1944, Hall advised the union's PACs: "Every candidate for the Legislature . . . should be asked to make a written commitment to our program." Meanwhile, at the local level, union leaders — Filipinos, Japanese, Chinese, and Hawaiian — went "directly to their own groups," recalled ILWU strategist Louis Goldblatt. "They were like party whips. For example, Filipino guys would go out and talk to

Filipino guys, house to house." After a union meeting, the workers would "break up into political rallies by language groups." At one of these rallies, Bert Nakano told his fellow workers: "Politics goes hand in hand with the labor movement. You got to strike together when it comes to voting." The message of the ILWU was clear: the voting booth would be labor's path to power.[3]

In October, Hall informed Goldblatt: "We are approaching our Territorial General Election Day, November 7th, with some confidence." On election day, sixteen out of the twenty-one candidates endorsed by PACs were elected to the House of Representatives and six out of the eight candidates endorsed by PACs won seats to the Senate. The new representatives included ILWU members Joseph Kaholokula, Jr., of Maui, and Amos Ignacio of the Big Island. "We really worked hard to get PACs candidates elected," said a Portuguese worker in 1945. Shortly after the election, Hall reported to Goldblatt: "I am quite confident that we will be able to push through a 'little Wagner Act' to protect agricultural workers and to compel employers to bargain collectively with their representatives. Nine of the fifteen Senators have pledged support on this measure, as have seventeen of the thirty House members." The next spring the legislature passed the act, extending to agricultural workers the right of collective bargaining — a right that had already been granted to industrial laborers by the National Labor Relations Law or the Wagner Act. The way was now open for strike action in 1946.[4]

What workers realized was the need to expand what scholar Richard Edwards has called the "contested terrain" from the workplace to the political arena. "One of the big factors in the strength of the union [in 1946] . . . was that we had established ourselves in political circles," explained a Nisei. "We set up PACs and we had a territory-wide political machine organized. We elected two members of the union to the House of Representatives. We gained respect because we could get votes for people who otherwise couldn't get elected. What we couldn't win across the bargaining table, we decided we'd seek through the Territorial Legislature."[5]

Once they had secured their right to collective bargaining through the legislature, the workers went out on strike for higher wages and a forty-hour work week. The *ILWU Dispatcher* declared: "This time, everybody is out with his union brothers and sisters — Japanese, Chinese, Filipino, Puerto Rican, Portuguese and Hawaiian. We have a united front against our bosses and they are not able to pit one group of us against another as they did in the old days."

Twenty-eight thousand striking laborers shut down thirty-three of the thirty-four plantations. After a long and bitter seventy-nine day strike, the workers won decisively. In a victory statement, the ILWU declared: "It is the first time in the history of Hawaii that a strike of sugar workers has been conducted where there has been no split among racial groups."[6]

Interethnic unity, especially between Filipinos and Japanese, made sense strategically. By the early 1940s, five out of ten laborers were Filipino and three were Japanese. The ILWU provided the leadership and ideology for interethnic unity and cooperation. "The ILWU told the people," recalled Jose Corpuz, "the ILWU is not looking at your ethnic background, racial background you had or what color you had. . . . The main fact is that we care only about you as a worker. As a worker, we have only one common goal." The union's strategy involved an affirmative-action program to integrate the labor movement's leadership in the islands. In October 1945 the ILWU instructed its officers at the local level: "The importance of racial unity in the Islands makes it imperative that steps be taken to put Filipinos, Hawaiians, Portuguese and others into prominent positions, even though in some cases they might not be as qualified or as capable as the Japanese. It may well mean that Japanese of considerable ability may have to step back and press, instead, for the election of individuals of other racial groups."[7]

But ILWU officers like Hall and Goldblatt worried about possible Japanese unwillingness to step back. In a confidential letter, February 7, 1946, regional director Hall informed Goldblatt that Yasu Arakaki, one of the local leaders, needed to be "educated" on the importance of the interethnic strategy and that his Japanese nationalism had to be curbed. At the time, Arakaki was in San Francisco attending the ILWU leadership training school. "Arakaki should be kept on the mainland for a complete cure or discharged as hopeless," advised Hall. "The nub is Arakaki's ambition, both personal and a desire to show everybody that those of Japanese ancestry are as good or better than any other race — primarily as a reflex against discrimination, particularly wartime."[8]

Possibly Arakaki was "educated," or he actually had already realized the need for interethnic cooperation and unity. As president of Local 148, Arakaki spearheaded efforts for the "forced integration" of Filipinos in the union leadership. In a memo to ILWU officer J. R. Robertson on June 26, 1946, Arakaki described the ways he had activated new Filipino laborers to be leaders: "We are making every effort in search of potential leaders from the different racial groups so they will be able to hold their own. In order to boost the morale of the Filipino brothers we are making every effort to send their leaders to Honolulu trips, attending meetings so that when they return they will have confidence in carrying out their work." Two months later, during the strike, president Arakaki told the Women's Auxiliary Strike Corps of Olaa Plantation: "Only through interrelations of all racial groups can we hope to gain what labor is demanding from the employers at present."[9]

To administer the program of "forced integration," Goldblatt sent Frank Thompson to oversee the elections of ILWU local officers. Thompson carried out his assignment with a heavy hand. If a Japanese were nominated for chairman, Thompson would say: "Okay, nominations are open for vice-chairman." And if another Japanese were nominated, he would drop the gavel and say: "No, he's not eligible." Some workers would then question: "What do you mean he's not eligible? He's one of the founders of the union; the guy worked his ass off, he's competent." And Thompson would then reply: "He's not eligible because my instructions are that we are going to have all nationalities. Pick somebody else but he can't be Japanese."[10]

The officers' roll calls of several local units reflected the success of the integration strategy:

> 142–3: Jose Avellino, President
> Harry Kusano, Secretary-Treasurer
> 142–6: Amos Ignacio, President
> Kazuto Nishioka, Treasurer
> 142–7: Daniel Frias, President
> Hajime Kawasaki, Treasurer
> 142–8: Jacinto Conol, President
> Noburo Motonaga, Treasurer[11]

The ILWU strategy of "forced integration" and interethnic cooperation found receptive conditions. Japanese ethnic nationalism was no longer as strong as it had been. By the 1940s, 80 percent of the Japanese plantation laborers were Nisei. American citizens by birth, they did not have a close attachment to Japan. They had attended public schools, where they sat in classes next to Filipino, Chinese, Portuguese, and Korean children, and where they played games with one another and spoke pidgin English. The new Nisei leadership was young: Yasu Arakaki, Saburo Fujisaki, Susumu

Maeda, and Bob Kunimura were only in their twenties. "Most of our leadership in the various Locals and units," reported ILWU organizer Frank Thompson to Morris Watson, editor of the *ILWU Dispatcher* on October 10, 1944, "are young people and plenty intelligent. They don't intend to lead the same kind of existence that their Mothers and Fathers did when they were brought over here as coolie labor."[12]

More importantly, both the Japanese and the Filipinos in Hawaii did not need the mainland ILWU to teach them about the importance of interethnic solidarity. They had acquired this knowledge from their own experiences and practices as laborers. "I came here in 1924," a Filipino worker told an interviewer in 1945. "I go out cut cane. Today, I still cut cane. I get $2 a day. Only enough for kau kau [food]. Nowadays, wartime, everything cost high — no can save. When they come ask me to join union, quick I join. I think union going help us. In 1924 Filipinos had strike for more pay, but that time only Filipinos strike. This time Filipino, Japanese, Portuguese, all join one union. More better that way." Saburo Fujisaki of the Olaa Plantation saw the situation similarly. "We learned the idea of racial integration from experience," he explained. "We learned it from our experiences in the work place — in the fields and the mills — where day-to-day all races worked on the job side-by-side. And so, when it came time to strike in 1946, the workers themselves knew they had to have what they called an 'all race strike.' "[13]

Under ILWU leadership, the workers finally realized the vision of the 1920 strike — the organization of a "big interracial union." "This victory makes Hawaii part of the United States for all Hawaiians, especially the workers," declared ILWU President Harry Bridges. "It is no longer a feudal colony." Likewise Fujisaki described the 1946 strike as "history making," setting "the machinery in motion to dismantle the power of the Big Five."[14]

Meanwhile, California had also become a terrain of contest and change. During the 1940s, the California Justice Department had been actively enforcing the alien land law and confiscating lands declared illegally held by Japanese. By the end of 1946 it had made claims against more than sixty Japanese landowners, including the Oyama family of San Diego.

In 1934 Kajiro and Kohide Oyama had purchased six acres of agricultural land in San Diego and recorded the title of the property in the name of their American-born six-year-old son, Fred, the court declaring the Oyamas the guardians of their son's estate. In 1944, while the Oyamas were in an internment camp, the Justice Department filed a court petition for the confiscation of the Oyamas' property, charging they had violated the alien land law. After the California Supreme Court upheld the state's case against them, the Oyamas appealed to the U.S. Supreme Court. Could California prohibit an alien ineligible to citizenship from conveying land as a gift to a citizen child? In 1948, the Supreme Court ruled that such a restriction was unconstitutional. The California law was "nothing more than outright racial discrimination," the Court declared. "The only basis for this discrimination against an American citizen was the fact that his father was Japanese, and not American, Russian, Chinese, or English." In fact, the Court added, the Fourteenth Amendment was "designed to bar States from denying to some groups, on account of race or color, any rights, privileges, and opportunities accorded to other groups." Significantly, the Court referred to the United Nations Charter and to the fight against racism abroad during World War II. How could this nation be "faithful" to the international pledge of the United Nations Charter of human rights and freedoms for all without distinctions of race, the Court asked, if America had state laws which barred land ownership on account of race? The alien land law was "an unhappy facsimile, a disheartening reminder, of the racial policy pursued by those forces of evil whose destruction recently necessitated a devastating war." The 1948 Supreme Court decision telegraphed a signal for challenging the alien land laws directly. Four years later, in the cases of Sei Fujii and Haruye Masaoka, the California Supreme Court ruled that the state laws could not deny landownership to aliens ineligible to citizenship.

> *Land laws faded out,*
> *It is comfortable now —*
> *This America.*[15]

The court rulings reflected changing popular sentiments, especially in California. In the November 1946 election, an initiative for the validation of the alien land law — Proposition 15 — was placed on the ballot. The Japanese American Citizens League highlighted the contributions of Japanese Americans and reminded voters of the Nisei soldiers' demonstrated loyalty. The voters turned down Proposition 15 resoundingly — 1,143,780 to 797,067. "The election results prove that most Californians feel that Japanese Americans and their Issei parents have earned the right to justice and fair treatment," declared JACL leader Mike Masaoka. "They provide the first real public opinion poll of California citizens on an issue involving the state's residents of Japanese ancestry since 1920. . . . The lesson of the vote on Proposition 15 is that the war is over and the people of California will not approve discriminatory and prejudiced treatment of persons of Japanese ancestry." Ten years later, the JACL went on the offensive and placed its own initiative on the California ballot: Proposition 13 provided for the repeal of the alien land law. Though the court had already ruled that state law could not prohibit aliens ineligible to citizenship from landownership, the JACL wanted to remove the restriction from the statutes and use the initiative in an educational campaign against racial prejudice. By then the Supreme Court decision of *Brown v. Board of Education* and the Montgomery bus boycott had ushered America into the Civil Rights Era. Progressive attitudes on race had begun to become more widely shared, and over two and a half million voters approved the repeal by a two-to-one majority. The JACL hailed the victory: "It was a tribute to the Issei whose love for the land kept them steadfast through years of discrimination. In only half a century the Issei had come full circle, accepted as equal citizens in the country they had adopted."[16]

Meanwhile the Issei had been made eligible to naturalized citizenship. The 1952 McCarran-Walter Act nullified the racial restriction of the 1790 naturalization law. Actively lobbying for its passage, the JACL stressed how the law would recognize the parents of the Nisei soldiers who had distinguished themselves during World War II, and how it would acknowledge the worthiness of the Issei to become citizens. The enactment of the McCarran-Walter Law evoked elation among Japanese Americans. "It was the culmination of our dreams," exclaimed Harry Takagi. "I can't think of any other legislative action that so united the JACL. The bill established our parents as the legal equal of other Americans; it gave the Japanese equality with all other immigrants, and that was a principle we had been struggling for from the very beginning."[17]

Elderly Issei, forced to be "strangers" in America, were eager to become citizens in their adopted country. By 1965, some 46,000 immigrant Japanese had taken their citizenship oaths. One of them was Fusayo Fukuda Kaya, whose story we have been following in this book. In 1953, thirty-four years after she had arrived as a picture bride, she formally became an American. "She studied hard for the citizenship exam," her daughter Aiko Mifune recalled. Magohichi

Sakaguchi told me why he became a citizen: "I was born in Japan in 1896 and came here in 1913. I was living here and planning to stay here. I wanted to have the right to vote." Citizenship for my aunt Mitsue Takaki culminated a decision she had made years earlier. In 1931, after she had learned her husband, Teizo, would be deported to Japan by the immigration authorities, she had decided to stay in Hawaii with her three children. Decades later, as a grandmother, she passed her citizenship examination, and her children remember how proudly she stood before a federal judge and took the oath of allegiance as a citizen of the United States. Many Issei were in the twilight of their lives, yet they wanted to be "extravagant," to become citizens. One of them felt an urge to celebrate the moment in poetry:

> Going steadily to study English,
> Even through the rain at night,
> I thus attain,
> Late in life,
> American citizenship.[18]

While Issei were choosing to become Americans, Chinese were being forced to prove their loyalty to America. In 1949 the Chinese Communists under the leadership of Mao Zedong emerged victorious in the civil war in China, and Chiang Kai-shek and his Koumintang forces fled to Taiwan. Developments in China splintered Chinese communities in America. The Chinese Left and workers' associations welcomed Mao's triumph. "Under the leadership of the Chinese Communist Party," the Chinese Workers' Mutual Aid Association declared in their congratulatory telegram, "the masses of Chinese people and the People's Liberation Army thoroughly unfettered the yoke of imperialism, destroyed the reactionary dictatorship of the inept and corrupt Koumintang and established people's rule." Meanwhile, the Chinese Six Companies aligned itself with the Koumintang and supported the campaign to overthrow Communist rule on mainland China.[19]

Soon the conflict in China was violently extended to Chinese America. In San Francisco's Chinatown on October 9, 1949, the Chinese Workers' Mutual Aid Association held a celebration at the Chinese American Citizens Alliance Hall to commemorate the founding of the People's Republic of China. Five hundred people were packed in the hall. "We filled the whole place, even the balcony," recalled Franklin Woo. "It was a pretty exciting moment. . . . But during the second speech we heard a shout from the door, then all of a sudden two lines of men ran through the aisles to the speakers' platform, tore down the red flag, knocked over the vases of flowers, and began throwing some kind of blue dye around the audience." People panicked. "After about fifteen minutes we pulled ourselves together, somebody began singing the 'March of Volunteers,' the Chinese national anthem, and we all joined in. But by that time a lot of people had left because the thing shook them up." Describing the disruption years later, Koumintang leader Pei Chi Liu admitted: "On October 9, they [the Communist supporters] rented the CACA Hall to hold a celebration of Communist victory in China. But some of our people went inside and beat them, you know, knocked them down."[20]

A year later, Chinese-Communist intervention in the Korean War set off hysterical anti-Chinese reactions in the United States. The new peril was seen as yellow in race and red in ideology. "The Korean War affected us at the beginning in that we were taken for Communists," recalled Betty Lee Sung. "People would look at you in the street and think, 'Well, you're one of the enemy.' " "The whole atmosphere here then was fear," remarked Franklin Woo. "If you weren't careful, you could be thrown into a concentration camp." Soon Chinese had reason to think they were not paranoid. In late 1950, Congress passed the McCarran Internal Security Act, which provided for the internment of Communists during a national emergency. Authorizing the Attorney General to detain all persons for whom there was "reasonable ground" for believing they would "probably" engage in espionage or sabotage, this law became an ominous and menacing reminder to the Chinese: what happened to the Japanese on the West Coast during World War II could happen to them during the Cold War.[21]

Within this context of political repression, the Six Companies of San Francisco and the Chinese Consolidated Benevolent Association of New York led anti-Communist campaigns in Chinatowns across the country. Anti-Communist organizations soon began to proliferate in Chinese communities. In 1951 the newly formed Anti-Communist Committee for Free China declared its unequivocal loyalty to the United States and denounced Communism as antithetical to Chinese culture. In 1954 the All-American Overseas Chinese Anti-Communist League was established in New York in order to assure the American people that the Chinese living among them were not Communists.

The anti-Communist witch hunt soon threatened to get out of control. In 1955, the American Consul in Hong Kong warned that Chinese Communist spies could use fraudulent citizenship papers to secure American passports and enter the United States. The federal authorities immediately began investigating thousands of Chinese Americans, charging they had obtained passports based on false birth certificates. As the government prosecuted and deported Chinese residents found guilty of fraud, waves of alarm and apprehension swept through Chinese communities. Everywhere "paper sons" felt vulnerable and terribly anxious. To coordinate and administer its investigations, the government created the "Confession Program": Chinese residing in the United States illegally were encouraged to come forward and confess their guilt to the Immigration and Naturalization Service. Confessors were required to give full disclosure on every relative and friend. A single confession could implicate scores of other individuals. In return, the government would give them legal status if they were not involved in subversive activities. Thousands participated in the program: in San Francisco alone, 10,000 Chinese confessed. Ninety-nine percent of all confessors were permitted to remain in the United States.[22]

The "Confession Program" gave the government a weapon to target certain Chinese residents. Confessions involved intelligence gathering as well as loyalty tests, and the INS and the FBI used this information to investigate and deport persons who supported the Chinese Communist government or who belonged to organizations deemed "subversive." The program spread poisonous divisions and distrust within the Chinese community. "We knew the FBI was keeping a close eye on us, and we even suspected there was an informer among us," said Franklin Woo, who was then a member of the Min Ching, an organization that supported the People's Republic. "I guess that's one thing all of us feel bad about now, that we had to be suspicious of each other." Entire families had to be fearful. "Say, if a Min Ching member is discovered to have false papers, his whole family will be affected because probably they didn't have the proper papers either," explained Woo. "So they'll go from you, to the uncle who brought you in, his wife, and it goes on and on."[23]

But while international developments generated repression at home, they also stimulated reform, especially revisions of the restrictive immigration laws. World War II had forced the United States to reopen its gates to the Chinese as well as to Filipinos and Asian

Indians. Its very claims of democracy required the country to remove the racism contained within immigration policies. "It is certainly improper to keep them out altogether, because they are Oriental," argued Congresswoman Clare Boothe Luce in her support for the Filipino immigration and naturalization bill in 1946. But as Congress lifted exclusion it imposed limits. Asians could come again, but only a handful of them. "We are utterly justified in controlling and keeping low Oriental immigration in terms of numbers," explained Luce, "because of the fact that they in too great numbers may undermine our way of life, our living standards." Altogether, Congress permitted the entry of only a token number of immigrants. While Japan and Korea still were not allowed to send any immigrants, the Philippines and India were each given a quota of only a hundred and China a quota of only 105. By contrast, Poland alone had a quota of 6,524.[24]

However, ways around the quotas were available to Asians. After World War II, the U.S. Navy continued to recruit sailors in the Philippines, and thousands of Filipinos entered the United States through the door provided by the navy. After the Communist victory in China, 5,000 Chinese professionals and students found themselves stranded in the United States, and most of them were permitted to stay as immigrants under the 1948 Displaced Persons Act and the 1953 Refugee Relief Act. The most important loophole was the War Brides Act, which allowed Asian wives and children of United States servicemen to enter as nonquota immigrants. "Since the War Bride Act," testified Lim P. Lee before a congressional committee hearing in 1947, "every ship arriving from Hong Kong or Canton carried about 200 to 250 war brides and their dependents." Facing a three to one male-female ratio in the Chinese community, thousands of Chinese-American soldiers married women in China and brought them to the United States. Between 1946 and 1953, over seven thousand Chinese entered as war brides. "Right after the war," remembered Harold Liu of New York's Chinatown, "guys came home from the army with wives from China." Filipinos, too, were bringing wives here. After becoming citizens through service in the U.S. Armed Forces, Filipino men sent for their families. Meanwhile the Korean War began a new Korean immigration: between 1950 and 1965, some 17,000 Koreans entered, most of them as nonquota spouses of American citizens.[25]

In the 1952 McCarran-Walter Act, Congress approved immigration from the "Asian-Pacific Triangle," a large geographical region including most of South and East Asia. While ending exclusion, this new law was still racially discriminatory in intent and design: countries within the triangle were allowed only one hundred immigrants each. Immigration from European countries, on the other hand, was determined by the national origins quotas of the 1924 immigration law.[26]

But the Cold War, which the McCarran-Walter Act reflected in its provisions for the screening of subversives and the deportation of immigrants with Communist affiliations, also increased pressure for the legislation of fair and just immigration policies. Seeking to promote anti-Communism abroad and to present itself as a democracy to peoples engaged in anticolonialist struggles in Latin America, Africa, and Asia, the United States felt compelled to abandon the national-origins quotas. In his support for immigration reform in 1964, Secretary of State Dean Rusk warned that the existing discriminatory system was detrimental to American foreign relations.

Meanwhile, the Civil Rights Movement had begun to awaken the moral conscience of America, condemning racism in all of its forms, including immigration policies. Blacks and progressive whites launched massive protests against racial segregation and discrimination. In 1954 the U.S. Supreme Court declared that segregated schools were unconstitutional; ten years later, after countless civil rights marches and demonstrations led by Martin Luther King and others, Congress outlawed racial discrimination. Equality for Americans logically implied equality for immigrants seeking entry to America. "Everywhere else in our national life, we have eliminated discrimination based on national origins," Attorney General Robert Kennedy told Congress in 1964. "Yet, this system is still the foundation of our immigration law."[27]

A year later, Congress considered immigration reform. Old nativist fears were stirred, and the Daughters of the American Revolution protested: "Abandonment of the national origins system would drastically alter the source of our immigration. Any such change would not take into consideration that those whose background and heritage most clearly resemble our own are most readily assimilable." But the momentum for change, driven by pressures produced by the Cold War and the Civil Rights Movement, could not be halted. "Just as we sought to eliminate discrimination in our land through the Civil Rights act," declared a congressman in support of the immigration reform bill, "today we seek by phasing out the national origins quota system to eliminate discrimination in immigration to this nation composed of the descendants of immigrants."[28]

The Immigration Act of 1965 abolished the national-origins quotas and provided for the annual admission of 170,000 immigrants from the Eastern Hemisphere and 120,000 from the Western Hemisphere. Twenty thousand immigrants per country would be allowed to enter from the Eastern Hemisphere; exempted from the quota would be immediate family members, specifically spouses, minor children, and parents of U.S. citizens. Immigrants from the Eastern Hemisphere were to be admitted on a first-come, first-served basis by preference categories for adult family members, professionals and artists, needed skilled and unskilled laborers, and refugees.[29]

The new law was not expected to make a drastic change in the complexion of future immigrants. The family-preference system, the *Wall Street Journal* predicted, "insured that the new immigration pattern would not stray radically from the old one." A spokesman for the American Legion explained why this would be so. The great bulk of immigrants would be relatives of our present citizens and thus they would come from European countries. This meant, he added, virtually no change in the actual number of Asian immigrants. "Asiatics having far fewer immediate family members now in the United States than southern Europeans, will automatically arrive in far fewer numbers than Italians, Greeks and other southern European stock." Urging his colleagues to vote for the bill, Representative Emanuel Celler of New York assured Congress that there would not be many Asian immigrants: "Since the people of . . . Asia have very few relatives here, comparatively few could immigrate from those countries because they have no family ties in the U.S." The numbers seemed to tell the tale. The total Asian population in the United States was only one half of one percent, and consequently there were actually very few Asian-American citizens qualified to bring relatives here. Aware of this demographic reality, the Japanese American Citizens League noted: "Although the immigration bill eliminated race as a matter of principle, in actual operation immigration will still be controlled by the now discredited national origins system and the general pattern of immigration which exists today will continue for many years to come."[30]

Still the new law represented a sharp ideological departure from the traditional view of America as a homogeneous white society — a perspective which was carried to the shores of the New World by European settlers aboard John Winthrop's *Arbella* and other ships, and which was affirmed again and again in public policies such as the Naturalization Law of 1790 and the 1922 *Ozawa* decision. The

Civil Rights Movement offered a countervision: the time had come
for revising America's immigration policy and the old notions of who
could become an American. Moreover, contrary to expectations and
predictions, the 1965 Immigration Act would in fact lead to a significant break from the historic pattern of immigration based on the
national-origins quota. It would transform this country again into a
golden door for immigrants from a "different shore," pushed from
their homelands in Asia by "necessity" and pulled to America by
"extravagance."

The Second Wave: The Recent Asian Immigration

The 1965 immigration law began a new chapter in the history of
Asians in America, for it opened the way for the second wave of Asian
immigration. For centuries, an overwhelming majority of America's
immigrants were European; currently one out of every two immigrants comes from Asia. Mainly as a result of this second wave, Asian
Americans have soared in numbers — from one million, or less than
one percent of the U.S. population in 1965 to five million, or 2 percent
in 1985. There were nearly four times more Asian immigrants during
this twenty-year period than during the entire span of more than a
hundred years between the gold rush of '49 and the passing of the
new immigration law. The second wave not only produced a massive
increase in Asian immigration but also recompositioned the Asian-
American population: in 1960, 52 percent were Japanese, 27 percent
Chinese, 20 percent Filipino, 1 percent Korean, and 1 percent Asian
Indian. Twenty-five years later, 21 percent of Asian Americans were
Chinese, 21 percent Filipino, 15 percent Japanese, 12 percent Vietnamese, 11 percent Korean, 10 percent Asian Indian, 4 percent Laotian, 3 percent Cambodian, and 3 percent "other."[31]

The second-wave newcomers are strikingly different from the
earlier immigrants. They include significant numbers of professionals
and people from the cities, in contrast to the farmers and rural folk
of the past. "The [recent-immigrant] Asians are the most highly
skilled of any immigrant group our country has ever had," observed
Rand Corporation demographer Kevin McCarthy in 1985. The post-
1965 Asian arrivals have been entering a high-technology, service
economy rather than an industrialized and agricultural one. They are
not becoming railroad workers and farm laborers in America. While
their non-English-speaking predecessors were employable in the economy they found here, the recent immigrants face English-language
barriers in the general labor market. They also, perhaps, view re-

stricted employment possibilities with greater anxiety than did the first-wave people, for they are arriving as families rather than as single men and as settlers rather than sojourners. They cannot simply say that the situation here is only temporary and count the days until their return home.[32]

The second wave of Asian immigration includes proportionately fewer Japanese. Only about 4,000 have been coming annually, far below the 20,000 quota allotted to Japan. Between 1965 and 1984, only 93,646 Japanese entered the United States, representing a mere 3 percent of all Asian immigrants. Their numbers have been declining: in the first half of the 1980s, Japanese immigrants dropped to only 1.7 percent of the total immigration from Asia. Japan's tremendous post–World War II economic expansion has generated a great demand for labor, and consequently the Japanese government and industries have not encouraged the overseas migration of workers. Without an influx of new immigrants from Japan, Japanese Americans have become predominantly a native-born population: in 1980, 72 percent were citizens by birth. Japanese Americans are largely English-speaking; in fact very few *Sansei* and *Yonsei* (third and fourth generation respectively) know any Japanese. And the Japantowns or Nihonmachis have not been culturally renewed, for they lack the large and reinvigorating presence of new immigrants. "Many second- and third-generation Japanese Americans have moved to the suburbs," observed Jeff Mori, executive director of the Japanese Youth Council in San Francisco. "And there are too few new immigrants from Japan to fill their places in Japantown." But while Japanese have not been flocking to the United States, immigrants from other Asian countries have been entering America in unprecedented numbers. Why have they been coming again and what is the significance of this new immigration?[33]

The recent Chinese newcomers are called *San Yi Man,* "new immigrants." They represent the third largest group of immigrants, after Mexicans and Filipinos. Between 1965 and 1984, they numbered 419,373 — almost as many as the 426,000 Chinese who came here between 1849 and 1930. In 1960 the Chinese population was only 237,000 — half the size of the Japanese population; twenty years later it had jumped to 812,200 and had surpassed the Japanese. The Chinese community had been radically transformed from 61 percent American-born to 63 percent foreign-born, becoming again mainly an immigrant community. Sixty percent of the second wave of Chinese immigrants settled in two states, California and New York, where they are revitalizing Chinatowns. New York City, the first choice of many new Chinese immigrants, has witnessed a virtual population explosion in its Chinatown. Before the 1965 Immigration Act, New York's Chinatown never had a population of more than 15,000 people; twenty years later, it had become the home of 100,000.

This tide of new immigrants from China was not anticipated at all when Congress passed the 1965 immigration law. The *Lo Wa Kiu* ("old overseas Chinese") had been here a long time, and most of them did not have immediate family members to bring to America. Surprisingly, the very family-unification provision of the law, designed to promote European immigration, opened the way for the entry of the *San Yi Man*. One of the doors for the beginning of this new immigration was the university. "My brother-in-law left his wife in Taiwan and came here as a student to get a Ph.D. in engineering," explained Subi Lin Felipe. "After he received his degree, he got a job in San Jose. Then he brought in a sister and his wife, who brought over one of her brothers and me. And my brother's wife then came."[34]

This family history is illustrative. During the 1960s, Chinese students flocked to the United States to pursue their education; in 1980 half of the 300,000 foreign students here were from China and other Asian countries. Thousands of Chinese students were able to find employment and then acquire Labor Department certification as immigrants under the preference category for skilled workers. In this way large numbers of Chinese were able to change their status from foreign students to immigrants. Once they had become immigrants, they could develop an expanding immigrant kin network under the family-preference categories of the 1965 law. They could bring their wives and children; then as U.S. citizens a few years later, the new immigrants, including both husbands and wives, could bring their parents here on a nonquota basis; they could also sponsor their brothers and sisters, who, in turn, could arrange for the entry of their spouses and children. Thus one immigrant coming originally as a student could develop what historian David Reimers has called "a chain migration."[35]

Unlike the *Lo Wa Kiu*, the second-wave immigrants have come mostly from urban areas. They include Mandarin as well as Cantonese speakers. Most were initially refugees from the People's Republic of China, and they usually emigrated from a second point of departure such as Hong Kong or Taiwan rather than directly from mainland China; after the normalization of relations between China and the United States in 1979, the People's Republic of China was allowed to have its own quota. While the old immigration was composed mostly of men, the new immigration has included more women than men. Fifty-two percent of Chinese arriving between 1966 and 1975 were female. While the earlier immigrants had been peasants, the recent immigrants have originated not only from the working class but also from the professional class. Between 1966 and 1975, 43 percent of the immigrants were operatives, clerks, crafts workers, and service workers, while 49 percent were managers, professionals, and technical workers. The number of scientists and engineers immigrating from Hong Kong and Taiwan skyrocketed from thirty-six in 1964 to 1,164 in 1970. Between 1969 and 1978, 75 percent of Chinese aliens became naturalized American citizens during their fifth to eighth year of residence. America, to the new Chinese immigrants, is not Gam Saan, a place to work temporarily, but a new home where they hope to find greater economic opportunities for themselves and educational advantages for their children.[36]

Behind this new immigration can be found a range of motives. Like many of the first-wave Chinese who fled from the turmoil of civil wars such as the Red Turban Rebellion, many recent newcomers have sought refuge from political conflict and instability in China. After the Revolution in 1949, Betty Chu accepted the idea of Communism, and became a high-school teacher. During the 1960s, however, she saw how people were beginning to live in fear. Individuals suspected of reactionary thoughts were being harassed by young Communists and sent to remote provinces. Worried about the rising political repression of the Cultural Revolution in China, Betty Chu and her husband made a "secret" decision to leave the country. Her husband secured a permit to visit his brother in Hong Kong and then stayed there; Betty Chu followed with her son. Her husband's brother, who had gone to the United States as a student years earlier, had become an American citizen, and he sponsored the Chu family as immigrants in 1969.[37]

Another second-wave immigrant, Xiu Zhen was not as fortunate as Betty Chu: she was not able to get out before the Cultural Revolution reached its zenith. A high-school teacher, she was accused by the Red Guards of being a spy. "Maybe I wrote some letters and mentioned something political," she explained later, "but I was not political at all." They cut off her hair and put her in jail. "Everybody was placed in this one room," she said. "I was there about one year and two months with fourteen other people. We didn't sleep there. We went home at night, but they made us work very hard. . . . Sometimes the Red Guards burned me with cigarettes. They kept saying, 'We have to wash your brains.' " In 1974, Xiu was allowed to visit her mother in Hong Kong. "I said I had to go to her because she was sick. Of course that was not the real reason." From Hong Kong, she came to the United States.[38]

Like the nineteenth-century pioneers seeking Gam Saan, the second-wave Chinese immigrants have also been pulled to America. "The people told me that coming to America will be just great," said Chin Moy Lee who came in 1968. "There was hot running water, cold water and even warm air [heating]. The water in the village countryside was filthy and very unsanitary, filled with pigs' and other animals' waste. Any place with 'clean water' must be like 'the sky above the sky.' America is 'Heaven.' " The immigrants of the second wave believed the chances of getting ahead would be better here and saw America as a place of possibilities. Wing Ng came to the United States in 1975 at the age of twenty-three. "The reason why I wanted to come to the United States is that I heard it is really freedom. That's the first thing. And the second was education. . . . When I was young, during the Cultural Revolution, there were no colleges to get into." Wing joined her father in Hong Kong but found educational as well as employment possibilities there extremely limited: "In Hong Kong it is difficult to go to college, too. Only two universities. Too many people. Too much competition for jobs. The people in Hong Kong don't like the others coming in and taking the jobs. So the only jobs you can get are in the factories."[39]

America would be a land of greater opportunity, the San Yi Man believed. But after arriving, they found impoverished China-towns in cities like San Francisco and New York. Shrouded behind the tourist image of Chinatown as a fascinating and charming mecca was the reality of the ghetto with its problems of poverty, unemployment, and crowded housing. In 1960, Chinese-male income was only 68 percent of white-male income in the San Francisco Bay Area and only 56 percent in the New York metropolitan area, and the income for Chinese women was significantly lower — 36 percent and 44 percent for each respective area. The unemployment rate for men in San Francisco's Chinatown was 12.8 percent, nearly double the 6.7 percent for the city. Thirty-seven percent of Chinese families in New York's Chinatown lived below the official poverty level. San Francisco's Chinatown had a population density of 885 persons per residential acre, compared to only eighty-two for the other sections of the city. Over half of the housing units in both Chinatowns were considered old, deteriorated, and substandard. Both communities had extremely high rates of suicide and tuberculosis. Many of its inhabitants were elderly men, "bachelors" living out the remainder of their lives in tiny eight-by-eight-foot rooms in dilapidated hotels. "They never revealed their feelings publicly," Ling-chi Wang of San Francisco sadly observed, "but not too infrequently one of them would be reported in the Chinese newspapers as having committed suicide, being robbed by a prostitute, sent to the state mental hospital, overdosed from heroin, or discovered dead for many days in his lonesome cubicle."[40]

The different class backgrounds of the new immigrants has led to the formation of a bipolar Chinese-American community — one divided between a colonized working class and an entrepreneurial-professional middle class. In 1980, 51 percent of the 77,829 employed Chinese immigrants were located in menial service and low-skilled, blue-collar work, while 42 percent were engaged in managerial and technical occupations. In New York City there are the "Downtown Chinese" of waiters and seamstresses as well as the affluent and professional "Uptown Chinese." In southern California, there are Chinatowns in central Los Angeles as well as in Monterey Park.[41]

"America's first suburban Chinatown," Monterey Park stands as a contrast to the old Chinatowns. As recently as 1960, the city had been 85 percent white, 12 percent Spanish-surname, and only 3 percent Asian and "other"; ten years later, Japanese represented 9 percent and Chinese 4 percent of the city's 49,166 residents. Since then the Chinese have become the largest ethnic group, totaling over 50 percent of the 61,000 residents in 1988. Most of them are from Hong Kong and Taiwan, and Monterey Park has come to be called "Little Taipei." During the early 1980s, the city elected its first Chinese mayor, Lilly Chen. But not everyone has welcomed the new Chinese presence. In 1986 a sign at a gas station near the city limits, for example, displayed two slanted eyes with the declaration: "Will the last American to leave Monterey Park please bring the flag."[42]

The Chinese residents of Monterey Park are not allowing such bigotry to discourage or deter them. They are building an American city in their image, and they have the capital to do so. In 1985 *Forbes* magazine estimated that $1.5 billion had been deposited in Monterey Park financial institutions during the year, or about $25,000 for every man, woman, and child. Some of the money represents capital flight from Hong Kong: nervous about the impending return of Hong Kong to the People's Republic of China in 1997, investors there have been transferring their capital to the United States, and Chinese realtors like Frederic Hsieh have been promoting Monterey Park as a "Chinese Beverly Hills." Many of the Chinese newcomers are wealthy professionals and businessmen, and their BMWs can be seen parked on the streets. The Chinese own two thirds of the property and business in the city. In Monterey Park can be found Chinese markets, restaurants, and retail stores as well as Chinese theaters, Chinese churches, and professional services of Chinese doctors and lawyers. "Today," observed sociologist Charles Choy Wong in 1988, "Monterey Park is institutionally complete for the Chinese community."[43]

But concentrations of the *San Yi Man* are also located in the old Chinatowns. Eighty percent of the population of New York's Chinatown, 74 percent of San Francisco's Chinatown, and 88 percent of Los Angeles's Chinatown are foreign-born. Unlike the suburban Chinese professionals, they are mostly low-wage laborers, employed as service workers and operatives. Forty to 50 percent of the workers in Chinatowns in San Francisco and Los Angeles and almost 70 percent of New York's Chinatown laborers are crowded into these two occupations.[44]

These workers belong to a colonized labor force. Most of them do not have even a high-school degree, and they also lack English-language skills. Fifty-five percent of the Chinese residents of New York's Chinatown do not speak English well or at all. "This does not mean that they are not trying to learn," explained Peter Kwong, who has worked as a community organizer for fifteen years. "In fact, there are at least two dozen English-language schools in the community. . . . Thousands of working people squeeze time out from their busy schedules to attend classes. However, the real problem is that they do not have the opportunity to use English on the job or with other Chinese immigrants. They soon forget the scant English they have learned." The problems of limited English-speaking ability and limited employment opportunities are self-reinforcing. "Chinese people have lower incomes because first, the language problem," explained Wing Ng. "If you know just a little English, you can go to an office and get a job cleaning up. It has more security, more benefits. But how are you going to get a job like that if you don't know a little English? And how are you going to learn English if you have to work twelve hours a day, six days a week and then come home and take care of your family?"[45]

Unable to speak English, many Chinese-immigrant women have no choice but to work as seamstresses. A study of garment workers in San Francisco's Chinatown found that 72 percent of them are secondary-wage earners. They have husbands who work, but they have to work too in order to contribute to the family income and to help the family barely to get by. Though they work for wages, most of the women are still solely responsible for all household chores. Carrying a double burden, they concentrate in the garment industry where they find flexible work hours and are allowed to bring their babies and let them sleep near them in the factory.[46]

The garment industry has exploited this supply of Chinese-female labor, transforming the Chinatowns of New York and San Francisco into industrial centers specializing in clothing production. "These factories are one of New York City's unknown industrial success stories," said Harry Schwartz, president of the Garment Industry Development Corporation. "You walk around the Garment District and ask, 'Where have the production shops gone?' Well, they've gone to Chinatown." In 1986 there were 550 unionized factories employing 22,000 workers in the Lower East Side and Chinatown. The garment factories in New York City provide immigrant-Chinese women with their main source of employment. A similar situation exists in San Francisco, where the manager of a garment factory said: "I guess almost all Chinese immigrant women who want to work come to the sewing shops." There, producing almost half of the total volume of apparel manufactured in San Francisco, they usually work for minimum wages and in a sweatshop environment. "The conditions in the factories are terrible," said Wing Ng. "Dirty air, long hours, from eight in the morning to eight at night, six days! They are paid by the piece and only a few can make good money. They don't protest because they don't know how to talk back and they don't know the law." Many actually do know the law, but they are afraid to protest and demand higher wages because they feel trapped: they know they cannot find employment outside of Chinatown if they are fired for striking or if they lose their jobs as a result of factory closures produced by high labor costs.[47]

While women are located largely in the garment industry, men are employed mainly in restaurants. S. L. Wong, the director of an English-language school in San Francisco's Chinatown, explained that recent immigrants find themselves locked in a low-wage restaurant labor market: "Most immigrants coming into Chinatown with a language barrier cannot go outside this confined area into the mainstream of American industry." Danny Lowe described what had happened to him: "Before I was a painter in Hong Kong, but I can't do it here. I got no license, no education. . . . I want a living, so it's dishwasher, janitor or cook."[48]

Chinatown garment and restaurant workers experience what can be called a "dual form of oppression." Denied entry into the mainstream labor market, they are forced to work in the Chinese ethnic economy. "It's really amazing how the Chinese exploit themselves," complained a garment worker. "The ones who are lucky enough to own a sewing factory or something, just go on and make more and more money for themselves." Most Chinese are not so fortunate, however. Economist Paul Ong found that "an overwhelming majority of the Chinatown immigrants who settled in San Francisco between 1962 and 1975 and who started in the ethnic labor market were confined to that market in 1980." Unemployment, high in Chinatown because of the continuing influx of new immigrant workers, disciplines the workers and keeps their labor "cheap." A waiter employed in a Chinatown restaurant usually works sixty hours a week for two hundred dollars a month, with no overtime pay, no health benefits, and no job security. A garment worker is on the job ten to twelve hours a day, six days a week, and makes only about $9,000 a year. In 1980, 25 percent of the New York Chinatown population lived below the poverty level, compared to 17 percent for the city.[49]

Chinatown workers have fought for higher wages and better working conditions. In San Francisco, for example, Jennie Lew sued her employer. For years she had been paid by factory owner Kim Wah Lee at a piecework rate but was required to fill out a biweekly time card certifying receipt of a minimum wage of $1.65 an hour; this illegal arrangement enabled Lee to increase the production of pieces per worker and pay less than the minimum wage. In 1971, Lew submitted evidence exposing her boss's corrupt practice and won a settlement that required him to pay a fine and also give her back pay for five years. Chinatown workers have also struggled collectively. In 1980 waiters at New York Chinatown's largest restaurant, the Silver Palace, organized a three-month-long strike and successfully forced the management to recognize their union and guarantee them a forty-hour week, minimum wage, overtime pay, paid holidays, and health benefits. In 1982, the garment workers of New York's Chinatown showed their militancy. When the Chinese garment factory owners refused to accept a new contract negotiated by the International Ladies Garment Workers' Union, 20,000 Chinese garment workers demonstrated and quickly won their contract. "We cannot accept any treatment that is inferior," declared leader Alice Tse. "Chinese workers are people, too! We should receive equal treatment."[50]

Whenever Chinatown workers have tried to organize themselves into a union, they have been told by their employers: "We are all Chinese and we should not fight among ourselves." "We are all immigrants in this country, trying to make a living. If we fight, we will lose our businesses to the whites and all of us will suffer." Ethnic solidarity has become an instrument of labor control. But workers seeking to unionize also have faced the iron fist of their employers. "Every time we get somewhere with our unionizing effort," complained a restaurant-labor organizer, "some tong member who claims to be an old friend of the management will approach and suggest we not push his friend too far and make him lose face, if we want to avoid unnecessary bloodshed among us Chinese."[51]

"Chinatown is like a warm bath — once a new immigrant decides to settle in, it is difficult to get out, even as the water slowly becomes cold," observed Peter Kwong. "However, once inside Chinatown, the immigrants find that mobility is limited. There is only one path upward: to become the owner of a business." Actually the opportunities to become the owner of a restaurant or garment factory are limited. The initial capital required is beyond the reach of most workers. New businesses are being opened in Chinatown, but they are owned by recent immigrants who come with financial resources. Many come from the professional class. Ask restaurant owners what they did for a living in China and many will say they had been engineers and even college professors. But business ownership is hazardous, and the turnover rate for Chinatown enterprises is extremely high: over a quarter of New York Chinatown's shops disappeared between 1980 and 1981, and over 30 percent of Chinatown garment factories in California registered by the Department of Employment in 1978 were closed, sold, or inactive by 1982.[52]

Occupational downgrading is a problem for many recent immigrants. "There are innumerable instances of former doctors, teachers, accountants, and engineers who took jobs as janitors and waiters when they first arrived," reported Betty Lee Sung. "Some stay in the rut because of language problems or because they are afraid to venture out and compete vigorously in the job market." In Canton, Winnie Wu had been a mathematics teacher and her husband a professor of Chinese at a university; in San Francisco, she works as an office clerk and he as a janitor in a hotel. Both want to get ahead and they study English late into the night, sometimes until 2 A.M. Similarly, Tom Wing Wah had been a professional with a college degree in physics. She arrived here in 1976 and went to work on an assembly line in a factory. "We are college graduates," she said, "but are working in sewing or electronic factories. We all have taken a big step backwards in our profession or work. Life cannot forever be like this — work, work, and work." Asked whether she hoped the day would come when she could use her physics training, Tom replied: "I have thought about this constantly — the day when I can work at a desk using a pen and not have to do physical labor. But I don't really know anymore. By the time I refresh my studies, I think I will be too old. I don't think like that anymore. I would be happy if I could just advance myself at my present job one step up." But even that one step has sometimes been difficult to get. "Sometimes even if we are on the same work level, the Caucasians would receive a bit more pay. They may not be the better worker; the Chinese may be the better worker, but the Chinese will receive less pay."[53]

Similarly Wei-Chi Poon and her husband, Boon Pui Poon, have experienced the problem of underemployment. Before they came in 1968, she had been a young biology professor and he had been an architect in the People's Republic of China. "We had a really hard time right after we got here," she said. "My husband was a very good architect, but because he couldn't speak English he could work only as a draftsman. His pay was so low that he had to work at two jobs, from eight in the morning till eleven o'clock at night." She worked in a laundry factory, packing uniforms into bags to be sent to Vietnam and earning only the minimum wage of $1.85 an hour. "The bags were at least 100 pounds each. At the time, I was one of the younger workers, so I had more strength than some of the others. I got scared, wondering, 'Will I be doing this for the rest of my life?' " She knew she would be trapped unless she learned English. "We were so busy working and so tired we had no time and energy to study English." A program funded by the Comprehensive Employment Training Act enabled her to take English classes and work as a library assistant in the Chinatown branch of the San Francisco Public Library. She enrolled in the city's junior college and did so well she was able to be admitted directly to graduate study in library science at San Jose State University. Currently Wei-Chi Poon is the head of the Asian American Studies Library of the University of California at Berkeley. She has mixed feelings about coming here. "Had we stayed in China," she said reflectively, "I would be a professor rather than a librarian and my husband a successful architect rather than a draftsman."[54]

The children of the second-wave Chinese face special difficulties and challenges. In Chinatown they feel the confinement and boundaries surrounding their lives and their parents. "For a while we lived in [New York] Chinatown on Bayard Street till I was two," a resident said. "I remember impressions from then. Like looking out the window a lot. I remember the sensation. It's like glass on my forehead. It's all this looking out of the window 'cause we couldn't go out. My mother and my sister who was a baby then were living in Chinatown in that apartment and my father was out in Queens starting the laundry then." For the Chinese of the younger generation, English is their second language, spoken outside the home. Many also feel a strong obligation to do well in school, particularly to please their parents. They are lectured by their parents, especially the college-educated parents who were professionals in China and Taiwan, that education is the key to employment opportunities in their newly adopted land. "Yes, with a good education, my children can find a better job," explained a Chinese mother, who had a college degree from a university in China and worked in a factory here. "I don't want them to be like the first generation of Chinese immigrants here. They have to work so hard in those slave labor jobs."[55]

Many of the young Chinese are high educational achievers, entering elite universities like Harvard and Berkeley and winning awards in competitions like the Westinghouse Science Talent Search. But there are others, especially the children of the "Downtown Chinese," who do not find promising futures ahead of them. Many are alienated and angry. Facing an English-language barrier and prospects of low-wage work in restaurants and laundries, they turn to gangs like the Ghost Shadows and Flying Dragons and force Chinese shopkeepers to give them extortion money. "A lot of the owners pay," a Chinese businessman explained. "They are afraid the gang will break their window or set fire to the store." Asked why he became involved in crime, a gang member replied: "To keep from being a waiter all my life."[56]

But regardless of their different class backgrounds, the *San Yi Man* often experience a shared sense of rejection by white society. "American students always picked on us, frightened us, made fun of us and laughed at our English," said immigrant student Christina

Tien of Los Angeles. "They broke our lockers, threw food on us in the cafeteria, said dirty words to us, pushed us on campus. Many times they shouted at me, 'Get out of here, you chink, go back to your country.'" The new immigrants have found themselves perceived as "strangers," like the Chinese of the first wave. "We are," remarked John Kuo Wei Tchen, "perceived as foreigners in a perpetual sense."[57]

Compared to the second-wave Chinese immigrants, the recent Filipino immigrants have been invisible. They have not concentrated in Manila Towns in the older sections of cities and have not built new Filipino suburban communities. Yet, the new Filipino immigration has been much larger than its Chinese counterpart: 664,938 entered between 1965 and 1984 — over 200,000 more than the Chinese. In 1990, Filipinos represented the second largest Asian group in the United States.

Over three fourths of the Filipino population in the 1980s were immigrants. Unlike the early Filipino immigrants, the second-wave Filipinos have come from the city rather than the country, and they have migrated as settlers rather than sojourners. Between 1969 and 1978, 60 percent of Filipino aliens became American citizens during their fifth to eighth year of residence. In striking contrast to the early, predominantly male immigration, the recent newcomers have been mostly women. Between 1966 and 1971, women far outnumbered men — 66,517 to 47,599. Unlike the first-wave Filipinos, the new immigrants have included professionals such as engineers, scientists, accountants, teachers, lawyers, nurses, and doctors. Between 1966 and 1970, of 39,705 Filipinos admitted under the occupational category, only 3,792, or 10 percent, were laborers, while 25,723, or 65 percent, were professional and technical workers.[58]

One of the factors driving this middle-class exodus was the repressive regime of President Ferdinand Marcos. Professionals in the Philippines became increasingly critical of Marcos's corruption and alarmed by his political repression and violations of human rights. Citing an Amnesty International report on the torture of political prisoners in the Philippines in 1976, a Filipino stockbroker here stated: "I know such things to be true." Business executive Froilan Aragon told the *New York Times* that the 1983 assassination of opposition leader Benigno Aquino played a key role in his decision to move to the United States with his family.[59]

But the push from the Philippines was also economic. Describing this "brain drain," Jack Foisie wrote in the *Los Angeles Times* in 1972: "There is an overabundance of a well-educated middle class in the Philippines, and a startling number of them cannot use their special learning after graduation. The Philippine government's own statistics indicate that only 60% of today's college graduates are employed in any more than menial jobs." In 1970 there were 732,868 students enrolled in colleges and universities, constituting 25 percent of the college-age population in the Philippines. In its ratio of higher education enrollment per 100,000 population, the Philippines rated second only to the United States. But college graduates there faced extremely limited employment prospects. A survey of the 1969 graduating class found that for every job requiring education there were one hundred to 150 applicants; in 1970, of the 1,000,135 persons with college diplomas only 610,000 were able to find suitable employment. "We have more than two hundred registered civil engineers in the city," said the mayor of Lucena City. "Where would I get them employed! So the problem is a surplus of professionals."[60]

College-educated Filipinos suffered not only from a scarcity of jobs but also from low wages. "Wages in Manila are barely enough to answer for my family's needs," said one immigrant. "I must go abroad to better my chances." A nurse compared wages in the two countries: "My one day's earning here in America is more than my one month's salary in Manila, especially when I do a plus eight [overtime]." Explaining why he and other professionals came to the United States, an accountant observed: "It is common [in the Philippines] for middle-class Filipinos to work at two or even three jobs because of the high cost of living. I have paid as much as $7.50 per pound for chicken there because food is not in abundance as it is here. . . . In the United States, hard work is rewarded. In the Philippines, it is part of the struggle to survive." Images of American abundance, carried home by the *Balikbayans,* or immigrants returning to their homeland for visits, have pulled frustrated Filipinos to this country. When Carlos Patalinghug went back for a visit in 1981 after working in the United States for ten years, he told his friends: "If you work, you'll get milk and honey in America." Other Balikbayans described the United States as a "paradise." "The Balikbayans," Governor Eladio Caliwara of Quezon Province reported, "say that in the United States people from the Philippines are given the opportunity to work for better pay, better medical conditions, better social security. . . . For example medical practitioners who migrate and become American citizens have very good opportunities in the United States, both personally and professionally."[61]

Indeed, most prominent among the professional immigrants have been nurses and doctors, who seem to be ubiquitous in the medical services in the United States. In 1974 there were more than 10,000 Filipino nurses. During the 1970s, of the 2,000 nurses who had graduated from schools in the Philippines each year, 20 percent came to the United States. Proportionately the flow of Filipino doctors has been even greater. Forty percent of all Filipino doctors in the world practice in the United States. The University of Santo Tomas medical school has been supplying more doctors to the United States than any other foreign medical school. In 1974 there were some 7,000 Filipino doctors in the United States, one thousand of them in New York alone where the total Filipino population was only 45,000. Filipino doctors are on the staff of every hospital in New York and New Jersey.[62]

In 1970, 24 percent of all foreign physicians entering the United States came from the Philippines, far ahead of Canada with 8 percent and Britain with 6 percent. Other Asian countries also trailed behind: India sent 8 percent and South Korea 7 percent. The oversupply of physicians was particularly acute in the Philippines. The problem stemmed not from too many doctors but from too many poor people. "75% of the people were poor, 23.5% middle class and 1.5% privileged rich," estimated Senator Benigno Aquino in 1972. In 1966 there were ten physicians for every 10,000 people in the Philippines, compared to twenty in the United States and only two in India and five in South Korea. What determined whether this ratio represented an under- or oversupply was the per capita income: in 1968, it was $180 in the Philippines, compared to $3,980 in the United States, $100 in India, and $180 in South Korea. The general pattern was that countries having incomes per capita ranging from $1,000 to $4,000 could afford twenty doctors per 10,000 people, while countries with incomes per capita below $200 could afford only two physicians per 10,000 people.[63]

But coming to America has not necessarily increased the opportunities for Filipino medical professionals. Here Filipino doctors must pass an examination administered by the Educational Council for Foreign Medical Graduates in order to qualify for private practice, internship, or hospital residence. The examination as well as additional state requirements often force Filipino doctors to do further study and find temporary employment as nurses' aids and laboratory assistants. "In Los Angeles, there are several hundred Filipino unlicensed physicians working in jobs that are totally unrelated to their knowledge and expertise," Dr. Jenny Batongmalaque stated in her testimony before the California Advisory Committee to the United States Commission on Civil Rights. "They have no opportunity to review or to attend review classes. They cannot afford to pay the tuition and they have no time because they have to earn a living to feed themselves and their children." Similarly attorney Leon Baringa told the committee: "Filipino doctors are accepted as professionals as defined by the Immigration and Naturalization Service and the Department of Labor. However, when they come here, they are not allowed to practice that profession under which they were granted the visa because of the State's strict licensing procedures. That's an inconsistency." This inconsistency forced one Filipino physician, a surgeon, to work in a restaurant as a meat cutter; he did not tell his employers he was a doctor. Later, in an interview he smiled as he remarked: "They thought I was very good at separating the meat from the bone."[64]

Foreign-educated pharmacists have encountered even more severe difficulties: they have not even been allowed to take the licensing examinations in many states. In California, for example, eligibility to take the state examination requires the candidate to be a graduate of a school on the Board of Pharmacy's list of accredited institutions, which has never included a foreign school. The board has been worried about an "oversupply." In 1973, Fred Willyeard, assistant executive secretary of the board, noted that "far too many schools were graduating far too many pharmacists." Hundreds of Filipino pharmacists have been excluded from the profession: in 1973 there were 350 to four hundred of them in Los Angeles and San Diego alone.[65]

Filipino professionals in veterinary medicine have also experienced obstacles. After arriving in America in 1973, a veterinarian explained that she had hoped to practice in her field. But she learned she would first have to pass an English test, satisfy a one-year clinical internship at an accredited veterinary hospital without pay, and pass the California state licensure examination. To support her family and herself while she prepared for the examination, she had to work as a clerk at the Aetna Life and Casualty Insurance Company. She was finally able to obtain her license seven years later. "Foreign educated or trained professionals are as good as the Americans," she said in an interview. "They set up these ridiculous prerequisites in order to discourage us from pursuing our license because they see foreigners as a viable competition to American graduates."[66]

As a result of these and other restrictions, many Filipino immigrants have found themselves underemployed. In Salinas, California, during the 1970s, more than half of the new immigrants who had been employed in professional and technical occupations in the Philippines worked as clerical, sales, and wage laborers. "When these ex-professionals get together," anthropologist Edwin Almirol observed, "they often tease [themselves] by calling each other by their former titles, such as 'doctor,' 'attorney,' 'engineer,' 'professor.' " The *New York Times* also noted this pattern of occupational downgrading: "[Filipino] lawyers work as file clerks, teachers as secretaries, dentists as aides, engineers as mechanics." Sometimes Filipino professionals found themselves steered toward manual employment simply because they were Filipino. A college-educated newcomer, for example, was directed to an agricultural job by an agent in a government employment office. "He simply asked me if I were a Filipino and without opening my folder," the disappointed job seeker said, "he gave me an address of a vegetable grower."[67]

Indeed, regardless of whether they are old-timers or recent immigrants, Filipinos have found themselves in a racially stratified labor market. In San Francisco in 1980, for example, both immigrant and American-born Filipino men were far below white men in participation in managerial and professional occupations — 16 percent for Filipinos, compared to 32 percent for whites. In the service occupations such as food, health, and cleaning, on the other hand, Filipino men had a much higher level of participation than white men — 12 percent for American-born Filipinos and 21 percent for immigrant Filipinos, compared to only 6 percent for whites. Because of their location in the lower strata of the labor-market structure, Filipino men earned only about two thirds of the average income of white men. But the problems of underemployment and discrimination in the labor market have not turned second-wave Filipinos toward ethnic enterprise. According to the 1980 census, Filipinos ranked fifteenth among seventeen recent immigrant groups in their rate of self-employment, while Koreans had the highest rate.[68]

Before the Immigration Act of 1965, Koreans were so small numerically and so spread out geographically they were a hidden minority. But the new Korean immigration has led to the dramatic emergence of Koreans as a very visible group in America, the Korean population having jumped from 10,000 in 1960 to half a million in 1985. Some 100,000 live in New York, where a cluster of Korean restaurants and stores suddenly appeared on Broadway between 23rd and 31st streets. In Los Angeles, the home of 150,000 Koreans, a new community has sprung up on Olympic Boulevard. "It's called Koreatown," *Newsweek* reported in 1975. "What used to be Mexican-American, Japanese and Jewish stores and businesses are now mostly Korean, with giant Oriental letters spread across their low-slung storefronts." This concentration of Korean-owned grocery stores, churches, gas stations, travel agencies, barbershops, insurance companies, restaurants, and nightclubs prompted a Korean immigrant to remark: "One does not feel that one lives in America when one lives on Olympic Boulevard."[69]

The recent Korean immigrants have generally come from the college-educated middle class rather than from the farming and working classes. Surveys of Korean householders in New York and Los Angeles found that about 70 percent came with college degrees. Seventy-one percent of Koreans entering through occupational categories between 1966 and 1968 had been professional and technical workers in Korea, though this percentage declined to 40 percent for the years 1974 to 1977. Unlike the first-wave Koreans, the new immigrants have been coming as settlers, *yimin,* and have been bringing their families to America. In 1975, 86 percent of Korean householders in New York were married. A majority of them apply for citizenship when they meet the five-year residence requirement. "The fascination of America for the Korean immigrants," observed Kim Ta Tai in 1975, "is to come to a free and abundant country, and breathe in its air of freedom, and make plans for a new life such that they are changing their destinies, which were fatalistically determined by tradition and history in the old country."[70]

The second-wave migration has been occurring within the context of rapid economic modernization in Korea. Under the control of Park Chung-hee's military dictatorship from 1961 to 1979, South Korea initiated a program of accelerated industrial modernization and developed an export-oriented economy. Between 1961 and 1977, exports jumped from $41 million to $10 billion. To keep the prices of its goods competitive in the international market, Korean industries depended on low-wage labor. The government assisted capital by prohibiting strikes and creating a surplus of workers. Government anti-inflation policies kept rice prices low and precipitated an agricultural crisis. Unable to survive in farm communities, millions of

Koreans moved to the cities. Between 1960 and 1975, the proportion of the population living in urban areas of 50,000 and more shot upward from 28 to 52 percent. Urbanization concentrated the people of South Korea at the very moment the country was experiencing a population explosion — from 25 million in 1960 to 35 million in 1975. "Korea's population density is one of the world's highest," explained Won Hoon Chung of the Korean Exchange Bank of California in 1976, "so the natural tendency is to seek some better opportunity than at home where competition is too keen." Covering a territory about the size of Maine, South Korea has a population density second only to Bangladesh.[71]

"I came to Seoul for a job," one of the migrants from a rural area explained. But Seoul, like other cities, did not have jobs for all of them. Neither were there sufficient employment opportunities for college-educated workers. Thousands of professionals began emigrating to West Germany, Brazil, Argentina, Canada, and the United States. "I could not find a job after obtaining my B.S. in chemical engineering at Chungnam University," said Hee-duck Lee. "Miserable" as an unemployed college graduate, he applied for an overseas labor contract and worked in West Germany as a miner for three years. "I was afraid that I would become unemployed again if I returned to the home country. I wandered through some European nations for a while, but I could not find a proper place to settle. Upon arriving in the United States, I found a lot of jobs waiting for me."[72]

Like the Filipinos, the recent Korean immigrants have included many medical professionals: between 1965 and 1977, over 13,000 Korean physicians, nurses, pharmacists, and dentists entered the United States. As South Korea modernized, it expanded its medical-training facilities. After 1966, twenty new nursing schools were established; by 1977 thirty-seven nursing colleges were graduating 2,500 nurses each year. The supply of nurses, however, exceeded the demand, and, in 1973, 59 percent of the graduating nurses were unemployed. "In the past ten years," observed a school dean in 1974, "there has been a tremendous increase in the number of young women seeking careers in nursing. Although modern medical centers absorbed many of these graduates, many have been unable to find work in Korea and so have sought employment overseas." Similarly, the number of Korean medical schools increased from eight to fifteen within ten years; by 1977 they were graduating some twelve hundred doctors annually. "The schools in Korea produce many qualified doctors," said Hyung Lum Kim, who sponsored as immigrants his brother and sister, both physicians. "The truth is they have more doctors in Korea than they can support — not more than they need, but American cities can use more too." Unable to secure positions in the major cities and unwilling to "go into exile" in the rural areas where the standard of living was low and work was less remunerative, many doctors emigrated to the United States.[73]

Here the Korean nurses and physicians were drawn to the eastern seaboard, where there was a shortage of medical workers. In 1980 New York City had a concentration of 20 to 25 percent of all Korean-immigrant nurses and doctors. "Korean doctors of New York," sociologist Ilsoo Kim observed, "are the most 'successful' of Korean immigrants. They represent the largest group of Korean suburban houseowners; most of the Korean residents of Scarsdale are immigrant doctors. With MD plates on their cars, the Korean doctors in New York can display their highly esteemed status in white suburban neighborhoods."[74]

Actually this appearance of status has shrouded some frustrating realities. Korean doctors often found themselves confined to inner-city hospitals and shunned by white doctors, and they tended to be in specializations such as anesthesiology and radiology rather than the more prestigious areas like surgery and internal medicine. Beginning in the late 1970s, Korean doctors also began encountering a declining demand for physicians and a new wave of discrimination against foreign doctors when they applied for internships and resident positions in hospitals. Furthermore, many Korean doctors have not been practicing medicine in the United States. They discovered they simply could not support a family and also prepare for the Visa Qualifying Examination, the English-language test, and the medical test in their field of specialization. Many Korean physicians, especially those with limited English-language skills, have been working as hospital orderlies and nurses' assistants. In southern California in the mid 1970s, some six hundred Korean physicians did not have licenses to practice medicine.[75]

Like their Filipino counterparts, Korean pharmacists found themselves excluded from taking the licensing examination in states like California. Seung Sook Myung, for example, had been a pharmacist in Korea for ten years. After arriving in Los Angeles in 1974, she became a knitting-machine operator at a plant where about 90 percent of the workers were Korean. Like many fellow educated and professional Koreans, Myung was locked in a low-wage working class. Unable to practice pharmacy, Kong Mook Lee of Los Angeles invested his money in a garment factory. "The only thing my wife knows is sewing," he said. "The only thing I know is pharmacy. Pharmacy is impossible; so sewing is the only way." Lee counted at least three hundred experienced Korean pharmacists in southern California alone who had to change occupations. "We never expected to lose our profession at the same time as we immigrated to this beautiful and wonderful country," he complained. "Today, most of us find ourselves in a job which is inconsistent with our qualification and experience. We are suffering from starvation wages."[76]

Korean immigrants educated in fields such as teaching and administration also have limited employment prospects. Occupational downgrading has been a widespread problem for Korean professionals: only 35 percent, a 1978 Los Angeles survey found, were able to enter professional occupations here. "In the Kent Village Apartments [near Washington, D.C.]," reported a Korean journalist in 1976, "about 90 percent of some 600 Korean residents are skilled workers; the remaining are salesmen. . . . About 50 percent of the Korean residents here are college graduates, most having studied social science." Formerly white-collar workers in their home country, Korean immigrants have become auto mechanics, welders, radio repairers, and television technicians as well as gas-station attendants, gardeners, and janitors.[77]

Korean immigrants have also become owners of wig shops, restaurants, liquor stores, and, most visibly, greengroceries. Commenting on the rise of "Korean" greengrocers, the *New York Times* observed in 1977: "In fruits and vegetables, traditionally an immigrant business, first it was Jews, when it centered in the Washington market area, then Italians. And now up in the Bronx, it's the Koreans." By 1983, Koreans dominated the retail produce business, owning three quarters of the twelve hundred greengroceries in New York City. In fact, there are so many Korean greengrocers they worry about competition from one another. "Across the street from me," remarked Kyu Suck Lee, the new owner of a store on East 170th Street in the South Bronx, "there is another Korean greengrocer; he bought his place from a Chinese four years ago. One block down, there's another Korean: he got his store from an old Jewish man who moved to Florida. Across from him, there's still another Korean. . . . Four Korean greengrocers in this crowded ghetto area!"[78]

Unlike recent Filipino immigrants, the Korean newcomers have a very high rate of self-employment, and this pattern has sometimes been attributed to the presence of a Confucian ethic in Korean culture, with its emphasis on industry, self-regulation, and family ties. But this notion overemphasizes the influence of the home country's culture. More important than the influence of Korean culture may be the development of Korean attitudinal and behavior responses to their particular immigrant conditions here in America. A study of Korean business owners showed that more than 90 percent of them worked harder and lived more frugally here than they had in Korea. In other words, explanations for the extensive involvement of Korean immigrants in small business are more likely to be found by examining their specific social and economic circumstances in the United States rather than the Confucian culture of the old country.[79]

Behind the making of Korean ethnic enterprise in America is a complex combination of factors. Significantly, the new Korean immigrants had not been shopkeepers in Korea. In the mid 1970s, only 6 percent of Korean householders in New York had been small-business owners in the old country. Yet, 34 percent were in the retail, wholesale, and catering businesses in New York. Like the first-wave Korean immigrants, they have been able to secure capital through the *kae,* or credit-rotating system brought here from Korea. But the new immigrants also have available funding from the Small Business Administration. Most importantly, they have brought capital with them to this country. "In the early 1970s," explained Sung Soo Kim, executive director of the Korean Produce Association, "they left their children in the care of grandparents . . . and came with money that ranged from the price of fare back home to $5,000, $10,000." Beginning in 1981, Korean immigrants have been allowed by the South Korean government to take a maximum of $100,000 to start a business here. Noting the expanding and visible presence of Korean entrepreneurs in Los Angeles, Professor Edna Bonacich explained: "They are more likely to come [to America] with money."[80]

Korean newcomers have become shopkeepers at a very opportune moment. Middle-class whites have been fleeing to the suburbs and abandoning the inner cities to blacks and Latinos, and older white merchants have been closing their businesses to retreat from the growing ghetto or to retire. "Before the Korean immigrants landed in this city, who were the greengrocers?" said Eugene Kang of New York's Korean Produce Association. "Most likely, they were Jewish and Italian, along with Greeks. The Jews and Italians and Greeks, they are third generation now. They want to go to law school.

They are no longer taking care of father's business, which was green-grocer." A niche in the retail economy has developed for Koreans to fill. Ironically, they had left white-collar jobs in a modernized economy in Korea and had become old-fashioned shopkeeping capitalists in America.[81]

Actually many Korean immigrants have also been pushed into self-employment. "What else can I do?" asked greengrocer Ill Y. Chung, the holder of master's degrees in both city planning, from a Korean university, and mechanical engineering, from the University of Hawaii. "I need money but there are not good jobs for Koreans." A majority of Korean small businessmen are college graduates: 78 percent of Korean greengrocers, a New York survey found, had college degrees. Many of them have sought refuge in small shopkeeping because of their limited English-language skills. According to a 1975 study of Korean immigrants over twenty-three years of age, only 10 percent had no difficulty with English. Forty percent spoke no English at all. "The language barrier," observed Kim Ha Tai, "virtually makes the newcomers deaf and dumb." Working long hours to survive, most Koreans have not been able to attend English classes. As greengrocers, they need only a minimal knowledge of English to operate their businesses.[82]

But Koreans have also been driven into shopkeeping by racial discrimination in the labor market. "When it comes to getting employment in American firms, factories, public and private institutions," charged Kim Ha Tai, "there is a great deal of difficulty in securing jobs due to discrimination and language barriers." Explaining why he resigned from a New York insurance company and became a greengrocer, Yun Pang, who holds an MBA from an American university, said: "When I began to work for the insurance company, I met an Asian co-worker. This man had been with the company for several years. He was born in the U.S. His English was perfect. He was a hard worker. But he received only token promotions and was regularly bypassed by the white American workers who joined the firm after he did. I thought, 'This guy is good. But if he's not making it, neither will I.' So I left. In the store, at least, I'm in control of my own future."[83]

Many Korean shopkeepers rely entirely on the family to operate the business. Korean women have no or little English-language skills, and, unlike Filipino immigrant women, who are usually English-speaking, and who represent a 67 percent labor-force participation rate, they have extremely limited access to the general labor market.

As spouses of Korean men who own small shops, they represent a source of unpaid labor. "In this business you can earn only labor costs," Korean shopkeepers say. By "labor," they mean their own time, and the hours of work by their wives and their children. In a Korean-owned family business, everyone works.[84]

"The work here is very hard," said Jeung Uen Choi, owner of a greengrocery. "My husband leaves for Hunts Point wholesale market before dawn. I get the children off to school and work in the store from eight to eight, then go home and make dinner. We work all the time." Indeed, the workday for Korean shopkeepers and their families begins early in the morning. "Mr. Kim bought his store two years ago from a Jewish American for a total payment of $15,000 — $10,000 for the store price and $5,000 in key money," a newspaper reported in 1977. "He and his son daily purchase vegetables· at four o'clock every morning when the dawn is coming, they get up and drive to Hunts Point in the Bronx, where a city-run wholesale market is located. . . . In the market they run and run in order to buy at low prices as many as one hundred and seventy different kinds of vegetables and fruits. All the transactions are made in cash. At 7 o'clock they return to the store and mobilize the rest of the family members in order to wash and trim vegetables."[85]

Out on the streets early in the morning darkness and at their stores until late at night, Korean greengrocers are open game for muggers and armed bandits, and many of them are murdered. The physical labor of the business is punishing. "No matter how much energy, health, and stamina one may have," a greengrocer said, "one cannot stand more than two years of this daily toil." They complain of backaches and blood in their urine. "Sometimes you get so tired," another sighed, "you cannot see the dollar in your hand." Some greengrocers make handsome profits, clearing over $100,000 a year. But, for all their hard work and long hours, most of them actually do not earn very much: $17,000 to $35,000 a year representing, on average, the income of the labor of an entire family.[86]

But they work hard, many Korean immigrants say, for their children: "The first generation must be sacrificed." The parents must struggle in order for the children to attend college and become professionals as their parents had been in Korea. Their own lives have become bleak in the United States, but they will do everything to brighten the futures of their children. In a poem describing the despair he felt for himself and the hope he nurtured for his child, a school janitor who had been a teacher in Korea wrote:

I do not see, although I have eyes.
Then, have I become blind? No, I have not.
I do not hear, although I have ears.
Then, have I become deaf? No, I have not.
I do not speak, although I have a mouth.
Then, have I lost my speech? No, I have not.
I have become an old stranger
  who wants to raise a young tree
  in this wealthy land.

Another former teacher in the old country, greengrocer Young Sop Kim of East 184th Street in the Bronx explained the purpose of his work and life: "The day before yesterday I kept my store closed all day long. That was my first day off since I started this business in 1976. My son, Jong Moon, graduated from Princeton University on that day. All my family members came. I am an old man, 65 years. I don't have a driver's license to get to the Hunts Point market. I can't run this business alone. But I have another son to help through college, Jong Won. I think I can last until both my sons go all the way up, to the highest educational degree."[87]

Reflecting on the rise of Korean ethnic enterprise, Christopher Kim explained: "The immigrants come with a lot of money — $100,000 and $200,000," said Kim, who has worked as a lawyer in Los Angeles's Koreatown for over a decade. "They sell their homes, everything they own in Korea and bring their cash with them. Many then open liquor stores in the black community. All their transactions are in cash. They are tough. They take risks and know they could get shot by robbers. But the pay off is large and rapid. They have homes in the Palos Verdes Estates and drive BMWs. The Korean businessmen are like the Jews of the 1930s. They are hardworking and aggressive, but because of color they never reach the place where the Jews have reached."[88]

To make their businesses profitable, many Korean entrepreneurs hire and exploit other Korean immigrants, requiring long working hours and paying low wages without vacations and health benefits. Korean employers have special access to the Korean work force because these workers are cut off from the general labor market as a result of discrimination and their limited knowledge of English. In 1978, 40 percent of Korean heads of households in Los Angeles County were self-employed, and they employed an additional 40 percent of Koreans. Fully 80 percent of employed Koreans worked within the Korean ethnic economy. The plight of Korean laborers has been often overlooked in the news media's celebration of Korean shopkeeping success. During the 1970s, Jung Sook Kim worked in a garment factory and her husband worked eleven hours a day in a New York fruit and vegetable store owned by another Korean. "We came for a better life," she complained, "but we have not found it better yet. It is work, work, work."[89]

Even more than the Koreans, Asian Indians had become a disappearing minority in the United States before World War II. In 1946 when the gates for Asian-Indian immigration were reopened, their population totaled a mere fifteen hundred. The new quota allowed only a token number to enter annually. Suddenly, after the 1965 Immigration Act, immigrants from southern Asia began coming to America in increasing numbers. By 1970, twenty-thousand had arrived from Pakistan, an independent nation carved from India in 1947 that includes part of the Punjab. Half of the Pakistani immigrants were Punjabis. But unlike the first-wave Punjabi farmers, the Pakistani newcomers were highly educated professionals from the major cities. Most of the post-1965 immigrants from South Asia have come from India, and the Asian-Indian population in America has climbed steeply from 10,000 in 1965 to 525,000 twenty years later. No longer a tiny minority isolated in the agricultural valleys of California, Asian Indians have become very visible, especially in the Northeast, where 34 percent of them live — 18 percent in New York alone. A section of Indian restaurants and stores on New York City's Sixth Street has come to be known as "Little India."[90]

The new immigrants are very different from their first-wave brethren. Unlike the early newcomers, who were virtually all male, the second wave has been equally divided between men and women. They also have arrived as settlers rather than sojourners: by 1980 50 to 60 percent of them had become naturalized citizens. English-speaking and educated, the second-wave immigrants come mostly from the professional class. "The first Indian immigrants and the post-1965 Indian immigrants are two separate worlds," a second-wave newcomer explained. "It is a class thing. They came from the farming, the lower class. We came from the educated middle class. We spoke English. We went to college. We were already assimilated in India, before we came here."[91]

But like the early Asian Indians, the second-wave immigrants have come here mainly for economic reasons. Employment prospects for them had been severely limited in India. The situation in the home country had pushed them out: in 1972, out of 288,460 educated unemployed Indians, 594 held doctorates, 39,820 had done post-graduate study, and 210,528 were college graduates. Unemployment was a particularly widespread problem for engineers and physicians. India had a "surplus" of 100,000 engineers in 1974 and 20,000 unemployed physicians in 1970. Between 1966 and 1977, 83 percent of Asian-Indian immigrants entering under an occupational category had been professionals and technical workers in India. Recently, however, immigrant professionals have been bringing their less-educated relatives.[92]

Most second-wave Asian Indians have found economic opportunities here to be much greater than in their home country. Of all Asian American groups, Asian Indians have the lowest percentage employed in services (8 percent) and the highest percentage employed as managers and professionals (47 percent). They include 25,000 physicians and dentists in practice, 40,000 engineers, 20,000 scientists with Ph.D.'s, 2,000 professionals in areas like law and finance. After arriving here, however, many Asian-Indian professionals have changed their occupations and are not employed in the fields of their training. College-educated, they can be found operating travel agencies, sari shops, and luncheonettes featuring pizza, souvlakia, and Indian "fast food." They are also newsstand operators in the subways of Manhattan. "You don't need a lot of capital to start," explained newsstand owner Bawnesh Kapoor. "You don't have inventory problems because you normally turn over your entire inventory in a week. You don't have accounts receivable problems. You don't have to worry about changes in fashion." Asian Indians have also found a niche in the motel business: they own fifteen thousand motels, or 28 percent of the nation's 53,629 hotels and motels.[93]

Asian-Indian Americans have been trying to define who they are in their adopted society. The issue of their identity was raised sharply in 1975. In a memorandum seeking to define the term "minority groups," the director of the Office of Federal Contract Compliance stated that persons of Asian-Indian descent "are regarded as white." Asian Indians like the leaders of the India League of America based in Chicago argued it would be a mistake for their group to claim minority-group status: "If employers find it possible to fill some kind of minority 'quota' by reporting high-level Indo-American employees, while continuing to discriminate against the truly disadvantaged minorities, we may find many Americans turning against us."

But many other Asian Indians believed Asian Indians should be considered a minority group. In a statement to the U.S. Civil Rights Commission in 1975, the Association of Indians in America declared: "The language of the Civil Rights Act clearly intends to protect those individuals who might be disadvantaged on the basis of appearance. It is undeniable that Indians are different in appearance; they are equally dark-skinned as other non-white individuals and are, therefore, subject to the same prejudices. . . . While it is commonly believed that the majority of Indians working in this country are well-educated and employed in jobs of a professional nature, their profiles are not at all unlike those of Korean and Japanese immigrants. Vis a vis other professionals, Indians are disadvantaged for reasons of racial discrimination." In 1976, leaders of the association participated in a government-sponsored meeting of Pacific Islanders and Asian Americans including Chinese, Japanese, Filipino, and Korean representatives to discuss the ethnic categories to be used for the 1980 census. A year later, the Bureau of the Census agreed to reclassify immigrants from India and their descendants from "white/Caucasian" to "Asian Indian."[94]

"Asian Indians," they also want to be identified as Americans. Hamida Chopra explained it this way. She came to the United States after 1965 to join her student husband, thinking her stay here would only be temporary. "America is my home," she said twenty-three years later. Though she has chosen not to become a citizen, she thinks of herself as "an American." But she is also Indian. She speaks only Urdu in her home and has taught her daughter the language and culture of the ancestral land. She always wears Indian clothing — the *dupatta, shalwar,* and *kameez,* for everyday dress, and the sari for formal occasions. When she first came, people looked at her as a "foreigner." "But now these days," she noted, smiling, "they look at me and have no curiosity. American society is open, able to absorb differences in cultures and dress. I feel that the definition of what is 'American' has become broader."[95]

Similarly Dr. S. Patel wants to have her identity both ways: "I am, I know, both Indian and American." When she arrived in 1967, she was planning to be here for only five years. "Mine was an arranged marriage," she said. "My husband was studying in the United States and I came here to be with him. We bought a house, saying we would sell it when we returned to India. But then my son was born. Meanwhile I also passed my examination for my medical license and did my internship. So one thing led to another. And five years extended into ten years. And we found ourselves staying permanently."[96]

Still Dr. Patel misses her homeland. They visit India every three years, taking their children with them. "When my husband and I pass away, I don't think my children will be visiting India," she remarked. "My children will probably give their children American names. I would like my son to marry an Indian, but I would let him make his own choice." She is concerned about divorce, however. "In an Indian marriage there is no divorce. Yes, marriage does have its ups and downs. But divorce is out of the question in Indian culture. So that is what I would worry about if my son did not marry an Indian woman."[97]

The second-wave immigrant generation, Dr. Patel observed, was too busy trying to survive after they had first arrived here to have time to think about their community or ethnicity. "But now we are established professionally, and we have time to think about our future in America." For her, ethnicity is political as well as personal. "Indians have to organize to be visible and to have influence. I am not political. I am too busy being a mother and working. But I am concerned about the tightening of laws about doctors from foreign countries practicing here. It would make it more difficult for doctors from India to come here. So we as Indians have to be concerned."[98]

Like virtually all second-wave Asian Indians, Dr. Patel has made America her home. But she admitted in a moment of reflection: "Now that I think about it I sometimes would like to move back to India. Why? Because there is too much individualism here in America. I am getting old and I am afraid my children will grow up and will not be near me. In India, children take care of their parents. This doesn't happen in this country. So there is a price to be paid for coming here. The family isn't as close here."[99]

Dr. Patel and her fellow newcomers from India as well as China, Korea, and the Philippines came to America as immigrants. Suddenly, beginning in 1975, hundreds of thousands of other Asians have arrived from Southeast Asia, not as immigrants but as refugees — as peoples fleeing from political persecution, and they have a very different story to tell.

Pushed by "Necessity": The Refugees from Southeast Asia

Twenty-five years ago, in 1964, there were only 603 Vietnamese living in the United States. They were students, language teachers, and diplomats. They were from South Vietnam, a country that had begun to receive increasing attention in the news. Vietnam had been a French colony since the late nineteenth century; beginning in World War II, the Vietminh, under the leadership of Ho Chi Minh, fought the French to regain their country's independence. This war culmi- nated in 1954 when the French forces were defeated at the battle of Dien Bien Phu. At Geneva shortly afterward, the French and Vietminh signed an agreement that provided for a temporary partition of Viet- nam at the seventeenth parallel and for an all-Vietnamese election in 1956. But a year after the Geneva conference, a new government was formed in the south headed by Ngo Dinh Diem, with the support of the United States, to counter the government in the north backed by China and the Soviet Union. The partition of Vietnam became permanent: the election was never held and civil war erupted. United States involvement in the conflict began to expand significantly in the early sixties when President John Kennedy sent Special Forces to Vietnam and when President Lyndon Johnson asked Congress to give him war powers in the 1964 Gulf of Tonkin Resolution. The war ended disastrously for South Vietnam and the United States eleven years later, precipitating a massive exodus of Vietnamese to the United States.[100]

Unlike the other Asian groups already in America, the 1975 wave of Vietnamese migrants did not choose to come here. In fact, they had no decision to make, for they were driven out by the pow- erful events surrounding them. Most of them were military personnel and their families, in flight from the North Vietnamese troops. A week before the collapse of the South Vietnamese government on April 29, ten to fifteen thousand people were evacuated; then in a frenzy during the last days of April, 86,000 Vietnamese were airlifted out of the besieged country. "That morning, April 29," former Pre- mier Nguyen Cao Ky recalled, describing his last hours in Saigon, "I found myself alone at the big headquarters of the general staff. . . . At noontime, all the American helicopters came in for the final, big evacuation. On the ground, there were hundreds of thousands of Vietnamese, running — right, left, every way, to find a way to escape. My bodyguards said to me, 'Well, General, it's time for us to go, too.' "[101]

At street level, panic gripped the people. "On those last days of April," remembered a refugee, "[there was] a lot of gunfire and bombing around the capital. People were running on chaotic streets. We got scared. . . . We went to an American building where a lot of Americans and their Vietnamese associates were ready to be picked up by American helicopters." They could "feel" the bombing. "Our houses were shaking," said Thai Dang. "Then afterwards we went outside and saw abandoned guns and army uniforms on the streets. The soldiers in flight had thrown away their weapons and taken off their clothes. Here and there we saw bodies."[102]

The city shuddered under relentless missile bombardments; homes and buildings were burning everywhere.

> *Fires spring up like dragon's teeth*
> *At the standpoints of the universe:*
> *A furious, acrid wind sweeps them toward us from all*
> *   sides. . . .*
> *All around, the horizon burns with the color of death.*

In a frenzy, frightened people rushed to get out of Saigon. From the roof of the American embassy, hundreds climbed frantically onto helicopters. Others drove to the airport, where they abandoned their cars with notes on the windshields: "For those who are left behind." Terrifying images had been seared into the minds of the refugees. "What was the one event during the trip [evacuation] you will never forget?" an interviewer asked a Vietnamese woman en route from the Philippines to the United States. "It was when all of these people were trying to get on the plane at the airport," she replied. "I saw people jamming the door and women and children could not get on. The shelling came closer and then the plane took off with people still hanging at the door."[103]

Others left by boat. "There was a lot of bombing during the night and the next morning people were rushing to the barges," said Linh Do. "My mother was carrying my two-year-old sister wrapped in a blanket. She had lost her shoes and was running barefoot." Another Vietnamese girl recalled how she and her family scrambled to board a small boat with fifty other people. "I could hear the noisy firing guns, screams from injured people on the beach, and cries of little children," she wrote later. "While standing on the boat, I couldn't think of anything. It was not until sunset, when it was dark, that I stopped staring back and started worrying about the waves. It rained all night. I was all wet and cold. Holding each other, my brother and I prayed. The next day at noon time, we reached an American ship. As soon as the ship lowered one of its stairs, everybody climbed up the stairs without any order. Men, women and children were pushed aside and dropped into the sea. Some were crushed between boats. I carried my youngest brother and went up that stairs with fear." During the next few weeks, forty to sixty thousand Vietnamese escaped in boats to the open sea, where they were picked up by American navy ships and transported to Guam and the Philippines.[104]

The refugees had no time to prepare psychologically for departure; more than half of the refugees later said they were given less than ten hours. "I was afraid of the killings when the Communists came to town," one of them explained, expressing the concern of most refugees. Some did not even know for certain who would be going and who would be staying: "Mother came along to the airport. Then at the last minute she stayed behind because the number of children staying was larger than those leaving." Others thought they would be gone for only a month or two: "My mother would never have left her other six children behind if she thought she wasn't coming back." Many did not even know they were leaving or where they were going. "I saw everyone running to the harbor, so I decided to go along," recalled a Vietnamese. After reaching the Philippines, a family learned they were bound for the United States; later they said: "We did not plan on taking this trip."[105]

Altogether some 130,000 Vietnamese refugees found sanctuary in the United States in 1975. The first-wave refugees generally came from the educated classes: 37 percent of the heads of households had completed high school and 16 percent had been to college. Almost two thirds could speak English well or with some fluency. Generally, the refugees came from the urban areas, especially Saigon; they were more westernized than the general population. They had worked with the French and then the Americans. About half of them were Christian, a group representing only 10 percent of the people in Vietnam. They came as family units rather than as young single men; almost half were female. After their arrival in the United States, the 1975 refugees were initially placed in processing camps like Pendleton in California and Fort Chaffee in Arkansas. From the camps they were spread throughout the country but they soon began to gather in communities such as Orange County, California.[106]

Meanwhile, in Vietnam the fighting had stopped and "everything had fallen into absolute silence, a silence that was so unusual." Then the new Communist government began the reconstruction of society. Businesses were nationalized and reeducation camps were instituted for individuals associated with the old regime. "New Economic Zones" were developed for the movement of the population to the countryside. Thousands of Vietnamese, particularly urban business and professional elites, were ordered to "go to the country to do labour, the hard jobs, to make the irrigation canals, sometimes for one month, sometimes for two, or three months." "I remember the choked mute lines of families trudging out of the cities to begin agricultural work in the countryside," said an ethnic-Chinese businessman. "They had no prior knowledge of how to do that job, yet they had no choice." One of them said: "Life was very hard for everybody. All had changed! . . . I could see no future for me in Vietnam, no better life! I wanted to escape."[107]

Thousands did escape — 21,000 in 1977, 106,500 in 1978, over 150,000 in 1979, and scores of thousands more later. The second-wave Vietnamese refugees took their wives and children and boarded crowded, leaky boats, risking their lives at sea where storms threatened to drown them and pirates waited to rob them and rape the women. Two thirds of the boats were attacked by pirates, each boat an average of more than two times.

> Can you imagine human hair
> Flowing all over the sea,
> Children's bodies ready to dissolve
> As human meat dinners of fish?
>
> But they keep on leaving
> As humanity turn their heads away
> And still they serenely
> Throw themselves into death.[108]

Thai Dang remembered how she left on February 19, 1981, when she was only thirteen years old. "I just wanted to embrace my dear friend, Trang, tightly, telling her that I would be leaving Saigon in an hour, that she would always remain my friend." But she had to keep her planned escape a secret. "So, I left briefly, as if chased by a ghost, before they could see my eyes getting red. . . . I was yearning to capture each familiar scene, each beloved face of the place I had lived and grown up." But as Dang and other refugees were on their way to the hiding place of the boat, they were "discovered and hunted like beasts" by the Vietnamese forces. "I ran, fell, and ran for my life in the unknown darkness of a strange forest, totally oblivious to my bleeding wounds." Her mother placed her on a small boat and waved good-bye, and Dang wondered: "Who was to guarantee that I would survive in the dark sea?" But at sea they were attacked by Thai pirates. "The pirates, wearing almost nothing but frightening tatoos, jumped into our boat with axes and guns to rob and beat us. The air was saturated with the most disheartening cries. . . . We were literally begging on our knees."[109]

Luong Bot Chau told a similar story. She and her husband, along with over two dozen refugees, had sailed away on a small, thirty-foot vessel. Off the coast of Thailand, their boat was attacked by Thai pirates. The pirates chopped off one of her husband's fingers to get his ring and then tried to slit his throat. "But the knife they had was too blunt," she said later. Instead they clubbed him to death and threw his body into the sea. Then they dragged the young girls up to the deck and systematically raped them. "We heard them scream and scream," Luong Bot Chau cried. "We could not get out, because the pirates had nailed down the hatch." Thirty-six-year-old Hue, who now lives in Sunnyvale, California, vividly remembered what happened to her on a boat in the Gulf of Thailand. When they saw the Thai pirates approaching their boat, Hue and the other women smeared their faces with engine oil and fish sauce to diminish their appeal. But the pirates ordered them to bathe and then raped them. Hue still wakes up screaming from nightmares of the experience — the "dark skinned men" encircling her, the knife at her throat, the hands that "clawed," and the teeth that "bit," mutilating her breasts. Two other women survivors recounted the horror they experienced: "The pirates tied them [the Vietnamese men] up and threw them into the water. The remaining people were tied up too, and locked in the hold after being stripped of their belongings. After this, the pirates came . . . to pillage and rape people. One person was killed after being dealt a blow with an iron bar. Another had his finger cut off because he was unable to pull off his wedding ring. When everything was looted, the pirates hurried to go. They released the men they kept in the hold and kicked them back to our boat. Some fell into the water and drowned with their hands bound behind their backs."[110]

The survivors floated to Thailand, where they were forced to live in squalid refugee camps for months (and in the case of many individuals, for years). From the camps they went to countries like Australia, Canada, and France. Most of them came to the United States. "In 1978 my sister, Nguyet, my brothers Tinh, Hung, my father, and I left the country," wrote Tuyet Ahn Nguyen in a letter to me. "My mom and sister and couple of brothers stayed in Vietnam. It was so hard for my family to suffer the separation." The second-wave refugees were diverse, including educated professionals as well as fishermen, farmers, and storekeepers from the rural areas and small coastal cities and villages. Unlike the earlier refugees from Saigon, most of them did not speak English. Approximately 40 percent of the second wave were ethnic-Chinese Vietnamese. They had experienced hostility from Vietnamese society for decades, and became targets for discrimination under the new Communist regime. The government's program of nationalizing the economy focused heavily on the ethnic Chinese. Constituting 7 percent of the country's population, they controlled about 80 percent of its retail trade. Furthermore, military conflict had broken out between China and Vietnam in 1979, and the ethnic Chinese in Vietnam found themselves caught in the political crossfire.[111]

In 1985 there were 643,200 Vietnamese in the United States. "Remember these are the people who were on our side," an American veteran of the Vietnam War said. "They have a right to come to this country as refugees. They just need a home." But often they do not feel welcome here. Like earlier Asian immigrants, the Vietnamese have felt the stings of racial slurs and have sometimes been called names like "Chink" and told to "go back to China." "The presence of the Vietnamese refugees," explained Chuong Hoang Chung, a lecturer at the University of California at Berkeley, "is viewed as a threat, such as being cheap labor when there is a scarcity of jobs. They are also viewed as a threat in places where the scarcity of low-income housing forces blacks and refugees to compete." On the Gulf Coast of Texas, Vietnamese fisherman have been the targets of Ku Klux Klan demonstrations and threats. Competition between Vietnamese and white fishermen has erupted in ugly confrontations and incidents of violence. "There's too many of them," a white fisherman declared, "and there's not enough room for them and there's going to be lots of hard feelings if they don't get some of them out of here and teach the ones that they leave how to act and how to get along. I think they ought to be put on a reservation somewhere or . . . in a compound to teach them our laws and our ways, the way we live, our courtesy as a people." But Vietnamese see their situation differently. "It's really hard for you [Americans] to understand us," said a Vietnamese immigrant, "and we don't expect you to, but we do expect you to treat us as human beings and not be prejudiced."[112]

Many Vietnamese, especially those who fought in the army, nurture a fierce determination not to let their loyalty to their homeland slip away. Their strong anti-Communism has led to a stifling of dissent within the Vietnamese community. "It is ironic that despite the struggle to escape what they considered tyranny in Vietnam," T. T. Nhu sadly commented in the *San Jose Mercury News* in 1988, "many refugees find that they face another tyranny in this country in the form of insistence on political conformity. . . . It is reminiscent of nightmarish times already experienced in this country during the McCarthy era." But the patriots refuse to acknowledge the end of the war. They lobby Congress to give military aid to the "freedom fighters" in Vietnam poised to overthrow the Communist government. They form organizations like the National United Front for the Liberation of Vietnam; in their official anthem, they declare: "Citizens, arise and respond to the call of the ancestorland. . . . Even at the cost of lying dead in heaps, we shall shed our blood to revenge our people." At Tet New Year celebrations, they gather under a banner trumpeting the slogan, *To Quoc Tren Het: Country Above All.* "We shall return," they shout as they pledge themselves to the "liberation of Vietnam." In 1983 former South Vietnamese Vice President Nguyen Cao Ky, who runs a liquor business in Huntington Beach, California, said that Vietnamese refugees were training in U.S. national parks in preparation to engage in armed struggle in their homeland. "Give me the guns," he promised, "and we'll kick them [the Communists] out." Former Vietnamese Army Colonel Pham Van Lieu predicted: "I think we will defeat them [the Communists] in three to five years, surely before the end of this decade."[113]

Many Vietnamese see themselves as sojourners, hopeful they can return to their country someday. A 1977 survey of household heads showed that 41 percent planned to return to Vietnam to live. Fewer have such plans today, but still strong attachments to the home country remain. "Vietnam is my home," said a refugee in 1988 as she described to me her determination to go back. She had been here for ten years and had even become a naturalized American citizen, but she adamantly claimed her Vietnamese identity. "I get angry, mad," she argued, "when I see Vietnamese children who can't speak Vietnamese." They include her own, born in the United States. "But what would happen to your children when you return to Vietnam?" I asked. "They will have to choose between the two countries," she replied. But others think the likelihood of returning to Vietnam is extremely remote, and they have begun to make America their new home. "If Vietnam were a free country," said Loan Vo Le, who fled from Saigon in April 1975, "I would like to go back. I miss my family so much. But we couldn't stay. I'm afraid we are too spoiled by life here, the conveniences, the opportunities, the education and the free-

dom. . . . I feel like a Vietnamese American, but inside I'm still Vietnamese." But others, like Linh Do, would like to have it both ways.
"Returning to Vietnam is not a choice," she explained. She had been
only a child when her family left in 1975. "Now I'm American
culturally. But the Vietnamese community in California has grown
so large that you almost don't have to go home to be home. Here
you can find Vietnamese food, dances, and culture."[114]

But Vietnamese culture, some realize, cannot be strictly maintained here, particularly in terms of gender roles. "In Vietnam, the
women usually were dependent on the husband a great deal," a
refugee explained. "Then when we came here, the Vietnamese women
had jobs. This made the men feel extremely insecure." But some men
have overcome this problem, he continued. "My wife didn't work
in Vietnam. Now because she is working, I start to help her with the
dishes and chores around the house. Sometimes when I am on vacation and she is working, I try new recipes so that when she comes
home the meals are ready. She never tells me that I should help her
but I think because she is working like me too, I should give her a
hand." Some of the women have found new opportunities for themselves in America. Winnie Che, for example, began working as a
waitress in 1981. "My first job I felt so happy," she said. "I can
work! Somebody will hire me here." Che saved her money and took
loans from family and friends and in 1983 opened a restaurant, the
Little Sai-Gon, in Carnation, Washington. "In Vietnam, I would be
just a housewife: clean up, cook dinner. Here, if you work hard, you
can do what you want." Vietnamese women like Winnie Che have
begun to stretch and feel the arches of their backs, freeing themselves
for new activities and identities. But this exercise of new freedom is
often accompanied by conflict within the family as college-educated
Vietnamese women seeking professional careers try to break through
the "riverbanks" of the arranged marriages planned for them by
parents and the roles traditionally assigned to women.[115]

Thrust abruptly into a very different culture, Vietnamese find
their traditional family ties severely strained. "Back in Vietnam the
family is something precious for us — father, mother, children," explained Tran Xuan Quang. "But in coming here, we saw that the
family here is too loose. The father works in one place, the mother
works in another and they don't see each other at all. Sometimes the
father works in the morning and the mother works in the afternoon
and the children go to school. When they get home, they hardly see
each other at all." Sometimes parents are disappointed and depressed

by the new behavior of their children. Living alone in Oakland's Chinatown, sixty-one-year-old Pham Hai is unemployed because of her poor English and fairly advanced age. "When I was in Vietnam I expected my children would take care of me when I got here," she explained. "But when I got here my children threw me out of their house a short time later. My children now sit around and smoke marijuana. This is very different from my life in Vietnam. I don't understand it. Many times I have thought of suicide." Many children have begun to lose their Vietnamese language. "I hated it when Americans teased me about my language," complained Mai Khanh Tran. "Maybe that's why I don't talk in Vietnamese in front of an American anymore. When I first came here, I used to talk in Vietnamese but ever since they teased me I don't feel comfortable doing it anymore. At home I do because my parents always talk Vietnamese and I'm trying to preserve what I have for as long as possible. But I can feel it's slipping away."[116]

While thousands of Vietnamese young people are entering universities as high achievers, others are on the streets. Many of them are unaccompanied minors. They came here alone, sent by parents seeking to keep their children from the draft and hoping they would have a chance to seek an education in America and to become citizens. The strategy is to "throw out the anchor": citizen children would be able to bring their parents to America. But, lacking families here, many of these children have difficulty surviving. They live in motels and hang out in places like the Midnight Cafe and the Saigon Center pool hall in the San Gabriel Valley east of Los Angeles.

Many of them join gangs. A gang member named Qui said his gang could steal an average of ten stereos a night and then sell them for fifty dollars each. "Then we go out, eat a big dinner and gamble. We can spend it all that night." But Vietnamese gang activity has not been limited to petty crime. In 1984, a gang attempted to rob the Jing Hing jewelry store in Los Angeles's Chinatown. Alerted by a silent alarm, two police officers arrived on the scene and a shootout left one officer wounded and the other officer and two holdup men dead. Sang Nam Chinh escaped with wounds but was later arrested and charged with the attempted robbery and the murder of the police officer. Chinh had left Vietnam with his sister and 350 refugees crowded on a boat in 1978, and after a year in a refugee camp in Malaysia he came to the United States. Chinh was placed in the ninth grade at Mark Keppel High School in Alhambra, but he was not prepared for schooling here. He had not been in a classroom for six years and was illiterate in his own language. "He really tried that first year," his sister said, "but he would come home and tell me that his classes were too hard. He said he needed help, but none of us knew English." Chinh dropped out of the eleventh grade and then worked for a while as a busboy and a delivery man; eventually he became involved in a group of young Chinese-Vietnamese known as the "Hac Qui Boys," or "black ghost" boys. Vietnamese teenagers like Chinh have become what has been called "a lost generation."[117]

Most refugees know they face adjustment problems in America and have begun the process of resettlement. "In their heart, they want to go back," observed Chuong Hoang Chung. "But reality has crept in and they know they will be here for a long time. They receive letters from home saying the conditions are terrible and don't come back. They are also having children born here." Many Vietnamese want to become part of American society. "I think it's necessary to acculturate to some degree in order to move up and most important to live within the society in harmony," said one of them. "For example, if we are strangers in the neighborhood, there might be some resistance from the natives. But if we become their friends and show them that we are nice people too, then their anti-Vietnamese attitude would alter. In fact, if different people understand each other, then there will be a lot less hatred between races." But many new settlers want the understanding to be based on accepting and appreciating them as Vietnamese as well as Americans. "We cannot look at the future without knowing who we are. We must remember our roots, our heritage," insisted Kien Pham. Confident Vietnamese Americans will make important contributions to their adopted country, he predicted: "I am sure we will have Vietnamese in Congress before the year 2000."[118]

But the Vietnamese are currently concentrating on more immediate economic needs. Many refugees have new jobs that do not have the remunerative rewards and status of the work they did in Vietnam. A study conducted in 1978 showed that 30 percent of the refugee heads of households had been professionals in Vietnam and another 15 percent had been managers; twenty-seven months after their entry in the United States, only 7 percent were professionals and 2 percent managers. Meanwhile the percentages of household heads jumped in other occupations — from 14 percent to 30 percent for crafts, 3 percent to 12 percent for operatives, and 14 percent to 24 percent for blue-collar work. This pattern has persisted: a 1983 study found that 19 percent of the men and women had been professional and technical workers in Vietnam but that here they represented only 6 and 9 percent respectively. Occupationally, Vietnamese became concentrated in craft, operative, and service employment. "In Vietnam I was a history and geography teacher," a refugee told an interviewer. "Here I worked on many different jobs — brick layer, carpenter, clerk typist, salesman, truck driver, delivery man. I felt frustrated and depressed because I had social status and possessions in Vietnam. Here I didn't have anything." The Vietnamese also experience problems of racial discrimination. A refugee employed by the Bank of America for several years said she believed white men in the bank were promoted faster and received higher salaries than she did: "I'm a U.S. citizen, but my physical appearance cannot change — I'm still yellow."[119]

"I am a patient man," a Vietnamese refugee said. "If I have to start over again, I believe I will make it someday. I believe I will become self-sufficient as an auto mechanic. Most refugees have only one hope: to have a job and become a tax payer." Actually, many Vietnamese have achieved much more. In California where the Vietnamese have concentrated and where 40 percent have made their homes, they have created their own Vietnamese colonies or ethnic enclaves. In 1988 the city council of Westminster, Orange County, officially designated the area along Bolsa Avenue from Magnolia to Bushard as "Little Saigon." This section constitutes a "large language island." "A walk down the Bolsa Avenue can testify to the extensive use and importance of Vietnamese," observed Chuong Hoang Chung. "A look at directories published in Vietnamese and distributed free to Vietnamese shoppers shows that any Vietnamese resident of Orange County can obtain all necessary services without ever having to use English. From social services to health care and other basic needs, Vietnamese speakers are at home."[120]

In Orange and Los Angeles counties, Vietnamese-owned businesses have proliferated. Vietnamese professionals are in abundance as doctors and dentists, and ethnic-Chinese Vietnamese are almost ubiquitous in restaurants and grocery stores. Their businesses are not just mom-and-pop stores. In fact, many of the retailers had been big merchants in Vietnam and had brought capital with them to the United States: here they own supermarket chains like Wai Wai Supermarkets and Man Wah Supermarkets. "For people who do business here, they feel as if they are doing business at home," said Hoang Giao of the Vietnamese Chamber of Commerce in Los Angeles. Most of the shop signs in Westminster are in Vietnamese only. But the merchants of "Little Saigon" have begun to reach out for a larger customer market. In some Vietnamese stores, signs announce: "Se habla español."[121]

In northern California, the Vietnamese have also begun to flourish as entrepreneurs, especially in San Jose. "Vietnamese now constitute 10 percent of San Jose's population and have moved into its commercial life in an aggressive way," reported T. T. Nhu in 1988. "Nearly forty percent of the retail business in downtown San Jose is Vietnamese. . . . The fact is that the Vietnamese have become an inescapable presence in San Jose. They want to become part of San Jose because they are here to stay." Downtown San Jose had been in decline until the arrival of the Vietnamese newcomers. "There's a new vitality downtown and it's the Vietnamese who have made it what it is today," stated Doanh Chau, executive director of the Vietnamese Chamber of Commerce. "It was abandoned. But the past few years has brought a new life to the area."[122]

The signs of Vietnamese-American settlement are certainly evident. Significantly, Vietnamese have recently begun coming to America as immigrants: they are entering under the Orderly Departure Program, a 1979 agreement between Vietnam and the United States, which allows 20,000 Vietnamese (family members of those who have already immigrated) to enter the United States annually.

Not as visible and not as well known as the Vietnamese are the refugees from Lan Xang, "Kingdom of the Million Elephants," as the land was called in the fourteenth century. An inland country wedged between Thailand and Vietnam, Laos was colonized by the French in 1893; after World War II, Laotian nationalists led by the Pathet Lao began their struggle to overthrow French colonialism. As soon as Laos was established as an independent state by the 1954 Geneva Accords, civil strife broke out between the Royal Lao and the Pathet Lao for control of the country. This internal conflict merged with developments in Vietnam: the Ho Chi Minh Trail, which North Vietnam used as a supply line to the south, ran through Laos. North Vietnam supported the Pathet Lao in order to protect the trail while the United States gave assistance to the Royal Lao and the Hmong and Mien in the highlands to interrupt the movement of troops and military supplies. By the 1960s, the Vietnam War had been extended into Laos, and the United States actively increased its operations there through the Agency for International Development and the Central Intelligence Agency. Suddenly, in 1975, after the

Pathet Lao had taken power and began a campaign of bloody repression, the groups supporting the United States scrambled in panic for safety. Seeking sanctuary as refugees, some 70,000 ethnic Lao, 10,000 Mien, and 60,000 Hmong fled to America.

"This is a good life here," said an ethnic Lao refugee. "No war. No death. No hunger. We like to stay here — for now." These last two words carry apprehension for their future here. Many Lao find the culture here nearly incomprehensible. "It is easier to move the mountains than get used to American culture," one of them observed. Another remarked: "We have been living in a jungle for a long time in Laos. This is another kind of jungle — a technological and bureaucratic jungle."[123]

Kimmakone Siharath knows how difficult the transition from Laos to America has been for his fellow ethnic Lao. His family had lived in a small farming village outside of Vientiane; his father had worked for the government military forces and was forced to escape to Thailand after the Pathet Lao victory. A year later, in 1976, his mother took Siharath and his younger sister across the Mekong River to reunite the family. In 1979 they migrated to the United States, where they lived in San Jose for two years before settling in Arvin, near Bakersfield, California.[124]

"Arvin is like Laos," said Siharath. "It is a small town, a farming community. I was the only Lao, only Asian in school. Most of the students were Mexican, and they called me 'Chino.' They thought I was Chinese." His father is employed as a custodian at a high school in Bakersfield, and his mother works on an assembly line in a factory manufacturing oxygen masks. "The old people miss their homeland," Siharath observed. "In Laos, they owned their land. They were independent and did their own farming. They worked for six months to grow the rice and then stored their crops. They would go hunting and fishing. There was plenty of fresh meat. But here life is stressful. Many Lao are on welfare, and others have low-wage jobs."[125]

"The old people would like to return to Laos," Siharath said. They find it hard to adjust. His father would go back if the Pathet Lao were no longer in power. "I would like to return too," Siharath added. "No matter how long you are here in America, you will always be an Asian, always an outsider, not an American." He has only a vague picture of the square bamboo house he had left. "Inside I wish I could really know where my homeland is. The little bit of memory from my childhood is burning inside me, and I want to be reunited with it." He has applied for United States citizenship. "But psychologically I don't feel I'm an American. I will be what I am only in Laos. America is not a bad place. Still I miss the closeness and friendship of village life in Laos where you could name everybody in the whole village." Indeed, life for Siharath here is very different than it would have been there. A genetics major at the University of California at Berkeley, he explained: "My parents pushed education. Here education is a necessity for survival. But if I were in Laos, I would not be in college. I would be a farmer now."[126]

The clash between cultures has been especially sharp and painful for two other refugee groups from Laos — the Mien and Hmong. They had been targeted for destruction by the Pathet Lao, for both had been recruited by the CIA to conduct American military operations in Laos. "From 1961 on," said Houa Thao Vang, now a resident of Fresno, California, "we worked for the CIA." "We Hmong fought what Americans call the secret war in Laos," revealed Dang Moua, now a pig farmer in Livingston, California. "It was no secret to us." Touly Xiong was one of the Hmong soldiers: "Every young man had to serve in the army. We had no choice. The village leader would come and get you." The war inflicted heavy casualties on the Hmong. "We had to move from camp to camp," said Xiong. "Our villages were bombed."[127]

The situation became extremely dangerous after the war ended in 1975. "The Pathet Lao wanted revenge, the extermination of the Hmong," explained Touly Xiong. "I left Laos on June 18, 1975. I had to go or else I would be killed." Xiong escaped alone; others went in groups. "I remember the first evening that people in my village, Ban Nam Hia, Sayaboury, Laos, fled to Thailand," said Ghen Vang. "Before making a decision to flee that evening in June, 1975, the entire village, young and old, men and women, over 1,000 people were outside. . . . They talked and discussed what to do. The goal was decided: Thailand and then America, but it was a dark and unseen goal. The decision was passed along from person to person. At 10:30 P.M. most of the villagers were gone. By midnight all had fled."[128]

The refugees trekked to the Mekong River, crossing it on bamboo rafts and rubber inner tubes to Thailand. Then from the crowded camps they were transported to the United States. The Mien have settled in Seattle, Portland, Sacramento, Oakland, San Jose, and Long Beach. Over half of the Hmong have congregated in California, especially in Fresno, but they are also located in places like Missoula,

Seattle, Providence, Minneapolis-St. Paul, La Crosse, and Eau Claire.

Life in America has been radically different for the Mien and Hmong. They feel intensely lost in America, where they have to figure out how to use toilets and gas stoves and how to fill out welfare forms. For them paying a telephone bill is an ordeal. First they have to figure out which number is the amount due and write a check or buy a money order. Then they have to tear the bill along the perforated line and fold it correctly so the company address shows through the envelope's window, and finally they need to get a stamp and place it in the proper corner.[129]

Mien and Hmong find that Americans generally do not know who they are or why they are here. They are often mistaken for Chinese and called "Chinks." In Eau Claire, Hmong names stand out in the telephone directory, and they get hostile phone calls. Angry voices tell them: "Go back to your country." "You eat dog." "I'm coming to kill you!" Chu Vue, who arrived here in 1978 when he was thirteen years old, said white students spat on him and the other Hmong students in junior high school. "One time they asked me whether I knew karate, and I told them, 'yes,' and they stopped pushing me around." Reflecting on the rejection the Hmong have experienced, Chou Lee of the Hmong Community Center in Eau Claire said: "Racism is like a wall. You cannot break through it."[130]

Learning English has also been trying and traumatic for them. Without the knowledge of English they cannot attend job-training programs and without job skills they cannot be employed. "The first year I spent in America, I made very little progress," said Tony Vang, the executive director of the Lao Family Community of Fresno. "Then I decided: I must forget Laotian. Forget the French I was educated in. Forget Hmong! I must think only in English, only about learning American ways. I struggled along OK in the daytime, but I dreamt every night in Hmong or Lao. It took me three years to dream in English, and those dreams, too, are about the refugee camps, about running away from my country." But Vang is one of very few educated Hmong. They came from a preliterate culture; they do not understand how signs and letters can carry meanings. The concept of written words and language is unfamiliar. The Hmong language was given written form only recently, by American and French missionaries in 1953, and most of the refugees — 70 percent — are not literate in their own language. In English classes offered at the Hmong Community Center in Eau Claire, the Hmong are first taught to read and write in Hmong. "We teach them ABCs and apply the alphabet to the Hmong language," explained Chou Lee. "Once they become literate in Hmong, then they can learn English and use the dictionary."[131]

But adjustment is not merely a matter of language. "When you pull a plant out of the ground without any soil around its roots — soil from where it was grown — and transplant it, the plant will have trouble surviving," explained Dang Moua, who became a hog farmer in California. "The Hmong never really thought about coming to America, never really believed they would have to leave Asia. Then suddenly we were here. . . . The technology and the Latin language of European or Mexican immigrants are much closer to America's. They have some dirt on their roots."[132]

Many Hmong are trying to plant their roots in new dirt by farming in Minnesota and California, especially in Fresno, where more than 20,000 Hmong live. But the slash-and-burn agricultural methods of the old country do not apply here. In the mountains of Laos where they grew corn and rice for food and poppies as a cash crop for opium, they were able to farm an area for two or three seasons and then move to another area after the soil had been exhausted. Here they discovered they had to use chemical fertilizers and also pesticides. "My people could not read English, couldn't follow instructions on pesticide packages," said Lang Lee, director of Fresno's United Lao Agricultural Association. "Many get sick from the spray." Hmong farmers have other problems, too, Lee continued. "We don't understand how to irrigate fields. In Laos, farmers just wait for rain. We don't understand marketing — one year farmers get high price for snow peas, next year almost nothing. . . . We thought to ourselves, if we farm, maybe we can be independent people again. But unfortunately, when we arrive in Central Valley [of California] we learn that you must have something else: lots of money."[133]

"We have no other skills but farming — except that we are not even farmers anymore," said a Hmong refugee. "We are just unemployed soldiers." But the American government, Hmong say, has an obligation to them. "We fought for 20 years side-by-side with the CIA in the 'secret war.' My brother was killed by North Vietnamese soldiers," said Touly Xiong. Almost every Hmong family here in America lost a father or one or more sons in America's "secret war." The Hmong remember the "promise" the CIA made to them: "The Americans in Laos had an agreement, a contract with us: 'You help us fight for your country, and if you can't win, we will take you with us and we will help you live.' " They were brought to America, but making a living here has been extremely difficult for them. "The Americans came to my country and built the war there. Now I have no country and have nothing," a refugee observed bitterly. "When I stayed in Laos I was a farmer. . . . I had all the things I wanted. I never begged anyone for food. Only when I came to the country of America I had to beg."[134]

Employment is a desperate problem for the Mien and Hmong. Some try to make ends meet by selling handicrafts like needlework, silver bracelets, and earrings and by doing housecleaning and yard work. Most do not have jobs: their rate of unemployment reaches as high as 90 percent. After fleeing from Laos in 1975 and living five years in a refugee camp in Thailand, Choy Sapha has had different jobs in Alabama and California. "I speak Lao, Thai, Mien, English, some Chinese, and Spanish swear words," he said, adding that he worked for a while as a mushroom picker with Mexicans in Pescadero, California, for Campbell's Soup. Unemployed, he is trying to learn more English, attending classes in community centers like the Harbor House in Oakland. The Hmong constitute what is becoming a permanent welfare class. A 1987 California study showed that three in ten refugee families have been on public assistance for four to ten years, and many of the long-term welfare families have been Hmong. Most Hmong are barely surviving.[135]

Some do not survive. Seemingly healthy Hmong men have died suddenly and mysteriously, their deaths medically unexplainable and called the "Hmong sudden-death syndrome." "The autopsies have been uniformly negative," stated medical examiner Michael McGee of St. Paul, Minnesota. "We're really quite baffled." Doctors have ruled out nerve gas — which was used in Laos — as a factor, for only men have been affected. "Over one hundred have died so far [1988] by the sudden death," said Kai Moua, director of the Hmong Community Center in Eau Claire. "They're all men, about 30–50 years old. They had been soldiers for 15–20 years. They don't know how to start life over again. They don't know how to farm or to work in a factory." They were also overcome with grief. Moua described what happened to a relative: "My cousin almost died one night. He was healthy, but he thought about his parents in Laos and missed them. When he was sleeping, he felt pressure like some air in his lung that went up to his heart and he couldn't breathe and he tried to push the air back down." Touly Xiong told me that his forty-eight-year-old brother-in-law died from sudden-death syndrome:

"My sister had gone to ESL [English as a second language] class that night and when she came home she found her husband depressed. He said he felt lonely and missed home. They went to bed and around 3 A.M. she woke up. Her husband was making a choking noise and then died." Hmong also suffer from "survivor guilt." "Why should I live while others died [in the war]?" asked Vang Xiong, who was stricken by the sudden-death syndrome but survived. Another wondered: "I shouldn't be alive while better men than me, like my elder brother, are dead."[136]

Relocation depression is widespread among the survivors, for all of them suffer from the stress of resettlement in a strange new environment. "The Hmong were kings of their area in the mountains," explained Tou-Fu Vang, a worker in a federal refugee resettlement program. "Now they find themselves in a situation that is completely out of their control." Many Hmong in Wisconsin sit by their window, feeling lonely and sobbing uncontrollably. "My father wakes up with nightmares about three nights a week," said Touly Xiong. "He is asleep and then I hear him screaming, 'Get out! Get out! The Communists are coming!' I would like to take him to a counselor. We keep our problems bottled up. Just to tell our stories and have someone listen would help us." But there is no counselor available for Hmong in Eau Claire. Sometimes they even feel a bit better when they tell their stories to an interested scholar. "We hope you will include our stories in your book," they said to me. "Americans need to understand us and what we have gone through." The Hmong need sensitive and understanding professional attention, for their psychological condition affects their ability to cope. "If people are depressed, how can they get a job or listen to an ESL teacher?" asked Sean-glim Bit, a counselor at the Asian American Medical Clinic in Oakland. In their struggle to live, to overcome their nightmares, the Hmong express their sorrow in song:

> Oh heaven, we Hmong did not want to flee from our
>   country to a new country
> So far that we can no longer see our land
> We hear the birds singing, they fly in the sky
> They make us feel so lonely
> The sun is shining brightly
> Are you as lonely as I am, or not?
> I still have relatives back in my native country
> I miss them more than most people can miss anyone.

> My life in this country is sunny; it makes me feel
>   like asking,
> "Should I continue to live or is it better to
>   die?"
> I have no parents or relatives, only myself alone
> Do you know how lonely I am?[137]

The Hmong and Mien worry about whether they will be able to preserve their culture here. "In America we don't wear our traditional clothing, not even grandmother," said one of them. "We only wear our traditional clothing on special days, and I will make my children only one set of clothes. When they grow up I don't know if they will marry American or Mien, so I will make only one set. Maybe when they grow up, they may forget our language." Another Mien predicted: "I am very positive the Mien will lose their traditional religion within the next ten years. There will be no more shamans. There will be no more scroll." In Mien homes they listen from cassettes to mournful ballads sung by relatives still in Thai camps, telling stories about how Mien villages had been destroyed and how they had become an uprooted people.[138]

Younger Hmong are gradually making an adjustment. They have learned to speak and write English, and many do not remember the old country. "Laos is like a dream," said Mao Yang, a college student in Wisconsin. She had escaped from Laos in 1976 when she was only eight years old. "I can remember fragments, details, but that's all." Her goal is to graduate with a degree in restaurant management and to own a restaurant in California someday. California appeals to young Hmong living in places like Wisconsin. Two Hmong interviewed together in Eau Claire explained to me why they felt this way about California. "There are more Asians there," said Chou Vue, who stands at five feet and who is a student at the University of Wisconsin. "People don't look at you. Also I feel much more taller in California." Hmong college student Nou Xiong said that she felt like an "outsider" in Wisconsin and "more blended" in California. Young people see themselves as Hmong Americans, and plan to make this country their permanent home. Asked if she would go back to Laos if her parents decided to return, Nou Xiong replied, "No." "But what if your future husband wanted to go back?" Chou Vue questioned her, and she smiled: "Oh, he can go."[139]

But the older Hmong and Mien spend much of their time in sadness. "Our village in Laos was ideal," an old Hmong grandfather recalled. "The mountains for rice fields were endless. There were big forests with game to hunt. Good streams. Bamboo. We never had to move far like other villages. Not until the Communists came." "What I miss the most from Laos is my cow," said a Mien refugee. "I raised cows in the mountains. . . . Sometimes they would come from the jungle, and I would ride on the back of one cow." The Hmong and Mien are deeply and spiritually attached to the land they were forced to leave. "In Laos we believed there were spirits in the mountains," a refugee in San Diego explained. "Here, maybe the American Indians believe in spirits, but those (pointing in the direction of the nearby Laguna range) are *their* mountains, not ours."[140]

Like the refugees from Laos, thousands of Cambodians had been violently uprooted, chased here under threat of death. Located south of Laos and between Thailand and South Vietnam, Cambodia had also been dragged into the Vietnam War. In 1965, the Cambodian government under the leadership of Norodom Sihanouk began to permit North Vietnamese troops to move supplies through Cambodia. Five years later, Sihanouk was deposed by General Lon Nol, and the United States extended the Vietnam War into Cambodia by sending bombers to destroy North Vietnamese supply lines and storage facilities. In April 1975, while the North Vietnamese stormed Saigon, the Khmer Rouge forces led by Pol Pot came to power and renamed the country Kampuchea. The new regime instituted a brutal program for the mass relocation of the urban population to the countryside and for the mass destruction of all Cambodians affiliated with the American-supported Lon Nol government. "Pol Pot killed all the educated and professional people — doctors, lawyers, teachers," said Vacchira Loth, a refugee now living in Rochester, Minnesota. "If they knew I had been a medical school student, I would have been killed right away." Under Khmer Rouge rule, some 2 million people, or about a third of the country's entire population, died, most of them by starvation and disease. Remembering the "killing fields" of her homeland, fifteen-year-old Channa Cheng wrote a poem in her ninth-grade class in Seattle:

> The people are hungry. The sun
>   is shining.
> The women are working in the rice field.
> The babies are crying for their mother's milk.
> The guards are standing with arms around guns.[141]

To escape from certain death, hundreds of thousands of Cambodians fled to Thailand when Vietnamese troops invaded Cambodia and overthrew Pol Pot in early 1979. "I am a Khmer refugee, age twenty-five," one of them wrote in a letter seeking sponsorship to the United States. "In the four years gone by I have lived in Pol Pot's regime. My uncle, my aunt, and my two brothers were killed and buried in the same hole because Pol Pot's elements knew that my relatives were soldiers. Pol Pot's men killed my older sister's husband because they accused him as a political man who betrayed their Communist Party. I live with wretchedness. . . . My parents, my older brother and sister died because the Thai sent them back into the mountains."[142]

From disease-infested and crowded camps, over 100,000 Cambodian refugees have been resettled in the United States. They include some educated people from the cities, but most of them are country folk, farmers from the rural areas who have a lower educational level than their counterparts from Vietnam. Many are women who had lost their husbands in the conflict and had come here with their children. All refugees carry the horrible psychological scars of the war and mass exterminations. "The tragedy during the war hurts inside when I remember what happened in the past," a tenth-grade Cambodian boy told an interviewer. "I try not to think about it, but at night I dream and see my brother who they killed. I dream about him trying to find us. I dream they keep shooting him and shooting him until I wake up."[143]

Many Cambodian refugees suffer from what psychiatrists call "post-traumatic stress disorder" — a depression that had also afflicted the survivors of the World War II Nazi concentration camps. A thirty-five-year-old Cambodian woman living in Oregon found she could not overcome the horror she had witnessed and experienced. After her husband had been executed and her eighteen-month-old daughter had starved to death, she escaped to Thailand with her remaining children. She had left the killing fields behind but the killing fields did not leave her. In Oregon each night "she would fall asleep, and in her dreams people came to kill her. During the day she was jumpy and easily startled, and when night came again she told herself to stay on guard and not fall asleep. Depressed, she was losing weight and had frequent thoughts of killing herself and her two children." With memories of the extermination still fresh in their minds, still haunting them, many Cambodians experience recurring nightmares, emotional numbness, loss of appetite, and withdrawal.[144]

Cambodians would like to return to their homeland someday, but they realize the possibility is remote. "We want a chance to become part of this country," said one refugee. "It is a chance for a new life. But, inside, the memories are still there. We won't ever forget." The younger refugees, however, are looking at the future rather than the past but often find themselves trapped between the two. Sathaya Tor, for example, had slaved for four years in a Khmer Rouge child-labor camp. In 1979, the twelve-year-old boy crossed mine fields in order to escape to Thailand; he came to the United States two years later. In 1988 he enrolled at Stanford University, where he is the only Cambodian except for a custodian. "Nowadays, sometimes I feel like a frog jumping from one world to the other: school, my family, being American, being Khmer," Sathaya reflected. "In a way to be assimilated in another culture, you have to give up your own culture. With one foot in each culture, the wider you have to spread your legs, the more you could lose your balance. I'm at a point in my life where for the first time I feel vulnerable, and it's scary." Fellow Cambodian refugee Chanthou Sam can understand Sathaya's feelings. She herself had arrived here in 1975 when she was only twelve years old. Six years later, in recognition of her scholastic achievement and personableness, she was elected by her fellow students to be the Rose Festival Princess in Portland, Oregon. Hoping to become an accountant, she realizes her ambitions are often at odds with her traditional culture: "A Cambodian woman is supposed to sit at home, cook, and clean house. I want to be somebody. I want my own job, house, and car before I marry. I want to be independent. It is very hard to be caught in the clash of cultures."[145]

The Southeast-Asian Americans themselves are very diverse. They have come from different countries, cultures, and classes. They include, for example, preliterate tribesmen from the mountains as well as college-educated professionals from the cities, welfare families as well as wealthy businessmen, and superachieving university students as well as members of youth gangs. But, despite the differences among themselves, the Southeast Asians share something unique, a fundamentally different experience from all of the other Asian groups: "necessity," not "extravagance," has defined their lives. They did not come here voluntarily, seeking Gam Saan or fortunes in America. In fact they are not immigrants. Except for the Vietnamese who have begun to enter recently under the Orderly Departure Program, the Southeast Asians in the United States were driven to America by the circumstances and powerful forces of war. They did not think and dream about coming; in fact, most of them had no time to plan and prepare for their movement to a new land. Fleeing from the horrors of war, they departed in panic not knowing the country of their destination. They experienced the trauma of refugee camps and the terrible feeling of wondering whether they would have a place to begin life again. They worried about how the receiving society would view them as unexpected guests and refugees rather than desired immigrants with skills. Unlike the Chinese, Japanese, and other Asian immigrants in America, they cannot go home. More so than the earlier groups of Asian immigrants, the refugees are truly the uprooted. The refugees are like "the homeless people," lamented one of them. "They have no place they can call their own. They feel no sense of belonging to this land." In Texas, another refugee wrote:

> *In the obscurity of the night, a refugee cries*
> *His tear of woe flooded on his eyes*
> *He sobs for homeless life,*
> *   the uncertainty of tomorrow. . . .*[146]

12

Breaking Silences
Community of Memory

Like Georg Simmel's "stranger," the early Asian immigrants found themselves viewed and treated as outsiders. As newcomers, they lacked organic and traditional ties to American society. But so did Irish, Jewish, Italian, and other European immigrants. All of them were members of a transnational "industrial reserve army." Coming from lands across the Pacific, however, Asians were "strangers from a different shore." They were "pushed," for "poverty hurt." They were also "pulled" here to meet the labor needs of America's railroads, plantations, mines, farms, and factories. Powered by "necessities" of the "modern world-system," the international labor migrations from Asia to the United States took place, to use Cheng and Bonacich's apt phrase, "under capitalism." But there was in addition "extravagance" — the desire for freedom, and the realization of potentials, for what Carlos Bulosan described as the "building of a new life with untried materials."[1]

America seemed to offer a unique place for such a pursuit, for society in this "fresh green breast of the new world" was still an unfinished one. The land was liminal. The "riverbanks" of centuries of customs and strictures had not yet been formed, inviting initiative and the exercise of imagination. "The country is open, go forward," they exclaimed. Their dreams inspired many to break from old patterns and to cross a wide ocean. But here the Asian newcomers encountered a prevailing vision of America as essentially a place where European immigrants would establish a homogeneous white society and where nonwhites would have to remain "strangers." Their distinguishing physical features became what Robert E. Park termed "racial uniforms," and they were placed in a racially stratified labor structure. In order to discipline labor and keep wages low, planters in Hawaii pitted workers of different Asian nationalities against each other, and employers on the mainland promoted "ethnic antagonism" between Asian and white workers.[2]

But the Asian immigrants chose not to let the course of their lives be determined completely by the "necessity" of race and class in America. While tensions did develop among the Asian groups in the islands, a remarkable degree of interethnic community emerged among them as they lived together in the camps, spoke the common language of pidgin English, and went out on strike together in 1920 and 1946. On the mainland, the various Asian groups were comparatively isolated from each other and struggled separately against racism and competition from a hostile white working class. Isolated as "strangers," first-wave Chinese and Japanese immigrants developed their own economic enclaves, which in turn provided an economic basis for ethnic solidarity. The early Korean, Asian Indian, and Filipino immigrants did not develop their own colonies. The post-1965 groups have also charted different directions for themselves: the Koreans, Chinese, and Vietnamese have concentrated their economic resources in their own ethnic communities, while the Asian Indians and Filipinos have tended to integrate themselves into American society.

Throughout their history in this country, Asians have been struggling in different ways to help America accept and appreciate its diversity. Gradually, through events like World War II as well as through struggles such as the labor strikes and the Civil Rights Movement, American society has been moving toward a racially inclusive countervision of democracy — the possible pluralistic America depicted by Walt Whitman and Carlos Bulosan. Today Asian Americans live in a very different America from the one the earlier immigrants entered. They are no longer the targets of anti-miscegenation laws: in California in 1980, the rate of marriages to whites for Japanese was 32 percent, Filipinos 24 percent, Asian Indians 23 percent, Koreans 19 percent, Vietnamese 15 percent, and Chinese 14 percent. Asian Americans are no longer victimized by legislation denying them naturalized citizenship and landownership. They have begun to exercise their political voices and have representatives in both houses of Congress as well as in state legislatures and on city councils. They enjoy much of the protection of civil rights laws that outlaw racial discrimination in employment as well as housing and that provide for affirmative action for racial minorities. They have greater freedom than did the earlier immigrants to embrace their own "diversity" — their own cultures as well as their own distinctive physical characteristics, such as their complexion and the shape of their eyes. Many Asian-American children have access to bilingual education and ESL programs, and in universities across the country, from Berkeley to Brown, students find curricula offering courses on Asian-American history. Previously the targets of exclusionist laws, Asian Americans are currently able to maintain the vitality of their communities by the continuing influx of new Asian immigrants. But in many painful ways, they still find themselves unjustly viewed and treated as "strangers from a different shore."

The Myth of the "Model Minority"

Today Asian Americans are celebrated as America's "model minority." In 1986, NBC *Nightly News* and the *McNeil/Lehrer Report* aired special news segments on Asian Americans and their success, and a year later, CBS's *60 Minutes* presented a glowing report on their stunning achievements in the academy. "Why are Asian Americans doing so exceptionally well in school?" Mike Wallace asked, and quickly added, "They must be doing something right. Let's bottle it." Meanwhile, *U.S. News & World Report* featured Asian-American advances in a cover story, and *Time* devoted an entire section on this meteoric minority in its special immigrants issue, "The Changing Face of America." Not to be outdone by its competitors, *Newsweek* titled the cover story of its college-campus magazine "Asian-Americans: The Drive to Excel" and a lead article of its weekly edition "Asian Americans: A 'Model Minority.'" *Fortune* went even further, applauding them as "America's Super Minority," and the *New Republic* extolled "The Triumph of Asian-Americans" as "America's greatest success story."[3]

The celebration of Asian-American achievements in the press has been echoed in the political realm. Congratulations have come even from the White House. In a speech presented to Asian and Pacific Americans in the chief executive's mansion in 1984, President Ronald Reagan explained the significance of their success. America has a rich and diverse heritage, Reagan declared, and Americans are all descendants of immigrants in search of the "American dream." He praised Asian and Pacific Americans for helping to "preserve that dream by living up to the bedrock values" of America — the principles of "the sacred worth of human life, religious faith, community spirit and the responsibility of parents and schools to be teachers of tolerance, hard work, fiscal responsibility, cooperation, and love." "It's no wonder," Reagan emphatically noted, "that the median incomes of Asian and Pacific-American families are much higher than the total American average." Hailing Asian and Pacific Americans as an example for all Americans, Reagan conveyed his gratitude to them: we need "your values, your hard work" expressed within "our political system."[4]

But in their celebration of this "model minority," the pundits and the politicians have exaggerated Asian-American "success" and have created a new myth. Their comparisons of incomes between Asians and whites fail to recognize the regional location of the Asian-American population. Concentrated in California, Hawaii, and New York, Asian Americans reside largely in states with higher incomes but also higher costs of living than the national average: 59 percent of all Asian Americans lived in these three states in 1980, compared to only 19 percent of the general population. The use of "family incomes" by Reagan and others has been very misleading, for Asian-American families have more persons working per family than white families. In 1980, white nuclear families in California had only 1.6 workers per family, compared to 2.1 for Japanese, 2.0 for immigrant Chinese, 2.2 for immigrant Filipino, and 1.8 for immigrant Korean (this last figure is actually higher, for many Korean women are unpaid family workers). Thus the family incomes of Asian Americans indicate the presence of more workers in each family, rather than higher incomes.[5]

Actually, in terms of personal incomes, Asian Americans have not reached equality. In 1980 the mean personal income for white men in California was $23,400. While Japanese men earned a comparable income, they did so only by acquiring more education (17.7 years compared to 16.8 years for white men twenty-five to forty-four years old) and by working more hours (2,160 hours compared to 2,120 hours for white men in the same age category). In reality, then, Japanese men were still behind Caucasian men. Income inequalities for other men were more evident: Korean men earned only $19,200, or 82 percent of the income of white men, Chinese men only $15,900 or 68 percent, and Filipino men only $14,500 or 62 percent. In New York the mean personal income for white men was $21,600, compared to only $18,900 or 88 percent for Korean men, $16,500 or 76 percent for Filipino men, and only $11,200 or 52 percent for Chinese men. In the San Francisco Bay Area, Chinese-immigrant men earned only 72 percent of what their white counterparts earned, Filipino-immigrant men 68 percent, Korean-immigrant men 69 percent, and Vietnamese-immigrant men 52 percent. The incomes of Asian-American men were close to and sometimes even below those of black men (68 percent) and Mexican-American men (71 percent).[6]

The patterns of income inequality for Asian men reflect a structural problem: Asians tend to be located in the labor market's secondary sector, where wages are low and promotional prospects minimal. Asian men are clustered as janitors, machinists, postal clerks, technicians, waiters, cooks, gardeners, and computer programmers; they can also be found in the primary sector, but here they are found mostly in the lower-tier levels as architects, engineers, computer-systems analysts, pharmacists, and schoolteachers, rather than in the upper-tier levels of management and decision making. "Labor market segmentation and restricted mobility between sectors," observed social scientists Amado Cabezas and Gary Kawaguchi, "help promote the economic interest and privilege of those with capital or those in the primary sector, who mostly are white men."[7]

This pattern of Asian absence from the higher levels of administration is characterized as "a glass ceiling" — a barrier through which top management positions can only be seen, but not reached, by Asian Americans. While they are increasing in numbers on university campuses as students, they are virtually nonexistent as administrators: at Berkeley's University of California campus where 25 percent of the students were Asian in 1987, only one out of 102 top-level administrators was an Asian. In the United States as a whole, only 8 percent of Asian Americans in 1988 were "officials" and "managers," as compared to 12 percent for all groups. Asian Americans are even more scarce in the upper strata of the corporate hierarchy: they constituted less than half of one percent of the 29,000 officers and directors of the nation's thousand largest companies. Though they are highly educated, Asian Americans are generally not present in positions of executive leadership and decision making. "Many Asian Americans hoping to climb the corporate ladder face an arduous ascent," the *Wall Street Journal* observed. "Ironically, the same companies that pursue them for technical jobs often shun them when filling managerial and executive positions."[8]

Asian Americans complain that they are often stereotyped as passive and told they lack the aggressiveness required in administration. The problem is not whether their culture encourages a reserved manner, they argue, but whether they have opportunities for social activities that have traditionally been the exclusive preserve of elite white men. "How do you get invited to the cocktail party and talk to the chairman?" asked Landy Eng, a former assistant vice president of Citibank. "It's a lot easier if your father or your uncle or his friend puts his arm around you at the party and says, 'Landy, let me introduce you to Walt.' " Excluded from the "old boy" network, Asian Americans are also told they are inarticulate and have an accent. Edwin Wong, a junior manager at Acurex, said: "I was given the equivalent of an ultimatum: 'Either you improve your accent or your future in getting promoted to senior management is in jeopardy.' " The accent was a perceived problem at work. "I felt that just because I had an accent a lot of Caucasians thought I was stupid." But whites with German, French, or English accents do not seem to be similarly handicapped. Asian Americans are frequently viewed as technicians rather than administrators. Thomas Campbell, a general manager at Westinghouse Electric Corp., said that Asian Americans would be happier staying in technical fields and that few of them are adept at sorting through the complexities of large-scale business. This very image can produce a reinforcing pattern: Asian-American professionals often find they "top out," reaching a promotional ceiling early in their careers. "The only jobs we could get were based on merit," explained Kumar Patel, head of the material science division at AT&T. "That is why you find most [Asian-Indian] professionals in technical rather than administrative or managerial positions." Similarly an Asian-Indian engineer who had worked for Kaiser for some twenty years told a friend: "They [management] never ever give you [Asian Indians] an executive position in the company. You can only go up so high and no more."[9]

Asian-American "success" has emerged as the new stereotype for this ethnic minority. While this image has led many teachers and employers to view Asians as intelligent and hardworking and has opened some opportunities, it has also been harmful. Asian Americans find their diversity as individuals denied: many feel forced to conform to the "model minority" mold and want more freedom to be their individual selves, to be "extravagant." Asian university students are concentrated in the sciences and technical fields, but many of them wish they had greater opportunities to major in the social sciences and humanities. "We are educating a generation of Asian technicians," observed an Asian-American professor at Berkeley, "but the communities also need their historians and poets." Asian Americans find themselves all lumped together and their diversity as groups overlooked. Groups that are not doing well, such as the un-employed Hmong, the Downtown Chinese, the elderly Japanese, the old Filipino farm laborers, and others, have been rendered invisible. To be out of sight is also to be without social services. Thinking Asian Americans have succeeded, government officials have some-times denied funding for social service programs designed to help Asian Americans learn English and find employment. Failing to re-alize that there are poor Asian families, college administrators have sometimes excluded Asian-American students from Educational Op-portunity Programs (EOP), which are intended for *all* students from low-income families. Asian Americans also find themselves pitted against and resented by other racial minorities and even whites. If Asian Americans can make it on their own, pundits are asking, why can't poor blacks and whites on welfare? Even middle-class whites, who are experiencing economic difficulties because of plant closures in a deindustrializing America and the expansion of low-wage service employment, have been urged to emulate the Asian-American "model minority" and to work harder.[10]

Indeed, the story of the Asian-American triumph offers ideo-logical affirmation of the American Dream in an era anxiously wit-nessing the decline of the United States in the international economy (due to its trade imbalance and its transformation from a creditor to a debtor nation), the emergence of a new black underclass (the per-centage of black female–headed families having almost doubled from 22 percent in 1960 to 40 percent in 1980), and a collapsing white middle class (the percentage of households earning a "middle-class" income falling from 28.7 percent in 1967 to 23.2 percent in 1983). Intellectually, it has been used to explain "losing ground" — why the situation of the poor has deteriorated during the last two decades of expanded government social services. According to this view, ad-vanced by pundits like Charles Murray, the interventionist federal state, operating on the "misguided wisdom" of the 1960s, made matters worse: it created a web of welfare dependency. But this analysis has overlooked the structural problems in society and our economy, and it has led to easy cultural explanations and quick-fix prescriptions. Our difficulties, we are sternly told, stem from our waywardness: Americans have strayed from the Puritan "errand into the wilderness." They have abandoned the old American "habits of the heart." Praise for Asian-American success is America's most re-cent jeremiad — a renewed commitment to make America number one again and a call for a rededication to the bedrock values of hard work, thrift, and industry. Like many congratulations, this one may veil a spirit of competition, even jealousy.[11]

Significantly, Asian-American "success" has been accompanied by the rise of a new wave of anti-Asian sentiment. On college campuses, racial slurs have surfaced in conversations on the quad: "Look out for the Asian Invasion." "M.I.T. means Made in Taiwan." "U.C.L.A. stands for University of Caucasians Living among Asians." Nasty anti-Asian graffiti have suddenly appeared on the walls of college dormitories and in the elevators of classroom buildings: "Chink, chink, cheating chink!" "Stop the Yellow Hordes." "Stop the Chinese before they flunk you out." Ugly racial incidents have broken out on college campuses. At the University of Connecticut, for example, eight Asian-American students experienced a nightmare of abuse in 1987. Four couples had boarded a college bus to attend a dance. "The dance was a formal and so we were wearing gowns," said Marta Ho, recalling the horrible evening with tears. "The bus was packed, and there was a rowdy bunch of white guys in the back of the bus. Suddenly I felt this warm sticky stuff on my hair. They were spitting on us! My friend was sitting sidewise and got hit on her face and she started screaming. Our boy friends turned around, and one of the white guys, a football player, shouted: 'You want to make something out of this, you Oriental faggots!' "[12]

Asian-American students at the University of Connecticut and other colleges are angry, arguing that there should be no place for racism on campus and that they have as much right as anyone else to be in the university. Many of them are children of recent immigrants who had been college-educated professionals in Asia. They see how their parents had to become greengrocers, restaurant operators, and storekeepers in America, and they want to have greater career choices for themselves. Hopeful a college education can help them overcome racial obstacles, they realize the need to be serious about their studies. But white college students complain: "Asian students are nerds." This very stereotype betrays nervousness — fears that Asian-American students are raising class grade curves. White parents, especially alumni, express concern about how Asian-American students are taking away "their" slots — admission places that should have gone to their children. "Legacy" admission slots reserved for children of alumni have come to function as a kind of invisible affirmative-action program for whites. A college education has always represented a valuable economic resource, credentialing individuals for high income and status employment, and the university has recently become a contested terrain of competition between whites and Asians. In paneled offices, university administrators meet to discuss the "problem" of Asian-American "over-representation" in enrollments.

Paralleling the complaint about the rising numbers of Asian-American students in the university is a growing worry that there are also "too many" immigrants coming from Asia. Recent efforts to "reform" the 1965 Immigration Act seem reminiscent of the nativism prevalent in the 1880s and the 1920s. Senator Alan K. Simpson of Wyoming, for example, noted how the great majority of the new immigrants were from Latin America and Asia, and how "a substantial portion" of them did not "integrate fully" into American society. "If language and cultural separatism rise above a certain level," he warned, "the unity and political stability of the Nation will — in time — be seriously eroded. Pluralism within a united American nation has been our greatest strength. The unity comes from a common language and a core public culture of certain shared values, beliefs, and customs, which make us distinctly 'Americans.' " In the view of many supporters of immigration reform, the post-1965 immigration from Asia and Latin America threatens the traditional unity and identity of the American people. "The immigration from the turn of the century was largely a continuation of immigration from previous years in that the European stock of Americans was being maintained," explained Steve Rosen, a member of an organization lobbying for changes in the current law. "Now, we are having a large influx of third-world people, which could be potentially disruptive of our whole Judeo-Christian heritage." Significantly, in March 1988, the Senate passed a bill that would limit the entry of family members and that would provide 55,000 new visas to be awarded to "independent immigrants" on the basis of education, work experience, occupations, and "English language skills."[13]

Political concerns usually have cultural representations. The entertainment media have begun marketing Asian stereotypes again: where Hollywood had earlier portrayed Asians as Charlie Chan displaying his wit and wisdom in his fortune cookie Confucian quotes and as the evil Fu Manchu threatening white women, the film industry has recently been presenting images of comic Asians (in *Sixteen Candles*) and criminal Asian aliens (in *Year of the Dragon*). Hollywood has entered the realm of foreign affairs. *The Deer Hunter* explained why the United States lost the war in Vietnam. In this story, young American men are sent to fight in Vietnam, but they are not psychologically prepared for the utter cruelty of physically disfigured Viet Cong clad in black pajamas. Shocked and disoriented, they collapse morally into a world of corruption, drugs, gambling, and Russian roulette. There seems to be something sinister in Asia and the people there that is beyond the capability of civilized Americans to comprehend. Upset after seeing this movie, refugee Thu-Thuy Truong exclaimed: "We didn't play Russian roulette games in Saigon! The whole thing was made up." Similarly *Apocalypse Now* portrayed lost innocence: Americans enter the heart of darkness in Vietnam and become possessed by madness (in the persona played by Marlon Brando) but are saved in the end by their own technology and violence (represented by Martin Sheen). Finally, in movies celebrating the exploits of Rambo, Hollywood has allowed Americans to win in fantasy the Vietnam War they had lost in reality. "Do we get to win this time?" snarls Rambo, our modern Natty Bumppo, a hero of limited conversation and immense patriotic rage.[14]

Meanwhile, anti-Asian feelings and misunderstandings have been exploding violently in communities across the country, from Philadelphia, Boston, and New York to Denver and Galveston, Seattle, Portland, Monterey, and San Francisco. In Jersey City, the home of 15,000 Asian Indians, a hate letter published in a local newspaper warned: "We will go to any extreme to get Indians to move out of Jersey City. If I'm walking down the street and I see a Hindu and the setting is right, I will just hit him or her. We plan some of our more extreme attacks such as breaking windows, breaking car windows and crashing family parties. We use the phone book and look up the name Patel. Have you seen how many there are?" The letter was reportedly written by the "Dotbusters," a cruel reference to the *bindi* some Indian women wear as a sign of sanctity. Actual attacks have taken place, ranging from verbal harassments and egg throwing to serious beatings. Outside a Hoboken restaurant on September 27, 1987, a gang of youths chanting "Hindu, Hindu" beat Navroz Mody to death. A grand jury has indicted four teenagers for the murder.[15]

Five years earlier a similarly brutal incident occurred in Detroit. There, in June, Vincent Chin, a young Chinese American, and two friends went to a bar in the late afternoon to celebrate his upcoming wedding. Two white autoworkers, Ronald Ebens and Michael Nitz, called Chin a "Jap" and cursed: "It's because of you motherfuckers that we're out of work." A fistfight broke out, and Chin then quickly left the bar. But Ebens and Nitz took out a baseball bat from the trunk of their car and chased Chin through the streets. They finally cornered him in front of a McDonald's restaurant. Nitz held Chin while Ebens swung the bat across the victim's shins and then bludgeoned Chin to death by shattering his skull. Allowed to plead guilty to manslaughter, Ebens and Nitz were sentenced to three years' probation and fined $3,780 each. But they have not spent a single night in jail for their bloody deed. "Three thousand dollars can't even buy a good used car these days," snapped a Chinese American, "and this was the price of a life." "What kind of law is this? What kind of justice?" cried Mrs. Lily Chin, the slain man's mother. "This happened because my son is Chinese. If two Chinese killed a white person, they must go to jail, maybe for their whole lives. . . . Something is wrong with this country."[16]

Vincent Chin was the only son of Lily and Hing Chin. Lily's great-grandfather had been an immigrant railroad laborer in the nineteenth century, and she remembers his tales about racial persecution. Hing Chin had arrived in the United States in 1922 at the age of seventeen and had served in the U.S. Army during World War II. After the war, both Lily and Hing Chin worked in a laundry, and Mrs. Chin became an assembly-plant worker after her husband died of a kidney disease in 1980. Their son had high hopes for a career. "When he was a child," Lily Chin recalled, "he wanted to be a writer. I said, 'Vincent, you can't make money at that.' Then he wanted to be a lawyer because he liked to talk. 'Ma, I want to be a lawyer.' 'Oh, you're Chinese, nobody'd believe you,' I said. Then he wanted to be a veterinarian. 'Oh, Vincent, you can't do that. You can't open up the animals, you're scared of blood.'" Vincent graduated from Oak Park High School and studied architecture at the Lawrence Institute of Technology. In the summer of 1982, he was working as a draftsman for Efficient Engineering when he was brutally murdered. "I don't understand how this could happen in America," Mrs. Chin cried out bitterly. "My husband fought for this country. We always paid our taxes and worked hard. Before I really loved America, but now this has made me very angry."[17]

The murder of Vincent Chin has aroused the anger and concern of Asian Americans across the country. They know he was killed because of his racial membership: Ebens and Nitz perceived Chin as a "stranger," a foreigner, for he did not look like an American. But why was Chin viewed as an alien? Asian Americans blame the educational system for not including their history in the curricula and for not teaching about U.S. society in all of its racial and cultural diversity. Why are the courses and books on American history so Eurocentric? they have asked teachers and scholars accusingly.

Asian Americans and supporters of justice for Vincent Chin have charged that the corporate executives of the auto industry must also be held accountable for Chin's death: the auto manufacturers should have been designing and building fuel-efficient cars twenty years ago, and now they are blaming Japan for Detroit's massive unemployment. "Unemployment is not caused by foreign competition," argued Newton Kamakane of UAW Local 1364 in Fremont, California. "It's the result of mistakes and poor planning of the multinational corporations — and General Motors is one of the biggest of them." Unfortunately, unemployment might not have been entirely the consequence of "mistakes and poor planning." American auto companies have been deliberately locating much of their production outside of the United States. They have assembly plants in places like Ciudad Juarez, Mexico, which has come to be called "Little Detroit." They have even invested in the Japanese auto companies themselves: General Motors owns 34 percent of Isuzu (which builds the Buick Opel), Ford 25 percent of Mazda (which makes transmissions for the Escort), and Chrysler 15 percent of Mitsubishi (which produces the Colt and Charger). In their television commercials and their promotional campaigns to "buy American," the automakers have contributed to the anti-Japan hysteria pervasive among American workers and to the proliferation of bumper stickers that scream "Unemployment — Made in Japan" and "Toyota-Datsun-Honda-and-Pearl Harbor."[18]

In their protests, Asian Americans recount a long, unhappy history: "The killing of Vincent Chin happened in 1982, not 1882—the year of the Chinese Exclusion Act!" They see a parallel between then and now. "What disturbs me," explained George Wong of the Asian American Federation of Union Membership, "is that the two men who brutally clubbed Vincent Chin to death in Detroit in 1982 were thinking the same thoughts as the lynch mob in San Francisco Chinatown one hundred years ago: 'Kill the foreigners to save our jobs! The Chinese must go!' When corporate heads tell frustrated workers that foreign imports are taking their jobs, then they are acting like an agitator of a lynch mob."[19]

The murder of Vincent Chin has underscored the need for Asian Americans to break silences. "For a long time we have not fought back," declared George Suey of San Francisco. "But this time we will

stand up and fight for our rights." Indeed all Asian Americans—
Chinese, Japanese, Koreans, Filipinos, Asian Indians, and Southeast
Asians — are standing up this time. They realize what happened to
Vincent Chin could happen to them — to anyone with Asian features.
"My blood boiled when I first learned that Vincent Chin was delib-
erately attacked and murdered as an act of racial hatred," growled
Harold Fong of the Chinese-American Citizens Alliance. "When the
word 'Jap' gets painted on a door or a man is murdered," declared
Congressman Norman Mineta of San Jose, "we ought to let the whole
world know." Though they represent diverse communities, Asian
Americans have come together and joined their voices in protest. Dr.
Marisa Chuang of the newly formed American Citizens for Justice
stated: "This is an historical moment for Asian Americans because
for the first time we are all united."[20]

Roots

To confront the current problems of racism, Asian Americans know
they must remember the past and break its silence. This need was
felt deeply by Japanese Americans during the hearings before the
commission reviewing the issue of redress and reparations for Japanese Americans interned during World War II. Memories of the
internment nightmare have haunted the older generation like ghosts.
But the former prisoners have been unable to exorcise them by speaking out and ventilating their anger.

> *When we were children,*
> *you spoke Japanese*
> *in lowered voices*
> *between yourselves.*
>
> *Once you uttered secrets*
> *which we should not know,*
> *were not to be heard by us.*
> *When you spoke*
> *of some dark secret*
> *you would admonish us,*
> *"Don't tell it to anyone else."*
> *It was a suffocated vow of silence.*[21]

"Stigmatized," the ex-internees have been carrying the "burden
of shame" for over forty painful years. "They felt like a rape victim,"

explained Congressman Norman Mineta, a former internee of the Heart Mountain internment camp. "They were accused of being disloyal. They were the victims but they were on trial and they did not want to talk about it." But Sansei, or third-generation Japanese Americans, want their elders to tell their story. Warren Furutani, for example, told the commissioners that young people like himself had been asking their parents to tell them about the concentration camps and to join them in pilgrimages to the internment camp at Manzanar. "Why? Why!" their parents would reply defensively. "Why would you want to know about it? It's not important, we don't need to talk about it." But, Furutani continued, they need to tell the world what happened during those years of infamy.[22]

Suddenly, during the commission hearings, scores of Issei and Nisei came forward and told their stories. "For over thirty-five years I have been the stereotype Japanese American," Alice Tanabe Nehira told the commission. "I've kept quiet, hoping in due time we will be justly compensated and recognized for our years of patient effort. By my passive attitude, I can reflect on my past years to conclude that it doesn't pay to remain silent." The act of speaking out has enabled the Japanese-American community to unburden itself of years of anger and anguish. Sometimes their testimonies before the commission were long and the chair urged them to conclude. But they insisted the time was theirs. "Mr. Commissioner," protested poet Janice Miri-kitani,

> So when you tell me my time is
> up I tell you this.
> Pride has kept my lips
> pinned by nails,
> my rage coffined.
> But I exhume my past
> to claim this time.[23]

The former internees finally had spoken, and their voices compelled the nation to redress the injustice of internment. In August 1988, Congress passed a bill giving an apology and a payment of $20,000 to each of the survivors of the internment camps. When President Ronald Reagan signed the bill into law, he admitted that the United States had committed "a grave wrong," for during World War II, Japanese Americans had remained "utterly loyal" to this country. "Indeed, scores of Japanese Americans volunteered for our Armed Forces — many stepping forward in the internment camps themselves. The 442nd Regimental Combat Team, made up entirely of Japanese Americans, served with immense distinction to defend this nation, their nation. Yet, back at home, the soldiers' families were being denied the very freedom for which so many of the soldiers themselves were laying down their lives." Then the president recalled an incident that happened forty-three years ago. At a ceremony to award the Distinguished Service Cross to Kazuo Masuda, who had been killed in action and whose family had been interned, a young actor paid tribute to the slain Nisei soldier. "The name of that young actor," remarked the president, who had been having trouble saying the Japanese names, " — I hope I pronounce this right — was Ronald Reagan." The time had come, the president acknowledged, to end "a sad chapter in American history."[24]

Asian Americans have begun to claim their time not only before the commission on redress and reparations but elsewhere as well— in the novels of Maxine Hong Kingston and Milton Murayama, the plays of Frank Chin and Philip Gotanda, the scholarly writings of Sucheng Chan and Elaine Kim, the films of Steve Okazaki and Wayne Wang, and the music of Hiroshima and Fred Houn. Others, too, have been breaking silences. Seventy-five-year-old Tomo Shoji, for example, had led a private life, but in 1981 she enrolled in an acting course because she wanted to try something frivolous and to take her mind off her husband's illness. In the beginning, Tomo was hesitant, awkward on the stage. "Be yourself," her teacher urged. Then suddenly she felt something surge through her, springing from deep within, and she began to tell funny and also sad stories about her life. Now Tomo tours the West Coast, a wonderful wordsmith giving one-woman shows to packed audiences of young Asian Americans. "Have we really told our children all we have gone through?" she asks. Telling one of her stories, Tomo recounts: "My parents came from Japan and I was born in a lumber camp. One day, at school, my class was going on a day trip to a show, and I was pulled aside and told I would have to stay behind. All the white kids went." Tomo shares stories about her husband: "When I first met him, I thought, 'wow.' Oh, he was so macho! And he wanted his wife to be a good submissive wife. But then he married me." Theirs had been at times a stormy marriage. "Culturally we were different because he was Issei and I was American, and we used to argue a lot. Well, one day in 1942 right after World War II had started he came home and told me we had to go to an internment camp. 'I'm not going to camp because I'm an American citizen,' I said to him. 'You have to go to camp, but not me.' Well, you know what, that was one time my husband was right!" Tomo remembers the camp: "We were housed in barracks, and we had no privacy. My husband and I had to share a room with another couple. So we hanged a blanket in the middle of the room as a partition. But you could hear everything from the other side. Well, one night, while we were in bed, my husband and I got into an argument, and I dumped him out of the bed. The other couple thought we were making violent love." As she stands on the stage and talks stories excitedly, Tomo cannot be contained: "We got such good, fantastic stories to tell. All our stories are different."[25]

Today, young Asian Americans want to listen to these stories—to shatter images of themselves and their ancestors as "strangers" and to understand who they are as Asian Americans. "What don't you know?" their elders ask. Their question seems to have a peculiar frame: it points to the blank areas of collective memory. And the young people reply that they want "to figure out how the invisible world the emigrants built around [their] childhoods fit in solid America." They want to know more about their "no name" Asian ancestors. They want to decipher the signs of the Asian presence here and there across the landscape of America — railroad tracks over high mountains, fields of cane virtually carpeting entire islands, and verdant agricultural lands.

> *Deserts to farmlands*
> *Japanese-American*
> *Page in history.*[26]

They want to know what is their history and "what is the movies." They want to trace the origins of terms applied to them. "Why are we called 'Oriental'?" they question, resenting the appellation that has identified Asians as exotic, mysterious, strange, and foreign. "The word 'orient' simply means 'east.' So why are Europeans 'West' and why are Asians 'East'? Why did empire-minded Englishmen in the sixteenth century determine that Asia was 'east' of London? Who decided what names would be given to the different regions and peoples of the world? Why does 'American' usually mean 'white'?" Weary of Eurocentric history, young Asian Americans want their Asian ancestral lives in America chronicled, "given the name of a place." They have earned the right to belong to specific places like Washington, California, Hawaii, Puunene, Promontory Point, North Adams, Manzanar, Doyers Street. "And today, after 125 years of our life here," one of them insists, "I do not want just a home that time allowed me to have." Seeking to lay claim to America, they realize they can no longer be indifferent to what happened in history, no longer embarrassed by the hardships and humiliations experienced by their grandparents and parents.

> My heart, once bent and cracked, once
> ashamed of your China ways.
> Ma, hear me now, tell me your story
> again and again.[27]

As they listen to the stories and become members of a "community of memory," they are recovering roots deep within this country and the homelands of their ancestors. Sometimes the journey leads them to discover rich and interesting things about themselves. Alfred Wong, for example, had been told repeatedly for years by his father: "Remember your Chinese name. Remember your village in Toishan. Remember you are Chinese. Remember all this and you will have a home." One reason why it was so important for the Chinese immigrants to remember was that they never felt sure of their status in America. "Unlike German and Scottish immigrants, the Chinese immigrants never felt comfortable here," Wong explained. "So they had a special need to know there was a place, a home for them somewhere."[28]

But Wong had a particular reason to remember. His father had married by mutual agreement two women on the same day in China and had come to America as a merchant in the 1920s. Later he brought over one of his wives. But she had to enter as a "paper wife," for he had given the immigration authorities the name of the wife he had left behind. Born here in 1938, Wong grew up knowing about his father's other wife and the other half of the family in China; his parents constantly talked about them and regularly sent money home to Quangdong. For years the "family plan" had been for him to visit China someday. In 1984 he traveled to his father's homeland, and there in the family home — the very house his father had left decades earlier — Alfred Wong was welcomed by his *Chung Gwok Mama* ("China Mama"). "You look just like I had imagined you would look," she remarked. On the walls of the house, he saw hundreds of photographs — of himself as well as sisters, nieces, nephews, and his own daughter — that had been placed there over the years. He suddenly realized how much he had always belonged there, and he felt a warm connectedness. "It's like you were told there was this box and there was a beautiful diamond in it," Wong said. "But for years and years you couldn't open the box. Then finally you got a chance to open the box and it was as wonderful as you had imagined it would be."[29]

Mine is a different yet similar story. My father, Toshio Takaki, died in 1945, when I was only five years old; my mother married Koon Keu Young about a year later, and I grew up knowing very little about my father. Many years later, in 1968, after my parents had moved to Los Angeles, my mother passed away and I had to clear out her room after the funeral. In one of her dresser drawers, I found an old photograph of my father as a teenager: it was his immigration photograph. I noticed some Japanese writing on the back. Later a friend translated: "This is Toshio Takaki, registered as an emigrant in Mifune, Kumamoto Prefecture, 1918." I wondered how young Toshio managed to come to the United States. Why did he go to Hawaii? Did he go alone? What dreams burned within the young boy? But a huge silence stood before me, and I could only speculate that he must have come alone and entered as a student, since the 1908 Gentlemen's Agreement had prohibited the immigration of Japanese laborers. In Hawaii, he met and married my mother, Catherine Okawa, a Nisei. I had no Takaki relatives in Hawaii, I thought.

Ten years later, while on a sabbatical in Hawaii, I was "talking story" with my uncle Richard Okawa. I was telling him about the book I was then writing — *Iron Cages,* a study of race and culture in America. Suddenly his eyes lit up as he exclaimed: "Hey, why you no go write a book about us, huh? About the Japanese in Hawaii. After all, your grandparents came here as plantation workers and your mother and all your aunts and uncles were born on the plantation." Smiling, I replied: "Why not?" I went on to write a history of the plantation laborers. The book was published in 1983, and I was featured on television news and educational programs in Hawaii. One of the programs was aired in January 1985; a plantation laborer on the Puunene Plantation, Maui, was watching the discussion on television when he exclaimed to his wife: "Hey, that's my cousin, Ronald!" "No joke with me," she said, and he replied: "No, for real, for real."

A few months later, in July, I happened to visit Maui to give a lecture on the plantation experience. While standing in the auditorium shortly before my presentation, I noticed two Japanese men approaching me. One of them draped a red carnation lei around my shoulders and smiled: "You remember me, don't you?" I had never seen this man before and was confused. Then he said again, "You remember me?" After he asked for the third time, he pulled a family photograph from a plastic shopping bag. I saw among the people in the picture my father as a young man, and burst out excitedly: "Oh, you're a Takaki!" He replied: "I'm your cousin, Minoru. I saw you on television last January and when I found out you were going to come here I wanted to see you again. You were five years old when I last saw you. I was in the army on my way to Japan and I came by your house in Palolo Valley. But I guess you don't remember. I've been wondering what happened to you for forty years." Our families had lost contact with each other because of the war, the isolation of the plantation located on another island, my father's death, and my mother's remarriage. Minoru introduced me to his brother Susumu and his son, Leighton, who works on the Puunene Plantation and represents the fourth generation of Takaki plantation workers. Afterward they took me to the Puunene Plantation, showing me McGerrow Camp, where my branch of the Takaki family had lived, and filling me with stories about the old days. "You also have two cousins, Jeanette and Lillian in Honolulu," Minoru said, "and a big Takaki family in Japan."

A year later I visited my Takaki family in Japan. On the day I arrived, my cousin Nobuo showed me a box of old photographs that had been kept for decades in an upstairs closet. "We don't know who this baby is," he said, pointing to a picture of a baby boy. "That's me!" I exclaimed in disbelief. The box contained many photographs of my father, mother, sister, and me. My father had been sending pictures to the family in Kumamoto. I felt a part of me had been there all along and I had in a sense come home. Nobuo's wife, Keiko, told me that I was *Kumamoto kenjin* — "one of the people of Kumamoto." During my visit, I was taken to the farm where my father was born. We drove up a narrow winding road past waterfalls and streams, tea farms, and rice paddies, to a village nestled high in the mountains. The scene reminded me of old Zen paintings of Japanese landscapes and evoked memories of my mother telling me the story of Momotaro. Toshino Watanabe, an old woman in her eighties, gave me a family portrait that her sister had sent in 1919: there they were in fading sepia — my uncle Teizo, grandfather Santaro, aunt Yukino, cousin Tsutako, uncle Nobuyoshi, and father, Toshio, just fourteen years old — in McGerrow Camp on the Puunene Plantation.

The stories of Alfred Wong and myself branch from the larger history of Asian Americans and America itself — from William Hooper and Aaron Palmer, westward expansion, the economic development of California and Hawaii, the Chinese Exclusion Act, the Gentlemen's Agreement. The history of America is essentially the story of immigrants, and many of them, coming from a "different shore" than their European brethren, had sailed east to this new world. After she had traveled across the vast Pacific Ocean and settled here, a woman captured the vision of the immigrants from Asia in haiku's seventeen syllables:

> *All the dreams of youth*
> *Shipped in emigration boats*
> *To reach this far shore.*

In America, Asian immigrants and their offspring have been actors in history — the first Chinese working on the plantations of Hawaii and in the gold fields of California, the early Japanese immigrants transforming the brown San Joaquin Valley into verdant farmlands, the Korean immigrants struggling to free their homeland from Japanese colonialism, the Filipino farm workers and busboys seeking the America in their hearts, the Asian-Indian immigrants picking fruit and erecting Sikh temples in the West, the American-born Asians like Jean Park and Jade Snow Wong and Monica Sone trying to find an identity for themselves as Asian Americans, the second-wave Asian immigrants bringing their skills and creating new communities as well as revitalizing old communities with culture and enterprise, and the refugees from the war-torn countries of Southeast Asia trying to put their shattered lives together and becoming our newest Asian Americans. Their dreams and hopes unfurled here before the wind, all of them — from the first Chinese miners sailing through the Golden Gate to the last Vietnamese boat people flying into Los Angeles International Airport — have been making history in America. And they have been telling us about it all along.[30]

13

One-Tenth of the Nation

Asian Americans in the Twenty-First Century

As I write this last chapter for the new edition, I realize that I have been teaching Asian-American history at Berkeley for twenty-five years. The enrollments in my classes have ranged from 10 to 350 students, and altogether I have taught more than 10,000 students. They have been white, black, Chicano, and Native American, but mostly Asian American. I have especially enjoyed teaching research seminars, where students have been encouraged to recover their parents' and grandparents' stories about coming from "a different shore" and creating new lives in America. In the retelling of these memories, many of these students have become my teachers. Challenging the ethnocentrism of E. D. Hirsch and Arthur Schlesinger, Jr., our research has taught us that "American" should not mean just white or European in origin. Transforming the understanding of our nation's past into a larger memory, our re-visioned history has enabled us to claim America for our communities. But, I wonder, what will the twenty-first century hold for the generation of Asian-American students I have taught?

A statistical profile of Asian Americans can offer some clues. In this last decade of the twentieth century, they continue to increase in numbers. In 1980, there were 3,500,000 Asian Americans; ten years later, they totaled 7,274,000 — a 108-percent increase, compared to 6 percent for whites, 13 percent for blacks, and 53 percent for Hispanics. In 1990, the Chinese represented the largest subgroup, with 23 percent, followed by Filipinos at 19 percent, the Japanese at 12 percent, Asian Indians at 11 percent, Koreans at 11 percent, the Vietnamese at 8 percent, Laotians at 2 percent, Cambodians at 2 percent, and the Thai and Hmong each at 1 percent. Asian Americans varied in terms of education: 58 percent of the Asian Indians were college graduates, 41 percent of the Chinese, 39 percent of the Filipinos, 34 percent of the Koreans, and 34 percent of the Japanese, but only 17 percent of the Vietnamese, 6 percent of the Cambodians, 5 percent of the Laotians, and 5 percent of the Hmong. Poverty rates ranged from 4 percent for the Japanese and 11 percent for the Chinese to 24 percent for the Vietnamese, 42 percent for Cambodians, and 62 percent for the Hmong, above the black poverty rate of 26 percent. Numbering 10 million in 1997, Asian Americans are projected to become 40 million by 2050 — 10 percent of the total U.S. population.[1]

But statistics do not stir insightful or imaginative thinking about what will happen to Asian Americans in the coming century. After all, numbers cannot capture and convey dynamic movements and changes, or extravagant as well as dashed dreams, or thoughts and feelings in ferment. More helpful are reflections on important events and developments of the 1990s. To end this study, we examine three of them — the 1992 Los Angeles riot, the linking of the Asian-American admissions controversy to the attack on affirmative action, and the increasingly complex identities among Asian Americans.

Redefining Race in America: The 1992 Los Angeles Riot

"Sa-i-gu," "April twenty-nine," is how Korean Americans painfully remember the violence and destruction of the 1992 Los Angeles riot. On that day, a California jury had announced its not-guilty verdict in the trial of four white police officers charged with beating Rodney King, a black man. The videotaped images of the policemen brutally subduing King had been beamed around the world. The jury's decision ignited an explosion of fury and violence in South Central Los Angeles and nearby Koreatown.

"Once again, young blacks are taking to the street to express their outrage at perceived injustice," *Newsweek* reported, "and once again, whites are fearful that The Fire Next Time will consume them." But this conflict was different from the 1965 Watts riot: it was not just between blacks and whites.[2]

The fire this time consumed the stores and dreams of Korean Americans. "April 29, 1992, the night the store burned down," merchant Young Soon Han recalled, "I didn't even know what was happening. I hadn't been paying much attention to the Rodney King verdict. I didn't think the issue was so serious. But some of the people from the neighborhood came into the store and said, 'Mrs. Han, you'd better run now! People are coming this way, and you will get hurt.' I said, 'Why? I haven't done anything wrong.' But they convinced me I was in danger, so I went home. That night, I kept in contact with the woman who lived in a house behind our store. She finally told me that the store had been burned to the ground."[3] Another Korean shopkeeper had been warned to stay away from her business. "We had two full-time black employees," she said. "And sometimes kids in the neighborhood worked for us too. They treated us like family." But, when the riot began, "our employees called and said people were looting. I asked if I should come. They said if you come now you will be beaten to death. We will do what we can to protect your store."[4]

The governor declared a state of emergency and ordered 6,000 National Guard troops into the city to restore order. When the unrest finally came to an end on May 1, entire areas of Los Angeles resembled a bombed-out city. The human toll was high: 58 deaths, 2,400 injuries, and 12,000 arrests. More than 3,000 businesses had been damaged by fire, vandalism, or looting, and losses totalled $800 million. Most of the businesses damaged or destroyed were Korean owned. In Koreatown, every building, row after row and block after block, had been reduced to rubble on both sides of the street.[5]

Tensions between blacks and Korean Americans had been volatile before the riot. Stereotypes influenced their perceptions of each other. In their homeland, Korean immigrants had seen Hollywood films and television news reports picturing blacks as poor, criminally inclined, welfare dependent, lazy, and violent. In the inner city, Korean encounters with underclass blacks seemed to confirm these negative depictions. On the other hand, many blacks saw Koreans as exploitative shopkeepers who would not hire blacks, and they considered the newcomers strange, rude, condescending, and unfriendly. There were misunderstandings on both sides: Koreans did not recognize the economic and social problems of blacks who were isolated in the inner cities, while blacks did not realize that the Korean-owned businesses depended on family workers and that Korean culture restricted friendliness to family and close friends.

Within this context of mutual cultural ignorance, African-American resentment had turned to rage in the spring of 1991, when a fifteen-year-old black girl named Latasha Harlins was shot and killed by Korean shopkeeper Soon Ja Du after a scuffle over a bottle of juice. Black anger seethed when Du was placed on probation rather than being sent to jail. The memory of Harlins' death was still vivid when the King verdict came down a year later. "We're mad for a whole lot of reasons," declared a young black man. "First that 15-year-old was killed and they got away with it. Then they beat Rodney King like a dog and the jury sets them free. The black people don't get no justice, nowhere, no time."[6]

After the riot, blacks and Koreans offered explanations for the days of fury and destruction. A black woman said that she understood why rioters had burned Korean stores: "Now the Koreans run the liquor store and don't let no black people work there, and they treat black people like their dogs. I stopped my grandchildren from going to the little Korean store up on the corner. They was talking to them like they was bad." A black businessman described the black rage: "I saw angry people. Furious people. I also saw people who were going to take advantage of the situation. . . . They were hitting Korean businesses. They were looking at people who had abused them in the past."[7] A Korean-American shopkeeper reflected on the looting by blacks: "I don't think Koreans are entirely blameless. In my opinion, those doing business in the black community don't have the proper understanding to do business there. They can't speak the language or understand black customs. So even if they don't mean to be that way, Korean merchants are perceived as being unfriendly. The way Koreans interact with each other doesn't work in America. On the other hand, the blacks ask us Koreans, 'Why don't you respect us?' But their young kids steal, and the older kids too. How can we respect them?"[8]

A black minister called for cross-cultural understanding between African Americans and Korean Americans. "If we could appreciate and affirm each other's histories," he explained, "there wouldn't be the generalizations and stigmatizations, and we would see that we have more in common."[9]

Economically, however, Koreans and blacks had little in common. For blacks in South Central, work had "disappeared."[10] In the 1970s, as scholar William Julius Wilson noted, corporations across America had relocated production to the suburbs and low-wage countries. In South Central Los Angeles, companies like General Motors, Goodyear, and Firestone closed plants that had provided jobs for blacks. In the wake of this deindustrialization came devastating poverty, increased welfare dependency, soaring high school dropout rates, and also anger.

"A riot," observed Martin Luther King, Jr., "is the language of the unheard."[11] The 1992 L.A. uprising expressed desperation and frustration. The poverty rate in South Central Los Angeles in 1990 was 30 percent — higher than the 27 percent during the 1965 Watts riot. "I don't think it's very difficult to figure out why the riots happened so intensely," said Ramona Ripston, executive director of the American Civil Liberties Union of Southern California. "As far as I can see, we have a lot of young people, 15, 16 years old, no programs to keep them in school, no jobs, no health care, no stake in society. It's a form of civil war."[12] A black gang member explained: "It was not a riot — it was class struggle that took place in south central. . . . It ain't just about Rodney King. He was the lighter and it blew up."[13] When the civil war and class struggle exploded, the Korean merchants happened to be there.

"At first I didn't notice," a Korean shopkeeper said, "but I slowly realized the looters were very poor. This riot happened because of the gap between rich and poor."[14] Reflecting on her losses, another Korean also understood the class-divided context for the rampage. "When I think about it," she commented, "I am most angry at white people. If the government had watched over the blacks better, this would not have happened to us."[15]

The destruction left many Korean Americans stunned, dazed. "It has been twenty years since Koreans came here," an immigrant woman reflected sadly. "Everything we worked for is now in flames. It burned in one day." As they stared in shock at the devastation, they grieved. "We Koreans worked hard to realize our dreams," one of them said. "Now nothing is left but ashes."[16]

Beyond the economic loss, there was the psychological pain. "Right after the riots," one Korean immigrant said, "we were anxious to solve the problems however we could. We wanted to grab onto something or somebody to survive. We were in shock. The main problem now is the aftershock syndrome. When you receive a big shock, you may not feel it right away because the shock is too great. The victims are wondering day in day out, where are we going to go from here? They have a lot of problems — depression, stress, loss of memory. I know because I am a typical case right now. I cannot remember anything most of the time. It's getting worse and worse. Some people have committed suicide or died of stress. I don't see any bright future at this moment. It seems hopeless now. I feel unworthy, desperate, miserable."[17]

Similarly, Susan Lee was unable to free herself from the riot's traumatic memories. During the days of fury and fire, she recalled, Koreatown "looked like it went to war." Smoke was rising from buildings, and Korean merchants were frantically trying to "salvage any remainings of their dreams." What she saw resembled a surrealistic scene from hell. "I couldn't believe what I was seeing, something from the movies. I felt like I was on the movie screen walking through a war zone and people in the movie theater were watching this." But she was not watching a Hollywood fantasy. "I honestly wasn't prepared for what I was about to see, in front of me was the remaining rubbles of the stores that I had poured my money, sweat, and time into. Everything that I had worked so hard to build was crumbled in front of me. I had spent my whole life building a dream that was destroyed in one night. . . . When my stores were destroyed, a part of me was destroyed. I died, not physically but emotionally."[18]

The L.A. riot of 1992 offered an eye-opening lesson: beyond and more important than racial and cultural differences was the perplexing problem of the deteriorating inner-city economy. For Koreans and blacks, the prospects of working it out and getting along in the twenty-first century are not promising. Korean employment of black youth will not generate enough jobs for blacks, and the jobs will be low paying. "Even if most of the Korean merchants hire one or two employees," explained scholar Edward Chang, "it's not going to make much of an economic impact in South Central L.A."[19] The executive director of the Asian Pacific American Legal Center, Stewart Kwoh, direly predicted that "the economic polarization between the 'haves' and 'have-nots'" would be "the main ingredient for future calamities."[20]

But fierce visions and thoughtful voices have emerged within the community to confront the racial fault lines of Los Angeles. "Many of us in the second generation," declared community leader Angela Oh on the fifth anniversary of Sa-i-gu, "believe there are a new set of progressive principles which must be adopted in our efforts to go forward as Korean Americans with a new vision. Those principles emphasize concepts of inclusiveness rather than exclusiveness, compassion rather than criticism, and a constant push toward social change for justice, not just for Korean Americans but for all people."[21] Out of the riot's ashes, there has arisen a spirit of refusal to allow grim conditions and unsolicited circumstances to rule the relations between blacks and Koreans in the twenty-first century.

A "Chain Reaction" of Issues:
From Asian-American Admissions to Affirmative Action

In 1984, while examining fall admissions data for the University of California at Berkeley, Professor Ling-chi Wang of Asian-American

Studies was surprised and disturbed to discover that the number of newly enrolled Asian Americans had declined precipitously by 21 percent — from 1,303 in 1983 to 1,031 a year later. Meanwhile, Asian Americans noticed parallel patterns at other universities, including Brown and Harvard. In 1986, a faculty committee at Stanford University reported that it had found "unaccountably lower admission rates for Asians than for whites."[22]

The University of California at Berkeley became the storm center of the Asian-American admissions controversy. Sharing his troubling statistics with Asian-American community leaders, Professor Wang helped organize the Asian American Task Force on University Admissions. In 1985, the task force released a report charging that the drop in Asian-American enrollment was due to a series of policy changes that discriminated against Asian-American applicants. The university administrators dismissed the charges. Three years later, however, evidence supporting the task force claims was produced at a subcommittee hearing of the State Assembly. Chancellor Michael Heyman apologized to the Asian-American community: "I wish we were more sensitive to the underlying concerns. While they did not manifest themselves as neatly as I now see them, Berkeley could have acted more openly and less defensively."[23]

By this time, however, the issue was no longer confined to the Berkeley campus. In December 1986, University of California President David Gardner addressed the controversy in an interview with the *San Diego Union*. He pointed out that Asian-American students were overrepresented in the university: Asians made up only 6 percent of the state's population, but they comprised more than 20 percent of UC's undergraduate enrollment. Gardner explained that efforts to redress earlier ethnic imbalances for blacks and Hispanics were being jeopardized by the new Asian-American presence. This change in the ethnic composition of the students was "causing unrest among some groups, including whites who [were] experiencing a decline in representation."[24]

Gardner's remarks offered, perhaps inadvertently, an initial link between two explosive issues — Asian-American admissions and affirmative action. During the 1980s, the University of California increased black and Latino enrollment by giving special consideration to "underrepresented minorities." This affirmative action was generating complaints that blacks were unfairly taking away admission slots from white students. Now Asian-American students were also being depicted as victims of "reverse discrimination."

The Asian-American admissions issue was quickly hijacked by conservatives for their own political purpose. "Beginning in late 1988," scholar Dana Takagi noted, "conservatives and neoconservatives suggested that discrimination against Asian Americans was symptomatic of a deeper problem at the university — affirmative action. According to conservatives, discrimination against Asians was the logical and inevitable outcome of preferences for 'other' minorities (that is, blacks and Chicanos/Latinos)." What had begun as a protest against discrimination in Asian-American admissions had turned into a "chain reaction" against affirmative action.[25]

In May 1988, during a signing ceremony for Asian Pacific American Heritage Week, President Ronald Reagan used the Asian-American admissions issue as an entering wedge against affirmative action. "I know," he stated, "there is growing concern that some universities may be discriminating against citizens of Asian and Pacific heritage, accepting a lower percentage of these applicants than get admitted from other groups, despite their academic qualifications. Well, to deny any individual access to higher education when it has been won on the basis of merit is a repudiation of everything America stands for."[26] Reagan had skillfully redefined the Asian-American admissions issue into a battle between "meritocracy" and affirmative action.

Six months later, Attorney William B. Reynolds, head of the Civil Rights Division of the Justice Department, announced that affirmative action should be blamed for discrimination against Asian-American students. "There is substantial statistical evidence," he argued, "that Asian American candidates face higher hurdles than academically less qualified candidates of other races, whether those candidates be minorities (black, Hispanic, Native American) or white." Reynolds identified affirmative action as the culprit. "The phenomenon of a 'ceiling' on Asian American admissions is the inevitable result of the 'floor' that has been built for a variety of other favored racial groups."[27]

The stage was set for a political assault on affirmative action itself. In the spring of 1995, Governor Pete Wilson of California used his opposition to affirmative action to launch his campaign for the Republican nomination for the presidency. His candidacy quickly faltered, but the conservative scrutiny of affirmative action opened the way for the Regents of the University of California to abolish affirmative action in admissions and employment. Their decision was made suddenly and unilaterally on July 20, while the faculty and stu-

dents were away from their campuses. This new policy was engi-
neered by Ward Connerly, a financial contributor to Governor Wilson's campaign fund and a Wilson appointee to the board of regents.

In his justification for dismantling affirmative action, Connerly
pointed out that "preferential treatment" for blacks constituted "reverse discrimination" against Asian Americans. "Ask the student
who works hard for four years to earn a 4.0 grade point average only
to be denied admission to Berkeley or UCLA in favor of someone
with a 3.0, merely because UC wants racial diversity, whether she
thinks we are being divisive," Connerly challenged. "Ask the poor
Vietnamese student who is turned away from Berkeley . . . , despite
his high grades, in favor of a wealthy underrepresented minority
whether he thinks we are being divisive. Ask him whether he is satisfied with the explanation that we are getting too many Asians at
those campuses."[28]

A year later, affirmative action exploded from a university issue
to the hottest political issue in California. Conservatives placed
Proposition 209 on the ballot. The proposed constitutional amendment would prohibit the state from discriminating against or granting "preferential treatment" to any individual or group on the basis
of race, sex, color, ethnicity, or national origin in employment and
education. This language left unstated its intended effect: the aboli-
tion of affirmative action. Connerly became the leader of the initiative's campaign, raising enormous amounts of money from the
Republican Party and wealthy conservatives.

For the Republican Party, the link between the Asian-American
admissions issue and Proposition 209 was strategically partisan.
"There's no doubt that Republicans can run on a platform of fairness
and use this issue to get the Asian vote," stated Jerry Reynolds of
the Center for Equal Opportunity, a conservative think tank. "Any
time racial preferences are used, there's a victim. And in California,
the victim often has an Asian face." Though Asian Americans represented only 1 percent of the electorate, he added, focusing on
the "Angry Yellow Male" inoculated the Republican Party's anti-
affirmative action crusade against charges of racism.[29] Significantly,
presidential candidate Bob Dole announced his endorsement of
Proposition 209 in Little Saigon, a Vietnamese-American community
in Orange County.

Connerly and his colleagues deliberately identified their proposition with Martin Luther King, Jr.'s "I have a dream" speech and his
famous phrase about judging people based on the content of their

character rather than the color of their skin. They also called Proposition 209 the "California Civil Rights Initiative." This deception confused many citizens into thinking that they were supporting King's dream and voting for civil rights. However, the initial strong support for the proposition began to slip as the election approached and as many voters began to realize that the initiative would abolish affirmative action. Alarmed, the Republican Party and Connerly unleashed an expensive television media blitz that saturated the electronic media the weekend before the election.

The proposition passed, 54 percent to 46 percent. An analysis of the votes by ethnic groups was revealing: according to the *Los Angeles Times*, 63 percent of whites favored it, while 74 percent of blacks and 76 percent of Latinos rejected it. The Asian-American vote was 61 percent against Proposition 209.[30]

Clearly, Asian Americans had shown their support for affirmative action. Through newsletters, newspapers like *Asianweek*, radio, and television, Asian-American civil rights organizations had effectively educated their communities. They pointed out that Asian Americans had benefited from affirmative action. Thanks to affirmative action set-aside programs, there were more minority-owned businesses among Asian Americans. Thanks to affirmative action employment programs, there were more Asian Americans in police and fire departments, government offices, the mass media, law firms, management, and university social science and humanities departments. But Asian Americans had yet to achieve equality: whites with college degrees earned 11 percent more than Asian Americans with comparable education, and white high school graduates made 26 percent more money than their Asian-American counterparts. Nationwide, Asian Americans constituted less than 1 percent of union construction workers, and they continued to hit the glass ceiling in management. Clearly, Asian Americans still needed affirmative action for themselves.

In their defense of affirmative action, however, Asian Americans were also reaching beyond their own ethnic interests. An Asian-American civil rights organization eloquently identified the moral issue facing voters: "In his widely quoted 'I have a dream' speech, Dr. Martin Luther King, Jr., envisioned a society which 'judged people based on the content of their character rather than the color of their skin.' Some Proposition 209 backers have claimed that Dr. King's remarks should be interpreted to mean that he would have opposed affirmative action because it violates the notion of a color-blind society.

This view fails to acknowledge the context of Dr. King's remarks, which envisioned a time when all races would be equal. Sadly enough, this equality has not been achieved in the three decades since Dr. King made that speech. For Proposition 209 supporters to suddenly call for a color-blind society is not only wrong, it insidiously undermines the spirit of Dr. King's message."[31]

Indeed, Asian Americans know that this society is still far from color-blind. They are continually being reminded of the persistence of prejudice in the anti-immigrant backlash and the high rate of hate crimes against them as people of color. Many of them also understand that affirmative action means more than addressing past discrimination: it seeks to challenge the institutional structures of education and employment that operate "naturally" and silently to discriminate against minorities. Moreover, Asian-American supporters of affirmative action are driven by a deep moral concern. Rejecting the resegregation of America, they are struggling to reaffirm the dream of Martin Luther King, Jr., and take all of us toward a twenty-first-century society that is truly color-blind.

Asian-American Multiplicity

There are no Asians in Asia, only people with national identities, such as Chinese, Japanese, Korean, Indian, Vietnamese, and Filipino. But on this side of the Pacific there are Asian Americans. This broader identity was forged in the crucible of racial discrimination and exclusion: their national origins did not matter as much as their race. Thus, out of "necessity," theirs became a community rooted in the struggle against racism. Shared resistance began with campaigns against the restrictions for naturalized citizenship and immigration that affected all Asian Americans. In the sixties, this common commitment to equality was strengthened by student movements demanding what they called "Asian American" studies, and was reinforced in the eighties by the pan–Asian American crusade for justice for Vincent Chin. From struggles emerged an "extravagance" — an Asian-American identity.

What does it mean to be Asian American in the 1990s? To answer this question, we need to recognize that ethnic identity is neither essentialist nor static: it is both "being" and "becoming." "The making of Asian American culture," scholar Lisa Lowe points out, "includes practices that are partly inherited, partly modified, as well as partly invented."[32] As we have learned throughout this book, Asian Americans have been constantly defining and redefining themselves in different times, places, and circumstances. Even before they left their homelands, they already had dreams about what they could and would become in America. After their arrival, they imagined the lives and futures they wanted for themselves and their children.

As they approach the twenty-first century, Asian Americans are continuing to modify their cultural inheritances and inventing new dimensions to their identities. Many of them are reaching toward what Yen Le Espiritu calls Asian-American panethnicity.[33] Including but also transcending specific nationalities, this new sense of community can be seen in celebrations for Asian Pacific American Heritage Month. In its 1997 program, for example, Oakland's Asian Culture Center featured a festival of music and dances from China, the Philippines, Korea, Polynesia, and India. This collective spirit is also reflected in newspapers like *Asianweek* of San Francisco, professional associations like Asian Americans in Higher Education and the Association of Asian/Pacific American Artists, political and community organizations like the Coalition of Asian Pacific Americans and the Asian Law Caucus of San Francisco, and media and performance arts groups like the National Asian American Telecommunications Association and the Asian American Theater Company.

In addition to associating with each other in the professions and organizations, Asian Americans are also marrying across their specific Asian nationalities. The 1990 census, according to sociologist Larry Shinagawa, showed that 30 percent of Asian-American marriages involved different Asian groups. This pattern was especially pronounced in California. Himself a Japanese American married to a Korean American, Shinagawa observed: Always "a harbinger of trends in the Asian American community," California "is currently the only place with large communities of every Asian group. There's just a larger possibility for interaction."[34] Nationally, the rate of interethnic marriages has been booming. "We are at the dawn of a new, truly pan-Asian American community," *Asianweek* announced in February 1997. "Asian American children can grow up with the comfort of being connected to their roots, but at the same time be accepted and honored as a uniquely American creation."[35]

An example of this coming together of different Asian cultures can be found in the family of Tim and Sharon Chan. During Chinese New Year's, they take their children to visit the home of Tim's mother for a dinner of *jai* (a vegetarian dish often served during holidays). In March, they watch the Cherry Blossom Festival parade in San Francisco's Japantown — an event that Sharon enjoyed as a Japanese American. "They [our children] enjoy learning about both sides [of their cultures]," said Tim Chan, "but they are very much American."[36]

Civil rights activists Hoyt Zia, a Chinese, and Leigh-Ann Miyasato, a Japanese, are another example of interethnic marriage. They met during a Christmas party sponsored by the Asian American Bar Association and started dating when their work paths crossed. For Zia's parents, their marriage affirmed the yielding of old-world memories to new-world experiences. "I think they [my parents] were just happy that I was marrying an Asian," Zia recalled. "At first I had some concerns because my parents lived through World War II in China and I didn't know how they would react. But they were happy." Marrying Leigh-Ann suited Hoyt just fine. "I think of myself as an Asian American before I think of myself as a Chinese American," he said. Their two children identify themselves as Asian American. "Our kids know that they are half-Japanese and half-Chinese. But I hope that we were able to show them that they should identify with pride that they are Asian American."[37]

Asian Americans are not only choosing partners from different Asian nationalities, Leigh-Ann Miyasato noted, they are also marrying interracially. "One of my sisters married a Caucasian and another an African American," she reported. "They [my parents] were attuned to the idea that their daughters were not going to marry Japanese Americans and it didn't bother them."[38] In 1990, 31 percent of Asian-American marriages were interracial, most of them to whites. *Newsweek* reported in 1997 that one in five Asian-Pacific Americans had a non-Asian spouse. These marriages produced nearly two million children under eighteen who were of mixed race.[39]

My own family reflects both of these trends of ethnic and racial mixtures. My father died when I was five years old, and my mother remarried a Chinese immigrant. My older sister married a Chinese American; one of their sons married a Vietnamese, and they have three children. After my sister and her husband divorced, he married a Mexican American, and they have two children. My younger Chinese/Japanese brother is married to a Caucasian, and they have a son. My wife is Caucasian, and we have three children; our two grandchildren are one-quarter Japanese.

This racial integration of Asian-American families is redefining race in America, moving us toward what historian David Hollinger calls a "postethnic" society of cosmopolitanism and multiple identities for groups and also individuals.[40] "The old labels of white and

black, of Hispanic and Asian become less and less useful," announced
Asianweek in January 1997, "as we embrace the promise of America
and move toward a multicultural society. . . . Since the 1970s, a multiracial baby boom has hit the country, with Asian Pacific Americans
among those leading the way and hapas — half- or part-APA, which
is derived from the Hawaiian term *hapa haole* [half white] — coming
of age. . . . As Asian Americans, we celebrate being not one or the
other but both; as hapas or others of mixed race, we can proudly em-
body the diversity that is America's greatest resource."[41]

"Hapa" has been redefined to mean all combinations of racial
mixtures. A leader of the Hapa Issues Forum, Greg Mayeda reflected
on the meaning of being multiracial: "There are negative views and
stereotypes of mixed-race people. To some, hapas represent the extinction of the community, when in actuality, they are the natural
step in the history of the Japanese American community."[42] The hapas have begun to discover and define their multiple identities. "As
the Asian American community expands in new directions," the
Hapa Issues Forum declared, "the culture will naturally evolve. Today, Asian Americans can have green eyes, red hair, and freckles.
Their last names can range from White to Wong. They can take pride
in multiple ethnicities. With equal enthusiasm, they can celebrate
Kwanzaa, Hanukkah, St. Patrick's Day, Cinco de Mayo, as well as
Chinese New Year, the Tet Festival, Choosuk, and the Cherry Blossom Festival.[43]

This fusion of races and cultures is being played out at family
gatherings. Asian-Indian immigrant Shashi Kalra described one of
them: "My niece is getting a divorce. She has two children. Her first
husband was European-American and her fiancé is Mexican. A few
weeks ago I went over to my sister's home to celebrate a birthday. At
the party we had our new Mexican side of the family as well as the
usual Indian crowd. My sister was in the kitchen cooking samosas.
There were other relatives there preparing a mixture of Indian and
Mexican food. In the center of the room there was a stereo. I sat there
in the other room looking through the glass partition at the people
dancing. Never before had I seen Indian people dancing to Spanish
music. I saw my nieces and my nephews dancing along with my own
children. Later in the evening the music changed and everyone began
dancing to Bungra music. I moved over into the other room with the
food and saw all the people trying to create a new type of meal with
this mixture of tortillas and curry."[44]

Many multiracial Americans of part-Asian descent have become celebrities, and the most famous is Tiger Woods. Reporting his victory on April 13, 1997, *USA Today* described the making of history on the golf course: "With thousands of cheering fans lining the lush fairways at Augusta National Golf Club Sunday, the 21-year-old Woods became the youngest man and the first of color — his father is black and his mother Thai — to win the coveted green jacket that goes with The Masters champion."[45] Also witnessing his triumph were Americans in eight million homes across the country and countless others all over the world.

But the mass media and most Americans viewed Woods as African American only. This one-dimensional representation of his ethnicity upset his mother, Kultida. "All the media try to put black in him," she complained in the March 27, 1995, issue of *Sports Illustrated.* "Why don't they ask who half of Tiger is from? In the United States, one little part black is *all black.* Nobody wants to listen to me. I've been trying to explain to people, but they don't understand. To say he is 100 percent black is to deny his heritage. To deny his grandmother and grandfather. To deny *me!* "[46]

Tiger Woods himself has clearly defined who he is. "My parents have taught me to always be proud of my ethnic background," he told the *New York Times.* "Please rest assured that is, and will be, the case, past, present and future. The various media have portrayed me as African-American, sometimes Asian. In fact, I am both. Yes I am the product of two great cultures, one African-American and the other Asian. On my father's side I'm African American. On my mother's side I am Thai. Truthfully, I feel very fortunate, and equally proud, to be both African-American and Asian!"[47]

For many multiracial Americans, the proclaiming of their complex identity has more than a cultural purpose. Politically, they are challenging the rigid categories and notions of race that have been socially constructed throughout history. The multiracial identity, explained Dr. Helena Jia Hershel, of Chinese and Austrian descent, is "the beginning of the destruction of the idea of race."[48]

Beyond erasing race, multiracial Americans of part Asian descent are also creating a new multiculturalism in the arts. One of the pathbreakers of this new fusion is musician Anthony Brown, son of a Japanese mother and an African-American/Choctow father. Brown's compositions bring together diverse instruments, like the saxophone and Japanese *taiko* drums, mixing Asian sounds with black jazz. "It's a new dialect," he said. "Personally, I look in the mirror every morning and I see it. I think the mixes are what bring out those things that are special. Jazz is a mix. And now it's universal." One of his pieces is entitled "E.O. 9066," a reference to President Roosevelt's executive order authorizing the internment of Japanese Americans. In San Francisco, Brown leads a multicultural musical ensemble called African Eurasian Eclipse. For Brown, identity is the dynamic interactivity of the varied parts of the total self. "The whole issue of whether you see yourself as Asian or black is the same as asking whether you're a father, husband, a brother, a musician, or a composer. We're all these different things. You can't decide ethnicities along one arbitrary line. That's what America is all about."[49]

This vibrant multiculturalism is also a liberating theme for Asian-American musicians who are not multiracial. A leading jazz musician, Jon Jang explained that his composition *Island: Immigrant Suite #2* was inspired by his study of the Chinese-immigrant experiences at Angel Island. He was emotionally moved by the poems inscribed on the walls of the immigration station — outcries of loneliness, anger, and dreams denied. Jang described his work as "musical language," trying to "recontextualize Chinese sorrow song within the modern jazz or new musical context, but from a Chinese American perspective." A third-generation Chinese American, he declared, "Music is an offering. With *Island*, I want the audience to experience the souls of people from the Chinese diaspora that have touched me and that I hope will bring a rediscovery about the humanity in all of us."[50]

Similarly, Miya Masaoka is also seeking to express a larger humanity through her music. Internationally recognized, she brilliantly weaves together *gagaku* (Japanese court orchestral music), jazz, and blues. As a teenager, Miya had been "a complete blues fanatic" because she "felt blues really expressed in a very effective, very pure way, the oppression of African Americans and by extension, all people of color, all oppressed people." In the 1980s, Miya began playing the *koto*. Remembering the koto music she had heard as a child in Buddhist temples, she discovered that this Japanese instrument could be a powerful way to convey her feelings and thoughts as a multicultural Asian American. At that time, Miya met musicians Anthony Brown and Jon Jang. "And then of course, things radically changed," Miya recalled excitedly. "They were forming Asian American music. I felt that it was becoming part of a movement because

until then the most interesting culture for me growing up in the suburbs was Black American writing, literature, plays, and music. So to
have something Asian American being developed and to be a part of
it, to transform it, to make a contribution to it was very empower-
ing."[51]

The Past as a Path to the Future

Finally, we reframe the question asked at the beginning of this chapter: What will the twenty-first century hold not only for my students
but also for all of us as Americans in our diverse society? The history
of Asian Americans teaches us that we hold the future in our own
hands: the men and women of our story made decisions about their
lives and communities, though usually in circumstances not of their
choosing. They struggled to change the world around them in order
to determine their future.

Indeed, throughout history, Asian Americans have been transforming America and also finding themselves being transformed by
America. Since the arrival of the first Chinese during the 1849 gold
rush, the interaction between Asian Americans and the larger society
has been dynamic and dialectical. Exploited as agricultural and industrial workers, they fought for justice through labor unions and
strikes. Victims of the "white"-only provision of 1790 Naturalization
Law, they organized campaigns that culminated in its nullification in
1952 — a victory that made political membership more inclusive and
the Statue of Liberty a more democratic symbol. Forced into segregated Chinatowns and internment camps, Asian Americans joined
the U.S. military during World War II and fought as "one people"
against fascism abroad and for equality at home. Excluded by racist
immigration laws like the 1882 Chinese Exclusion Act and the 1924
National Origins Act, they helped end this discrimination with the
1965 Immigration Act. Denied their cultures in a Eurocentric society,
Asian Americans sought to preserve their heritages by creating communities like Chinatowns as well as Nihonmachis (Japantowns), organizing festivals, and founding language schools as well as churches
and temples. Rendered invisible in mainstream history textbooks and
courses, they established their own historical societies and museums
and also organized exhibits for the Smithsonian Institution. And
through a student activism that emerged in the sixties and resurged in
the nineties, they innovated new curriculums in Asian-American
studies at universities across America — from Berkeley and UCLA to
Minnesota and Michigan to Cornell, Columbia, and Princeton.

These struggles of Asian Americans have been a continuous rebellion against the exclusive constructions of "we, the people" and a constant resolve to help make this "a more perfect union," an ethnically diverse yet united society. The recovering and sharing of their stories can help all Americans understand why these immigrants who went east to America should have been viewed and treated not as "strangers," but as Americans "from a different shore." The history of Asian Americans offers all of us an opportunity to carry into the coming century a larger memory of America's past.

A Note of Appreciation

Many people participated in this enterprise of "extravagance." My colleagues Amado Cabezas, Roberto Haro, Franklin Odo, Him Mark Lai, Judy Yung, Edward Chang, Jane Singh, Jerry Takahashi, Chuong Chung, and Hyung-chan Kim read different parts of the manuscript, giving criticisms and providing additional information. Gary Okihiro helpfully raised some theoretical issues. Wei-Chi Poon was always there to assist with translations for Chinese terms. Chuong Chung gladly reproduced most of the photographs used as illustrations in the book. Judy Yung provided indispensable support as my research assistant. She gathered documents and also scouted collections in the Bancroft Library and the Hoover Institution Archives. Sau-ling Wong shared her insightful interpretation of Maxine Hong Kingston's terms and themes of "extravagance" and "necessity." While I have defined and used both of them in my own way, I found Wong's essay on the subject and our discussion seminal. My longtime friend and colleague, Larry Friedman read an early draft of the entire manuscript and sent me flying back to the conceptual drawing board. Richard Balkin gave frank advice at a timely moment. Jennifer Josephy, my editor at Little, Brown and Company, offered the critical encouragement I needed to pursue "what persisted" and the freeing of the study's themes. Carol Takaki deserves special thanks. She went through every chapter line by line at least twice. Fortunately I had the manuscript on a word processor, for her compelling editorial suggestions for changes and revisions were myriad. Finally, my deepest thanks to all the people who told me their stories and enabled me to write their book, for in the telling and retelling of our stories we create our "community of memory" and reclaim the authorship of our own history.

Notes

Preface. Confronting "Cultural Literacy"

1. E. D. Hirsch, Jr., *Cultural Literacy: What Every American Needs to Know* (Boston, 1987).
2. Arthur Schlesinger, Jr., *The Disuniting of America: Reflections on a Multicultural Society* (New York, 1992), pp. 16, 17, 112, 113, 117, 127.
3. Oscar Handlin, *The Uprooted: The Epic Story of the Great Migrations That Made the American People* (New York, 1951).
4. Walt Whitman, *Leaves of Grass and Selected Prose* (New York, 1958), p. 343.
5. Thomas Jefferson, *Notes on the State of Virginia* (New York, 1964), pp. 138–139; *Debates and Proceedings in the Congress of the United States, 1789–1791*, 2 vols. (Washington, D.C., 1834), vol. 1, pp. 998, 1284; vol. 2, pp. 1148–1156, 2264.
6. Abraham Lincoln, "Address delivered at the dedication of the cemetery at Gettysburg," November 19, 1863, reprinted in Gary Wills, *Lincoln at Gettysburg: The Words That Remade America* (New York, 1992), p. 263.
7. Yan Phou Lee, "The Chinese Must Stay," *North American Review,* vol. 148, no. 398 (April 1889), p. 476. Gary Okihiro also makes this point about the Asian-American struggle for democracy in his *Margins and Mainstreams: Asians in American History and Culture* (Seattle, 1994).
8. Andrew Lind, *Hawaii's Japanese: An Experiment in Democracy* (Princeton, 1946), pp. 161–162.
9. Robert A. Wilson and Bill Hosokawa, *East to America: A History of the Japanese in the United States* (New York, 1980), p. 279.
10. David Reimers, *Still the Golden Door: The Third World Comes to America* (New York, 1985), p. 67.

1. From a Different Shore

1. Leonard Greenwood, "El Centro's Community of Sikhs Dying Out," *Los Angeles Times,* December 28, 1966.
2. West Coast premiere of David Hwang's *Family Devotions*, San Francisco State University, February 1987.
3. Albert Scardino, "Commercial Rents in Chinatown Soar as Hong Kong Exodus

Grows," *New York Times*, December 25, 1986; Douglas Martin, "Living in Two Worlds: Chinese of New York City," *New York Times*, February 19, 1988; Mark Arax, "Asian Influx Alters Life in Suburbia," *Los Angeles Times*, April 5, 1987; Robert Reinhold, "Flow of 3d World Immigrants Alters Weave of U.S. Society," *New York Times*, June 30, 1986.

4. Data from Cary Davis, Carl Haub, and JoAnne Willette, *U.S. Hispanics: Changing the Face of America*, a publication of the Population Reference Bureau, vol. 38, no. 3 (June 1983), p. 8; Robert W. Gardner, Bryant Robey, and Peter C. Smith, *Asian Americans: Growth, Change, and Diversity*, a publication of the Population Reference Bureau, vol. 40, no. 4 (October 1985), pp. 2, 3, 5, 7, 8.

5. William Wong, "Racial Taunts of Inonye Are a Chilling Reminder," *East/West*, July 23, 1987.

6. Congressman Norman Mineta, from the Foreword, in Timothy J. Lukes and Gary Y. Okihiro, *Japanese Legacy: Farming and Community Life in California's Santa Clara Valley* (Cupertino, Calif., 1985).

7. *The Californians*, May/June 1987, p. 5; Oscar Handlin, *The Uprooted: The Epic Story of the Great Migrations That Made the American People* (New York, 1951).

8. Maxine Hong Kingston, *China Men* (New York, 1980), pp. 100, 101, 102, 114, 117.

9. Mr. Yip, in Him Mark Lai, Genny Lim, Judy Yung (eds.), *Island: Poetry and History of Chinese Immigrants on Angel Island, 1910-1940* (San Francisco, 1980), p. 136; poem, ibid., p. 40. "Flowery Flag" is a reference to the United States. For the need to study the excluded as well as the excluders, see Roger Daniels, "Westerners from the East: Oriental Immigrants Reappraised," *Pacific Historical Review*, vol. 35 (1966), pp. 373–383, and "American Historians and East Asian Immigrants," *Pacific Historical Review*, vol. 43 (1974), pp. 449–472.

10. Interview with Jean Park (pseudonym), Prologue of "The Autobiography of a Second Generation Korean American," in Christopher Kim, "Three Generations of Koreans in America," Asian American Studies 199 paper, University of California, Berkeley, 1976, pp. 42–44; interview with Suen Hoon Sum, in Jeff Gillenkirk and James Matlow, *Bitter Melon: Stories from the Last Rural Chinese Town in America* (Seattle, 1987), p. 56, interview with Filipino immigrant in Virgilio Menor Felipe, "Hawaii: A Pilipino Dream," M.A. thesis, University of Hawaii, 1972, Prologue, p. iii; Virginia Cerenio, "you lovely people," in Joseph Bruche, *Breaking Silence: An Anthology of Contemporary Asian American Poets* (Greenfield Center, N.Y., 1983), p. 11.

11. My thanks to Joy Kogawa for this phrase, in Joy Kogawa, *Obasan* (Boston, 1982), opening page; "Social Document of Pany Lowe, Interviewed by C. H. Burnett, Seattle, July 5, 1924," p. 6, Survey of Race Relations, Stanford University, Hoover Institution Archives; Dennis Akizuki, "Low-Cost Housing for Elderly Pilipinos Delayed," *Daily Caiifornian*, November 1, 1974; interview with Toden Higa, in Ethnic Studies Oral History Project, *Uchinanchu: A History of Okinawans in Hawaii* (Honolulu, 1981), p. 520; Keiko Teshirogi, poem, in Kazuo Ito, *Issei: A History of Japanese Immigrants in North America* (Seattle, 1973), p. 480; Robert Bellah, et al., *Habits of the Heart: Individualism and Commitment in American Life* (Berkeley, 1985), p. 153.

12. Folk song, translation, in Marlon K. Hom (ea. and trans.), *Songs of Gold Mountain: Cantonese Rhymes from San Francisco Chinatown* (Berkeley, 1987), p. 134; "When I Journeyed from America," in Harriet M. Pawlowska (ed.), *Merrily We Sing: One Hundred Five Polish Folk Songs* (Detroit, 1961), pp. 154–155.

13. Rowland Berthoff, *British Immigrants in Industrial America,* 1750–1950 (Cambridge, Mass., 1953), p. 10; Frances Kraljic, *Croatian Migration to and from the United States, 1900–1914* (Palo Alto, 1978), pp. 29, 46; Caroline Golab, *Immigrant Destinations* (Philadelphia, 1977), pp. 48, 58; Victor Von Borosini, "Home-Going Italians," *Survey,* September 28, 1912, p. 792; Theodore Saloutos, *They Remember America: The Story of the Repatriated Greek-Americans* (Berkeley, 1956), p. 50; Theodore Saloutos, "Causes and Patterns of Greek Emigration to the United States," *Perspectives in American History,* vol. 7 (1973), pp. 411, 417, 421, 423, and 436; Thomas J. Archdeacon, *Becoming American: An Ethnic History* (New York, 1983), pp. 138–139.

14. Michael Moore, "Pride and Prejudice," *Image: The Magazine of Northern California,* in *San Francisco Examiner,* November 15, 1987, p. 17.

15. Georg Simmel, "Der Fremde" or "The Stranger," in Simmel, *On Individuality and Social Forms,* edited by Donald N. Levine (Chicago, 1971), pp. 143–149. For suggestive discussions of Simmel, see Franklin Ng, "The Sojourner, Return Migration, and Immigration History," in Chinese Historical Society of America, *Chinese America: History and Perspectives,* 1987 (San Francisco, 1987), pp. 53–72; Stanford M. Lyman, "The Chinese Diaspora in America, 1850–1943," in Chinese Historical Society of America, *The Life, Influence and Role of the Chinese in the United States, 1776–1960* (San Francisco, 1976), pp. 131–134.

16. John Higham, *Strangers in the Land: Patterns of American Nativism, 1860–1925* (New York, 1966), F. Scott Fitzgerald, *The Great Gatsby* (rpt. New York, 1953); Stanley Lieberson, *A Piece of the Pie: Black and White Immigrants since 1880* (Berkeley, 1980), p. 33; J. N. Hook, *Family Names: How Our Surnames Came to America* (New York, 1982), pp. 351, 322–325. It would be difficult to count the number of people who changed their family names, but it may have been extensive. In western Pennsylvania, for example, 76 percent of Ukrainian names were changed by the third generation. Ibid., p. 322.

17. Robert E. Park, "Human Migration and the Marginal Man," *American Journal of Sociology,* vol. 33, no. 6 (May 1928), p. 890; Robert E. Park, "Racial Assimilation in Secondary Groups with Particular Reference to the Negro," *Papers and Proceedings, Eighth Annual Meeting of the American Sociological Society, 1913,* vol. 8 (Chicago, 1914), p. 71.

18. Robert Blauner, "Colonized and Immigrant Minorities," in Ronald Takaki (ed.), *From Different Shores: Perspectives on Race and Ethnicity in America* (New York, 1987), pp. 149–160; Edna Bonacich, "A Theory of Ethnic Antagonism: The Split Labor Market," *American Sociological Review,* vol. 37, no. 5 (October 1972), pp. 547–559. For the concept of the industrial reserve army, see Karl Marx, *Capital: A Critique of Political Economy* (New York, 1906), pp. 689–703; I have expanded this concept to include the racial and transnational dimensions of this labor reserve.

19. Victor and Bret de Bary Nee, "Growing Up in a Chinatown Grocery Store: Interview with Frank Ng," in Emma Gee (ed.), *Counterpoint: Perspectives on Asian America* (Los Angeles, 1978), p. 346; Edna Bonacich and John Modell, *The Economic Basis of Ethnic Solidarity: Small Business in the Japanese American Community* (Berkeley, 1980).

20. For quotas, see Proclamation 2283 of President Franklin D. Roosevelt, *Code of Federal Regulations* (Title 3—The President, 1936–38 Compilation), pp. 140–141; 1924 Immigration Act, section 13, reprinted in Eliot G. Mears, *Resident Orientals on the American Pacific Coast: Their Legal and Economic Status* (New York,

1927), appendix, p. 515. The 1924 law was amended in 1930 to allow the entry of Asian wives of American citizens married after June 1930.

21. *Debates and Proceedings in the Congress of the United States, 1789–1791,* 2 vols. (Washington, D.C., 1834), vol. 1, pp. 998, 1284; vol. 2, pp. 1148– 1156, 1162, 2264; Cable Act, 42 U.S. *Stat* 1021; Yamato Ichihashi, *Japanese in the United States* (Stanford, 1932), pp. 324–325. The Cable Act was amended in 1931, permitting an American woman who married an alien ineligible to citizenship to retain her U.S. citizenship.

22. Robert Mirak, "Armenians," in Stephan Thernstrom, *Harvard Encyclopedia of American Ethnic Croups* (Cambridge, Mass., 1980), pp. 139, 141, 143; Mr. G. Sato, in David Mas Masumoto, *Country Voices: The Oral History of a Japanese American Family Farm Community* (Del Ray, Calif., 1987), p. 13.

23. Roger Daniels, *Concentration Camps USA: Japanese Americans and World War II* (New York, 1971); Peter Irons, *Justice At War: The Story of the Japanese American Internment Cases* (New York, 1983).

24. Perry Miller, *Errand into the Wilderness* (New York, 1956); John Winthrop, in Ronald Takaki, *Iron Cages: Race and Culture in Nineteenth–Century America* (New York, 1979), p. 21; Winthrop Jordan, *White over Black: American Attitudes Toward the Negro, 1550–1812* (Chapel Hill, N.C., 1968), p. xiv; Benjamin Franklin, *Observations Concerning the Increase of Mankind* (1751), in Leonard W. Labaree (ed.), *The Papers of Benjamin Franklin* (New Haven, 1959–), vol. 4, p. 234; *Federalist Papers,* in Stephen Steinberg, *The Ethnic Myth* (New York, 1981), p. 9; Jefferson to Monroe, November 24, 1801, in Paul L. Ford (ed.), *The Works of Thomas Jefferson* (New York, 1892–1899), vol. 9, p. 317; Jefferson, *Notes on the State of Virginia* (rpt. New York, 1964, originally published in 1781), p. 119; Jefferson to George Flower, September 12, 1817, in H. A. Washington (ed.), *The Writings of Thomas Jefferson* (Washington, D.C., 1853–1854), vol. 7, p. 84; U.S. v. Bhagat Singh Thind, 261 U.S. 215 (1923).

25. Walt Whitman, "By Blue Ontario's Shore" and "Passage to India," in Whitman, *Leaves of Grass* (rpt. New York, 1958), pp. 284, 340–343; Walt Whitman, in Horace Traubel, *With Walt Whitman in Canada,* 2 vols. (New York, 1915), vol. 2, pp. 34–35; Herman Melville, *Moby-Dick* (rpt. Boston, 1956), pp. 105, 182, 253, 322–323; Ito, *Issei,* p. 497; Carlos Bulosan, *America Is in the Heart: A Personal History* (rpt. Seattle, 1981, originally published in 1946), pp. 188–189.

26. Fitzgerald, *The Great Gatsby,* p. 182.

27. Maxine Hong Kingston, *The Woman Warrior: Memoirs of a Girlhood Among Ghosts* (New York, 1976), p. 9; Park, "Human Migration and the Marginal Man," pp. 881–893; Victor Turner, *Dramas, Fields, and Metaphors: Symbolic Action in Human Society* (Ithaca, N.Y., 1974), pp. 232, 237; Arnold Van Gennep, *The Rites of Passage* (rpt. Chicago, 1960); John Locke, *Of Civil Government: Second Treatise* (rpt. Chicago, 1955), p. 39; Bulosan, *America Is in the Heart,* pp. 104, 66, 251.

I. Extravagance

1. Carlos Bulosan, *America Is in the Heart: A Personal History* (rpt. Seattle, 1981, originally published in 1946), p. 97; Sing Kum, "Letter by a Chinese Girl," January 4, 1876, reprinted in O. Gibson, *The Chinese in America* (Cincinnati, 1877), p. 220; poem by Ichiyo, in Kazuo Ito, *Issei: A History of Japanese Immigrants in North America* (Seattle, 1973), p. 20.

2. Overblown with Hope

1. William Hooper to Ladd and Company, March 28, 1835, William Hooper Papers, Hawaiian Collection, University of Hawaii Library, Honolulu.

2. Hooper, diary, September 12, 1835, and September 12, 1836, Hooper Papers.

3. William Hooper to Ladd and Company, November 15, 1836, and December 1, 1838, Hooper Papers.

4. Aaron H. Palmer, *Memoir, geographical, political, and commercial, on the present state, productive resources, and capabilities for commerce, of Siberia, Manchuria and the Asiatic Islands of the Northern Pacific Ocean; and on the importance of opening commercial intercourse with those countries, March 8, 1848.* U.S. Cong., Senate, 30th Cong., 1st sess., Senate misc. no. 80, pp. 1, 52, 60, 61.

5. Ronald Takaki, *Iron Cages: Race and Culture in Nineteenth-Century America* (New York, 1979), p. 269; Perry Miller, *Errand into the Wilderness* (New York, 1956); Max Weber, *The Protestant Ethic and the Spirit of Capitalism* (rpt. New York, 1958, originally published in 1930); Robert A. Wilson and Bill Hosokawa, *East to America: A History of the Japanese in the United States* (New York, 1980), p. 21.

6. Mark Twain, *A Connecticut Yankee in King Arthur's Court* (rpt. New York, 1963, originally published in 1889).

7. *Pacific Commercial Advertiser,* April 25, 1874; *Pacific Commercial Advertiser,* June 9, 1877; for a study of the political economy of Hawaii's sugar industry, see Nod Kent, *Hawai: Islands Under the Influence* (New York, 1983).

8. *Royal Hawaiian Agricultural Society Transactions,* vol. 1, no. 5 (June 1852), pp. 6–7.

9. Theo. H. Davies and Company to C. McLennan, July 2, 1890; January 3, 1898, Laupahoehoe Plantation Records, microfilm, University of Hawaii Library; William G. Irwin and Company to George D. Hewitt, October 12, 1894, Hutchinson Plantation Records, microfilm, University of Hawaii Library; vice president of H. Hackfield and Company to G. N. Wilcox, May 5, 1908, Grove Farm Plantation Records, Grove Farm Plantation, Kauai.

10. *Royal Hawaiian Agricultural Society Transactions,* vol. 1, no. 5 (June 1852), pp. 6, 7, 70.

11. *Planters' Monthly,* vol. 2, no. 11 (November 1883), pp. 177, 245–247; A. S. Cleghorn, in Republic of Hawaii, *Report of the Bureau of Immigration* (Honolulu 1895), pp. 256–257; U.S. Commissioner of Labor Carroll Wright, in *Honolulu Record,* January 12, 1950.

12. G. C. Hewitt to W. G. Irwin and Company, March 16,1896, Hutchinson Plantation Records; Robert Hall, George F. Renton, and George H. Fairfield, in Republic of Hawaii, *Report of the Labor Commission on Strikes and Arbitration* (Honolulu 1895), pp. 23–24, 28, 36, respectively; H. Hackfield and Company to George Wilcox, September 26, 1896, Grove Farm Plantation Records.

13. H. Hackfield and Company to George Wilcox, December 22, 1900, Grove Farm Plantation Records.

14. "Report of the Commission of Labor," in *Planters' Monthly,* vol. 22, no. 7 (July 1903), p. 296; Walter Giffard to manager of the Hutchinson Sugar Plantation, October 3, 1898, in Wayne K. Patterson, "The Korean Frontier in America: Immigration to Hawaii, 1896–1910," unpublished Ph.D. thesis, University of Pennsylvania, 1977, p. 100; Theo. H. Davies and Company to C. McLennan, n.d., Laupahoehoe Plantation Records; manager of the Hutchinson Sugar Plantation to W. G. Irwin and Company, April 11, 1905, Hutchinson Plantation Records.

15. Judd, in *Pacific Commercial Advertiser,* December 21, 1906, labor committee of the Hawaiian Sugar Planters' Association to the trustees, July 28, 1909, Grove Farm Plantation Records; manager of the Hawaiian Agricultural Company to C. Brewer and Company, August 7 and 27, 1913, Hawaiian Agricultural Company Records, microfilm, University of Hawaii Library.

16. *Report of the Joint Special Committee to Investigate Chinese Immigration,* Senate Report No. 689, 44th Cong., 2nd sess., 1876–1877, pp. 679, 680; A. W. Loomis "How Our Chinamen Are Employed," *Overland Monthly,* vol. 2 (March 1869), p. 240; Charles W. Brooks, "The Chinese Labor Problem," *Overland Monthly,* vol. 3 (November 1869), p. 407; Samuel Bowles, *Our New West* (Hartford, Conn., 1869), p. 414; *The Nation,* vol. 11 (July 14, 1870), pp. 18–19; Henry Robinson "Our Manufacturing Era," *Overland Monthly,* vol. 2 (March 1869), pp. 280–284; Otis Gibson, *The Chinese in America* (Cincinnati, 1877), pp. 99, 57.

17. Robinson, "Our Manufacturing Era," p. 282; Crocker, testimony, *Report of the . . . Committee to Investigate Chinese Immigration,* p. 667.

18. Godkin, "Editorial," *The Nation,* vol. 10 (June 23, 1870), p. 397; John Todd, *The Sunset Land* (Boston, 1870), p. 283. See Karl Marx, *Capital: A Critique of Political Economy* (New York, 1906), pp. 689–703, and Edna Bonacich, "A Theory of Ethnic Antagonism: The Split Labor Market," *American Sociological Review,* vol. 37, no. 5 (October 1972), pp. 547–559.

19. Carey McWilliams, *Factories in the Field: The Story of Migratory Farm Labor in California* (Santa Barbara, Calif., 1971), pp. 106, 86, 107.

20. Sucheta Mazumdar, "Punjabi Agricultural Workers in California, 1905–1945," in Lucie Cheng and Edna Bonacich (eds.), *Labor Immigration Under Capitalism: Asian Workers in the United States before World War II* (Berkeley, 1984), pp. 552–553; U.S. Immigration Commission, *Japanese and Other Immigrant Races in the Pacific Coast and Rocky Mountain States,* vol. 1, *Japanese and East Indians* (Washington D.C., 1911), p. 333; McWilliams, *Factories in the Field,* p. 86.

21. McWilliams, *Factories in the Field, pp.* 127–128, 131; Bruno Lasker, *Filipino Immigration* (Chicago, 1931), p. 302; Carey McWilliams, "Exit the Filipino," *The Nation,* September 4, 1935, p. 265; Mrs. Thorburn of the Watsonville Chamber of Commerce, interview, Wood interview notes, p. 70, James Earl Wood Collection Bancroft Library, University of California, Berkeley.

22. Frank Waterman, interview, Wood interview notes, p. 15, envelope 3, Wood Collection; Department of Industrial Relations, State of California, *Facts about Filipino Immigration into California,* Special Bulletin No. 3 (San Francisco, 1930), pp. 60–61.

23. Marx, *Capital: A Critique,* pp. 689–703; Cheng and Bonacich (eds.), *Labor Immigration Under Capitalism;* Immanuel Wallerstein, *The Modern World-System* (New York, 1974); Robert Blauner, *Racial Oppression in America* (New York, 1972); Georg Simmel, "Der Fremde" or "The Stranger," in Simmel, *On Individuality and Social Forms,* edited by Donald N. Levine (Chicago, 1971), pp. 143–149.

24. Maxine Hong Kingston, *The Woman Warrior: Memoirs of a Girlhood Among Ghosts* (New York, 1976), pp. 6, 7; poem, in Kazuo Ito, *Issei: A History of Japanese Immigrants in North America* (Seattle, 1973), p. 20. I am grateful to Kingston for the terms "necessity" and "extravagance," which I define and use in my own way; Sau-ling Wong brilliantly paired the terms in "Necessity and Extravagance in Maxine Hong Kingston's *The Woman Warrior*: Art and the Ethnic Experience," *MELUS* (forthcoming).

25. June Mei, "Socioeconomic Origins of Emigration: Guandong to California,

1850–1882," in Cheng and Bonacich (eds.), *Labor Immigration Under Capitalism,* p. 232.

26. Elizabeth Wong, "Leaves from the Life History of a Chinese Immigrant," *Social Process in Hawaii,* vol. 2 (1936), pp. 39–42; Huie Kin, *Reminiscences* (Peiping, 1932), p. 17.

27. Kil Young Zo, *Chinese Emigration into the United States, 1850–1880* (New York, 1971), p. 62; "The Celestials at Home and Abroad," in *Littel's Living Age,* August 14, 1852, p. 294; Clarence E. Glick, *Sojourners and Settlers: Chinese Migrants in Hawaii* (Honolulu, 1980).

28. Zo, *Chinese Emigration,* p. 83; "Celestials at Home and Abroad," p. 294.

29. Circular, translation, in Diane Mei Lin Mark and Ginger Chih, *A Place Called Chinese America* (Dubuque, Iowa, 1982), p. 5; Lee Chew, interview, "Life Story of a Chinaman," in Hamilton Holt (ed.), *The Life Stories of Undistinguished Americans as Told by Themselves* (New York, 1906), pp. 287–288.

30. Mr. Quan, interview, in Him Mark Lai, Genny Lim, Judy Yung (eds.) *Island: Poetry and History of Chinese Immigrants on Angel Island, 1910–1940* (San Francisco, 1980), p. 48; popular saying, in Mark and Chih, *A Place Called Chinese America,* p. 6; Chinese sojourner to Henryk Sienkiewicz, in Sienkiewicz, "The Chinese in California," translated by Charles Morley, reprinted in *California Historical Quarterly,* vol. 34 (December 1955), p. 309; folk song, translation, in Marlon K. Hom (ea. and trans.), *Songs of Gold Mountain: Cantonese Rhymes from San Francisco Chinatown* (Berkeley, 1987), p. 39.

31. Edward Beechert, *Working in Hawaii: A Labor History* (Honolulu, 1985), p. 65; Chung Kun Ai, *My Seventy-Nine Years in Hawaii* (Hong Kong, 1960), p. 16.

32 "Letter of the Chinamen to His Excellency, Gov. Bigler," San Francisco, April 28, 1852, reprinted in *Littel's Living Age,* July 3, 1852, pp. 32–34; message from Dr. Bowring to Lord Malmesbury, January 5, 1853, in Zo, *Chinese Emigration,* p. 86; William Speer, *The Oldest and the Newest Empire: China and the United States* (Hartford, Conn., 1870), pp. 475–478.

33. Raymond Len, letters to the author, May 3, 1987, and October 8, 1987; Len Mau Yun, daughter-in-law of Len Wai, interview, July 13, 1988; Ginger Chih, "Immigration of Chinese Women to the U.S.A., 1900–1940," unpublished M.A. thesis, Sarah Lawrence College, 1977, p. 11.

34. Judy Yung, *Chinese Women of America: A Pictorial History* (Seattle, 1986), p. 11; Lai Chun-Chuen, *Remarks of the Chinese Merchants of San Francisco, upon Governor Bigler's Message* (San Francisco, 1855), p. 3.

35. Victor Nee and Herbert Y. Wong, "Asian American Socioeconomic Achievement: The Strength of the Family Bond," *Sociological Perspectives,* vol. 28, no. 3 (July 1985), pp. 288–289; Len Mau Yun, interview with author, July 13, 1988.

36. *Pacific Commercial Advertiser,* April 23, 1864, and August 25, 1877; Tin-Yuke Char, *The Sandalwood Mountains: Readings and Stories of the Early Chinese in Hawaii* (Honolulu, 1975), pp. 204–205; Frank Damon, "Homes for the Homeless: A Plea for Chinese Females Immigration," in *The Friend,* vol. 38, no. 11 (1881), p. 98.

37. H. M. Whitney to Dr. Damon, November 21, 1881, in *The Friend,* vol. 38, no. 12 (1881), p. 104; Hillebrand, in *Report of the President of the Bureau of Immigration to the Legislative Assembly of 1886* (Honolulu, 1886), p. 23.

38. *The Friend,* January 1880, p. 6.

39. George Anthony Peffer, "Forbidden Families: Emigration Experiences of Chinese

Women Under the Page Law, 1875–1882," in *Journal of American Ethnic History,* vol. 6 (1986), pp. 28–46.

40. In Re Ah Moy, on Habeas Corpus, Circuit Court, District of California, in Robert Desty (ed.), *Federal Reporter: Circuit and District Courts of the United States, August–November,* 1884 (Saint Paul, 1884), pp. 785–789. On the exclusion of Chinese wives, see Megumi Dick Osumi, "Asians and California's Anti-Miscegenation Laws," in Nobuya Tsuchida (ed.), *Asian and Pacific American Experiences: Women's Perspectives* (Minneapolis, 1982), p. 7; the 1882 and 1888 acts are reprinted in Cheng-Tsu Wu, *Chink! A Documentary History of Anti-Chinese Prejudice in America* (New York, 1972), pp. 70–75, 80–85.

41. Lucie Cheng Hirata, "Chinese Immigrant Women in Nineteenth-Century California," in Tsuchida (ed.), *Asian and Pacific American Experiences,* p. 46.

42. Lilac Chen, interview, in Victor and Brett de Bary Nee, *Longtime Californ': A Documentary Study of an American Chinatown* (New York, 1972), p. 84; "Story of Wong Ah So," in Social Science Institute, Fiske University, *Orientals and Their Cultural Adjustment* (Nashville, 1946), pp. 31–33.

43. Folk song, in Hom (ed. and trans.), *Songs of Gold Mountain,* p. 146; Hakka folk song, in Char, *The Sandalwood Mountains,* p. 67.

44. Poem, in Ito, *Issei,* p. 29.

45. Alan Moriyama, "The Causes of Emigration: The Background to Japanese Emigration to Hawaii, 1885 to 1894," in Cheng and Bonacich (eds.), *Labor Immigration Under Capitalism,* pp. 250–254; *Japan Weekly Mail,* December 20, 1884, reprinted in Nippu Jiji, *Golden Jubilee of the Japanese in Hawaii, 1885–1935* (Honolulu, 1935).

46. Yamaguchi newspaper, in Yuji Ichioka, *The Issei: The World of the First Generation Japanese Immigrants, 1885–1924* (New York, 1988), p. 45.

47. Moriyama, "Causes of Emigration," pp. 259–262.

48. John Modell, "Tradition and Opportunity: The Japanese Immigrant in America," *Pacific Historical Review,* vol. 40, no. 2 (1971), pp. 164–165; Yasuo Wakatsuki, "Japanese Emigration to the United States, 1866–1924," in *Perspectives in American History,* vol. 12 (1979), pp. 452–453; Ito, *Issei, p.* 36.

49. Daniel K. Inouye, *Journey to Washington* (Englewood Cliffs, N.J., 1967), pp. 3–7; Ito, *Issei,* pp. 30, 771.

50. Richard Okawa, interview with author, July 1980; poem, in Ito, *Issei,* p. 29; Alan Moriyama, *Imingaisha: Japanese Emigration Companies and Hawaii, 1894–1908* (Honolulu, 1985), pp. 73, 85.

51. Interviews, in Ito, *Issei,* pp. 33, 27, 38.

52. Richard Okawa, interview with author, July 1980; Moriyama, "Causes of Emigration," pp. 264–266.

53. Japanese Consul Takahashi Shinkichi, official message, February 13, 1884, and Japanese Consul Chinda Sutemi, confidential memorandum, April 25, 1891, in Wilson and Hosokawa, *East to America,* pp. 47, 113–114.

54. Minoru Takaki, interview with author, on Puunene Plantation, Maui, July 1985; Takeo Takaki, interview with author, in Kumamoto, Japan, May 1986; Toshino Watanabe Utano, interview with author, in Kumamoto, Japan, May 1986; Lillian Takaki Ota, letter to the author, May 19, 1987; Toshino Watanabe Utano, interview with author, in Kumamoto, Japan, May 1986; Minoru Takaki, interview with author, July 1986.

55. Ai Miyasaki and Riyo Orite, interviews, in Eileen Sunada Sarasohn (ed.), *The Issei: Portrait of a Pioneer, An Oral History* (Palo Alto, Calif., 1983), pp. 44, 31–32.

56. Thomas C. Smith, *Nakahara: Family Farming and Population in a Japanese Village, 1717–1830* (Stanford, 1977), pp. 134, 152, 153; Sheila Matsumoto, "Women in Factories," in Joyce Lebra et al. (eds.), *Women in Changing Japan* (Boulder, Colo., 1976), pp. 51–53; Sharon L. Sievers, *Flowers in Salt: The Beginnings of Feminist Consciousness in Modern Japan* (Stanford, 1983), pp. 55, 62, 66, 84; Yukiko Hanawa, "The Several Worlds of Issei Women," unpublished M.A. thesis, California State University, Long Beach, 1982, pp. 31–34; Wakatsuki, "Japanese Emigration to the United States," pp. 401, 404; Wilson and Hosokawa, *East to America*, p. 42.

57. Hanawa, "The Several Worlds of Issei Women," pp. 13–16; Emperor Meiji, quoted in Susan McCoin Kataoka, "Issei Women: A Study in Subordinate Status," unpublished Ph.D. thesis, University of California, Los Angeles, 1977, p. 6; Akemi Kikumura, *Through Harsh Winters: The Life of a Japanese Immigrant Woman* (Novato, Calif., 1981), pp. 18, 25; Emma Gee, "Issei: The First Women," in Emma Gee (ed.), *Asian Women* (Berkeley, 1971), p. 11.

58. Tsuru Yamauchi, interview, in Ethnic Studies Oral History Project, *Uchinanchu: A History of Okinawans in Hawaii* (Honolulu, 1981), pp. 490, 491; folk saying, in Tadashi Fukutake, *Japanese Rural Society* (Ithaca, N.Y., 1967), p. 47.

59. Fukutake, *Japanese Rural Society,* pp. 6, 7, 39, 40, 42; Nee and Wong, "Asian American Socioeconomic Achievement," p. 292; Ito, *Issei,* p. 33.

60. Lillian Takaki Ota, daughter of Nobuyoshi Takaki, interview with author, July 1980; Wakatsuki, "Japanese Emigration to the United States, 1866–1924," p. 510.

61. H. A. Millis, *The Japanese Problem in the United States* (New York, 1915), p. 86.

62. Katherine Coman, *The History of Contract Labor in the Hawaiian Islands* (New York, 1903), p. 42; Moriyama, "Causes of Emigration," p. 273; Republic of Hawaii, Bureau of Immigration, *Report* (Honolulu, 1886), p. 256.

63. Manager of the Hutchinson Sugar Company to W. G. Irwin and Company, February 5, 1902, and January 25, 1905, Hutchinson Plantation Records; Aiko Mifune, granddaughter of the Fukudas, interviews with author, February 18, 1988, and March 29, 1988.

64. Yuji Ichioka, "Ameyuki-san: Japanese Prostitutes in Nineteenth-Century America," *Amerasia,* vol. 4, no. 1 (1977), pp. 6–7.

65. Riyo Orite, interview, in Sarasohn (ed.), *Issei,* p. 34; Ito, *Issei,* pp. 11, 34.

66. Ayako, interview, in Yuriko Sato, "Emigration of Issei Women," unpublished paper, Asian American Studies, University of California, Berkeley, 1982, p. 12; Ito, *Issei,* pp. 38, 248.

67. Frank S. Miyamoto, "Views from Within," Symposium on the Japanese American Internment Experience, University of California, Berkeley, September 20, 1987; Ito, *Issei,* p. 34; William C. Smith, *Americans in Process: A Study of Citizens of Oriental Ancestry* (Ann Arbor, 1937), p. 163. In his survey of Issei men, "Tradition and Opportunity: The Japanese Immigrant in America," pp. 166–168, John Modell found that only 15 percent of those who entered before 1907 intended upon arrival to stay in the United States permanently, and that 36 percent of those who arrived after 1909 came with intentions of settlement.

68. Ito, *Issei,* p. 49.

69. Patterson, "The Korean Frontier in America," p. 453; Hyung-chan Kim, "The History and Role of the Church in the Korean American Community," in Hyung-chan Kim (ed.), *The Korean Diaspora: Historical and Sociological Studies of Korean Im-*

migration and Assimilation in North America (Santa Barbara, Calif., 1977), pp. 49, 50.

70. Patterson, "The Korean Frontier in America," pp. 460–461, 467; Adelaide Kim, "The Place of the Korean in the Industrial Life of Los Angeles," circa 1924, p. 2, Survey of Race Relations, Stanford University, Hoover Institution Archives.

71. Interview, in Brenda Sunoo (ed.), *Korean American Writings: Selected Material From Insight, Korean American Bimonthly,* New York, 1975, pp. 24–25; interview, in Christopher Kim, "Three Generations of Koreans in America," unpublished paper, Asian American Studies 199, University of California, Berkeley, 1976, pp. 5, 8, 9.

72. Patterson, "The Korean Frontier in America," pp. 275, 284–285; Lee Houchins and Chang-su Houchins, "The Korean Experience in America, 1903–1924," *Pacific Historical Review,* vol. 43, no. 4 (November 1974), p. 552.

73. Hyung June Moon, "The Korean Immigrants in America: The Quest for Identity in the Formative Years, 1903–1918," unpublished Ph.D. thesis, University of Nevada, Reno, 1976, p. 61; Harold and Sonia Sunoo, "The Heritage of the First Korean Women Immigrants to the United States: 1903–1924," paper presented at the 10th Annual Conference of the Association of Korean Christian Scholars of North America, Chicago, April 1976, p. 11; Morris Pang, "A Korean Immigrant," in Hyung-chan Kim and Wayne Patterson (eds.), *The Koreans in America, 1882–1974* (New York, 1974), p. 118.

74. Patterson, "The Korean Frontier in America," pp. 386, 252; Moon, "The Korean Immigrants in America," pp. 60, 64; Bong-Youn Choy, *Koreans in America* (Chicago, 1977), pp. 293, 321.

75. Kyung Sook Cho Gregor, "Korean Immigrants in Gresham, Oregon: Community Life and Social Adjustment," M.A. thesis, University of Oregon, 1963, pp. 15, 16, 25.

76. Alice Chai, "A Picture Bride from Korea: The Life History of a Korean American Woman in Hawaii," in *Bridge* (Winter 1978), p. 37.

77. Patterson, "The Korean Frontier in America," p. 252.

78. Phillip V. Vera Cruz, interview, in Asian Americans for Community Involvement, *Why America?* (n.p., 1987), p. 5.

79. Salvador del Fierro, quoted in Hilda Bryant, "The Filipinos of Seattle," *Seattle Post-Intelligencer,* March 31, 1971; Angeles Amoroso Mendoza Jucutan, interview with author, June 6, 1987; Donald Anthony, "Filipino Labor in Central California," *Sociology and Social Research,* vol. 16 (September 1931), pp. 149–150; Francisco Carino, "My Life History," August 1924, pp. 1–2, 8, Survey of Race Relations, Stanford University, Hoover Institution Archives; *The Philippine Advocate,* July 1, 1931, in envelope 16, Wood Collection; Antenorcruze, interview, Wood interview notes, p. 162, envelope 10, Wood Collection.

80. Genevieve O. Laigo, interview, May 12, 1975, pp. 3, 4, Washington State Oral/Aural History Program, Washington State Archives, Olympia, Wash.

81. R. D. Mead to H. Hackfield and Company, 1916, Grove Farm Plantation Records.

82. Virgilio Menor Felipe, "Hawaii: A Pilipino Dream," unpublished M.A. thesis, University of Hawaii, 1972, p. 68; Carlos Bulosan, "My Father Was a Working Man," reprinted in Susan Evangelista, *Carlos Bulosan and His Poetry: A Biography and Anthology* (Seattle, 1985), p. 77; Felipe, "Hawaii: A Pilipino Dream," pp. 142–143.

83. Carlos Bulosan, *America Is in the Heart: A Personal History* (rpt. Seattle, 1981, originally published in 1946), pp. 23, 58, 55; Dolores Quinto, "Life Story of a Filipino Immigrant," *Social Process in Hawaii,* vol. 4 (1938), pp. 71–72, H. Brett Me-

lendy, *Asians in America: Filipinos, Koreans, and East Indians* (Boston, 1977), p. 38.

84. Bulosan, *America Is in the Heart,* p. 58.

85. Felipe, "Hawaii: A Pilipino Dream," pp. 121, 155–156; Quinto, "Filipino Immigrant," pp. 72–73.

86. Fred Cordova, *Filipinos: Forgotten Asian Americans* (Dubuque, Iowa, 1983), p. 11; Lasker, *Filipino Immigration,* pp. 204, 233, 256; Jacqueline Frost, "Old-Timers Live Simply: Forgotten Workers—The First Filipino-Americans," *Stockton Record,* November 25, 1985.

87. Reuben R. Alcantara, *Sakada: Filipino Adaptation in Hawaii* (Washington, D.C., 1981), p. 11; Felipe, "Hawaii: A Pilipino Dream," p. 158.

88. Manuel Buaken, *I Have Lived with the American People* (Caldwell, Idaho, 1948), p. 37; Quinto, "Filipino Immigrant," p. 71; Bulosan, *America Is in the Heart,* p. 88.

89. Rufina Clemente Jenkins, interview, November 10, 1975, pp. 1–4, Washington State Oral/Aural History Program, Washington State Archives, Olympia, Wash.; Pete Silifan, interview, in Asian Americans for Community Involvement, *Why America?,* p. 13; Angeles Amoroso Mendoza Jucutan, interview with author, June 14, 1987.

90. Fred Lockley, "The Hindu Invasion: A New Immigration Problem," *Pacific Monthly Magazine* (May 1907), p. 593; Bruce La Brack, "Immigration Law and the Revitalization Process: The Case of the California Sikhs," in S. Chandrasekhar (ed.), *From India to America: A Brief History of Immigration, Admission and Assimilation* (La Jolla, Calif., 1982), p. 60.

91. Sucheta Mazumdar, "Colonial Impact and Punjabi Emigration to the United States," in Cheng and Bonacich (eds.), *Labor Immigration Under Capitalism,* p. 320; McWilliams, *Factories in the Field,* p. 117; Saint N. Singh, "The Picturesque Immigrant from India's Coral Strand," *Out West,* vol. 30 (1909), pp. 43–44.

92. Lockley, "The Hindu Invasion," p. 595.

93. Sucheta Mazumdar, "Punjabi Agricultural Workers in California, 1905–1945," p. 551; Lockley, "The Hindu Invasion," p. 590; Mazumdar, "Colonial Impact," p. 330.

94. "Biographical Sketch of Deal Singh Madhas," based on interviews, in Allan Miller, "An Ethnographic Report on the Sikh (East) Indians of the Sacramento Valley," Anthropology 299 paper, University of California, Berkeley, 1950, appendix, pp. 106–107; Jane Singh, daughter of Puna Singh, interview with author, June 2, 1988; Sucha Singh, interview, August 8, 1924, Survey of Race Relations, Stanford University, Hoover Institution Archives; Bruce La Brack, "The Sikhs of Northern California: A Socio-Historical Study," unpublished Ph.D. thesis, Syracuse University, 1980, pp. iv, 74, 105; U.S. Immigration Commission, *Japanese and East Indians,* pp. 327, 348; Bruce La Brack, "Occupational Specialization among Rural California Sikhs: The Interplay of Culture and Economics," *Amerasia,* vol. 9, no. 2 (1982), p. 32.

95. Moola Singh, in Karen Leonard, "Immigrant Punjabis in Early Twentieth-Century California," in Sucheng Chan (ed.), *Social and Gender Boundaries in the United States* (Lewiston, New York, 1989), p. 108.

96. Victor Turner, *Dramas, Fields, and Metaphors: Symbolic Action in Human Society* (Ithaca, N.Y., 1974), pp. 232, 237; Robert E. Park, "Human Migration and the Marginal Man," *American Journal of Sociology,* vol. 33, no. 6 (May 1928), pp. 881–893; Kingston, *The Woman Warrior,* p. 9. Maxine Hong Kingston, *China Men* (New York, 1980), p. 90, also uses the term "immensity."

97. Choki Oshiro, interview, in Ethnic Studies Oral History Project, *Uchinanchu,* p. 404; Hanayo Inouye, interview, in Sarasohn (ed.) *Issei,* p. 37; Alicia Mendoza, "My Grandmother's Experiences as a First Wave Filipina Immigrant to the United States," term paper for Asian American Studies 124, Spring 1986, pp. 1–2.

98. Glick, *Sojourners and Settlers,* p. 27; Ito, *Issei,* p. 51; Hitomi Maoki, autobiography, in East Bay Japanese For Action, *Our Recollections* (Berkeley, 1986), p. 281; Felipe, "Hawaii: A Pilipino Dream," p. 160; Bulosan, *America Is in the Heart,* p. 93. I am indebted to Marina Feleo-Gonzalez and Frank Megino for the song "Kamakaway Ka Pa, Irog" ("You Were Waving Goodbye, Beloved").

99. Quinto, "Filipino Immigrant," p. 75; Francisco Carino, "My Life History," p. 3, Survey of Race Relations, Stanford University, Hoover Institution Archives; Bulosan, *America Is in the Heart,* pp. 97–98.

100. Lee Chew, "Life Story of a Chinaman," p. 289; Ito, *Issei,* pp. 13, 42, 29; Buaken, *I Have Lived with the American People,* p. 46; Quinto, "Filipino Immigrant," p. 75.

101. Poem, in Him Mark Lai, Genny Lim, Judy Yung (eds.), *Island,* p. 38; Ito, *Issei,* pp. 32, 43; Patterson, "The Korean Frontier in America," p. 398; James Okahata (ed.), *A History of Japanese in Hawaii, 1885–1935* (Honolulu, 1971), pp. 94–95; Benny F. Feria, *Filipino Son* (Boston, 1954), p. 41.

102. Ito, *Issei,* p. 41; Bulosan, *America Is in the Heart,* pp. 97–98.

103. Bill Hosokawa, *Nisei: The Quiet Americans* (New York, 1969), p. 48; Yang, interview, in Choy, *Koreans in America,* p. 294; Bulosan, *America Is in the Heart,* p. 97.

104. Poems, in Ito, *Issei,* pp. 51, 37.

105. Albert S. Evans, "From the Orient Direct," *Atlantic Monthly,* vol. 24 (1869), pp. 543–547; Otis Gibson, *The Chinese in America* (Cincinnati, 1877), pp. 46, 50, 53.

106. Moon, "The Korean Immigrants in America," p. 149; Felipe, "Hawaii: A Pilipino Dream," pp. 165–167; Huie Kin, *Reminiscences* (Peiping, 1932), p. 24.

107. Rose Hum Lee, "The Growth and Decline of Chinese Communities in the Rocky Mountain Region," unpublished Ph.D. thesis, University of Chicago, 1947, pp. 249–250; Rikae Inouye, interview, in Sarasohn (ed.), *Issei,* p. 51; Choy, *Koreans in America,* pp. 88–89; Aiko Mifune, daughter of Fusayo Fukuda, interviews with author, February 18, 1988, and March 29, 1988.

108. Choy, *Koreans in America,* pp. 320–322; Patterson, "The Korean Frontier in America," pp. 457–458; Linda Pomerantz, "The Background of Korean Emigration," in Cheng and Bonacich (eds.), *Labor Immigration Under Capitalism,* p. 307; Emma Gee, "Issei Women," in Gee (ed.), *Counterpoint* (Los Angeles, 1976), pp. 362–363.

109. Rose Hum Lee, "Chinese Dilemma," *Phylon* (1949), p. 139; Chew, "Story of a Chinaman," p. 285; Gibson, *The Chinese in America,* p. 53; John Jeong, interview, in Nee, *Longtime Californ',* p. 73; Nisuke Mitsumori, interview, in Sarasohn (ed.), *Issei,* p. 59; interview with Kwang-son Lee, in Sonia Sunoo, *Korea Kaleidoscope: Oral Histories,* vol. 1, *Early Korean Pioneers in the U.S.A.* (Davis, Calif., 1982), p. 92; "Biographical Sketch of Munshi Singh Thiara," based on interviews, in Miller, "An Ethnographic Report on the Sikh (East) Indians of the Sacramento Valley," appendix, p. 80.

110. Bulosan, *America Is in the Heart,* p. 97; Chiyo Okuye, in Kesa Noda, *Yamato Colony: 1906–1960, Livingston, California* (Livingston, Calif., 1981), p. 57; Carlos Bulosan, "Patterns in Black and White," reprinted in Evangelista, *Bulosan and His Poetry,* p. 164.

111. Poems in Ito, *Issei,* pp. 49, 32; Bulosan, *America Is in the Heart,* pp. 197–198, 97; Turner, *Dramas, Fields, and Metaphors,* pp. 232, 237; Simmel, "The Stranger," pp. 143–149.

II. Strangers

1. Letter from Saum Song Bo in *American Missionary* (October 1885), reprinted in *East /West,* June 26, 1986.

3. Gam Saan Haak

1. Georg Simmel, "Der Fremde" or "The Stranger," in Simmel, *On Individuality and Social Forms,* edited by Donald N. Levine (Chicago, 1971), pp. 143–149.

2. *Daily Alta California,* May 12, 1852; Lai Chun-Chuen, *Remarks* of *the Chinese Merchants* of *San Francisco, upon Governor Bigler's Message* (San Francisco, 1855), p. 4.

3. Mary Coolidge, *Chinese Immigration* (New York, 1909), pp. 22, 23; As-sing, in Ching Chao Wu, "Chinatowns: A Study of Symbiosis and Assimilation," unpublished Ph.D. thesis, University of Chicago, 1928, p. 15; Charles J. McClain, Jr., "The Chinese Struggle for Civil Rights in Nineteenth Century America: The First Phase, 1850–1870," *California Law Review,* vol. 72 (1984), p. 535.

4. *Assembly Committee on Mines and Mining Interests, Report,* Cal. Assembly, 3rd Sess., Appendix to the Journals, 829 (1852), p. 834; "Governor's Special Message," *Daily Alta California,* April 25, 1852; McClain, "Chinese Struggle for Civil Rights," pp. 536–537.

5. McClain, "Chinese Struggle for Civil Rights," pp. 544, 555.

6. Sucheng Chan, "Chinese Livelihood in Rural California: The Impact of Economic Change, 1860–1880," in *Pacific Historical Review,* vol. 53, no. 3 (1984), pp. 281–282.

7. Gunther Barth, *Bitter Strength: A History of the Chinese in the United States, 1850–1870* (Cambridge, Mass., 1964), pp. 114, 115; Otis Gibson, *The Chinese in America* (Cincinnati, 1877), p. 234.

8. Barth, *Bitter Strength,* p. 114; telegrams reprinted in Albert Dressler (ed.), *California Chinese Chatter* (San Francisco, 1927), pp. 2, 3, 9.

9. Barth, *Bitter Strength,* p. 115; Alexander Saxton, *The Indispensable Enemy: Labor and the Anti-Chinese Movement in California* (Berkeley, 1971), p. 58.

10. Chan, "Chinese Livelihood in Rural California," p. 297.

11. E. L. Sabin, *Building the Pacific Railway* (Philadelphia, 1919), p. 111; Corrine K. Hoexter, *From Canton to California: The Epic of Chinese Immigration* (New York, 1976), p. 73; Jack Chen, *The Chinese in America* (New York, 1981), p. 67.

12. Thomas Chinn, H. M. Lai, and Philip Choy, *A History of the Chinese in California* (San Francisco, 1969), p. 45.

13. Albert P. Richardson, *Beyond the Mississippi* (Hartford, 1867), p. 462; Saxton, *Indispensable Enemy,* p. 65.

14. Thomas W. Chinn (ed.), *A History of the Chinese in California* (San Francisco, 1969), p. 46; *San Francisco Alta,* July 1 and 3, 1867; Sabin, *Building the Pacific Railway,* p. 111.

15. Aaron Palmer, *Memorial,* March 8, 1848, U.S. Cong., Senate, 30th Cong., 1st sess., Senate misc. no. 80, p. 1; F. F. Victor, "Manifest Destiny in the West," *Overland Monthly,* vol. 3 (August 1869), pp. 148–149; Robert L. Harris, "The Pacific Railroad—Unopen," *Overland Monthly,* vol. 3 (September 1869), p. 252.

16. Paul M. Ong, "Chinese Labor in Early San Francisco: Racial Segmentation and Industrial Expansion," *Amerasia,* vol. 8, no. 1 (1981), pp. 70–75.

17. *San Francisco Morning Call,* May 27, 1873, reprinted in Henry J. West, *The Chinese Invasion* (San Francisco, 1873).

18. Ong, "Chinese Labor in Early San Francisco," pp. 75–77.

19. A. W. Loomis, "How Our Chinamen Are Employed," *Overland Monthly,* vol. 2 (March 1869), pp. 233–236; O. Gibson, *Chinaman or White Man, Which?* (San Francisco, 1873), p. 10; McClellan, in Coolidge, *Chinese Immigration,* p. 357.

20. Carey McWilliams, *Factories in the Field: The Story of Migratory Farm Labor in California* (Santa Barbara, 1971), pp. 67, 71.

21. Loomis, "How Our Chinamen Are Employed," p. 237; Sandy Lydon, *Chinese Gold: The Chinese in the Monterey Bay Region* (Capitola, Calif., 1985), p. 286.

22. Sucheng Chan, *This Bitter-sweet Soil: The Chinese in California Agriculture, 1860–1910* (Berkeley, 1986), p. 176.

23. Based on figures from tables in appendix, Chan, "Chinese Livelihood in Rural California," pp. 300–307; Chan, "Chinese Livelihood in Rural California," pp. 288–289, 296; Loomis, "How Our Chinamen Are Employed," p. 234.

24. Linda Perrin, *Coming to America: Immigrants from the Far East* (New York, 1980), p. 25; Loomis, "How Our Chinamen Are Employed," pp. 233–234; Chan, *Bittersweet Soil,* p. 242.

25. Calculations in Chan, *Bitter-sweet Soil,* pp. 305–307, 316–317; Henryk Sienkiewicz, "The Chinese in California," translated by Charles Morley, reprinted in *California Historical Society Quarterly,* vol. 34 (December 1955), p. 309; McWilliams, *Factories in the Field,* p. 71.

26. Chan, *Bitter-sweet Soil,* p. 328.

27. Ibid., pp. 332–333.

28. McWilliams, *Factories in the Field,* p. 74.

29. Paul Ong, "Chinese Laundries as an Urban Occupation in Nineteenth Century California," *The Annals of the Chinese Historical Society of the Pacific Northwest* (Seattle, 1983), p. 72.

30. Lee Chew, "The Life Story of a Chinaman," in Hamilton Holt (ed.), *The Life Stories of Undistinguished Americans as Told by Themselves* (New York, 1906), pp. 289–290; Wong Chin Foo, "The Chinese in New York," *The Cosmopolitan,* vol. 5, no. 4 (June 1888), p. 298.

31. Paul Siu, "The Chinese Laundryman: A Study of Social Isolation," unpublished Ph.D. thesis, University of Chicago, 1953, pp. 168, 63.

32. Lee Chew, "Life Story of a Chinaman," p. 296; Ong, "Chinese Laundries as an Urban Occupation," pp. 69, 70, 74; Victor and Brett de Bary Nee, *Longtime Californ': A Documentary Study of an American Chinatown* (New York, 1972), p. 22; Ng Poon Chew, "The Chinaman in America," *Chautauquan,* vol. 9, no. 4 (January 1889), p. 802.

33. Lee Chew, "Life Story of a Chinaman," pp. 291–294.

34. *Vicksburg Times,* June 30, 1869, in James W. Loewen, *The Mississippi Chinese: Between Black and White* (Cambridge, Mass., 1971), p. 22; planters' convention report, reprinted in John R. Commons et al. (eds.), *A Documentary History of American Industrial Society* (Cleveland, 1910–1911), vol. 9, p. 81.

35. John Todd, *The Sunset Land* (Boston, 1870), pp. 284–285; Lucy M. Cohen, *Chinese in the Post-Civil War South: A People Without a History* (Baton Rouge, La., 1984), p. 109; Loewen, *The Mississippi Chinese,* p. 23.

36. Loewen, *The Mississippi Chinese,* p. 24; Ralph Keeler, "The 'Heathen Chinee' in the South," *Every Saturday,* vol. 3, no. 83 (July 29, 1871), p. 117; Cohen, *Chinese in the Post–Civil War South,* pp. 123–124.

37. Cohen, *Chinese in the Post–Civil War South,* p. 136.

38. *Harper's New Monthly Magazine* (December 1870), p. 138.

39. William Shanks, "Chinese Skilled Labor," *Scribner's Monthly*, vol. 2 (September 1871), p. 495; Washington Gladden, *From the Hub to the Hudson* (Greenfield, Wis., 1870), p. 107; *North Adams Transcript*, in Frederick Rudolph, "Chinamen in Yankeedom: Anti-Unionism in Massachusetts in 1870," *American Historical Review*, vol. 53, no. 1 (October 1947), pp. 4, 8, 9.

40. Rudolph, "Chinamen in Yankeedom," p. 10.

41. *The Nation*, vol. 10 (June 23, 1870), p. 397; *Boston Commonwealth*, June 25, 1870; *Springfield Republican*, June 17, 1870.

42. *The Nation*, vol. 10 (June 23, 1870), p. 397; *Harper's New Monthly Magazine* (December 1870), p. 138; Shanks, "Chinese Skilled Labor," pp. 495–496.

43. *The Nation*, vol. 10 (June 30, 1870), p. 412; Rudolph, "Chinamen in Yankeedom," p. 23.

44. Frank Norton, "Our Labor System and the Chinese," *Scribner's Monthly*, vol. 2 (May 1871), p. 70.

45. Samuel Bowles, *Our New West* (Hartford, 1869), p. 414.

46. Crocker, testimony, *Report of the Joint Special Committee to Investigate Chinese Immigration*, Senate Report No. 689, 44th Cong., 2nd sess., 1876–1877, pp. 679, 680; Karl Marx, *Capital: A Critique of Political Economy* (New York, 1906), pp. 689–703; Robert Blauner, *Racial Oppression in America* (New York, 1972).

47. Simmel, "Der Fremde" or "The Stranger," pp. 143–149.

48. Hinton Rowan Helper, *The Land of Gold: Reality Versus Fiction* (Baltimore, 1855), p. 96.

49. *New York Times*, September 3, 1865; *San Francisco Chronicle*, Mar. 6, 1879.

50. *San Francisco Alta*, June 4, 1853; *Hutching's California Magazine*, vol. 1 (March 1857), p. 387; *New York Times*, December 26, 1873; *The Wasp Magazine*, vol. 30 (January–June 1893), pp. 10–11; *Report of the Joint Special Committee to Investigate Chinese Immigration*, p. vi; Dan Caldwell, "The Negroization of the Chinese Stereotype in California," *Southern California Quarterly*, vol. 53 (June 1971), pp. 123–131.

51. Megumi Dick Osumi, "Asians and California's Anti-Miscegenation Laws," in Nobuya Tsuchida (ed.), *Asian and Pacific American Experiences: Women's Perspectives* (Minneapolis, 1982), pp. 2, 6.

52. *California Marin Journal*, April 13, 1876; Seymour, in *New York Times*, August 6, 1870; *The Nation*, vol. 9 (July 15, 1869), p. 445; *Congressional Record*, 47th Cong., 1st sees., p. 3267.

53. California Supreme Court, The People v. Hall, October 1, 1854, in Robert F. Heizer and Alan F. Almquist, *The Other Californians* (Berkeley, 1971), p. 229.

54. Stanford Lyman, "Strangers in the City: The Chinese in the Urban Frontier," in Franklin Odo (ed.), *Roots: An Asian American Reader* (Los Angeles, 1971), p. 175; Stuart C. Miller, *The Unwelcome Immigrant: The American Image of the Chinese, 1752–1882* (Berkeley, 1969), p. 190.

55. Perrin, *Coming to America*, pp. 32–33.

56. Henry Grimm, *"The Chinese Must Go": A Farce in Four Acts* (San Francisco, 1879), pp. 3, 4, 8.

57. Ibid., p. 19.

58. Bret Harte, "Plain Language from Truthful James," *Overland Monthly*, vol. 5 (September 1870), pp. 287–288; *New York Globe*, January 7, 1871, in George R. Stewart, Jr., *Bret Harte: Argonaut and Exile* (Boston, 1931), p. 180; *Springfield Re-*

publican, in Margaret Duckett, *Mark Twain and Bret Harte* (Norman, Okla., 1964), p. 38.

59. Harte, "Plain Language," pp. 287–288.

60. Harte to Mrs. M. Sherwood, in *New York Times*, May 10, 1902, in Stewart, *Harte*, p. 181.

61. Harte, "Wan Lee, the Pagan," in Harte, *Harte's Complete Works*, 20 vols. (Boston, 1929), vol. 3, pp. 262–279.

62. Harte, "See Yup," ibid., vol. 7, pp. 144–160.

63. Henry George, speech, February 4, 1890, in Henry George, Jr., *The Life of Henry George* (New York, 1930), p. 100; George, ibid., p. 210; George, speech, February 4, 1890, ibid., p. 80.

64. Henry George, diary, January 1, February 21, 22, 1865, Henry George Papers, New York Public Library, New York, New York.

65. George, "What the Railroad Will Bring Us," *Overland Monthly*, vol. 1 (October 1868), pp. 297–306.

66. George, "The Chinese on the Pacific Coast," *New York Tribune*, May 1, 1869, reprinted in A. M. Winn, *Valedictory Address, January 11, 1871, at Excelsior Hall, San Francisco, to the Mechanics' State Council of California* (San Francisco, 1871), pp. 13–19.

67. A. J. Steers of the editorial department to W. H. Appleton, 1880(?), in George Papers, New York Public Library.

68. Henry George, *Progress and Poverty: An Inquiry into the Cause of Industrial Depressions and of Increase of Want with Increase of Wealth. The Remedy.* (New York, 1879), pp. 3, 6, 280, 325, 326, 390, 388, 492, 475, 480, 496.

69. John A. Garraty, *Unemployment in History: Economic Thought and Public Policy* (New York, 1978), pp. 103–109.

70. *The Nation* (March 16, 1882), p. 222; *Congressional Record*, 47th Cong., 1st sess., pp. 2973–4, 2033, 3310, 3265, 3268; appendix, pp. 48, 89, 21.

71. Chinese Exclusion Act of 1888, reprinted in Cheng-Tsu Wu, *"Chink!": A Documentary History of Anti-Chinese Prejudice in America* (New York, 1972), pp. 82–83.

72. Letter, reprinted in Paul Jacobs and Saul Landau, *To Serve the Devil: Colonials and Sojourners* (New York, 1971), vol. 2, pp. 66–67.

73. "To His Excellency Governor Bigler from Norman Asing," in *Daily Alta California*, May 5, 1852; Lai Chun-Chuen, *Remarks of the Chinese Merchants of San Francisco*, p. 5.

74. "Memorial of the Chinese Six Companies," in *San Francisco Alta*, May 28, 1876; Chinese Six Companies, letter to A. J. Bryant, Mayor of San Francisco, published in *San Francisco Call*, November 2, 1877.

75. Hoexter, *From Canton to California*, p. 44; McClain, "Chinese Struggle for Civil Rights," pp. 555–557.

76. McClain, "Chinese Struggle for Civil Rights," pp. 561–563.

77. Fung Tang, "Address to the Committee by the Chinese Merchants," *Daily Alta California*, June 26, 1869; McClain, "Chinese Struggle for Civil Rights," pp. 564–567.

78. Lee Chew, "Life Story of a Chinaman," p. 298; Kwang Chang Ling, *Why Should the Chinese Go? A Pertinent Inquiry from a Mandarin High in Authority* (San Francisco, 1878), p. 16; "Life History and Social Document of Mr. J. S. Look," Au-

gust 13, 1924, p. 1, Survey of Race Relations, Stanford University, Hoover Institution Archives; "Life History and Social Document of Law Yow," August 12, 1924, p. 3, ibid.; "Life History and Social Document of Andrew Kan," August 22, 1924, p. 2, ibid.; Huie Kin, *Reminiscences* (Peiping, 1932), p. 27.

79. Kil Young Zo, *Chinese Emigration into the United States, 1850–1890* (New York, 1978), p. 181; Lee Chew, "Life Story of a Chinaman," pp. 298–299.

80. Ginn Wall, in Nee, *Longtime Californ'*, p. 27.

81. Lai Chun-Chuen, *Remarks of the Chinese Merchants*, pp. 3, 6. Since the total Chinese population in the United States at any time in the nineteenth century did not exceed 110,000, these figures must have included migrants who left and then reentered the country.

82. Stanford Lyman, *Chinatown and Little Tokyo* (New York, 1986), pp. 171–172; The Six Companies, "To the American Public," April 1, 1876, reprinted in Gibson, *The Chinese in America*, p. 300.

83. Chinn et al., *Chinese in California*, p. 10; Huie Kin, *Reminiscences*, pp. 25, 28; A. W. Loomis, "The Old East in the New West," *Overland Monthly*, vol. 1 (October 1868), p. 364.

84. Gibson, *The Chinese in America*, p. 14.

85. A. W. Loomis, "Chinese in California: Their Sign-Board Literature," *Overland Monthly*, vol. 2 (August 1868), pp. 152–155.

86. Based on tables in Chan, "Chinese Livelihood in Rural California," appendix, pp. 300–307.

87. "Interview with Chinese Tong Members in Chicago," January 1925, and letter by C. O. M., a laundry worker, December 14, 1913, in "Segregation folder," box 1, Survey of Race Relations, Stanford University, Hoover Institution Archives; interview by C. H. Burnett, August 9, 1924, ibid., p. 5.

88. A. W. Loomis, "Holiday in the Chinese Quarter," *Overland Monthly*, vol. 2 (February 1869), pp. 148, 149, 151; poem, in Marlon K. Hom (ea. and trans.), *Songs of Gold Mountain: Cantonese Rhymes from San Francisco Chinatown* (Berkeley, 1987), p. 195.

89. Diane Mei Lin Mark and Ginger Chih, *A Place Called Chinese America* (Dubuque, Iowa, 1982), pp. 69–70.

90. Lucie Cheng Hirata, "Chinese Immigrant Women in Nineteenth-Century California," in Carol Berkin and Mary Norton (eds.), *Women of America* (Boston, 1979), pp. 243–244.

91. Hom (ed. and trans.), *Songs of Gold Mountain*, p. 309; Lilac Chen, interview, in Nee, *Longtime Californ'*, p. 85; Judy Yung, *Chinese Women of America: A Pictorial History* (Seattle, 1986), p. 23; Hirata, "Chinese Immigrant Women," p. 234.

92. Perrin, *Coming to America*, p. 19; Sing Kum, "Letter by a Chinese Girl," reprinted in Gibson, *The Chinese in America*, pp. 220–221; "Story of Wong Ah So—Experiences as a Prostitute," in Social Science Institute, *Orientals and Their Cultural Adjustment* (Nashville, 1946), pp. 31–32; "Story of Exslave, and Slave Owner," in "Two Schools for Chinese" by Mrs. Park, August 1924, pp. 3–4, Survey of Race Relations, Stanford University, Hoover Institution Archives.

93. Folk song, translation, Hom (ea. and trans.), *Songs of Gold Mountain*, p. 321.

94. Jack Chew, interview, in Peter C. Y. Leung, *One Day, One Dollar: Locke, California and the Chinese Farming Experience in the Sacramento Delta* (El Cerrito, Calif., 1984), appendix, p. 68; Willard G. Jue, "Chin Gee-Hee, Chinese Pioneer Entrepreneur in Seattle and Toishan," in Douglas W. Lee (ed.), *The Annals of the*

Chinese Historical Society of the Pacific Northwest (Seattle, 1983), p. 32; A. W. Loomis, "Chinese Women in California," vol. 2 *Overland Monthly* (April 1869), pp. 349–350.

95. Lydon, *Chinese Gold*, pp. 156–158; "Memorial of the Chinese Six Companies," 1876, reprinted in Gibson, *The Chinese in America*, p. 318.

96. Telegrams reprinted in Dressler (ed.), *California Chinese Chatter*, pp. 12–22.

97. Lee Chew, "Life Story of a Chinaman," p. 295; "Life History of Mr. Woo Gen," July 29, 1924, p. 16, Survey of Race Relations, Stanford University, Hoover Institution Archives; "Conversation with waiter, International Chop Suey," February 2, 1924, ibid.

98. Markie Tom to Lung On, October 16, 1905, in the Kam Wah Chung Company, John Day, Oregon, papers, translation by Chia-Lin Chen on microfilm, Asian American Studies Library, University of California, Berkeley; "Life History and Social Document of Albert King of Seattle," July 21, 1924, p. 13, Survey of Race Relations, Stanford University, Hoover Institution Archives; Chin Chao Wu, "Chinatowns," p. 300; Wong, "The Chinese in New York," p. 308; Lee Chew, "Life Story of a Chinaman," pp. 296, 299.

99. "An Interracial Romance," interview conducted in 1924, interviewee's name not to be published, Box 27, Folder 178, Survey of Race Relations, Stanford University, Hoover Institution Archives.

100. Chinese rhyme, in Hom (ea. and trans.), *Songs of Gold Mountain*, p. 90; Gibson, *The Chinese in America*, pp. 15–16; Loomis, "The Old East in the New West," p. 364; Lee Chew, "Life Story of a Chinaman," p. 294; "Conversation with waiter, International Chop Suey," February 2, 1924, Survey of Race Relations, Stanford University, Hoover Institution Archives; "Interview with Tom Lee, Cook for Dr. N. C. Peterson," circa 1924, p. 2, ibid.

101. Mark and Chih, *A Place Called Chinese America*, p. 52.

102. Robert Stewart Culin, in Lyman, *Chinatown and Little Tokyo*, p. 123; Robert Culin, "Customs of the Chinese in America," *Journal of American Folklore* (July–September 1890), pp. 191, 193; "The Sound of the Slippers," in Paul Radin (ed.), *The Golden Mountain: Chinese Tales Told in California*, collected by Jon Lee in Oakland and translated by Lee (Taipei, 1971), p. 5.

103. Wong Sam and Assistants, *An English–Chinese Phrase Book* (San Francisco, 1875), pp. 13, 14, 16, 18, 20, 22, 52, 56, 106, 108, 113, 122, 128, 155, 219, 232.

104. Culin, in Lyman, *Chinatown and Little Tokyo*, p. 123; Culin, "Customs of the Chinese in America," pp. 191, 193; Pardee Lowe, *Father and Glorious Descendant* (Boston, 1943), p. 98; Wong, "The Chinese in New York," p. 301.

105. Translated and reprinted in Loomis, "The Old East in the New West," p. 362.

106. Personal letter in Chinese collected by Paul C. P. Siu, in Siu, "The Sojourner," *American Journal of Sociology*, vol. 58 (July 1952), pp. 35–36; Ing Weh-teh to Ing Pang-chi, June 16, 1897; Liang Zu-teh to Liang Kau-tsi, November 28, 1902, Kam Wah Chung Company Papers.

107. Hom (ed. and trans.), *Songs of Gold Mountain*, p. 294.

108. Rose Hum Lee, "Chinese Dilemma," *Phylon* (1949), p. 139; Him Mark Lai, Genny Lim, and Judy Yung (eds.), *Island: Poetry and History of Chinese Immigrants on Angel Island* (San Francisco, 1980), p. 12; interview with old laundryman, in "Interviews with Two Chinese," circa 1924, Box 326, folder 325, Survey of Race Relations, Stanford University, Hoover Institution Archives; "Life History and Social Document of Andrew Kan," p. 11, Survey of Race Relations, Stanford University, Hoover Institution Archives.

109. Victor Turner, *Dramas, Fields, and Metaphors: Symbolic Action in Human Society* (Ithaca N.Y., 1974), pp. 232, 237. I am indebted to Judy Yung for telling me about the Chinese phrase, *Jo lui jai;* Yung, interview with author, November 30, 1987.

4. Raising Cane

1. *Hawaiian Gazette,* June 27, 1877.
2. Plantation work song, in *Hawaii Herald,* February 2, 1973; Maxine Hong Kingston, *The Woman Warrior: Memoirs of a Girlhood Among Ghosts* (New York, 1976), pp. 6–7.
3. Ethnic Studies Oral History Project, *Stores and Storekeepers of Paia and Puunene, Maui* (Honolulu, 1980), p. 399.
4. "The Five O'Clock Whistle," in the *Kohala Midget,* April 27, 1910.
5. Korean woman, in Eun Sik Yang, "Korean Women of America: From Subordination to Partnership, 1903–1930," *Amerasia,* vol. 11, no. 2 (1984), p. 5; Ethnic Studies Oral History Project, *The 1924 Filipino Strike on Kanai* (Honolulu, 1979), vol. 2, p. 662.
6. "Plantation Work Begins, Silently, In Early Morn," *Honolulu Star Bulletin,* January 13, 1934; Minnie Caroline Grant, *Scenes in Hawaii* (Toronto, 1888), pp. 140–142.
7. Lillian Ota Takaki, daughter of Yukino Takaki, letter to the author, August 10, 1985.
8. Richard Okawa, interview with the author, July 1980; Harold and Sonia Sunoo, "The Heritage of the First Korean Women Immigrants to the United States, 1903–1924," paper presented at the 10th Annual Conference of the Association of Korean Christian Scholars of North America, Chicago, April 8–10, 1976, p. 10.
9. Ethnic Studies Oral History Project, *Uchinanchu: A History of Okinawans in Hawaii* (Honolulu, 1981), pp. 360, 520, 513; Korean woman, in Harold and Sonia Sunoo, "The Heritage of the First Korean Women Immigrants," p. 12.
10. H. Brett Melendy, *Asians in America: Filipinos, Koreans, and East Indians* (Boston, 1977), pp. 86–87; Ethnic Studies Oral History Project, *Uchinanchu,* p. 488; Andrew Lind, *An Island Community* (Chicago, 1938), pp. 240–241; song, in *Hawaii Herald,* February 2 and October 26, 1973.
11. Kim Hyung-soon, interview, in Bong-Youn Choy, *Koreans in America* (Chicago, 1979), p. 303; Ethnic Studies Oral History Project, *Waialua and Haleiwa: The People Tell Their Story* (Honolulu, 1977), vol. 8, p. 149.
12. Mary H. Drout, *Hawaii and a Revolution* (New York, 1898), pp. 237–238.
13. Ethnic Studies Oral History Project, *Waialua and Haleiwa,* vol. 8, p. 167; Yako Morishita, poem, in Jiro Nakano, "History of Japanese Short Poems (Tanka, Haiku and Senryu) in Hawaii," unpublished manuscript, 1986, p. 46.
14. Interview, in Choy, *Koreans in America,* p. 321; song, in Yukuo Uyehara, "The Horehore-Bushi: A Type of Japanese Folksong Developed and Sung Among the Early Immigrants in Hawaii," in *Social Process in Hawaii,* vol. 28 (1980–1981), p. 114.
15. Ethnic Studies Oral History Project, *Uchinanchu,* p. 369.
16. Song, in Uyehara, "The Horehore-Bushi," p. 114.
17. *Pacific Commercial Advertiser,* May 30, 1874; David Bowman to James Campsie, May 3, 1920, Hawaiian Agricultural Company Records.
18. Republic of Hawaii, *Report of the Labor Commission on Strikes and Arbitration* (Honolulu, 1895), p. 16; Hawaiian Sugar Planters' Association, *The Sugar Industry of Hawaii and the Labor Shortage* (Honolulu, 1921), p. 37.

19. Director of Theo. H. Davies and Company to C. McLennan, February 15, 1904, Laupahoehoe Plantation Records; Hawaiian Sugar Planters' Association, Bureau of Labor Statistics, memo to plantations, February 12, 1918, Grove Farm Plantation Records; vice president of H. Hackfield and Company to George Wilcox, September 24, 1910, Grove Farm Plantation Records; Hawaiian Sugar Planters' Association, *Sugar Industry,* pp. 5, 15, 31, 43.

20. *Pacific Commercial Advertiser,* July 26, 1904; William Henry Taylor, "The Hawaiian Sugar Industry," unpublished Ph.D. thesis, University of California, Berkeley, 1935, p. 99.

21. Clarence Glick, *Sojourners and Settlers: Chinese Migrants in Hawaii* (Honolulu, 1980), pp. 34–35; Republic of Hawaii, *Report of the Labor Commission,* pp. 11–13; Bureau of Labor Statistics, *Report of the Commissioner of Labor* (Washington, 1905), pp. 96–97.

22. Planter and Goo Kim, in *Honolulu Record,* October 18, 1951; Lee, in Choy, *Koreans in America,* pp. 95–96; *Pacific Commercial Advertiser,* September 5, 1868; A. Moore, in *Report of the Labor Commission,* pp. 11–13; George Dole to William G. Irwin, August 22, 1879, letterbook, in Kauai Museum, Lihue, Kauai; Kim, interview, in Choy, *Koreans in America,* p. 303; Yukiko Kimura, "Sociohistorical Background of the Okinawans in Hawaii," unpublished paper, University of Hawaii, 1962, p. 5.

23. Hawaiian Sugar Planters' Association, resolution of trustees, November 18, 1904, Grove Farm Plantation Records; *Planters' Monthly,* vol. 1, no. 7 (October 1882), p. 242; Bureau of Labor Statistics, *Report of the Commissioner of Labor on Hawaii* (Washington, D.C., 1916), pp. 120–153; Machiyo Mitamura, "Life on a Hawaiian Plantation: An Interview," in *Social Process in Hawaii,* vol. 6 (1940), p. 51.

24. Hawaiian Sugar Planters' Association to "Our Plantation Managers," July 24, 1901; Hawaiian Sugar Planters' Association, circular letter, August 22, 1910, Grove Farm Plantation Records; Hawaiian Sugar Planters' Association, *The Sugar Industry of Hawaii,* pp. 38, 39; manager of the Hawaiian Agricultural Company Plantation to C. Brewer and Company, December 20, 1911, Hawaiian Agricultural Company Records.

25. Hawaiian Sugar Planters' Association, circular, "The Labor Question," May 7, 1917, Grove Farm Plantation Records; Virgilio Felipe, "Hawaii: A Pilipino Dream," unpublished M.A. thesis, University of Hawaii, 1972, p. 177.

26. James J. Jarvis, *Scenes and Scenery in the Sandwich Islands* (London, 1844), p. 97; William Hooper, diary, William Hooper Papers, Hawaiian Collection, University of Hawaii Library, June 11, 1836; Ladd and Company to William Henry N. Hooper, printer and brother of William Hooper, November 15, 1837, Hooper Papers; Hooper to Ladd and Company, January 5, 1839 and April 7, 1839, Hooper Papers.

27. Isabella Bird, *Six Months in the Sandwich Islands* (Honolulu, 1964), p. 77; song, in Uyehara, "Horehore-Bushi," p. 116; Jack Hall, *A Luna's Log* (Kohala, 1927), p. 6.

28. Clarence E. Glick, "The Chinese Migrant in Hawaii," unpublished Ph.D. thesis, University of Chicago, 1938, p. 42; Yasutaro Soga, in *Honolulu Record,* October 27, 1949; Felipe, "Hawaii: A Pilipino Dream," p. 208.

29. *Kohala Midget,* July 12, 1911; *Hawaiian Gazette,* June 6, 1877; *Planters' Monthly,* vol. 1, no. 1 (April 1882), p. 20.

30. Glick, "Chinese Migrant," p. 48; Chung Kun Ai, *My Seventy-Nine Years in Hawaii* (Hong Kong, 1960), p. 99; Felipe, "Hawaii: A Pilipino Dream," pp. 208, 227.

31. *Hawaii Herald,* February 2, 1973.

32. *Pacific Commercial Advertiser,* August 14, 1880; Anton Cropp, diary, 1892, pp. 4, 12, 13, Grove Farm Plantation Records.

33. *Polynesian,* December 3, 1859; Ewald Kleinau, Diary. January 11, 1882, Bancroft Library, University of California, Berkeley; Raymond Len, letter to author, May 3, 1987; Len Too Shing, interview, July 13, 1988.

34. *Maui News,* August 18, 1900; *Hawaiian Star,* March 17, 1906; Miki Sato, circular, September 21, 1903, in Grove Farm Plantation Records.

35. Tamashiro, interview, in Ethnic Studies Oral History Project, *Uchinanchu,* p. 364; John Reinecke, *Feigned Necessity: Hawaii's Attempt to Obtain Chinese Contract Labor, 1921–1923* (San Francisco, 1979), p. 27.

36. *Pacific Commercial Advertiser,* September 7, 1891.

37. *Honolulu Record,* April 28, 1949; president of the Planters' Association of Maui, letter to the trustees of the Hawaiian Sugar Planters' Association, May 1900, Grove Farm Plantation Records.

38. *The Higher Wage Question,* excerpts reprinted in Bureau of Labor Statistics, *Report of the Commissioner of Labor on Hawaii* (Washington, D.C., 1910), p. 76.

39. Soga, in *Honolulu Record,* July 7, 1949; Allan Beekman, "Hawaii's Great Japanese Strike," reprinted in Dennis Ogawa (ed.), *Kodomo no tame ni* (Honolulu, 1978), p. 158.

40. Letter to plantation manager E. K. Bull, signed by ninety-two strikers, May 19, 1909, reprinted in Bureau of Labor Statistics, *Report of the Commissioner of Labor,* p. 80; Higher Wage Association, statement, ibid., p. 68; *Higher Wage Question,* ibid., pp. 77–78.

41. Takashi Tsutsumi, *History of Hawaii Laborers' Movement,* translation (Honolulu, 1922), pp. 194–198.

42. Ibid., p. 175.

43. Ibid., pp. 217, 224, 238, 240, 241, 242, 243.

44. President of C. Brewer and Company to James Campsie, manager of the Hawaiian Agricultural Company, February 3, 1920, Hawaiian Agricultural Company Records; R. D. Mead, director of the Labor Bureau, to manager of Grove Farm Plantation, February 13, 1920, Grove Farm Plantation Records.

45. Hyung June Moon, "The Korean Immigrants in America: The Quest for Identity in the Formative Years, 1903–1918," unpublished Ph.D. thesis, University of Nevada, Reno, 1976, p. 290.

46. Tadao Okada, interview with author, July 1980.

47. Hawaii Laborers' Association, *Facts about the Strike on Sugar Plantations in Hawaii* (Honolulu, 1920), p. 1.

48. Tsutsumi, *Hawaii Laborers' Movement,* pp. 12, 44, 17, 13, 22.

49. Milton Murayama, *All I Asking for Is My Body* (rpt. San Francisco, 1975), p. 34.

50. Murayama, *All I Asking for Is My Body,* pp. 28, 96.

51. Jared C. Smith, *Plantation Sketches* (Honolulu, 1924), p. 17; Minoru Takaki, interview with author, July 1985; Morris Pang, "A Korean Immigrant," *Social Process in Hawaii,* vol. 13 (1949), p. 114.

52. Richard Okawa, interviews with author, February 1978 and July 1980; Minoru Takaki, interview with author, July 1985.

53. Dolores Quinto, "The Life Story of a Filipino Immigrant," *Social Process in Hawaii,* vol. 4 (1938), p. 77.

54. William W. Goodale to E. D. Tenney, January 26, 1903, Grove Farm Plantation Records; Kosuke Teruya, interview, in Ethnic Studies Oral History Project, *Uchinanchu,* p. 523; Smith, *Plantation Sketches,* p. 51.

55. Dr. Charles A. Peterson, circular, October 26, 1899, reprinted in *Honolulu Record,* December 1, 1949; M. Lord to E. D. Tenney, July 21, 1916, Grove Farm Plantation Records.

56. Yasutaro Soga, *Looking Backward 50 Years in Hawaii,* reprinted in *Honolulu Record,* March 31, 1949; Ethnic Studies Oral History Project, *Uchinanchu,* pp. 363, 489; Hyon Sun, in Koh Seung-jae, "A Study of Korean Immigrants to Hawaii," *Journal of Social Sciences and Humanities,* no. 38 (June 1973), p. 27; Ruben Alcantara, *Sakada: Filipino Adaptation in Hawaii* (Washington, 1981), p. 32.

57. Vice president of H. Hackfeld and Company, with circular attached, to G. Wilcox, September 24, 1910, Grove Farm Plantation Records.

58. C. Brewer and Company to W. G. Ogg, August 2, 1916, Hawaiian Agricultural Company Records; Donald S. Bowman to Grove Farm Plantation, September 15, 1920, Grove Farm Plantation Records; W. Pfotenhauser, "President's Address," *The Hawaiian Planters' Record,* vol. 4, no. 1 (January 1911), p. 4; Donald S. Bowman, "Housing the Plantation Worker," ibid., vol. 22, no. 4 (April 1920), pp. 202–203.

59. Ray Stannard Baker, "Human Nature in Hawaii: How the Few Want the Many to Work for Them—Perpetually, and at Low Wages," *American Magazine,* vol. 73 (January 1912), p. 33; Ethnic Studies Oral History Project, *Uchinanchu,* p. 382; Kazuo Ito, *Issei: A History of Japanese Immigrants in North America* (Seattle, 1973), p. 21; manager of Hawaiian Agricultural Company to C. Brewer and Company, March 19, 1913, Hawaiian Agricultural Company Records.

60. C. S. Childs, "Report on Welfare Investigation: Grove Farm Plantation, Kauai," 1919, Grove Farm Plantation Records; Ethnic Studies Oral History Project, *Uchinanchu,* p. 65.

61. Murayama, *All I Asking for Is My Body,* p. 45.

62. Felipe, "Hawaii: A Pilipino Dream," p. 189; Ethnic Studies Oral History Project, *Uchinanchu,* p. 523.

63. Soga, in *Honolulu Record,* October 27, 1949; Ewald Kleinau, "Diary of Operations in the Sugar Refinery, Paauhau Plantation, Hawaii," September 2, 1881, Bancroft Library, University of California, Berkeley; James Okahata (ed.), *A History of Japanese in Hawaii* (Honolulu, 1971), p. 122; Ethnic Studies Oral History Project, *Uchinanchu,* p. 371; Felipe, "Hawaii: A Pilipino Dream," p. 189; *Hawaii Herald,* February 2, 1973.

64. Ethnic Studies Oral History Project, *The 1924 Filipino Strike on Kauai,* vol. 2, p. 675.

65. Vice president of H. Hackfeld and Company to George Wilcox, September 24, 1910, with circulars attached, Grove Farm Plantation Records; manager of Hawaiian Agricultural Company to the Hawaiian Sugar Planters' Association, April 5, 1919, Hawaiian Agricultural Company Records.

66. Tin-Yuke Char, *The Sandalwood Mountains: Readings and Stories of Early Chinese in Hawaii* (Honolulu, 1975), p. 216.

67. S. P. Aheong, in Tin-Yuke Char, *The Bamboo Path: Life and Writings of a Chinese in Hawaii* (Honolulu, 1977), pp. 234, 235.

68. Homer Hulbert, "The Koreans in Hawaii," *Korea Review,* vol. 5, no. 11 (November 1905), p. 412; George H. Jones, "Koreans Abroad," *Korea Review,* vol. 6, no. 12 (December 1906), p. 451; Moon, "The Korean Immigrants in America," pp. 226, 227.

69. Director of Theo. H. Davies and Company to C. McLennan, February 10, 1902, Laupahoehoe Plantation Records.

70. *Hawaiian Gazette,* February 6, 1867; Kleinau, "Diary," February 17, 1882; Grant, *Scenes in Hawaii,* pp. 65, 68, 69.

71. Manager of the Hawaiian Agricultural Company to C. Brewer and Company, October 17 and November 2, 1911, Hawaiian Agricultural Company Records; H. Hackfield and Company to George Wilcox, April 25, 1900, Grove Farm Plantation Records; Ethnic Studies Oral History Project, *Uchinanchu,* pp. 383, 472.

72. Director, Bureau of Labor, Hawaiian Sugar Planters' Association, to manager of the Hawaiian Agricultural Company, December 4, 1920, Hawaiian Agricultural Company Records; Felipe, "Hawaii: A Pilipino Dream," pp. 134–135.

73. Ethnic Studies Oral History Project, *Uchinanchu,* p. 387.

74. Mrs. Joe Rapozo, in *Honolulu Advertiser,* July 6, 1973; Ethnic Studies Oral History Project, *Waialua and Haleiwa,* vol. 8, p. 64, and vol. 9, p. 223.

75. Manager of the Hawaiian Agricultural Company to Bureau of Labor, Hawaiian Sugar Planters' Association, April 5, 1919, Hawaiian Agricultural Company Records.

76. John E. Reinecke, "'Pidgin English' in Hawaii: A Local Study in the Sociology of Language," *American Journal of Sociology,* vol. 43, no. 5 (March 1938), reprinted in Dennis Ogawa, ea., *Kodomo no tame ni,* p. 212.

77. Interviews, in Ethnic Studies Oral History Project, *Uchinanchu,* pp. 415, 470; William C. Smith, "Pidgin English in Hawaii," *American Speech,* vols. 8–9 (February 1933), pp. 15–19.

78. Ethnic Studies Oral History Project, *Waialua and Haleiwa,* vol. 3, p. 11; Anna Choi, interview, in Choy, *Koreans in America,* p. 322.

79. Nobuo Takaki, grandson of Nobuyoshi Takaki, interview with author, in Kumamoto, Japan, May 1986.

80. Aheong, in Ah Jook Ku, "The Pioneer Women," in United Chinese Penman Clubs, *The Chinese of Hawaii, 1956–1957* (Honolulu, 1957), p. 22.

81. Raymond Len, letter to the author, May 3, 1987; Glick, *Sojourners and Settlers,* p. 163; Len Too Shing, interview with author, July 13, 1988.

82. Len Mau Yun, interview with the author, July 13, 1988; Doris M. Lorden, "The Chinese-Hawaiian Family," *American Journal of Sociology,* vol. 40 January 1935), p. 460.

83. William C. Smith, *Americans in Process: A Study of Our Citizens of Oriental Ancestry* (Ann Arbor, 1937), pp. 34–38; song, in *Hawaii Herald,* February 2, 1973.

84. Richard Okawa, interview with author, July 1980; Daniel K. Inouye, *Journey to Washington* (Englewood Cliffs, N.J., 1967), pp. 24–25; Kazuo Miyamoto, *Hawaii: End of the Rainbow* (Rutland, Vt., 1968), p. 23; "The History of My Life," by a Korean student, document number N-49, William C. Smith Documents Collection, Special Collections, University of Oregon Library, Eugene, Oregon; Aiko Mifune, interview with author, February 18, 1988.

85. Yamauchi, interview, in Ethnic Studies Oral History Project, *Uchinanchu,* p. 499.

86. Minoru Takaki and Susumu Takaki, interview with author on the Puunene Plantation, July 1985; Jeanette Takaki Watanabe, interview with author, March 14, 1987.

87. Smith, *Americans in Process,* pp. 294, 283, 321; Lawrence H. Fuchs, *Hawaii Pono: A Social History* (New York, 1961), p. 293.

88. Ray Stannard Baker, "Human Nature in Hawaii," p. 330.

89. Curtis Aller, "The Evolution of Hawaiian Labor Relations: From Benevolent Paternalism to Mature Collective Bargaining," unpublished Ph.D. thesis, Harvard University, 1958, p. 39.

90. Lillian Takaki Ota, interview with author, May 1986; Ellen Kasai, interview with author, August 1986.

91. Murayama, *All I Asking for Is My Body*, pp. 28, 96; Fuchs, *Hawaii Pono: A Social History*, pp. 288–289; William C. Smith, *The Second Generation Oriental in America* (Honolulu, 1927), p. 16; Smith, *Americans in Process*, pp. 55–57, 161–162.

92. Smith, *Americans in Process*, p. 52.

93. Letters from my mother, December 11, 1957; November 30, 1958; February 28, 1959.

94. Ethnic Studies Oral History Project, *Uchinanchu*, p. 488; songs, in *Hawaii Herald*, February 2 and October 26, 1973.

95. Victor Turner, *Dramas, Fields, and Metaphors: Symbolic Action in Human Society* (Ithaca, N.Y., 1974), pp. 232, 237; Felipe, "Hawaii: A Pilipino Dream," p. v.

96. Edna Bonacich, "A Theory of Ethnic Antagonism: The Split Labor Market," *American Sociological Review*, vol. 37, no. 5 (October 1972), pp. 547–559; Georg Simmel, "Der Fremde" or "The Stranger," in Simmel, *On Indiuiduality and Social Forms*, edited by Donald N. Levine (Chicago, 1971), pp. 143–149.

III. Necessity

1. Dhan Gopal Mukerji, *Caste and Outcast* (New York, 1923), p. 269; Do-Yun Yoon, in Sonia Sunoo, *Korea Kaleidoscope: Oral Histories*, vol. 1: *Early Korean Pioneers in the U.S.A.* (Davis, Calif., 1982), p. 69; Kazuo Ito, *Issei: A History of Japanese Immigrants in North America* (Seattle, 1973), p. 250.

5. Ethnic Solidarity

1. William C. Smith, *The Second Generation Oriental in America* (Honolulu, 1927), p. 21.

2. Maxine Hong Kingston, *The Woman Warrior: Memoirs of a Girlhood Among Ghosts* (New York, 1976), pp. 7–8.

3. Edna Bonacich, "A Theory of Ethnic Antagonism: The Split Labor Market," *American Sociological Review*, vol. 37, no. 5 (October 1972), pp. 547–559; David J. O'Brien and Stephen S. Fugita, "Middleman Minority Concept: Its Explanatory Value in the Case of the Japanese in California Agriculture," *Pacific Sociological Review*, vol. 25, no. 2 (April 1982), pp. 190, 198, 199; Kazuo Ito, *Issei: A History of Japanese Immigrants in North America* (Seattle, 1973), p. 446; Edna Bonacich and John Modell, *The Economic Basis of Ethnic Solidarity: Small Business in the Japanese American Community* (Berkeley, 1980).

4. Minoru Iino, "My Life History," April 12,1926, pp. 3–4, Survey of Race Relations, Stanford University, Hoover Institution Archives.

5. Ito, *Issei*, pp. 93, 95, 99, 100, 127, 129, 130; Shiki Ito, "My Sixty-Four Years in America," in East Bay Japanese For Action (ed.), *"Our Recollections"* (Berkeley, 1986), p. 125; Bill Hosokawa, *Nisei: The Quiet Americans* (New York, 1969), p. 136; "Life History of Sakoe Tsuboi," p. 3, Survey of Race Relations, 1924, Stanford University, Hoover Institution Archives; Kesa Noda, *Yamato Colony, 1906–1960* (Livingston, Calif., 1981), p. 84.

6. Ito, *Issei*, pp. 94, 96, 98, 127, 128, 133, 134, 135; Kiyoshi Kawakami, "How California Treats the Japanese," *The Independent*, vol. 74 (May 8, 1913), p. 1020;

Eileen Sunada Sarasohn (ed.), *The Issei: Portrait of a Pioneer, An Oral History* (Palo Alto, Calif., 1983), pp. 64, 67.

7. Sarasohn (ed.), *Issei*, p. 61; Ito, *Issei*, p. 129.

8. Yamato Ichihashi, *Japanese in the United States* (rpt. New York, 1969, originally published in 1932), p. 140, U.S. Immigration Commission, *Japanese and Other Immigrant Races in the Pacific Coast and Rocky Mountain States* (Washington, D.C., 1911), vol. 1, pp. 33–46.

9. Ito, *Issei*, pp. 317, 362.

10. Ibid., pp. 435, 312, 343.

11. Ibid., pp. 335, 409, 442; Yuji Ichioka, *The Issei: The World of the First Generation Japanese Immigrants, 1885–1924* (New York, 1988), pp. 72–73.

12. Ichioka, *Issei*, p. 83; Ito, *Issei*, pp. 293, 299, 294.

13. Ito, *Issei*, pp. 294, 301.

14. Ichioka, *Issei*, pp. 86, 90.

15. Ito, *Issei*, pp. 539, 248.

16. Ichioka, *Issei*, pp. 62–63.

17. Yamato Ichihashi, *Japanese in the United States* (Stanford, 1932), p. 110.

18. Ichihashi, *Japanese*, pp. 119, 120, 121, 129.

19. Ito, *Issei*, p. 710.

20. Ibid., pp. 703–705.

21. Ibid., p. 722.

22. Ichihashi, *Japanese*, pp. 162–163.

23. Immigration Commission, *Japanese and Other Immigrant Races*, vol. 1, p. 80.

24. Ichioka, *Issei*, p. 121.

25. Paul S. Taylor and Tom Vasey, "Historical Background of California Farm Labor," *Rural Sociology*, vol. 1 (September 1936), p. 286; Gerald D. Nash, "Stages of California's Economic Growth, 1870–1970: An Interpretation," *California Historical Quarterly* (Winter 1972), pp. 318–319.

26. Chieko Sano, "Recollections," in East Bay Japanese for Action (ed.), *"Our Recollections,"* p. 179; Ito, *Issei*, pp. 260, 498.

27. Ito, *Issei*, pp. 250, 280.

28. Ibid., pp. 251, 442.

29. Ibid., pp. 251, 255, 282; Yukiko Hanawa, "The Several Worlds of Issei Women," unpublished M.A. thesis, California State University, Long Beach, 1982, p. 86.

30. "Interview with Mr. S. Nitta," 1924, p. 2, Survey of Race Relations, Stanford University, Hoover Institution Archives; Bill Hosokawa, *Nisei*, p. 61.

31. Kiyoshi K. Kawakami, *Asia at the Door: A Study of the Japanese Question in Continental United States, Hawaii and Canada* (New York, 1914), p. 99; *San Francisco Chronicle*, June 25, 1912; Kawakami, "How California Treats the Japanese," p. 1020; "Visit with Mr. George Shima, 'Potato King' of California," interview, July 14, 1924, pp. 1–3, Survey of Race Relations, Stanford University, Hoover Institution Archives.

32. Noda, *Yamato Colony*, pp. 44, 45.

33. Sarasohn (ed.), *Issei*, p. 87.

34. Ito, *Issei*, pp. 11, 168, 40.

35. Ichioka, *Issei*, p. 61.

36. Ibid., pp. 147, 148.
37. Noda, *Yamato Colony,* p. 18.
38. Ibid.
39. Ichioka, *Issei,* p. 148; Noda, *Yamato Colony,* pp. 10, 18, 40, 65, 174; Ito, *Issei,* p. 132.
40. Tomas Almaguer, "Racial Domination and Class Conflict in Capitalist Agriculture: The Oxnard Sugar Beet Workers' Strike of 1903," *Labor History,* vol. 25, no. 3 (Summer 1984), p. 334.
41. Ichioka, *Issei,* pp. 98–99.
42. Almaguer, "Racial Domination," pp. 346, 347.
43. American Federation of Labor, *Proceedings* (1904), p. 100; Augusta Pio, "Exclude Japanese Labor," *American Federationist,* vol. 12, no. 3 (March 1905), pp. 275–276.
44. Ichihashi, *Japanese,* p. 231; "Asiatic Exclusion League of North America, Preamble and Constitution, 1905," reprinted in Eliot Mears, *Resident Orientals on the American Pacific Coast* (New York, 1927), appendix, p. 435; Roger Daniels, *The Politics of Prejudice: The Anti-Japanese Movement in California and the Struggle for Japanese Exclusion* (New York, 1968), p. 85.
45. Ichihashi, *Japanese,* p. 236.
46. Theodore Roosevelt to George Kennan, May 6, 1905, in Elting E. Morison (ed.) *The Letters of Theodore Roosevelt* (Cambridge, Mass., 1951), vol. 4, pp. 1168–1169; Roosevelt to Harrison Gray Otis, January 8, 1907, ibid., vol. 5, p. 542; Roosevelt to Elihu Root, July 26, 1907, ibid., vol.5, p. 729; "Extract from President Roosevelt's Message to Congress Concerning the Japanese Question, December 3, 1906," reprinted in Mears, *Resident Orientals,* appendix, pp. 438–442.
47. Roosevelt, "National Life and Character," *Sewanee Review,* August 1894, reprinted in Theodore Roosevelt, *American Ideals* (New York, 1904), pp. 307, 311, 312; Roosevelt to Theodore Roosevelt, Jr., February 13, 1909, in Morison, *Letters,* vol. 6, p. 1521; Roosevelt to Philander C. Knox, February 8, 1909, ibid., vol. 6, p. 1512; Roosevelt to James Wilson, February 3, 1903, ibid., vol. 3, p. 416.
48. Ichihashi, *Japanese,* p. 244; "The Gentlemen's Agreement," from *Report of Commissioner General of Immigration,* reprinted in Mears, *Resident Orientals,* appendix, p. 443.
49. Roger Daniels, *Concentration Camps USA: Japanese Americans and World War II* (New York, 1971), p. 12; Ito, *Issei,* p. 105.
50. Chapter 113, California Statutes 1913.
51. Spencer Olin, Jr., "European Immigrant and Oriental Alien: Acceptance and Rejection by the California Legislature of 1913," *Pacipc Historical Review,* vol. 25 (August 1966), p. 311; Ichihashi, *Japanese,* p. 275.
52. Eliot Mears, *Resident Orientals,* p. 146; *Sacramento Bee,* May 1, 1913, in Susan McCoin Kataoka, "Issei Women: A Study in Subordinate Status," unpublished Ph.D. thesis, University of California, Los Angeles, 1977, p. 38; Noda, *Yamato Colony,* p. 81; "How to Survive Racism in America's Free Society," a lecture by Togo Tanaka, April 3, 1973, published in Arthur A. Hansen and Betty E. Mitson (eds.), *Voices Long Silent: An Oral Inquiry into the Japanese American Evacuation* (Fullerton, Calif., 1974), p. 85.
53. Ichioka, *Issei,* p. 153; "Interview with M. Sasaki," 1924, pp. 2–3, Survey of Race Relations, Stanford University, Hoover Institution Archives; Kawakami, *Asia at the Door,* pp. 110–111.

54. Timothy J. Lukes and Gary Y. Okihiro, *Japanese Legacy: Farming and Community Life in California's Santa Clara Valley* (Cupertino, Calif., 1985), p. 59; "Interview with Mr. S. Nitta," December 16, 1924, p. 1, Survey of Race Relations, Stanford University, Hoover Institution Archives; Sarasohn (ed.), *Issei*, p. 87.

55. Ichioka, *Issei*, pp. 150, 155; Ichihashi, *Japanese*, p. 279; Robert Higgs, "Landless by Law: Japanese Immigrants in California Agriculture to 1941," *Journal of Economic History*, vol. 38, no. 1 (March 1978), pp. 220–221; Ito, *Issei*, p. 165.

56. Ito, *Issei*, p. 165.

57. Noda, *Yamato Colony*, pp. 47, 69; Ito, *Issei*, pp. 165, 166, 270; Kazuo Miyamoto, *Hawaii: End of the Rainbow* (Rutland, Vt., 1964), p. 239.

58. "Life History of a Japanese Man at Santa Paula, California," December 29, 1924, p. 3, Survey of Race Relations, Stanford University, Hoover Institution Archives.

59. In 1850 Hikozo, a shipwrecked fisherman from Japan, arrived in San Francisco and became an American citizen. The 1910 census showed 420 Japanese-born American citizens. See Bradford Smith, *Americans from Japan* (New York, 1948), p. 148.

60. Ichioka, *Issei*, p. 215; *Review of Reviews*, June 1913, in H. A. Millis, *The Japanese Problem in the United States* (New York, 1915), p. 251; Kawakami, *Asia at the Door*, pp. 68–69.

61. Kiichi Kanzaki, "Is the Japanese Menace in America a Reality?" in *The Annals of the American Academy of Political and Social Sciences* (1921), pp. 96–97.

62. Yuji Ichioka, "The Early Japanese Immigrant Quest for Citizenship: The Background of the 1922 Ozawa Case," *Amerasia*, vol. 4, no. 2 (1977), p. 12.

63. Ichioka, "Early Japanese Immigrant Quest for Citizenship," pp. 10, 11, 17; Ichihashi, *Japanese*, p. 298; Ozawa v. United States, Decision of the Court, November 13, 1922, reprinted in Mears, *Resident Orientals*, appendix, pp. 509, 513, 514.

64. Section 13 of the 1924 Immigration Act, reprinted in Mears, *Resident Orientals*, appendix, p. 515; "Life History and Social Document of Andrew Kan," August 22, 1924, pp. 12–13, Survey of Race Relations, Stanford University, Hoover Institution Archives; Ichihashi, *Japanese*, p. 303.

65. *Japanese American Courier*, January 21, 1933; Ichioka, *Issei*, p. 247; "Message from Japan to America," *Japan Times and Mail*, October 1, 1924, reprinted in Mears, *Resident Orientals*, appendix, pp. 516–518; "Interview with R. Ode, Japanese foreman," 1924, pp. 12, 18, Survey of Race Relations, Stanford University, Hoover Institution Archives.

66. Robert E. Park, "Racial Assimilation in Secondary Groups with Particular Reference to the Negro," *Papers and Proceedings, Eighth Annual Meeting of the American Sociological Society, 1913*, vol. 8 (Chicago, 1914), p. 71.

67. Mears, *Resident Orientals*, p. 342; Ichihashi, *Japanese*, p. 312.

68. Ito, *Issei*, pp. 884, 429, 491, 889, 454, 270, 156; Victor Turner, *Dramas, Fields, and Metaphors: Symbolic Action in Human Society* (Ithaca, N.Y., 1974), pp. 232, 237.

69. "Interview with S. Nitta," January 7, 1925, pp. 2–3, Survey of Race Relations, Stanford University, Hoover Institution Archives; "Interview with Mrs. Florence Kojima," December 11, 1924, ibid., p. 3; "Interview with Mr. T. Torikai," August 7, 1924, ibid., p. 2; "Life History of a Japanese Man at Santa Paula, California," December 29, 1924, ibid., p. 4.

70. "A Farmer's View of the Question," by George Shima, reprinted in Mears, *Resident Orientals*, appendix, p. 471.

71. *Taihoku Nippo,* in Ichioka, *Issei,* p. 253; Ito, *Issei,* p. 602.

72. "American-Born Japanese in Interstitial Position Say League President," *Japanese American Courier,* April 17, 1928; "Life History of Kazuo Kawai," March 2, 1925, p. 17, Survey of Race Relations, Stanford University, Hoover Institution Archives; "Interview with Mr. S. Nitta," January 7, 1925, ibid., p. 2; Yuji Ichioka, "A Study in Dualism: James Yoshinori Sakamoto and the *Japanese American Courier,* 1928–1942," *Amerasia,* vol. 13, no. 2 (1986–87), p. 57.

73. Ito, *Issei,* pp. 535, 987.

74. *Japanese American Courier,* January 21, 1933; Ito, *Issei,* pp. 274, 449, 497; "Life History of Dr. Peter S——— of Los Angeles," 1925, pp. 2–3, Survey of Race Relations, Stanford University, Hoover Institution Archives; "Interview with Yamato Ichihashi," ibid., p. 1; "Life History of a Japanese Man at Santa Paula, California," December 29, 1924, ibid., p. 2, S. Morris Morishita in William C. Smith, *Americans in Process: A Study of Our Citizens of Oriental Ancestry* (Ann Arbor, 1937), p. 112; Hosokawa, *Nisei,* p. 136.

75. Ichihashi, *Japanese,* pp. 321–322; Jerrold Takahashi, "Changing Responses to Racial Subordination: An Exploratory Study of Japanese American Political Styles," unpublished Ph.D. thesis, University of California, Berkeley, 1980, p. 107.

76. Noriko Bridges, interview with author, March 18, 1988; Lindbergh S. Sata, "Musings of a Hyphenated American," in Stanley Sue and Nathaniel Wagner, *Asian-American Psychological Perspectives* (Palo Alto, Calif., 1973), pp. 150–155; Frank Miyamoto, interview with author, March 25, 1988.

77. Hosokawa, *Nisei,* p. 160; Aiji Tashiro, "The Rising Son of the Rising Sun," *New Outlook* (September 1934), p. 37; "A Picture Bride: Interview with Mrs. K. Nakashima," April 15, 1924, pp. 4, 6, Survey of Race Relations, Stanford University, Hoover Institution Archives; Betty Yamaguchi, interview with author, June 2, 1988.

78. Tanaka, "How to Survive Racism in America's Free Society," p. 85; Monica Sone, *Nisei Daughter* (Boston, 1953), p. 22.

79. John Okada, *No-No Boy* (rpt. San Francisco, 1976, originally published in 1957), pp. 15–16.

80. "Interview with Yamato Ichihashi," p. 1, Survey of Race Relations, Stanford University, Hoover Institution Archives; Tanaka, "How to Survive Racism in America's Free Society," p. 87; see William C. Smith, *Americans in Process,* p. 134, for dual citizenship of children of European-immigrant parents.

81. William C. Smith, "Born American, But—," *Survey Graphic* (May 1926), p. 168.

82. Yori Wada, "Growing Up in Central California," *Amerasia,* vol. 13, no. 2 (1986–87), p. 8; Hosokawa, *Nisei,* p. 161.

83. Fred Korematsu, "Views from Within," A Symposium on the Japanese American Internment Experience, University of California, Berkeley, September 19, 1987; Kay Yasui, " 'Jap!' 'Jap!' 'Jap!'," *Pacific Citizen,* January 15, 1931; interviews with Mary Tsukamoto and Donald Nakahata, in John Tateishi, *And Justice for All: An Oral History of the Japanese American Detention Camps* (New York, 1984), pp. 5, 36; Tanaka, "How to Survive Racism in America's Free Society," pp. 84, 90; "An American Born Japanese in America," an interview with J. Sato, pp. 2–3, Survey of Race Relations, Stanford University, Hoover Institution Archives.

84. *Japanese American Courier,* January 1,1930; "How to Survive Racism in America's Free Society," by Tanaka, p. 85; W. C. Smith, *The Second Generation Oriental in America,* p. 24; Morishita, in Smith, *Americans in Process,* p. 112.

85. Report on Vocational Guidance Issue by Kojiro Unoura, in *Japanese American Courier,* September 10, 1938; Mears, *Resident Orientals,* pp. 199, 200.

86. Miss Okamura, Japanese Center, YWCA, Oakland, interview, "Segregation folder," Survey of Race Relations, Stanford University, Hoover Institution Archives; Kazuo Kawai, "Three Roads, and None Easy: An American-born Japanese Looks at Life," *Survey* (May 1, 1926), pp. 164, 165; "Interview with U——Z——," August 21, 1924, pp. 2–3, Survey of Race Relations, Stanford University, Hoover Institution Archives; Yoshiko Uchida, Desert Exile: *The Uprooting of a Japanese American Family* (Seattle, 1982), pp. 44–45; John Modell, *The Economics and Politics of Racial Accommodation: The Japanese of Los Angeles, 1900-1942* (Urbana, Ill., 1977), p. 133.

87. Bradford Smith, *Americans from Japan,* pp. 248–249.

88. Modell, *Economics and Politics of Racial Accommodation,* p. 132; Wada, "Growing Up in Central California," p. 12; "Interview with Miss Esther B. Bartlett of Y.W.C.A.," December 12, 1924, p. 5, Survey of Race Relations, Stanford University, Hoover Institution Archives.

89. Tashiro, "The Rising Son of the Rising Sun," p. 36; Kawai, "Three Roads," p. 165; "An American Born Japanese in America," an interview with J. Sato, p. 5, Survey of Race Relations, Stanford University, Hoover Institution Archives.

90. Modell, *Economics and Politics of Racial Accommodation,* pp. 137–138.

91. Tashiro, "The Rising Son of the Rising Sun," pp. 36, 40.

92. Takahashi, *Changing Responses,* pp. 139–152; Los Angeles *Doho,* November 1, 1938.

93. *Japanese American Courier,* August 31, 1929, January 1, 1928; Takahashi, *Changing Responses,* p. 119.

94. Takahashi, *Changing Responses,* p. 122; *Japanese American Courier,* April 13, 1929.

95. *Japanese American Courier,* March 31, 1928, September 12, 1936, July 24, 1937; *Nikkei Shimin,* July 15, 1930, in Edward K. Strong, *The Second Generation Japanese Problem* (Stanford, 1934), p. 13.

96. Ichioka, "Sakamoto and the *Japanese American Courier,*" p. 52, *Japanese American Courier,* January 1, 1938; Hosokawa, *Nisei,* pp. 197, 201; *Pacific Citizen,* November 1932 and November 1936.

97. *Rafu Shimpo,* December 29, 1940; Smith, *Americans in Process,* p. 138.

98. *Japanese American News (Nichi Bei),* in Bradford Smith, *Americans from Japan,* pp. 244–245.

99. Tashiro, "Rising Son of the Rising Sun," p. 37; W. C. Smith, *The Second Generation Oriental in America,* pp. 23, 5.

100. Ichioka, "Sakamoto and the *Japanese American Courier,*" p. 59, "Life History of Kazuo Kawai," March 2, 1925, pp. 5, 12, 13, 15–17, Survey of Race Relations, Stanford University, Hoover Institution Archives.

101. Sone, *Nisei Daughter,* pp. 8–10.

102. Ibid., pp. 10, 11, 22.

103. Ibid., pp. 3, 18.

104. Ibid., pp. 60–63.

105. Ibid., pp. 70, 52.

106. Ibid., pp. 87, 90, 91, 93, 97.

107. Ibid., p. 107.
108. Ibid., pp. 38, 114, 115, 119, 122.
109. Ibid., pp. 121, 133.
110. Ibid., pp. 131–132.
111. Ibid., pp. 124, 144.

6. Ethnic Islands

1. F. L., "The Life History of a Hawaiian-Born Chinese Girl," circa 1924, pp. 3–11, Survey of Race Relations, Stanford University, Hoover Institution Archives.

2. Jacob Riis, *How the Other Half Lives: Studies Among the Tenements of New York* (rpt. Cambridge, Mass., 1970), p. 69.

3. Folk songs, in Him Mark Lai, Joe Huang, and Don Wong, *The Chinese of America 1785–1980* (San Francisco, 1980), p. 51; Diane Mei Lin Mark and Ginger Chih, *A Place Called Chinese America* (Dubuque, Iowa, 1982), p. 52.

4. Folk song, translation, Marlon K. Hom (ed. and trans.), *Songs of Gold Mountain: Cantonese Rhymes from San Francisco and Chinatown* (Berkeley, 1987), p. 45. Such songs were likely written by men using female personae.

5. Chinese rhyme, Hom (ed. and trans.), *Songs of Gold Mountain*, p. 124; letter by unknown Chinese migrant, in the Kam Wah Chung Company Papers, John Day, Oregon.

6. Chu-chia to Lung On, July 1899; wife to Lung On, n.d.; Lung On to Liang Kwan-jin, March 2, 1905; Liang Kwan-jin to Lung On, March 4, 1905; Ing Du-hsio to Ing Hay, April 9, no year, translations by Chia-Lin Chen, Kam Wah Chung Company Papers.

7. Mrs. John W. Murray to Chia-Lin Chen, October 30, 1971, reprinted in Chen, "A Gold Dream in the Blue Mountains: A Study of the Chinese Immigrants in the John Day Area, Oregon, 1870–1910," unpublished M.A. thesis, Portland State University, 1972, pp. 123–124.

8. Folk song, translation, Hom (ed. and trans.), *Songs of Gold Mountain*, p. 96.

9. Esther Wong, "The History and Problem of Angel Island," March 1924, pp. 7–8, Survey of Race Relations, Stanford University, Hoover Institution Archives; "Interview with Mr. Faris, Deputy Commissioner of Immigration in Seattle," ibid., pp. 2–11.

10. H. K. Wong, *Gum Sahn Yun: Gold Mountain Men* (San Francisco, 1987), p. 187; Alice Fun, interview, February 28, 1982, Chinese Women of America Research Project, Chinese Culture Foundation of San Francisco, p. 3, Victor and Brett de Bary Nee, *Longtime Californ': A Documentary Study of an American Chinatown* (New York, 1972), p. 63.

11. Eliot G. Mears, *Resident Orientals on the American Pacific Coast* (Chicago, 1928), p. 408; Helen Chen, "Chinese Immigration into the United States: An Analysis of Changes in Immigration Policies," unpublished Ph.D. thesis, Brandeis University, 1980, p. 105; Nee, *Longtime Californ'*, p. 25; R. D. McKenzie, *Oriental Exclusion: The Effect of American Immigration Laws, Regulations, and Judicial Decisions upon the Chinese and Japanese on the American Pacific Coast* (Chicago, 1928) pp. 46, 94, 192, 194; S. W. Kung, *Chinese in American Life: Some Aspects of Their History, Status, Problems, and Contributions* (Seattle, 1962), pp. 92, 100, 192–195; Wen-Hsien Chen, "Chinese Under Both Exclusion and Immigration Laws," unpublished Ph.D. thesis, University of Chicago, 1940, pp. 28–29. In a note to the author, July 1988, H. M. Lai points out that Chinese from remote areas like Grass Valley were also able to secure forged birth certificates.

12. Richard Kock Dare, "The Economic and Social Adjustment of the San Francisco

Chinese for the Past Fifty Years," unpublished M.A. thesis, University of California Berkeley, 1959, p. 54.

13. Him Mark Lai, Genny Lim, Judy Yung (eds.), *Island: Poetry and History of Chinese Immigrants on Angel Island, 1910–1940* (San Francisco, 1980), p. 44, Mark and Chih, *A Place Called Chinese America*, pp. 47–48; Shih-Shan Henry Tsai, *The Chinese Experience in America* (Bloomington, Ind., 1986), p. 101.

14. Paul Siu, "The Chinese Laundryman: A Study of Social Isolation," unpublished Ph.D. thesis, University of Chicago, 1953, pp. 239, 241; Judy Yung, interview with author, November 11, 1987; funeral announcements for Sen Hin Yung (Yip Jing Tom) in *San Francisco Sunday Examiner and Chronicle*, November 29, 1987, and *Chinese Times*, December 1–3, 1987; Him Mark Lai, interview with author, December 18, 1987; Ruthanne Lum McCunn, *Chinese American Portraits: Personal Histories, 1828–1988* (San Francisco, 1988), pp. 108–109; Alfred Wong, interviewed by Carol Takaki, April 11, 1988.

15. Chinese rhymes, in Hom (ed. and trans.), *Songs of Gold Mountain*, pp. 74, 78; Esther Wong, "The History and Problem of Angel Island," March 1924, pp. 1–4, Survey of Race Relations, Stanford University, Hoover Institution Archives; Lai, Lim, Yung (eds.), *Island*, pp. 72, 74, 28, 68; Mary Naka, "Angel Island Immigration Station," 1922, Survey of Race Relations, Stanford University, Hoover Institution Archives.

16. Lai, Lim, Yung (eds.), *Island*, pp. 126, 150, 94.

17. Fuju Liu, "A Comparative Demographic Study of Native-Born and Foreign-Born Chinese Populations in the United States," unpublished Ph.D. thesis, Michigan State College, 1953, pp. 96, 97. "Urban area," as defined by the 1940 census report, "is made up for the most part of cities and other incorporated places having 2,500 inhabitants or more." *Sixteenth Census of the United States, 1940, Population*, vol. 2, part 1, p. 8.

18. Rose Hum Lee, "The Decline of Chinatowns in the U.S.," *American Journal of Sociology*, vol. 54, no. 5 (March 1949), pp. 425, 427; Nee, *Longtime Californ'*, pp. 26–27.

19. Peter Wong, in Linda Perrin, *Coming to America: Immigrants from the Far East* (New York, 1980), p. 46; Nee, *Longtime Californ'*, p. 22; Ching Chao Wu, "Chinatowns: A Study of Symbiosis and Assimilation," unpublished Ph.D. thesis, University of Chicago, 1928, pp. 86–93.

20. Siu, "Chinese Laundryman," pp. 25, 146; Kung, *Chinese in American Life*, p. 57; Peter Kwong, *Chinatown, N.Y.: Labor & Politics, 1930–1950* (New York, 1979), p. 61; Wong Wee Ying, interview, May 7, 1982, Chinese Women of America Research Project, Chinese Culture Foundation of San Francisco, p. 4.

21. Siu, "Chinese Laundryman," pp. 10–13.

22. Dare, "Economic and Social Adjustment of the San Francisco Chinese," pp. 12–13.

23. Siu, "Chinese Laundryman," pp. 88–89.

24. Loy Wong, interview, April 26, 1982, p. 7, New York Chinatown History Project; Siu, "Chinese Laundryman," pp. 162, 159; "Xi yi qu" (laundry song) by Wen Yiduo, an art student living in New York, circa 1925. I am indebted to Marlon Hom for sharing this poem with me.

25. Siu, "Chinese Laundryman," pp. 150, 154.

26. Ibid., pp. 151, 302, 308, 312, 319.

27. Yuan Liang, "The Chinese Family in Chicago," unpublished M.A. thesis, University of Chicago, 1951, p. 28.

28. Siu, "Chinese Laundryman," pp. 210, 215–217.

29. Ibid., pp. 161, 156, 287.

30. Kwong, *Chinatown, N.Y.,* pp. 63–64.

31. Ibid., pp. 65–66.

32. Lee, "Decline of Chinatowns," p. 428; Nee, *Longtime Californ',* p. 62.

33. Ng Poon Chew, "The Chinaman in America," *Chautauquan, vol. 9,* no. 4 (January 1889), p. 802; Esther Wong, "The History and Problem of Angel Island," March 1924, p. 11, Survey of Race Relations, Stanford University, Hoover Institution Archives; Nee, *Longtime Californ',* p. 64; Esther Lum, "Chinese During Depression," *Chinese Digest,* vol. 1, no. 2 (November 22, 1935); Ling-chi Wang, "Politics of Assimilation and Repression: History of the Chinese in the United States, 1940 to 1970," unpublished manuscript, Asian American Studies Library, University of California, Berkeley, pp. 40–45.

34. Lim P. Lee, "The Need for Better Housing in Chinatown," *Chinese Digest,* December 1938, p. 7; Carey McWilliams, *Brothers Under the Skin* (rpt. Boston, 1964, originally published in 1942), pp. 108–110; "The Life Story of Edward L. C. as written by himself," circa 1924, p. 5, Survey of Race Relations, Stanford University, Hoover Institution Archives.

35. Herman Scheffaner, "The Old Chinese Quarter," *Living Age* (August 10, 1907) pp. 360, 362; "Historic Chinatown," *San Francisco Chronicle,* October 1, 1917 and December 24, 1917.

36. Ivan Light, "From Vice District to Tourist Attraction: The Moral Career of American Chinatowns, 1880–1940," *Pacific Historical Review,* vol. 43, no. 3 (August 1974), p. 381; Pardee Lowe, "Chinatown's Last Stand," *Survey Graphic,* vol. 25 no. 2 (February 1936), pp. 88, 89.

37. "Historic Chinatown," *San Francisco Chronicle,* December 24, 1917; "Historic Chinatown," *San Francisco Chronicle,* October 1, 1917.

38. Dare, "Economic and Social Adjustment of the San Francisco Chinese," pp. 19, 56, 57; Grayline advertisement, in *Chinese Digest,* December 13, 1935, *Chinese Digest,* February 1938, p. 2; Ruth Hall Whitfield, "Public Opinion and the Chinese Question in San Francisco, 1900–1947," unpublished M.A. thesis, University of California, Berkeley, 1947, pp. 52–56, 88.

39. Nee, *Longtime Californ',* p. 428; *Chinese Digest,* December 20, 1935, p. 8; ibid., November 22, 1935, p. 10, and January 31, 1936, p. 11.

40. Whitfield, "Public Opinion and the Chinese Question," pp. 51, 52, 55; Herbert Ashbury, *The Barbary Coast: An Informal History of the San Francisco Underworld* (New York, 1933), p. 166; Scheffaner, "Old Chinese Quarter," p. 362; Charles C. Dobie, *San Francisco's Chinatown* (New York, 1936), p. 253; Esther Wong, "The History and Problem of Angel Island," pp. 11–12.

41. Nee, *Longtime Californ',* p. 71; Florence Chinn, "Religious Education in the Chinese Community of San Francisco," unpublished M.A. thesis, University of Chicago, 1920, p. 30; Light, "From Vice District to Tourist Attraction," p. 390; Esther Wong, "The History and Problem of Angel Island," pp. 11–12.

42. Frank W. White, "Last Days of Chinatown in New York," *Harper's Weekly,* vol. 51 (1907), p. 1208; Mark and Chih, *A Place Called Chinese America,* p. 51; Tsu Cheng Wu, "Chinese People and Chinatown in New York City," unpublished Ph.D. thesis, Clark University, 1958, pp. 28–30; Kian Moon Kwan, "Assimilation of the Chinese in the United States: An Exploratory Study in California," unpublished Ph.D. thesis, University of California, Berkeley, 1958, p. 62.

43. Wong Chin Foo, "The Chinese in New York," *The Cosmopolitan,* vol. 5, no. 4 (June 1888), p. 299, 302; Light, "From Vice District to Tourist Attraction," pp.

382, 389, 390, 387; T. C. Wu, "Chinese People and Chinatown in New York City," p. 59; "Chinatown Housing Study Begun For State by Locality Volunteers," *New York Times,* June 15, 1950.

44. H. M. Lai, note to author, July 1988; Rose Hum Lee, "Chinese in the U.S. Today: The War Has Changed Their Lives," *Survey Graphic,* October 1942, p. 419.

45. Mark and Chih, *A Place Called Chinese America,* p. 58; Whitfield, "Public Opinion and the Chinese Question," p. 41; Dean Lan, "Chinatown Sweatshops," in Emma Gee (ed.), *Counterpoint: Perspectives on Asian America* (Los Angeles, 1976), p. 352; "Toggery Trouble," *Time,* vol. 31, no. 13 (March 28, 1938), pp. 54, 56.

46. "Toggery Trouble," *Time,* p. 56.

47. Wang, "Politics of Assimilation and Repression," pp. 63, 69; Judy Yung, *Chinese Women of America: A Pictorial History* (Seattle, 1986), appendix H, p. 124; Lao Mei, "Memory of Something Tragic," *China Daily News,* January 4, 1941, translation by Marlon Hom, reprinted in *Bu Gao Ban,* newsletter of the New York Chinatown History Project, Fall 1988, p. 8.

48. C. C. Wu, "Chinatowns," pp. 158, 160, 179, 180, 181, 185; Wong Chin Foo, "The Chinese in New York," pp. 299, 302, 304; Lao Mei, "A Chapter of Life," *China Daily News,* August 27, 1940, translation by Marlon Hom, reprinted in *Bu Gao Ban,* newsletter of the New York Chinatown History Project, Fall 1988, p. 9.

49. Kwan, "Assimilation of the Chinese," p. 62; Nee, *Longtime Californ',* p. 148; Wong Chin Foo, "The Chinese in New York," p. 308; Rose Hum Lee, *The Chinese in the U.S.A.* (Hong Kong, 1960), pp. 40, 41; Ling-chi Wang, "Politics of Assimilation and Repression," p. 47. Even the 52 percent figure would not have been reached had it not also been for the 90,299 Chinese who returned to their homeland between 1908 and 1943. See Kung, *Chinese in American Life,* p. 94.

50. Nee, *Longtime Californ',* p. 148; Nee, "Growing Up in a Chinatown Grocery Store," p. 345; Effie Lai, interview, in Jeff Gillenkirk and James Motlow, *Bitter Melon: Stories from the Last Rural Chinese Town in America* (Seattle, 1987), p. 68.

51. Nee, *Longtime Californ',* pp. 150, 180; Nee, "Growing Up in a Chinatown Grocery Store," p. 346; Victor Wong, "Childhood 1930s," in Nick Harvey (ed.), *Ting: The Cauldron: Chinese Art and Identity in San Francisco* (San Francisco, 1970), p. 15.

52. Nee, *Longtime Californ',* p. 60; Peter Wong, in Perrin, Coming *to America,* p. 45; "Life History and Social Document of Albert King," July 31, 1924, p. 7, Survey of Race Relations, Stanford University, Hoover Institution Archives.

53. Mark and Chih, *A Place Called Chinese America,* p. 74.

54. Alice Fong Yu and Jack Don, in Mark and Chih, *A Place Called Chinese America,* pp. 74, 75; "Interview with Lillie Leung," August 12, 1924, p. 3, Survey of Race Relations, Stanford University, Hoover Institution Archives; Him Mark Lai, interview with author, April 22, 1988; Nee, *Longtime Californ',* p. 152; "Interview with Sun (Peter) Lee," August 13, 1924, Survey of Race Relations, Stanford University, Hoover Institution Archives.

55. Victor Wong, "Childhood II," in Harvey (ed.), *Ting,* p. 71.

56. Loy Wong, interview, April 26, 1982, New York Chinatown History Project, p. 5; Rose Hum Lee, "Chinese Dilemma," *Phylon* (1949), p. 139; Mark and Chih, *A Place Called Chinese America,* p. 75.

57. Ginger Chih, "Immigration of Chinese Women to the U.S.A., 1900–1940," unpublished M.A. thesis, Sarah Lawrence College, 1977, p. 33; "The Life Story of

Edward L. C. as written by himself," circa 1924, pp. 2, 7, Race Relations Survey, Stanford University, Hoover Institution Archives; Victor Wong, "Childhood II," in Harvey, *Ting,* p. 70.

58. "The Life Story of Edward L. C.," pp. 2, 7; Julia I. Hsuan Chen, "The Chinese Community in New York: A Study in Their Cultural Adjustment, 1920–1940," unpublished Ph.D. thesis, American University, Washington, D.C., 1941, p. 80; Thomas W. Chinn, "A Chinese 49er Daughter in American Life," in H. K. Wong, *Gum Sahn Yun,* p. 204.

59. Kit King Louis, "Problems of Second Generation Chinese," *Sociology and Social Research* (January–February 1932), p. 251; Julia Chen, *Chinese Community in New York,* p. 80; "Interview with Mrs. E. M. Findlay," Survey of Race Relations, Stanford University, Hoover Institution Archives; interview with Priscilla Fong, in Nee, *Longtime Californ',* p. 179; "Interview with Flora Belle Jan, Daughter of Proprietor of the Yet Far Low Chop Suey Restaurant," circa 1924, p. 1, Survey of Race Relations, Stanford University, Hoover Institution Archives; "Life History of Grace Wen," in Florence Brugger, "The Chinese-American Girl: A Study in Cultural Conflicts," unpublished M.A. thesis, New York University, 1935, p. 129. I am indebted to Judy Yung and Him Mark Lai for information about the changing of given names among second-generation Chinese.

60. Robert Dunn, "Does My Future Lie in China or America?" *Chinese Digest,* 1936, reprinted in *Bulletin* of the Chinese Historical Society of America, vol. 8, no. 1 (January 1973), p. 40; Kwan, "Assimilation of the Chinese," p. 245; anonymous, "Chinese Girls: Two Types, Being the Personal Observations of an American-born Chinese," *Chinese Digest,* March–April 1939, p. 10.

61. C. C. Wu, "Chinatowns," p. 258; Interview with Betty Lee Sung, January 4, 1982, Chinese Women of America Research Project, Chinese Culture Foundation of San Francisco, p. 4; Mark and Chih, *A Place Called Chinese America,* p. 85; "Interview with Lillie Leung," pp. 1–2.

62. Louis, "Problems of Second Generation Chinese," p. 257; Victor Wong, "Childhood II," p. 71.

63. "The Life Story of Edward L. C.," p. 5.

64. Jade Snow Wong, *Fifth Chinese Daughter* (rpt. New York, 1950), pp. 74, 51, 4.

65. Ibid., pp. 29, 51, 110.

66. Ibid., pp. 27, 111.

67. Ibid., pp. 74, 36, 109.

68. Ibid., pp. 15, 23.

69. Ibid., pp. 73, 70.

70. Ibid., p. 120.

71. Ibid., pp. 126, 129.

72. Ibid., pp. 129, 131, 169.

73. Ibid., pp. 179, 180, 181.

74. Ibid., pp. 188, 233.

75. Ibid., p. 234.

76. Ibid., pp. 245, 246.

77. Ibid., p. 155; for median years of school completed for men and women over twenty-five years of age, see Wang, "Politics of Assimilation and Repression," p. 67; Julia Chen, *Chinese Community in New York,* p. 84.

78. William C. Smith, *Americans in Process: A Study of Our Citizens of Oriental An-*

cestry (Ann Arbor, 1937), p. 298; Lowe, "Chinatown's Last Stand," p. 90; Louis, "Problems of Second Generation Chinese," pp. 252–253.

79. Mark and Chih, *A Place Called Chinese America,* pp. 88, 89; Pardee Lowe, *Father and Glorious Descendant* (Boston, 1943), pp. 191–192; "Life History and Social Document of Fred Wong," August 29, 1924, p. 6, Survey of Race Relations, Stanford University, Hoover Institution Archives; "Interview with Peter Soohoo," August 7, 1925, p. 1, Survey of Race Relations, Stanford University, Hoover Institution Archives; Julia Chen, *Chinese Community in New York,* pp. 90–91; Dunn, "Does My Future Lie in China or America?" p. 41; Flora Belle Jan, "An American-Born Looks at Young Chinatown," *Chinese Christian Student,* January 1931, p. 7, in Julia Chen, *Chinese Community in New York,* p. 92; see also Grace Wang, "A Speech on Second-Generation Chinese in U.S.A.," *Chinese Digest,* August 7, 1936, pp. 6, 14.

80. Laura McKeen to Dr. Eliot G. Mears, May 27, 1927, in Box 16, folder on "Community Contacts," Survey of Race Relations, Stanford University, Hoover Institution Archives; Nee, *Longtime Californ',* p. 154; Kwan, "Assimilation of the Chinese," p. 176.

81. Miss Wong, Chinese YWCA, San Francisco, 1927, "Segregation folder," Survey of Race Relations, Stanford University, Hoover Institution Archives, Alice Fun, interview, Chinese Women of America Research Project, p. 20; Brugger "The Chinese-American Girl," p. 82; McWilliams, *Brothers Under the Skin,* p. 111, Nate R. White, "Crisis in Chinatown," *Christian Science Monitor,* February 2, 1941; Mark and Chih, *A Place Called Chinese America,* p. 89; Dean Lan, "Chinatown Sweatshops," in Gee (ed.), *Counterpoint,* pp. 351–352.

82. *Chung Sai Yat Po,* August 17, 1933, and June 25, 1935, translated and quoted in Dare, "Economic and Social Adjustment of the San Francisco Chinese," p. 62; Mears, *Resident Orientals,* p. 202; Kaye Hong, "Does My Future Lie in China or America?" in *Chinese Digest,* May 22, 1936, p. 3; "Interview with Louise Leung," August 13, 1924, Survey of Race Relations, Stanford University, Hoover Institution Archives; Smith, *Americans in Process,* p. 95.

83. Victor Wong, "Childhood II," p. 70; Louis, "Problems of Second Generation Chinese," p. 256; Simmel, "Der Fremde" or "The Stranger," in Simmel, *On Individuality and Social Forms,* edited by Donald N. Levine (Chicago, 1971), pp. 143–149.

84. James Low, oral history, in Nee, *Longtime Californ',* p. 170.

85. J. S. Wong, *Fifth Chinese Daughter,* p. 178.

7. Struggling Against Colonialism

1. Wayne K. Patterson, "The Korean Frontier in America: Immigration to Hawaii, 1896–1910," unpublished Ph.D. thesis, University of Pennsylvania, 1977, p. 252; interview, in Sonia Sunoo, *Korea Kaleidoscope: Oral Histories,* vol. 1, *Early Korean Pioneers in the U.S.A.* (Davis, Calif., 1982), p. 77.

2. Adelaide Kim, "The Place of the Korean in the Industrial Life of Los Angeles," circa 1924, pp. 2, 3, Survey of Race Relations, Stanford University, Hoover Institution Archives; "Life History of J. Lim," 1924–25, p. 3, Survey of Race Relations, Stanford University, Hoover Institution Archives; interview, in Sunoo, *Korea Kaleidoscope,* p. 69.

3. "Life History of Mr. Hong, Korean," circa 1924, p. 2, Survey of Race Relations, Stanford University, Hoover Institution Archives; interview, in Sunoo, *Korea Kaleidoscope,* p. 69; Bong Youn Choy, *Koreans in America* (Chicago, 1979), pp. 109–110.

4. Choy, *Koreans in America*, p. 109.

5. H. Brett Melendy, *Asians in America: Filipinos, Koreans, and East Indians* (Boston, 1977), pp. 133–134.

6. Sun Bin Yim, "The Social Structure of Korean Communities in California, 1903–1920," in Lucie Cheng and Edna Bonacich (eds.), *Labor Immigration Under Capitalism: Asian Workers in the United States before World War II* (Berkeley, 1984), p. 529; interview, in Sunoo, *Korea Kaleidoscope*, p. 69; Melendy, *Asians in America*, p. 136.

7. Interviews, in Sunoo, *Korea Kaleidoscope*, pp. 77, 118; interview of Mrs. Myung ja Sur, in Christopher Kim, "Three Generations of Koreans in America," Asian American Studies 199 paper, University of California, Berkeley, 1976, p. 2. I am indebted to Gin Pang for the Korean terms *chong gak* and *horlebees*, interview with author, February 23, 1988.

8. Interview, in Brenda Sunoo, *Korean American Writings: Selected Material From Insight, Korean American Bimonthly* (New York, 1975), p. 25; Yim, "Social Structure of Korean Communities," p. 528.

9. Hyung-chan Kim, note to author, June 20, 1988; Choy, *Koreans in America*, p. 106; Edna Bonacich and John Modell, *The Economic Basis of Ethnic Solidarity: Small Business in the Japanese American Community* (Berkeley, 1980).

10. Korean immigrant and the *New Korea*, quoted in Yim, "Social Structure of Korean Communities," p. 519.

11. Interview with Jean Park (pseudonym), Prologue of "The Autobiography of a Second Generation Korean American," in Kim, "Three Generations of Koreans in America," Asian American Studies 199 paper, University of California, Berkeley, 1976, pp. 42–44.

12. Ibid.

13. Choy, *Koreans in America*, pp. 301–302.

14. Yim, "Social Structure of Korean Communities," p. 523; Ivan H. Light, *Ethnic Enterprise in America: Business and Welfare Among Chinese, Japanese, and Blacks* (Berkeley, 1972).

15. Interview, in Choy, *Koreans in America*, p. 304.

16. Hyung June Moon, "The Korean Immigrants in America: The Quest of Identity in the Formative Years, 1903–1918," unpublished Ph.D. thesis, University of Nevada, Reno, 1976, p. 199.

17. *Sinhan Minbo*, editorial, in Moon, "Korean Immigrants in America," p. 157.

18. Moon, "Korean Immigrants in America," pp. 157–159.

19. Choy, *Koreans in America*, p. 110; Moon, "Korean Immigrants in America," p. 295; Adelaide Kim, "The Place of the Korean," p. 3.

20. Interview, in Choy, *Koreans in America*, p. 305.

21. Elaine Kim, *Asian American Literature* (Philadelphia, 1982), p. 37; Harold and Sonia Sunoo, "The Heritage of the First Korean Women Immigrants in the United States: 1903–1924," paper presented at the 10th Annual Conference of the Association of Korean Christian Scholars of North America, Chicago, 1976, p. 21.

22. Moon, "Korean Immigrants in America," pp. 229, 139; Park, interview, p. 37; Louise Yim, *My Forty Year Fight for Korea* (New York, 1951), p. 167.

23. Eun Sik Yang, "Koreans in America, 1903–1945," in Eui-Young Yu et al. (eds.), *Koreans in Los Angeles: Prospects and Promises* (Los Angeles, 1982), p.17; Moon, "Korean Immigrants in America," pp. 253, 119; for illiteracy rates, see Moon, "Korean Immigrants in America," p. 269.

24. Gloria Hahn, interview, in Choy, *Koreans in America*, p. 310.

25. Moon, "Korean Immigrants in America," p. 303.

26. Moon, "Korean Immigrants in America," p. 316; Wilson Hong, in Dale White, "Koreans in Montana," *Asia and the Americas*, vol. 45, no. 3 (March 1945), p. 156.

27. *Sinhan Minbo*, editorial, in Moon, "Korean Immigrants in America," p. 283; advertisement, in Eun Sik Yang, "Korean Women of America: From Subordination to Partnership, 1903–1930," *Amerasia Journal*, vol. 11, no. 2 (1984), p. 17; Melendy, *Asians in America*, p. 135.

28. Moon, "Korean Immigrants in America," pp. 85, 86.

29. *Sinhan Minbo*, editorial, in Moon, "Korean Immigrants in America," p. 87.

30. Moon, "Korean Immigrants in America," p. 161.

31. Ibid., p. 286.

32. Ibid., p. 331.

33. Choy, *Koreans in America*, p. 148; Moon, "Korean Immigrants in America," pp. 328, 354, 314.

34. Younghill Kang, *East Goes West* (New York, 1937), pp. 74, 58.

35. Ibid., pp. 61, 74.

36. Ibid., p. 73.

37. Ibid., p. 383.

38. Ibid., pp. 73, 400, 401.

39. Ibid., p. 74; Moon, "Korean Immigrants in America," p. 118; Whang, Sa Sun, interview, in Sunoo, *Korean American Writings*, p. 25.

40. Park, interview, pp. 6, 1, 7, 18.

41. Ibid., pp. 4, 6, 7; Myung ja Sur, interview, in Kim, "Three Generations of Koreans," p. 10.

42. Park, interview, p. 14; Myung ja Sur, interview, p. 2.

43. Park, interview, pp. 2, 3.

44. Ibid., p. 15.

45. Ibid.

46. Ibid., pp. 16, 19.

47. Ibid., pp. 21, 36.

48. Ibid., pp. 22, 38, 23.

49. Ibid., p. 36.

50. Ibid., pp. 17, 38, 37.

51. Ibid., pp. 24, 25.

52. Ibid., pp. 36, 24, 25, 30, 31.

53. Ibid., pp. 17, 18, 22.

54. Ibid., pp. 39, 41, 37.

55. Ibid., p. 38; Ilsoo Kim, *New Urban Immigrants: The Korean Community of New York* (Princeton, 1981), pp. 18, 24.

56. Melendy, *Asians in America*, pp. 144–145; Kyung Sook Cho Gregor, "Korean Immigrants in Gresham, Oregon: Community Life and Social Adjustment," unpublished M.A. thesis, University of Oregon, 1963, pp. 53–54; Moon, "Korean Immigrants in America," pp. 116, 119, 120; "Life History of J. Lim," 1924–1925, p. 1, Survey of Race Relations, Stanford University, Hoover Institution Archives; William C. Smith, *The Second Generation Oriental in America* (Honolulu, 1927), p. 7.

8. "The Tide of Turbans"

1. Ralph S. Kuykendall, *The Hawaiian Kingdom, 1854–1874, Twenty Critical Years*, vol. 2 (Honolulu, 1953), pp. 179–181; Ralph S. Kuykendall, *The Hawaiian Kingdom, 1874–1893, The Kalakaua Dynasty*, vol. 3 (Honolulu, 1967), pp. 43, 118, 129–132; Katherine Coman, *The History of Contract Labor in the Hawaiian Islands* (New York, 1903), p. 32.

2. Saint Nihal Singh, "The Picturesque Immigrant from India's Coral Strand," in *Out West*, vol. 30 (1909), pp. 44–45.

3. Leonard Greenwood, "El Centro's Community of Sikhs Dying Out," *Los Angeles Times*, December 28, 1966; Agnes Foster Buchanan, "The West and the Hindu Invasion," in *Overland Monthly*, vol. 51, no. 4 (April 1908), pp. 308–313.

4. H. A. Millis, "East Indian Immigration to the Pacific Coast," in *Survey*, vol. 28, no. 9 (June 1912), p. 379; Herman Scheffauer, "The Tide of Turbans," *Forum*, vol. 43 (June 1910), pp. 616–618; Bruce La Brack, "The Sikhs of Northern California: A Socio-historical Study," unpublished Ph.D. thesis, Syracuse University, 1980, p. 130.

5. Joan M. Jensen, *Passage from India: Asian Indian Immigrants in North America* (New Haven, 1988), p. 113; Samuel Gompers and Herman Gutstadt, *Meat vs. Rice: American Manhood against Asiatic Coolieism, Which Shall Survive?* (San Francisco, 1908), p. 17; H. Brett Melendy, *Asians in America: Filipinos, Koreans, and East Indians* (Boston, 1977), pp. 192–193; "Hindu Invasion," *Collier's Weekly*, vol. 45 (March 26, 1910), p. 15.

6. Buchanan, "The West and the Hindu Invasion," pp. 308–313.

7. Scheffauer, "Tide of Turbans," pp. 616–617.

8. "The Hindoo Question in California," in *Proceedings of the Asiatic Exclusion League* (San Francisco, February 1908), pp. 8–10.

9. *Survey*, vol. 25 (1910), p. 3; Melendy, *Asians in America*, p. 223.

10. *Proceedings of the Asiatic Exclusion League* (San Francisco, April 1910), p. 8.

11. Jensen, *Passage from India*, p. 248; Gary Hess, "The Forgotten Asian Americans: The East Indian Community in the United States," in Norris Hundley (ed.), *The Asian American: The Historical Experience* (Santa Barbara, 1976), pp. 169–170.

12. U.S. v. Bhagat Singh Thind, 261 U.S. 204–215 (Washington, D.C., 1923); Gurdial Singh, "East Indians in the United States," *Sociology and Social Research*, vol. 30 (January–February 1946), p. 212.

13. Jane Singh, interview with author, June 2, 1988; Aseem Chhabra, "How the West Was Won: A Veteran Recalls the Pleasures and Pains of Putting Roots," *India Abroad*, July 4, 1986, p. 11.

14. Melendy, *Asians in America*, p. 221.

15. Jensen, *Passage from India*, p. 265; Salim Khan, "A Brief History of Pakistanis in the Western United States," M.A. thesis, Sacramento State University, 1981, p. 43.

16. Hess, "Forgotten Asian Americans," pp. 166–167; Ved Prakash Vatuk and Sylvia Vatuk, "Protest Songs of East Indians on the West Coast, U.S.A.," in Ved Prakash Vatuk (ed.), *Thieves in My House: Four Studies in Indian Folklore of Protest and Change* (Bhairavanath, Varanasi, India, 1969), pp. 71, 72.

17. Rev. E. M. Wherry, "Hindu Immigrants in America," in *Missionary Review of the World*, vol. 30 (December 1907), pp. 918–919.

18. Scheffauer, "Tide of Turbans," p. 617.

19. Melendy, *Asians in America*, p. 227; Millis, "East Indian Immigration," pp. 384–385.

20. Mr. Cook, Bridge Land and Navigation Company, interview, Wood interview notes, p. 48, envelope 3, James Earl Wood Collection, Bancroft Library, University of California, Berkeley.

21. Annette Thackwell Johnson, "'Ragheads'—A Picture of America's East Indians," in the *Independent,* vol. 109 (October 28, 1922), p. 234; Bruce La Brack, "Occupational Specialization among Rural California Sikhs: The Interplay of Culture and Economics," in *Amerasia,* vol. 9, no. 2 (1982), p. 39.

22. Dhan Gopal Mukerji, *Caste and Outcast* (New York, 1923), pp. 269–270.

23. Mukerji, *Caste and Outcast,* pp. 275–276; Jensen, *Passage from India,* p. 40.

24. Mukerji, *Caste and Outcast,* pp. 281–282.

25. "Interview with Inder Singh," May 31, 1924, p. 2, Survey of Race Relations, Stanford University, Hoover Institution Archives; Millis, "East Indian Immigration," pp. 384–385; Mary Paik Lee, "A Korean/Californian Girlhood," edited by Sucheng Chan, in *California History,* March 1988, p. 54; Allan Miller, "An Ethnographic Report on the Sikh (East) Indians of the Sacramento Valley," pp. 57–59; Scheffauer, "Tide of Turbans," p. 618.

26. Bruce La Brack, "Occupational Specialization among Rural California Sikhs," p. 34.

27. Rajani K. Das, *Hindustani Workers on the Pacific Coast* (Berlin, 1923), p. 93; D. S. Saund, *Congressman from India* (New York, 1960), p. 45.

28. "Biographical Sketch of Harnam Singh Sidhu," in Miller, "Ethnographic Report," p. 101; see Karen Leonard, "Punjabi Farmers and California's Alien Land Law," *Agricultural History,* vol. 59, no. 4 (October 1985), p. 550 for quote, and pp. 549–562 for Punjabi farming practices.

29. Sucha Singh, interview, August 8, 1924, Survey of Race Relations, Stanford University, Hoover Institution Archives; Leonard, "Punjabi Farmers and California's Alien Land Law," pp. 552–555; text based on interviews, in Khan, "Pakistanis in the Western United States," pp. 39, 41; Greenwood, "El Centro's Community of Sikhs Dying Out"; "Biographical Sketch of Munshi Singh Thiara" and "Biographical Sketch of Harnam Singh Sidhu," based on interviews, in Miller, "An Ethnographic Report on the Sikh (East) Indians of the Sacramento Valley," Anthropology 299 paper, University of California, Berkeley, 1950, appendix pp. 81 and 104 respectively; D. P. Pandia and Mme. Kamaladevi, "Justice for Hindus in America," *The Christian Century,* vol. 57 (March 13, 1940), p. 357.

30. This comparison is developed in Leonard, "Punjabi Farmers and California's Alien Land Law," pp. 559–561.

31. U.S. Immigration Commission, *Japanese and Other Immigrant Races in the Pacific Coast and Rocky Mountain States,* vol. 1, *Japanese and East Indians* (Washington, 1911), p. 348; Johnson, "'Ragheads,'" p. 234.

32. Bruce La Brack, "Immigration Law and the Revitalization Process: The Case of the California Sikhs," in S. Chandrasekhar (ed.), *From India to America: A Brief History of Immigration, Admission and Assimilation* (La Jolla, 1982), p. 60; U.S. Immigration Commission, *Japanese and East Indians,* p. 339; Saint Nihal Singh, "The Picturesque Immigrant from India's Coral Strand," p. 45.

33. V. V. Raman, "The Pioneer Woman: Making a Home in What Was a Social Wilderness," *India Abroad,* July 4, 1986, p. iv.

34. Moola Singh, in Karen Leonard, "Immigrant Punjabis in Early Twentieth-Century California," in Sucheng Chan (ed.), *Social and Gender Boundaries in the United States* (Lewiston, New York, 1989), pp. 108–109; Bill Strobel, "California's Sikhs: The Pride and the Prejudice," in *California Today,* the magazine of the *San Jose*

Mercury News, May 27, 1979; Greenwood, "El Centro's Community of Sikhs Dying Out"; Sucheta Mazumdar, "Punjabi Agricultural Workers in California, 1905–1945," in Lucie Cheng and Edna Bonacich (eds.), *Labor Immigration Under Capitalism: Asian Workers in the United States before World War II* (Berkeley, 1984), p. 572.

35. *Sutter County Farmer,* May 29, 1923, in La Brack, "The Sikhs of Northern California," p. 156.

36. For statistics on marriages, see Bruce La Brack and Karen Leonard, "Conflict and Compatibility in Punjabi-Mexican Immigrant Families in Rural California, 1915–1965," in *Journal of Marriage and the Family,* vol. 46 (1984), p. 528; Das, *Hindustani Workers on the Pacific Coast,* p. 110; information about Lohar Bupara from Roberto Haro, interview with author, September 6, 1988; "Interview with Inder Singh," p. 1, Survey of Race Relations, Stanford University, Hoover Institution Archives; Khan, "Pakistanis in the Western United States," p. 46; Leonard, "Immigrant Punjabis," p. 110; Sucha Singh, interview, August 8, 1924, Survey of Race Relations, Stanford University, Hoover Institution Archives.

37. "Interview with Inder Singh," May 31, 1924, p. 2, Survey of Race Relations, Stanford University, Hoover Institution Archives; Karen Leonard, "Marriage and Family Life Among Early Asian Indian Immigrants," in S. Chandrasekhar, *From India to America* (La Jolla, 1982), p. 72.

38. Leonard, "Marriage and Family Life Among Early Asian Indian Immigrants," p. 73; Haro, interview with author, September 6, 1988; Bruce La Brack and Karen Leonard, "Conflict and Compatibility in Punjabi-Mexican Immigrant Families in Rural California, 1915–1965," *Journal of Marriage and the Family,* vol. 46 (August 1984), p. 530; Leonard, "Changes in Meaning for Immigrant Punjabis," pp. 114–115; Sucha Singh, interview, Survey of Race Relations, Stanford University, Hoover Institution Archives.

39. Mukerji, *Caste and Outcast,* p. 277.

40. Mazumdar, "Punjabi Agricultural Workers," p. 572; Das, *Hindustani Workers on the Pacific Coast,* p. 84; Mukerji, *Caste and Outcast,* pp. 270, 277; "Hindus of Los Angeles," p. 25, Survey of Race Relations, Stanford University, Hoover Institution Archives.

41. Das, *Hindustani Workers on the Pacific Coast,* p. 82.

42. Mukerji, *Caste and Outcast,* pp. 279–281.

43. Das, *Hindustani Workers on the Pacific Coast,* p. 80.

44. S. Chandrasekhar, "The Indian Community in the United States," in *Far Eastern Survey,* June 6, 1945, p. 149.

9. Dollar a Day, Dime a Dance

1. Geoffrey Dunn and Mark Schwartz, *Dollar a Day, 10¢ a Dance: An Historic Portrait of Filipino Farmworkers in America,* film and video (San Francisco, 1985); interview, Wood interview notes, p. 90, envelop 10, James Earl Wood Collection, Bancroft Library, University of California, Berkeley.

2. Manuel Buaken, *I Have Lived with the American People* (Caldwell, Idaho, 1948), p. 353; "I Am Only a Foreigner — So This Is America," letter written by a Filipino to an Americanization teacher in Los Angeles, circa 1924, p. 1, survey of Race Relations, Stanford University, Hoover Institution Archives.

3. Fred Cordova, *Filipinos: Forgotten Asian Americans, A Pictorial Essay, 1763–circa 1963* (Seattle, 1983), p. 39; Buaken, *I Have Lived with the American People,* p. 61.

4. Angeles Amoroso Mendoza Jucutan, interview with author, June 14, 1987; Buaken, *I Have Lived with the American People*, pp. 188, 82; hotel manager, interview, Wood, "Earning a Living," p. 3, envelope 9, Wood Collection.

5. Cordova, *Filipinos*, p. 22.

6. "Canta Ti Alaskero," by Trinidad A. Rojo. A university student, Rojo worked in Alaska for ten summers. Translation from Ilocano to English by Sebastian S. Abella. Song reprinted in Lauren Wilde Casady, "Labor Unrest and the Labor Movement in the Salmon Industry of the Pacific Coast," unpublished Ph.D. thesis, University of California, 1938, pp. 137–138.

7. Cordova, *Filipinos*, p. 65; John Castillo, interview, July 29, 1975, pp. 11–12, Washington State Oral/Aural History Program, Washington State Archives, Olympia, Washington.

8. Cordova, *Filipinos*, pp. 46, 41.

9. Filipino Oral History Project, *Voices: A Filipino American Oral History* (Stockton, Calif., 1984), n.pp.; Cordova, *Filipinos*, pp. 38, 40.

10. Frank Waterman, interview, Wood interview notes, p. 16, envelope 3, Wood Collection; Cordova, *Filipinos*, pp. 40; Bauken, *I Have Lived with the American People*, pp. 194–195.

11. Cordova, *Filipinos*, pp. 38, 41.

12. Harry Hammond, editor of *Byron Times*, interview, Wood interview notes, pp. 52–53, envelope 3, Wood Collection; Mr. Oku, Japanese grower, interview, Wood interview notes, pp. 10–11, envelope 10, Wood Collection; Filipino laborer, interview, Wood interview notes, p. 69, envelope 10, Wood Collection.

13. Buaken, *I Have Lived with the American People*, p. 63; Cordova, *Filipinos*, p. 38.

14. Juanita Salvador Burris, "Ti Isuda Ti Imuda . . . 'Those Who Came First,'" *Bridge: An Asian American Perspective*, Winter 1977, p. 57; Carlos Bulosan, *America Is in the Heart: A Personal History* (rpt. Seattle, 1981, originally published in 1946), p. 158; Mr. Oku, Japanese grower, interview, Wood interview notes, pp. 10–11, envelope 10, Wood Collection; Filipino Oral History Project, *Voices*, n.pp.; Cordova, *Filipinos*, pp. 43, 39.

15. Emory Bogardus, "American Attitudes Towards Filipinos," *Sociology and Social Research*, vol. 14 (September 1929), pp. 65–66; H. Brett Melendy, *Asians in America: Filipinos, Koreans, and East Indians* (Boston, 1977), pp. 78, 79, 77.

16. Buaken, *I Have Lived with the American People*, pp. 61–62.

17. Ibid., p. 357; *San Francisco Chronicle*, August 29, 1934.

18. *San Francisco Chronicle*, September 6, 7, 1934; Melendy, *Asians in America*, p. 81; Howard DeWitt, "The Filipino Labor Union: The Salinas Lettuce Strike of 1934," in *Amerasia*, vol. 5, no. 2 (1978), p. 15.

19. Carey McWilliams, "Exit the Filipino," *Nation*, September 4, 1935, p. 265; Cordova, *Filipinos*, p. 73; Bulosan, *America Is in the Heart*, p. 104.

20. Stuart C. Miller, *"Benevolent Assimilation": The American Conquest of the Philippines*, 1899–1903 (New Haven, 1982), p. 24; secretary, interview by James Earl Wood, Wood interview notes, "Immigration of Filipinos into California," p. 8, envelope 2, Wood Collection.

21. "A Native Filipino's Impressions of America" and "Experiences and Opinions of a Filipino," in Fisk University Social Science Institute, *Orientals and Their Cultural Adjustment* (Nashville, Tenn., 1946), p. 113; Felicidad Acena, interview, July 28, 1975, p. 3, Washington State Oral/Aural History Program, Washington State Archives, Olympia, Washington; Francisco Carino, "My Life History," August

1924, p. 5, Survey of Race Relations, Stanford University, Hoover Institution Archives; Magdaleno Abaya, "A Thumb Portrait of My Life History in Relation to America," circa 1924, ibid.; Cordova, *Filipinos*, p. 191; autobiography, in Roberto V. Vallangca, *Pinoy: The First Wave, 1898–1941* (San Francisco, 1977).

22. Manuel Buaken, *I Have Lived with the American People* (Caldwell, Idaho, 1948), pp. 68–69; Cordova, *Filipinos*, p. 144; Angeles Amoroso Mendoza Jucutan, interview with author, June 14, 1987.

23. Buaken, *I Have Lived with the American People*, p. 147; C. M. Goethe, "Filipino Immigration Viewed as a Peril," in *Current History*, vol. 34 (June 1931), p. 353; Carino, "My Life History;" p. 2, Survey of Race Relations, Stanford University, Hoover Institution Archives; Melendy, *Asians in America*, p. 66; John Castillo, interview, July 29, 1975, p. 7, Washington State Oral/Aural History Program, Washington State Archives, Olympia, Washington; Bogardus, "American Attitudes Towards Filipinos," *Sociology and Social Research*, vol. 14 (September 1929), p. 64; Cordova, *Filipinos*, p. 115; Donald Anthony, "Filipino Labor in Central California," *Sociology and Social Research*, vol. 16 (September 1931), p. 151.

24. Edna Bonacich, "A Theory of Ethnic Antagonism: The Split Labor Market," *American Sociological Review*, vol. 37, no. 5 (October 1972), pp. 547–559; Sonia E. Wallovits, *The Filipinos in California* (San Francisco, 1972), p. 41; Buaken, *I Have Lived with the American People*, pp. 94–95.

25. *Evening Pajaronian*, October 30, 1929, in envelope 9, Wood Collection; letter addressed to Chief of Police, Sunnyvale, postmarked August 5, 1930, and handwritten note to farmer, in envelope 15, Wood Collection; *Fresno Republican*, August 19, 1930; *Reedley Mailbag*, August 22, 1930; H. C. Peterson, interview, Wood interview notes, p. 93, envelope 10, Wood Collection; Cordova, *Filipinos*, p. 116. "Aresto Lande" was Aristo E. Lampky.

26. "Common white laborer," interview, Wood interview notes, pp. 70–72, envelope 3, Wood Collection.

27. *Evening Pajaronian*, December 5, 1929, in envelope 9, Wood Collection; Resolution of the Chamber of Commerce of Northern Monterey County, December 6, 1929, copy in envelope 1, Wood Collection; Melendy, *Asians in America*, p. 55.

28. Interview with Rohrback by James Earl Wood, circa 1930–1931, in Wood, "A Record of Conflict," unpublished notes, p. 21, envelope 9, Wood Collection; Duncan Aikman of the *Baltimore Sun*, in *Literary Digest*, February 15, 1930, p. 12.

29. Mr. Tinkham, interview, Wood interview notes, p. 42, envelope 3, Wood Collection; Melendy, *Asians in America*, p. 67.

30. Mr. Moody, deputy labor commissioner, interview, Wood interview notes, p. 16, envelope 10, Wood Collection; D. Crowell, interview, February 22, 1930, Wood interview notes, p. 35, envelope 3, Wood Collection; *Time*, vol. 28 (April 13, 1936), p. 17.

31. David Barrows, "The Desirability of the Filipino," in *The Commonwealth*, vol. 5, no. 45, November 5, 1929, pp. 321–326.

32. Megumi Dick Osumi, "Asians and California's Anti–Miscegenation Laws," in Nobuya Tsuchida (ed.), *Asian and Pacific American Experiences: Women's Perspectives* (Minneapolis, 1982), pp. 17, 18; Wallovits, *Filipinos in California*, p. 6.

33. "Lovers' Departure," *Time*, vol. 28 (April 13, 1936), p. 17; Ernest Ilustre, "Great Lovers," in *Time*, vol. 28 (April 27, 1936), p. 6.

34. Cordova, *Filipinos*, pp. 115, 116; Filipino Oral History Project, *Voices*, n.pp.

35. *Stockton Record*, March 6, 1930, in envelope 10, Wood Collection; letter of

Charles Martin, *Dinuba Sentinel*, August 8, 1928, in envelope 10, Wood Collection; *San Francisco News*, November 13, 1929, in envelope 4, Wood Collection.

36. *Sacramento Bee*, March 30, 1933; Osumi, "Asians and California's Anti-Miscegenation Laws," pp. 19–21; Bulosan, *America Is in the Heart*, p. 143.

37. U.S. Supreme Court, in Wallovits, *Filipinos in California*, p. 3; Julian Ilar, "Who Is the Filipino?" *Filipino Nation*, November 1930, p. 13.

38. Anthony, "Filipino Labor in Central California," p. 149.

39. "Every Cause Has Its Effect," *Filipino Nation*, July 1931, p. 5; Senator Tydings, in Wallovits, *Filipinos in California*, p. 5.

40. Benicio T. Catapusan, "Filipino Immigrants and Public Relief in the United States," *Sociology and Social Research*, vol. 23 (July–August 1939), pp. 546–554.

41. Honorante Mariano, *The Filipino Immigrants in the United States* (San Francisco, 1972), p. 68.

42. *Los Angeles Herald*, April 16, 1934; *Los Angeles Times*, July 31, 1936.

43. McWilliams, "Exit the Filipino," p. 265.

44. Casiano Pagilao Coloma, "A Study of the Filipino Repatriation Movement," unpublished M.S. thesis, University of Southern California, 1939, pp. 40–41, 44; "Lover's Departure," *Time*, p. 17.

45. Anthony, "Filipino Labor in Central California," p. 150; Buaken, *I Have Lived with the American People*, pp. 355, 358; Emory S. Bogardus, "Filipino Repatriation," *Sociology and Social Research*, vol. 21 (September–October 1936), pp. 67–71.

46. Virgilio Menor Felipe, "Hawaii: A Pilipino Dream," unpublished M.A. thesis, University of Hawaii, 1972, p. 68; Royal F. Morales, *Makibaka: The Pilipino-American Struggle* (Los Angeles, 1974), pp. 52, 53. I am indebted to Frank Megino for the song, "Kumakaway Ka Pa, Irog" ("You were Waving Goodbye, Beloved").

47. Interview, Wood interview notes, p. 99, envelope 10, Wood Collection; Midi Yanez, "Filipinos and the Depression," *Filipino Nation*, November 1932, p. 14; Aurelio Bulosan, interview, in *Amerasia*, vol. 6, no. 1 (May 1979), p. 160; Morales, *Makibaka*, p. 57; Bulosan, *America Is in the Heart*, p. 124.

48. Wallace Stegner, in Royal F. Morales, *Makibaka*, p. 47; Buaken, *I Have Lived with the American People*, p. 357; Rojo, "Canta Ti Alaskero," in Casady, *Labor Unrest and the Labor Movement in the Salmon Industry*, pp. 137–138; Bulosan, *America Is in the Heart*, pp. 255, 108. I am indebted to Frank Megino for the songs.

49. Elena S. H. Yu, "Filipino Migration and Community Organizations in the United States," *California Sociologist*, vol. 3, no. 2 (Summer 1980), p. 84.

50. Pyong Gap Min, "Filipino and Korean Immigrants in Small Business: A Comparative Analysis," *Amerasia*, vol. 13, no. 1 (1986–87), pp. 53–72.

51. Hilario Moncado, "Philippine Independence Before Filipino Exclusion," *Filipino Nation*, May 1931, p. 9.

52. Felix Tapiz, Wood interview notes, p. 38, envelope 3, Wood Collection; Cordova, *Filipinos*, pp. 191, 109, 212.

53. Luis Agudo, interview, Wood interview notes, p. 95, envelope 10, Wood Collection; Cordova, *Filipinos*, pp. 212, 214; "Passage From Life," by Carlos Bulosan, in Susan Evangelista, *Carlos Bulosan and His Poetry: A Biography and Anthology* (Seattle, 1985), p. 144; Filipino Oral History Project, *Voices*, n.p.

54. Charles F. Crook, deputy labor commissioner of San Joaquin Country, interview, February 21, 1930, Wood interview notes, pp. 25, 26, envelope 3, Wood Collec-

tion; Buaken, *I Have Lived with the American People*, pp. 116–117; Carlos Bulosan, *America Is in the Heart*, p. 274; Vallangca, *Pinoy*, p. 96.

55. Paul Cressey, *The Taxi-Dance Hall: A Sociological Study in Commercialized Recreation and City Life* (Chicago, 1932), pp. 10–11; Cordova, *Filipinos*, pp. 89–90.

56. Vallangca, *Pinoy*, pp. 87, 96.

57. Cordova, *Filipinos*, p. 211; Vallangca, *Pinoy*, pp. 51, 78; Benicio T. Catapusan, "The Filipino Occupational and Recreational Activities in Los Angeles," unpublished M.A. thesis, University of Southern California, 1934, p. 73.

58. Alfredo Munoz, *The Filipinos in America* (Los Angeles, 1972), p. 89.

59. Morales, *Makibaka*, p. 51; Jacqueline Frost, "Old-Timers Live Simply: Forgotten Workers—The First Filipino-Americans," *Stockton Record,* November 25, 1985; Cordova, *Filipinos*, pp. 147, 152. I am indebted to Frank Megino for the song "Dalagang Pilipina."

60. Wood, field notes, envelope 3, Wood Collection; Cordova, *Filipinos*, pp. 153, 109; Maria Abastilla Beltran, May 5, 1975, p. 13, Washington State Oral/Aural History Program, Washington State Archives, Olympia, Washington.

61. Filipino labor contractor, interview, Wood interview notes, p. 121, envelope 10, Wood Collection; Cordova, *Filipinos*, p. 141; Bruno Lasker, *Filipino Immigration* (Chicago, 1931), p. 119.

62. Luis Agudo, interview, Wood interview notes, p. 94, envelope 10, Wood Collection; Anthony, "Filipino Labor in Central California," pp. 149–150.

63. Cordova, *Filipinos*, p. 141; *Berkeley Gazette*, August 1930, UP story dated August 11, 1930, clipping in envelope 16, Wood Collection.

64. Cressey, *Taxi-Dance Hall*, pp. 171–172; Mr. Escalanta, interview, Wood interview notes, p. 24, envelope 10, Wood Collection; Lorraine Libadia, interview, October 22, 1975, p. 2, Washington State Oral/Aural History Program, Washington State Archives, Olympia, Washington; Cordova, *Filipinos*, pp. 143, 158.

65. Benicio T. Catapusan, "Filipino Intermarriage Problems in the United States," *Sociology and Social Research*, vol. 22 (1938), p. 270.

66. Cordova, *Filipinos*, p. 161; Liz Megino, interview with author, April 28, 1988; Filipino Oral History Project, *Voices*, n.pp.

67. Cordova, *Filipinos,* pp. 158, 159, 134.

68. Bulosan, *America Is in the Heart*, p. 88; Bulosan, letter dated April 27, 1941, excerpt reprinted in *Amerasia Journal*, vol. 6, no. 1 (May 1979), p. 144; Bulosan, "My Education," reprinted ibid., p.117; Bulosan, letter dated May 2,1938, excerpt reprinted ibid., p.143. Bulosan used pseudonyms for the individuals in his narrative.

69. Bulosan, *America Is in the Heart*, pp. 14, 17, 18, 24.

70. Ibid., p. 67.

71. Ibid., pp. 69–70.

72. Ibid., pp. 99–101.

73. Ibid., pp. 101–102, 149, 161.

74. Ibid., pp. 146, 170, 105, 116, 120.

75. Ibid., p. 134.

76. Ibid., pp. 256, 258, 144, 145, 277, 253.

77. Ibid., pp. 156, 157, 112, 207–209.

78. Ibid., p. 147.

79. Ibid., pp. 198–203.
80. Ibid., pp. 209–216, 301, 303, 235.
81. Ibid., pp. 114–115, 230, 242, 247, 189.
82. Ibid., pp. 307–308.
83. Ibid., pp. 56–57.
84. Ibid., pp. 265, 139.
85. Ibid., pp. 180, 183, 187.
86. Ibid., pp. 172–173.
87. Ibid., p. 224.
88. Ibid., p. 235.
89. Ibid., pp. 312, 289, 189, 230, 146, 195–196.
90. Ibid., pp. 313–314, 310–312.

IV. Diversity

1. Carlos Bulosan, *America Is in the Heart: A Personal History* (rpt. Seattle, 1981, originally published in 1946), pp. 313–314.

10. The Watershed of World War II: Democracy and Race

1. Carlos Bulosan, *America Is in the Heart: A Personal History* (rpt. Seattle, 1981, originally published in 1946), pp. 315–316, 324.
2. Georg Simmel, "Der Fremde" or "The Stranger," in Simmel, *On Individuality and Social Forms*, edited by Donald N. Levine (Chicago, 1971), pp. 143–149.
3. Apolinaria Gusman Oclaray, oral history, in Roberto V. Vallangca, *Pinoy: The First Wave, 1898–1941* (San Francisco, 1977), p. 100.
4. Manuel Buaken, *I Have Lived with the American People* (Caldwell, Idaho, 1948), pp. 321–323; Carlos Bulosan, "The Voice of Bataan," in Susan Evangelista, *Carlos Bulosan and His Poetry: A Biography and Anthology* (Seattle, 1985), p. 121.
5. Buaken, *I Have Lived with the American People*, pp. 322–323; James G. Wingo, "The First Filipino Regiment and Its Racial Strains," *Asia*, October 1942, p. 562; see also R. T. Feria, "War and the Status of Filipino Immigrants," *Sociology and Social Research*, vol. 31 (1946–47), p. 52.
6. Bulosan, *America Is in the Heart*, p. 318.
7. Bienvenido Santos, "Filipinos in War," *Far Eastern Survey*, vol. 11 (November 30, 1942), p. 249.
8. F. Shor, "See You in Manila," condensed from *The American Legion Magazine*, March 1943, in *Reader's Digest*, March 1943, p. 117; Doroteo Vite, "A Filipino Rookie in Uncle Sam's Army," *Asia*, October 1942, pp. 564, 566.
9. Fred Cordova, *Filipinos: Forgotten Asian Americans, A Pictorial Essay, 1763–circa 1963* (Seattle, 1983), pp. 218, 219; Lorraine Jacobs Crouchett, *Filipinos in California: From the Days of the Galleons to the Present* (El Cerrito, Calif., 1982), p. 53.
10. Iris Brown Buaken, "My Brave New World," *Asia*, May 1943, p. 269; F. A. Taggaoa, "No Cause for Regret," *Asia*, October 1942, p. 567.
11. Manuel Buaken, "Life in the Armed Forces," *New Republic*, vol. 100 (August 30, 1943), p. 278.
12. Manuel Buaken, "Our Fighting Love of Freedom," *Asia*, October 1942, p. 88.
13. Liz Megino, interview with author, April 28, 1988; Buaken, *I Have Lived with the*

American People, pp. 323, 324; H. Brett Melendy, *Asians in America: Filipinos, Koreans, and East Indians* (Boston, 1977), p. 51.

14. Crouchett, *Filipinos in California*, pp. 58–59; Taggaoa, "No Cause for Regret," p. 567.

15. Bulosan, *America Is in the Heart*, pp. 319; Feria, "War and the Status of Filipino Immigrants," pp. 50, 51, 53.

16. Buaken, "Life in the Armed Forces," p. 279; Liz Megino, interview with author, April 28, 1988; "Filipino Baiting in California," *Nation*, July 28, 1945, p. 71.

17. Bong-Youn Choy, *Koreans in America* (Chicago, 1979), p. 172.

18. Hyung-chan Kim and Wayne Patterson, *The Koreans in America, 1882–1974* (Dobbs Ferry, N.Y., 1974), p. 45.

19. Choy, *Koreans in America*, p. 170; *Korean National Herald-Pacific Weekly*, February 25, 1942, in Lauriel Eubank, "The Effects of the First Six Months of World War II on the Attitudes of Koreans and Filipinos toward the Japanese in Hawaii," unpublished M.A. thesis, University of Hawaii, 1943, p. 73.

20. Interview with Jean Park (pseudonym), Prologue of "The Autobiography of a Second Generation Korean American," in Christopher Kim, "Three Generations of Koreans in America," Asian American Studies 199 paper, University of California, Berkeley, 1976, pp. 46–47.

21. Melendy, *Asians in America*, pp. 156–158; Eubank, "Effects of the First Six Months of World War II on the Attitudes of Koreans and Filipinos toward the Japanese in Hawaii," pp. 73, 86.

22. Park, in Kim, "Three Generations of Koreans in America," section on Park, p. 46; Eubank, "Effects of the First Six Months of World War II on the Attitudes of Koreans and Filipinos toward the Japanese in Hawaii," p. 68.

23. Melendy, *Asians in America*, p. 155.

24. Melendy, *Asians in America*, p. 157; Choy, *Koreans in America*, p. 326.

25. Choy, *Koreans in America*, pp. 173–175, 280.

26. Melendy, *Asians in America*, pp. 224, 225.

27. Fred Riggs, *Pressures on Congress: A Study of the Repeal of Chinese Exclusion* (New York, 1950), pp. 164–165; David Reimers, *Still the Golden Door: The Third World Comes to America* (New York, 1985), p. 15.

28. S. Chandrasekhar, "Indian Immigration in America," *Far Eastern Survey*, July 26, 1944, pp. 142, 143.

29. Gary Hess, "The Asian Indian Immigrants in the United States: The Early Phase, 1900–65," *Population Review*, vol. 25 (1982), p. 32; Jane Singh, interview with author, June 2, 1988.

30. D. S. Saund, *Congressman from India* (New York, 1960), pp. 72–75.

31. Lonnie Quan, interview, October 15, 1982, Chinese Women of America Research Project, Chinese Culture Foundation of San Francisco, p. 11.

32. *Time*, December 22, 1941, p. 33.

33. *Congressional Record*, 78th Congress, 1st sess. 1943, vol. 89, part 6, p. 8594; Ling-chi Wang, "Politics of Assimilation and Repression: History of the Chinese in the United States, 1940 to 1970," unpublished manuscript, Asian American Studies Library, University of California, Berkeley, pp. 167–168; Nellie Wong, *Dreams in Harrison Railroad Park* (Berkeley, 1977), p. 16.

34. Quoted in Paul Siu, "The Chinese Laundryman: A Study of Social Isolation," unpublished Ph.D. thesis, University of Chicago, 1953, p. 130; Lao Mei, "On Mother's Day," in *China Daily News*, May 15, 1941, translated by Marlon Hom,

reprinted in *Bu Gao Ban*, newsletter of the New York Chinatown History Project, Fall 1988, pp. 9–10.

35. "A Memo to Mr. Hider, Hirohito & Co.," *Chinese Press*, May 8, 1942; Rose Hum Lee, "Chinese in the United States Today: The War Has Changed Their Lives," *Survey Graphic*, October 1942, p. 444.

36. Peter Kwong, *Chinatown, N.Y.: Labor and Politics, 1930–1950* (New York, 1979), pp. 114–115.

37. Florence Gee, "I Am an American—How Can I Help Win This War?" *Chinese Press*, May 15, 1942; "Women in the War," *Chinese Press*, March 24, 1943; "First Chinese WAAC: New York's Emily Lee Shak," *Chinese Press*, September 25, 1942; Lee, "Chinese in the United States Today," p. 444.

38. Victor and Brett de Bary Nee, *Longtime Californ': A Documentary Study of an American Chinatown* (New York, 1972), pp. 154–155; Diane Mei Lin Mark and Ginger Chih, *A Place Called Chinese America* (Dubuque, Iowa, 1982), pp. 97–98.

39. Lee, "Chinese in the United States Today," p. 419; "Give 'Em Wings: The Story of the Part Played in Aircraft by L.A. Chinese," *Chinese Press*, April 2, 1943.

40. Arthur Wong, oral history, in Joan Morrison and Charlotte Fox Zabusky (eds.), *American Mosaic: The Immigrant Experience in the Words of Those Who Lived It* (New York, 1980), p. 78; "All Chinatown Responds to War Needs," *Chinese Press*, January 2, 1942; Calvin F. Schmid and Charles E. Noble, "Socioeconomic Differentials Among Nonwhite Races," *American Sociological Review*, vol. 30, no. 6 (December 1965), p. 916.

41. Jade Snow Wong, *Fifth Chinese Daughter* (rpt. New York, 1965, originally published in 1945), p. 189; "Chinese Career Girls: They Help Run the Vital 'Behind-the-Line' Business of the United States at War," *Chinese Press*, May 29, 1942; "Women in the War," *Chinese Press*, March 26, 1943.

42. Lee, "Chinese in the United States Today," pp. 419, 444.

43. Ibid., p. 444; Wang, "Politics of Assimilation and Repression," p. 202.

44. Riggs, *Pressures on Congress*, pp. 111, 112, 116; "A Chinese Youth Meeting," *Chinese Press*, October 1, 1943.

45. Riggs, *Pressures on Congress*, pp. 112–113.

46. Franklin D. Roosevelt, "Message from the President of the United States Favoring Repeal of the Chinese Exclusion Laws," October 11, 1943, in Riggs, *Pressures on Congress*, appendix, pp. 210–211.

47. John W. Dower, *War Without Mercy: Race and Power in the Pacific War* (New York, 1986), p. 167; Riggs, *Pressures on Congress*, pp. 161–162.

48. Dower, *War Without Mercy*, pp. 164–169; *Congressional Record*, 78th Congress, 1st sess. 1943, vol. 89, part 6, pp. 8580, 8581, 8597.

49. Jade Snow Wong, "Puritans from the Orient: A Chinese Evolution," in Thomas C. Wheeler (ed.), *The Immigrant Experience: The Anguish of Becoming American* (New York, 1971), p. 130.

50. Seichin Nagayama, interview, in Ethnic Studies Oral History Project, *Uchinanchu: A History of Okinawans in Hawaii* (Honolulu, 1981), p. 479; Mary Tsukamoto, interview, in John Tateishi, *And Justice for All: An Oral History of the Japanese American Detention Camps* (New York, 1984), p. 6.

51. Tsukamoto, in Tateishi, *And Justice for All*, p. 10; Simmel, "The Stranger," pp. 143–149.

52. Robert A. Wilson and Bill Hosokawa, *East to America: A History of the Japanese in the United States* (New York, 1980), p. 154; Commission on Wartime Reloca-

tion and Internment of Civilians, *Personal Justice Denied: Report of the Commission on Wartime Relocation and Internment of Civilians* (Washington, D.C., 1982), p. 264.

53. Commission on Wartime Relocation, *Personal Justice Denied*, p. 265.
54. Ibid., p. 269.
55. Ibid., p. 270.
56. Ibid., pp. 270, 272.
57. Ibid., p. 274.
58. Albert Horlings, "Hawaii's 150,000 Japanese," *The Nation* (July 1942), pp. 69–70.
59. Lawrence Fuchs, *Hawaii Pono: A Social History* (New York, 1961), p.302; Andrew Lind, *Hawaii's Japanese: An Experiment in Democracy* (Princeton, 1946), p. 64.
60. Jacobus tenBroek, Edward Barnhart, and Floyd Matson, *Prejudice, War and the Constitution: Causes and Consequences of the Evacuation of the Japanese Americans in World War II* (Berkeley, 1970), p. 117; Bradford Smith, *Americans From Japan* (Philadelphia, 1948), pp. 171–172; Lind, *Hawaii's Japanese*, p. 63.
61. Dennis Ogawa, *Kodomo no tame ni: For the sake of the children* (Honolulu, 1978), pp. 279– 280; Lind, *Hawaii's Japanese*, p. 42.
62. Smith, *Americans From Japan*, p. 180.
63. Lind, *Hawaii's Japanese*, p. 122.
64. Gavan Daws, *Shoal of Time: A History of the Hawaiian Islands* (rpt. Honolulu, 1977), p. 339.
65. Ogawa, *Kodomo no tame ni*, pp. 315, 320; Commission on Wartime Relocation, *Personal Justice Denied*, p. 280; Minoru Hinahara, interview with author, July 3, 1988.
66. Commission on Wartime Relocation, *Personal Justice Denied*, p. 48.
67. Ibid., pp. 52–53.
68. Ibid., p. 55.
69. Roger Daniels, *Concentration Camps USA: Japanese Americans and World War II* (New York, 1971), pp. 45–46.
70. Commission on Wartime Relocation, *Personal Justice Denied*, pp. 64, 73.
71. Ibid., pp. 56, 71–72, 80; Lind, *Hawaii's Japanese*, p. 49; Daniels, *Concentration Camps USA*, p. 62; tenBroek, Barnhart, and Matson, *Prejudice, War and the Constitution*, p. 75; Gary Y. Okihiro and Julie Sly, "The Press, Japanese Americans, and the Concentration Camps," *Phylon*, vol. 44, no. 1 (1983), pp. 66–69.
72. tenBroek, Barnhart, and Matson, *Prejudice, War and the Constitution*, pp. 79–80.
73. Ibid., p. 80.
74. Ibid., p. 83; Commission on Wartime Relocation, *Personal Justice Denied*, pp. 70–71.
75. Commission on Wartime Relocation, *Personal Justice Denied*, pp. 75, 78.
76. Ibid., pp. 78, 79.
77. Peter Irons, *Justice At War: The Story of the Japanese American Internment Cases* (New York, 1983), p. 20.
78. Daniels, *Concentration Camps USA*, p. 65; Commission on Wartime Relocation, *Personal Justice Denied*, p. 66.
79. Commission on Wartime Relocation, *Personal Justice Denied*, pp. 83, 84.
80. Ibid., p. 85.

81. Ibid., pp. 111, 121; Congressman Robert Matsui, speech in the House of Representatives on the 442 bill for redress and reparations, September 17, 1987, *Congressional Record* (Washington, D.C., 1987), p. 7584; Monica Sone, *Nisei Daughter* (Boston, 1953), p. 158; Takae Washizu, interview, in Eileen Sunada Sarasohn (ed.), *The Issei: Portrait of a Pioneer* (Palo Alto, Calif., 1983), p. 166; poem by Sojin, in Constance Hayashi and Keiho Yamanaka, "Footprints: Poetry of the American Relocation Camp Experience," *Amerasia*, vol. 3, no. 2 (1976), p. 115.

82. Minoru Yasui, interview, Tateishi, *And Justice for All*, pp. 70–71; Gordon Hirabayashi, "Growing Up American in Washington," the Spring 1988 Pettyjohn Distinguished Lecture, Washington State University, March 24, 1988; Hirabayashi, interview with author, March 24, 1988.

83. Tom Hayase, in Sarasohn (ed.), *Issei*, p. 166; Commission on Wartime Relocation, *Personal Justice Denied*, p. 132.

84. Sone, *Nisei Daughter*, p. 166; poem by Keiho Soga, in Jiro Nakano and Kay Nakano (eds. and trans.), *Poets Behind Barbed Wire* (Honolulu, 1983), p. 19; letter by Congressman Norman Mineta's father, quoted in his speech to the House of Representatives, September 17, 1987, *Congressional Record* (Washington, D.C., 1987), p. 7585; Commission on Wartime Relocation, *Personal Justice Denied*, p. 135.

85. Yasui and Tsukamoto, interviews, in Tateishi, *And Justice for All*, pp. 73, 12, 74; poem by Hakujaku, in Hayashi and Yamanaka, "Footprints," p. 116; Commission on Wartime Relocation, *Personal Justice Denied*, pp. 139, 142, 147.

86. Poems by Hibutsu and Sasabune, in Hayashi and Yamanaka, "Footprints," p. 115.

87. Yasui, interview, in Tateishi, *And Justice for All*, p. 76; poem by Sojin Takei, in Nakano and Nakano (eds. and trans.), *Poets Behind Barbed Wire*, p. 35; Sone, *Nisei Daughter*, p. 192.

88. Commission on Wartime Relocation, *Personal Justice Denied*, p. 160; poem by Nikaido Gensui, in Hayashi and Yamanaka, "Footprints," p. 116.

89. Commission on Wartime Relocation, *Personal Justice Denied*, pp. 169, 172, 176.

90. Poems by Taisanboku Mori and Keiho Soga, in Nakano and Nakano, *Poets Behind Barbed Wire*, pp. 25, 57.

91. Poem by Sadae Takizawa, in Sarasohn, *Issei*, p. 184; Miyo Senzaki, interview, in Tateishi, *And Justice For All*, p. 104.

92. tenBroek, Barnhart, and Matson, *Prejudice, War and the Constitution*, p. 150; Commission on Wartime Relocation, *Personal Justice Denied*, pp. 189, 191.

93. Commission on Wartime Relocation, *Personal Justice Denied*, pp. 191–192.

94. Poem by Sunada Toshu, in Hayashi and Yamanaka, "Footprints," p. 116; Commission on Wartime Relocation, *Personal Justice Denied*, p. 195; Sone, *Nisei Daughter*, p. 198.

95. Frank S. Emi, "Draft Resistance at the Heart Mountain Concentration Camp and the Fair Play Committee," paper presented at the Fifth National Conference of the Association for Asian American Studies, Washington State University, March 24–26, 1988, pp. 2–4; Frank S. Emi, interview with author, March 26, 1986; Kiyoshi Okamoto, "We Should Know," typed speech, February 25, 1944, copy given to the author by Frank S. Emi.

96. Commission on Wartime Relocation, *Personal Justice Denied*, p. 195; Emi, "Draft Resistance at the Heart Mountain Concentration Camp," p. 4.

97. James Omura, "Japanese American Journalism During World War II," paper presented at the Fifth National Conference of the Association for Asian American

Studies, Washington State University, March 24–26, 1988; Emi, "Draft Resistance at the Heart Mountain Concentration Camp," pp. 6–8; Emi, interview with author, March 26, 1988; typed statement by the Fair Play Committee for the meeting on March 5, 1944, copy given to the author by Frank S. Emi.

98. Emi, interview with the author, March 26, 1988; reported by Yasui, interview, Tateishi, *And Justice for All*, p. 86.

99. Lind, *Hawaii's Japanese*, p. 161; interview with Hiroshi Kobashigawa, April 15, 1988, by Ben Kobashigawa, transcript in author's possession.

100. Shig Doi, interview, in Tateishi, *And Justice for All*, pp. 165–166; Chester Tanaka, *Go For Broke: A Pictorial History of the Japanese American 100th Infantry Battalion and the 442d Regimental Combat Team* (Richmond, Calif., 1982), p. 100.

101. Daniel K. Inouye, *Journey to Washington* (Englewood Cliffs, N.J., 1967), pp. 151–152.

102. Shig Doi, interview, in Tateishi, *And Justice for All*, p. 161; Lind, *Hawaii's Japanese*, p. 158.

103. Lind, *Hawaii's Japanese*, pp. 161–162.

104. Commission on Wartime Relocation, *Personal Justice Denied*, p. 260; Ronald Reagan, quoted in *Pacific Citizen*, December 1945, pp. 19–26, requoted in "Text of Reagan's Remarks," *Pacific Citizen*, August 1988, p. 5.

105. Silvestre Pulmano, in Tricia Knoll, *Becoming Americans: Asian Sojourners, Immigrants, and Refugees in the Western United States* (Portland, Oreg., 1982), pp. 104–105; Tanaka, *Go For Broke*, p. 171.

106. Frank Chuman, *The Bamboo People: The Law and Japanese–Americans* (Del Mar, Calif., 1976), pp. 343–344; Lind, *Hawaii's Japanese*, p. 166.

107. Commission on Wartime Relocation, *Personal Justice Denied*, p. 92.

108. Helen Murao, interview, in Tateishi, *And Justice for All*, p. 48; Commission on Wartime Relocation, *Personal Justice Denied*, p. 233.

109. Aiko Mifune, interviews with author, February 18, 1988 and March 29, 1988; Timothy Lukes and Gary Okihiro, *Japanese Legacy: Farming and Community Life in California's Santa Clara Valley* (Cupertino, Calif., 1985), p. 137; Commission on Wartime Relocation, *Personal Justice Denied*, p. 242; poem by Keiho Soga, in Nakano and Nakano (eds. and trans.), *Poets Behind Barbed Wire*, p. 64.

11. "Strangers" at the Gates Again

1. Frank Chuman, *The Bamboo People: The Law and Japanese–Americans* (Del Mar, Calif., 1976), pp. 334, 338.

2. Hall to Goldblatt, June 15, 1944, in Hall Files, Anne Rand Library, International Longshoremen's and Warehousemen's Union, San Francisco; Hall to Goldblatt, August 22, 1944, in Hall Files, Anne Rand Library.

3. Sanford Zalburg, *A Spark Is Struck! Jack Hall & the ILWU in Hawaii* (Honolulu, 1979), p. 118; Yasu Arakaki to Jack Kawano, April 26, 1946, and minutes of meeting, "Discussion of Political Action," April 25, 1946, in file on "Notes on Negotiation and Strike Strategy Meeting," in author's personal possession; Goldblatt, "Working Class Leader," p. 346; document entitled "Mass Rally," October 26, 1946, Hawaii Files, Anne Rand Library.

4. Hall to Goldblatt, October 23, 1944 and November 27, 1944, Hall Files, Anne Rand Library; K. K. Lane and C. Ogata, "Change of Attitudes Among Plantation Workers," *Social Process in Hawaii*, vols. 9–10 (1945), p. 96; Honolulu *Star-Bulletin*, November 9, 1944.

5. Lance Fujisaki, "Saburo Fujisaki: An Oral History," Asian American Studies 129 paper, Spring 1983, University of California, Berkeley, p. 27.

6. *ILWU Dispatcher*, September 6, 1946; ILWU Territorial Sugar Negotiating Committee, "A Statement to All Locals, Units and the Membership of the ILWU Engaged in the Sugar Strike," November 15, 1946, in Hawaii File, Anne Rand Library.

7. Jose Corpuz, in LeiAnn Corpuz, "Filipino Labor History in Hawaii: A Case Example of Mr. Jose Corpuz," term paper for Asian American Studies 124, Spring 1987, p. 7; ILWU memorandum, October 1945, in Hawaii File, Anne Rand Library.

8. Louis Goldblatt to Jack Hall, August 20, 1945, in Jack Hall Files, Anne Rand Library; Jack Hall to Louis Goldblatt, February 7, 1946, in Jack Hall Files, Anne Rand Library.

9. Yasu Arakaki to J. R. Robertson, June 26, 1946, in file on "Notes on Negotiation and Strike Strategy Meeting, 1946 August to October," given to author by Saburo Fujisaki, in author's personal possession; ILWU (CIO) Local 148, Women's Auxiliary Corps, Minutes, September 4, 1946, p. 2, in file on "Notes on Negotiation and Strike Strategy Meeting."

10. Louis Goldblatt, interviewed by Estolv Ward in 1977–1979, entitled "Working Class Leader in the ILWU, 1935–1977," Bancroft Library, University of California, Berkeley, pp. 319–320.

11. *ILWU Dispatcher*, March 8, 1946.

12. Frank Thompson to Morris Watson, October 10, 1944, Local 142 Files, Anne Rand Library.

13. Lane and Ogata, "Change of Attitudes Among Plantation Workers," p. 96; Fujisaki, "Saburo Fujisaki: An Oral History," p. 11; Fujisaki, interview with author, July 24, 1985.

14. Noel Kent, *Hawaii: Islands under the Influence* (New York, 1983), p.135; Fujisaki, "Saburo Fujisaki: An Oral History," p. 5.

15. Frank Chuman, *The Bamboo People*, pp. 209–218; Kazuo Ito, *Issei: A History of Japanese Immigrants in North America* (Seattle, 1973), p. 585.

16. Chuman, *Bamboo People*, pp. 206, 222.

17. Ibid., p. 312; Robert A. Wilson and Bill Hosokawa, *East to America: A History of the Japanese in the United States* (New York, 1980), p. 279.

18. Aiko Mifune, interview with author, March 29, 1988; Magohichi and Tazue Sakaguchi, interview with author, June 2, 1988; Jeanette Takaki Watanabe, interview with author, March 14, 1987; poem by Kiyoko Meda, in Lucille Nixon and Tomoe Tana (eds. and trans.), *Sounds From the Unknown: A Collection of Japanese American Tanka* (Denver, 1963), p. 49.

19. Ling-chi Wang, "Politics of Assimilation and Repression: History of the Chinese in the United States, 1940 to 1970," unpublished manuscript, Asian American Studies Library, University of California, Berkeley, pp. 392, 394.

20. Victor and Brett de Bary Nee, *Longtime Californ': A Documentary Study of an American Chinatown* (New York, 1972), pp. 214–215, 219.

21. Judy Yung, *Chinese Women of America: A Pictorial History* (Seattle, 1986), p. 83; Nee, *Longtime Californ'*, p. 216; Wang, "Politics of Assimilation and Repression," p. 405.

22. Shih-Shan Henry Tsai, *The Chinese Experience in America* (Bloomington, 1986), pp. 135–136.

23. Nee, *Longtime Californ'*, p. 216.

24. David Reimers, *Still the Golden Door: The Third World Comes to America* (New York, 1985), p. 16.

25. Wang, "Politics of Assimilation and Repression," p. 287; Diane Mei Lin Mark and Ginger Chih, *A Place Called Chinese America* (Dubuque, Iowa, 1982), p. 100.

26. David Reimers, *Still the Golden Door*, pp. 17–21.

27. Ibid., p. 67.

28. Ibid., pp. 83, 70, 71.

29. Ibid., p. 82.

30. Ibid., pp. 85, 75, 76.

31. Robert W. Gardner, Bryant Robey, and Peter C. Smith, *Asian Americans: Growth, Change, and Diversity*, a publication of the Population Reference Bureau, vol. 40, no. 4 (October 1985), p. 5.

32. William Doerner, "Asians: To America with Skills," *Time*, vol. 126, no. 1 (July 8, 1985), p. 43.

33. Fred Arnold, Urmil Minocha, and James T. Fawcett, "The Changing Face of Asian Immigration to the United States," in James T. Fawcett and Benjamin V. Carino (eds.), *Pacific Bridges: The New Immigration from Asia and the Pacific Islands* (New York, 1987), pp. 131, 132; Ernesto Pernia, "The Question of the Brain Drain from the Philippines," *International Migration Review*, vol. 10, no. 1 (Spring 1976), pp. 64–69; James Leung, "Japantown is Rapidly Losing its Japanese Identity," *San Francisco Chronicle*, May 16, 1988.

34. Subi Lin Felipe, interview with author, July 24, 1988.

35. Reimers, *Still the Golden Door*, pp. 95–96.

36. Elliot R Barkan, "Whom Shall We Integrate?: A Comparative Analysis of the Immigration and Naturalization Trends of Asians before and after the 1965 Immigration Act," *Journal of American Ethnic History*, vol. 3, no. 1 (Fall 1983), p. 48; Arnold, Minocha, and Fawcett, "The Changing Face of Asian Immigration to the United States," in Fawcett and Carino, *Pacific Bridges*, pp. 126–127, 130; Bernard P. Wong, *Chinatown: Economic Adaptation and Ethnic Identity of the Chinese* (New York, 1982), pp. 28–29; Betty Lee Sung, "Polarity in the Makeup of Chinese Immigrants," in Roy Simon Bryce-Laporte (ed.), *Source Book on the New Immigration* (New Brunswick, N.J., 1980), pp. 40–48; Reimers, *Still the Golden Door*, pp. 103, 104.

37. Betty Chu, oral history, in Joan Morrison and Charlotte Fox Zabusky (eds.), *American Mosaic: The Immigrant Experience in the Words of Those Who Lived It* (New York, 1980), pp. 305–314.

38. Xiu Zhen, in Thomas Kessner and Betty Boyd Caroli, *Today's Immigrants, Their Stories: A New Look at the Newest Americans* (New York, 1981), pp. 251–252.

39. Chin Moy Lee, interview, January 8, 1982, Chinese Women of America Research Project, Chinese Culture Foundation of San Francisco, p. 1; Kessner and Caroli, *Today's Immigrants*, p. 253.

40. Dean Lan, "Chinatown Sweatshops," in Emma Gee (ed.), *Counterpoint: Perspectives on Asian America* (Los Angeles, 1976), pp. 352–353; Wang, "Politics of Assimilation and Repression," pp. 501, 504, 506, 510, 515, 512.

41. Peter Kwong, *The New Chinatown* (New York, 1987), p. 5; Charles Choy Wong, "Monterey Park: A Community in Transition," paper presented at the Fifth National Conference of the Association for Asian American Studies, March 24–27, Washington State University, p. 2.

42. Wong, "Monterey Park: A Community in Transition," pp. 3–9; Evelyn Hsu, "Influx of Asians Stirs Up L.A. Area's 'Little Taipei,'" *San Francisco Chronicle*, August 1, 1986; Thomas Elias, "Anti–Asian Bigotry Apparently," *Houston Chronicle*, July 28, 1985.

43. Mark Arax, "Asian Influx Alters Life in Suburbia," *Los Angeles Times*, April 5, 1987; Hsu, "Influx of Asians"; Wong, "Monterey Park: A Community in Transition," pp. 8–15.

44. Paul Ong, "Chinatown Unemployment and the Ethnic Labor Market," *Amerasia*, vol. 11, no. 1 (1984), p. 45.

45. Kwong, *New Chinatown*, p. 36; Kessner and Caroli, *Today's Immigrants*, p. 256.

46. Lan, "Chinatown Sweatshops," p. 354; Ong, "Chinatown Unemployment and the Ethnic Labor Market," p. 51.

47. Alexander Reid, "New Asian Immigrants, New Garment Center," *New York Times*, October 5, 1986; Ilsoo Kim, "Korea and East Asia: Premigration Factors and U.S. Immigration Policy," in Fawcett and Carino (eds.), *Pacific Bridges*, p. 332; Reimers, *Still the Golden Door*, p. 107; Kessner and Caroli, *Today's Immigrants*, p. 257.

48. Nee, *Longtime Californ'*, pp. 282, 285.

49. Kwong, *New Chinatown*, pp. 6, 58; Nee, *Longtime Californ'*, p. 311; Ong, "Chinatown Unemployment and the Ethnic Labor Market," pp. 37–45.

50. Nee, *Longtime Californ'*, pp. 290–295; Kwong, *New Chinatown*, pp. 143–145, 151–152.

51. Kwong, *New Chinatown*, pp. 9, 30, 94, 123, 148.

52. Ibid., p. 67; Ong, "Chinatown Unemployment and the Ethnic Labor Market," pp. 46–48.

53. Sung, "Polarity in the Makeup of Chinese Immigrants," p. 48; Karen Ringuette, "Asian Immigrants: Debunking the Myths," *East/West*, October 23, 1986, p. 9; Tom Wing Wah, interview, September 5, 1982, Chinese Women of America Research Project, Chinese Culture Foundation of San Francisco, pp. 3–4.

54. Wei-Chi Poon, interviews with author, January 27 and February 2, 1988; Wei-Chi Poon, interview, January 18, 1983, Chinese Women of America Research Project, Chinese Culture Foundation of San Francisco, p. 3.

55. Tom Wing Wah, interview, Chinese Women of America Research Project, p. 2; Fay Chiang, interview, October 7, 1982, Chinese Women of America Research Project, Chinese Culture Foundation of San Francisco, p. 9.

56. Reimers, *Still the Golden Door*, p 106; Kessner and Caroli, *Today's Immigrants*, p. 240.

57. Christina Tien, in Laurie Olsen, Project Director, *Crossing the Schoolhouse Border: Immigrant Students and the California Public Schools*, a California Tomorrow Policy Research Report (San Francisco, 1988), p. 34; John Kuo Wei Tchen, in Douglas Martin, "Living in Two Worlds: Chinese of New York City," *New York Times*, February 19, 1988.

58. Arnold, Minocha, and Fawcett, "The Changing Face of Asian Immigration to the United States," pp. 130, 131; Barkan, "Whom Shall We Integrate?," p. 48; Charles B. Keely, "Philippine Migration: Internal Movements and Emigration to the United States," *International Migration Review*, vol. 7 (September 1973), pp. 182–183.

59. Michael Sterne, "Manila Strip on Ninth Avenue is Bit of Home for Filipinos," *New York Times*, December 30, 1976; Steve Lohr, "Filipinos Flock to U.S. as

Manila Woes Grow," *New York Times*, clipping file, "Immigrant Filipino Americans," Asian American Studies Library, University of California, Berkeley.

60. Jack Foisie, "2000 Filipinos a Day Ask for Visa to the U.S.," *Los Angeles Times*, October 9, 1972; Frank Denton, with Victoria Villena-Denton, *Filipino Views of America: Warm Memories, Cold Realities* (Washington, D.C., 1986), p. 126.

61. Linda Perrin, *Coming to America: Immigrants from the Far East* (New York, 1980), p. 129; "New Faces: How They're Changing U.S.," U.S. *News & World Report*, February 20, 1978, p. 32; Alfredo Munoz, *The Filipinos in America* (Los Angeles, 1972), p. 29; Denton, *Filipino Views of America*, pp. 114, 148, 103.

62. For information on Filipino doctors, see "Over-Seas Filipinos: A New Breed of Professionals," *Archipelago*, June 1974, pp. 10–15; Pernia, "Question of the Brain Drain from the Philippines," pp. 64–65; Reimers, *Still the Golden Door*, p. 101.

63. Royal F. Morales, *Makibaka: The Pilipino-American Struggle* (Los Angeles, 1974), p. 79; Pernia, "Question of the Brain Drain," pp. 68–69.

64. California Advisory Committee to the U.S. Commission on Civil Rights, *Asian Americans and Pacific Peoples: A Case of Mistaken Identity* (Washington, D.C., 1975), pp. 47, 48; Perrin, *Coming to America*, p. 130.

65. California Advisory Committee to the U.S. Commission on Civil Rights, *A Dream Unfulfilled: Korean and Pilipino Health Professionals in California* (Washington, D.C., 1975), pp. 16, 17.

66. Wilhelm Quejada, "The Brain Drain Phenomenon," Asian American Studies 124 Paper, Spring 1987, University of California, Berkeley.

67. Edwin Almirol, "Social Stigma and Economic Status among Filipinos in California," unpublished paper, University of California, Davis, pp. 16, 17; Earl Caldwell, "Filipinos: A Fast-Growing U.S. Minority," *New York Times*, March 5, 1971.

68. Amado Cabezas, Larry Hajime Shinagawa, and Gary Kawaguchi, "New Inquiries into the Socioeconomic Status of Pilipino Americans in California," *Amerasia*, vol. 13, no. 1 (1986–87), pp. 3–7; Pyong Gap Min, "Filipino and Korean Immigrants in Small Business: A Comparative Analysis," *Amerasia*, vol. 13, no. 1 (1986–87), p. 54.

69. "The Pioneers," *Newsweek*, May 26, 1975, p. 10; Bong-youn Choy, *Koreans in America* (Chicago, 1979), p. 249.

70. Eui-Young Yu, "Korean Communities in America: Past, Present, and Future," *Amerasia*, vol. 10, no. 2 (1983), p. 29; Ilsoo Kim, *New Urban Immigrants: The Korean Community in New York* (Princeton, 1981), p. 18; Pyong Gap Min, "From White–Collar Occupations to Small Business: Korean Immigrants' Occupational Adjustment," *Sociological Quarterly*, vol. 25 (Summer 1984), p. 341; Kim Ha Tai, "Koreans in S. California," *New Korea*, March 6, 1975.

71. Kim, *New Urban Immigrants*, pp. 49, 72; Nancy Yoshihara, "Koreans Find Riches, Faded Dreams in L.A.," *Los Angeles Times*, February 1, 1976.

72. Kim, *New Urban Immigrants*, pp. 73, 77, 40.

73. Kim, *New Urban Immigrants*, pp. 148, 167, 163; Tomoji Ishi, "International Linkage and National Class Conflict: The Migration of Korean Nurses to the United States," *Amerasia*, vol. 14, no. 1 (1988), pp. 23–50; Kessner and Caroli, *Today's Immigrants*, p. 130.

74. Kim, *New Urban Immigrants*, p. 169.

75. Ibid., pp. 158, 165, 172.

76. Yoshihara, "Koreans Find Riches, Faded Dreams in L.A."; Kessner and Caroli,

Today's Immigrants, pp. 132, 133; California Advisory Committee to the U.S. Commission on Civil Rights, *A Dream Unfulfilled*, pp. 16, 13; "The Pioneers," *Newsweek*, p. 100.

77. Yu, "Korean Communities," p. 34; Kim, *New Urban Immigrants*, pp. 96, 97.

78. Marlys Harris, "Making It: How the Koreans Won the Green-Grocer Wars," *Money*, March 1983, p.192; Ilsoo Kim, "The Big Apple Goes Bananas Over Korean Fruit Stands," *Asia* (September/October 1981), p. 51.

79. Pyong Gap Min, "Filipino and Korean Immigrants in Small Business," pp. 54, 58.

80. Kim, *New Urban Immigrants*, pp. 40, 102; JoAn Paganetti, "Korean Greengrocers Thrive in New York," *Advertising Age*, April 18, 1985, p. 42; Jesus Sanchez, "L.A. Top Choice for Koreans in Business in U.S.," *Los Angeles Times*, June 6, 1987.

81. Elizabeth Mehren, "Success Saga in America: Korean Style," *Los Angeles Times*, August 12, 1987; Ivan H. Light, "Asian Enterprise in America: Chinese, Japanese, and Koreans in Small Business," in Scott Cummings, *Self-Help in Urban America: Patterns of Minority Business Enterprise* (Port Washington, N.Y., 1980), pp. 38–55.

82. Kim, *New Urban Immigrants*, p. 113; Kwang Chung Kim and Won Moo Hurh, "Korean Americans and the 'Success' Image: A Critique," *Amerasia*, vol. 10, no. 2 (1983), p. 14; Philip K. Y. Young, "Family Labor, Sacrifice and Competition: Korean Greengrocers in New York City," *Amerasia*, vol. 10, no. 2 (1983), p. 57; Choy, *Koreans in America*, p. 248; Tai, "Koreans in S. California."

83. Kim Ha Tai, in *The New Korea*, March 13, 1975, quoted in Edna Bonacich, Ivan Light, and Charles Choy Wong, "Korean Immigrant: Small Business in Los Angeles," in Bryce-Laporte (ed.), *Source Book on the New Immigration*, p. 179; Kim, "Big Apple Goes Bananas," p. 50.

84. Kim, "Big Apple Goes Bananas," p. 51.

85. Min, "Filipino and Korean Immigrants in Small Business," p. 56; Kim, *New Urban Immigrants*, pp. 112, 114.

86. Kim, *New Urban Immigrants*, p. 120; Harris, "Making It: How the Koreans Won the Green-Grocer Wars," p. 198.

87. Choy, *Koreans in America*, p. 248; Kim, "Big Apple Goes Bananas," p. 51.

88. Christopher Kim, interview with author, June 19, 1988.

89. Ivan Light, "Immigrant Entrepreneurs in America: Koreans in Los Angeles," in Nathan Glazer, *Clamor at the Gates: The New American Immigration* (San Francisco, 1985), p. 162; Barbara Basler, "Koreans Find New York Is a Place of Opportunity," *New York Times*, October 2, 1979.

90. Gardner, Robey, and Smith, *Asian Americans*, p. 5; Reimers, *Still the Golden Door*, p. 115.

91. Barkan, "Whom Shall We Integrate?," p. 48; Dr. S. Patel (pseudonym), interview with author, October 24, 1986.

92. B. N. Ghosh, "Some Economic Aspects of India's Brain Drain into the U.S.A.," *International Migration*, vol. 17, no. 3–4 (1979), p. 281; Maxine P. Fisher, "Creating Ethnic Identity: Asian Indians in the New York City Area," *Urban Anthropology*, vol. 7, no. 3 (1978), p. 273; Philip Leonhard-Spark and Parmatma Saran, "The Indian Immigrant in America: A Demographic Profile," in Parmatma Saran and Edwin Eames, *The New Ethnics: Asian Indians in the United States* (New York, 1980), pp. 152, 145.

93. Martin Gottlieb, "New Seekers of the Dream: Immigrants from South Asia," *New*

York Times, January 3, 1986; "Indian Immigrants Prosper as Owners of Motels," *New York Times*, June 22, 1985; Maxine P. Fisher, *The Indians of New York City: A Study of Immigrants from India* (Columbia, Mo., 1980), pp. 18–19; "Surge in Indian Immigration," *Asian Week*, May 22, 1987; "Indians Discuss Assimilation," *Asian Week*, October 10, 1986.

94. Fisher, *Indians of New York City*, pp. 119–130; Fisher, "Creating Ethnic Identity," p. 280.

95. Hamida Chopra, interview with author, September 12, 1988.

96. Dr. S. Patel (pseudonym), interview with author, October 24, 1986.

97. Ibid.

98. Ibid.

99. Ibid.

100. Arnold, Minocha, Fawcett, "The Changing Face of Asian Immigration to the United States," p. 130; Gardner, Robey, and Smith, *Asian Americans*, p. 5.

101. Nguyen Cao Ky, in Morrison and Zabusky (eds.), *American Mosaic*, p. 418.

102. Student paper, name withheld, "Vietnamese Refugee," Asian American Studies 126, Spring 1987, University of California, Berkeley, pp. 1–2; Thai Dang, interview with author, April 28, 1988.

103. Thai Dang, interview with author, April 28, 1988; Thich Nhat Hanh, *The Cry of Vietnam*, in Thomas Bentz, *New Immigrants: Portraits in Passage* (New York, 1981), p. 145; William T. Liu, *Transition to Nowhere: Vietnamese Refugees in America* (Nashville, Tenn., 1979), p. 78.

104. Linh Do, interview with author, November 10, 1988; Vietnamese student, name withheld, "A Confused Time," Asian American Studies 20A, Spring 1980, University of California, Berkeley, pp. 1–2.

105. "New Immigrants' Quest: Refugees from Saigon," *New York Times*, July 2, 1986; Liu, *Transition to Nowhere*, pp. 21, 15, 19.

106. Liu, *Transition to Nowhere*, p. 55; Kenneth Skinner, "Vietnamese in America: Diversity in Adaptation," *California Sociologist*, vol. 3, no. 2 (Summer 1980), p. 105; Barry N. Stein, "Occupational Adjustment of Refugees: The Vietnamese in the United States," *International Migration Review*, vol. 13, no. 1 (Spring 1979), p. 40.

107. Lesleyanne Hawthorne, *Refugee: The Vietnamese Experience* (Melbourne, Australia, 1982), pp. 97, 214, 221, 237.

108. Du Tu Le, "Binh Minh Nhan Loai Moi," "Dawn of a New Humanity," *Dat Moi*, April 1979, p. 9.

109. Thai Dang, interview with author, April 28, 1988; Thai Dang, diary, November 1986, copy given to the author; Thai Dang, letter to U.S. senator, January 20, 1988, copy given to the author.

110. Barry Wain, *The Refused: The Agony of the Indochina Refugees* (New York, 1981), pp. 72, 73; Michael Dorgan, "Attacks Leave Scars that Will Not Fade," *San Jose Mercury News*, April 10, 1987; Bruce Grant, *The Boat People: An 'Age' Investigation* (New York, 1979), pp. 65, 66.

111. Tuyet Anh Nguyen, letter to the author, May 2, 1988; Chuong Hoang Chung, "The Language Situation of Vietnamese Americans," in Sandra McKay and Sau Ling Wong (eds.), *Language Diversity: Problem or Resource?* (New York, 1988), p. 277.

112. Alan Hope, "Language, Culture are Biggest Hurdles for Vietnamese," *Gainesville* (Ga.) *Times*, March 31, 1985; Edward Iwata, "Ugly Tangle over Foreign Fishing

Ways," *San Francisco Chronicle*, September 10, 1983, p. 28; Karen Ringuette, "Asian Immigrants: Debunking the Myths," p. 9; Tricia Knoll, *Becoming Americans: Asian Sojourners, Immigrants and Refugees in the Western United States* (Portland, Oreg., 1982), pp. 196, 192.

113. T. T. Nhu, "Old Feuds Still Disrupt Peace among Vietnamese," *San Jose Mercury News*, March 2, 1988; Katherine Bishop, "Refugees Press on with Vietnam War," *New York Times*, August 3, 1987, pp. 1, 8; Cheryl Romo, "The War away from Home," *In These Times*, August 10–23, 1983, pp. 12–13, 22; Marvine Howe, "Vietnamese Celebrate Traditional New Year," *New York Times*, February 1, 1987; Joanne Omang, "Dreaming of a Return to Vietnam," *San Francisco Chronicle*, March 9, 1983.

114. Skinner, "Vietnamese in America," p. 111; interview with Vietnamese woman, name withheld, field notes, February 27, 1988; Bentz, *New Immigrants*, p. 154; Linh Do, interview with author, November 28, 1988.

115. Student paper, name withheld, "Vietnamese Refugee," Asian American Studies 126, Spring 1987, University of California, Berkeley, pp. 7–8; Ashley Dunn, "Legacy Comes Home: The Land of Opportunity Offers Refugees a New Life," *Seattle Times Post-Intelligencer*, April 28, 1985.

116. Michael McCabe and L. A. Chung, "Facing the Hopes and Fears of Assimilation," *San Francisco Chronicle*, July 25, 1988; Knoll, *Becoming Americans*, pp. 188, 186.

117. Mark Arax, "Lost in L.A.," *Los Angeles Times Magazine*, December 15, 1987, pp. 10–18, 42–48.

118. Chung, interview with author, March 24, 1988; student paper, name withheld, "Vietnamese Refugee," Asian American Studies 126, Spring 1987, University of California, Berkeley, p. 10; Dexter Waugh, "Southeast Asians in U.S.: Refugees 'No More,'" *San Francisco Examiner*, November 25, 1985.

119. Stein, "Occupational Adjustment of Refugees, p. 29; David Haines, "Vietnamese Refugee Women in the U.S. Labor Force: Continuity or Change?" in Rita James Simon and Caroline Brettell (eds.), *International Migration: The Female Experience* (Totowa, N.J., 1986), p. 73; Khanh Ninh, interview with a middle-aged Vietnamese woman, October 23, 1982, paper for Asian American Studies 125, Fall 1982, University of California, Berkeley, p. 14; student paper, name withheld, "Vietnamese Refugee," Asian American Studies 126, Spring 1987, University of California, Berkeley, p. 4.

120. "Duke Points the Way to Little Saigon," *East/West*, June 30, 1988; Chung, "Language Situation of Vietnamese Americans," pp. 276, 285, 289.

121. Liu, *Transition to Nowhere*, p. 170; Anh K. Tran, "Adaptational Strategy of Chinese-Vietnamese in the United States," paper presented at the Fifth National Conference of the Association for Asian American Studies, March 24–27, 1988, Washington State University, p. 30; Julie Rees, "Striving for the American Dream," *Long Beach Press-Telegram*, May 6, 1985.

122. Patrick Anderson, "Asians Revive Tenderloin," *Asian Week*, April 17, 1987; Raymond Lou, "The Vietnamese Business Community of San Jose," paper presented at the Fifth National Conference of the Association for Asian American Studies, March 24–27, 1988, Washington State University, pp. 3, 4; Judith Lyons, "72,000 Viets with 320 Firms Spark New Life in San Jose," *Asian Week*, June 19, 1987.

123. Judy Keen, "Viet War—It Won't Go Away," *Stockton* (Calif.) *Record*, April 28, 1985; Knoll, *Becoming Americans*, p. 164; Jeffrey Kaye, "Yearning to Breathe Free," *New West*, April 7, 1980, p. 57.

124. Kimmakone Siharath, interview with author, October 17, 1988.

125. Ibid.

126. Ibid.

127. Frank Viviano, "Strangers in the Promised Land," *Image*, August 31, 1986, in *San Francisco Chronicle*, August 31, 1986, p. 19; Touly Xiong, interview, April 25, 1988.

128. Touly Xiong, interview with author, April 24, 1988; Knoll, *Becoming Americans*, p. 242.

129. Carol Takaki, report on visit to service center for Mien at Harbor House in Oakland, California, March 28, 1988.

130. Touly Xiong, interview with author, April 24, 1988; Chou Vue, interview with author, April 14, 1988; Chou Lee, interview with author, April 25, 1988.

131. Viviano, "Strangers in the Promised Land," p. 17; "A Note on Hmong Orthography," in Bruce Downing and Douglas Olney (eds.), *The Hmong in the West: Observations and Reports* (Minneapolis, 1982), p. 217; Bruce Thowpaou Bilatout et al., *Handbook for Teaching Hmong-Speaking Students* (Folsom, Calif., 1988), p. 28; Chou Lee, interview with author, April 15, 1988.

132. Viviano, "Strangers in the Promised Land," p. 18.

133. Ibid., pp. 18–19.

134. Chou Lee, interview with author, April 25, 1988; Touly Xiong, interview with author, April 24, 1988; Viviano, "Strangers in the Promised Land," pp. 19, 21.

135. Nou Xiong, interview with author, April 24, 1988; T. T. Nhu, "Work Ethic and Need Motivate Welfare Cheaters," *San Jose Mercury News*, April 7, 1988; Choy Sapha, interviewed by Carol Takaki, March 28, 1988.

136. Eliot Marshall, "The Hmong: Dying of Culture Shock?" *Science*, May 29, 1981, p. 1008; Jean Seligmann, "The Curse of the Hmong," and Louise Woo, "Mental Health Services Scarce for Asian Settlers," *Oakland Tribune*, October 29, 1987; *Newsweek*, August 10, 1981, p. 47; "Mystery Deaths in the Night," *Time*, February 23, 1981, p. 102; Kai Moua, interview with author, April 25, 1988; Touly Xiong, interview with author, April 25, 1988; Joseph J. Tobin and Joan Friedman, "Spirits, Shamans, and Nightmare Death: Survivor Stress in a Hmong Refugee," *American Journal of Orthopsychiatry*, vol. 53, July 1983, pp. 443–445.

137. Tobin and Friedman, "Spirits, Shamans, and Nightmare Death," pp. 445; Touly Xiong, interview with author, April 25, 1988; Woo, "Mental Health Services"; Amy R. Catlin, "Speech Surrogate Systems of the Hmong: From Singing Voices to Talking Reeds," in Downing and Olney (eds.), *The Hmong in the West*, p. 189.

138. Carol Colley, "Iu Mien Voices," paper for Asian American Studies 126, Spring 1987, University of California, Berkeley, p. 7; Knoll, *Becoming Americans*, pp. 225, 226; Eric Crystal, "Pride and Survival in an Alien World," *San Francisco Chronicle and Examiner*, May 24, 1981.

139. Mao Yang, interview with author, April 23, 1988; Chou Vue and Nou Xiong, interview with author, April 24, 1988.

140. John Everingham, "One Family's Odyssey to America," *National Geographic*, vol. 157, no. 5 (May 1980), p. 646; Colley, "Iu Mien Voices," p. 10; George M. Scott, Jr., "A New Year in a New Land: Religious Change among the Lao Hmong Refugees in San Diego," in Downing and Olney, *The Hmong in the West*, p. 83.

141. Ken McCracken, "Surviving Khmer Rouge: Refugee Details Life in Cambodia during Pol Pot Regime," *Rochester* (Minn.) *Post-Bulletin*, June 6, 1985; Con Duncan, "Cambodia Has Left a Refugee Teen-ager Much Older than Her Peers," *Seattle Times Post-Intelligencer*, May 26, 1985.

142. Knoll, *Becoming Americans*, p. 284.

143. Chung, interview with author, March 24, 1988; Cambodian boy, quoted in Laurie Olsen, Project Director, *Crossing the Schoolhouse Border: Immigrant Students and the California Public Schools*, a California Tomorrow Policy Research Report (San Francisco, 1988), p. 22.

144. Phil Manzano, "Clinic Provides Help to Soothe Refugees' 'Scars,' " *Portland Oregonian*, November 9, 1986.

145. T. T. Nhu, "A Survivor of the Hell of Khmer Rouge Cambodia," *San Jose Mercury News*, May 4, 1988; Knoll, *Becoming Americans*, pp. 296, 165.

146. Chi Huynh, "Even Success Has Its Price," paper, Asian American Studies 126, Spring 1987, University of California, Berkeley, p. 4; Khoi Tien Bui, "The Refugee," in *Houston Post*, January 8, 1985.

12. Breaking Silences

1. Georg Simmel, "Der Fremde" or "The Stranger," in Simmel, *On Individuality and Social Forms*, edited by Donald N. Levine (Chicago, 1971), pp. 143–149; Karl Marx, *Capital: A Critique of Political Economy* (New York, 1906), pp. 689–703; Immanuel Wallerstein, *The Modern World-System* (New York, 1974); Lucie Cheng and Edna Bonacich (eds.), *Labor Immigration Under Capitalism: Asian Workers in the United States before World War II* (Berkeley, 1984); Robert E. Park, "Human Migration and the Marginal Man," *American Journal of Sociology*, vol. 33, no. 6 (May 1928), p. 890; Carlos Bulosan, *America Is in the Heart: A Personal History* (rpt. Seattle, 1981, originally published in 1946), p. 104.

2. F. Scott Fitzgerald, *The Great Gatsby* (rpt. New York, 1953), p. 182; Victor Turner, *Dramas, Fields, and Metaphors: Symbolic Action in Human Society* (Ithaca, N.Y., 1974), pp. 232, 237; Wayne K. Patterson, "The Korean Frontier in America: Immigration to Hawaii, 1896–1910," unpublished Ph.D. thesis, University of Pennsylvania, 1977, p. 252; Maxine Hong Kingston, *The Woman Warrior: Memoirs of a Girlhood Among Ghosts* (New York, 1976), p. 6; Robert E. Park, "Racial Assimilation in Secondary Groups with Particular Reference to the Negro," *Papers and Proceedings, Eighth Annual Meeting of the American Sociological Society, 1913*, vol. 8 (Chicago, 1914), p. 71; Edna Bonacich, "A Theory of Ethnic Antagonism: The Split Labor Market," *American Sociological Review*, vol. 37, no. 5 (October 1972), pp. 547–559.

3. CBS, *60 Minutes*, "The Model Minority," February 1, 1987; "Asian-Americans: Are They Making the Grade?" *U.S. News & World Report*, April 2, 1984, pp. 41–47; "The Changing Face of America," Special Immigrants Issue, *Time*, July 8, 1985, pp. 24–101; "Asian-Americans: The Drive to Excel," *Newsweek on Campus*, April 1984, pp. 4–15; "Asian-Americans: A 'Model Minority,' " *Newsweek*, December 6, 1982, pp. 40–51; "America's Super Minority," *Fortune*, November 26, 1986; David A. Bell, "The Triumph of Asian-Americans: America's Greatest Success Story," *New Republic*, July 15 and 22, 1985, pp. 24–31.

4. President Ronald Reagan, speech to a group of Asian and Pacific Americans in the White House, February 23, 1984, reprinted in *Asian Week*, March 2, 1984.

5. Ronald Takaki, "Have Asian Americans Made It?" *San Francisco Examiner*, January 10, 1984; Ronald Takaki, "Comparisons between Blacks and Asian Americans Unfair," *Seattle Post-Intelligencer*, March 21, 1985.

6. Amado Cabezas and Gary Kawaguchi, "Empirical Evidence for Continuing Asian American Income Inequality: The Human Capital Model and Labor Market Segmentation," in Gary Y. Okihiro et al. (eds.), *Reflections on Shattered Windows:*

Promises and Prospects for Asian American Studies (Pullman, Wash., 1988), pp. 148, 154; Amado Cabezas, "The Asian American Today as an Economic Success Model: Some Myths and Realities," paper presented at "Break the Silence: A Conference on Anti-Asian Violence, Examining the Growth and Nature of the Problem and Finding Solutions," May 10, 1986, University of California, Berkeley, pp. 6, 8, 9; Amado Cabezas, Larry Hajime Shinagawa, and Gary Kawaguchi, "A Study of Income Differentials Among Asian Americans, Blacks, and Whites in the SMSAs of San Francisco–Oakland–San Jose and Los Angeles–Long Beach in 1980," paper presented at the "All-UC Invitational Conference on the Comparative Study of Race, Ethnicity, Gender, and Class," May 30 and 31, 1986, University of California, Santa Cruz, pp. 9, 10.

7. Cabezas and Kawaguchi, "Empirical Evidence for Continuing Asian American Income Inequality," pp. 156–157.

8. U.S. Equal Employment Opportunity Commission, report, summary in Laird Harrison, "U.S. Study Finds Few Asians in Management," *Asian Week*, May 13, 1988; Winfred Yu, "Asian-Americans Charge Prejudice Slows Climb to Management Ranks," *Wall Street Journal*, September 11, 1985; editorial, *East/West*, June 30, 1988.

9. L. A. Chung and Michael McCabe, "Bay Area Asians Counting on Economic Success, Poll Says," *San Francisco Chronicle*, July 26,1988; L. A. Chung, "Shedding an Accent to Attain Success," ibid.; John Schwartz, "A 'Superminority' Tops Out," *Newsweek*, May 11, 1987, pp. 48–49; Aprajita Sikri, "Latent Prejudice, Envy Now," *India Abroad*, December 25, 1987; Hamida Chopra, interview with author, September 12, 1988.

10. Ronald Takaki, "Asian Americans in the University," *San Francisco Examiner*, April 16, 1984; William Raspberry, "Beyond Racism (Cont'd.)," *Washington Post*, November 19, 1984; Barry Bluestone and Bennett Harrison, *The Deindustrialization of America* (New York, 1982).

11. Peter Schmeisser, "Is America in Decline?" *The New York Times Magazine*, April 17, 1988; Paul Kennedy, *The Rise and Fall of the Great Powers* (New York, 1987); William Julius Wilson, *The Truly Disadvantaged: The Inner City, the Underclass, and Public Policy* (Chicago, 1987), p. 65; Chris Tilly, "U-Turn on Equality: The Puzzle of Middle Class Decline," *Dollars & Sense*, May 1986, p. 11 ("middle-class" income is defined as between 75 percent and 125 percent of median household income); Bob Kuttner, "The Declining Middle," *The Atlantic Monthly*, July 1983, pp. 60–72; Barbara Ehrenreich, "Is the Middle Class Doomed?" *The New York Times Magazine*, September 7, 1986, pp. 44, 50, 62; Tom Wicker, "Let 'Em Eat Swiss Cheese," *New York Times*, September 2, 1988; Don Wydiff, "Why the Underclass Is Still Under," *New York Times*, November 16, 1987; Charles Murray, *Losing Ground: American Social Policy, 1950–1980* (New York, 1984), pp. 32, 146, 220, 227; Ronald Takaki, "Poverty Is Thriving Under Reagan," *New York Times*, March 3, 1986.

12. Marta Ho, interview with author, November 5, 1988.

13. Tom Surh, "U.S. Policy on Asian Immigration," *East Wind*, vol. 1, no. 2 (Fall/Winter 1982), pp. 27–28; Zita Arocha, " '80s Immigration Matching the Record 1901–10 Flood," Honolulu *Star-Bulletin and Advertiser*, July 24, 1988; Susan Rasky, "Senate, 88 to 4, Passes Bill Setting Immigration Limits," *New York Times*, March 16, 1988.

14. Thu-Thuy Truong, panel discussion, Asian American Studies 20A, Spring 1980, University of California, Berkeley; *Rambo: First Blood Part II* (HBO video, New York, 1985).

15. Jean Daskais, "Jersey City Indians Battle Hate," *India West,* October 16, 1987; Savyasaachi Jain, "Threats of Racial Violence Alarm Indians in Jersey City," *India Abroad,* October 2, 1987; "Irregularities Reported in Jersey Asian Slaying Trial," *Asianweek,* September 23, 1988.

16. Ronald Takaki, "Who Really Killed Vincent Chin" *San Francisco Examiner,* September 21, 1983.

17. Takaki, "Who Really Killed Vincent Chin?"

18. David Smollar, "U.S. Asians Feel Trade Backlash," *Los Angeles Times,* September 14, 1983; Robert Christopher, "Don't Blame the Japanese," *The New York Times Magazine,* October 19, 1986; Ronald Takaki, "I am not a 'Jap'; I am a man," *In These Times,* October 19–25, 1983; Gordon Martin, "Links Between Detroit, Japan?" *San Francisco Chronicle,* September 8, 1983; John Holusha, "The Disappearing 'U.S. Car,' " *New York Times,* August 10, 1985.

19. Takaki, "Who Really Killed Vincent Chin?"

20. Takaki, "Who Really Killed Vincent Chin?"; Smollar, "U.S. Asians Feel Trade Backlash."

21. Richard Oyama, poem published in *Transfer 38* (San Francisco, 1979), p. 43, reprinted in Elaine Kim, *Asian American Literature: An Introduction to the Writings and Their Social Context* (Philadelphia, 1982), pp. 308–309.

22. Congressman Robert Matsui, speech in the House of Representatives on bill 442 for redress and reparations, September 17, 1987, *Congressional Record* (Washington, 1987), p. 7584; Congressman Norman Mineta, inteniew with author, March 26, 1988; Warren Furutani, testimony, reprinted in *Amerasia,* vol. 8, no. 2 (1981), p. 104.

23. Alice Tanabe Nehira, testimony, reprinted in *Amerasia,* vol. 8, no. 2 (1981), p. 93; Janice Mirikitani, "Breaking Silences," reprinted ibid., p. 109.

24. "Text of Reagan's Remarks," reprinted in *Pacific Citizen,* August 19–26, 1988, p. 5; *San Francisco Chronicle,* August 5 and 11, 1988.

25. Tomo Shoji, "Born Too Soon . . . It's Never Too Late: Growing Up Nisei in Early Washington," presentations at the University of California, Berkeley, September 19, 1987, and the Ohana Cultural Center, Oakland, California, March 4, 1988.

26. Kingston, *The Woman Warrior,* p. 6; poem in Kazuo Ito, *Issei: A History of Japanese Immigrants in North America* (Seattle, 1973), p. 493.

27. Kingston, *The Woman Warrior,* p. 6; Robert Kwan, "Asian v. Oriental: A Difference that Counts," *Pacific Citizen,* April 25, 1980; Sir James Augustus Henry Murry (ed.), *The Oxford English Dictionary* (Oxford, 1933), vol. 7, p. 200; Aminur Rahim, "Is Oriental an Occident?" in *The Asiandian,* vol. 5, no. 1, April 1983, p. 20; Shawn Wong, *Homebase* (New York, 1979), p. 111; Nellie Wong, "From a Heart of Rice Straw," in Nellie Wong, *Dreams in Harrison Railroad Park* (Berkeley, 1977), p. 41.

28. Robert Bellah et al., *Habits of the Heart: Individualism and Commitment in American Life* (Berkeley, 1985), p. 153; Alfred Wong, interviewed by Carol Takaki, April 6 and 13, 1988.

29. Ibid.

30. Poem by Shigeko, in Kazuo Ito, *Issei,* p. 40.

13. One-Tenth of the Nation

1. U.S. Commission on Civil Rights, *Civil Rights Issues Facing Asian Americans in the 1990s* (February 1992), pp. 15, 17; "The APA Population Report," *Asianweek,* January 19, 1996.

2. "Beyond Black and White," *Newsweek,* May 18, 1992, p. 28.

3. Elaine Kim and Eui-Young Yu, *East to America: Korean American Life Stories* (New York, 1996), p. 246.

4. "Sa-I-Gu," PBS broadcast, 1994.

5. Description based on an account by Troy Takaki, who drove through the area shortly after the riot. Shared with the author on June 21, 1997.

6. *New York Times,* May 3, 1992.

7. Ronald Takaki, *From the Land of Morning Calm: The Koreans in America* (New York, 1994), p. 114.

8. Ibid.

9. *San Francisco Chronicle,* May 4, 1992.

10. William Julius Wilson, *When Work Disappears: The World of the New Urban Poor* (New York, 1996).

11. *San Francisco Examiner,* May 3, 1992.

12. *New York Times,* May 3, 1992.

13. *San Francisco Examiner,* May 31, 1992.

14. "Sa-I-Gu," PBS broadcast, 1994.

15. Ibid.

16. Ibid.

17. Kim and Yu, *East to America,* pp. 249–250.

18. Samantha Lee, "Life of Susan Lee," Asian American Studies 120 paper, University of California, Berkeley, 1997, pp. 17–18.

19. *Asianweek,* June 19, 1992.

20. Sam Chu Lin, "Hope and Resignation in L.A.," *Asianweek,* April 25, 1997.

21. Frank Wu, "A Long Time Coming: Two Key Appointments Go to APAs," *Asianweek,* June 20, 1997. In his major speech on race given in California on June 14, 1997, President Bill Clinton announced that he had appointed Oh to the seven-member advisory board for "One America in the 21st Century: The President's Initiative on Race."

22. Dana Takagi, *The Retreat from Race: Asian American Admissions and Racial Politics* (New Brunswick, N.J., 1992), pp. 25, 30, 49.

23. "Asian American Admissions: Chancellor Heyman's Remarks before the Hayden Committee," *Berkeleyan,* February 10–23, 1988.

24. Michael Scott-Blair, "Ethnic Imbalance Shifts at UC," *San Diego Union,* December 11, 1986.

25. Takagi, *Retreat from Race,* p. 9; Thomas Edsall and Mary Edsall, *Chain Reaction: The Impact of Race, Rights, and Taxes on American Politics* (New York, 1991). The Edsalls use the phrase "chain reaction" to describe the ways conservatives have exploited liberal issues to advance their own agenda on race and politics.

26. Takagi, *Retreat from Race,* p. 100.

27. Ibid., pp. 103–104.

28. Ward Connerly, "With Liberty and Justice For All," Heritage Lecture no. 560, The Heritage Foundation *Lectures and Educational Programs,* March 8, 1996.

29. Jerry Reynolds, quoted in "Evaluation of Community Education Efforts in the Anti-Prop 209 Campaign Within the Asian Pacific American Community in Southern California" (Asian Pacific American Legal Center of Southern California, Los Angeles, 1997).

30. "Affirmative Action Controversy in California," *Crosscurrents: Newsmagazine of the UCLA Asian American Studies Center*, vol. 19, no. 2 (fall/winter, 1996), p. 1; Connie Rice, "Toward Affirmative Reaction," *Nation* (January 13/20, 1997), p. 23.

31. "In Support of Civil Rights: Taking on the Initiative" (Special Report, Leadership Education for Asian Pacifics, October 1996).

32. Lisa Lowe, *Immigrant Acts: On Asian American Cultural Politics* (Durham, 1996), pp. 64–65.

33. Yen Le Espiritu, *Asian American Panethnicity: Bridging Institutions and Identities* (Philadelphia, 1992).

34. Alethea Yip, "Pan-Asian Bonds of Matrimony," *Asianweek*, February 14, 1997.

35. "Pan-Asian Vows," *Asianweek*, February 14, 1997.

36. Yip, "Pan-Asian Bonds."

37. Ibid.

38. Ibid.

39. John Leland and Gregory Beals, "In Living Colors," *Newsweek*, May 5, 1997, p. 59.

40. David Hollinger, *Postethnic America: Beyond Multiculturalism* (New York, 1995).

41. "The Multicultural Society Is Here," *Asianweek*, January 3, 1997.

42. Alethea Yip, "One or the Other," *Asianweek*, January 3, 1997.

43. Hapa Issues Forum brochure (Berkeley, Calif., 1996).

44. Gaurav Kalra, "Life Story of Shashi Kalra," Asian American Studies 120 paper, University of California, Berkeley, 1997, p. 18.

45. "Charismatic young champ raises golf's level and increases its lure," *USA Today*, April 14, 1997.

46. Greg Mayeda, "Golf Phenomenon Asserts Mixed Race Identity," *What's Hapa'ning: The Hapa Issues Forum Newsletter*, vol. 3, no. 2 (summer 1995), Berkeley, Calif.

47. Ibid.

48. Helena Jia Hershel, panel discussion, Hapa Issues Forum, Fourth Annual Conference, University of California, Berkeley, April 26, 1997.

49. Nina Wu, "Bridging Cultural Boundaries," *Asianweek*, March 21, 1997.

50. Oliver Wang, "A Bitter Suite," *Asianweek*, May 31, 1996.

51. Sylvia Chan, "Constructing New Realities: Conversations with Musician/Composer/Performer Miya Masaoka," Ethnic Studies 195 paper, University of California, Berkeley, 1996, pp. 6, 10, 11, 12.

Index

About the Author

Ronald Takaki is professor of Ethnic Studies at the University of California, Berkeley, where he has been teaching for more than two decades. The grandson of Japanese immigrant plantation laborers in Hawaii, he has a Ph.D. in American history from Berkeley. The Berkeley faculty has honored Takaki with a Distinguished Teaching Award, and the Society of American Historians has elected him to be a fellow. He designed and then directed Berkeley's Ethnic Studies Ph.D. program, the first of its kind in the nation. He was instrumental in the institution of Berkeley's American Cultures graduation requirement for understanding our society's racial and ethnic diversity. He has lectured in Japan, Russia, Armenia, and South Africa. Takaki's approach in his scholarship is truly comparative and multicultural. His *Iron Cages: Race and Culture in Nineteenth-Century America* has been critically acclaimed, and his prize-winning *A Different Mirror: A History of Multicultural America* has been hailed by *Publishers Weekly* as "a brilliant revisionist history of America that is likely to become a classic of multicultural studies."